WORKS ISSUED BY
THE HAKLUYT SOCIETY

―――――

Series Editors
Gloria Clifton
Joyce Lorimer

―――――

A SCIENTIFIC, ANTIQUARIAN AND PICTURESQUE TOUR:
JOHN (FIOTT) LEE IN IRELAND, ENGLAND AND WALES,
1806–1807

THIRD SERIES
NO. 34

THE HAKLUYT SOCIETY
Trustees of the Hakluyt Society 2018–2019

PRESIDENT
Professor Jim Bennett

VICE-PRESIDENTS

Professor Felipe Fernández-Armesto
Captain Michael K. Barritt RN
Professor Roy Bridges
Professor Will F. Ryan FBA
Professor Suzanne Schwarz
Dr Sarah Tyacke CB
Professor Glyndwr Williams

COUNCIL
(with date of election)

Dr Megan Barford (2018)
Dr Jack Benson (co-opted)
Professor Michael Brennan (2018)
Professor Daniel Carey (2014)
Dr Natalie Cox (Royal Geographical Society Representative, 2017)
Professor Nandini Das (2014)
Dr Nicholas Evans (2016)
Dr Bronwen Everill (2017)
Dr John McAleer (2015)
Dr Guido van Meersbergen (co-opted)
Professor Ladan Niayesh (2017)
Professor Joan-Pau Rubiés (2016)
Dr John Smedley (2018)
Dr Edmond Smith (2017)
Professor Sebastian Sobecki (2015)
Dr Felicity Stout (2017)

HONORARY TREASURER
Mr Alastair Bridges

HONORARY JOINT SERIES EDITORS
Dr Gloria Clifton   Professor Joyce Lorimer

HONORARY EDITOR (ONLINE PUBLICATIONS)
Mr Raymond Howgego FRGS

HONORARY ADMINISTRATIVE EDITOR
Dr Katherine Parker

HONORARY ARCHIVIST
Dr Margaret Makepeace

HONORARY ADVISER (CONTRACTS)
Mr Bruce Hunter

ADMINISTRATION
(to which enquiries and applications for membership may be made)
Telephone: +44 (0) 07568 468066   Email: office@hakluyt.com

Postal Address only
The Hakluyt Society, c/o Map Library, The British Library,
96 Euston Road, London NW1 2DB, UK

Website: http://www.hakluyt.com

Registered Charity No. 313168   VAT No. GB 233 4481 77

INTERNATIONAL REPRESENTATIVES OF THE HAKLUYT SOCIETY

Australia	Dr Martin Woods, Curator of Maps, National Library of Australia, Canberra, ACT 2601
Canada	Professor Cheryl A. Fury, Department of History and Politics, University of New Brunswick Saint John, PO 5050, Saint John, NB, Canada, E2L 4L5
Central America	Dr Stewart D. Redwood, P.O. Box 0832-1784, World Trade Center, Panama City, Republic of Panama
France	Contre-amiral François Bellec, 1 place Henri Barbusse, F92300 Levallois
Germany	Monika Knaden, Lichtenradenstrasse 40, 12049 Berlin
Iceland	Professor Anna Agnarsdóttir, Department of History and Philosophy, University of Iceland, Reykjavík 101
Japan	Dr Derek Massarella, Faculty of Economics, Chuo University, Higashinakano 742–1, Hachioji-shi, Tokyo 192–03
Netherlands	Dr Anita van Dissel, Room number 2.66a, Johan Huizingagebouw, Doezensteeg 16, 2311 VL Leiden
New Zealand	John C. Robson, Map Librarian, University of Waikato Library, Private Bag 3105, Hamilton
Portugal	Dr Manuel Ramos, Av. Elias Garcia 187, 3Dt, 1050 Lisbon
Russia	Professor Alexei V. Postnikov, Institute of the History of Science and Technology, Russian Academy of Sciences, 1/5 Staropanskii per., Moscow 103012
Spain	Ambassador Dámaso de Lario, Glorieta López de Hoyos, 4, 28002 Madrid
Switzerland	Dr Tanja Bührer, Universität Bern, Historisches Institut, Unitobler, Länggasstrasse 49, 3000 Bern 9
USA	Professor Mary C. Fuller, Literature Section, 14N-405, Massachusetts Institute of Technology, 77 Massachusetts Avenue, Cambridge, MA, 02139-4207

Portrait of John Lee (né Fiott), by Thomas Herbert Maguire, 1849.
Copyright National Portrait Gallery, London (NPG D37240).

A SCIENTIFIC, ANTIQUARIAN AND PICTURESQUE TOUR

JOHN (FIOTT) LEE IN IRELAND, ENGLAND AND WALES, 1806–1807

Edited by
ANGELA BYRNE

Published by
Routledge
for
THE HAKLUYT SOCIETY
LONDON
2018

First published 2018 for the Hakluyt Society by
Routledge
2 Park Square, Milton Park, Abingdon, Oxon OX14 4RN

and by Routledge
711 Third Avenue, New York, NY 10017

Routledge is an imprint of the Taylor & Francis Group, an informa business

© 2018 The Hakluyt Society

The right of Angela Byrne to be identified as author of this work has been asserted by her in accordance with sections 77 and 78 of the Copyright, Designs and Patents Act 1988.

All rights reserved. No part of this book may be reprinted or reproduced or utilized in any form or by any electronic, mechanical, or other means, now known or hereafter invented, including photocopying and recording, or in any information storage or retrieval system, without permission in writing from the publishers.

Trademark notice: Product or corporate names may be trademarks or registered trademarks, and are used only for identification and explanation without intent to infringe.

British Library Cataloguing-in-Publication Data
A catalogue record for this book is available from the British Library

Library of Congress Cataloging-in-Publication Data
A catalog record for this book has been requested

ISBN: 978-1-138-49200-4 (hbk)
ISBN: 978-0-429-42689-6 (ebk)

Typeset in Garamond Premier Pro
by Waveney Typesetters, Wymondham, Norfolk

Routledge website: http://www.routledge.com
Hakluyt Society website: http://www.hakluyt.com

 Printed in the United Kingdom by Henry Ling Limited

For Micheál

CONTENTS

List of Maps and Illustrations	x
Preface	xii
Acknowledgements	xiii
List of Abbreviations	xv
Symbols, Weights, Measurements and Currency	xvi
Itinerary	xvii

INTRODUCTION 1
1. Brief Biography of John Lee, né Fiott (1783–1866) 2
2. Lee's Walking Tour of Ireland, England and Wales 7
3. Landscapes of the Home Tour 10
4. The Tour in Ireland 12
    a. History and Antiquities 16
    b. Memories of 1798 and 1803 in Lee's Diaries 18
5. Lee as a Scientific Traveller 20
6. Textual Introduction 22
    a. The Text 22
    b. Editorial Conventions 24
    c. Critical Apparatus 24

DIARIES OF A TOUR OF IRELAND, ENGLAND AND WALES IN 1806–1807
1. Tour from London to Holywell in Wales 35
2. Tour from Holywell to Dublin and Fermoy 88
3. Mallow to Bantry 179
4. Bantry to Castlemain 196
5. Killarney to Dublin 234

APPENDIX 1. Sketchbooks of Lee's Tour in Ireland, England and Wales 309
6. Sketchbook, 1806 309
7. Sketchbook, 1806–7 319
8. Sketchbook, 1807 329

APPENDIX 2. Correspondence of John Lee (né Fiott) Relating to Visits to Ireland in 1806–7 and 1857 340

BIBLIOGRAPHY 345

INDEX 366

LIST OF MAPS AND ILLUSTRATIONS

Maps

Map 1.	Lee's route through England and Wales, 31 July–29 August 1806.	26
Map 2.	Lee's route through Ireland, 30 August 1806–6 March 1807.	27
Map 3.	Lee's route through Ireland, detail. Showing his route from Dublin to Ninemilehouse, 5–19 September 1806; and from Castletown to Dublin, 29–30 January 1807.	28
Map 4.	Lee's route through Ireland, detail. Showing his route from Clonmel to Mallow, 19–30 September 1806; from Mallow to Inchigeelagh, 1–9 October 1806; and from Loghill to Roscrea, 20 November 1806–29 January 1807.	29
Map 5.	Lee's route through Ireland, detail. Showing his route from Inchigeelagh to Bantry, 8–10 October 1806; from Bantry to Killarney, 11–30 October 1806; and from Killarney to Loghill, 30 October–20 November 1806.	30
Map 6.	Lee's route through Ireland, detail. Showing his route from Dublin to Ninemilehouse, 5–19 September 1806; from Castletown to Dublin and Drogheda, 29–30 January 1807; and from Dublin to Drogheda, 18–19 February 1807.	31

Illustrations

Frontispiece: Portrait of John Lee (né Fiott), by Thomas Herbert Maguire, 1849. Copyright National Portrait Gallery, London (NPG D37240).

Figures 1–14 are reproduced by kind permission of the Master and Fellows of St John's College, Cambridge.

Figure 1.	'Sketch of w*ha*t seems to be the plan of the Physic garden at Cambridge'. By John Lee, 31 July 1806. Lee seems to have titled the sketch at a later date and in fact it matches his description of the garden at Oxford (SJC, MS U.30 (1), f. 8v).	39
Figure 2.	Two sketches of moulds seen at the Royal China Manufactory, Worcester. By John Lee, 4 August 1806 (SJC, MS U.30 (1), f. 21v).	48
Figure 3.	Sketches of furnaces seen at the Royal China Manufactory, Worcester. By John Lee, 4 August 1806 (SJC, MS U.30 (1), f. 22v).	49
Figure 4.	'Sketch of the Country round the Wrekin as seen from the Top'. By John Lee, 8 August 1806 (SJC, MS U.30 (1), f. 44v).	67

LIST OF MAPS AND ILLUSTRATIONS

Figure 5. Sketch of ruined church and churchyard at Old Connaught, Co. Wicklow, as described in SJC, MS U.30 (2), f. 37v (p. 107). By John Lee, 3 September 1806 (SJC, MS U.30 (6), f. 47r). 108

Figure 6. 'View on the road within 3 miles of Blessingtown of the Welp [Whelp] rock from some cottages[.] At this spot the shower came on and while my companions the soldiers were sheltering themselves, this was scetched [sic]', as described in SJC, MS U.30 (2), f. 56v (p. 121). By John Lee, 8 September 1806 (SJC, MS U.30 (6), f. 54r). 122

Figure 7. 'Curious holly at 7 Churches [Glendalough]', as described in SJC, MS U.30 (2), f. 68v (p. 129). By John Lee, 11 September 1806 (SJC, MS U.30 (6), f. 61r). 130

Figure 8. Two sketch maps of roads around Annamoe, Co. Wicklow, showing relative locations of Annamoe Bridge, Roundwood, and the nearby barracks, as described in SJC, MS U.30 (2), ff. 69v–70v (pp. 129, 131). The map on the right is a magnification of a section of the map on the left. By John Lee, 11 September 1806 (SJC, MS U.30 (2), f. 90r). 131

Figure 9. Plan of Carlow castle. By John Lee, 17 September 1806 (SJC, MS U.30 (2), f. 102r). 147

Figure 10. Sketch of water pump mechanism in Youghal baths, as described in SJC, MS U.30 (2), ff. 126v–127v (pp. 158–60). By John Lee, 23 September 1806 (SJC, MS U.30 (2), f. 127v). 159

Figure 11. 'View of a white rock and bridge over the river which runs through Lord Mount Cashels grounds. The road to Fermoy from Kilworth September 28'. The scene is described in SJC, MS U.30 (2), f. 145v (p. 171). By John Lee, 28 September 1806 (SJC, MS U.30 (2), f. 103r). 172

Figure 12. 'Tower in Lord Mount Cashel grounds near Fermoy September 28'. The scene is described in SJC, MS U.30 (2), f. 145v (pp. 171, 174). By John Lee, 28 September 1806 (SJC, MS U.30 (2), f. 121r). 173

Figure 13. 'Views of the horse bridge on the Bank of the river going up to Killaloe January 27'. Killaloe is described at SJC, MS U.30 (5), f. 51v (pp. 276, 278). By John Lee, 27 January 1807 (SJC, MS U.30 (8), ff. 6v–7r). 277

Figure 14. Sketch, 'Tower at Roscrea January 30 February 4', described in SJC, MS U.30 (5), f. 55v (p. 281). The date of the sketch is more likely 29 January 1807, as recorded in Lee's diary. By John Lee (SJC, MS U.30 (8), ff. 32v–33r). 282

Figure 15. Illustrated heading of a letter from John Lee to Joseph Bonomi, 14 September 1857, with an engraving of 'THE MONSTER TELESCOPE' at Parsonstown (Cambridge University Library, Add. 9389/2/L/97). 343

PREFACE

This book is an edited and annotated transcription of five manuscript diaries created by John Lee, né Fiott (1783–1866) during a walking tour through parts of England, Wales and Ireland between 31 July 1806 and 6 March 1807. It also includes, as appendices, three sketchbooks and two letters relating to that walking tour, and a letter relating to a return visit to Ireland in 1857. The original manuscript diaries and sketchbooks are held at St John's College Library, University of Cambridge ('Diaries and Sketchbooks of Tour from London to Ireland, August 1806–March 1807', SJC, MSS U.30 (1–8)). This is the first time that these diaries have been published. The numbered titles Lee gave to each of his eight diaries, written in ink inside their front covers, are retained in this edition as chapter headings.

Lee had just completed a BA degree at Cambridge when he made this tour. He departed from London and travelled through Oxford, along the Severn and through the Vale of Llangollen, before crossing the Irish Sea to Dublin. From there, he went south through the Wicklow Mountains and on to the cities of Kilkenny, Waterford, Cork and Limerick, and the celebrated Lakes of Killarney. His private observations form a useful addition to the existing corpus of early nineteenth-century accounts of Ireland. The memory of the 1798 rebellion is vivid in Lee's diaries, as he records the stories and experiences of those who participated in or witnessed violent events. Those events played a key part in Ireland's accession to the Union in 1801, and Lee's diaries demonstrate his engagement with the new, fourth, kingdom of the Union. Despite this political unification, as discussed further in the Introduction, the continuing cultural, social and economic distance between Britain and Ireland in the period is well borne out in Lee's account.

This edition aims to present the original text as accurately as possible, but is not a facsimile version. As explained in detail in the Introduction, the presentation of Lee's diaries posed a range of challenges for the editor, not least his fondness for abbreviations and symbols, his use of a numerical code, and his varying pagination systems. Every effort has been made in the explanatory notes to identify for the reader the people and places Lee mentions, but in some cases this has not been possible. The absence of an explanatory note indicates that no useful additional information was found. The editor offers the text as a resource upon which local historians and other researchers may build.

ACKNOWLEDGEMENTS

This project has received generous assistance from institutions in the United Kingdom, Canada and Ireland. An Overseas Visiting Scholarship at St John's College, University of Cambridge (2010) facilitated the initial transcription of the manuscript diaries. The project advanced with the support of a Marie Curie COFUND/Irish Research Council postdoctoral mobility fellowship (2010–13) held at the Institute for the History and Philosophy of Science and Technology at University of Toronto in 2010–12, and at the History Department at National University of Ireland Maynooth in 2012–13. The University of Greenwich provided research support in 2014–15, and the Hakluyt Society generously provided research funding in the project's final stages.

These diaries and letters are published by permission of the Master and Fellows of St John's College, Cambridge. Kathryn McKee and her colleagues were always welcoming and helpful during my many enjoyable visits to St John's College library over the life of this project. I also benefited from the expertise and patience of staff at the following libraries: the British Library; the Caird Library at the National Maritime Museum, Greenwich; Cambridge University Library; the Centre for Buckinghamshire Studies, Aylesbury; and the National Library of Ireland, Dublin.

For long-term mentorship, encouragement and guidance, I sincerely thank Professor R. V. Comerford, Dr David Lederer, Professor Anngret Simms, and Dr Jacinta Prunty, who first introduced me to Lee's diaries. Dr Robin Glasscock read an early draft of the Welsh and English sections of the text and was a kindly guide and sponsor during my fellowship at St John's. Dr Liam Chambers generously read and commented on the introduction. For help with Welsh place names, I thank Dr David Parsons of the Place-Names of Wales Project at University of Wales Centre for Advanced Welsh and Celtic Studies. I am particularly grateful to Dr Chris L. Nighman, Associate Professor in the History Department and coordinator of the Medieval Studies Program, Wilfrid Laurier University, Waterloo, Ontario, Canada, who helped with transcription of the Latin passages and provided translations. Other help with epitaphs was provided by Joyce Lorimer, Hakluyt Society series editor, and Thari Zweers. I am indebted to the expertise, advice and guidance of Hakluyt Society editor Gloria Clifton, and thank David Cox for professionally and efficiently translating my hand-drawn route maps into a useful and readable format. Any errors that remain are my own.

In late 2010, I had the pleasure of discussing Lee with the late Professor W. R. Mead in the warm surroundings of the Centre for Buckinghamshire Studies. Then, and in our subsequent correspondence, I was greatly encouraged by Professor Mead's enthusiasm for this project and his conviction of the importance of Lee's travel diaries and sketchbooks as a historical source. I regret that he did not live to see this edition published.

For moral support, encouragement, hospitality and welcome distractions, I thank my family, Dr Susan Grant, Dr Georgina Laragy and Dr David Murphy, Dr Shane

McCorristine and Corinna Connolly, Roisín Thurstan, and former colleagues at the Department of History, Politics and Social Studies at the University of Greenwich. Micheál Lavelle has lived with John Lee for as long as I have, and I thank him for retracing some of Lee's steps around Ireland and Wales with me.

LIST OF ABBREVIATIONS

BAAS	British Association for the Advancement of Science
BCE	before Christian era
BL	British Library
CBS	Centre for Buckinghamshire Studies, Aylesbury
CE	Christian era
Co.	County
CUL	Cambridge University Library
cwt	hundredweight, equal to 112 lb or 50.8 kg
d	*denarii*, penny or pence
DIB	*Cambridge Dictionary of Irish Biography*, online edition
dwt(s)	pennyweight(s)
E	East
G, gs	guinea, guineas
ha	hectare
IHTA	*Irish Historic Towns Atlas*
Ir.	Irish language (Gaeilge)
km	kilometres
L	left
l	*libri*, pounds (currency)
lb(s)	pound(s) (weight)
LED	Landed Estates Database
MS, MSS	manuscript, manuscripts
N	North
NIAH	National Inventory of Architectural Heritage
no, nos	number, numbers
ODNB	*Oxford Dictionary of National Biography*, online edition
OED	*Oxford English Dictionary*, online edition
OS	Ordnance Survey
penny/p~ wt(s)	pennyweight(s)
R, Rt	right
S, Shgs, Ss	shilling(s)
S	South
SE	South-east
SW	South-west
SJC	St John's College Library, Cambridge
U	you
W	West
Yd, yds	yard, yards

SYMBOLS, WEIGHTS, MEASURES AND CURRENCY

Symbols

O^r	circular
÷, ÷d	divides, divided
=	equal, equal to
N°	number
∥	parallel
⊥^{r}	perpendicular
∴	therefore
Δ	triangular

Weights and Measures

English mile	=	1.61 kilometres
Foot	=	30.48 centimetres
Gallon	=	4.55 litres
Hogshead	=	a unit of measurement for liquids (*OED*), varying according to the liquid
Inch	=	2.54 centimetres
Irish mile	=	the customary length of a mile in Ireland, approx. 2,048 metres (*OED*)
Ounce	=	28.35 grams
Perch	=	5.5 yards = 5.03 metres
Pint	=	0.57 litres
Pound	=	453.59 grams
Ton	=	1,015.87 kilograms
Yard	=	91.44 centimetres

Currency

The British currency in John Lee's time divided the pound sterling into 20 shillings, each shilling consisting of 12 pence, or 240 pence to a pound.

Farthing	=	a quarter of a penny
Guinea	=	one pound and one shilling

ITINERARY

Uncertain overnight stops are given in square brackets.

1. Tour from London to Holywell in Wales

31 July 1806, Thursday. London — Hounslow — Slough — Maidenhead — Marlow — Oxford
1 August 1806, Friday. Oxford
2 August 1806, Saturday. Oxford — Woodstock — Chipping Norton — Broadway Hill — Worcester
3–4 August 1806, Sunday–Monday. Worcester
5 August 1806, Tuesday. Worcester — Henwick Hill — Hallow Park — Holt — Stourport — Bewdley
6 August 1806, Wednesday. Bewdley — Hampton Lode — Bridgnorth — Apley — Coalport — Coalbrook Dale — Iron Bridge
7 August 1806, Thursday. Iron Bridge — Coalbrook Dale
8 August 1806, Friday. Coalbrook Dale — Buildwas — Wrekin — Atcham
9 August 1806, Saturday. Atcham — Shrewsbury — Nesscliffe — Shrewsbury
10 August 1806, Sunday. Shrewsbury — Oswestry — Selattyn — Chirk — Oswestry — Whittington
11 August 1806, Monday. Whittington — Oswestry — Chirk Castle — Llangollen
12 August 1806, Tuesday. Llangollen — Llantysilio — Pontcysyllte — Cefn Mawr — Wynnstay — Ruabon
14 August 1806, Thursday. Ruabon — Wrexham
15 August 1806, Friday. Wrexham — Acton Park — Gresford — Wrexham
16 August 1806, Saturday. Wrexham — Caergwrle — Mold — Holywell

2. Tour from Holywell to Dublin and Fermoy

22 August 1806, Friday. Holywell — Mostyn — Trelawnyd — Gwaenysgor — Dyserth Castle — Rhuddlan — St Asaph
23 August 1806, Saturday. St Asaph — Abergele — Conwy
24 August 1806, Sunday. Conwy
25 August 1806, Monday. Conwy — Llandudno
26 August 1806, Tuesday. Llandudno — Dwygyfylchi — Penmaenmawr — Conwy
27 August 1806, Wednesday. Conwy — Tal-y-Cafn — Caerhun — Llanbedr-y-Cennin — Gwydir Castle — Llanrwst
28 August 1806, Thursday. Llanrwst — Gwydir — Pont-y-Pair — Rhyd-Lanfair
29 August 1806, Friday. Rhyd-Lanfair — Capel Curig — Bangor — Holyhead — sail to Dublin
30 August 1806, Saturday. Dublin Bay — Dublin

xvii

JOHN (FIOTT) LEE IN IRELAND, ENGLAND AND WALES, 1806–1807

31 August 1806, Sunday. Dublin
1 September 1806, Monday. Dublin — Malahide
2 September 1806, Tuesday. Malahide — Dublin
3 September 1806, Wednesday. Dublin — Taney — Kilgobbin — Bray
5 September 1806, Friday. Bray — Powerscourt — Lovers Leap — Bray
6 September 1806, Saturday. Bray — Kilmacanogue — Delgany — Newtownmountkennedy
7 September 1806, Sunday. Newtownmountkennedy — Luggala Lodge
8 September 1806, Monday. Luggala Lodge — Oldcourt — Blessington — Ballymore Eustace
9 September 1806, Tuesday. Ballymore Eustace — Russborough House — Poulaphouca — Russborough House
10 September 1806, Wednesday. Russborough House — Blessington — Luggala Lodge
11 September 1806, Thursday. Luggala Lodge — Glenmacnass — Glendalough — Roundwood — Annamoe — Newtownmountkennedy
12 September 1806, Friday. Newtownmountkennedy — Dunran Demesne — Killiskey — Devils Glen — Rathnew
13 September 1806, Saturday. Rathnew — Rathdrum — Cronebane mine — Arklow
14 September 1806, Sunday. Arklow
15 September 1806, Monday. Arklow — Kilbride — Pollahoney Bridge — Rostygah — Ballinasilloge — Moneyteige — Kilpipe — Tinahely
16 September 1806, Tuesday. Tinahely — Clonmore — Acaun Bridge — Rathmore Bridge — Carlow
17 September 1806, Wednesday. Carlow — Leighlinbridge — Royal Oak — Kilkenny
18 September 1806, Thursday. Kilkenny — Dunmore Cave — Kilkenny
19 September 1806, Friday. Kilkenny — Callan — Ninemilehouse — Clonmel
20–21 September 1806, Saturday–Sunday. Clonmel
22 September 1806, Monday. Clonmel — Newcastle — Cappoquin (onwards by boat) — Dromana —Villierstown — Youghal
23–24 September 1806, Tuesday–Wednesday. Youghal
25 September 1806, Thursday. Youghal — Cappoquin — Lismore
26 September 1806, Friday. Lismore — Owennashad Glen — Lismore
27 September 1806, Saturday. Lismore — Castle Richards — Fermoy
28 September 1806, Sunday. Fermoy — Moorepark — Kilworth — Fermoy
29 September 1806, Monday. Fermoy — Tobernahulla — Kilworth — Fermoy
30 September 1806, Tuesday. Fermoy — Ballyhooly — Killavullen — Ballymagooly — Mallow

3. Mallow to Bantry

1 October 1806, Wednesday. Mallow
2 October 1806, Thursday. Mallow — Ballynamona — Ballyclough — Bottlehill — Sixmilewater — Carrignavar — Cork
3 October 1806, Friday. Cork — Lapps Island — Glanmire — Little Island — Hop Island — Passage West — Haulbowline Island — Cobh — Spike Island — Cobh — Cork
4 October 1806, Saturday. Cork — Glanmire — Cork
5 October 1806, Sunday. Cork — Sundays Well — Cork

6 List October 1806, Monday. Cork — Blarney — Iniscarra — Ovens
7 October 1806, Tuesday. Ovens — Kilcrea — Cronody — Dripsey Castle — [Clashanure]
8 October 1806, Wednesday. [Clashanure] — Carrigadrohid — Caum — Inchigeelagh — Kilbarry
9 October 1806, Thursday. Kilbarry — Inchigeelagh — Kilmore — Gougane Barra — Ballingeary
10 October 1806, Friday. Ballingeary — Doughill — Inchiroe — Bantry

4. Bantry to Castlemain

11 October 1806, Saturday. Bantry — Glengarriff — Bantry
12 October 1806, Sunday. Bantry — Chapel Island — Whiddy Island — Bantry
13 October 1806, Monday. Bantry — Glengarriff — Bantry
14 October 1806, Tuesday. Bantry and surrounding area
15 October 1806, Wednesday. Bantry — Kenmare by boat
16 October 1806, Thursday. Kenmare — Killarney
17 October 1806, Friday. Killarney and surrounding area
18–19 October 1806, Saturday–Sunday. Killarney
20 October 1806, Monday. Killarney — Gap of Dunloe — Killarney
21 October 1806, Tuesday. Killarney and surrounding area
22 October 1806, Wednesday. Killarney — Dunloe Castle — Foiladuane — Killarney
23 October 1806, Thursday. Killarney — Mangerton — Killarney
24–27 October 1806, Friday–Monday. Killarney
28 October 1806, Tuesday. Killarney — Dinis Island — Eagle's Nest — Killarney
29 October 1806, Wednesday. Killarney
30 October 1806, Thursday. Killarney — Tralee
31 October 1806, Friday. Tralee — Derrymore — Killelton — Kilgobbin Church — Cappaclough — Castlegregory — Killiney — Stradbally — Liscarney — Cloghane
1 November 1806, Saturday. Cloghane — Connor Hill — Dingle
2 November 1806, Sunday. Dingle
3 November 1806, Monday. Dingle — Ventry — Dunquin
4 November 1806, Tuesday. Dunquin — Dunmore Head — Dunquin
5 November 1806, Wednesday. Dunquin — Blasket Islands — Dunquin — Ventry — Dingle
6 November 1806, Thursday. Dingle — Ballinclare
7 November 1806, Friday. Ballinclare
8 November 1806, Saturday. Ballinclare — Castlemaine — Milltown
9 November 1806, Sunday. Milltown — Killarney
10 November 1806, Monday. Killarney

5. Killarney to Dublin

14 November 1806, Friday. Killarney — Tralee — Ardfert
15 November 1806, Saturday. Ardfert — Ballyheige — Ballingarry Island — Kerry Head
16 November 1806, Sunday. Kerry Head — Ballyheige — Ardfert
17 November 1806, Monday. Ardfert — Tralee
18 November 1806, Tuesday. Tralee — Abbeydorney — Listowel

19 November 1806, Wednesday. Listowel — Newtown Sandes (Moyvane) — Glin
20 November 1806, Thursday. Glin — Loghill — Cappagh — Askeaton
21 November 1806, Friday. Askeaton — Adare — Limerick
22–27 November 1806, Saturday–Thursday. Limerick
28 November 1806, Friday. Limerick — Doneraile — Clogheen
29 November 1806, Saturday. Clogheen — Doneraile — Clogheen
30 November 1806, Sunday. Clogheen — Doneraile — Clogheen
1 December 1806, Monday. Clogheen — Doneraile — Clogheen
2 December 1806, Tuesday. Clogheen — Twopothouse — Buttevant — Clogheen
3 December 1806, Wednesday. Clogheen — Doneraile — Castletownroche — Doneraile
4 December 1806, Thursday. Doneraile — Mallow — Millstreet — Sixmilebridge — Killarney
5–8 December 1806, Friday–Monday. Killarney
9 December 1806, Tuesday. Killarney — Millstreet — Ten Mile House
10–11 December 1806, Wednesday–Thursday. Ten Mile House
12 December 1806, Friday. Ten Mile House — Dripsey — Athnowen
13 December 1806, Saturday. Athnowen — Ovens — Cork
14 December 1806, Sunday–10 January 1807, Saturday. Cork
11 January 1807, Sunday. Cork — Ten Mile House — Blarney — Cork
12–14 January 1807, Monday–Wednesday. Cork
15 January 1807, Thursday. Cork — Glanmire — Midleton — Youghal
16 January 1807, Friday. Youghal — Clashmore — Dungarvan
17 January 1807, Saturday. Dungarvan — Kilmacthomas — Newtown
18 January 1807, Sunday. Newtown — Waterford
19 January 1807, Monday. Waterford
20 January 1807, Tuesday. Waterford — Carrick-on-Suir — Clonmel
21 January 1807, Wednesday. Clonmel — Cashel
22 January 1807, Thursday. Cashel — Lisheen
23 January 1807, Friday. Lisheen — Holycross — [Cashel]
24 January 1807, Saturday. [Cashel] — Golden — Thomastown — Dundrum — [Lisheen]
25 January 1807, Sunday. [Lisheen] — Pallas — Limerick
26 January 1807, Monday. Limerick
27 January 1807, Tuesday. Limerick — Anacotty — Castleconnell — O'Briens Bridge — Killaloe
28 January 1807, Wednesday. Killaloe — Nenagh
29 January 1807, Thursday. Nenagh — Toomyvara — Moneygall — Dunkerrin — Roscrea — Castletown — Maryborough (Portlaoise)
30 January 1807, Friday. Maryborough (Portlaoise) — Monasterevin — Kildare — Curragh — Naas — Clondalkin — Dublin
31 January 1807, Saturday–17 February 1807, Tuesday. Dublin
18 February 1807, Wednesday. Dublin — Drogheda — site of Battle of Boyne — Drogheda
19 February 1807, Thursday. Drogheda — Dublin
20 February 1807, Friday–6 March 1807, Friday. Dublin

INTRODUCTION

In its long history, the Hakluyt Society has published critical editions of remarkable accounts of modern and early modern travels on all continents and oceans of the world. A 'home tour' of England, Wales and Ireland in 1806–7 may seem anomalous in such a series. However, during his walking tour of Ireland John Lee (né Fiott) experienced people and histories far removed from those with which he was familiar, and that exerted no small influence over British political and cultural life in the period. English observations on Ireland in the years immediately following the Act of Union (1801) have taken on a new significance in recent years. This is due in no small part to the development of the 'four nations' approach to British history, generating new critical approaches to the ways in which distinctive regional identities were fashioned and negotiated within Britain, both in terms of differences and similarities.[1]

Historic travel accounts have undergone a reappraisal in recent years, attracting new attention from scholars for their depth and breadth of content, as records of intercultural contact and as invaluable sources for local history, folklore, the natural sciences, and more. Lee's diaries are no exception. Rich in detail and thematic scope, they record a wealth of experiences and observations, from the colleges of Oxford to the backstreets of Dublin, from the mines of Wales to the remains of Ireland's early Christian monasteries. Lee described and sketched sites of antiquarian interest and peasant cabins. He recorded his conversations with landowners, labourers, rural children, innkeepers and market sellers, reflecting the varied nature of his interactions with a spectrum of English, Welsh and Irish society. In Dublin, he was introduced to the highest echelons of the British administration, enjoying an audience with the Lord-lieutenant at Dublin Castle, but he spent most of his time in Ireland in the company of military men, middling gentry and farmers. The variety of his experiences reflects the strong local and provincial identities of early nineteenth-century Britain. Lee hinted at the continued ubiquity of the Welsh and Irish languages in rural areas and took lessons in the Irish language during his stay in Cork city, but he was surprised to encounter Irish speakers in urban areas.[2] The uncertainty and idiosyncrasy of his rendering of Irish- and Welsh-language place names is a reminder that Lee made his tour three decades before the Ordnance Survey standardized and Anglicized these place names.

Lee wrote almost every day for just over seven months, detailing everything from industry to natural resources, from recent history to architecture, from the agricultural economy to private art collections. This array of information is crammed into five small pocket notebooks, in a tight scrawl alternating between ink and pencil. His diaries are

---

[1] Smyth, 'Introduction', p. 10.
[2] In the south, south-west and west of Ireland, up to 90% of the population born in 1771–81 were Irish-speaking; the figures in Leinster were lower. See FitzGerald, 'Estimates for Baronies'.

extremely dense, both in terms of content and presentation. His handwriting is small and he was fond of abbreviations, but as many folios remain blank this does not seem to have been motivated by a concern to economize on paper. Some of his experiences and impressions are recounted in brief, tantalizing glimpses, demonstrating the personal nature of the manuscript and the immediate function of the diaries as an aid to memory. He also occasionally made rough, fragmentary notes or memoranda in pencil with the intention of translating them into longhand narrative at a later date. These disjointed notes are retained in this edition and are indicated to the reader by a footnote. Their value lies in their status as immediate, on-the-spot observations – ephemeral notes that are usually lost during the publication process. On other occasions, Lee employed a numerical code that has been reproduced in full in this edition, but has not been solved. This code may record activities that would have met with disapproval or censure.

This edition contains reproductions of a selection of Lee's many on-the-spot sketches, which were made in his five diaries and three sketchbooks. It has not been possible to reproduce all of his many sketches in this book because of their number and because the majority were left unfinished. Rough but detailed notes and descriptions accompany the sketches, supplementing Lee's written observations and providing more detail on the landscapes he valued as picturesque, beautiful or sublime (discussed in more detail below). His notes detail the qualities of the foreground, middle ground and background to each scene, and indicate the presence of focal points like ruins or towers. Most importantly, the sketchbooks indicate a never-realized intention to complete the sketches at a later date.

1. Brief Biography of John Lee, né Fiott (1783–1866)

John Lee was born John Fiott in Totteridge, Hertfordshire, on 28 April 1783. He was the eldest son of John Fiott, a merchant, and Harriet Lee of Hartwell, Buckinghamshire. Harriet Lee died in 1794, followed by John Fiott in 1797, leaving their seven surviving children under the guardianship of their uncle, William Lee Antonie of Colworth House, Bedfordshire (1764–1815). In 1815, in fulfilment of the requirements of an inheritance from Lee Antonie, John Fiott assumed the name of Lee by royal licence. His full, busy and varied life is detailed in the *ODNB* and in Hanley's pamphlet *Dr John Lee* (1983). Therefore, this brief biography will only cover details relevant to the diaries annotated in this book and to his life's travels.

In 1801, Lee entered the University of Cambridge, graduating BA in 1806. Surviving personal correspondence of spring 1806 indicates that he had hoped to secure a fellowship at Cambridge immediately, but his friends thought that it was more likely that he would be successful in the following year.[1] It seems that his failure to secure a fellowship in 1806 precipitated his decision to embark on the tour described in this book.

This was the first of at least four tours that Lee made in his life. He later travelled in Scandinavia, the Mediterranean and the Middle East (as described in more detail below). He also returned to Ireland on 2–14 September 1857, a short visit recorded in a letter to

---

[1] St John's College, Cambridge [hereafter SJC], Letter of T. F. Twigge to John Lee, 27 Feb. 1806, MS Box 1a, Doc. 18; SJC, Letter of Thomas Barber to John Lee, 18 Mar. 1806, MS Box 1a, Doc. 19.

INTRODUCTION

the sculptor and Egyptologist Joseph Bonomi (1796–1878).[1] The stationery Lee used was appropriately decorative, headed by a lithograph of the 'Leviathan of Parsonstown' (Figure 15), the six-foot telescope constructed at Birr Castle in 1845 by William Parsons, 3rd Earl of Rosse (1800–1867), with whom Lee had at least a little subsequent correspondence.[2] Accompanying Lee was one 'Mr Ellis FRAS', probably the astronomer William Ellis (1828–1916). The visit appears to have had two objectives. The first was to attend the twenty-seventh meeting of the British Association for the Advancement of Science (BAAS) in Dublin (26 August–6 September 1857), one of the most important forums for the physical sciences and just one of the many societies in which Lee was active.[3] The second object was to visit observatories. The pair visited Edward Joshua Cooper's (1798–1863) observatory at Markree Castle, Co. Sligo and the Birr Leviathan, where the weather was unfortunately 'very unfavourable for observation'. Their route from Sligo to Birr diverted westwards to Connemara through Castlebar (Co. Mayo), Clifden and Portumna (Co. Galway). Connemara had been absent from Lee's 1806–7 itinerary and had, in the intervening fifty years, developed as a destination for travellers. It is unfortunate that no more detailed account of this short visit has been located, as Lee may have found Ireland greatly changed since 1806–7, particularly given the enormous socio-economic consequences of the Great Famine of 1845–52.

Shortly after completing his walking tour of England, Wales and Ireland, Lee embarked on a two-year residence in Scandinavia, supported by a travelling bachelorship from the University of Cambridge. The fellowship required Lee to write monthly reports in Latin, detailing the 'religion, learning, laws, politics, customs, manners and rarities, natural and artificial, which [he] shall find worth observing', but he appears to have written only one such report.[4] His travels in Scandinavia – including the cities of Copenhagen, Stockholm and Gothenburg – and the year he spent at Uppsala University are described in five notebooks and sketchbooks (BL, Add MS 47493 B–D; SJC, MSS U.30 (9–10). Lee described his activities in Scandinavia to his peer at St John's College, Hugh Percy (1785–1847, later 3rd Duke of Northumberland) in letters now preserved on microfilm at the British Library. Lee did keep a diary in Scandinavia – he referred to it in his letters to Percy and it is cited in the traveller and mineralogist Edward Daniel Clarke's *Travels in Scandinavia* – but it has unfortunately been lost.[5] He returned to Cambridge in June 1809 to take his MA degree.

In 1810, Lee set out on a five-year tour of the Eastern Mediterranean. Visiting Gibraltar, Malta, Smyrna, Constantinople, Greece, Egypt, the Levant and the Holy Land,

---

[1] Cambridge University Library [hereafter CUL], John Lee to Joseph Bonomi, 14 Sept. 1857, Add MS 9389/2/L/97. See Appendix 2.

[2] Lambeth Palace, Correspondence of John Lee with William Parsons, 3rd Earl of Rosse, 16 Mar. 1864, MS 2879, f. 301. For Figure 15, see below, p. 343.

[3] See below, p. 5.

[4] Hanley, *Dr John Lee*, p. 4; CUL, Fiott, Documents relating to Worts bequest, 1808–9, MS Oo.6.96 (19).

[5] British Library, London [hereafter BL], Letter of John Fiott to Lord Percy, 22 May 1808, MSS of the Duke of Northumberland, Letters and Papers, vol. 65, 1808–9, Alnwick Castle, no. 65, 23/1. BL microfilm no. 311 (hereafter Alnwick papers). Clarke, *Travels in Scandinavia*, II, pp. 84–5n, 241n, 402n, 516–17n; III, pp. 3, 12n, 20n, 24n, 112n, 237n, 353n. An appendix to Clarke's account, a note on the mine at Falun, was translated by Lee (ibid., II, pp. 578–80). A sketch by Lee is reproduced in ibid., III, p. 1. On Lee's residence in Scandinavia, see Mead, 'The Finnish Journey'; 'Dr John Lee of Hartwell and his Swedish Journey'; 'A British Visitor to Skåne'; and Schiötz, *Utlenders Reiser i Norge*, pp. 120–21.

he collected antiquities and artefacts which would later form part of his renowned personal library and museum at Hartwell House.[1] Lee joined the circle of British Romantics in the Mediterranean and enjoyed the company of Lord Byron during three months in Athens.[2] The architect Charles Robert Cockerell (1788–1863) claimed in December 1811 to have found Lee's name (as Fiott) carved in a cave on Mount Ida, Crete.[3] The ancient riches of Egypt were first revealed to Europeans following Napoleon's invasion in 1798, and Lee joined in the subsequent hunt for Egyptian and Greco-Roman antiquities.[4] In May 1811, he became the first European to sketch the tombs around the pyramids of Giza. These sketches were later reproduced in the German periodical, *Jahrbücher der Literatur* in 1838.[5] He continued on through the Holy Land, Tripoli and Aleppo to Same in the Ionian Islands, where he made archaeological excavations that would later be published in a short twelve-page pamphlet.[6]

Lee's travels in the Mediterranean and Near East formed the basis of his private museum and contributed materially to the establishment of his reputation as an authority on antiquities. Throughout his life he corresponded with leading international scholars, while receiving Greek, Arabic and hieroglyphic manuscripts and inscriptions from antiquaries working in the Near East.[7] His private museum was sufficiently respected to attract donations of curiosities from the likes of John Ross, the Arctic explorer.[8] The international reach of Lee's scholarly network, with correspondents across Europe, South Africa and the Middle East, reflects the transnationalism of imperial science and the connections by which it was underpinned.

The death of William Lee Antonie in September 1815 saw John Lee inherit a number of estates, but their encumbrances led him to return to Cambridge. He graduated LLD and gained admission to Doctors' Commons in 1816. An important change occurred in 1827, when he inherited Hartwell House, the seat of his mother's family since 1617. This marked the beginning of a very different period in his life, during which he chose to maintain his practice in ecclesiastical law and his country estates while simultaneously making Hartwell House a centre of scientific and antiquarian inquiry, with its observatory and museum. He now possessed the means necessary to pursue his antiquarian and scientific interests.

The figure of the 'gentleman of science' can be idealized in histories of science. With independent means, such individuals were free to pursue the avenues of inquiry they wished, seemingly free of state or other influences. Lee fits the profile of the disinterested polymath, selflessly granting access to his observatory, library and museum to others. His home served as an unofficial research institute that hosted visiting scholars, as the founding site of a number of scholarly societies and as a gathering-place for the learned. From the 1830s, Lee devoted enormous energy to scholarship and was active in an array

---

[1] On the contents of Lee's library and museum, see Bonomi, *Catalogue of the Egyptian Antiquities*; *Catalogue of Theological Books*; Filippoupoliti, 'Specializing the Private Collection'; McAlpine, *A Catalogue of the Law Library*; [Lee], *Oriental Manuscripts*; Sharpe, *The Triple Mummy Case*; Smyth, *Descriptive Catalogue*.
[2] Hanley, *Dr John Lee*, pp. 5–6; *The Georgian Era*, III, p. 470.
[3] Tregaskis, *Beyond the Grand Tour*, p. 182, n. 32.
[4] See Tregaskis, *Beyond the Grand Tour* and Angelomatis-Tsougarakis, *The Eve of the Greek Revival*.
[5] 'Übersicht von zwanzig Reisen in die Türken', facing p. 44.
[6] Lee, *Antiquarian Researches*.
[7] BL, General correspondence of John Lee, 1809–39, Add MS 47490, ff. 67–241b.
[8] See Byrne, *Geographies of the Romantic North*, pp. 93–6.

INTRODUCTION

of societies. He was a founding member of the Astronomical Society, the British Meteorological Society, the Royal Geographical Society and the Chronological Society. He was also a member of the Royal Society, the Society of Antiquaries, the Royal Numismatic Society, the Society of Arts, the Geological Society, the British Archaeological Association, the Syro-Egyptian Society, the Asiatic Society of Bengal and the Buckinghamshire Architectural and Archaeological Society, and he regularly attended BAAS meetings. While he published very little of his own work, his encouragement and facilitation of the work of others did not go unrecognized. Edward Daniel Clarke named a 'red siliceous substance from Gryphytta' *Leeite*, as Lee was the first to bring a sample to Britain.[1] In July 1817, *The Gentleman's Magazine* publicized Lee's donation of three Greco-Roman antiquities to the Fitzwilliam Museum, Cambridge.[2] In 1852, he featured in Thomas Herbert Maguire's series of lithograph portraits of 'celebrated scientific men,'[3] alongside Charles Darwin, the astronomer Sir George Biddell Airy (1801–92), the botanists Sir William Jackson Hooker (1785–1865) and Joseph Dalton Hooker (1817–1911), the geologists Sir Charles Lyell (1797–1875) and Sir Roderick Murchison (1792–1871), the polar explorer Sir James Clark Ross (1800–1862) and the physicist Sir Edward Sabine (1788–1883).[4] Finally, Lee was, somewhat controversially, elected president of the Royal Astronomical Society in 1861 in preference to George Airy. Constance, Lady Battersea (1843–1931), recalled a childhood visit to Hartwell:

> Hartwell House was an attraction to us in our young years, and we used periodically to visit its strange old owner, the learned Dr. Lee. He would take us into his wonderful and crowded museum, where on one occasion he presented me with a little stuffed bird, hoping that it might prove the forerunner of a collection of my own, for he said that the pleasure of collecting, no matter what, was one of the chief roads that led to a happy life. On one unforgettable starlight night we were admitted to his famous observatory, and invited to look through the telescope, receiving much valuable information at the time. To us the astronomer seemed a very old man, and when, in company with one of his own years, he came to dine at Aston Clinton, we were not astonished at seeing the two aged guests of my parents dropping placidly off to sleep after their repast.[5]

In parallel to his scientific and antiquarian interests, and despite the large sums he expended on travel and the acquisition of artefacts and scientific instruments, in his later years Lee was a social reformer and enlightened philanthropist who gave generously to charitable causes and to the tenants on his estate. He was the driving force behind the foundation of the county infirmary in Aylesbury in 1833 and in 1848 he assisted the endowment of the Aylesbury Mechanics' Institute, with its reading room, library and occasional lectures. He has been remembered as 'a model landlord'[6] who provided new cottages and allotments for his tenants and assisted elective emigration to North America and South Africa. For example, in 1834 he arranged for T. W. Bowler (1812–69), grandson of his housekeeper at Hartwell, to travel to Cape Town as observatory assistant to Sir Thomas Maclear (1794–1879). While Bowler was not suited to astronomy, he did

---

[1] Clarke, 'Further Account of Petalite'.
[2] *The Gentleman's Magazine*, July 1817, p. 58. Lee was referred to as 'Dr Fiott Lee of St John's College'.
[3] See frontispiece.
[4] Exhibition advertised in *The Athenaeum*, 1414, 2 Dec. 1854, p. 1469.
[5] Battersea, *Reminiscences*, pp. 139–40.
[6] Hanley, *Dr John Lee*, p. 10.

go on to become one of the Cape's most noteworthy nineteenth-century landscape artists.[1]

Lee's international network extended beyond the sciences and antiquarianism. He was a committed advocate for temperance and pacifism, particularly from the 1840s onward. In 1848, he organized a temperance meeting at Hartwell, which developed into the annual Hartwell Peace and Temperance Festival and continued for some twenty years, featuring such speakers as the American pacifist Elihu Burritt (1810–79) and the temperance lecturer John Bartholomew Gough (1817–86).[2] He also chaired the committee of the Peace Society for a time.[3] Despite his promotion of temperance and pacifism, in his youth Lee regularly consumed porter, wine and cider, so that his uncle reprimanded him for his wine bill at Cambridge; displayed an active interest in military affairs; and enjoyed associating with active servicemen.[4] His surviving Scandinavian letters and sketchbooks focused largely on military matters, with Lee going so far as to offer his services to the Swedish military (the offer was not accepted).[5] He considered the Irish peasant over-fond of spirituous liquor, but on several occasions he gave money to the poor despite being aware that it would be used for the purchase of whiskey.

In 1833, Lee married Cecilia Rutter, whom he and a contemporary respectively described as a 'person of humble station but of excellent character and good disposition' and as 'a most estimable middle-aged lady'.[6] She died at Hartwell on 1 April 1854, and in November 1855 Lee married Louise Catherine Wilkinson, a woman almost forty years his junior and the eldest daughter of his friend Robert Wilkinson, who ran a private boarding school at Totteridge Park, the old Lee family seat. There was no issue from either marriage. While it was not uncommon for married couples to collaborate on scientific work, only scant evidence has been found of the participation of his first wife in the work ongoing at Hartwell observatory, and none of his second wife. Henry Lawson (1774–1855), who had a private observatory at his home in Hereford, acknowledged Cecilia (née Rutter) Lee's hospitality during his visits to Hartwell, and she communicated remarks made by the well-known chronometer maker Edward John Dent (1790–1853) in relation to his famous instruments to James Epps (1773–1840), assistant astronomer at Hartwell.[7] While Lee advocated female suffrage as an electoral candidate later in life, the early diaries published here contain only a few scattered references to rural women's domestic work, some moral judgments on impoverished urban women and a few remarks on the physical attractiveness of young Irish women.

Lee's obituary emphasized his 'persistence and industry… diligence and ability' and that he was 'emphatically a man of moral courage'.[8] He faded into obscurity rather quickly, but

---

[1] Evans, 'Maclear, Sir Thomas (1794–1879)'.

[2] Hanley, *Dr John Lee*, p. 20. See also the contemporary account of 'The Hartwell Festival' published in *The Colonial Intelligencer*, 41, June 1851, pp. 280–88.

[3] Ceadel, *The Origins of War Prevention*, pp. 193, 301.

[4] Bedfordshire Archives and Records Service, William Lee Antonie to John Fiott, undated letter, Unilever Colworth Estate, Sharnbrook fonds, UN494.

[5] BL, Alnwick papers, John Fiott to Lord Percy, Stockholm, 23 May 1808.

[6] Hanley, *Dr John Lee*, p. 11; Fowler, *Records of Old Times*, pp. 75–6.

[7] Centre for Buckinghamshire Studies, Aylesbury [hereafter CBS], Letter of Henry Lawson to Lee, 24 July 1842, D/X720/6; CBS, Letter of James Epps to Lee, 27 Nov. 1838, D/X720/2. On marital collaboration in the sciences, see Abir-Am and Outram, eds, *Uneasy Careers and Intimate Lives*.

[8] Buxton, 'Obituary', pp. 215, 235.

the bicentenary of his birth in 1983 presented an opportunity to revisit his life and his role in nineteenth-century science. *New Scientist* magazine credited him with 'organising what might be considered the forerunners of today's scientific conferences' and Sir Patrick Moore formally opened a special exhibition at the Centre for Buckinghamshire Studies (then Buckinghamshire Record Office).[1] Despite the popular and local interest in Lee prompted by the bicentenary, the depth and breadth of his scholarly interests is not reflected in published scholarship. The late W. R. Mead uncovered aspects of Lee's Scandinavian tour in a series of published articles, and Lee's private collections are the subject of a detailed essay by Anastasia Filippoupoliti, but the scope of his scientific, antiquarian, political and social interests merits much more attention.[2] It is hoped that this volume will help to ignite increased scholarly interest in his life and work.

Despite the scope of surviving archival resources relating to Lee's life, much of his correspondence is scholarly in nature, revealing little of his personality. The diaries presented here open a window on his beliefs and personality, revealing a romantic wanderer with a mischievous sense of humour, a keen eye for detail and a humane interest in people of all backgrounds.

2. Lee's Walking Tour of Ireland, England and Wales

Lee's diaries never refer directly to Rousseau, that pioneer of romantic solitary walking but, like him, Lee travelled mostly alone and on foot, struggling through bogs and mountains, or enjoying the gentle and easily negotiated towing paths of Ireland's growing canal network. Occasionally, when the landscape became too challenging or time was pressing, he hitched lifts on farmers' and tradesmen's carts, preferring these to the more comfortable coach-and-four usually favoured by genteel travellers, for experience more than economy. (His dash from Limerick to Dublin by post-chaise is the exception, discussed later.) He also enjoyed travelling by boat along the Rivers Severn, Blackwater and Kenmare. His prolonged contact with the landscape in all kinds of weather made his experiences deeply personal and subjective.

He relished solitary contemplation of the landscapes through which he walked, granting as it did the impression of being the first person at a particular spot, or one of only a few to have been there. For example, near Lovers' Leap in Wicklow, he 'went ... a long way back by a path w*hi*ch seems as if on*ly* 6 people had ever been there before'.[3] Any desire for company faded as his tour progressed. In the vicinity of Pontcysyllte aqueduct, he 'wished for a companion to address', but by the time he reached Killarney he had developed a better appreciation for solitude. He so enjoyed the approach to the Lakes of Killarney – 'What can be more grand, more magnificent more sublime more surpassing all the powers of description or narration' – that he concluded, 'A companion here would spoil one to this, for no person could share time to speak the mind and soul is so wrapt up in itself and so full of the sensations which the surrounding objects excite.'[4]

[1] *New Scientist*, 98/1356, 5 May 1983, p. 320.
[2] Mead, 'The Finnish Journey'; 'The Mineralogical Collection'; 'Dr John Lee of Hartwell and his Swedish Journey'; 'A British Visitor to Skåne'. Filippoupoliti, 'Specializing the Private Collection'.
[3] SJC, MS U.30 (2), f. 40v, p. 110.
[4] SJC, MS U.30 (1), f. 61v, p. 82; SJC, MS U.30 (4), f. 10v, p. 203.

The personal motivation behind Lee's walking tour of England, Wales and Ireland in July 1806 to March 1807 was later ascribed to a 'furor for rambling'.[1] Surviving correspondence reveals that Lee's uncle and guardian, William Lee Antonie did not approve of his seemingly aimless wandering. Lee Antonie wrote on 28 December 1806 on the subject of 'money concerns', a subject that the younger man had, in his view, 'taken no notice of'. His uncle's accusation lends added significance to Lee's regular record of expenditure, jotted throughout the diaries.

> I wish to know from you the great advantage you have deriv'd of either, [improvement and economy] from your present residence in Ireland and what are your expectations of your continued residence there to go through the remainder of the Country and in the spring to cross over to Scotland? I perfectly know that travelling over different Country's is a most amusing way of passing the time But without you have a plan in view, for so doing, and without the Means of executing that plan without occurring of great expence when compar'd to the Income of defraying of more expences and above all others at a time when the greatest economy should and must be attended to – I am sure that you will reflect more seriously upon this subject especially when you find that notwithstanding your strict attention to economy you have Bills sent to you to your great surprize, of <u>half as much more</u> as you had suppos'd.[2]

It is possible that, having been forwarded, Antonie's letter may have found Lee at leisure in Cork – where he stayed for four weeks – and that it may have been the cause of his comparatively hasty journey from Limerick to Dublin, made by post-chaise rather than on foot. Lee dashed through the Irish midlands with an altogether different approach than the commitment to pedestrianism that he had previously demonstrated. It appears that he did not make it to Scotland, and it is certain that he was back in Cambridge by July 1807 at the latest, to receive his fellowship and embark for Scandinavia.

From the 1770s, the figure of the pedestrian traveller emerged. Famously, Dorothea and William Wordsworth, Samuel Taylor Coleridge and Robert Southey walked in England, Scotland and Wales from the mid-1790s, and John Thelwall's *The Peripatetic* (1793) elucidated the political and philosophical uses of walking. However, and as Lee found, the pedestrian was not everywhere a lauded figure and commonly aroused suspicion. As Anne Wallace states, their 'mode of travel proclaimed their poverty and therefore the greater probability of their being wanderers with some illicit or economically disruptive motive'.[3] Within his own circle – 'the noblest and most hospitable' – Lee grew irritated by the ubiquity of the opinion that travelling on horseback would be faster and not much more expensive than walking, as they 'Never consider[ed] the independance [sic] of my method of travelling'. He confided to his diary that he preferred being in the open air, 'and have my thoughts and body free instead of being parked up in a cage and travelling like a dead body in a hearse', independent in his thoughts and itinerary. He also argued that walking was faster, what with the trouble

---

[1] Bedfordshire Archives and Records Service, Reverend John Webster Hawksley to William Lee Antonie, undated letter, Unilever Colworth Estate, Sharnbrook fonds, UN319, quoted in Hanley, *Dr John Lee*, p. 4.

[2] SJC, William Lee Antonie to John Fiott, 28 Dec. 1806, MS Box 1a, Doc. 22. This is one of only two extant letters sent to Lee in the period 31 July 1806–6 Mar. 1807, and is reproduced in full at pp. 341–2.

[3] SJC, MS U.30 (5), ff. 13r–13v, p. 244; Wallace, *Walking*, p. 29. See also Jarvis, *Romantic Writing*, and Solnit, *Wanderlust*.

INTRODUCTION

of ordering a carriage, awaiting its preparation, depending on unreliable drivers and negotiating the often-treacherous Irish roads.[1] His mode of travelling attracted some gentle teasing from a friend:

> How goes on your Tour? do your legs last out, or has a poney the honour of bearing you about? Have you learned to bide the pelting of the pitiless storms which have been so numerous, and has the lightning taken no notice of the brass head or foot shall I call it of your umbrella? Do Snowdon's lofty summits, the awful, wild and vast forms of Cader [Cadair] Idris, Carnarvon Castle and Conway's 'foaming flood' answer your expectations? And do you imagine that after your eye has been accustomed for weeks to rove over so unbounded a variety of romantic scenery, you can look with satisfaction on the tame hills at Totteridge, or endure a glance at the flats of Cambridgeshire?[2]

The mental stimulation and creativity engendered by walking are examined elsewhere.[3] The ideals underlying Lee's tour are evident in his self-reflexive comments after long solitary walks. For example, crossing the mountains between Killarney and Kenmare, he revealed:

> Tried in this wild sequestered place to walk barefoot and did for a long way with ease but it delayed me too long to continue so. I have no idea of not being able to do *what* the common people do every day, and *what* Adam did before me.[4]

Taken together with the focus of Longley's teasing letter, this instance reveals a romantic vision of commune with nature and experiencing the simplicity of rural life.

While Lee's tour sits within the romantic context of domestic travel, it must also be understood within the European Enlightenment context of global exploration. Expedition narratives burst onto the book trade in the wake of Cook's first Pacific expedition (1768–71) and would retain a strong hold over the reading public into the twentieth century. Lee makes no direct reference in his diaries to such publications, but it is unlikely that a person with his education and interests should not have read or owned at least some. In later life, Lee donated to John Ross's search for the missing Franklin expedition in 1850, and carried on a lengthy correspondence with Ross.[5] The eighteenth- and nineteenth-century reading public was captivated by expedition accounts, the reach and audience of such books extending so that they came to encompass not only the details of an expedition's course and tables of scientific observations, but also subjective, experiential and personal narratives of peoples and places encountered. Lee's diaries follow this model and his opportunities for such encounters were maximized by his mode of travel. His pedestrianism was ideally suited to the aesthetic and literary values underpinning his tour. As his tour progressed, as he travelled farther west into Wales and farther into Ireland's mountain ranges, he found more opportunities for solitary reflection. His experiences as a solitary pedestrian are expressions of the sublime, which is discussed in the following section.

---

[1] SJC, MS U.30 (5), f. 13r–v, p. 244.
[2] SJC, William Longley to John Fiott, 23 Aug. 1806, MS Box 1a, Doc. 21. This is one of only two extant letters sent to Lee in the period 31 July 1806–6 Mar. 1807, and is reproduced in full at pp. 340–41.
[3] Gros, *A Philosophy of Walking*, pp. 19–21.
[4] SJC, MS U.30 (4), f. 9r, p. 202.
[5] National Maritime Museum, London, John Ross and John Lee, Letters Relating to Franklin Search Expeditions and Learned Societies, 1850–56, HAR/301–359.

As a pedestrian traveller, Lee developed a close relationship with the weather during his walking tour. Until winter had fully set in, Lee only described weather conditions on occasion – for example, a particularly hot day – but from 15 November 1806 he kept a daily weather log, noting the preceding day's conditions at the beginning of each entry. While not sufficiently methodical or prolonged to contribute materially to our understanding of weather patterns in the British Isles in 1806–7, his record provides a level of daily detail that may usefully supplement such generalized records as William Wilde's long-term report on the Irish climate.[1] Wilde informs us that the mean temperature in Ireland in 1806 was 49.2°F (9.4°C) and 47.9°F (8.8°C) in 1807. Lee described the temperature as 'cold' or 'freezing' on 27 separate days during his Irish tour, 18 of which occurred between November and February. Local observations recorded in Lee's diaries corroborate Wilde's record that there were 208 rainy days in 1806: 'The People in Limerick say they never knew such a wet winter as this has been for many years indeed. Although this season is generally wet yet this is incomparable.'[2] On several days in December 1806, the quantity of rain forced Lee to remain indoors all day, or allowed him to venture out-of-doors for only a short time (e.g. 1 December, 16 December). Heavy rains had their advantages, however, in showing the lakes and waterfalls of Kerry at their best.[3] Lee's interest in weather and climate would endure beyond his pedestrian tour, with the British Meteorological Society being founded at Hartwell House in 1850.

3. Landscapes of the Home Tour

This brief introduction does not intend to conflate experiences of England, Wales and Ireland, which meant very different things to travellers and could be presented in very different ways. As a whole, however, Lee's itinerary included some of the standard features of the 'home tour', the key sites of Conwy and Llangollen in Wales, and Killarney in Ireland. The home tour responded to the realities of Continental upheaval and war from 1789 onwards, but has a longer, prior history emerging from domestic British circumstances. From the mid-to-late eighteenth century, travellers and travel writers began to shift their focus from the Continent to Britain and Ireland, illustrating the importance of travel in identity formation and in the construction of nationhood, particularly in relation to Ireland and Scotland.[4]

Interest in the domestic British and Irish landscape had its conception in the emergence of new aesthetic priorities – the picturesque, sublime and beautiful – as articulated in Edmund Burke's *A Philosophical Enquiry into the Origin of our Ideas of the Sublime and Beautiful* (1757) and William Gilpin's picturesque travel writing in *Observations, Made in the Year 1772, on Several Parts of England* (1786). Lee's walk took place against a backdrop of rapidly developing interest in Britain's picturesque, sublime and beautiful landscapes as landscape painters, gothic writers and travellers embraced the reconceptualization of the domestic landscape. The fetishization of the domestic landscape was conceived early on in

---

[1] Wilde, 'Tables of Deaths', p. 168.
[2] SJC, MS U.30 (5), f. 14v, p. 245.
[3] SJC, MS U.30 (4), f. 11v, p. 203.
[4] For more on the home tour, see: Ousby, *The Englishman's England*; Andrews, *The Search for the Picturesque*; Kinsley, *Women Writing the Home Tour*.

Arthur Young's *Six Weeks' Tour through the Southern Counties of England and Wales* (1769) and was later developed in Coleridge and Wordsworth's *Lyrical Ballads* (1798). The decade before and after Lee's walking tour saw the publication of a flurry of tours and scientific travels in England and Wales, including Thomas Pennant's *A Tour in Wales* (1778), Ann Radcliffe's influential *Observations during a Tour to the Lakes of Lancashire, Westmoreland, and Cumberland* (1795) and William Hutton's *Remarks upon North Wales* (1803).

Pre-Christian antiquities and medieval ruins punctuate Lee's journey, providing focal points for his sketches (and presenting opportunities for gathering folklore and local histories). His register of landscape description sits comfortably within the genre of picturesque travel, with its emphasis on experiencing 'an ideal form of nature' at vantage points and at ruins. This 'ideal form' was that established by landscape painters like Gilpin, who provided the medium through which Lee evaluated British and Irish landscapes. He remarked that the scenery on the approach to Henley 'reminds us of those views which one sometimes sees of places abroad, which are selected as most proper for beautiful landscapes'.[1] Near Killarney, he found a scene that 'puts one in mind of forest scenery or of … descriptions of Jaques', meaning the landscape artist, Jacques d'Arthois.[2] At Ardfert, a vista of orderly estate lands and crumbling medieval ruins combined to 'fill the mind with many pleasing reflections'.[3] Notably, Lee carried a Claude glass, a slightly convex tinted mirror that translated the living landscape into a version of nature in keeping with the tone of the landscape paintings of the celebrated seventeenth-century artist, Claude Lorrain, and providing the illusion of seeing the landscape through Claude's eyes. The landscape could thus be appreciated as truly 'picture-esque' – as being like a picture. He applied his Claude glass to the scenes on the River Severn as he travelled by wherry from Bewdley to Bridgnorth.[4]

Despite being largely unfinished, Lee's annotated sketches demonstrate a concern for composition in keeping with the standards set in landscape painting by Claude Lorrain. Lorrain's paintings were composed of distinct layers or *coulisses* – a wooded foreground, a middle distance, a mountain backdrop and sky – and spatial depth was established with the use of 'transitional objects' such as bridges or temples.[5] Lee's sketches demonstrate the same use of framing, textures and spatial depth, portraying wooded foregrounds with bridges, villages, church towers or ruins; textured middle distances; and mountains in the background. So, too, do his textual descriptions. At Evesham, he found that 'the Bridge over the Avon with the surrounding scenery forms a very picturesque appearance'.[6] Similarly, at Penmachno mill, the impression made by following a 'roaring' river enhanced the 'most picturesque and beautiful' scene, with its 'Waterfall tremendous and sublime to look at'.[7] His imprecision with terminology reflects the internalisation of the effects of

---

[1] SJC, MS U.30 (1), f. 4r, p. 36.
[2] SJC, MS U.30 (4), f. 28r, p. 214.
[3] SJC, MS U.30 (5), f. 3r, p. 235.
[4] SJC, MS U.30 (1), f. 37v, p. 58; Hooper, 'The Isles/Ireland', p. 174. The difference between perception and reality of the Welsh landscape in the period is studied in Zaring, 'The Romantic Face of Wales'; Marshall, 'The Problem of the Picturesque' examines the relationship between evaluations of real landscapes and the qualities sought in picturesque landscape paintings, whereby nature was expected to mimic art.
[5] Axton, 'Victorian Landscape Painting', p. 282.
[6] SJC, MS U.30 (1), f. 16r, p. 43.
[7] SJC, MS U.30 (2), f. 21r, p. 97.

landscape. His lists of the contents of art collections at the great houses he visited are further evidence of his fashionable taste, his broad knowledge of art history and his consciousness of the role of the visual experience in touring.

The emotional experience of the sublime seasoned the aesthetic pleasure of touring the domestic landscape. Walking from Pont-y-Pair to Rhyd-Lanfair, Lee paused to admire a swollen watercourse against a backdrop of cloud-capped mountains, through a dimming mist of rain, concluding that 'No body *coul*d feel the situation untill exactly in similar one'.[1] He sought out the wild and untamed, eager to experience Burke's 'sort of delightful horror, a sort of tranquillity tinged with terror; which, as it belongs to self-preservation, is one of the strongest of all the passions. Its object is the sublime.'[2] He also wished to experience extreme sensations, acutely expressed in his disappointment at the celebrated Powerscourt waterfall in Wicklow, which he found 'excessively tame and looks like [a] place where one *coul*d have said a gentleman has shewed his taste in making a waterfall more than a fine bold work of nature'.[3] By the time he reached Killarney – by then an established destination for the landscape tourist – he thrilled at prospect of rocks falling on him as he roamed the surrounding mountains: 'M*ountai*ns [are] wonderfully ragged and and [*sic*] loose stones appear hanging over the tops as if ready to fall. I must leave off and go on or they will certainly come down on me.'[4]

4. The Tour in Ireland

Lee's tour of Ireland began with his arrival in Dublin on 30 August 1806, having sailed from Holyhead through a 'high swell'. Richard Colt Hoare recorded in his *Journal of a Tour in Ireland* (1807) that he had a 'rough and tedious passage' of 23 hours from Holyhead to Dublin in June 1806. Given that Lee also made his crossing in summer and that he records a 'high swell', it may be assumed that his crossing took around the same length of time.[5] Lee's convoluted itinerary led him south from Dublin to Wicklow, Kilkenny, Cork, Killarney, Waterford, the Dingle Peninsula and Blasket Islands, north into Limerick and briefly through the midlands, back to Dublin and, briefly, a little north to Drogheda. It was confined to the southern counties of Ireland, the most common route at the time for its better roads, staging posts, and for the access it provided to the celebrated destinations of Wicklow and Killarney, two of the three principal sites of interest to visitors to eighteenth- and nineteenth-century Ireland (the third being the Giant's Causeway, which he did not visit). Colt Hoare's 'southern tour' (as he named it) also brought him from Dublin through the midlands, his itinerary overlapping with Lee's through Nenagh, Killaloe, Limerick, Adare, Askeaton, Glin, Listowel, Tralee, Ardfert, Killarney, Millstreet, Cork, Youghal, Lismore, Fermoy, Mallow, Cashel, Kildare and Dublin. Colt Hoare's tour was, however, performed in a counter-clockwise direction and with some differences in diversions from Lee's main route. Coincidentally, Lee and Colt Hoare stayed at the same lodgings in Nenagh (Cantrell's inn) and Limerick (Swinburne's

---

[1] SJC, MS U.30 (2), f. 20r, p. 96.
[2] Burke, *A Philosophical Enquiry*, p. 257.
[3] SJC, MS U.30 (2), f. 41v, p. 110.
[4] SJC, MS U.30 (4), f. 11v, pp. 203–4.
[5] Hoare, *Journal of a Tour*, p. 1.

hotel). Lee's overall itinerary was also similar to John Carr's, who likewise recorded some of his impressions of Wales in the first chapter of *The Stranger in Ireland* (1806).

While many guidebooks conformed to providing the traveller with a standard itinerary that enabled them to efficiently visit the most famous sites, the traveller and antiquary Richard Pococke (1704–65), for one, has been remembered for showing 'little respect for "accepted" routes'.[1] Pococke's expertise in antiquities would have been indispensable to Lee, but his Irish tours lay unpublished until 1891, so it is likely that it was the steward on-site who informed him of the fact that like Lee himself, Pococke could not read a faded old inscription at Ardfert friary. Incidentally, the popular *Post-Chaise Companion* – the first such pocket book for travellers in Ireland – made a similar remark.[2] In any event, Lee's convoluted itinerary struck a balance between already well-established visitor sites and lesser-visited regions. Lee may have been the first (or at least, one of the first) non-Irish visitor to record a visit to the Blasket Islands, but the lakes of Killarney were already well established as a tourist site thirty years before he got there.[3]

While the Napoleonic Wars impacted on British travellers' access to the Continent in the late eighteenth and early nineteenth centuries, other factors had contributed to making Ireland a destination from the mid-eighteenth century onwards. Road transportation improved, canals extended westwards, and more, better-quality guidebooks were published. Finally, as Glenn Hooper has pointed out, Ireland presented a solution to an 'epistemological vacuum'.[4] Ireland's accession to the United Kingdom in 1801 attracted English visitors eager to familiarize themselves with their 'Sister Isle', even if writers were prone to overstate the extent of the island's unfamiliarity to the English. Two decades prior to the Union of 1801, the Irish clergyman and writer Thomas Campbell stated (having assumed the persona of an English author for the purposes of his *Philosophical Survey*), 'There is, perhaps, no country dependent on the British Crown, which Englishmen know less of than Ireland; and yet it may safely be affirmed, there is none which has a fairer and a stronger claim to their attention.'[5] In 1806, Richard Colt Hoare referred to Ireland's 'neglected shores', claiming that the island still 'remained unvisited and unknown ... Because of the want of books, and living information, we have been led to suppose its country rude, its inhabitants savage, its paths dangerous.'[6] It is worth noting at this point that around a hundred travel accounts of Ireland had been published in the second half of the eighteenth century.[7] Some counties had been scientifically described and their topographical features codified in Charles Smith's mid-eighteenth-century *Antient and Present State* series, and scientific travel accounts of

---

[1] Hadfield and McVeagh, *Strangers to that Land*, p. 135.

[2] SJC, MS U.30 (5), f. 3r, p. 235; Wilson, *Post-Chaise Companion*, p. 182. Pococke's Irish tours were first published as Stokes, ed., *Pococke's Tour*.

[3] Neither of the two most comprehensive annotated bibliographies of travels in Ireland cites any pre-20th-century visitor to the Blasket Islands; see McVeagh, *Irish Travel Writing* and Woods, *Travellers' Accounts*. See also Williams, *Creating Irish Tourism*, pp. 129–50; Gibbons, 'Topographies of Terror', pp. 23–44; Zuelow, *Making Ireland Irish*, p. xviii.

[4] Hooper, *Travel Writing and Ireland*, pp. 2–3; this book provides an excellent survey of British tours in Ireland in 1760–1860. Another valuable recent addition to the study of Irish travel and tourism in the period 1850–1914 is James, *Tourism, Land, and Landscape*.

[5] [Campbell], *A Philosophical Survey*, p. iii.

[6] Hoare, *Journal of a Tour*, pp. i, ii.

[7] Williams, *Creating Irish Tourism*, p. xiv.

Ireland appeared from the 1770s, including the agricultural reformer Arthur Young's *A Tour in Ireland ... in the Years 1776, 1777 and 1778* (1780).[1]

Lee usually eschewed guidebooks in favour of recording oral testimony gathered from local informants. His diaries refer to only a small number of guidebooks, including [A Gentleman of Oxford], *The New Oxford Guide* (1759); Cooke, *Topographical and Statistical Description of the County of Salop* (*c*. 1805); and [Green], *A Brief History of Worcester; or, 'Worcester Guide'* (1806). A book Lee refers to as 'Roads of Ireland' is probably George Taylor and Andrew Skinner's useful volume, *Maps of the Roads of Ireland* (1778), published as part of a series that included volumes on the roads of Scotland and England in 1776–83.[2] Lee remained only three nights at Limerick, but he did buy or at least have access to Ferrar's *An History of the City of Limerick* (1767), the first published history of the city. It is not possible to say with certainty whether Lee read any other travel accounts before his departure or during his tour. As noted above, the best-known accounts of Ireland contemporaneous with Lee's tour are John Carr's *The Stranger in Ireland* (1806) and Richard Colt Hoare's *Journal of a Tour in Ireland* (1807). Carr made his tour in 1805, but because *The Stranger in Ireland* was published in August 1806, just as Lee was embarking on his Irish tour, it is unlikely that Lee could have read it until after his return to England in spring 1807.[3] Even if Lee had had access to Carr's book, its deficiencies in detail and originality would have limited its value.

Lee's account conforms well with late eighteenth- and early nineteenth-century published surveys of Ireland, attempting as they did to elucidate the island's politics, social conditions, history and economy. Where Lee's account differs from the published accounts is in its status as a set of private, on-the-spot observations, unabridged and unfiltered. Lee did not need to mediate the content of his diaries, or to rationalize his inclusion of folklore, mythology and idiosyncratic material. The Scottish natural historian and geologist Robert Jameson (1774–1854) excluded such matter from his *Mineralogy of the Scottish Isles* as 'not worthy of serious attention'.[4] Thomas Pennant recorded Highland traditions in his *Tour of Scotland and Voyage to the Hebrides*, but with the defence that it was necessary 'lest their memory should be lost'.[5] Lee was free to detail in his unpublished diaries his interactions with all sorts of people – landowners and middling gentry, merchants, shopkeepers, innkeepers and beggars – even recording their anecdotes and the turns of phrase that appeared to him characteristic of the Irish lexicon. These snippets reveal aspects of these people's lives and priorities, as well as the accessible exoticism of Irish rural life.

Lee's status as a pedestrian traveller made him more likely to interact with the rural poor, and made him dependent upon their hospitality. A girl named 'Peggey' conducted him across a 'horrible frightful' mountain road to the farmhouse of one James Cronin near Gougane Barra Lake, where Lee stayed one night. Cronin and his family welcomed

---

[1] Between 1744 and 1756, Smith published *Antient and Present State* volumes for the counties (and cities) of Cork, Down, Kerry and Waterford on behalf of the Physico-Historical Society; see Magennis, '"A Land of Milk and Honey"'.

[2] Taylor and Skinner, *Survey and Maps of the Roads of North Britain*, London, 1776, and *Survey of the Great Post Roads between London, Bath and Bristol*, London, 1776.

[3] 'Mr. Carr's *Stranger in Ireland* is published, and shall be reviewed next month.' *The Monthly Mirror*, Aug. 1806, p. 74.

[4] Jameson, *Mineralogy of the Scottish Isles*, II, pp. 2–3.

[5] Pennant, *Tour in Scotland and the Hebrides*, I, p. 108.

Lee warmly, sharing their plain fare of potatoes and milk. Cronin guided Lee over the mountain to the lake, relating local history, traditions and folklore. Interesting insight is provided in Lee's description of the toilet facilities and sleeping arrangements at the farmhouse, with Lee sharing a room with James Cronin, his wife, and their six children.[1] Other opportunities to acquaint himself with local people arose when Lee hired boys to porter his luggage, or when he asked for directions. He had one particularly striking interaction with a boy in the Knockmealdown Mountains, the relationship between the young man and the child painted in terms not dissimilar to descriptions of explorers' interactions with global indigenous peoples. The pair communicated by signs and intonation. The boy 'jabbered' in Irish, expressing wonder and surprise at the fruits of his rummage through Lee's knapsack: bread (not likely to have been a staple of his diet), a piece of slate and a spyglass.[2]

Coupled with his anti-revolutionary liberal politics, Lee's account takes on a gothic register through the combination of his antiquarianism, his taste for the sublime, his fascination with Ireland's recent history and his descriptions of what he saw as the disgusting personal habits of the Irish (detailed below). At once fascinated and repulsed by the Irish peasant, Lee's characterisations of their manners, customs and ways of life construct an accessible 'other'. The levels of scholarship and linguistic ability he found among the poor impressed him: 'many poor peasants in Ireland who in this point *would* put their [England's] best scholars right not only in the pronunciation but in speaking the [Latin] language itself'.[3] He found the Irish peasant and labourer occasionally entertaining company, but ultimately symptomatic of the island's social and economic backwardness. The traveller expects locals to furnish local knowledge, but Lee frequently found people unable (or unwilling?) to provide with any degree of accuracy such basic information as the distance to the next town. The 'friendly interest' of Dubliners irritated Lee, their questions and curiosity appearing impertinent, but it was he who posed curious questions in rural Wicklow, persistently asking the ages of the boys who guided him around bogs and mountains. (They rarely had the answer.) The proliferation of holy wells and 'pattern days' (days of devotion to a local saint) further signalled to him ignorance and superstition. Lee describes pilgrims walking and crawling around St Michael's well in Co. Waterford, while festivities carried on nearby with 'all the appearance of a fair', with people gaming, drinking whiskey and brawling, despite the fact that it was both a Sunday and a holy day.[4] Lee adopted an uncharacteristically mocking tone in his account of interviewing local people in relation to the efficacy of the healing waters. The Irish language placed further distance between Lee and the Irish people. Despite hearing it in use in places, he treated the language as a curio, a quaint antiquity that signified the progress of his journey in both space and time. In Cork, he purchased copies of Irish manuscripts and took lessons in the Irish language and Gaelic script from a shopkeeper and bookseller, in much the same way that he would later investigate and collect ancient papyri. Lee's diaries provide a tantalizing glimpse into the life of the language before the increase in bilingualism and the retreat of fluent, quotidian use of Irish to the western

---

[1] SJC, MS U.30 (3), ff. 14r–16v, pp. 191–2, 193–4.
[2] SJC, MS U.30 (2), f. 137r, p. 166.
[3] SJC, MS U.30 (5), ff. 13v–14r, p. 244.
[4] SJC, MS U.30 (2), f. 147v, pp. 175–6. Into the 19th century, '[f]olk religion was centred on holy wells, local saints, the kin-group, and the home, rather than on church buildings' (Bourke, *The Burning*, p. 11).

fringes of the island.[1] While he did comment on hearing the 'chattering of Welsh' for the first time, the evidence does not suggest that he engaged with that language in the same way that he did with Irish.[2]

Lee found Dublin's urban poor in worse condition than their English counterparts, and he was just one of the many visitors to nineteenth-century Ireland who noted the poverty rife across the island.[3] The material standard of living appeared very low. He did not find the population hungry, but rather in a state of passivity and lassitude, and it seemed to him that 'They have by habit got settled in filth and dirt and smoke'.[4] The public display of poor Irish bodies and their openness about bodily functions repulsed and fascinated Lee. Near Callan, a child emerged from a cabin to '[do] its affairs' before Lee's eyes in a hedge and, on first arriving in Cork, he was greeted by the sight of 'a silly woman sitting d*ow*n on the paveme*nt* side, ½ covered but many parts of her body to be seen' and by people walking barefoot in the muddy streets.[5] His observations on the norms observed in the use of privies at inns are brief and ambiguous, but nevertheless communicate difference. At Nenagh, he indicated that the innkeeper did not reserve the privy for paying guests and, cryptically, that he 'met with a bad reception' when he attempted to use it.[6] The dung heaps piled outside rural cabins – for convenience and to protect this valuable fertilizer from theft – disgusted Lee, but out of fascination and a love of detail, he included them in his sketches.[7]

a. History and Antiquities

Travellers' interest in folklore was not coincidental to Ireland's reputation as a landscape richly populated by the material remains of the past, due in part to a lack of economic development. A predominantly rural, agrarian economy and, in the south and west, a largely Gaelic-speaking population, were situated within a landscape scattered with the fragmentary remains of antiquity. The emphasis on history was not unique to Lee's account of Ireland. In his popular *The Stranger in Ireland*, John Carr attempted to distance the latest member of the United Kingdom from its terrible recent past by 'evoking a general historical condition of melancholy ruin and decay'.[8] Carr's politicization of the Irish landscape is mirrored in Lee's delineation of the Irish landscape as a series of demesnes and estates; in his emphasis on ruins and 'Danish mounds' (tumuli); and in his understanding of topography and geology.

Lee's diaries read at times like a gazetteer of landed estates – what William H. A. Williams terms 'estate tourism'. Estates and country houses were among the earliest tourist attractions and, by the late eighteenth century, it was commonplace for their housekeepers in England, Wales and Ireland to admit visitors.[9] Lee's enumeration of the names of estates and their proprietors, and his evaluations of the topographical and architectural features

---

[1] See Kelly, 'Irish Protestants and the Irish Language'.
[2] SJC, MS U.30 (1), f. 52r, p. 77.
[3] Ó Gráda, 'Poverty, Population, and Agriculture', pp. 108–33. See also the chapter on poverty in Williams, *Tourism, Landscape, and the Irish Character*, pp. 80–104.
[4] SJC, MS U.30 (2), f. 118r, p. 155.
[5] SJC, MS U.30 (2), f. 114v, p. 153; SJC, MS U.30 (3), ff. 3v–4r, p. 182.
[6] SJC, MS U.30 (5), f. 54v, p. 280.
[7] SJC, MS U.30 (8), ff. 60v–61r, p. 338. Sketch not reproduced.
[8] Bohls and Duncan, eds, *Travel Writing 1700–1830*, p. 122.
[9] Williams, *Creating Irish Tourism*, pp. 49–65. See also Anderson, 'Remaking the Space'.

of those estates, inscribes onto the Irish rural landscape a triumphant reading of the island's recent history and a limited optimism. Despite increasing absenteeism – which did not escape Lee's notice – estates signalled the possibility of economic and social improvement of bleak boglands and impoverished tenants.[1] He experienced Ireland during a period of transition. Large landowners had already become, to a large extent, an absentee class, while the urban middle class thrived as some landowners, like the Barrys of Cork, poured investment into the regions.[2] Alongside these signals of progress, everyday life in provincial and rural Ireland continued to be ruled by 'superstition', religious observance and the farming calendar, as evident in Lee's descriptions of funeral rites and 'pattern days'. Lee's close observation of the landscape and his interest in local histories and folklore informed his record of the activities of the improving landlords in the south of Ireland. His consciousness of the destruction of ancient ringforts was tempered by his eye for the 'beautiful' and the ways in which landowner 'taste and elegance' provided a 'wonderful assist[ance]' to nature. He selected the mines at Ross Island in Co. Kerry as an example. Criticized by others for their effect on the landscape, Lee defended the appearance of the mines, saying 'It makes the scenery more beautiful increases the contrast and variety for which Kerry [is] celebrated'.[3]

Lee's first impressions of Ireland were informed by his arrival in Dublin, and betray conflicting expectations. Late eighteenth- and early nineteenth-century antiquaries and travellers who sought signals of Ireland's former status as a light in the 'Dark Ages' were disappointed to find that Dublin had 'preserved less of the "light of other days"' than other European cities, its medieval fabric largely buried beneath modern buildings.[4] While Lee admired the city's modern features, particularly James Gandon's celebrated Custom House, he was unimpressed with its remaining medieval buildings. He complained that Christchurch Cathedral was 'situated in a very bad and narrow part of the town' – the heart of the medieval city – and described the building itself as 'very narrow and much inferior to all the cathedrals I ever saw in England'.[5] He did not have to travel far from the city to have his appetite for antiquities and ruins satisfied. Co. Wicklow provided ruins set amid picturesque and sublime scenery within a short distance of the city. As he travelled further south into Munster, Lee sketched in words and images the many ruined abbeys and castles scattered throughout the country. He also noted the abundance of 'Danish mounds' or earthen forts and mounds. A gothic fascination with ruins is in strong evidence in Lee's account, but his (mostly) brief impressions do not extend further than recording unusual architectural features or inscriptions.

Lee's eye for the gothic translated to his engagement with Ireland's geology and mineralogy, particularly at Dunmore cave, Co. Kilkenny. The cave developed a reputation as a sublime and gothic attraction having been first described in 1708 by Kilkenny native George Berkeley as 'one of the rarities of this kingdom … [a] remarkable place'. Writing seven years retrospectively, Berkeley reflected that the 'dismal solitude, the fearful darkness, and vast silence … have left lasting impressions'.[6] Lee described the stalagmites

---

[1] SJC, MS U.30 (2), ff. 116r–117r, pp. 154–5.
[2] Dickson, *Old World Colony*, paints a lively picture of such developments in Munster in the period.
[3] SJC, MS U.30 (5), f. 43v, p. 270.
[4] Prunty, 'Nineteenth-Century Antiquarian Accounts', pp. 482–4.
[5] SJC, MS U.30 (2), f. 27r, p. 99.
[6] Berkeley, 'Description of the Cave of Dunmore', p. 503.

as 'a mass of petrefaction [*sic*]', a static matter forming the underbelly of the Irish landscape, mirroring the economic stagnation he witnessed on the island. A gleaming underground cathedral was illuminated by Lee's torch, and was at once sullied by its smoke. The mineral formations at Dunmore were naturally of interest to travellers, but the cave's reputation was chiefly founded upon the human remains found in its darkest recesses. Early modern Irish annals record that a massacre of 1,000 people took place in the cave in 928 CE. Various theories have been proposed on the origins of these remains, but archaeologists now broadly agree that the victims likely died while seeking refuge from Viking attacks. Dunmore's significance in Lee's account lies in its position in a genealogy of violence stretching back hundreds of years, and continuing into the present.[1]

b. *Memories of 1798 and 1803 in Lee's Diaries*

The 1798 and 1803 rebellions cast a shadow over early nineteenth-century travel accounts, as pointed out elsewhere.[2] This section can only provide an introductory overview to these events, broadly to contextualize Lee's record of eyewitness accounts.[3] Throughout the Irish portion of his diaries, Lee paid a great deal of attention to the late rebellions and savoured them with gothic relish, recording their events as related to him by participants and witnesses on both sides. Historians continue to debate the causes of the 1798 rebellion. It came at the end of a decade marked by a political crisis that saw a stalling of moves for parity of status for catholics, agrarian disturbances arising from economic grievances, and the activities of the Society of United Irishmen, founded in Belfast in 1791 and suppressed in 1794. Government intelligence in relation to a planned rebellion led to the arrest of most of the Society's leaders in March 1798. On the night of 23–24 May 1798, the uprising was launched, despite the absence by imprisonment of most of the Society's leaders. Sporadic fighting erupted around the country, particularly in counties Carlow, Kildare, Meath, Wicklow and Wexford, followed by Antrim and Down. Wexford saw a brutal backlash by the North Cork Militia, and summary executions spread into neighbouring Wicklow. On 22 August, a French fleet with 1,000 troops landed on the Co. Mayo coast, but on 8 September its forces were defeated in Longford (events related to Lee by an eyewitness).[4] The rebellion resulted in an estimated (and disputed) 20,000–30,000 deaths and the imprisonment and exile of thousands.[5] It was also a deciding factor in the dissolution of the Dublin parliament and the establishment of the United Kingdom of Great Britain and Ireland in 1801. Furthermore, the threat from Napoleon's France remained, and Lee visited some of the Martello towers and other defensive structures erected along the Irish coast as part of Britain's defence strategy.

In 1799, the United Irishmen began to rebuild their organization, but on a smaller scale than before. By early 1803, a fresh revolution was being planned under the

[1] See Byrne, 'A Previously Unknown Traveller's Account'.

[2] Hooper, 'The Isles/Ireland', p. 179. See Killeen, *Gothic Ireland*, for more on the impact of violence on Anglo-Irish writing and identity in the period 1641–1801.

[3] Detailed studies of the 1798 and 1803 rebellions include: Dickson, Keogh and Whelan, *The United Irishmen*; Elliott, *Robert Emmet*; Geoghegan, *Robert Emmet*; Smyth, *Revolution, Counter-Revolution and Union*; Whelan, *The Tree of Liberty*.

[4] See SJC, MS U.30 (2), ff. 52r–53v, pp. 117–18.

[5] Smyth, *Men of No Property*, p. 178.

INTRODUCTION

leadership of Robert Emmet (1778–1803). The capture of strategic positions in Dublin was to coincide with the arrival of a French fleet. Fearing discovery, a scaled-down rising was called prematurely for 23 July 1803. The rebels were ill equipped, possessing many more pikes than firearms, and many volunteers failed to present themselves. The uprising's minor but fatal affrays – see Lee's account of the murder of Viscount Kilwarden and his nephew[1] – were easily suppressed, and Emmet went into hiding. He was arrested on 25 August and executed on 20 September; 21 other participants were also executed. This spelled the end of the Society of United Irishmen, and continuing popular and agrarian unrest in Ireland in the years that followed was mainly focused on economic issues.

The memories of 1798 and 1803 lived on, however, in popular song and in opposition to the establishment. Lee's record of eyewitness accounts of 1798 in particular is significant because accounts of its events carried political currency right into the nineteenth century; '[t]he struggle for control of the meaning of the 1790s was also a struggle for political legitimacy'.[2] Parties on all sides produced conflicting accounts of events for political ends and for self-justification.[3] The raw memories of 1798 permeated Lee's experiences in Leinster in particular, altering the tone of the tour from the romantic solitude Lee enjoyed in rural England and Wales, to a gothic tone of violence and unspecified threats. On his first day in Dublin, his host related stories of treacherous servants; on his second day, he visited Thomas Street, where Emmet launched the uprising of 1803. Walking through part of the Wicklow Mountains in the company of soldiers, Lee heard the stories embedded in that landscape and saw the remains of abandoned rebel camps and the burnt-out remains of landowners' houses.[4] He also spent a number of days in the company of Sir Thomas Judkin 'Flogging' Fitzgerald, who brutally targeted and interrogated suspected rebels in Tipperary in 1798. Lee demonstrated clear admiration for Fitzgerald and his actions, despite his own admission that he was 'a most violent man and therefore dangerous'.[5]

Lee's short trip north to Drogheda with the purpose of visiting the site of the Battle of the Boyne, is further evidence of his understanding of Ireland as a space inhabited by its own troubled history. James II's defeat at the hands of William III in 1690, and the subsequent treaties made in 1691, drove Stuart sympathizers or 'Jacobites' to the Continent and buttressed the economic and legal position of Anglican landowners. Lee made detailed sketches of the site and the surrounding area, paying particular attention to battlefield archaeology. Lee reserved judgment on the events at the Boyne, his pilgrimage to the site speaking for itself and sitting in juxtaposition to his entertainment that evening by some of the last great harpers in the Irish tradition.[6]

Nourished by tales of the recent rebellions and the otherness of the Irish, Lee's gothic imagination indulged in night-walking fantasies. Walking alone through lonely,

---

[1] SJC, MS U.30 (2), f. 33v, p. 105.
[2] Whelan, *The Tree of Liberty*, p. 133.
[3] On the writing and commemoration of 1798 in the 19th century, see Beiner, *Remembering the Year of the French*; Whelan, *The Tree of Liberty*, pp. 133–75; and Ian McBride, C. J. Woods and Dáire Keogh's essays in Bartlett et al. eds, *1798: a Bicentenary Perspective*, pp. 469–528.
[4] SJC, MS U.30 (2), ff. 56v–57v, p. 121.
[5] SJC, MS U.30 (5), ff. 38v–49r, pp. 267–75.
[6] SJC, MS U.30 (5), ff. 75r–78v, pp. 302–3.

isolated mountain bogs, Lee feared robbery and attack. Returning late to Bray from a day's walk in the Wicklow Mountains over a 'Horrible lonely and gloomy lane', Lee felt 'Benighted' by the inability to find his way. Six days later, walking at dusk near Roundwood, Co. Wicklow, one young man's desire for company on the road made Lee fearful and suspicious, so he prepared to use his umbrella and geologist's hammer for self-defence.[1]

5. Lee as a Scientific Traveller

Lee's early travels were formative experiences, rounding off his exclusive education and laying the foundations for his later antiquarian and scientific interests. Up to at least the 1830s, science was a 'gentlemanly' pursuit cultivated through travel and networks.[2] Lee's interests in geology, mineralogy and botany are clearly in evidence in the diaries published in this book. Completing most of his tour alone and on foot gave Lee the time and autonomy to observe close at hand the variety of landscapes through which he travelled. He clambered over stiles and struggled across bogs to experience romantic solitude, while recording the plants, trees, animals and geological features that captured his attention. Where possible, in this edition Latin and/or common names are provided in square brackets for the flora and fauna that he named or described in his diaries.

Lee's walking tour has a strongly scientific character in keeping with the contemporary figure of the scientific traveller. Scientific travellers joined in the new appeal of British and Irish landscapes, particularly those of Scotland and Ireland, as presenting fresh fields of study. Provincial scientific studies appealed to the reading public. They contained 'new' information and often included lavish illustrations and maps, all presented in tandem with observations on the exotic Celts who inhabited Ireland, Wales and the Scottish Highlands and islands.[3] British scientific travellers employed the unifying language of the Linnaean taxonomy to symbolically connect the geographical and climatic diversity of the natural history of imperial territories and colonies. The Welsh-born naturalist Thomas Pennant (1726–98) is an excellent example of the emerging genre of domestic British scientific description. Taken as a whole, his works positioned Scottish and Irish natural history within a broader, global context, but more significantly, his *A Tour in Scotland* (1771) and *A Tour in Scotland and Voyage to the Hebrides* (1774) communicated his own original observations, unlike his *Indian Zoology* (1769) and *Arctic Zoology* (1784). (He never travelled to either the Arctic or India.) It is therefore significant that Lee referenced Pennant's history of his local parish in Wales, indicating that Lee was at least acquainted with current trends in domestic scientific travel and its methodologies.

Early on, Lee's tour developed a focus on the science of industry. This was as much due to geographical accident (his track through Wales) as it was to the fact that these

---

[1] SJC, MS U.30 (2), ff. 42v, 70v, pp. 111, 132.
[2] On amateurism and professionalism in the sciences, see Barton, '"Men of Science"'; Barton, '"Huxley, Lubbock"'; Elliott, 'The Origins of the Creative Class'.
[3] See Byrne, 'Imagining the Celtic North'.

INTRODUCTION

industries represented a marriage of his interests in mathematics and mineralogy. A visit to the Royal China Manufactory at Worcester is described in detail, taking the reader through every stage of the production process, aided by sketches of the moulds used in the manufactory (Figures 2 and 3, reproduced at pp. 48 and 49). Approaching Iron Bridge after dark, Lee conjures a magical picture of distant lights discerned through a drizzle, and the clanging sound of hammers at the ironworks.[1] The following day, Lee engaged a local guide and received a thorough tour of Darby's famous ironworks at Coalbrook Dale. Visits to mines gave Lee an opportunity to observe geological strata – his sketches speak to his interest in those – and to gather mineralogical and geological specimens. Lee noted the qualities of the various rocks, minerals and geological formations he found on mountainsides and in mineshafts, even collecting so many mineralogical specimens during one day's walk that he had to hire two boys to help carry his heavy bags.[2] He requested that the proprietor of a marble works in Kilkenny would forward samples to him, as he had not time for a visit.[3] Lee's museum at Hartwell House was later renowned for the mineralogical collection he amassed during his own travels and through correspondents, and he was elected to the Geological Society in 1841. It has been suggested that his love of mineralogy and specimen collecting began during his visit to Sweden in 1807–9,[4] but the diaries published in this book clearly indicate his strong interest in that science at an earlier stage. Long before the establishment of his own private museum, Lee enjoyed a visit to the Dublin Society's premises. He found that three and a half hours was only sufficient for a cursory examination of its lecture room, library, museum and laboratory. He enjoyed the numismatic, paleontological and zoological collections, thought the mineralogical collection was 'a most beautiful sight', and noted the collection of Irish mineral specimens, arranged by county. He made two further visits to the museum at the close of his tour, five months later.[5]

The diaries also detail the plant life Lee found in the mountains and valleys through which he walked. His scientific concern with systematic classification is reflected in his use of the Linnaean binomial system. At the beginning of his tour, he made a detailed record of his visit to Oxford University's botanic garden, sketching its ground plan and giving a detailed textual description of the relative positions of the groups of plants and the irrigation system. He admired the botanical library but indicated that it was a little out-of-date, with most of the books being over a century old. He returned to the garden at 10:30 that night to see the night-blooming cactus, *Cereus*, but elected not to return at half past midnight to witness it in full bloom. The attention Lee paid to plants and flowers reveals his eye for detail and the sensory nature of the pedestrian tour. He recorded trees and plants with care, detailing their locations and even preserving one leaf that he found covered in aphids between the leaves of his first diary, where its reddish-brown imprint still remains.[6]

---

[1] SJC, MS U.30 (1), f. 41r, p. 60.
[2] SJC, MS U.30 (2), f. 83v, p. 138.
[3] SJC, MS U.30 (2), f. 109v, p. 152.
[4] Mead, 'Dr John Lee of Hartwell and his Swedish Journey', p. 16. See also Mead, 'The Mineralogical Collection'.
[5] SJC, MS U.30 (2), f. 32v, p. 103; SJC, MS U.30 (5), f. 60v, p. 287.
[6] SJC, MS U.30 (6), flyleaf and f. 1r, p. 309.

6. Textual Introduction

After the sale of some of the Hartwell papers at Sotheby's in 1941, the remainder of the collection was handed to the British Records Association for distribution among the most appropriate archives. Ethel Stokes, secretary of the Association, wrote with a somewhat irritated tone that Lee had 'kept almost every scrap of written paper that came to him'.[1] His extensive archive of correspondence, personal papers and scientific notes is now spread across at least eighteen repositories in Australia, Britain, Canada, Sweden and the USA.[2] For Lee's early life, however, the records are patchier, possibly due to the unreliability of the post during the Napoleonic Wars. The only two surviving letters that he received during the execution of the tour described in this book are published in Appendix 2.

The five diaries and three sketchbooks created by Lee during this walking tour and published in this volume are held at St John's College, Cambridge (SJC, MS U.30 (1–8)). The eight original notebooks are, for the most part, unpaginated and total 610 manuscript folios, many but not all written on both sides. The reader is alerted to blank folios as they appear in the text with a note in square brackets. The number of lines per page is not consistent and the notebooks vary greatly in length.[3]

Tour from London to Holywell in Wales	68 ff.	25,960 words	SJC, MS U.30 (1)
Tour from Holywell to Dublin and Fermoy	153 ff.	44,330 words	SJC, MS U.30 (2)
Mallow to Bantry	17 ff.	8,960 words	SJC, MS U.30 (3)
Bantry to Castlemain	59 ff.	23,340 words	SJC, MS U.30 (4)
Killarney to Dublin	88 ff.	35,700 words	SJC, MS U.30 (5)
Sketchbook, 1806	64 ff.	3,680 words	SJC, MS U.30 (6)
Sketchbook, 1806–7	68 ff.	3,290 words	SJC, MS U.30 (7)
Sketchbook, 1807	93 ff.	3,580 words	SJC, MS U.30 (8)

a. The Text

The diaries presented here are all as penned by Lee in 1806–7, and have been subjected to no editorial or other intervention since. In keeping with the objectives of the Hakluyt Society, this edition does not aim for facsimile reproduction of the original journals, but the full text has been transcribed without any omissions. This edition is divided into five sections, preserving the original titles provided by Lee inside the front cover of each of his notebooks. The titles are provided in bold at the beginning of each section. The text retains Lee's original paragraphing and the solid lines he occasionally drew between daily

---

[1] SJC, Letter of Ethel Stokes, 17 July 1941, MS Box 1a.

[2] The following list is indicative, not comprehensive: Beinecke Library, Yale University; BL; CUL; CBS; Hertfordshire Archives and Local Studies; Institution of Engineering and Technology Archives, London; Lambeth Palace; Library and Archives Canada, Ottawa; Museum of the History of Science, Oxford; National Library of Australia, Canberra; National Maritime Museum, Greenwich; National Meteorological Archive, Exeter; Parliamentary Archives (UK); Royal Astronomical Society; Royal Society; Senate House Library, University of London; SJC; State Library of New South Wales, Sydney; Uppsala University Library, Sweden. Lee's mineralogical collection is at Buckinghamshire County Museum. See also list of manuscript sources, p. 345.

[3] Folio counts provided in the following list include blank folios and folios which have been cut or torn out, where definite, countable evidence of the folio remains within the binding. Word counts are to the nearest ten.

INTRODUCTION

entries. Where Lee dated his diary entries these dates have been retained, but have been rendered in bold type to aid the reader. Where Lee did not provide a full date at the beginning of a diary entry, the editor has supplied the missing information in square brackets or as an italicized editorial intervention.

Lee's handwriting was small and close, he was fond of abbreviations and he often wrote in pencil. Every effort has been made to transcribe the text as accurately as possible, but some uncertainties unfortunately remain. Uncertain transcriptions are given in square brackets followed by a question mark; illegible words are represented by asterisks in square brackets. Much of journal SJC, MS U.30 (3) was written in pencil and some of the pages are badly smudged, meaning some of the text is now illegible; the reader is alerted to the affected pages in the footnotes. Lee's spelling was consistent with normal nineteenth-century usage, but individual instances of unusual spellings are followed by a clarification in square brackets or by [*sic*]. Lee's abbreviations are expanded in italic font, except for the commonly used ones listed above (p. xv). Superscripts used in abbreviations have been silently lowered (e.g. M^r), with the following exceptions: N° (meaning 'number'), O^r (meaning 'circular'), $\perp^r$ (meaning 'perpendicular') and the unit abbreviations 's' (*solidi*, shillings) and 'd' (*denarii*, pence). Lee corrected some errors and omissions in the text himself, apparently at the time of writing; his own deletions and insertions are retained in this edition. He made some of these corrections above his scored-out text, while others follow immediately in the same line. Lee refrained from using much punctuation; to aid the reader, the editor has inserted punctuation as appropriate, in square brackets. Occasionally, proper nouns and other pieces of information are represented in the text by a dash, suggesting memory lapses by Lee; the missing information is provided in a footnote, where possible.

Lee peppered his narrative with sketches of varying detail, quality and finish. Many were simple aides-memoire, for example, to supplement a technical description or a description of the layout of a building. Others were more detailed and better-finished drawings of ruins or scenes that Lee evidently intended to complete later, but never did (if he did, they do not survive). His three sketchbooks – journals SJC, MSS U.30 (6), (7) and (8) – complement his five written diaries. Many of the sketches are quite heavily annotated. While the large number of sketches and their varying quality meant that it was possible to reproduce only a selection of them in this volume, Lee's annotations have been transcribed as appendices to the diaries. These notes often take the form of long titles or captions and as such are published in full. Lee also tended to write brief, one-word annotations within the sketches, indicating a never-realized intention to complete the sketches later. These very brief annotations have not been transcribed, given their limited value when the sketch itself is not available to the reader. In sketchbook SJC, MS U.30 (7), Lee often made initial captions and other notes in pencil, later writing these over in ink. Where the pencil notes are the same as the ink notes, they have not been transcribed.

Lee experimented with different ways of writing up his journal. The folios in journals SJC, MSS U.30 (1), (2) and (3) were not always written up in order, so the original text has been reordered to avoid confusion. The footnotes indicate where this has been done, and the original order of writing will be evident to the reader by following the folio numbers provided in square brackets. In journal SJC, MS U.30 (2), Lee briefly flirted with numbering the pages himself; these numbers are included as marginal notes. In sketchbook SJC, MS U.30 (6), delicate blotting sheets remain between most of the folios – these are blank and have not been counted as folios. Finally, in parts of journals SJC, MSS U.30 (4) and (5), Lee wrote across facing verso and recto folios, so that the text runs right across both pages; the reader is alerted to these sections in the footnotes.

b. Editorial Conventions

The following conventions have been employed in the text:
a) [text in square brackets] – editorial interpolation and/or addition;
b) (text in parentheses) – word(s) inserted in the original by the author, either above the line or within the main text;
c) text struck through – words or phrases crossed out by the author in the original manuscript, but which remain legible. In the case of illegible strikethroughs, the number of words or lines is noted in square brackets;
d) Lee made extensive use of the runic thorn (ye, yt, yr, ys), which is silently modernized;
e) missing letters are inserted and abbreviations are expanded as editorial interpolations in italics;
f) &c is silently modernized to etc.;
g) Lee's use of symbols has been retained and is explained in the list of symbols (see p. xvi);
h) & is silently replaced by 'and';
i) when Lee intended to correct the word order of a phrase, he underlined and/or numbered the relevant words. These word-order changes have been implemented by the editor and are indicated by a footnote;
j) Lee's use of punctuation was minimal. To aid the reader, punctuation has been added where necessary, in square brackets;
k) an illegible word is represented by three asterisks in square brackets [***]; where there is more than one illegible word in succession, the second and subsequent words are represented by one asterisk each;
l) Lee's use of capital letters was inconsistent, as was common at the time. The first word of each sentence and proper names are silently corrected to upper case to aid the reader, but otherwise his use of capitals has been retained;
m) words split by a line-break in the original are silently rejoined;
n) ships' names, Latin names for flora and fauna, words in languages other than English, and titles of books and dramatic works are silently italicized.

c. Critical Apparatus

The critical apparatus to this text includes footnotes on points of geography, history, language, biography and natural history. These notes are intended to provide basic information on people, places and events mentioned, and to explain terms that may be unfamiliar to the reader. The editor has intentionally kept these notes brief, so they should not be considered comprehensive. Footnotes and clarifications in square brackets only appear on first mention of the person, place or event, but a cross-reference to the first mention is provided if mention is made in more than one of the diaries.

Lee made his journey some thirty years prior to the Ordnance Survey's standardization of Irish- and Welsh-language place names. Every effort has been made to identify places mentioned, but this has not been possible in all cases. The Irish-language version of a given place name is provided in square brackets where it helps to clarify or explain Lee's rendition of the name, and when a place is located within the modern Irish-speaking regions (*Gaeltacht*). Lee's often-idiosyncratic spelling of place names has been retained, with the modern spelling provided in square brackets on the first mention only.

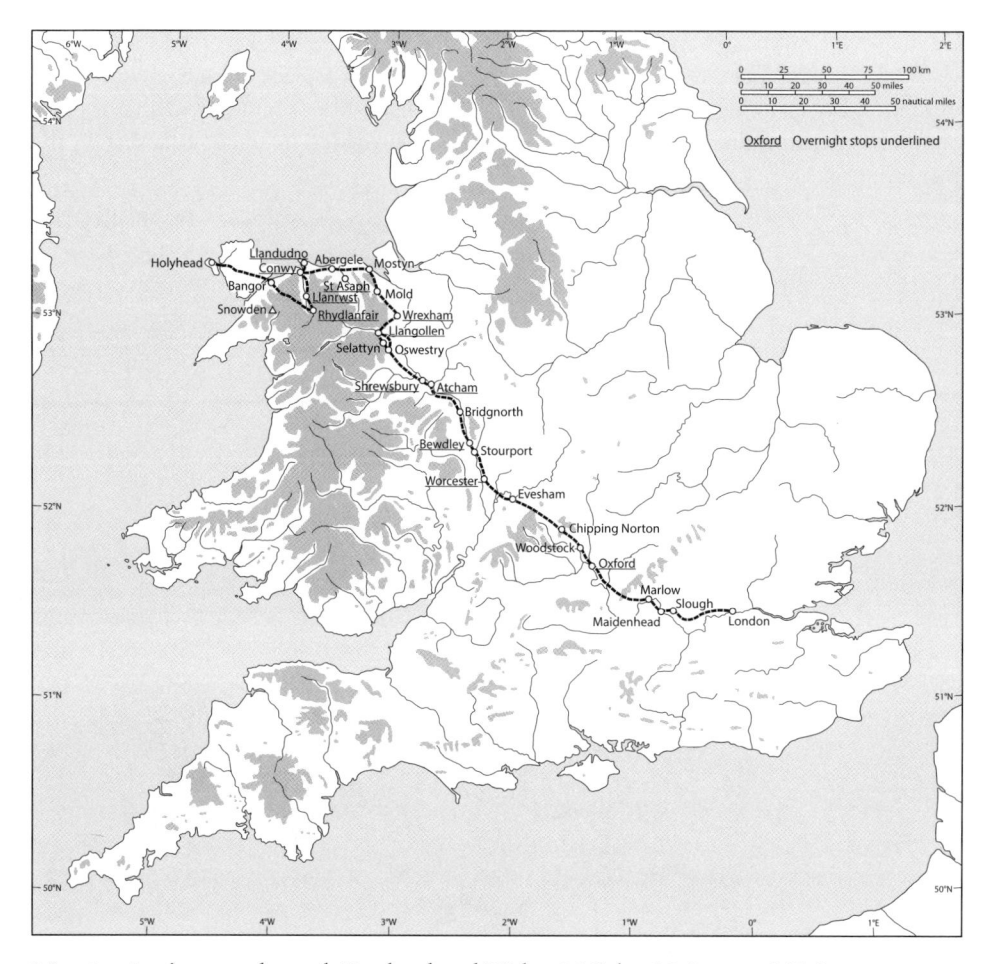

Map 1. Lee's route through England and Wales, 31 July–29 August 1806.

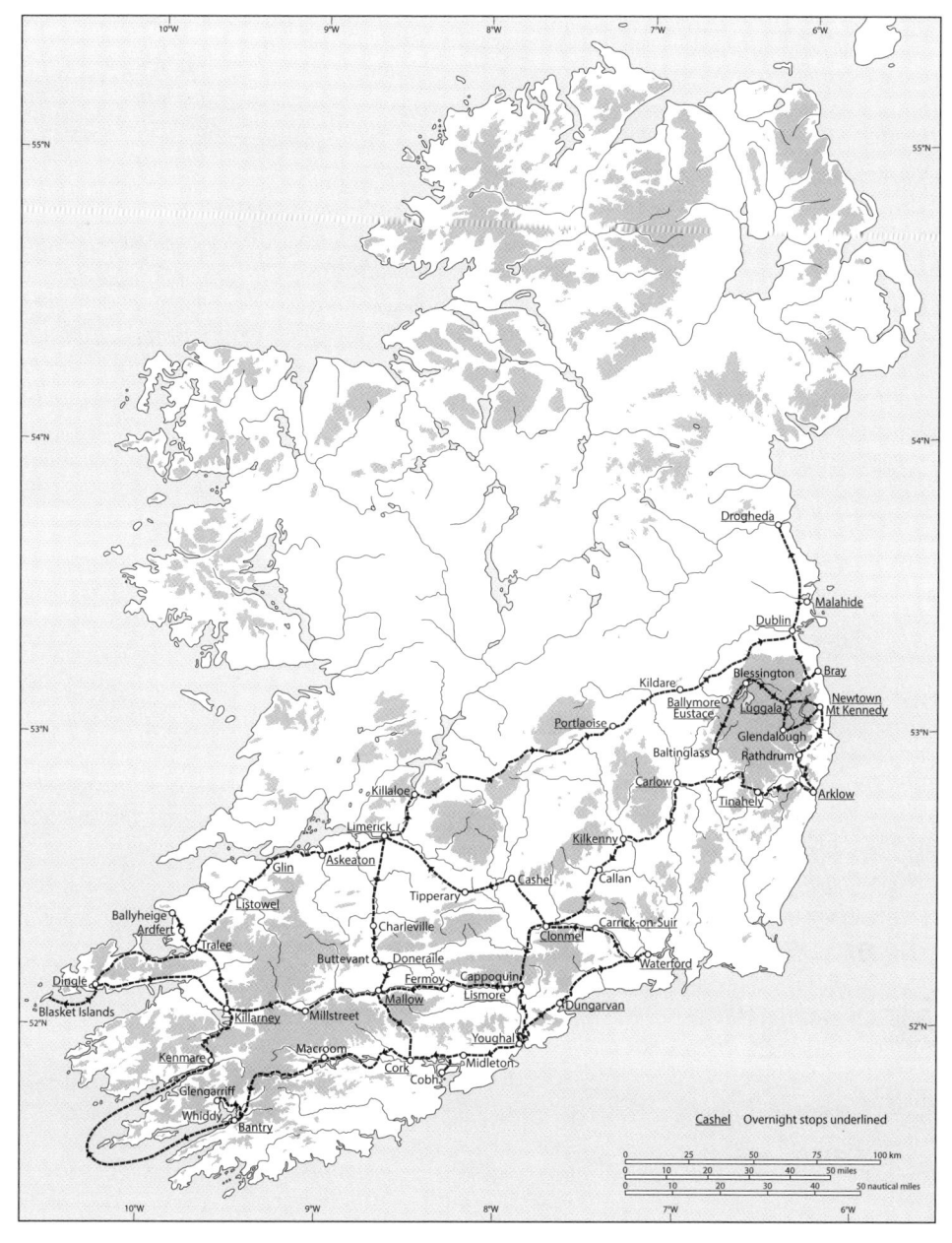

Map 2.   Lee's route through Ireland, 30 August 1806–6 March 1807.

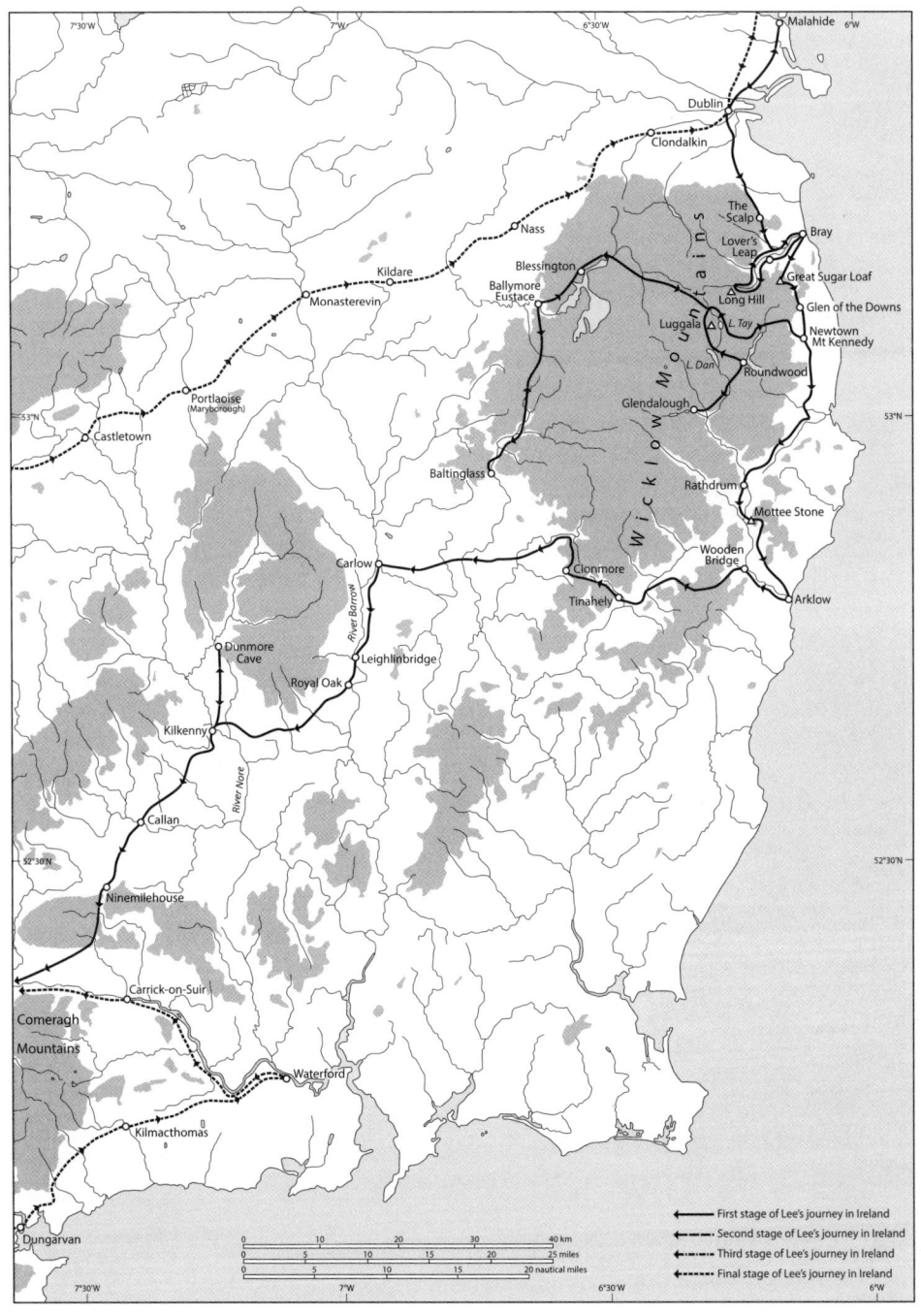

Map 3. Lee's route through Ireland, detail. Showing his route from Dublin to Ninemilehouse, 5–19 September 1806 (solid line); and from Castletown to Dublin, 29–30 January 1807 (broken line).

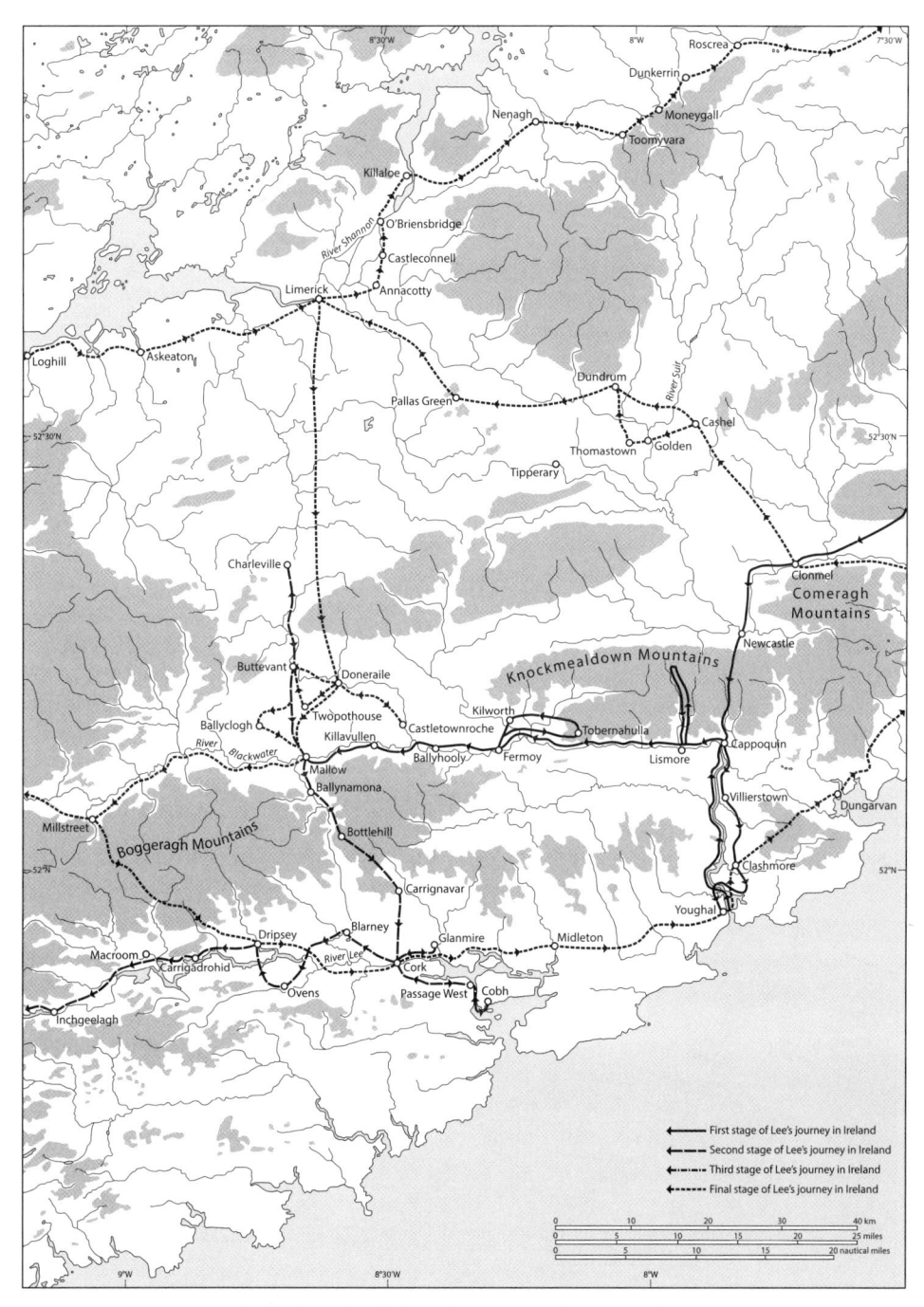

Map 4. Lee's route through Ireland, detail. Showing his route from Clonmel to Mallow, 19–30 September 1806 (solid line); from Mallow to Inchigeelagh, 1–9 October 1806 (chain line); and from Loghill to Roscrea, 20 November 1806–29 January 1807 (long broken line).

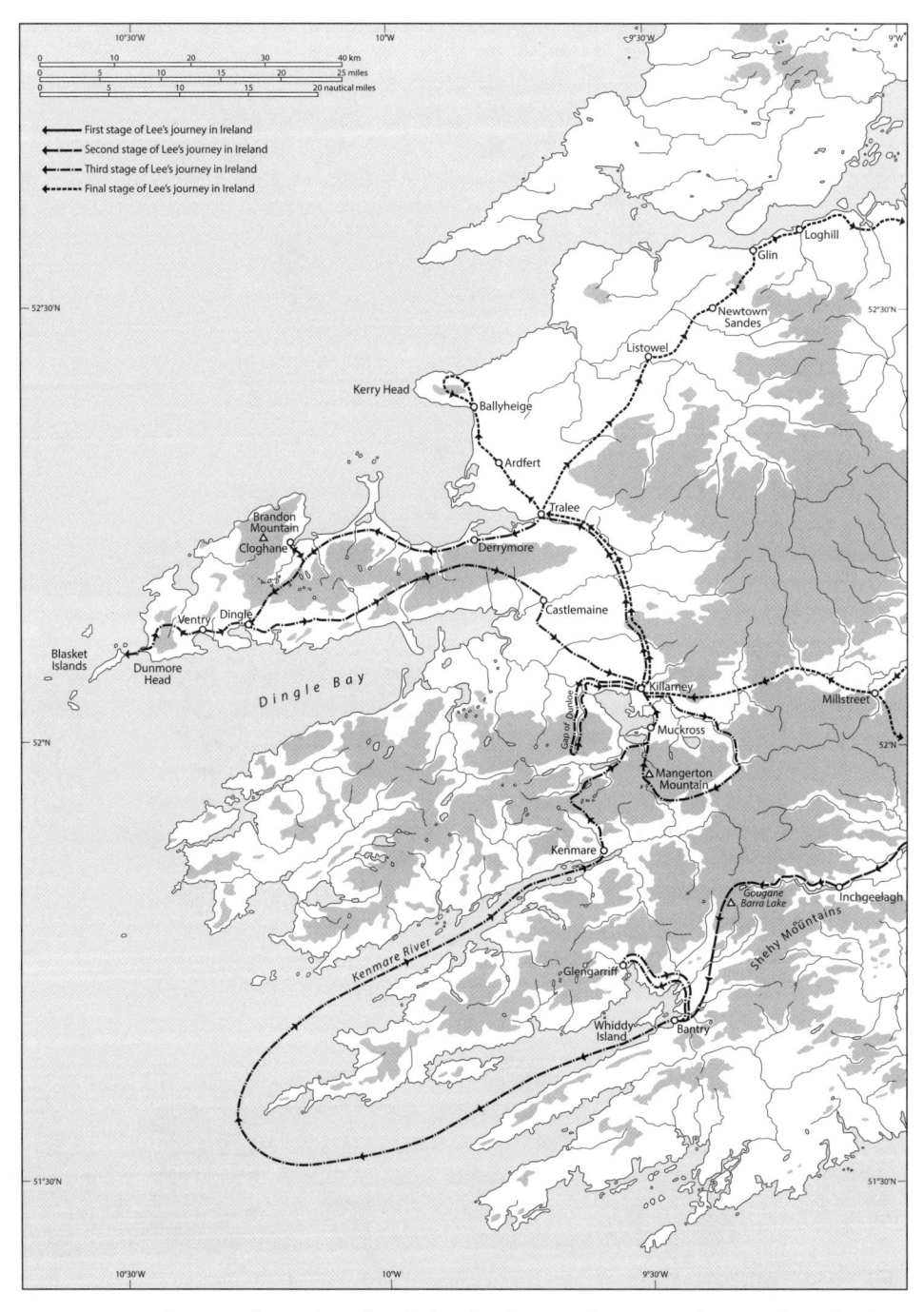

Map 5. Lee's route through Ireland, detail. Showing his route from Inchigeelagh to Bantry, 8–10 October 1806 (chain line); from Bantry to Killarney, 11–30 October 1806 (short and long broken line); and from Killarney to Loghill, 30 October–20 November 1806 (broken line).

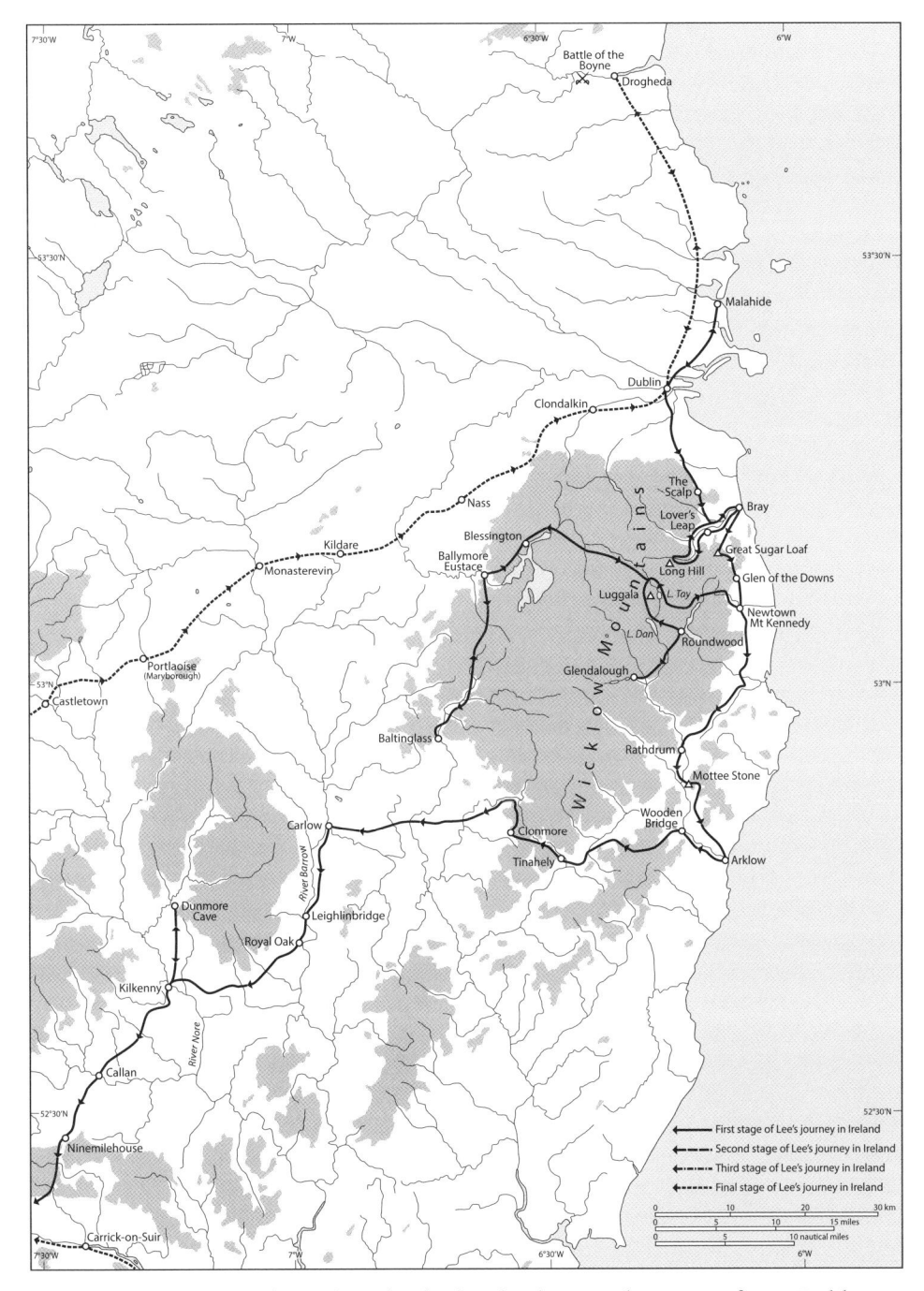

Map 6. Lee's route through Ireland, detail. Showing his route from Dublin to Ninemilehouse, 5–19 September 1806 (solid line); from Castletown to Dublin and Drogheda, 29–30 January 1807; and from Dublin to Drogheda, 18–19 February 1807 (broken line).

DIARIES OF A TOUR
OF IRELAND, ENGLAND AND WALES
IN 1806–1807

1. TOUR FROM LONDON TO HOLYWELL IN WALES[1]

[SJC, MS U.30 (1)]
[f. 1 *cut out*]

[f. 2r] **[31 July 1806, Thursday]**
We started f*ro*m the Whitehorse Cellar at 10 M*inu*tes past 9 and arrived in Oxford at ¼ past 5[.][2] Betw*ee*n Hounslow and ~~Slough~~ (Oxford) the crops of Oats and corn were remarkably fine and they were in many parts cut[.] The sickle was basely employed on both sides of the road all the way and we were informed that the crops when down did not ~~deceive~~ fall short of wh*at* they appeared when standing. The reapers frequently work with their left hands as well as with the right w*hi*ch must be a very desirable art as the labor must be rendered much more easy. About the neighbourhood of Town the 2nd Crops of Clover looked very well and some were cut[.]

Having in this stage f*ro*m Hounslow to Slough two leaders very unequal to each other, their traces were observed to be crossed and the coachman informed us that they by that means wou*l*d enable the horses to draw better together. I doubt it much[.] The road about 16 Miles from town begins to be uncommonly interesting and the traveller may at a distance observe the venerable turrets of Windsor rearing their antique heads above the trees. From Slough[,] w*hi*ch is not more than a mile f*ro*m Windsor[,] the Castle is fairly seen and ~~casts~~ strikes the spectator with wonder as he considers its magnificent and regal appearance and with astonishment as he considers the many laborious hours w*hi*ch have in diff*eren*t centuries been spent in its erection. Nothing can be more noble than the appearance of the two f*ro*m from [*sic*] this road. Eton College immediately reminds the beholder (who has been accustomed to the sights and) who has ever gazed with delight on the magnificent Building at ~~Kings College~~ (Cambridge) of Kings College chapel, of w*hi*ch it seems to be a correct yet a smaller resemblance[.] [f. 3r] We could only observe on its top two of those lofty towers w*hi*ch are in general called by the name of the larger pepper boxes. The road from there [Windsor] to Marlow is very engaging. The Woods w*hi*ch crown the hill and skirt in all variety of form*s* the cornfields of w*hi*ch some have parted with their produce and some are ready to resign their produce[.] The Beautiful winding vallies and the winding streams all unite to produce the most pleasing sensations in the mind of a person, who is delighted with view*in*g the landscapes of nature. The view of Marlow f*ro*m the hill opens most suddenly and beautifully[.] The Church[,] the Town[,] the river [Thames] winding along the valley from it, and the foreground to the

---

[1] Note inside front cover by Lee.
[2] Lee commenced his journey in London: the White Horse Cellar Coach Office was in Piccadilly (*Topography of London*, n.p.). While he uses first person plural pronouns on occasion, he does not name his companion, if any.

scene made by the wood hanging from the hills opposite to the town, are indescribably beautiful and the whole road to Henley is more like the picture which we form in our ideas when the Elysian Gardens are brought to the recollection[.] If any thing can Equal or if any thing can nearly approach the view of Marlow as a candidate for effect it is the View of Henley when you have just got halfway down the Hill between Lord Malmsburys[1] Lodge and the Town[.][2]

[f. 3v] [*margin: Small ink sketch of ladder, annotated,* remarkable good constructed high ladders broad and the wood stouter at the bottom and fine light and tapering towards the top][3]

Most of the names of Villages or hamlets or Gentlemens houses are illspelt or wrong named no doubt as well as the names of the Inhabitants for we found great difficulty in understanding the sounds and many we could not make out and very few persons could spell the names to us when we requested them[.]

[f. 2v] [*margin:* August 1. Thermometer at 4 [o'clock]. 67
[August] 2. At 7 OClock Thermometer 60″[4]]

[f. 4r] It reminds us of those views which one sometimes sees of places abroad, which are selected as most proper for beautiful landscapes. [Upon?] looking behind the hill has a good effect and the large patches of lavender about 20 Acres in all with their (dark) blue flowers form a variety to the landscape such as is hardly ever seen in this country[.]

Passing through Maidenhead at one Extremity of the town a Boy asked the Coachman whether Old Hodges was going up to Town today, 'Yes you will see him presently'[5] was the answer. And upon asking what the boy meant we were told that about half a year ago Old Hodges as he was driving along through the town whipped one of the boys who was playing at marbles in the middle of the street, he only just gave him one cut and told him to keep out of the way. However the whole of the party were exasperated at their companion being thus treated and they have ever since every day whenever he goes through the town been followed by all the boys who hallow and howl at him, calling him names as their ingenuity suggests to them Old Hog[,] O Hodge[,] etc[.] They have done it so long that he is teased to death by them, Thus it seems that like a parcel of hens they are initable[6] and that boys may not be hurt with impunity. This shews to what a degree, a [spirit?] exists in the mind of the youth of this Kingdom [f. 4v *blank*] [f. 5r] who all take his part because they think him to have been injured. The crops looked remarkably fine all the way down to Oxford and the scattered fields of hops which were just in flower and had grown beyond the height of their poles and were twining round each other in all the gay luxuriance of prosperity was a sufficient proof that their buds were no longer in

---

[1] James Harris, 1st Earl of Malmesbury (1746–1820), diplomatist (Scott, 'Harris, James (1746–1820)'); proprietor of Park Place, near Henley-on-Thames.

[2] Narrative continues at f. 4r, below.

[3] In the page margin, Lee made a small ink sketch of the ladder, not reproduced here. It is not clear where he saw it.

[4] ″ normally signifies seconds, but Lee used it in place of a degree sign.

[5] Quotation marks added.

[6] Lee probably means 'inimitable'.

danger from the detrimental fly [aphids]. For some miles between Marlow and Henley every turn of the road presented us with a view of hanging (beech) woods[,] hop grounds, and here and there a field of clover in little heaps reminded me of many a waistcoat whose pattern of various and well transfused spots has been probably originated from some idea of this sort. Nothing can exceed the windings of the river [Thames] at Henley for beauty and elegance[.] Had not we passed by the Lodge of Lord Harcourt[1] before we come to the two rows of cottages which skirt the road, one would have been led, by the great appearance of neatness and comfort which they show, to imagine that the house₁ of some₂[2] nobleman, who consults the happiness and welfare of his labourers and of the poor, was situated very near. Every cottage had a garden and a stack [f. 5v *Sketch of church among trees, ink, captioned*] View near Oxford [f. 6r] of wood close adjoining to the house which they are probably allowed to pick up (out of the wood) or perhaps his lordships munificence allows them some proportion of wood according to the size of their families. The [borows?][3] of lofty trees on the sides of the road add to the comfort as well as to the beauty of the cottages, by the shelter they afford and by the liveliness of their foliage. The gardens were ornamented with flowers according to the taste of the owners or engaged with furnishing the common necessaries which the poor so seldom can obtain. In short from their appearance they seem to be models for any cottages which a gentleman might wish to have upon his estate both for their neatness and seeming convenience and comfort.

Considering myself as by no means an impartial observer of the merits of the 2 Universities it was not my intention to make any remarks upon Oxford (which I should ever venture to produce among my friends) and therefore as we came along on the coach my determination was to pass over negligently every thing I saw and to make not one comparison between any thing here or at Cambridge.[4] But in spite of my resolution upon passing over Magdalen Bridge, I could not help feeling some [f. 6v *blank*] [f. 7r] sensations of pleasure and surprise which were well worth a guinea a second. Upon going into the Angel Yard and just casting a view towards a College opposite it struck me that it must be the well known Christ College[5] which we had so often heard mentioned but upon buying an Oxford Guide[6] and starting out my mistake was soon discovered. Of course no one can deny but that the streets and City of Oxford upon the whole are infinitely superior to that of Cambridge and in spite of our (primary) intentions not to enter into any comparisons, which intentions we now found would be extremely politic, still we could not help drawing comparisons every step we went and notwithstanding our prejudices which were ardently called to our aid, all the results turned out in favor of the place we were in. We first bent our steps to Christ Church to survey that Monster of Greatness which we had so often heard celebrated. Its entrance certainly surpasses that of Trinity.[7] Its Court is inferior. Its Library is inferior. The Halls are nearly on a par for

---

[1] Possibly William, 3rd Earl Harcourt (d. 1830).
[2] The word order has been reversed here, as indicated by Lee's subscript numbering.
[3] Boughs.
[4] Lee was a Cambridge graduate.
[5] Christ Church College.
[6] Possibly [A Gentleman of Oxford], *The New Oxford Guide*. The first edition was published in 1759; Lee may have used the recent 1805 or 1806 editions.
[7] Trinity College, Cambridge.

although Christ Church appears smaller yet the magnificent ascent to it makes up for the deficiency. We could not find out the Chapel[.] The Court is curious and has a more ~~magnificent~~ (venerable) appearance than Trinity[.] The Buildings of the latter look too mean for the size. The high [f. 8r] walk all round the Square is grand and upon the whole the Court if well examined may be superior to Trinity although the style of the windows is very unbecoming and trivial[.] Yet the Peckwater Square[1] is certainly inferior to the Second Court at Trinity[.] The Walks at Christ Church are certainly beautiful and the river bounds them most advantageously. The Grand Gravel Walk[,] which by stepping it appeared to be about 502 Yards[,] exceeds in grandeur any one in Cambridge and the whole of the grounds are infinitely superior to those of Trinity. The river[,] although it did not seem to pass through much of the town or to afford much advantage to it by its beauty[,] certainly excells [sic] the Cam. The Town Hall is far superior to that of Cambridge. The Rad cliffe [sic] Library can be compared to nothing at Cambridge which we could think off [sic]. But the Schools are far finer than ours and from the (External) appearance of the library above (and the Picture Gallery) it must be considered as surpassing the Public Library in Cambridge. The Market also ought not to be put on a par with that of Cambridge and no impartial observer would offer it such an insult[.] It would be too ludicrous to put into the scales of comparison a pound weight and a feather and to consider the University Pressing House here and the Press at Cambridge as opponents would be a consideration quite as absurd. We had better therefore allow it to be one of those things with which we have nothing to compare[.]

[f. 7v] Comparison between Oxford and Cambridge

Oxford		Cambridge
Christ. Church. Front	beats	Ditto Trinity
Hall	=	Hall
1 Court	beats	1 Court
Peckwater	yields to	2 Court
Library	Ditto –	Library
Walks	beat	Walks
River Isis	Ditto –	Cam
Schools	Ditto –	Schools
Market	Ditto –	Market
Radcliffe Library } Clarendon Press }	Nothing at Cambridge to compare with them	
Botanic Garden	yields to –	Cambridge Botanic Garden
Magdalen	superior to –	St Johns
New College	equal to	Emmanuel.
Trinity College	superior to	Jesus Cambridge
Wadham	superior to	Magdalen

[f. 8v] Sketch of what seems to be the plan of the Physic garden at Cambridge[2]

[1] Peckwater Quadrangle.
[2] Lee meant the garden at Oxford; the sketch corresponds to his written description on 1 Aug. The sketch is reproduced at p. 39 (Figure 1).

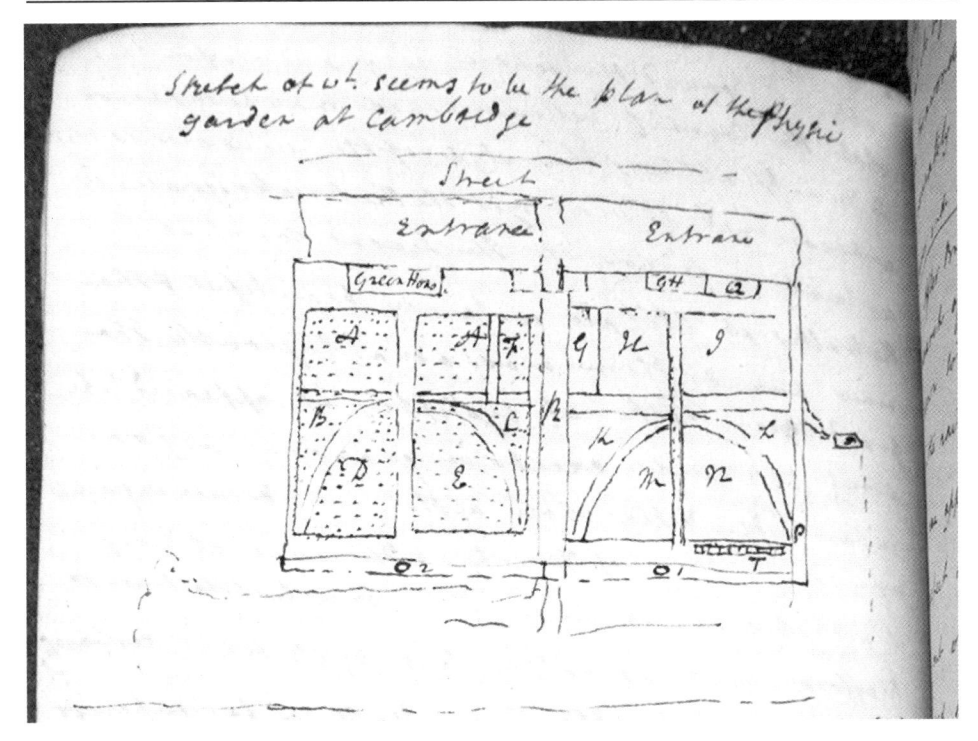

Figure 1. 'Sketch of what seems to be the plan of the Physic garden at Cambridge'. By John Lee, 31 July 1806. Lee seems to have titled the sketch at a later date and in fact it matches his description of the garden at Oxford (SJC, MS U.30 (1), f. 8v). Reproduced by kind permission of the Master and Fellows of St John's College, Cambridge.

R	is the Great Walk which separates the 2 Parts of the Garden there is a green house at the top of each and on one side is Q the Library
AA	are the *Planta Europa perennes* crossing over the road in regular order from one row to the other
B:	*Arboretum asiaticum* [Asian arboretum]
C.	*Arboretum Americanum* [American arboretum]
D.	*Planta asiatics Perennes* [Asian perennial plants]
E.	— *americans Perennes* [American perennial plants]
F.	*Gramina Exotica* [exotic grasses]
G.	— *Britannica* [British grasses]
H, I	*Planta Britannica perennes* [British perennial plants]
K.	*Planta Exotica Annua* [exotic annual plants]
L.	— *Britannica* — [British annual plants]
M.	*Arboretum Europeum* [European arboretum]
N.	— *Britannicum* [British arboretum]
OO.	*Planta diversa parva etc velut*[1] *Perguiclil Asplenium* [fern] *Lycopodia*. [*Lycopodium*, clubmoss] *Scirpi*. [scirpus] *Cerastia*. [*Cerastium*, mouse-ear chickweed]

[1] 'Various small plants such as'.

Draba[1] *Cardamine* [bittercress] – In O.2.[2] *sunt Alyssum Saxifrage* [rockfoil]. *Heliconias.*[3] *et Osillarum minutum.*[4]

[f. 9r] The tone of the G*rea*t Bell Tom[5] was not so loud as we had expected to hear it, but its softness made up for the deficiency of the sound[.] For a wonder we counted the 101 Times of its Tolling accurately although a Mail Coach was coming up the lower end of the Town at the time.

August 1. [Friday]
After Breakfast we sallied forth from our Inn in search of new adventure and directed our earliest steps down to the Botanical Garden, where we rambled about in the rain for some time, Perceiving a Gentleman there we approached him and requested some information with respect to the manner in w*hich* the grounds were laid out w*hich* he readily and handsomely gave and conducted us round the grounds. The plants in the beds are arranged according to the Linnean System[6] but those of diff*eren*t countries are kept in some deg*ree* separate. The American Bed and the European plants are on the Right hand as you enter the gate[.] The English plants are on the left, where also are all the Grasses of all countries together. The smaller plants begin [in] rows from the Green houses ~~on~~ crossing the middle paths and go backwa*r*ds and forwards each alternate row. The next Class are the plants of larger size and contain the shrubs arranged in the same manner. At the Bottom of the Garden under the wall and for its whole length are small divisions for those plants w*hich* require shade and [f. 9v *blank*] [f. 10r] moisture and w*hich* are small. Most of the *Carex*[,][7] hebe[8] etc and all the small plants[.] These divisions of two rows run the whole length of the wall at Bottom and there are a great many divisions. At the left corner are the *Orchis Ophrys*[,][9] (*Satyrium*[10]) etc classes and there are elevated long[,] narrow troughs for the water plants, these are also divided into 2 divisions abreast and the water is comm*unicat*ed f*ro*m one to the other by means of holes in the separate squares.[11] The hothouses are small and not in very good repair. The walk down the middle is formal. The method of having the water plants in boxes is very convenient for the person who wishes to inspect them but is not so good as the pond in the Garden at Camb*ri*dge and many will not live in them[.] The preceding Evening a night Blowing *Cereus*[12] had been in flower and there will be one tonight w*hich* we were offered permission to see. The Library is very convenient and contains an admirable collection of Botanical Books w*hich* were coll*ect*ed an 100 Yea*r*s ago[.] No very great additions were made to them since that

[1] A genus of plants in the mustard family.
[2] In reference to the sketch plan of the garden. *Sunt* is Latin for 'are'.
[3] A genus of tropical flowering plants.
[4] *Oscillatoria,* a genus of algae, including *oscillatoria minuta*.
[5] Great Tom, the bell in Tom Tower, Oxford, rings out 101 chimes to mark a curfew at 21:05 every night.
[6] The Linnaean taxonomy, established by the Swedish botanist Carl Linnaeus (1707–78) in 1735.
[7] A large genus of grassy plants.
[8] A genus of plants native to the South Pacific and South America.
[9] A large genus of orchid.
[10] A genus of orchid.
[11] Divisions are illustrated by a small, rough sketch of the grid structure in the text, not reproduced here.
[12] A cactus, the short-lived flower of which blooms at night.

time. Dr Sipthorpe[1] left a few. There is also a most valuable *Hortus Siccus*[2] which was not all collected by *Sipthorpe* but great many plants were sent to him by foreign Botanists as was the custom in those times[.]

NB. The *Ochis bicornis* [*Anacamptis pyramidalis*, pyramidal orchid] is not in the Hothouse here.

This Garden is not (no) finer [*sic*] than the Cambridge one[.]

[f. 10v *blank*]

[f. 11r] From thence we proceeded to Magdalen College which is altogether with its walks (spire and Bridge and meadows) and park more than a match for St Johns College Cambridge with its accompanying Gateway, Bridge and Garden[.] The park is most truly magnificent and the deer of which we counted about 28 are seen to great advantage from the meadow beneath the boles of the trees which even seem in height to rival those of St Johns[.] New College will bear comparison with Emmanuel Cambridge without blushing and the mound covered with shrubs and trees has a prodigiously noble effect between the 2 Rows of trees. Wadham will best compare with Magdalen Cambridge with regard to its size and although the Buildings of the latter are inferior to those of the former yet the Bibliotheca Pepesyana[3] will bring this difference down very much[.] The Gardens of Magdalen are evidently inferior to those of Wadham[.] If we grant that the whole of one is about sufficient to counter between the advantages of the other, such a concession is in favor of the Cambridge college. ~~Jesus College~~ Trinity College will from its three sided Court ~~will~~ and the Entrance in the other side through the Gateway bears great resemblance to Jesus Cambridge. But its buildings are vastly superior and the walks [f. 11v *blank*] [f. 12r] are extremely singular and fine, the two fences of Yew are cut into the shapes of columns which are at short distances from each other[4] and at the Ends the trees are cut into the shape of round columns. The whole is far finer than the college to which it will bear to be compared. The Senate House however looks to far better effect than does the Theatre, and one might compare several other colleges but still there will remain many for which there is nothing to shew in Cambridge against it[.] Kings College Chapel is without a rival, no chapel here being at all = to it. The Chapel or rather church of Christ Church is a very fine old Building but nothing equal to Kings. The Row of trees by St Johns makes that entrance into the town very beautiful[.] Balliol Brazenhoze [Brasenose], Corpus Christi and Oriel are each well worthy of observations[.] The High street from the foot of the Bridge to the church at the top where Fish Street [St Aldate's St] crosses it is said to be a mile long but by pacing it it was 853 steps or not quite so many yards. We paid a second visit (at 8 oclock) to the Physic Garden to see the night blowing *Cereus* which was half open and which both looked and smelt most beautifully. It was of a size not so large [f. 12v *blank*] [f. 13r] as they generally grow as we were informed, the plant being not in a very healthy state.

About ½ past ten we paid a second visit to the Physic garden to see the *Cereus* which was not at that time incompletely opened. The Stamina were arranged in elegant order around the inside of the Bell but there were a great many which had not arrived at their proper places. The odor which was diffused from the plant was extremely powerful and

---

[1] Humphrey Sipthorpe or Sibthorpe (1712–97), Sheridan Professor of Botany at Oxford 1747–84 (Newton and Hannah, *The Deserted Village*, p. 185).

[2] A collection of dried botanical specimens.

[3] The Samuel Pepys Library, Magdalene College, Cambridge.

[4] Illustrated by small, rough sketch of three columns in the text, not reproduced here.

might be sensibly perceived upon entering the planthouse. We were invited to come again in two hours time when the flower would have been in its highest state of maturity but on account of our intended early departure on the preceeding [*sic*] morning we declined the invitation[.]

August 2. [Saturday]
At seven OClock we mounted the Worcester Coach but found a very material difference in the expedition of the Journey although the fare was by some means contrived to be the same at [*sic*] that from Town and the distance was less[.] We did not arrive in Worcester before ¼ before 6. At Anston[1] 14 Miles from Oxford we were to Breakfast when going into the parlour we perceived two Tea Tables one for our Coach and one for the Birmingham which arrived at the same time, each had one plate of Bread and Butter on the Table and the other things were a coming [f. 13v *blank*] [f. 14r] upon which not liking the appearance of affairs we went into the Kitchen, Called for our Basons[2] of Milk and helping ourselves to the loaf we sat down before the kitchen fire whose warmth was by no means unacceptable as the wind had been high and the storms frequent. Besides the comfort of the kitchen we had opportunity of laying an embargo upon all the goods which were going to the parlour when we pleased and by that means were well supplied with Eggs[,] etc [and] Toast. As we passed through Woodstock we had but just time to cast a view up the Park[3] for we were at the time more intent at parrying the attacks of a shower with our umbrellas than were in making observations and had we been inclined to look around us all attempts would have been in vain; from the deep thick plantations of fir excluding all insight into the grounds[.]

At Chipping Norton the view is very fine and you may command a sight of the country for miles[.] At Morton in the Marsh the second stage, the road ascends a very long steep Hill from the summitt [*sic*] of which you may look back and have a fine view of all the tract of country though which you have been passing[.]

[f. 14v] Gazabow or the 2$\underline{10}$2. 1$\overline{1}$45$\overline{3}$. 345$\underline{6}$2.[4]

[f. 15r] The road from thence passes over downs for a considerable length untill it comes to Broadway Hill from the summit of which the view into Worcester shire and the whole country around is prodigiously fine, and cannot be described. At the Base of the Hill is the village which runs for some length, yet every house from the appearing intervention of trees, seems to be separated from the others. In the front is the great Bredon Hill on the left of which are the (~~Coles hall~~) (Cotswold) Hills and beyond these appearing over their summits and extended to the right are the Malvern hills in the background, on the right the country is extended as far as the sight can reach but the Day not being very fine We could not discern the minuter objects. On the summit of the (Broadway) Hill is a tall prospect house built by Lord Coventry[5] whose estate lies there and from this the view must be almost boundless[.] On Breedon Hill a chasm has within these few years opened and which extends to a very considerable depth[.] On the side of

---

[1] Probably Enstone.

[2] Lee often uses the spelling 'bason' for basin.

[3] The park of Blenheim Palace, home of the Dukes of Marlborough.

[4] This folly is mentioned again later in this entry. This is the first of a number of instances where Lee uses a numerical code which has not been deciphered.

[5] Broadway Tower, a folly built by George, 6th Earl of Coventry (1722–1809) in 1798.

this hill we were informed that a Mr Parsons had built a small prospect house w*hich* the com*mon* people in the neighbourhood not perhaps understanding the object of it or thinking it ridiculous, in general call the Gazabou.[1] From w*hich* Danish or Saxon words this term is derived, we shall leave to the curious in Etymological Enquiries to make out, it certainly [f. 15v *blank*] [f. 16r] may be ~~drawn from~~ (well and clearly) explained[.][2] The whole of this part of the country is called the Vale of Avesham [Evesham] the village of w*hich* lies on the road and the Bridge over the Avon with the surrounding scenery forms a very picturesque appearance[.]

(Star and Garter Inn Worcester)

The latter part of the Eveni*ng from* 6 to 10 was chiefly employed in walking about the town [Worcester] and its environs and the High Street with its continuation, although it is not so broad and although it does not possess those advantages of public Buildings w*hich* render Oxford so eminent yet is certainly superior to that of Oxford in its length and the neatness and Elegance of the Houses[.] The lower part is chiefly occupied with shops but the North End seems to be the most fashionable part of the Town. There are several walks in the environs of the place w*hich* are not only useful but from w*hich* the Town may be seen to great advantage[.] Those on the riversides are the foremost in their No^3 and several beautiful views may be obtained *from* its side.[4] The race ground is very eligibly situated and what is an advantage that so few possess is its being so close to the Town. From the Bank on the oppo*site* side of the river the races might be viewed to as great advantage as on the ground itself[.] The river [Severn] skirts one side of the Town. In the Eveni*ng* we visited the Theatre at halfprice more from curiosity to see the place and [f. 17r] the style of its furniture than to attend to the performance but we were very agreeably surprised to find ourselves well amused and entertained by Miss Duncan[5] in *The Romp*[6] The ~~house~~ farce for the Eveni*ng*[.] The house is extremely small and by no means so convenient or built on so modern a plan as we sh*oul*d have expected to have found in Worcester.

[f. 16v] In the Cloisters[7] are many tombstones most of wh(ose legends) are now worn away. There were several so modest that they ought to be preserved[.] On two stones near each other were the foll*owing* short inscriptions

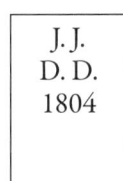

A M J. 1799	J. J. D. D. 1804	Lady Bourchier B^d in June 1726 son John Richard Esqr B^d in December 1728

---

[1] Parsons' Folly, built in the 18th century.
[2] Gazebo, 'C18: perh. humorously from GAZE, in imitation of L. future tenses ending in *-ebo*: cf. LAVABO' (*OED*).
[3] Number. This abbreviation is used throughout the diaries.
[4] Lee may have made the sketch at SJC, MS U.30 (6), f. 2r (see p. 309) at this point. This sketch is not reproduced here.
[5] Probably Maria Rebecca Davison (née Duncan, 1780x83–1858), an actress who played from an early age in theatres in England and Dublin, until 1829 (Knight, 'Davison [née Duncan], Maria Rebecca').
[6] Isaac Bickerstaff, *The Romp*, London, 1786.
[7] Worcester Cathedral; original Romanesque church built in 1084 with later additions, alterations and repairs (Engel, *Worcester Cathedral*, p. 13).

[*Small, rough ink sketch of rectangular structure in bottom corner of folio.*]

[f. 17r] **August 3. [Sunday]**
In the Morning after Breakfast (at 11 OClock) we went to the Cathedral to hear the service performed, and to our surprise the service began with the Litany and then followed the Communion. The rest of the Prayers had been performed at an Earlier Hour in the Morning[.] The Cathedral is here called the College[.] From where the name originates we could not learn. There is a small square behind it called College Green and some college formerly might have been in existence there. At one End of the College Green is a very fine old Gateway, much impaired by time[,] on the front of which is a figure in stone of King Edgar and two female figures[.] Under him is the date 957. The Gateway is divided in the middle by a Gate and the roofs of the two parts are different[.] By going down the Alley on the right hand as you come out of the College gate, at the farthest end are two curious figures in the lane in the front of a house[,] large as life or larger, one of which holds a sword in its hand and the other a pillar of stone[.]

[f. 17v] All the 4 Corners the same[.][1]

> Here lieth the Body
> of Ms Lucy Fox
> Daughter of Charles Fox Esquire
> of Chacomb
> In the County of Northampton
> She died November 19. 1766
> Also Mrs Cordelia Fox her
> Sister who died December 15. 1788.

> *H.S.E. [Hic Sepultus Est]*
> *Juxta matris venerandae Cineres*
> *Henricus Barton AM [Artium Magister]*
> *Excelsia Parochialis de Churchill*
> *Pastor Bonus*
> *Vir multiplice doctrina*
> *Singulare pietate, industria, fide,*
> *Prudens, frugi, sanctus, severus*
> *Neq:[Neque] contentus virtute saeculi sui*
> *Ita deniq:[denique] vixit*
> *Tanquam coram Deo, supremo judice*
> *Et in conspectu demum angelorum*
> *Rationem redditurus*
> *Obiit variolarum morbo abreptus.*
> *Die Septembris 23º AD 1745. AEt.[Aetatis] 61*

---

[1] Lee refers to a decorative feature of the headstone, a small sketch of which he made alongside his transcription of the epitaph (following). The sketch is not reproduced here.

> *Hic etiam in pace quiescit*
> *Beatam expectans resurrectionem*
> *Sara Barton*
> *Johannis Bourne armigeri filia*
> *Et Materfamilias sanctissimis moribus*
> *Que se ab aegroto marito*
> *Nullis suorum precibus*
> *Nullis lachrymis avelli passa*
> *Paucis admodum diebus*
> *Individua mortis ejusdem comes*
> *In eodem etiam tumulo sepeliri voluit*
> *Obiit*
> *Die Octobris primo, AD 1745 AEt.[Aetatis] 55*

Parentis optime meriti
Pietas liberorum posuit[1]

[f. 18r] For what reasons they [two figures] were put there we could not learn, they are not far from the waters Edge[.] In the cloisters are several stones containing the written accounts of the exits of persons buried there but as they are in the pavement a great many of them are completely obliterated by the attrition arising merely from the steps of those who pass over them and some it is impossible to read[.] Two or three struck our notice and as we were moralizing on the short lived Epitaphs we resolved to save some from immediate oblivion and accordingly took down the sentences and they are upon the opposite pages. The name of Fox (merely) induced us to preserve one, as every thing relating to that name now becomes a relic.[2] Two others were copied as they <u>were written in Latin</u>, and (every thing) in that language has some claims to our respect and attention.[3] One in remembrance of Daniel Collins AM[4] and another of Elizabeth Wife of John Perrot are still in good order. Within the Cathedral are a great many monuments of which incorrect and vague accounts are given in the Worcester Guide.[5] That of Sir Thomas

---

[1] Translation: 'Here lies buried, near the remains of his venerable mother, Henry Barton, Master of Arts, the good shepherd of the parish church of Churchill.

A man of manifold learning, singular piety, diligence, and faith, he was prudent, frugal, holy and strict, and not content with the morals of his times.

Thus, he indeed lived in such as way as to give an account in the end before God, the supreme judge, and in the presence of the angels.

He died suddenly of smallpox on the 23rd day of September, 1745 AD, at the age of 61.

Here also lies in peace, awaiting her blessed resurrection, Sara Barton, daughter of John Bourne, Esq., and a matriarch with the most holy morals, who, deprived of her sick husband a few days before, passed away without his tears or prayers. The inseparable companion of his death, she wished to be buried also in the same tomb. She died on the first day of October, 1745 AD, at the age of 55.

The piety of the children established this monument on behalf of the best parent.'

[2] Charles James Fox (1749–1806), politician, died on 13 Sept. 1806 after a long illness; he was still alive when Lee made this remark. Lee may refer here to Fox's failed attempt to forge peace with France in the months leading up to his death (*Mitchell, 'Fox, Charles James'*). The inscription to which Lee refers is at f. 17v, p. 44.

[3] This refers to the inscriptions above, f. 17v, pp. 44–5.

[4] Master of Arts (*artium magister*).

[5] Possibly [Green], *A Brief History of Worcester*, pp. 65–81.

Street[1] is finely done and the Boy over the tomb weeping is well executed as (are) the pair of scales on the left side. A Book is open on the right in w*h*ich are the words *Articuli Magnae chartae liberatum*[.][2] The Monlim*en*t [monument] was erected [f. 18v *blank*] [f. 19r] lately by one of his descend*a*nt*s* Thom*a*s Combe in 1774. The Monlim*en*t opposite to this of Bishop Hough[3] is very well described in the Guide. The *Alto Relievo*[4] beneath of the Bishop defending the articles before the three commissioners sent d*o*wn to Oxford is worth observation[.] The figures are well placed[,] even the room and the fire place are well executed[.] There formerly was a very fine copy of the descent of C*h*rist *fr*om the cross from Rubens, done by — but this staid [stayed] only for about four years when the Dean and Chapter had it taken down and put into their Library.[5] After w*h*ich the Gent*leman* who gave it for the altar piece requested to have it back and probably it was sent to him for it is not visible in the Library at present.

On the opposite side of the C*h*ur*c*h is a Mon*ume*nt of Bishop Maddox[6] done by Prince Hoare and a good representation beneath of the Good Samaritan healing the wound of the Pharisee. The figure on the left hand looks very awkward and has nothing to correspond with it[.]

Bust of Bishop Johnson by Nollekins[.][7]

Over the Entrance into the body of the C*h*ur*c*h and directly under the Organ are the Coats of arms of 56 Persons in two rows who contributed to the Building of the Gallery[,] in the Centre the arms of the Bishop and of the Dean and Chapter having 2 rows of 14 on each side of them. The Date is 1614 –

[f. 19v] In the Evening we took a walk over the river up to Porto Bello Gardens w*h*ich are about a Mile *fr*om the Town. They are placed on an eminence contiguous to the Banks of the River Severn and the windings of it down to Worcester with a view of the Town beyond the race Ground and the circumadjacent country form a pleasing and amusing view. We went to the Lower Gardens as they are called w*h*ich in fact are nothing but Benches (for smoking) surrounded with shrubs and very confined and from thence we returned to the town crossing the ferry over the race Ground[.]

(Aug*ust* 4) [Monday]

At the Star and Garter Inn where we are staying there are no ManServants, all are females and this has been the custom for many years. They all wear the same kind of dress and the same bonnets and a sort of ruffle comes down *fr*om the 2 Ends of the bonnet like a bridle[.][8]

---

[1] Sir Thomas Street (*c.*1625–96), judge and MP (*Halliday, 'Street, Sir Thomas'*).

[2] Representing the Magna Carta, agreed by King John in 1215: 'Articles of the Great Charter of Liberties'.

[3] John Hough (1651–1743), college head and bishop of Worcester; the monument is by L. F. Roubiliac (Lock, 'Hough, John').

[4] 'Carving, moulding, or stamping in which the sculptured shapes project from the plane surface to at least half their actual depth in the round' (*OED*).

[5] A copy of Rubens' 'Descent of Christ from the Cross' was commissioned for Worcester Cathedral by the engraver Valentine Green, from the Worcestershire portrait painter Thomas Phillips (1770–1845) (Peach, 'Phillips, Thomas'). Lee has evidently forgotten the artist's name, represented by a dash.

[6] Isaac Maddox (1697–1759), bishop of Worcester (Haydon, 'Maddox, Isaac').

[7] James Johnson (*c.*1705–74), bishop of Worcester; Joseph Nollekens (1737–1823), sculptor (Haydon, 'Johnson, James'; Kenworthy-Browne, 'Nollekens, Joseph').

[8] Lee sketched the bonnet on the following folio and at SJC, MS U.30 (6), f. 3r (p. 309), not reproduced here.

After Breakfast we went to see the China works of Messrs Joseph Flight and Martin Barry[.][1] We were obliged to call at the China Shop Nº 45. High Street for a Ticket without which no person can gain admission to the Workshops which are separate from the House and in Palace Row. The Clay is formed from the rude materials by the Masters who have a room set apart on purpose who mix it up there in the proper proportions[.] What the composition (of the clay) is remains a secret. A great Quantity of Soapstone [f. 20r] from Penzance and the Lands End forms a chief ingredient. ~~In this~~ The ingredients are first ground down and then all brought to this room where they are mixed and from thence the composition is taken in a soft state and measured out and put into a large Kiln (for 3 Days and 3 Nights) where[,] being exposed to an immense heat[,] it vitrifies and forms one solid mass from whence it is broken out in large pieces and then hammered into small pieces. It is then reduced to powder and afterwards [*Sketch of a woman, side profile, in an elaborate bonnet.*[2]] is put in a trough and with water and ground again[.] When in the lump[,] it appears of a Glassy form and of a fine blue intermixed with white and very [f. 20v *Three sketches, ink, of troughs*] [f. 21r] hard. When ground with water it loses the blue and is reduced to a kind of watery pulp which is then passed through a sieve and then through a finer [sieve]. This is then placed in troughs (Nº 1)[3] and under these are flues proceeding from a fire at one End (Nº 2)[.] Thus the moisture evaporates and the clay gets formed into hard cakes and as it is forming they cut it into squares with large knives to let it dry better and to be more convenient. While drying the dust settles on the top and dirties it[.] This is therefore scraped off and the whole of the upper surfaces are put into a water trough and cleaned and the stuff then goes through the seives [*sic*] as before. In the solid the composition was chiefly blue but in the grinding and drying it loses that color and becomes beautifully white. It is then taken into a cold room with a stone floor and cases and beaten with great hammers to temper it and to give it consistency and to drive out probably all the particles of air which may have been settled in it in drying[.] After it has been thus beaten it is trod under foot by persons with their bare feet, who do this at all seasons[,] winter and summer[,] on a stone floor. (The cold to which they subject themselves must be intense[.]) This is said to finish the tempering of it[.] The clay is then taken up to be worked[.] [f. 21v *Two sketches, ink*[4]] [f. 22r] The first hand into which it goes is the thrower who throws it on a wheel and at his pleasure forms a cup or saucer or teapot in a most elegant manner as the wheel goes round by his fingers alone. He has a piece of metal which he puts inside to smooth it in some cases. To see the clay rise up into any form is beautiful and to observe its swellings out into a Teapot and the contracting for the top is Elegant[.] The top is then formed in the same manner and the extraordinary degree to which it fits the Pot shews the skill of the man. These are then taken to a second person The Turner who fixes them on a lathe and turns them finer in the same manner as wood is done. They are then put into a room moderately warm to give them some consistency[,] from which they are taken down to the furnace[.] In an adjoining room are the models for handles and for those things which cannot be thrown

---

[1] This china manufactory was first established as the Worcester Porcelain Company in 1751 and in 1788 became the first Royal China Manufactory ([Green], *A Brief History of Worcester*, pp. 56–7).
[2] This sketch is similar to that at SJC, MS U.30 (6), f. 3r, and is as described in the previous paragraph.
[3] The figures in this paragraph refer to three sketches by Lee at f. 20v, not reproduced here.
[4] Reproduced at p. 48 (Figure 2).

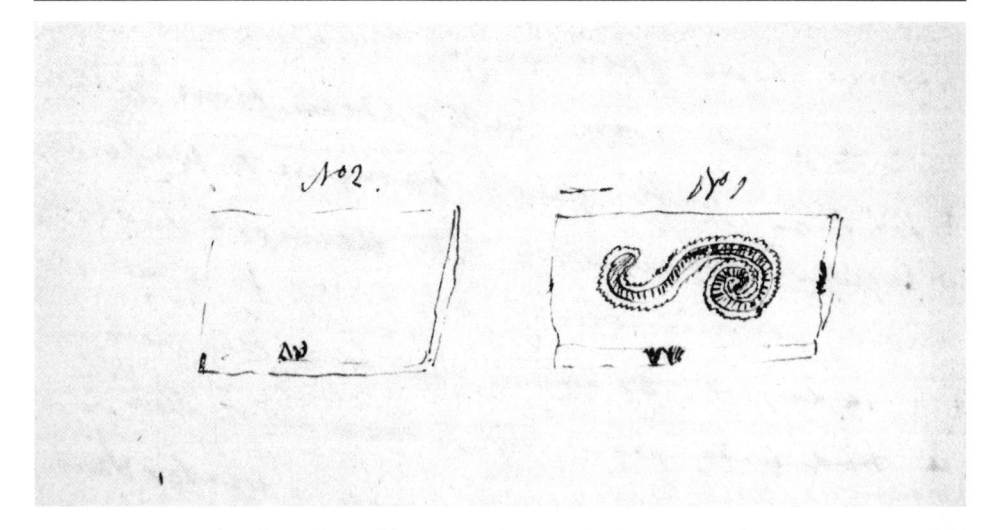

Figure 2. Two sketches of moulds seen at the Royal China Manufactory, Worcester. By John Lee, 4 August 1806 (SJC, MS U.30 (1), f. 21v). Reproduced by kind permission of the Master and Fellows of St John's College, Cambridge.

(all O^{r1} things are done by the thrower) as Ovals[,] etc. These models are made of plaister of paris and the figure as a handle of a Teapot or any extraneous ornament is formed in it and the clay is put into this (N° 1) and then the top being put on all the Extra clay is pressed into two canals on Each side of the model. Letting the top stay on about 10 Minutes the figure may [f. 22v *Four sketches, ink*²] [f. 23r] then to be taken out having acquired a degree of consistency and it is then ready for the furnace. The first furnace has six flues which go up the Inside and communicate with fires made all round the outside. As the coal sinks more is put on[,] thus heat is admitted into the furnace without any smoke or dirt. The cups and saucers are placed on cases which contain one or two or 3 things according to the size[.] These cases are called sagars³ and are made of the Stourbridge clay which stands the heat well. Some of the plates etc are placed on calcined flint and the Cups when put into the furnace have a ring put round each to keep their form and to hinder them from bulging when in [the] furnace[.] When the furnace is filled the mouth is shut and bricked up and heated for 37 hours, and then it is opened and all the things taken out. They can tell when the things are enough burnt by trial cups which they put in the furnace in different places and by taking these out and by their sound and if they appear clear the whole is enough baked. They are then ready to have the blue color put on which is done after which they are all exposed to a second Baking in the [f. 23v *blank*] [f. 24r] same manner in a larger furnace containing 7 flues and which will hold about 1500 Sagars[.] Here the Baking is for about 30 hours. The Glass [glaze] is a mixture of a milky appearance into which all the things are ~~placed~~ dipped and then Baked in the same furnace as before for 30 hours. The blue when put on is of a dirty color but after

---

[1] Circular. This symbol is repeated throughout the diaries.
[2] Reproduced at p. 49 (Figure 3).
[3] Saggar or sagger, 'a protecting case of baked fire-proof clay in which the finer ceramic wares are enclosed while baking in the kiln' (*OED*).

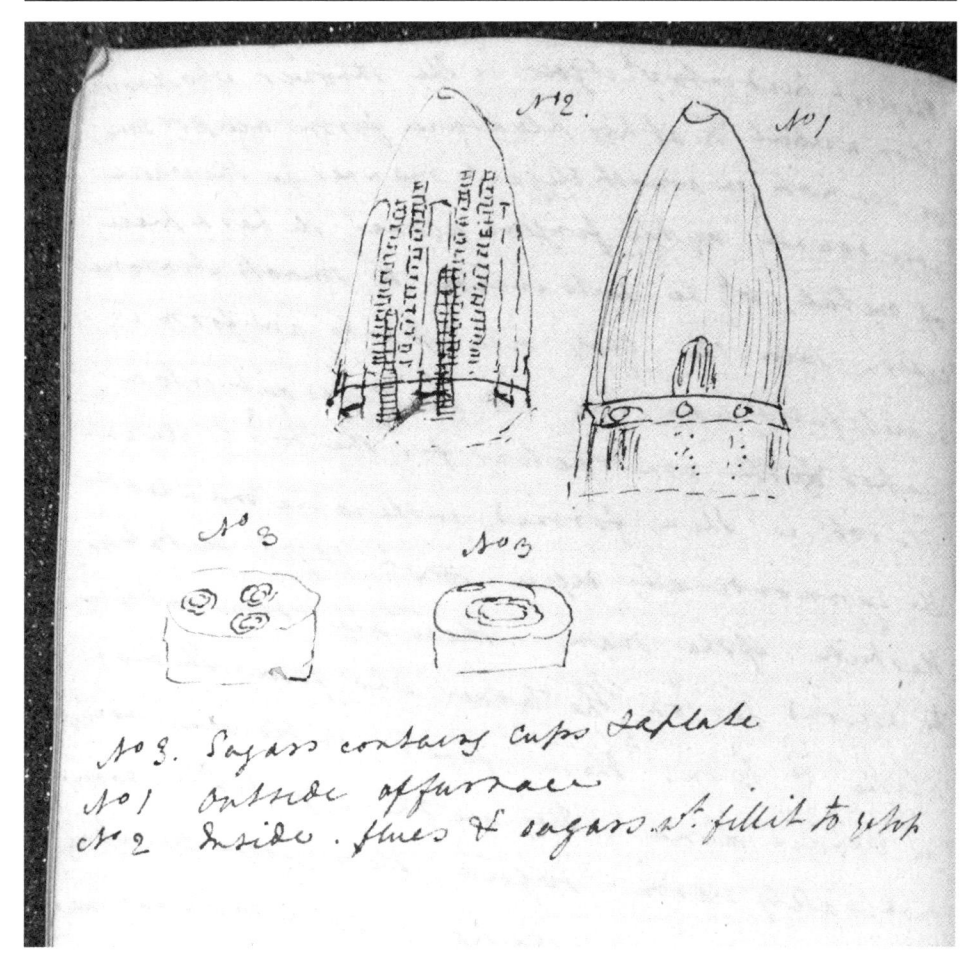

Figure 3. Sketches of furnaces seen at the Royal China Manufactory, Worcester. By John Lee, 4 August 1806 (SJC, MS U.30 (1), f. 22v). Reproduced by kind permission of the Master and Fellows of St John's College, Cambridge.

coming out this third time and being glossed is a beautiful shining appearance. The coloring is then done by different workmen up stairs who paint in most exquisite manner and the gold is then put on which is prepared by the Master and mixed with Spirits of Turpentine[.] After this the Cups are put into a fire for about 6 hours and then burnished by Women and girls with Derbyshire stones and the hand[.][1] There were about 25 painters at work and about 30 Women burnishing. The [*breaks off*]

The Sagars are made of the Stourbridge Clay and this is all ground under a great wheel of iron weighing 2 ton 17 Cwt to a powder as all (the materials) are ground by it. The Soap stone comes in small Chests from Cornwall[.] The lower workmen such as those who tread the mixture do not earn more than 9 or 10S a week, but some of the Painters who

---

[1] Lee seems to mean that the burnishing is done by hand using Derbyshire stone.

have learnt before [f. 24v *blank*] [f. 25r][1] They come there and then are apprenticed will earn from 2Gs to 3 a Week[.]

The room on the floor of the Town Hall is a fine spacious place[.] There are at Each End three pictures[,] at the N End is in the middle the picture of some Queen[2] with this inscription at the Bottom

E Dono Johannis Packington Baronnetti de Westwood in Com Wigorn –[3]

On the right hand side is a picture of some furious gentleman[4] and although it would not command ones attention from the elegance and style of the painting yet the figure and ludicrous appearance of it will certainly not allow it to be passed over. It is done by Thomas Shutor 1725[.] On one side is a court [*sic*] of arms on the Top are 3 Stars in the middle the bloody hand and below 3 Gloves[.][5]

The other picture is also a work of Thomas Shuter the Date 1725, this is some Earl probably one of the Coventry family[.] In the middle of the Court of arms are the 3 Gloves as in the former[,] its 2 Supporters are 2 Unicorns and above is an Earls Coronet. Its Motto *Je me fie in Dieu*[.][6]

At the other End in the middle appears the picture of some person probably belonging to the town[,] some former Mayor[,] but there is no name nor date to it[.] It appears a modern performance[.]

[f. 25v *blank*]

[f. 26r] On the right side is a picture of Thomas Lord Coventry[7] and on the left is one of the Rt Hon. Thomas Winnington Esquire, Cofferer to his Majesties Household and one of his Majesty's <u>most honorable</u> privy council[,] etc etc[,] as the cover of a letter informs us which is in his hand. It is a painting of B. Vanloos.[8]

Opposite the door are what we imagined to be the Arms of the town with the following inscription at the top[,] *Civitas in Bello. In pace fidelis.*[9] The motto below is *Mutare sperno.*[10] On the opposite side of the door going up to the Council Chamber is an old Inscription beginning with some thing about The first Year of the reign of Queen Mary[11] which those who have good eyes and time to spare may read[.] Upstairs is a good picture of the present King.[12] There are 12 Water Buckets in three Rows hanging in the room marked WC.

From the Town Hall we took a walk over the River to see the Distillery of Mr Williams which is close to the riverside. It was then repairing and the whole of the steam Engine by which it was worked was taking down for another which will supply its place. This distillery

---

[1] Ff. 24v and 25r are stained with the imprint of a leaf or fern pressed between the pages.
[2] A portrait of Queen Anne (*Sketch of the Antiquities of the Ancient City of Worcester*, p. 14).
[3] One of the portraits was of Sir John Packington, recorder of Worcester (*Sketch of the Antiquities of the Ancient City of Worcester*, p. 14). The translation of the Latin caption is: 'From the gift of John Packington, Baronet of Westwood in the County of Worcester'.
[4] 'An earl of Plymouth' (*Sketch of the Antiquities of the Ancient City of Worcester*, p. 14).
[5] In the page margin, Lee made a small ink sketch of the coat of arms as described, not reproduced here.
[6] 'I trust in God.' In the page margin, Lee made a small ink sketch, probably of this coat of arms, not reproduced here.
[7] Probably Thomas, 1st Baron Coventry (1578–1640).
[8] Thomas Winnington (1696–1746), politician; the portrait by J. B. van Loo remains at Worcester Corporation (*Courtney, 'Winnington, Thomas'*).
[9] 'The city faithful in war and in peace'.
[10] 'I scorn change'.
[11] Mary I, r. 1553–8.
[12] George III, r. 1760–1820.

is the largest in the Kingdom w*hi*ch is conducted by one man[.] The stills are of a very large size and the worms are of a great length. The Diam*ete*r of the worm at the bottom was ab*ou*t 2½ Inches and the top was to all appearances more than double that size. The Diam*ete*r of the Hollow w*hi*ch was formed by the spiral worm [f. 26v] at Bottom was 12 feet and the Diam*ete*r at top about 10½ feet[.] Hence the circumference of the whole worm w*hi*ch consists of 16 rounds is nearly ab*ou*t 11¼ × 16 Yards or 180 Yards in Length. The worm with the Tub in w*hi*ch it is placed (must have) cost about £1000. It is made of black tin. There were 3 worms and three stills all turned by steam. The Boiler is immense. In the Back room were about 14 or 15 immense large tubs containing some 10000 Gallons of waste in the winter season when the whole is at work. The liquor to be distilled is called wash and consists of ground Barley and malt and water[.] This is fermented and the yeast used to ferment this costs between £6 and 700 a year and w*hi*ch is sent f*ro*m all the brewhouses in the Country. The Wash is distilled 2 [twice] a day and the refuse goes to the pigs for w*hi*ch there are styes w*hi*ch will hold (betw*ee*n 600 and) 700[.] They are kept quite clean and the styes cleaned once a day and they do not lie on straw or any bed. The styes go all round the back of the premises and the dung is sold at ½ Guinea a load. The Duty upon an average is near £1000 or £950 a week w*hi*ch is paid Ev*er*y Saturday for the Distillery and the last week of working[.] This summer it came to £1115:14:10 as appeared in the Book of the Clerk to the Premises[.] There was a store room w*hi*ch at that time was not well filled but w*hi*ch contained 4 large Vessels of 3927. 3977. 3943. [and] 5973 Gallons of spirits[.]

[f. 27r] The spirit in its first state is very raw, it is distilled again for Hollands[1] and several times for making spirits of wine[,] Brandy[,] etc. We were informed that the Utensils alone empty on the premises were not worth less than £12000[.] In the Evening we again visited the Theatre in consequence of another Roscious of 7 Years of age being announced.[2] Master Dawson had played at the Academie Theatre[,] Leicester Square[,] London with great applause and had acted before His Majesty and the Royal Family, but as we expected a Betty[3] we were disappointed with him contrary perhaps to reason. He acted with a great deal of life and was perfect in his parts, but not altogether to the sense of the character although he made as good a Scrub in the *Beaux Stratagem*[4] as most boys of his age w*oul*d. It was obvious to see that Every attitude and gesture had been taught him and there was not the least nature in his performance[.] But however he might act in Town certainly it w*oul*d be unfair to judge of him by his performance at Worcester where his companions were all (bad) but Archer. Mr Stanwix the most despicable pantomimus we ever beheld and w*oul*d almost disgrace [f. 28r] a bern.[5] It w*oul*d therefore be time lost to stay and criticize the play.

August 5. [Tuesday]

In the morning previous to our departure we paid a visit to Mr F. Sheriff[6] a curiosity monger who had formerly been a Tailor but had left off business. We were informed that he was the only antiquary in the Town and understood that a visit to him w*oul*d not be unacceptable.

[1] A grain spirit (*OED*).
[2] Lee compares a new, young actor in Worcester to Quintus Roscius Gallus, the most celebrated Roman actor (*c.*126–62 BCE).
[3] Lee indicates that he was expecting to see a female actor.
[4] George Farquhar, *The Beaux' Stratagem*, London, 1707.
[5] Possibly intended as 'bairn', child (*OED*).
[6] Reference is also made to Mr Sheriff's collection of Roman coins found in Worcester, in Green, *History and Antiquities*, II, p. 107.

He kindly shewed us his Roman Coins[,] a few good[,] but he seemed to value some, for having had them for so many years. Some 30, 20[,] etc[,] and [made] a shew because Mr etc had given them to him. His passion for antiques could not be called Taste it was only a Turn, for he only knew the names of a few and that they were all different[.] He had a bag full of this sort and a bag full of that and being asked why he did not put them into order and sort them replied he had no time[.] He had a collection of shells which he valued highly but we were too ignorant of their value. He had also a very large collection of fossils and spars as he told us above ½ a Cwt, very curious and he seemed to set great store on an Old Roman Tile[,] quadrangular[,] hollow and very massy and upon a large snake stone about 2 foot Diameter which he [f. 27v] brought (from) above 100 Miles off. He offered to shew us a Shoe of Charles 2 and a Slipper of Elizabeth[,] etc[,] which we declined seeing as our time began to get short. And we did not Examine his prints for the same reason. We bought 2 Roman rings of him which he bought also about 12 Months ago at Liverpool at Mr Bullock's[1] sale who had many curiosities as well as these which were found at and sent over to him from Herculaneum. After seeing a piece of Pompys Pillar[2] we retired thanking him for his civility yet laughing at the idea of so many things all falling together into the hands of this curious virtuoso who knew no more about them than we did. After Breakfast (at ten OClock) having delivered our portmanteau into the Hands of Mr Fieldhouse the hospitable Landlord of the Star and Garter to be sent by the Coach to Shrewsbury before us. We took up our knapsacks and walked down to the Green Dragon, St Clements Gate from whence the werry[3] for Bewdley sets off. We here put the knapsacks on board it and began our walk intending to walk up the Severn side to Shrewsbury. At Henwick Hill after walking across the race Ground we crossed the river at the ferry there and continued our walk following the track up the water side which the horses [f. 29r] which tow the boats go. The werry was drawn by 3 Men and this we let pass us to walk at our leisure knowing that if we were tired we could easily over take it. The current of the River is extremely rapid and barges make their way slowly up it[.] They can sail up with wind SE or SW all the way[.] In the race week the Wherry comes up and down from Worcester every day for the 8 days and at other times it goes only Tuesdays[,] Thursdays, and Saturdays. About a mile and ½ up the stream is on the left a seat of (Mr Liggins [Lygon] of Matchfield) as we were told it is called Hallow Park[4] and looks very well from the river, a (fine) view of which it must command for a great length. Saw a woman with a swelled neck as big as an Egg. The meadows on the Left bank are very beautiful and look extremely fertile, the Hill bounds them for a very long way. The Banks of the river are very high, much more so than any we ever saw before. The river winds gently and very little of it is seen at a time. A little higher up (on the L Bank) is a spot called Camps consisting of two or 3 houses. On the opposite Bank is a house now building of Mr (Forsan) Spiggits, which will view the river very well but it forms no very advantageous [f. 30r] appearance from the ~~road~~ path. On the Pathside a little higher up was a crop of oats and wheat mixed[.] The outside land immediately struck our attention. We thought it was all accidental but the whole field was the same, and the

[1] William Bullock (bap. 1773, d. 1849), naturalist and antiquary, established museums or 'cabinets of curiosities' in Liverpool and Birmingham containing works of art, armoury, natural history specimens and curiosities from the Pacific (Baigent, 'Bullock, William').

[2] Approximately 86.5 feet (27m) in height, the ancient monument Pompey's Pillar was erected by the people of Alexandria in honour of Diocletian.

[3] Wherry, a light rowing-boat used chiefly on rivers (*OED*).

[4] Lee sketched the house at SJC, MS U.30 (6), f. 8v (p. 310), not reproduced here.

DIARY 1: TOUR FROM LONDON TO HOLYWELL IN WALES

reason of it we could not guess and there was nobody in sight to tell us. The Brick kiln of Mr Evans[1] at the turn of the river where it forms an island looks very pretty and the rock opposite has a good effect (*Vide* scetch).[2] There are here for some way up several Brick kilns. They were filling one which would hold 15000 Bricks.

[f. 28v] [*margin:* John Field owner of the Bewdley Wherry]

Plants
- Common *Silene*[3] all the way to Holt
- Large blue Geraniums all up to Stourport
- *Linum Perenne* [blue flax] ⎫
- Com*mon* Oxalis [common wood sorrel] ⎬ at Holt Banks
- *Convol*[*vulus*] *Minor* [*convolvulus tricolour*, dwarf morning glory or bindweed] white ⎭
- Hearts Ease [*Viola tricolor*] above Stourport
- Plenty of digitalis [foxglove] up to Bewdley
- *Resida* [*Reseda*, mignonette]
- *Symphytum* com*frey* Every where

[f. 29v] Bill at Worcester[,] Star and Garter. Mr Fieldhouse

2 Oct*ober*.	Coffee		:1	:6
	Sandwich		1	–
	Bed		1	
3.	Break*fast*		1	:6
	Dinner		4	:6
	Cyder		1	:6
	Sandwich		1	–
	Bed		1	–
4	Break*fast*		1	:6
	Dinner		4	–
	Cyder		1	:6
	Beer			4
	Sandwich		1.	–
	Bed		1	
		1	:2	:4
	Washing	–	–	6
		1	:2	:10
5.	Break*fast*		1	:6
		1	:4	:4
	Ch*amber* maid		3.	
	Waiter		3	
	Book		1	
		2	:1	:4

[1] Probably the brickworks on the bank of the Severn at Ribbesford.
[2] This sketch is at SJC, MS U.30 (6), f. 9r–v (p. 310), not reproduced here.
[3] A genus of flowering plants in the *Caryophyllaceae* family. In this case it was probably bladder campion (*Silene vulgaris*).

[f. 30r] We here observed a curious insect on the leaves of the plant — and only on the old leaves[.] Happening to gather a leaf our hands were suddenly stained with red like blood and we saw hundreds on the other side of it. The taste of the insect thus killed was rather acid akin [to] red currants to which the stain exactly corresponds[.] For the color *vide* Scetch Book.[1] The wind got up and being nearly south several Barges came along passing us majestically with their two sails[.][2] They are long and narrow and about 40 Tons or a little more. A great many passed us in [*sic*] the way to Bewdley[.] They are chiefly [f. 30v *blank*] [f. 31r] drawn by 3 or 4 Men when there is no wind and we only saw one horse employed the whole way up to Bewdley and that was only from Stourport at one of the kilns belonging to a Mr Evans of Hallow[.] The man said he believed the great kiln held near 50000 Brick. The common Bricks sell for 30 Shillings a 1000. The 2nd finer sort or the Stock or Fronting Brick about 33Ss. The 3rd Sort or paving Brick 35Ss. There is a larger sort of this best Paving Brick which sells for about 40S. The workmen Earn from 15S to 21S a week the Brick maker gets the latter. Boys about 7S[.] Some Temper The Clay: others carry it etc. On the right side the river is sheltered by ~~Bank~~ a ridge of hill which is almost Entirely covered with trees and which winds nearly with the river: nothing can be more beautiful. Going up to the House at (Painters Roving) ([Forsan?]) We were saluted by the attack of a large dog which immediately collected around us a host of labourers from the adjoining brick kiln[.] Some advised us to cross the river here, others dissuaded us and said if we could get over a brook just above we should meet with no more impediments all the way to Holt. This seemed the most adventurous plan and we therefore set out to meet the Brook, which by partly getting [f. 31v *blank*] [f. 32r] in we safely got over[,] then found the rest of the path not only good as we had been led to expect but also beautiful. The sides of the Hills looked just the same[,] as beautifull as wood can make them[,] and the flowery Banks of the winding and (gracefully) twisting stream, whose waters were often heard to murmur or to bustle at the windings[,] were as much as the eye could desire. The woods and Hills then become on the R of the meadows on the L. We left the Bank of the Severn to wind up the circling path which conducts up the hill on which stands Holt Castle Seat of Chillingsworth Esquire and which formerly belonged to the Earl of Coventry as the place informed us.[3] The Church was the object of our search and the curious old Gateway on the West side of the House[.] In the Church Yard is a Monument to the Memory of a Countess Dowager of Coventry Daughter of Sir Steynsham Master of Cadnor in the County of Derby etc Aged 86, 1788[.][4] And of her 2 Husbands Gilbert Earl of Coventry of Coome in this County and Edmund Pytts her second Husband[.][5] After viewing the venerable building we left the house and followed the path to the town through a range of <u>young trees</u>,[6] when coming to a field at the End of which was a kind of mount we made [f. 33r]

---

[1] These may have been clover mites (*Bryobia praetiosa*) or another small aphid, with their characteristic red pigmentation. SJC, MS U.30 (6), flyleaf and f. 1r (p. 309), are stained by the pressed leaf of this plant.

[2] The barge is illustrated in a small, rough ink sketch in the bottom corner of the page, not reproduced here.

[3] Holt Castle, originally built in the late 11th century and with later additions (Brooks and Pevsner, *The Buildings of England: Worcestershire*, pp. 380–82); Henry Chillingworth (d. *c.*1841) (*The Gentleman's Magazine*, new ser., 16, July–Dec. 1841, p. 109).

[4] Anne, daughter of Sir Streynsham Master (1640–1724) of Codnor Castle.

[5] Gilbert, 4th Earl of Coventry (1666–1719); and Edmund Pytts (1696?–1753) of Kyre, MP for Worcestershire in 1741–53 (History of Parliament Online).

[6] Word order has been changed here as Lee intended by underlining.

directly tow*ar*ds it and ascend*ing* had a pretty view of Holt, the River [Severn] and the oppo*site* (small) hills. We stood on a little precipice w*hic*h we then descended to the path w*hic*h led us to the Village where we were glad at two OClock to get a dinner off [*sic*] some cold Beef and ham. Holt is 6 Miles f*ro*m Worcester[.] *Linum perenne, Convolvolus miner* [*sic*], *Oxalis* common. We here crossed the river at the ferry paying the common Charons[1] fare ½. The Stream is about 3 Miles an hour. From this place [is] a long row of high (bare) hill continuous on the L w*hic*h is here and there cov*er*ed with a few trees just suff*icien*t to give it variety. A range of beautiful meadows as usual are on the oppo*site* side. The Parts of the hills all up where uncovered with verdure are of a dark red color and are a soft stone. The Woods and High ridge of hills change about a mile up, to the [R again?]. Mare's Tail [*Hippuris vulgaris*]. Rain about 3 in showers to 5 O Clock[.] On the left a field or two of hops shewed to great advantage from their diff*eren*t color and their arrangement and formed a pleasing variety. In this part of the river sev*eral* parties fishing and from their songs, ~~they~~ w*hic*h might ill agree with their sport we c*oul*d learn that their hearts [f. 33v blank] [f. 34r] were light although their sport might be not so[.] We now were treated with a variety of landscape[.] Hitherto we had had a hill on one side and meadows on the other, now meadows on each side and these narrow and bounded by high hill cov*er*ed with trees, except here and there an opening of red rock[.] The white stems of the delicately dressed Birch [*Betula*] were ambitious of distinguishing themselves among the rest and did so. On the right a little higher up were the first cornfields we met in the vales w*hic*h were between the meadows and skirted the ~~rock~~ rocky hills in every fantastic form (At Hampsted(\ture)[2] Mr Stringers)[.] The view is very fine[.][3] About a mile from Stourport or 5 from Holt is a curious rock on the left side w*hic*h comes close to the waters edge and is called the Redstone rock[4] w*hic*h name corresponds with [the] color[.] We saw several houses in the rock and their chimneys came out at the top[.] The river is here about 2 feet 6 or 8 [inches] deep in the channel ab*ou*t this time of year[.] 6 Miles up above Holt is Stourport where the Stour joins the Severn[.] There are 2 Basons w*hic*h have been lately made and w*hic*h communicate by [f. 35r] canals with the Birmingham, Grand Junction and Stourbridge works. There is a large Steam Engine w*hic*h is built on the Edge of a bason filled f*ro*m the Severn and this water is worked up by the Engine into a Bason[.] The Boats go ~~the~~ into a lock f*ro*m thence into one one [*sic*] Bason. Then into another Lock and into a 2*nd* Bason. The whole fall is <u>about 20 feet</u> (a man guessed so). The Engine throws up 5 Hogsheads at a stroke and moves in general 14 Strokes a Minute, but they can work near 16. Of the Coal called Slack (f*ro*m B*eeston*) the fire consumes 2 ton in 12 Hours of of [*sic*] the Beeston best coal 30 Cwt in 12 hours[.]

Slack costs 11.6 Shgs a ton }
Beeston Coal 14 –   } The Engine is one of Boltons[5] and when delivered on the w*ha*rf cost £2600 and the Cost when put up was 3000 as near as possible[.] It has been

---

[1] Charon was the character in Greek mythology who ferried the dead to Hades.
[2] Possibly Hampstall Inn, on the Severn. Lee indicates that he was unsure of the name.
[3] Lee made sketches in this area, at SJC, MS U.30 (6), ff. 10r, 10v (p. 310), not reproduced here.
[4] A river cliff of grained red sandstone, just south of Stourport on the Severn (Hull, *Memoirs of the Geological Survey*, p. 62).
[5] Boulton, Watt and Co. steam engine manufactories and foundries, established by Matthew Boulton (1728–1809), manufacturer and entrepreneur, and James Watt (1736–1819), engineer and scientist (Tann, 'Boulton, Matthew').

up 2 Years nearly. Boiler 19 feet to 9[.] The wharfs were all filled with Coal, Iron, Stone and had Every appearance of a flourishing place. This is the only place which communicates with canals on the Severn (~~above Worcester~~ (Quere [Query])). There were an amazing n° of Boats and the basons are not sufficiently capacious[.] They lack of Enlarging it[.] This place was till lately a village. They have a curious Iron Bridge, of 1 Arch over the river but [f. 34v] on the right side are 3 Stone Arches on the shore and then 29 small Brick ones. On the opposite side where the toll gate is are 3 large Brick Ditto [arches] and then 8 small ones. Pay 1^d. Wild hearts ease, Digitalis. The path is now on the L and winds up a rock impending over the river called Benbows Hill, from where you command a beautiful view up and down the river. A short distance up you come opposite Squire Follets house (formerly lived there a Lord Follet) called the Licky [Lickhill House.][1] Hills are now on the left to a great height and [there is a] small one on [the] R. But the most beautiful spot we had hitherto seen was Mr Prattlesons of Ripsford [Ribbesford].[2] The House is on the ~~left~~ (R as you look down) and at the side of hill which runs along and ends in the distance on the left. The river winds at the Edge of its meadows and on the opposite side are smaller hills which meet the opposite range.[3]

Just above the House the Hills rise high and [are] all covered with trees and on the opposite side are fine bold red rocks coming boldly and slipping into the water. The valley is also most beautiful and the spot is a paradise[.] Just above on the top of the hills is the house of Sir Thomas Winning[4] ~~of~~ (called) <u>Winterdene</u> Hill [Winterdyne], and this joins the Town of Bewdley which is 4 Miles above Stourport[.]

[f. 35v] [*margin*: Bewdley forest on the left up the river]

[f. 36r] At Bewdley we arrived about 7 OClock after having had a most delightful walk and we were directed by the persons of the Wherry to the Saracens Head which is by no means the largest inn. But a very good reception will await the tired traveller and although the appearance bespeaks poverty yet we got ~~a~~ good beds and a comfortable and cheap entertainment[.] It is close by the bridge and looking over the water[.]

[f. 32v]	Dinner	1	3½
	Ferry		½
	Bridge at Stourport	1	
	Stourport Ale		1½

[*margin*: Written in the Bridgenorth [Bridgnorth] Wherry – From Holt cross river and for 3 Miles Ombersley Parish. Then Hartlebury. ~~Then Metton~~ (To the Stour) Stourport etc all in Mytton [Mitton] Parish[.] Stourport Bason cost £105000 opened in 1771]

August 6. [Wednesday]

At 8 OClock this morning we started in the wherry for the sake of variety and to see how the river and its boundaries would look from the water[.] Just above Bewdley is

---

[1] 'Squire Follet' was John Folliott (d. 1814). In Mar. 1716–17 the barony of Folliott became extinct on the death of Henry, 3rd Lord Folliott (*Victoria County History: Worcester*, III, pp. 158–73).

[2] William Prattinton, father of Peter Prattinton, antiquary (*Victoria County History: Worcester*, IV, pp. 297–317).

[3] Lee sketched the scene at SJC, MS U.30 (6), f. 14r–v (p. 311), not reproduced here.

[4] Sir Thomas Edward Winnington (1779–1839), politician (History of Parliament Online).

DIARY 1: TOUR FROM LONDON TO HOLYWELL IN WALES

Bowles [Dowles] village, Church[1] and Brook which falls into the Severn on the L about 1 Mile from Bewdley. This is in Shropshire and the opposite Hills are in Worcestershire. Here are some Aqua fortis and vitriol Works and in ~~one of~~ the (biggest) Kilns we were told that there are 48 fires at work. The smaller was for grinding the sulphur etc[.] The Whole of the Manor except 2 Houses which belong to Mr George Baye is the property of Mrs Kaye (of Spring Grove).[2] Baye was a clerk to (the late) Mr Kaye[.] Just above are the Flemings Mill Rocks which take their name from a man of that name who had some time ago a Mill there.[3] These are not quite 2 Mile up the river. Above these are the Lower$_1$ and Upper$_2$[4] Paymore [Painsmore] Rocks[.] The lower are on the R and the [f. 37r] Upper on the left and the navigation is difficult to get between them. The men call them in general the Roundstone rocks. Above these are the Ground Shaking rocks, the most part of which at low water are bare and there is just room for a boat to pass, the stream is extremely hard and the water flows with great violence[.] The pass is rather on the left side. The river becomes here extremely steep and the appearance down it is like looking down an inclined plane. A man informed us that Mr Young[5] of Worcester who has often gone up and measured the level of the river as far as Colebrook [Coalbrookdale] says these rocks are on a level with the top of St Andrews Church steeple, Worcester[.] The river looks so rapid and the falls are so frequent that we inquired if it was frozen over. 'Yes (Sir) often. About 15 Years ago [it was] hard frozen and a sheep was roasted on it and the people walked on the ice as to a wake.'[6] About 66 Years ago an old Woman said it was very hard frozen and the same recurred. The views of the river about Tickley Hill are very fine[.][7] The path for the men who tow the boat is cut on the side of a rock and is a considerable height above the water. It is a cliff, yet sometime ago it was about 30 feet higher up and has been lowered by the Owners of the Boats at the permission [f. 36v] of Lord Valentia[8] to whom all this belongs and who has a house up at Areley [Arley] which is a very pretty village on the waterside on the R 4 Miles above Bewdley. These rocks between here and Bewdley are advantageous notwithstanding their difficulties for if they were any of them cut away they would render the river impassable over the others above and the fall is extremely great. The river is much wider up here than it is at Worcester 20 Miles below. And the current is very rapid indeed for these four miles[.] Most boats get if they can an additional man and we had 5 to pull us along in the wherry. Men are always employed to haul it, as it is too light for horses, yet we saw not above ½ Dozen horses at work all the way up to Colebrook in the barges. Why not we could not divine. A man for hauling [lead?] from Worcester to Bewdley [gets] 4Ss a day and a pint o' Beer = 3^d the same from Bewdley to

---

[1] St Andrew's Church, Dowles, originally built in the 15th century and rebuilt in 1789 (*Victoria County History: Worcester*, IV, pp. 262–5).

[2] Mary, Louisa and Caroline Skey inherited Spring Grove after the death of their brother Samuel in 1806, probably the 'late Mr Kaye' referred to by Lee (*Victoria County History: Worcester*, IV, pp. 262–5).

[3] Possibly Worralls corn mill on a tributary of the Severn, to the south of Upper Arley (*Victoria County History: Worcester*, III, pp. 5–10). This mill was disused by the late 19th century (OS 1st ser., Shropshire sheet LXXIV, SW, surveyed 1882–3, revised 1902).

[4] The word order has been reversed here, as indicated by Lee's subscript numbering.

[5] Possibly the same George Young who published a map of Worcester in 1810.

[6] Quotation marks added.

[7] Lee sketched this view at SJC, MS U.30 (6), f. 15r–v (p. 311), not reproduced here.

[8] George Annesley, Viscount Valentia (1770–1844) of Arley Hall, Bewdley (History of Parliament Online).

Bridgenorth. In winter they will not work [for] under 4:6 and a pint. The fare to Bewdley is 1S *from* thence to BridgeN*orth* 2S on account of the increased no. of men necessary to draw the boats. Just above Areley that part of the river is called Areley Lake. About a Mile [f. 38r] farther up is a ferry called Bar Gate [Bargate] and on the oppos*ite* side is — Childs Esq*uire* of <u>Kinlet</u>.[1] Billingsley Collieries close by.[2] Stanley Collieries are just above and which belong to Mr Benjamin Thomson.[3]

[f. 37v] [*Here follows one page of rough pencil notes that form the basis for Lee's diary entries around this time.*]

Men have for hauling *from* Worcester to Bewdley 4S and a pot of ale 3^d. *Ditt*o to Bridge North *from* Bewdley[.] In Winter they wont do it under 4:6 a day[.]

Just above Harley the river is called Harley Lake. About a mile [on] is Bar Gate a boat house and opposite 2 Miles to Child Esq*uire* of Kinlet[.]

Stanley Colliers[,] Mr Benjamin Thompson[,] Potters Load [Pottersload] a passage house just below the Ray [Rhea] Farm wh*ich* belongs to Mr Lewis attorney[4] [bends?][.][5] For 4 Miles from Bewdley the river is so rapid that they are obliged to have an extra man[.] We were drawn by 5 men[.] Sit in the wherry and by the help of a Claude Glass[6] see the Views up and down the river country changing[.] ½ p*ast* 1 shower[.]

Hamptons Load [Hampton Loade], Got some bread and cheese and treated the men S2:6 at a H*ous*e on the L[.]

Building new boat 60 ton. Heard noise of iron bars at distance and find them throwing them off the Key at the rocks[.]

Hole thro*ugh* rock bring iron and coal and [lake black?][.] Canal comes thro*ugh* rock overshot wheel[.] Excavations in rock storehouses. Iron rolled out into bars. [*End of page of rough pencil notes.*]

[f. 38r] Potters Load a passage house, just below the Ray Farm wh*ich* belongs to Mr Lewis an attorney at Law[.] The river is here very beautifully wooded on each side all the way up and we did not see one view wh*ich* was not beautiful[.] By sitting in the Wherry we co*uld* see all the views up the river and by fixing a Claude Glass to the Umbrella we co*uld* see all the prospect below to advantage. At 6 Miles further up or 10 from Bridgenorth we stopped at Hamptons Load [Hampton Loade] a few scattered houses and in one got some bread, and cheese and ale and in order to encourage the men to get on as fast as they co*uld* we treated them with ale for wh*ich* we had the 'Yes Sure' turned into the more dignified title of 'Yes Sir There is a ferry there.'[7] The House of best entertainment is on the L. We walked on from thence purposely to see about 2

---

[1] William Lacon-Childe of Kinlet (1786–1880) (History of Parliament Online). Lee left a dash in place of Childe's first name.

[2] A large coal works was present at Billingsley by 1796, connected to the River Severn by a horse drawn railway, run by a local businessman in 1803–10 (Evans, et al., 'Forest of Wyre').

[3] Stanley Collieries started in around 1803/4, owned by John and Benjamin Thompson, ironmasters and entrepreneurs (Poyner and Evans, 'Survey of Stanley Colliery', p. 66).

[4] Possibly the Mr Lewis, Bridgnorth attorney, who purchased Deuxhill estate (4 miles (6.5km) south-south-west of Bridgnorth) *c*.1784 (*Victoria County History: Shropshire*, X, pp. 293–300).

[5] Possibly a note referring to bends in the River Severn.

[6] A slightly convex tinted mirror, used to help produce artwork similar to that of Claude Lorrain (1600–1682), a leading 17th-century landscape artist.

[7] Quotation marks added.

Miles further up the river Yerton ford where are some iron works[1] and where there is a long passage cut thro*ugh* a Hill for boats to pass to another ford ab*ou*t 3 Quarters of a mile off where there are other works and where a *different* part of the process is carried on. The passage thro*ugh* the rock is extremely narrow and we were told that there is 6 foot water [f. 39r] in it[.] Above the water there hardly appears room for a person to stand upright in it. The iron is brought *from* the other ford here where it is put into the great fires and rolled and cut into bars and thin lengths and then sent d*ow*n the Severn. Thro*ugh* the rock is a bason[,] the water of wh*ich* comes along the canal here and this falls in some proportion and turns the great overshot wheel wh*ich* sets the whole works a going. Excavations are made in the rock *from* wh*ich* sand wh*ich* is used in the works is got and they make storehouses etc of the hollow parts[.] It is a curious looking place, and we heard the noise of iron Bars falling at a great distance and wh*ich* noise upon near approaching arose *from* their throwing these down *from* the Key on the shore for the boats. They were building a boat of 60 Tons there. The advantage of this canal is that it gives a ready communi*cation* between the 2 Works wh*ich* belong to the same man and they are easily connected with the Severn. Looking up the hollow canal the light is just visible at the farther end. The Great wheel was cased with sheet iron[.] There is a great deal of otter hunting in the basons and brooks near the river and the otters abound. 4 or 5 couple of dogs [is] enough. Otter does not run far. Dives perhaps 30 Yards. Bites terribly and will sometimes almost kill a dog with a lick of its tail. Teeth and tail its chief weapons. Bridgenorth looks very well *from* the river[.]

[f. 38v] The <u>low Ch*urch*</u> as it is called or St Marys[2] looks a fine object. The bridge next meets the view. And and then the ~~aqueduct~~ reservoir wh*ich* contains about 60 or 70 hogsheads of water. This part of the Town is Entirely built on a rock high, and many houses are cut out of it wh*ich* are inhabited by the poorer people who hold them and pay a trifling acknowledgem*ent* to the corporation. Near the C*hur*ch is a bit of an old castle[3] wh*ich* looks singular enough[.] In the other end of the Town is St Leonards or the High Church, a fine old Building.[4] It is curious to see the smoke *from* the chimneys com*ing* out of the rock. We saw here a very large Barge of[5] Bark 70 Tons to our surprise and understood that it waits for a flood or when the river is ab*ou*t 5 foot 3 or 4 Inches when it can get down to Worcester. These large boats seize these opportunitys[.] Shield the owner of the wherry has a Trow[6] of 70 tons loaded with Welsh Slate now at Shrewsbury waiting in the same manner for water about 5:5 or 6 (foot) and within these 10 Days the water has been once within 5 or 6 Inches of the mark[.]

We arrived at Bridge North ab*ou*t 5 and immediately we set out for the Iron Bridge at Cole Brook Dale [Coalbrookdale] hav*ing* been informed that ab*ou*t four miles up we shou*ld* pass a wooden Bridge and 4 miles Beyond was the Tontine Inn at the foot of the

---

[1] Possibly Eardington iron works, established in the late 18th century and closed in 1889; see Wood, *Abandoned and Vanished Canals*.

[2] Church of St Mary Magdalene, Bridgnorth, built in 1792 (Pevsner, *Shropshire*, p. 80).

[3] Bridgnorth Castle, built in 1098–1101 (Pevsner, *Shropshire*, pp. 82–3).

[4] St Leonard's Church, Bridgnorth, a medieval church with later additions; little of what Lee saw remains following extensive rebuilding in 1860–62 (Pevsner, *Shropshire*, p. 79).

[5] Lee probably means 'or'.

[6] A large flat-bottomed sailing barge on the Severn (*OED*).

Iron Bridge. About a mile up is a very fine Bold rock called the High Rock[1] and we were told a story of a taylor being on the top and dropping down his needle and fall*ing* after it and breaking his neck and when we laughed, we were again told it was true[.] The rocks are very bold here close to the rivers edge and in the rock are sev*era*l houses built[.] Trees and wood cover the rock very richly. The fish were jumping very much between the showers. Com*mon* scabious frequent. The rocks are very fine and bold[.] We were told hereabouts that it was 2½ [miles] to the wooden Bridge and were walking very quick indeed, [f. 40r] soon after we passed Th*omas* Whitmores House at Hapley [Apley][2] on the R a beautiful place and well surr*ou*nded with hills c*o*vered with trees. Opposite on the side where the path is is the Wrens nest ford[3] and ab*ou*t a mile up is the Roving House[.][4] Mr Browns of Cofley [Caughley][5] is just beyond. We f*ou*nd that the time ran away very quick. We set out at five and it was near 2 hours that we had been walking very quick and we were surprised that the wooden Bridge did not appear as we had gone more than 2½ miles since we inquired. At last 2¼ [hours] were passed and no Bridge appeared and the miles seemed the longest we had ever walked, and if the next four miles were as long as these had been we sh*ould* have had a great inclination to stop at the wooden Bridge but just before we came to it, meeting an old man and asking him he told us we had come 7 Miles and that it was ab*out* ¾ of a mile to the Bridge and that it was only a mile from Bridge to Bridge. Never were wearied travellers more happy at hearing that news for we had been 2 hours and 20 minutes coming and had walked 3½ an hour allowing some time for tak*ing* 2 Views and as this acc*ou*nt made the whole distance 8 M*i*les, as we had learnt at 1st: we gave credit to it and therefore set forth to walk this mile easy, but alas, this mile swelled out into 3 Nearly and it was past 8 before we got to the Tontine Inn at the foot of the wooden Bridge. It had rained nearly all the time f*ro*m 5 OClock to 8. The people here have no idea of distance. And when at wooden bridge some [f. 41r] told us it was 2 others a mile to the Iron Bridge[.][6]

Coalport is a*n* airly looking struggling place[.] On the R are a great many stacks of coal arranged in [*in ordere lorgo*?][7] on the riverside in battalions of black array for some distance. We crossed the river ab*ou*t 3 meadows above the Bridge at a horse ferry and then supposing it only a mile walked leisurely and sauntering on with umbrella fixed to guard off the rain and to go in cool. The night was dizzy [drizzly] and the smoke and rain had a very curious effect as we walked up to the Iron Bridge[.] It was too thick clearly to distinguish the riverside on the Edges of the hills but here and there the fires cast a clear light on the side of some houses and shewed us that there were plenty of others on the banks side.[8] The sounds of the furnaces saluted our ears and the hammers were heard at a distance[.] The whole had a curious effect and being ab*out* ½ p*a*st 8 the darkness added

---

[1] Lee sketched this rock at SJC, MS U.30 (6), ff. 20r, 21r (p. 312), not reproduced here.

[2] Apley Park near Stockton, a Georgian house replaced in 1811 by a Gothic mansion (Pevsner, *Shropshire*, p. 60). Thomas Whitmore (1782–1846) was MP for Bridgnorth 1806–31 (History of Parliament Online).

[3] Lee means 'forge'. Iron smithing sites along the lower Linley Brook were known collectively as the 'Wrens Nest forge' in 1808 (*Victoria County History: Shropshire*, X, pp. 348–54).

[4] The Rovings public house on the bank of the Severn (*Victoria County History: Shropshire*, X, pp. 233–40).

[5] The Browne estate at Caughley (*Victoria County History: Shropshire*, X, pp. 233–40).

[6] Lee means that some said it was one mile to the Iron Bridge, but others said it was two miles.

[7] This phrase is difficult to decipher but may be *in ordine longo*, 'in a long line'.

[8] Lee sketched this scene at SJC, MS U.30 (6), f. 23r (p. 312), not reproduced here.

DIARY 1: TOUR FROM LONDON TO HOLYWELL IN WALES

to the singularity of the scene. We got safe from the rain to the inn but found our 1 Mile had been 3 good ones[.]

[f. 39v] ~~We arrived~~ Squire Whitmores[1] about 4 Miles above Bridgenorth[.] Opposite *Squire* Whitmores some hay was not got in so late as this time. It was in small cocks[.]

Just above his house is the forge and several iron railways[.] Just above these is a brick kiln on the R.

About ¾ of a mile up are some white cottages on the L which look pretty – and just above this some great red brick works on the R.

Arely called (from map) over Areley. Above on opposite side pass by Bore [Borle] Brook which runs in to River.

Higher up on L is Hig-ley [Highley.] Just above the Rea [Rhea.] Just above on opposite side Alveley[.] Just above on R hill house[.] Just above Hampton Boat ford above on L. The Ray [River]. Above on R [is] Quatford[2] just ~~below~~ (above) Bridge North. On [the] opposite side [of Bridgnorth] [the] plan is called Lower Town. Above the High Rock is Burest mill[.][3] Above on L [is] Astley Abbot [Astley Abbots]. Above lower Green opposite Apley Hall. Whitmores.[4] Corfley [Caughley] above.

~~Where~~ The hill where the Stone mines we entered is called Benthal Edge.[5] Bildwas [Buildwas][.]

Bill at Iron Bridge[6]

August. 6.	Supper.	2	
	Ale –		: 8
	Bed	1	–
[August] 7.	Breakfast	1	: 6
	Eggs		: 4
	Lunch –		: 8
	Dinner	2	: 6
	Ale	8	
	Cyder	1	: 6
	Supper	1	–
	Bed –	1	–
	Ale for Men etc	5	
		17	:10
	Waiter	2	
	Chamber Maid	2	
		21	–

---

[1] William Whitmore of Dudmaston Hall, a 17th-century house now in the care of the National Trust.
[2] Lee sketched views of Quatford at SJC, MS U.30 (6), ff. 16r, 16v, 18r (pp. 311–12), not reproduced here.
[3] Possibly Pendlestone Mills on the right bank of the Severn immediately above Bridgnorth and High Rock (OS 1st series, Shropshire sheet LVIII, NE; surveyed 1882, revised 1901).
[4] See n. 1 above.
[5] Benthall Edge, a wooded outcrop of Silurian limestone on the right bank of the River Severn and to the west of Ironbridge (*Victoria County History: Shropshire*, X, pp. 247–57).
[6] This list of expenses is written perpendicular to the main text, in a box at the bottom of the folio.

[f. 41r] **Aug*u*st: 7: [Thursday]**
About ½ past 8 We started from the Inn having got hold of a very intelligent fellow who amongst his other various and numerous occupations acts as hairdresser and so genera*lly* esquires the company about the works. The first place we went to see was about 500 Yds up the riverside where the rock is cut into most curious forms[.] Pillows are left in ev*ery* direction and shape and the caverns are *from* 40 to 50 feet high. We then went *from* thence ~~where we were~~ (after seeing) [f. 40v] their parlour a place where they have a fire in winter and they smoke[.] The man who walked ab*out* with us lost his eye there some time ago as he was filling up a Hole with powder. The battering set fire to the powder and blew the rock to pieces and (Mr Williams) he lost his eye[.] A piece of the roof fell in at my feet while we were talking in the cave[.] The man said they were expecting a great deal down for some time as the roof was weak there. F*rom* thence went to the Entrance of CoalBrook dale up the Iron rail work called Ginny Ball Bee worked at first down hillsides by Jennys.[1] The crosses where the roads pass for diff*eren*t carriages are called Pass Bys[.] The modern railways were invented ab*out* 26 Y*ea*rs ago by Mr John Curr Bell Vue House Sheffield.[2] The old ways are extremely heavy and broad and a great deal of iron below ground and a complete floor under that. The new have no iron but what you see and only cross bars of wood at the joints. They last better than the old ones[.]

1 Horse will draw 10 Ton in a road declining 1 Inch in a Yd. The <u>switch</u> in the <u>Pass by</u>.[3] Got to Mr Derbys Ironworks.[4] Went into the works. Saw the Molds for Casting. First sand and powdered charcoal. Then charcoal [is] rubbed over. Then [the] edges [are] sprinkled with water to give the sand a consistency and to prevent [the] edges breaking off. Grate models, bars, Large pots etc. Furnace Tapped, holds 1½ or 3 Ton at times at once. 30 Ton of flowing Iron a week. He has 1300 Men at work. Beautiful to see the air burn in the molds when [the] metal [is] poured in[.] Small explosions f*rom* the air wh*ic*h brings d*ow*n the dust only[.] The furnaces have sometimes Stuff put in 3 times an hour[.] A charge, consists of 1st, 6 Baskets Coke, then 8½ small D*itt*o ironstone. But equal Quant*iti*es then 4 Boxes Limestone ½ W*eigh*t of the other[.] They tap at 10 and at 5 in Even*ing* if nec*essary* [to an hour or so?]. Furnace 40 hours before the top materials get to bottom. Mr D*er*by has coal works and iron stone but buys the lime stone. In another place [are] wheels grinding the smooth*ing* stone. Taylors Geese[5] and Iron pipes cast in another. In another a mold for p*ar*ts of an iron bridge. The bearer was 54 feet long and ribs weigh 4 Ton for a Brid*ge* at Bristol. Curious and massy Boxes for molds for Pipes. Curious massy stock[6] for a great iron wheel at Swinney mills, of cast iron[.] The wooden [arches?] w*oul*d be filled in. Diam*ete*r to be 80 feet[.] No other such in the Kingdom or in Gr*ea*t Britain[.]

There are many pits all over the neighb*our*hood and some 200 yds deep[.] In some which are not very safe the men are not all*ow*ed to have lights and they work in the dark,

---

[1] 'The Curr-type railways in Shropshire seem generally to have been called Ginney, Jinney or Jenny rails' (Trinder, *Industrial Revolution*, p. 124).

[2] John Curr, railway innovator (*c*.1756–1823).

[3] 'A place on a railway where vehicles can pass one another' (*OED*).

[4] Edmund Darby's ironworks at Coalbrookdale. In the following paragraph, Lee describes the smelting process at Darby's coke blast furnace.

[5] A tailor's goose is a smoothing iron. The correct plural is gooses.

[6] The 'hub' of a wheel (*OED*).

DIARY 1: TOUR FROM LONDON TO HOLYWELL IN WALES

for fear of the lamps [with*in*?] the lower forge where Mr Derbys forge hammer is at work[.]

[f. 42r] There is close by a large cast iron wheel cov*er*ed with plates of iron on the ~~wheels~~ teeth of the wheel. This is for turning the ins*trument* which bores the pipes of iron smo*oth*. A process exactly like that of boring cannon. The water w*hi*ch turns this wheel falls into a large bason *from* wh*ich* it is worked by a steam engine back again to the head of all the works and passes thro*ugh* a passage in the hill of 1000 Yds in length[.] Coal Brook dale or that p*art* wh*ich* is called by that name is up a separate valley *from* the river and ~~how and~~ Mr Edmund Derbys works are all in it[.] The whole of the rest of the place which in gen*era*l goes by that name is called the Iron Bridge or the Parish of Maidley [Madley.] In going down a mine here of ab*out* 200 Yds the Corfs[1] are 3 Minutes[.] Near Newcastle is a mine of coal 250 Yds Deep, *from* the bottom of which they will draw a corf in ¾ of a minute by a steam engine whose Cy*lin*der is 30 Inches Diam*ete*r.

From the Colebrook Dale we crossed the ferry to go and look at the limestone rock directly opposite where there is a very steep inclined plane cut d*ow*n the rock side[.] To all appearanc*es* it was not steep and we began running up very briskly and when we got wh*at* we thought [was] ½ way up we rested, completely beaten and blown, we then got on little and little and thought we sh*ould* never get to the top wh*ich* however we reached after a deal of labor and fatigue. From setting out hard at first, 3. 4̄6̄2̄6̄11̄4̄2̄4̄0̄6̄2̄5̄4 and 5̄5̄1̄6̄ 3̄1̄8̄2̄9̄. 3̄5̄5. 5̄5̄3̄2̄9̄. 3̄ 1̄1̄4̄2. 3̄4 the 3̄4̄9̄.

[f. 43r] The Buckets which go up and down were worked by a Jenny. And the Diam*ete*r of the wheel was ab*out* 5 feet and there were 33 rounds of chain on it[.] Therefore The length of [the] inclined plane [is] ab*out* 166 Yds down and very steep. About 23 Yds of ⊥^{r} rock is on one side [of] the place the men where [*sic*] work*ing* in the open day. The 13 first Yds was plane earth then a stratum of 10 Yds of stone. The rock is generally let out to a n^o [2] of men who go shares in the work done and if one is ill still he has his share. Fresh parties are called by the term <u>Butties</u> and some works have 2 or 3 Butties[.] At this Work were 2 Butties who have 10^d a ton for the stone they laid at the bottom of the In*clined* plane. 3 Ton makes wh*at* they call a Load. They had a labouring man to whom they give 2:6 a day and 2 Boys. They buy only powder for Blasting[,] *every* thing else is fo*und* there. There is a saying here that 'no man is so dry as a limestone digger'[3] and accordingly we sent for some ale wh*ich* was brought to them, and then 2 blasts were prepared. <u>One</u> in some rock wh*ich* had been loosened before and therefore only wanted breaking. The man takes an iron crow or spear with a sharp edge and straight at [the] bottom and beat*ing* on the rock and turning it about it makes a n^o of lines in ev*ery* direction which form a circular hole as he wears the rock away. This hole was <u>churned</u>[,] as the phrase is[,] to 6 Inches deep. He then poured 1 Inch of powder in and putting down a thin iron rod to the powder he filled the sides of it up with dust and then rammed this down hard (etc) untill it was filled[.] The Iron rod is then drawn out and a straw filled with powder put in and a piece of torch paper being lighted *every* body gets out of the way and off she goes. The other blast was made in a piece of (the solid) rock ~~that was~~ the hole was 16 Inches deep. The first part of the Hole was made in the same manner as above then when ab*out* 6 Inches deep,

---

[1] A large, strong basket formerly used in carrying ore or coal from the working place in a mine to the surface (*OED*).

[2] Number. This abbreviation is repeated throughout the diaries.

[3] Quotation marks added.

they pour water in and with a sharper pointed tool work it about[,] putting a little hay in at the top of the bale to hinder the water *from* flying ab*ou*t[.] The hole when made [is] then dried by putting (hay) down it and all the dirt being cleared out [f. 44r] of it[.] 5 Inches of powder were put in and done as before[.] The blast did not make a great noise and the large one loosened ab*ou*t 1 Ton of rock. From thence we went over the water to the Stone quarry in the rock to see 2 Blasts in the caves. The process [is] the same as this only the Explosion is greater. Since our absence, A great part of the ceiling had fallen in[,] about 4 Tons w*eigh*t[,] where the piece came down w*hich* fell at our feet!! Lucky Escape! No person was hurt[.] A Limestone lever will drink 2[1] as much in a day as a coal lever. The being out in the air may cause this and its being a more healthy Labor[.] We then walked to the inn ab*ou*t 2 OClock for a little refreshment and then proceeded over the river Paying ½ each. This bridge shewed great symptoms of decay some time ago and they repaired it and have built a pillar to strengthen it[.] We proceeded to an Ironstone mine where the Entrance was in horizontal. We took off our coats and hats and put handkerchiefs *roun*d our head and each with a candle in his hand marched in[.] The horse road was ab*ou*t 5 feet high and near 90 Yds long. This appeared awkward to go along[.] We passed the horse and his cart and got to the end where the branches began[.] These were extremely narrow (and low) and in many parts we were obliged to crawl on our hands and knees[.] They were ab*ou*t 2 foot high[.] We passed 3 men who were at work[.] They lay down on their Bases and leaning along on their sides pick at the layer w*hich* was thin and all the time make a horrible sort of groan.[2] We went to the End and shaking hands with one and smoking a minute with another we returned to the Horse road which we afterw*ar*ds thought [an] excellent road. We then sent for some beer and all drank together. The Cart is brought to the End of the road and there are small Boxes into w*hich* the boys pull gr*ea*t lumps of stone and then by a chain fastened round the middle and pass*ing* throu*gh* their legs they drag like ponies these boxes into the cart.[3] The workmen have flannel drawers on. Here were 4 Butties[,] a young man who has 3S a day and 2 Boys. ~~Candles~~ They have 22S. for 42 Cwt and are payed ev*ery* fortnight. An Experienced man has 3:6 or 4S a day. It is a good days work when they get [f. 45r] 42 Cwt or a stack and ¼th [fourth]. They use 2lb of Candles and 2lb of Powder a day. One branch is 500 yds[,] the other shorter. In a great mine ~~there is at the~~ the owner lets it out to so many Butties who Employ other men. At the Bottom of most pits is a small house like a store house where the pitmaster called the <u>chorlter</u> master keeps his candles[,] etc etc. They are quite safe. He then delivers out these to the men in their proper times and proportions[.] Some veins are not above 1 foot and ¼ and men must work under these. Each labouring man has so much work alloted [*sic*] to him in many works and when he has done it he leaves off whether in 2 hours or in 10. Men often lay great wagers about doing their work amo*ng*st themselves[.] Got a few specimens. We then walked up to the top of the rock and saw down a coal mine w*hich* was work*ing* but did not go down as the work wo*ul*d be just the same as in the other where they find some times a little coal also[.] We then went home to dinner and afterw*ar*ds at 6 OClock took a boat and went down the Severn to the China Works w*hich* are 2 Miles or more below the Iron Bridge. The process of throwing is similar

---

[1] Twice.
[2] Referred to again below, at f. 42v (p. 65).
[3] Lee drew a small rough sketch of a 'Boy dragging the Box in the mine' at f. 41v (p. 65), not reproduced here.

to that of Worcester but the man is not ½ so clever[.] They then dry the ware a little and after put it into a sort of mould and turn it afresh which gives it a scollop shape[.] A man then pares the Edges with a Knife. And the ware is put into the furnace for the 1st time and stays for about 40 hours[.] This [is] then taken to the Painting Shop, where there are a variety of copper plates and the impression is first taken off on a thin piece of paper almost as fine as silver paper. The mixture is a secret but is very sticky and these papers are then laid on the cups etc and are rubbed with the end of a piece of flannel rolled up[.] This fixes the color on the ware and does not rub off the paper but soon after the ware is taken and being put under water and rubbed the paper comes off and the colors and patterns are finely left[.] The ware is then put in the furnace which has 6 fires for about 18 or 20 hours and then it is taken out again and glazed and burnt for about [*margin:* Go to page on L after Boy dragging][1] [f. 42v] 18 Hours more. The Making [of] the molds is as curious a process as any. They first form the thing in clay just as they wish the thing to be sold to be and then take off this in plaster of paris cutting the clay (one) in halves. Thus 2 plaister molds are formed of the thing[.] In this they put the clay after rolling it and treating it exactly as dough for a pie. All oval or differently formed things which cannot be made by a circular lathe are thus done such as handles[,] Tool spouts etc. They would not tell us any of the materials which are used in the work, But Cornwall Clay, Burnt Bones and Flint are materials. Gave man 2S.

Close by is an inclined Plane down a hill down where boats come to a canal at [the] Bottom leading to the China Manufactory[.] The Boats are nearly flat Bottomed and are put into a sort of cradle going on wheels[2] and whose Weight keeps it of such a depth in the water that boats are easily shoved on it and then fastened on. There is a great engine which then pulls the cradle and boat up the plane. The rope is 2½ Inches thick and we were told that the plane was near 300 Yds long. As 1 Boat goes up 1 Plane close by another goes down and if the Boat going down [is to] be loaded to 5 Ton it will pull up 3 Ton in the return Boat. At the Top is a canal which goes up the country and about 2 Miles off we were told that there was another Inclined Plane 500 Yds long but not quite so steep for which the canal is carried into the country. As the friction arising from the rope on the ground would be considerable there are 45 ~~pullies~~ rollers all along the middle of the plane, which allow these to run much more easily. There is a cradle at top into which the boats descend from the upper canal. Our walk during the day had been very hot and close and as we were on the move from 6 to near four and from 6 to 9 we calculated our steps at not less than 22 Miles –

Why do Coal men make that noise?[3]

[f. 41v] Instruments for boring. N° 1. The tool for cutting the hole. N° 2. The sharper pointed Ditto. N° 3. Instrument for clearing out the pole. N° 4 A representation of the blast when filled the powder. Its [thassel?] for the straw and the paper.[4] [*Sketch, ink, captioned:* 'Boy dragging the Box in the mine']

---

[1] As noted in the Introduction, Lee's diary is not always written on continuous pages. Helpfully, he directs the reader in this instance to the point where the narrative continues, but this is not usually the case. Here, his marginal note refers to a small sketch of a boy dragging a load of stone, as described at f. 41v (p. 65).

[2] Lee made a rough ink sketch of the device in the page margin, not reproduced here.

[3] Reference to earlier description of miners groaning while at their work (see f. 44r, p. 64).

[4] In the original, four rough ink sketches of the instruments accompany this description, but they are not reproduced here.

[f. 43v] **August 8 [Friday]**
From thence at 7 OClock leaving the Tontine at the foot of the Iron Bridge with a guide walked up the meadows to Bildwas [Buildwas][,] 2 Miles[,] to Breakfast intending then to leave the river and to go to see the famous Wrekin glory of Salop. At Bild*wa*s is a remarkable neat commodious inn at [the] foot of Iron Bridge. Built by Cole Brook Dale Comp*any* 1796. Very fine arch and stand. Well and fern[.] A former stone bridge gave way and fell in all together at a flood[.] Between Collbrook Dale and Bildwas there was on 27 May 1773 a great rend and slip of the rock and side of hill tow*ar*ds the river, at a place called the Beeches [The Birches] on the Estate of Walter Seton Mosely.[1] The old course of the Severn was filled up and the road removed many yds in some parts and fields with their crop removed. Ab*out* 22 A*cr*es of land removed and damaged[.] The chasm was in some parts 8½[,] 10 and 12 Yds deep[.] Pillars of Earth were left standing in some p*ar*ts of the chasm and some of them ab*out* 4 feet higher than they formerly stood[.] Some of the insulated parts of land in the (diff*erent* p*ar*ts of the) chasm were raised 4 and some 8 feet. The chasm was about ½ mile in the longest part. Bildwas Abbey[2] looks well over the water[.] Our guide was John Howlas[,] Hair dresser at the Iron Bridge[,] a very intelligent person and who knows all the country[.] Hav*ing* laid in a stock of provisions start for the undertak*ing*[.] The day was beautiful but intolerably hot and soon made us feel its effects and proceeded gently according*ly*. We proceeded along the high road and pass The direction Post[,] on one arm wh*ich* points to Much Wenlock is the Foll*owing* direction[:] To M Wenlock[.] Our umbrellas were erected to keep off the sun. A little dist*ance* beyond the Ch*urch* Turn up a horse road thro*ugh* some fields wh*ich* brings to a small wood here The sun so powerful that we were obliged in the wood to change or rather thin our dress. Waistcoat neckcloths etc taken off. March on thro*ugh* fields to a white house before us, Wavers farm. This is a Beaut*iful* view. From thence make to the L rather along a path above the house lead*ing* to Leighton Lane[.] Pass by W. Davis Cottage. Leave Mr Williams (white) house much to the right. From thence cross the lane for the Waterspout lane [Spout Lane] at the end of wh*ich* is a spring of water. Very refreshing and welcome. Then leave Wrekin coppices to the R and make for the bottom of the hill cross*ing* a rail fence. The path winds gently up as if going to the left of the hill above is a fine old spreading yew tree wh*ich* is first to be joined[.] Leav*ing* this rather on the R wind up the edge of the hill to some rocks above and then the ascent is not very steep and brings you to the Bladder Stone rock so called. Walk on the top: on [f. 44v] the R is the Ravens Cup [Raven's Bowl] a large rock at the top of wh*ich* is a small hole ab*out* size of a Bason wh*ich* may be found by actually search*ing* for it and in this after rain is gen*era*lly some water. Reascend*ing* the Edge of Hill walk forw*ar*d and you come to the highest land. All ab*out* are O[r] places in wh*ich* were formerly fir trees but not thriv*ing* cut down[.] At the farther end nearly are 2 little hills wh*ich* are called Heavens Gates and beyond but lower 2 More at the End of the Hill called Hell Di*tt*o [Hell's Gates] by the People frequent*ing* the place[.] [*Sketch map and key, ink, reproduced at p. 67*]

---

[1] See Bowen, 'Getting into the Archive'.
[2] The Cistercian abbey at Buildwas, founded in 1134/5 (*Victoria County History: Shropshire*, II, pp. 50–59).

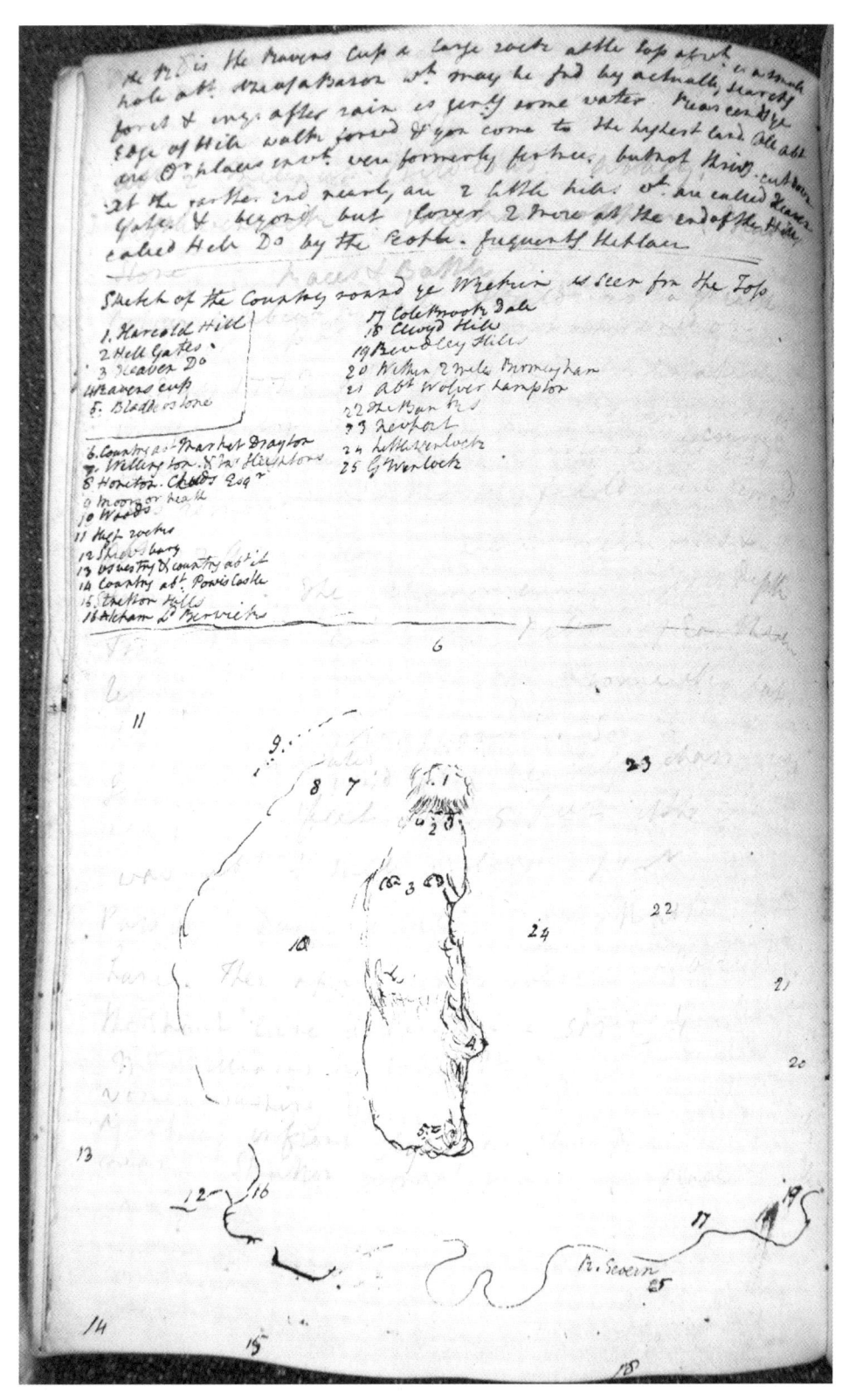

Figure 4. 'Sketch of the Country round the Wrekin as seen from the Top'. By John Lee, 8 August 1806 (SJC, MS U.30 (1), f. 44v). Reproduced by kind permission of the Master and Fellows of St John's College, Cambridge.

[f. 45v] [*margin:* The Ladies of the Cottage[1] will confer a very great obligation upon a stranger rambling from Cambridge if they will grant him permission to visit their cottage which he has always understood to be one the most beautiful features of Llangollen – (A message was sent back by the bearer saying it required) no answer]

[*margin:* Bilberries grow on Top of hill]
[f. 46r] We could not see Colebrook dale or Bridge but the Hills close round were very visible. The river winds all up the South side of the Wrekin and shores for the first time were plain [to be seen] – The river Tarn [Tern] is not visible all the way as marked but runs some where in that direction[.] We sat on Heaven Gates and looked around and then returned to the Bladderstone and examined that side. Day excessive hot[,] no bearing ones clothes on[.] The coppices at the bottom of the hillsides look well. The guide took off his shoes and advised us to ascend for security without ours but after disregarding his advice with a little slipping etc got up safe. But was obliged to take them off to come down, [it was] so slippery. About N° 10[2] are some woods and cornfields mixed and a farm in the middle of the woods looking well. Formerly there were races round the Wrekin. How the horses could run I do not know. 18 Hours more

In the year — upon the kings recovery when he went to St Pauls and all the Country [was] illuminated for joy,[3] a Waggon load of coal was drawn up from a farm house at the foot of the hill on the E side by 11 Horses. 4 Men attended it. One wheel was locked and they ascended at the north End and went up to the Bladderstone. A bonfire was made. A post was fixed[,] a [farmer?] set on the top[,] faggots etc. The farmers name is Daniel Rogers and many persons have doubted the truth of this and bets have been made but the farmer and the driver are now alive and many persons who saw it. A sheep was roasted and as much drink given as was desired by the Gentlemen of Millington[4] where 8 sheep were roasted at the same time. There is a grand wake on the 1 Sunday before May Day. On May Day and on the Sunday after May day. A great deal of company always comes and the hill appears like a great fair[.] The principal Booth close by Bladderstone. About 21 Years ago May day happening on a Sunday was fought a Battle between the colliers and the farming people in which the farming people were licked and many persons were so wounded that they were carried off the hill and many died.[5] The following Sunday the parties came in stronger N^os resolving to have another battle. The farming people armed with clubs etc came up the S side of the hill. The colliers [came] by the N but the latter were not half so numerous as their opponents and therefore did not risk a battle but retreated into the coppice below the hill which was surrounded and they then retreated to Little Wenlock. Expecting succours from Colebrook but not being sufficiently strong the Day ended without another battle. All the magistrates on [*sic*] the county were

---

[1] Eleanor Butler and Sarah Ponsonby, the 'ladies of Llangollen', whose residence, Plas Newydd, became an attraction due to the celebrity and scandal surrounding the women. See Mavor, *The Ladies of Llangollen*. This is a copy of a note Lee sent to them.

[2] Reference to Lee's sketch map at f. 44v and reproduced at p. 67 (Figure 4).

[3] Lee left the date blank (represented by a dash), but he refers to the recovery of George III from mental illness in 1789.

[4] Lee may mean the town of Wellington.

[5] At May Day wakes on the Wrekin, it was customary for colliers and farmers to 'battle' for possession of the summit, into the early 19th century (Stevenson, *Popular Disturbances*, p. 63).

assembled on the hill to stop any battle had it commenced. The Battle began with sticks and fists and then got to stones etc. We descended by the same path so we ascended to the Yew trees, then making for Coon Lane House on the river we crossed the little hill with firs on the top and descended this towards a farm house by which is a lane. Following this it brings out on the road where is a hand Post guiding to Shrewsbury and to 2 other directions as 3 roads meet. Passing on the road opposite the Wrekin go by Squire Jenkins of Chalton Hall[1] which stands on the hill on the R. A [f. 47r] coalpit is opposite on the L. Aquices[2] nest or wood Pidgeons. From Colebrook to Buildwas 2 Mile. To Bottom of Wrekin 4 [miles]. Up 1. Length 1 and Back again 1: To turn pike road 4 [miles]. Cross the road at about 6¼ [miles] from Iron Bridge and go up the opposite lane. A coal pit 40 Yds Deep on the L and 6 feet Diameter. An air pipe comes up the Mouth of the shaft. This lane brings [you] to a guide post. Leave the lane and go by the road through the field to Mr Symonds of Dryton. Pass down a lane from the house which will bring [you] to some cottages at [the] bottom, then cross the fields to another farm house before you. At it cross the lane and go down the meadow and come to [the] river opposite which is Coon Lane House. From Wrekin to Coon Lane house [is] 5 Miles. There [have] dinner. [Eel?] Pie[,] Cold Beef, Ham[,] Currant Pie and Cream. Got there at 4. The day was intolerably hot and ∴ staid till six for the cool evening. Here parted with my Guide and gave him 10:6 for his trouble. Dinner at 6. Cross [the] river. Ferry 2^d and go up [the] side of [the] river through [the] fields. [The] Path winds through long grass and bushes under a red rock. Then come to a style. Here you cannot keep [to the] river bank. Fine large red stone in river. Ascend a steep cliff. A fine view opposite is Mrs Pelhams old red house and grounds. [This was] The highest cliff over the river which [I] had passed over since Worcester. Hearts Ease and small convolvolus in abundance[.] Behind Mrs Pelhams house [are] Bold Hills. The path is obscure but keep as close to the river for [the] sake of [the] beauty of the views[.] After walking over several fields come to one field at [the] top of which the church of Wroxeter appears very pretty and a white house [is] close by in [the] trees. The miles are very long and although we were told it was but 3 Miles from Coon Lane it cannot be less than 5. The road to Atcham is to the left and it is 2 Miles from Wroxeter to Atcham[.] At the post shewing 9½ from Colebrook Vale is a neat lodge to Lord Berwicks Park[3] and the grounds are pretty[.] Cross a fine bridge over the Scarn which joins below the Severn but which is here as large as the Severn. About ½ past 8 reached the Talbot at Atcham, the situation of which is most beautiful. Bridge over Severn in front[,] on one side Church[4] surrounded with trees except on the bank of the river. Inn is excellent[,] good accommodation: Very nice Garden. Just the spot a person would like to live at. ~~The~~

August 9. [Saturday]
The Church is a very beautiful object from the bridge and all around [and] in it are some old monuments of the Burton family. They were just putting up a very old one which we were told came from St Chads Shrewsbury[.] It was broken in many pieces[,] was much defaced and the lines of 2 figures were just visible on ~~two~~ Pieces were in the old letter. *Hic*

---

[1] Edward Jenkins of Charlton Hill (d. 1820) (*Burke's Peerage*, 1853, III, p. 180).
[2] A queest is a dialect name for a ring dove or wood pigeon.
[3] Attingham Park, near Shrewsbury.
[4] Lee sketched this church at SJC, MS U.30 (6), f. 26r (p. 312); not reproduced here.

jacent corpora Edwardi Burton Et Josili uxoris[,] etc.[1] The Church is very neat and in the Chief pew in the place is a stone or common fire place which must [f. 46v] [*margin:* (Mr Dodson of Coon Lane House)[2]] make it very comfortable for the Lord of the Manor in Winter. In a frame hung up in one of the Pews is a curious Epitaph or Epicedium in a glass case and it has 2 doors[.] It consists of drawings and verses and some in print. The following will convey some small idea of it[.]

Parts 1 Contains the following Verses	N° 2 the following[3]
As men to the meridian come	To mortals why should Death be strange
So they decline as doth the Sun	Whilst like the Moon we often change
Which soon obscures itself from Sight	And find no sublunary stay;
And turns the longest day to night	Cause Time doth fly so fast away

N° 3 represents the moon over a crown and N° 4 A moon with very coarse features indeed and a very long nose, over a circle or the world probably[.]

N° 5 is a Cross on 3 Steps with a Snake or Serpent winding on it representing probably Time[.]

N° 6 is a very broad dark black border and goes all round the lower part of the picture. On the outside is a thin very narrow line just touching the waves of the former[.]

N° 7. is a rather smaller and more narrow border which does not meet at top to make room for a Sceleton [*sic*] who is treading on a woman in a coffin[.] He has a spear in the Right hand and between is a broad spade[.] On the opposite side is one rounded at the bottom.

N° 8 contains [f. 47v] the following Verses thus arranged)

Death in ambush	N° 9 contains the following
Doth sculking stand	Spade work lodgings
Ready to smite	Must needs be many
With dart in hand	Because that Death
And when there with	Neer spareth any
He gives a wound	*Ad mortem sic Vita fluit*[4]
No art to cure it	*Velut ad mare Flumen*[5]
Can be found	The sting of Death is Sin

Below is written on one side the Coffin or Shroud
AN EPITAPH or EPICEDIVM. } and on the opposite side   PENNED as a cautionary Farewell to a sinful world
                                                                                              by T Lyster

N° 11 and 12 contain the following lines
Soho! Passenger stay turn thine Eye   ∴ no more be seen to woe it
And see how here these Bones doe lie   But quit thy love and liking to it

---

[1] The translation of the inscription is 'Here lie the bodies of Edward Burton and of Joseli, his wife'; perhaps Lee made an error in copying it as it refers to the tomb of Edward Burton (d. 1524) and his wife Jocosa Coyney, removed from St Chad's in Shrewsbury to St Eata's in Atcham in 1788 (Newman and Pevsner, *Shropshire*, p. 125; *Burke's Landed Gentry*, 1847, I, p. 167).

[2] Not identified. Lee had dined there on the previous day.

[3] Numbers 1 and 2 refer to Lee's sketch plan of the church, not reproduced here.

[4] Life flows so to death.

[5] Like a river to the sea.

Much Toile and Trouble Envie and Strife
Doth still disturb thy mortal Life
But in this grot is now thy bed
Where I at rest have laid my head
As tis appointed thus thou must
Be reacquainted with the dust
———

Trust not the world before thou try it
For most men are deluded by it
Much like unto a Syrens Song
Which tempts to steer the Course thats wrong
Its vaine delights if that thou mind them
At last thou shall deceitful find them
Those seeming joys which thou art craving
Are painted toyes not worth the having
All filled with snares with nets and ginns
For to entangle thee in sins

For if the longest life of man
Is but in length but like a span
Then he that stands most surely shall
God knows how quickly have a fall
Then pause a while and learn of me
That in my case thou soon shalt be
And now prepare thyself for heaven
Before Deaths fatal stroke be given
———

It is not bones beneath a stone
That can doe good when life is gone
The greatest good thou here can have
is a remembrance of thy Grave
And Brittle state, which understood
And Pondered well may doe thee good
But Gods Good word all truth doth tell
And if in peace thou thinkst to dwell
Beg Grace and doe it
And Farewell

On the two doors of this were also verses etc. The doors (each) of course were ½ the width of the glass frame. On the R door in the middle [f. 48r] was a deaths head and below it 2 crossed shinbones in a circle, with 2 Moons on the sides. On the right of this on a separate piece of paper pasted on a coronet with a pair of wings and on the other side a sun or moon in a circle.[1] Below was ~~the~~ written 'The projection of the sphere for the lat*itude* of 53 Deg*rees*.' and at the Bottom the persons name 'By Tho*mas* Lyster 1685'[.] These were all drawn and on the opposite paper were Verses 'On Time' to the foll*owin*g effect

In rapid motion still the sun
With Time away is hasting
And shews how fast our Glass doth run
And how our days are wasting
Yet few of us have been so wise
As to regard how fast it flies

———

Unless it be a plot for pleasure.
Or hoard up trash to leave behind
We make such chaff our chiefest treasure
W*hic*h heirs will scatter with the wind
And for it wish us in our grave
And thats the thanks we often have

———

That Monarch w*hic*h bears greatest sway
And wears the richest golden crown
Could never court him long to stay

---

[1] Lee roughly sketched both the right and left doors, not reproduced here.

But trips his heels and throws him down
Into the [dust?] and silent Grave
Which is the lot we all must have

Below these verses is the picture of some old Gentleman with a fine wig and long [pendant?] cravat, some com*mon* priest and Below is the following Acrostic
Father requests I'll daly [*sic*] make thee
That into Favor thou woudst take me
For to they mercy I will fly
And in thy hands will live and dy:
Then safe, secure I [ever?] shall be
Whilst I my soul commend to thee
Then of thy Mercy not my Merit
In to thy hands receive my Spirit

Upon the top of the left door is written 'Three Entire triangles entirely in one Figure and one Entire triangle entirely in every one of the three'. Below is a heart with triangles in it and in the Top is written '*Pater*'. Middle '*Deus*'. Right '*Spiritus Sanctus*' on the Left '*Filius*'.[1] On the Adjacent paper a coat of arms with a sort of crown above[.] Below 'An Acrostic on the Holy Bible'
The trees therein whereon all Truth is growing
Health, Wealth, and Wisdom all thence are flowing
Our Shield and safetys there and sure defense
Most Joyful Tidings also come from thence
A touchstones there by w*hi*ch our steps are try'd
Salvations lamp is there to be our guide.
———————

Lost Pilgrims have a harbour there of rest
Yea comforts there for all with great oppressed
Such fruit is there for them in faith that crave it
That no things wanting but they there may have it
Enrich us Lord with this whose heavenly store
Remains when Earthly Things shall be no more.
———————

Another which may be wrot [*sic*] upon a blank leaf at the End of the Bible
The hungry Soul may here be always fed
Heres living water or heres dayly bread
Or life or strength or the right way to bless
My hearts delight also here placed is
[f. 49r] a Glass also to here whereby I find
Such things as please or do disease my mind
———————

Love joy and peace and all things to content me
You here may see from Heaven I have sent me

---

[1] The Latin words mean 'Father', 'God', 'Holy Spirit', 'Son'.

So lock them in my heart with Davids Key
That they from thence Lord neer bestolen away
Eternal praise and thanks then shall there be
Returned to God who gives such gifts to me

Below is "the projection of the Number Eight"

The Bill at Atcham where the accommodations were very Good was for Supper a Bed and Breakfast 4S[,] Waiter 1S. Cross the river and leave the turnpike road as soon as possible wh*ich* a path allows you to do. Above Atcham [is] a very pretty bend in the river and the woods hang well. Leave Chilton to the L. Farther on pass some cottages wh*ich* is Emstree [Emstrey Cottages] and beyond it, as we were told the river is bare and very tame, we struck off to the public road from wh*ich* are sev*eral* beautiful views all around. The Wrekin looks very venerable. Pass by St Giles old Church[1] and get to Shrewsbury wh*ich* is a very old Town. Saw much of the *Reseda* every where and some of the *Chenopodium* [goose foot] wh*ich* grows behind Sapsfords[.]

The streets are but very poor and the pavement is very rare[.] The streets all together are almost ½ as bad as those of Norwich. We intended to stay the rest of the day and all Sunday here ~~but on an~~ and had walked very leisurely in the morning nor did we leave Atcham until Eleven, but coming into Shrewsbury at 1 we fo*u*nd the place filled with company[.] Market Day and the Assizes were beginning. No room was to be had and beds were scarce. In consequence of wh*ich* after staying 2 hours there we resolved to go on 8 Miles to Neslip [Nesscliffe]. Some heavy thunder storms came on and much rain[.] Talbot Inn, civil treatment. The Town Hall looks a very old build*ing* and [the] Market [was] crowded. Altering Buckles of Knapsack 4^d. Socks 1(S):7. Trunk sending to Oswestry 1^S: Salop Guide[2] 2:6 A Porter 3^d. Bill at Talbot 4:3. Waiter 6^d. After the Thunder storm marched forward and another ab*out* a mile fr*om* the Town Passed by a good H*o*use At the End of the Town wh*ich* we were told was Dr Derwins.[3] Mr Powis house of Berwick[4] on the Rt am*ong* the trees over the river. The road mends the farther you get from Shrewsbury. Market women [f. 50r] mostly riding by 1 or 2 fr*om* market, great numbers of them Between the 3 and 4 Milestones bey*o*nd Salop[.] Very fine views into Wales. Hill appears beyond hill and some very great ones near on the Left. Pass over (I think) Montfords [Montford] Bridge and a Turn pike close by. Betwe*en* 7 and 8 Milestone [the] road [is] very rural[,] well wooded [on] each side[.] 2 long red hill*s* on the right[,] the Base cov*ere*d with groves. Come to the New Inn at Neslip, at 6 OClock. A small house[,] indifferent accommodation. Only 1 room for travellers. Appearances better with*ou*t than within. But remarkably civil people. In the front of the House are some Mountains[,] in the distance on the top of one called the Brithing [Breidden Hill] is a Mon*ume*nt erected

---

[1] The foundations of the medieval St Giles Church were still visible in the early 19th century (*Victoria County History: Shropshire*, II, pp. 105–8).

[2] Possibly George Alexander Cooke, *Topographical and Statistical Description of the County of Salop: Containing an Account of its Situation, Extent, Towns, Roads, Rivers ...; to which is Prefixed a Copious Travelling Guide ... Illustrated with a Map of the County*, London, [1805?].

[3] Robert Waring Darwin (1766–1848) of The Mount, Shrewsbury; physician and father of Charles Darwin (Desmond, Moore and Browne, 'Darwin, Charles Robert (1809–1882)').

[4] Probably Thomas Jelf Powys (d. 1805) of Berwick House, Shrewsbury.

to the memory of Admiral Rodney.[1] The names of the 4 Hills were repeated as if they were usually mentioned in some sort of (intended) rhyme by the people[:]

Mălăgōlvĭn [Moel-y-golfa] and the ~~Knitting~~ Kñithiñg [Cefn-eithin]

Kĕvĕnly Kĕskūth [Cefn-y-castell] and the Brīthiñg

Behind the New Inn is Nescliff hill[,] the hill which looked so well from the road[.] It belongs to Lord Bradford[2] and is all Limestone of which there are three fine pits[.] In the cliffs of this rock is a curious cave up 26 narrow steps of stone. This cave is said to have been made by a great Robber of the Name of Kynnaston Where he lived with his 2 horses and it is called Kynnaston cave, whether a horse ever went in seems doubtful but the persons there shew the place where the horses were tied up and where he slept.[3] This fellow[,] according to report and which reports are firmly believed by the people[,] made this cave himself and no one dare attack him there. He robbed all the Gentry of the neighbourhood for 20 Miles and if he saw any poor person he would give them what he had [f. 49v] despoiled from the rich so that they were all his friends and wished him well. He performed wonders on these horses. He had a fine bald horse and a brown mare. On the bald horse he took a famous leap of 16½ Yds at a place called the Low Bank from 1 Rock to Another[.] He was asleep[.] Above 20 persons came to take him[.] His horse puts down its head and wakes him up he gets and leaps from rock to rock. He was once beset both ways on Montford Bridge by persons to catch him and what does he do but he leaps over the battlements on his horse and rides away down the river[.] Upon asking where he bought these nags we were told Oh they were <u>enchanted</u>. The mare was not so tall as the horse nor so powerful and as he was riding the horse and exercising the mare leading her one day. [He was] Pursued and obliged to let go the mare and she was taken. He never did a poor man harm. He and his horse were both found dead in the cave and supposed to have been ill and died and horse died for sorrow[.] (Probably for want of food[.]) The door of his cave is now the door of the Gaol at Shrewsbury[.]

Thus far Story. An Elderly woman now lives in the cave which consists of 1 Moderate size apartment, and behind the door is a recess where a bed is placed. A pillar is cut in the rock and shelves for holding etcs[4] are made in it[.] On this Pillar are the letters | HK 1564 | cut which is all whereon hangs the tale. Nevertheless we were shewn where <u>Was formerly</u> the manger and the woman sleeps where the robber is said to have slept and in a very good place for him behind the door. The cave all smoked black, for the chimney smokes as it is so much sheltered, by the rock[.] No window. 'But' said the woman 'a Lady called here last week and has given me some money to have a window cut and the chimney altered and they are coming to see me again when it [f. 51r] is done.'[5] She was very much afraid they would come before it was done and that they would then accuse her of neglect. She said they had promised to have a fine painting stuck up in the road to bring her more company. We thought these very kind Ladies and understand they were Lord and Lady Bradford but she had misnamed them. 4̈04̇632̈92̇6̈ 13̇ 55̇13̇315̇52̈1̇ 732̇6̈. Lord Bradfords

---

[1] Rodney's Pillar, erected in 1782 at the top of Breidden Hill, Powys, Wales.

[2] Orlando Bridgeman, 1st Earl of Bradford (1762–1825), MP for Wigan (1784–1800) and agricultural improver (History of Parliament Online).

[3] Humphrey Kynaston (c.1468–1534), a highwayman who operated in the Shropshire area. The cave is still known as Kynaston's Cave.

[4] Probably meaning small, miscellaneous items.

[5] Quotation marks added.

House[1] [is] about 4 Miles off. Mr Williams[,] owner of the Quarries walked over [the] hill with us[.] Hill [is] 164 Acres. Ascend part of the hill well known by the name of the "Black" Steps[,] 47 in No. Get to top of Big Head Quarry. Precipice [is] 37 Yds high. Tremendous and quite ⊥^{r}. His father rented the same Quarries. Rent £19 per annum and Duty and Taxes on stone near £6 a year more. Duty 4^d a ton. Labourers [get] from 10 to 16 Shgs a week[.] He pays sometimes [£]6 or [£]8 or near £10 a week in wages[,] They (sometimes) get 10 Stone a day[,] some times not 1. As they loosen it [they] throw it down the precipice, so that the precipice now decreases. They sell it for about 6:8 or 7 or 8S^s a Ton but in general 4^d a (solid) foot which is S6:8 a ton. Mr Williams[,] some Beer = 9^d. Supper Milk and Bed 1^S: There is a very comfortable school erected in the Village with a neat clock in front. The foundation was the scite [sic] formerly of a chapel as these verses on the front declare

God prosper and prolong this public good
A School erected where a Chapel stood

[f. 50v] Walked all over the Hill Top which commands a most extensive view of all the circumadjacent Country but it was too late to see it to perfection. Saw the other 2 Quarries[,] the School Quarry and the Bridge Quarry from their directions[.]

Quantities of Bilberries growing there and hundreds of measures are annually gathered. Foresters House very snug in the trees[.]

[*margin*: Coach fare to Oswestry 3:6. Porter for trunk 2^d]

[f. 48v] [*margin*: Bill at Shrewsbury. Cold Eating 2. Porter 5. Carriage for Portmanteau from Worcester 1^S:10^d = 4:3]

Sunday 10. [August]
At six oClock mounted the Holy head Coach which leaves Salop about 4, and rode to Oswestry. Pass through Felton [West Felton] 4 Miles farther on. A hamlet. Oswestry. 6 Miles farther on. 4236104492 49347 4414113 24392 34 3625192. Very pretty place[.] Cross Foxes a capital Inn. Fine Bowling green[,] Church neat and elegant with trees[.] Wrote to Sir B.H.[2] taken by them to Sellatyn [Selattyn] to Church 3 long miles from Oswestry lanes very pretty. Pass by — House an Heiress. Pass by Mr — House. Sellatyn on the Mountain side [f. 54r] [is seen] very advantageously from hence[.] Follow lane to (the left) all the way[.] On the L is [sic] up the mountain is a farm house called Gai Gwinnlan or the white fields because there the snow lies longer than any where else in the neighbourhood. From several gates along the lane side are very fine views in to the vale and country we had left. Chirk Church cuts a distinguished figure from its white washed steeple[.] The Evening was very dull which diminished the views otherwise they are extensive and most abundant all along the lane which winds most advantageously along the side of the Mountain about ½ way or more up. At the farthest end of the Mountain the lane ascends considerably and comes to the Fron Farm[,] Mr Jones[.] And from a rising ground advancing a little in front (rather to the L) of the house a most extensive and wonderful

---

[1] Weston Park; for Lord Bradford see p. 74, n. 2.
[2] Not identified.

view, full of variety[.] Great part of the (1)¹ Vale of Llangollen and the neighbouring hills, river Dee running beneath among the groves. Hills leading to Llangollen spotted with white houses. Eglwsg [Eglwyseg] Rocks[,]² (2) Rhuabon (3) hills Beyond Hope (4) Hill. 5 Wynstay [Wynnstay]. 6 Wrexham[,] 7 Past the Bellan rocks and immense woods. Beyond Stafford shire and other counties without End[.] More to the Right 8 St Martins. 9 Wrekin Hills[,] 10 Shrewsbury. 11 Chirk, 12 Hills about Colebrook dale. Rodneys Pillar³ and Kynsaston [sic] Hills[,] 13 Bishops castle neighbourhood[,] 14 The Clay Hills beyond 15 Chirk castle and woods. The castle ½ appearing above the hill[.] Nothing can Exceed this view for to the Left are [Mountains?][,] in the middle Immense plains and wood and to the R hills again[.] The aqueduct and canal looks also to advantage and the river running along its woody Banks between it[.] From here may be seen Lancashire[,] Yorkshire, Derbyshire, Cheshire[,] Salop[,] Flintshire[,] Herefordshire[,] Staffordshire[,] Warwickshire[,] Denbeighshire[,] Merionethshire[,] Montgomery. Forest of Delamer [Delamere] and forsaw Northumberland⁴ with several others[.]

[f. 52r] Church⁵ very pretty and looks to advantage with the fine trees behind it. Beautiful Vale behind Church, and bold hills. Its name is — Vale. Returned to Oswestry and from thence to Wittington [Whittington] 2 Miles further. Vicarage a very neat spot. House newly built, 2 Capital Rooms[,] Dining Room and Study. The comfortable mansion of a hospitable man. Fine large old yew Tree. Grounds laid out with as much taste as (the) space and a few years residence there would or could allow[.] Fine charming man. In person like Sir J. Dyke⁶ only about 30 Years younger[.]

Monday 11. [August]
Brought by Mr Davis⁷ to Oswestry. Found letters from Town there. Wrote to my Uncle.⁸ Bill at Oswestry 3S. Evans map [of] N Wales 18S.⁹ Paper Book 3S. Bishop and all the Clergy in Oswestry. Ordination. Started at 2 OClock[.] Pale *Malva* [mallow], *Geran[ium] Robertianum* [herb Robert] and Digitalis hereabouts in plenty. Also Flower growing at Stanford yellow. 2 Sorts tall and short. Beyond Turn pike a Hand post guides to Chirk which is distant from Oswestry 5½ Miles. 2 Miles on cross a pretty wooded brook. Bare hills on the L. A most delightful prospect presents itself from the Bridge over the canal¹⁰ near Chirk. In front [are the] Church and village on opposite hill, river running rolling over the pebbly course in the bottom and fine woods on the R beyond it in the distance to the R. Fine country. On the L [are] the meadow and brook and over it the Aqueduct¹¹ and Hills beyond it. Subjects for 2 Good pictures. The road from thence to

---

¹ The numbers in the text refer to Lee's sketch in the page margin, not reproduced here.
² Lee compared a view near Dungarvan, Co. Waterford, to these rocks at SJC, MS U.30 (7), ff. 57v–58r (p. 326).
³ See p. 74, n. 1.
⁴ Lee may mean that he imagined being able to see as far as Northumberland from this vantage point.
⁵ Lee may mean Chirk.
⁶ Possibly Sir John Dixon Dyke, 3rd Baronet (1732–1810).
⁷ Probably his host at Whittington.
⁸ William Lee Antonie (see Introduction, p. 2).
⁹ John Evans (1723–95), cartographer. His map of North Wales was published in 1795 in nine sheets at a scale of almost one inch to the mile. A smaller-scale edition was published posthumously, in 1797.
¹⁰ Shropshire Union Canal, built in 1772–9 (Fisher, *The Canals of Britain*, p. 177).
¹¹ Chirk aqueduct, built in 1796–1801.

DIARY 1: TOUR FROM LONDON TO HOLYWELL IN WALES

the Town winds very neatly, but we left [the] road and turn to [the] left along side of [the] Canal. Pass Coal Pits[.] ~~Here~~ On the Bridge heard the first chattering of Welsh between 2 Old Women[.] Go over the Aqueduct. Such a view from it. The Bridge[1]

[f. 51v] [*margin*: Bill at Oswestry[,] Breakfast on 10th 1S: A porter to Wellington 9d[,] Waiter 1:3 = 3S]

---

below over the brook which was partly diverted from its course as it appeared to irrigate the meadows in the bottom[.] Church and Town on the Left. Hill and Coal Works and canal on the right in the distance. Woody banks and distant country beyond[.][2]

Ten noble Arches. Could not learn the particular of Aqueduct. Went through the Tunnel. Said to be 470 Yds[.]

View up the Vale from the Aqueduct was[:]

1. Meadows cut in all directions for the water to run. 2 and 3 Two high ranges of hills wooded and bounded by No 4. A high hill cultivated to near the top. 5 Course of the brook[.][3] This would make a fine view.

Length of the Aqueduct from the top of 1st Arch to the other at the End, 202 Paces. Said to be 60 feet high. Information doubtful. About here *Anagallis*[4] and *Cucubalus Behen*.[5] The passage for horses under the tunnel is fenced from the waters by a rail yet in the middle it is so dark that one cannot see it and Dropping of water through the top. Things like icicles and hollow hang from top and streams of white stuff like freezing water streams of the same stuff down the side probably the salts of the bricks and the earth. Walked after passing through [the] Tunnel by the lane up to the Mountain which is at the Top. Here we dined[.] Bill 3S and at 4 OClock started with a Guide to see the Castle.[6] Crossed over the End of the Tunnel and follow [the] road, untill a style [stile] presents itself which [we] cross over and go up it all the way through the fields bearing to the L. At last come to some pleasure grounds on the Left and [a] park which leads up to the House, which is not seen untill you are close by it. It presents a most venerable appearance. Its grand large towers and ancient gateway [are] very fine. Porticullis place of. Enter in gate. Long square of a college appearance, rather going to decay from want of being inhabited and neglect. On 1 Side Arches and chapel. On a stone over the door to the kitchen is [f. 52v *blank*] [f. 53r] the following inscription

THIS NEW BVILDING AND THE TOWRE WAS BVILT ALL IN ONE YEARE BY THOMAS. MYDDLETON KNIGHT 1636. But as no one part of the Building appeared to us in accurately observing it to have been built later than the rest, It may mean the whole Building was built at that time. If so[,] a good years work. From the gate we were shewn many counties, Cheshire[,] Derbyshire[,] Yorkshire[,] Lancashire[,] Denbeighshire[,] etc[,] but the view does not seem to be so extensive as that at the Fron farm farther on. In the Kitchen is an ~~old~~ antiquated picture of some old Butler with a smiling countenance with a jug in his hands and a mug. On one side is written [Decus

---

[1] Narrative continues below the solid line, at 'below over the brook'.
[2] Lee roughly sketched a map of the scene, 'Subject for a fine picture', in ink in the page margin; not reproduced here.
[3] The numbers refer to a sketch by Lee, not reproduced here.
[4] A perennial of the *Primulaceae* family, possibly scarlet pimpernel.
[5] Of the 'pink' family, bladder campion.
[6] Chirk Castle, Wrexham, Wales.

Calino?]. This place we were told had been in the Family of the Myddletons for this 3 last centuries and that by them the Estate was bought of the crown[.] Hall Staircase, Very good. Breakfast Room (as we were told) [contains] 4 Landscapes by Poussin. Painting by Guido[1] of a female. Battle of Belgrade by <u>Rembran*d*t</u>!! A holy Family <u>by Carrachi</u>[.] Picture of Sir H. Vane by Sir G. Kneller.[2] Rubens by himself In the long Gallery.[3] A Teniers.[4] Sir Orlando Bridgeman by *Sir* G K*neller*:[5] Sir Tho*ma*s and Lady Mydd*leto*n (By Vandyke!)[6] in Ol*iver* Cromwells Time[.] 5 of King Charles Beauties[.] James 2. Ch*arles* 2. William and Mary and D*uke* of Monmouth by Sir G K*neller*[.] *Duke* of Ormond and his Son[.] Lord Ossory by Sir G K*neller*. The long Gallery is filled with pictures of the family and is 100 feet by 22[.] Chapel. State bed I sho*uld* be sorry to sleep a night in[.] It is the worst I ever saw. House supplied with water fr*om* a neighbo*uring* hill. Thus far goes the Story of the old House keeper, we were shewn fr*om* whence Ol*iver* Crom*well* battered down the Old Castle. The scenery around is truly magnificent and as fine a spot for a palace as any w*hich* co*uld* be fo*und*. On one side [is] a fine range of Mountain all in grass[,] on the other [an] immense command of country. We left the Castle directly in front a long road untill come to a gate wh*ere* get over[,] cross a field and gett*ing* over a gate get into a lane. A fine farm lies just to the L. Sir Watkins took[7]

[f. 53v] [*margin:* The Welsh for a <u>Bull</u> is something like *Taurus* and for a <u>Window</u> something like *Fenestrum*[8]]

34 or 35 Y*ears* ago the Common opposite w*hich* is now co*vered* with colliers houses and coalpits had not a house upon it [when he took it]. Mr Jones had some coalpits, called the Acre Vaser [Acrefair] C*oal* Pits and as we intended going down some, we intended upon leav*ing* Llangollen for Rhuabon [Ruabon] to visit them as [they were] not 100 Yds out of road[.] He made us go into [the] House and take something and shewed the prospect thro*ugh* his telescope. Upon thank*ing* him for his hospitality [he] said he never let a stranger go by witho*ut* offer*ing* him something. The descent down the mountain here [is] very romantic and a many streams and rills of water come into the lane among the rocks. Come at length to some limepits and get into the Llangollen road. But although near 8 yet curiosity tempted us to go and look at the Aqueduct w*hich* we were told was 1033 Yds long fr*om* End to End[.] So it might [be] but the ironwork from pacing it is ab*out* 400 Yds (350 paces). The view below is enough to alarm and turn any body giddy, but it being late, darkish and mistly [*sic*] we did not see it to advantage[.] Crossing the

---

[1] Guido Reni (1575–1642).
[2] Called Sir Henry ('Harry') Vane (1613–62), artist not attributed, National Trust Inventory Number 1171137 (National Trust Inventory).
[3] Self-portrait (after Rubens), National Trust Inventory Number 1171178 (National Trust Inventory).
[4] David Teniers II (1610–90).
[5] Probably Sir Orlando Bridgeman, 1st Baronet (1609–74) by Pieter Borsselaer (fl. 1664–87), *c*.1670, National Trust Inventory Number 1171152 (National Trust Inventory). There are other paintings by Kneller in the collection but none fitting this description.
[6] Possibly Mary Napier, Lady Myddelton (1598–1675) as a Widow, *c*.1670, attributed to 'British school', National Trust Inventory Number 1171113, and Sir Thomas II Myddelton (1586–1666), *c*.1670, attributed to 'British school', National Trust Inventory Number 1171114 (National Trust Inventory).
[7] Narrative continues below, after solid horizontal line.
[8] In Welsh, bull is *tarw* and window is *ffenster*. Lee repeats this note at SJC, MS U.30 (2), p. 95.

DIARY 1: TOUR FROM LONDON TO HOLYWELL IN WALES

Canal at the bridge got into the road (4¼ to Llangollen) by the turnpike lead*ing* f*rom* Rhuabon and follow up the vale to Llangollen. The appearance of Llangollen by night did not strike [us] as fine and the canal at [the] side w*hi*ch was digging in sev*er*al places took away f*rom* its grandeur. Still the high mountains Dinas Bran[1] and the Cefn Uchaf looked grand. Got to the place after 9 but *coul*d not see much of the river, only heard it[.] Kings head Inn [of] Mr Mace is not the grand inn, but much the best for persons with*out* carriages. We had a very good sitt*ing* room and capital bedroom[,] Red paper, Scarlet Curtains and D*itt*o Window Curtains, and most civil treatment[.]

[f. 54v] **Tuesday 12. [August]**
Llangollen bridge. Slate bed of river[.] Go up the water side or here and there in it[,] not deep[.] ~~Keep~~ Come to cottages on [the] R[,] these go within a Yd of water under trees[.]

Large masses of slate river running bet*wee*n and over these fine hills and woods, Keep close to the river[.]

[f. 55r] 5 Miles f*rom* Langollen [is] Acre Vroer [Acrefair] Coal pit[,] 6 Yds deep[.]

[f. 55v] Started at 11. [Chester and Ellesmere] Canal on the R. Come to a Tannery.[2] 2 Bridges close by pass under them and ~~cross the water and~~ go along the side of the new making canal w*hi*ch is cut thro*ugh* a bed of slate rock. Astonishing bed[.] Come to a Wood of Birch[.] Beautiful prospect around. Water dashing over the rocks loudly[.] Climb along the bank side am*ong* the trees[.] At last come to a gate[,] leave the road side[,] go thro*ugh* it and a <u>VIEW</u> indescribable.[3]

The feeder.[4] There [will be?] a bason close by to supply Lime and Coal for Bala, 22 Miles off. This Bason will save them 8 Miles[.] The canal runs to Llangollen[,] Chirk[,] Ellesmere[,] Whitchurch [and] Nantwich[,] communicates with a line of 20 miles old Chester Canal, Then runs for 9 [miles] upon its own principle to the river Mersey not far f*rom* Liverpool[,] 12 [miles]. Here to the Chester Canal [is] 40 Miles. 69 Miles in all of 1 Line. It costs 18^d a Yd [cube?] for labor and 6^d for powder and tools[.] Now the boats carry 12 ton and by this bason they will carry 24 Ton. 15 Mile with*out* a lock and then 2 Locks 6 foot each. Then none to Witchurch[,] then 15 or 16. 6 foot each. 300 feet fall f*rom* there to Low Water mark at River Dee at Chester. The Highest Lock is 6 Inches [f. 56r] above the head of the canal[.]

[f. 56v] Bala Pool[,] 1115 Acres of water. Raise it 1 foot by a Dam for a reservoir. And in the dry season take off ¼ Inch a day[.] Will supply the canal and <u>river</u>[,] 48 days to run it off. Then showers will recover the head of water. So [the] river will have nearly its usual Qu*anti*ty of water[.][5]

Rocks all mountain Shale[,] all the slate family[.] *Ch*ur*ch* Yard on the R.[6] Tombstones on 6 Pillars with a stone at bottom. Here lieth the Body of Edw*ard* LEWYS of MAES Y [RUTHIN?]. He was interred on the 17 Day of Sept*ember*. *Anno Domini* 1690 *Aetatis suae* [aged] 86.

---

[1] Castell Dinas Bran, an iron-age hillfort and 13th-century castle (Pettifer, *Welsh Castles*, pp. 59–60).
[2] Possibly the spot where Lee made the sketch at SJC, MS U.30 (6), f. 31r–31v (p. 313), not reproduced here.
[3] Possibly the spot where Lee made the sketch at SJC, MS U.30 (6), f. 32v (pp. 313–14), not reproduced here.
[4] The feeder to the canal at Llangollen.
[5] Bala Lake or Llyn Tegid, the levels of which were raised as part of the construction of the Ellesmere Canal by the Scottish civil engineer Thomas Telford (1757–1834).
[6] Probably St Tysilio's church, Llantysilio.

Margaret Gryffith late wife to Edward Lewis was buried here THE Third day of September 1664 and 2 others – Tombstone of Thomas Jones of the Hall 1761. 44. An Urn. Five Years Old. Sun dial. Grave with flower stuck in it[.] An Arch.

//

From a mean of 4 Barometrical Observations made in the Alcove in Llandsilio [Llantysilio] Garden.[1] The Barometer cistern being 2 feet above the flag stone floor and another barometer. Observed at the same time upon the summit of Moel Morfydd [Llantysilio Mountain]. It appears the Hill is 1523 (Feet). 46 above the alcove Floor[.]

2 Observations an hour after were made upon Moel Maen Goron [Maen-y-goron] but as an accurate observation below was not made exactly at the same time and the mercury falling at the time and a great gust of wind happening at the Instant. May The given height in [f. 57r *blank*] [f. 57v] this instance may not be exactly accurate but such as it was the Height of that hill is 1509.64 Feet or 503 Yds 7 Inches ¾ nearly[.]

During the observations the variation in the height of the Mercury below was 0.044 (Inch). Above 0.040. Mean of Thermometer below 76°.5[.] Mean of Thermometer above 62°.5[.]

Curious Wainscoat [*sic*] Room[,] pictures by Wilson [a] Landscape Drawer[2] and by Lewis 1734[.][3]

8 Pictures[,] one with his cravat through the buttonhole[.] View up and down the river from the Nantsilio [Llantysilio] trees groves the hill above[.]

Curious Chimney piece. Old Tombstone *Hic Jacet NR. EILIA. RVRVET*[.][4]

10 Steps up to the Peep Hole[.]

43 Steps up a Tower.[5] Aniseed or Irish Parsley *Circea Lutetiana* [*Circaea lutetiana*, enchanter's nightshade] Pillar Elisig[.][6] Cross a fine Brook winding up the opposite hill. Peep at the castle[,] go along 2 fields then take a path to the Left for Dinas Bran[.]

Din Bren House[.] Front the Dinas Bran[.] Continue along the lane[,] come to 2 roads[,] go between these then a wicket Gate into [a] fir plantation. Pass through and follow [the] path to [the] hill side[.] Ascend, on top [are] Ruins of an oblong shape. Several doors and arches still left. A circular Tower [points?] towards Llangollen. Some pits in the middle. [f. 58r *blank*] [f. 58v] Appearance of a fosse all round S side. Great and small arches. And an arched passage at one end about 11 Yds long with 3 regular O^r holes at tops[.] At the S end is a O^r Turret close by a round hollow part of a Tower with a gradual descent to the bottom. Fosse round the S and E sides[.]

---

[1] The 18th-century house and gardens at Llantysilio Hall, prior to rebuilding in the later 19th century.

[2] Richard Wilson (1712/13–82), Welsh landscape painter (Solkin, 'Wilson, Richard').

[3] Features of Llantysilio Hall.

[4] 'Here Lies' [followed by the name]. This inscription seems to have been badly worn, with some disagreement over the correct reading. Pennant's reading ('ARVRVET', given in *A Tour in Wales*, p. 372) was disputed when a later archaeologist found traces of a letter 'M' and argued that the name of the deceased was probably 'Marred' or 'Margaret' (Palmer, 'Notice', p. 65). A modern Latinist suggests '*Hic Iacet N[oste]r Filia RVRVET*', 'Here lies our daughter Rurvet'. This tombstone was taken from the Valle Crucis abbey graveyard and placed in a dwelling house on abbey lands as a chimneypiece, as described in Williams, *A Brief Account*, pp. 14–15. Lee sketched a view of the abbey at SJC, MS U.30 (6), 33r–34v (p. 314).

[5] Possibly 'The Tower' near Llangollen, a late medieval tower house with later additions.

[6] The 9th-century Pillar of Eliseg, Denbighshire.

About 60 Yds by 22. The appearance of walls across the middle and an apartment to the Llandilio side and one on the L*l*angol*len* side or else double walls. 2 Arches at these Ends. Latitude of Llangoll*en* 53.

Civil treatment at the Kings Head. Mr Mace had a good room and a nice scarlet Bed~~room~~ D*itt*o Curtains D*itt*o. Out of [the] windows see the sun tip the oppos*ite* hills and hear the river murmuring Close by [the] bridge[.]

Bill at Llangollen. Washing a Shirt[,] 2 Hand*kerchiefs* and Waistcoat 9^d. As it rained hard all morning brought up my Journal. Started at 1. Clouds below mountain top. Plant w*hich* the Cambridgeshire shepherds smoak. Fine grass road[.] River at foot of hill winding. Pretty white house.[1] Oppos*ite* bank strewed with white houses[.] Follow old road course. Pretty recluse waterfall rippling d*ow*n among trees. The views f*ro*m the end of the Chirk road lead*ing* to Llangollen are the finest that can be conceived. The winding river[,] the Hills and Dinas Bran[,] the island by [Major? Sims?][,] the [f. 59v] aqueduct[.] The whole country around w*oul*d form some studies [for painters] but sketches are useless[.][2]

[f. 59r] [*margin:* Mr Edward The Eagles Rhuabon[.] Wrexham Red Lion]

[f. 59v] Aqueduct Base of 3 Pillar 6 Yds by 3y*ards*. 2 Inches

7 Pillar 6 Yds 3 Inch by 3 Yds

9 Pillar 6⅓ by 3 Yds 1/6

The Nobility and Gentry of / The adjacent Counties / Hav*ing* united their effort with / The great commercial Interest of this country / in creating an intercourse and union betw*een* / England and N W*ales* / by a navigable commun*ication* of the 3 Rivers / Severne Dee and Mersey / for the mutual benefit of agriculture and trade / caused the 1 Stone of this aqueduct of / Pontcysyllty / to be laid on the 25 day of July 1795 / when Ric*hard* Myddleton of Chirk Esq*uire* MP / One of the original Patrons of the / Ellesmere Canal / was lord of this Manor / and in the reign of our Sovereign / George the 3 / when the Equity of the laws and / the security of property / promoted the gen*er*al welfare of the nation / while the arts and sciences flourished / by his patronage and / the conduct of civil life was improved / by his Example.[3]

4 Arches with abutments thro*ugh* w*hich* river runs[.]

[f. 60r *blank*]

[f. 60v] Fine grove and walk thro*ugh* it. 19 Arches in Aqueduct. Fine old Bridge with circular abutments[.][4] Trees and water and wood charming. Cross the canal and go down lane. Pass by scattered houses on Cefn Mawr by a stone quarry. Women washing in a brook with fire at side. Charity [Welsh?] School[.] Go on and come to a road. Turn to Left, plenty [of] cottages. Making Large Parkgates[.]

Foal 2 Y*ea*rs old last month. By Woodpecker out of *an* Eclipse mare. ½ mile further on [is] Another Lodge[,] go in and make across the park rather to the L for a gate. Go thro*ugh* it and [*ecce?* here is] Brook[,] gave Shepherd 3½. Cross brook and ascend hill[.] At [the] top [the] grounds [are] very parkish. Plenty deer and hill with wood. Descend to the

---

[1] This may be the house Lee sketched at SJC, MS U.30 (6), f. 29r–v (p. 313), not reproduced here.

[2] Lee made two sketches near Llangollen, at SJC, MS U.30 (1), ff. 29r–v and 30r–v (p. 313), not reproduced here.

[3] Lee's transcription of the text on the foundation stone of the Pontcysyllte aqueduct, built 1795–1805.

[4] Possibly the scenes sketched at SJC, MS U.30 (6), ff. 35r, 36r, 36v, 37r (p. 314), not reproduced here.

gravel walk and follow it. Man said by brook [that I] could not miss [my] way but [it was] a damned long way and by a odd direction[,] across [the] path [would be] only 1 Mile. As if distance was my object. Path divides[,] 1 Top and other bottom. Wooden bridge on [the] R. Pass on[.] Come to a gate leading into a dingle. Beautifully broken ground. Brook through a fantastic arbour of trees. Several Walks. Keep [to] the lowest. Low bench on which [I] sat down with thankfulness. *Circea* [probably *Circaea lutetiana,* enchanter's nightshade]. Just further path falls into a broader, big enough [for a] carriage with a dexterous driver. Leave it for ~~the~~ (a) lower path[,] ~~seat~~ (bench) of wood. Fine rocks [on] sides of brook[.] Seat[.] 2 paths. Lower.[1] Cross Brook[.] [f. 61r *blank*] [f. 61v] Boards under bridge drawn[.] Tall trees on opposite high bank. Rock and Steps formed in it[.] Fine tree over hanging brook at bottom[.] Brook very low at ones feet. Opposite hill covered with fine shrubs and trees and at top [are] high trees. Here I wished for a companion to address. Murmuring brook, most lovely scenery, board to sit on[,] gazed and gazed and gazed again. Come by brook side again but immediately ascend and go forward to a fine stone seat with a romantic view before it. Wild strawberry growing on seat. A man would run over its beauties without allowing himself time to view who went a step an hour.[2] Bridge and steps on opposite side. Seat above most exquisitely placed. Thats enough described[.] Farther on a seat with an opening (to opposite bank) and bold trees hanging over. A seat and bridge over rock water course and pretty peep at path on opposite side. Steps up R bank to a bench surrounded with heath in flower and a fine environs of tree and wood. Beautiful and grand. Descend steps. Little path just below underneath bridge and path over it and seat, but go on R bank up steps winding much round. Opens a field and fine woody hill opposite. Steps up and down. Bold rocks and little cascade. Seat under trees down bridge steps. Arch and bridge road over it[.] Water roars, bold scenery[.] Wood more open[,] mount the [Lap?] hill and between the woods see the rock and Welsh hills downwards[,] Woods on 2 Hills and river in bottom. Higher up whole [f. 62r *blank*] [f. 62v] coursing river and more hills. View bolder and bolder. Higher up [the] rock [is] cut and [presents] view between view. Summer house above. [vale?] 3 miles below wooded. 2 miles to Rhuabon from Summer House. Return to summer House[.] It would have done me shame to try to [sublet?] it Ann Martyn. We have some ale coming from Rhuabon and [here? persons?] may have some, and when we are very poor of bread we cannot give every body some.[3] [Rough?]

Fine prospect of the Welsh Hills. Chirk etc

Cefn Uchan [Uchaf]. Fine House. Water [Goats?]. Between House and water [go?]. Fine turf. Ice house. Pillar.

To the memory of / Sir Watkins William Wynn Bart who died 29 Day of July / 1789 / This column was erected by his affectionate Brother / Francis Williams Wynn. *Filio optimo / mater / Eheu superstes* /[4]

---

[1] Lee abbreviates here, meaning, of two paths, he took the lower one.
[2] Lee means: Some travellers would run over its beauties without allowing themselves time to view them, unlike the person travelling more slowly ('a step an hour').
[3] Here, Lee recounts a fragment of conversation with (possibly) local farmers.
[4] Inscription on the Doric column memorial to Sir Watkin Williams-Wynn, 4th Baronet (1749–89), Welsh politician, in Wynnstay Park, Denbighshire. The translation of the Latin inscription is 'Alas! The mother survives her most excellent son'. Lee sketched this memorial at SJC, MS U.30 (6), f. 39r (p. 314), not reproduced here.

About 19 Yds Square
23 Yds ½. 144 Steps up
Circum*ference* at Rails at top 8 Yds 15 Inches
13 at a time and then broad step.[1]
Great [Base?] 8 foot and a trifle. Height 34 Yds
[f. 63r *blank*]
[f. 63v] Fine old Oak [*Quercus*] 11 Yds 2 feet [and] about 4 feet *from* ground[.] About 8 Inches *from* ground[,] 17 Yds round nearly[.] Both fine[.] Wild Ducks. Rhuabon. Brook. Fine old Bridge and view of mon*ument* and rocky brook[.]

Old Woman for Bread and Butter 6. Boy 1. Man for shew*ing* Obelisk 1. Got to Eagles at Rhuabon at 6½.

---

[14] Aug*ust* Thursday.
Bill. 4S. Mend*ing* Gaitors 4[d][.]

Mr Davis supported the harmony of W*elsh* Language and said w*hich* have [*sic*] a worth of 7 Cons*on*ants to 1 Vowel (strength). Facetiously. 1 Mile *from* Wynn stay to Ruabon Ch*urc*h. Started ½ p*ast* 9.

Fine open country on the R –

Noble woods of Erdigg [Erddig]. Wrexham Ch*urc*h in front[.] Tall convol*vulus*[.] 1 Bell[,] 5 Edges. About 2 foot high and thin narrow leaves with little ones at the joints[.]

W ⎫
7 E ⎬ Curious figures on house
1691 ⎭

Very fine mon*ument* of Mrs Mary Myddleton by Roubilliac[,] a pyramid falling and she rising at the trumpet blow*ing* by a cherub.[2] Picture of last supper given by Eliugh Yale Esq*uire*[.][3]

Stone mon*ument* of Bishop of Chester[4] in Queen Eliz*a*beth's time *Spe certa gloriosae resurrectionis hic in domino obdormivit reverendus in Christo / Pater D*[ominus] *Hugo Bellot Sacre Theologiae Doctor ex antiqua familia Bellotorum De Morton / in comitatu Cestriae oriundus, quem ob singularem* [f. 64v] *in Deum pietatem vita / integritatem prudentiam et doctrinam Elisabetha Regina primum ad Episcopatum / Bangorensem (2) in quo X annos sedit postea ad episcopatum Cestrensem transtulit / Ex quo post paucos menses Christus in celestem patriam evocavit / Anno domini 1596 Aetatis suae 54 / Cuthbertus Bellot fratri optimo & charissimo moestissimus posuit*[.][5]

---

[1] Here, Lee provides dimensions of the Wynnstay column, including its internal spiral staircase.
[2] Monument to Mary Myddelton (1688–1747), Church of St Giles, Wrexham, designed in 1751–2 by Louis-François Roubiliac.
[3] Elihu Yale (1649–1721), Welsh merchant and founder of Yale College in America.
[4] Hugh Bellot, DD (1542–96) (Williams, 'Bellot, Hugh').
[5] Translation: 'In certain hope of a glorious resurrection, here went to sleep in the Lord the reverend father in Christ Lord Hugh Bellot, doctor of sacred theology, born in the county of Chester from the ancient family of Bellot from Morton, whom by reason of his remarkable piety of life in God, his integrity, prudence and learning Queen Elizabeth first made Bishop of Bangor, in which he stayed for 10 years, and then transferred him to the bishopric of Chester, from which Christ called him to heaven after a few months, in the year of the Lord 1596 at the age of 54. His most mournful [brother] Cuthbert Bellot placed this monument to the best and dearest brother'. See also the version of this text in Cooper, *Athenae Cantabrigienses*, II, *1586–1609*, p. 204.

[f. 64r] [margin: Coach from Oswestry [***][1] Feathers]

[f. 64v] Curious old monument in Wood framed. Frame adorned with gilt cross bones. Coat [of] arms[,] 8 quarters 2 Crests

Here lyeth the Body of John Trevor / of Trevor in the County of Denb: Esquire / who married Mary Daughter of John Eylon / of Lleswood [Leeswood] Esquire by whom he had / issue 8 Sons and 5 daughters he di/ed 13 March 1682 Aged 64 yeares

Monument of Most of Owen Bold.
Small monument like a shell[2]
Feb 28: 1743 Obiit / Reverendus Gulielmus[3] Lewis / vir eruditus affabilis et eruditus (benevolus) / qui nil turpe vel in fe admisit / vel fovit in aliis /

Curious old heads of stone with some with arms and on these curious old Coat [of] arms in a few on the R. 6 quantitys different helmet. Lion crest on one side[,] deaths head on a coat [of] arms / opposite cross bones on Ditto.

15 Coats [of] arms round the great one and these two pillars beyond. On 1 a [Time?] Glass
Return of King David
[f. 65r blank]
[f. 65v Monument of an old Clerk
Daniel Jones died the 13 Day February 1668
Here lies interred beneath these stones
The beard the flesh and eke the bones
Of Wrexham Clerk old Daniel Jones
Philip Jones his son succeeded him and was interred
15 March 1720

Will Jones Clerk Son / of Philip Jones Clarke /
Died June 10: 1735 / Aged 39
Pig sucking its young ones

Born in America in Europe Bred
In Africa travelled and in Asia wed
Where long he lived and thrived in London died
Much good, some ill he did so hope all's even
and that his Soul through mercys gone to heaven
You that survive and read this tale take care
For this most certain exit to prepare
Where blest in peace the actions of the just

---

[1] This word has been scribbled over, making it illegible.
[2] The monument to Reverend William Lewis in Wrexham church; inscription follows.
[3] Pennant, *A Tour in Wales*, I, p. 293, has 'Guliel'. Translation: 'On February 28: 1743 died Reverend William Lewis, an erudite, affable and good-willed man, who neither did anything shameful himself nor encouraged it in others'.

Smell sweet and blossom on the silent dust
   on the oppo*site* side
IHS[1] / Eliugh Yale Esq*uire* / was buried the 22 of July / The year of our Lord / 1721

Fine steeple and tower. Old papers[.] No. of figures[.] Washing shirt[,] Drawers. Stock*ings*. Socks[,] Cravat[,] P*ocket* H*andkerchief* = 1^S.

[Friday 15 August]
Friday spent at Acton.[2] Gressford [Gresford]

[16 August] Saturday.
Bill at Wrexham 12:6. Trunk f*ro*m Oswestry 1:8. Wash*ing*. Shirt[,] Drawers[,] Stock*ings* and Socks[,] 2 Cravat*s* 1^S. Watch ribbon 3^d[.] Seeing Church 1^S. Man for note to Acton 1^S. Started at ½ p*as*t 6. Pass ab*out* 2½ Miles a few houses called the Wheat sheaf. Cole [coal] pits and houses on the L here and there. Bee orchid [*Ophrys apifera*] at Acton bog[.]
   [f. 66r *blank*]
   [f. 66v] Cross a Bridge[.][3] Woods on R. Pretty road. Just on the hill see a bridge in the Vale to the R. On [the] road to Chester [is a] lovely vale[,] great inclination to follow a path thro*ugh* [the] woods on the R. *Reseda*[,] *Anagallis* [pimpernel], Honeysuckle. Ascend Caergwle [Caergwrle] Ruins.[4] 3 pieces of wall. Cement consists of entirely small alabaster pebbles in 1 Rock[.] No perfect window or door. Part of a round Tower[.]
   4½ a Cwt coals here. View f*ro*m top of Castle ruins. Got to Caergwle at 9. Set out at 10[.] Leave Turnpike for the hill[.] Go thro*ugh* Caergwle[.] Get over styles and follow path[.] Come to a pretty wooded (bank) brook. Beyond a Bridge where road goes over. View of Caergwle Ruins. Follow it a little way. A style and path wh*ich* seems as if it wo*uld* save one some walk*ing*[.] Go over and it does save a turn in the road[,] nothing fine lost[.] ~~but for a~~ White <u>violet</u> heartsease small flower in hedges[.] See Smoke of Liverpool f*ro*m Caergwle hill[.] Plas Cyn.[5] Mr Eytons and the Straight brook. Ch*urch* mon*ument* of Mr Davis [G*wysaney*? latter*ly*?] of Whitehall[.][6] *Davis H Chiere Fecit*.[7] Standing leaning on an urn[.] Pews all marked. North Aile [*sic*] carved wood *H Chiere fecit*. To the memo*ry* of Rob*er*t Davies of Llanerch Esq*uire*[8] once possess'd of all the sociall Virtues / wh*ich* adorn the fine Gent*le*man / and of all the Moral Duties / which establish the good Man // In his person and behaviour elegant / In his convers*at*ion free and lively / In the conduct of Life ever = / Ever beyond exception generous / [f. 67r] As he was well k*now*n in the more private Light / Of the friend the Husband and the father / He was not less conspicuous / in being the avowed son / of the Ch*urch* of England / He was born Sept*ember* 2 1684 He died May 22 1728 /

---

[1] A Christogram representing the name 'Jesus' in Christianity.
[2] Acton Park near Wrexham, site of Acton Hall (no longer extant).
[3] Possibly the bridge sketched at SJC, MS U.30 (6), f. 42r (p. 315), not reproduced here.
[4] Caergwrle castle, begun in 1277 (Pettifer, *Welsh Castles*, p. 70). Lee sketched the ruins at SJC, MS U.30 (6), f. 43r (p. 315), not reproduced here.
[5] This could refer to a number of possible locations in and around Caergwrle.
[6] Probably Robert Davies of Gwysaney (1616–66) (see p. 86, n. 1, below).
[7] "H. Chiere made this." The sculptor was Henry Cheere (1702–81).
[8] Robert Davies of Llanerch, high sheriff of Flintshire (1684–1728) (Dictionary of Welsh Biography online).

This mon*ume*nt was erected at the cost of his faithful Wife Anne / the D*aught*er of John Brockholes of Claughton in Lancashire Esq*uire* / and Anne his wife interred near the commun*ion* rails in this / Church. The foresaid Rob*er*t had issue by Anne his Wife Rob*er*t Anne John Rich*ar*d Mary Peter and Elizabeth

---

*Mori quod potuit / Roberti Davies de Gwysaney / in com*itatu *Flint Armigeri / Hic expectat Beatam Resur*rectione*ᵐ / Filius fuit unicus Roberti / Filius Roberti Filius Johannes Filius Davidis / Uxorem duxit annam / Petri Mutton de Llannerch / in Com*itatu *Denb. Militis Filiam ac Heredem / Illum numerosa quae auxit prole / viz. sex maribus feminisque octo / Obiit vir integessimus A*nno Do*m*ini *1666*[1]

*Huic proxime sepulta / quorum et vixerat conjunctisimi / supra dicta eius uxor / postquam 21 annos preregerat / Viduam omnino ut dicebat Christianam / Matrona pius / Gentilibus suis componitur / Muttonus Davies Arm*iger */ praedictorum Rober*ti *et Annae / filius primogenitus / Cujus conjunx Elizabetha / Thomae Wilbraham de Woodley / in com*itatu *Palatino Cestri Barone*ti *filia unica / Hadleia in com*itatu *Middlesex / juxta avum suum sortitur sepulcrum / Ubi feminae lactissimae memoriam / marmori commisit maritus morens / Suscepit ab illa filios quinque: filiasque:totidem / Decessit vir vere Generosus / 1684*[2]

Below
*Hoc breve spatium / tam docto nomine heu quam indignum vitae, pro sua modestia assignavit / Rober*to *Davies arm*ige*ro / Muttoni Fil*ius [natum?] *Obiit Juli 8 1710 AE*tatis *52*[3]

[f. 67v] On a plate
Near the E end of this Chancel / in the C*hur*ch Y*ar*d with / the Pious and charitable / the Rever*en*d Mr Rich*ar*d Davies / Vicar of Rhuabon / Precentor of Brecon / Canon of St Asaph and St David / 5 and Youngest Son of Mutton / Davies of Gwyssaney Esq*uire* / Died May 25 1746 / Aged 73.

William Wynne of Tower DD / Some time Fellow of All Souls coll*ege* in Oxford / & rector of Llanvechen in this Diocese / Departed this life 3 March 1776 / Aged 77 / In conformity to ancient usage / from a proper regard to Decency / and a concern for the

---

[1] This inscription refers to Robert Davies of Gwysaney (1616–66) (Dictionary of Welsh Biography online). Translation: 'Here lie the remains of Robert Davies Esquire, of Gwysaney, in the County of Flint, where he awaits his Blessed Resurrection. He was the only son of Robert, who was the son of Robert, the son of John, the son of David. He took as his wife Anna, daughter and heiress of Peter Mutton of Llannerch, a knight of the County of Denbigh, who moreover gave him many children, namely six sons and eight daughters. This most complete man died in the Year of Our Lord 1666.'

[2] This inscription seems to refer to Mutton Davies of Gwysaney (1634–84) (Dictionary of Welsh Biography online). Translation: 'Buried close by this place the aforesaid wife of the closest one had lived; after 21 years she had continued as a thoroughly Christian widow, as they said. This pious matron was laid to rest by her family. Mutton Davies, Esquire, the eldest son of the aforementioned Robert and Anna, whose wife Elizabeth, the only daughter of Thomas Wilbraham of Woodley in the County Palatine of Chester, chose a tomb near her ancestor at Hadley in the County of Middlesex, where her husband sadly committed the memory of this most excellent woman to marble. He received from her five sons and and the same number of daughters. This truly generous man died in 1684.'

[3] Lee's transcription is difficult to decipher here. Possible translation: 'This small space was assigned to Robert Davies Esquire, born the son of Mutton, for his modesty; oh how very unworthy for the learned reputation of his life. He died July 8 1710 aged 52.'

Health of his / Fellow creatures he was moved to give / particular directions for being buried / in the adjoining C*hur*ch Y*ar*d / and not in the C*hur*ch / and as he scorned flattering others / while living he has took [*sic*] care to prevent / being flattered himself when dead / by causing this small memorial to be / set up in his life time / God be merciful to me a sinner

In the mid aile

IHS / Underneath lies interred / Mr John Davies 5 Son of / Robe*r*t Davies of Gwissaney Esq*uire* / by Anne his wife D*aughte*r and Heir / of Sir Peter Mutton of Llannerch / in this county of Denbeigh Kn*igh*t / he departed this life the 28 of Nov*embe*r / In the year of our Lord / 1705[1] / – Here under also lies interred / Mr Peter Davies 6 Son / of the above ment*ione*d / who died 16 December 1716[2] / – Below Mrs Anne Davies[3] and Mrs Mary Holland / Wife of the Reve*ren*d Mr Thos Holland / of Berow in the County of Anglesey[4] / caused this mon*umen*t out of their / love and gratitude to their affectionate / Uncles to be erected

[f. 68r] Mold Inferior to Wrexham and Gresham Churches[.] Start across the Mountain for Holy well. Pass Cotton factory. M*ess*rs Ridman and [Knight?] of Manchester 6 × 15 windows on 1 Side.[5] Head of water. Cross brook by turnpike Sign of Greyhounds [coursing?]

[Success?] to the Greyhounds / Good ale by / Cath Williams / Near this place within a Vault / There is rich liquor fixt / Youll say that Water Hops and malt / Was never better mixt /

Go up the lane bey*on*d the Public H*ouse* and follow it untill the Barn on the R hand[,] go up there. Road goes between some cottages and round above Hill. Lane continues for a very long way ascending. Come to a common[,] cross it and go up a lane wh*ere* the causeway leads to ab*out* ¼ Mile up a farm and old Lime Kiln and *fr*om top of it a most magnificent view of the sea (a branch)[,] beyond it land and beyond another branch of the sea[.][6]

---

[1] The monument in Mold Church to John Davies (1653–1705; *Burke's Landed Gentry*, 1852, I, p. 255), son of Robert Davies of Gwysaney (see p. 86, n. 1) and Anne, daughter of Sir Peter Mutton (Dictionary of Welsh Biography online).

[2] The above-mentioned monument in Mold Church includes an inscription to Peter Davies (1667–1716), son of Robert Davies (see also p. 86, n. 1) (*Burke's Landed Gentry*, 1852, I, p. 255).

[3] The above-mentioned monument in Mold Church includes an inscription to Anne Davies, eldest daughter of Robert Davies (see p. 86, n. 1) and wife of John Thelwall of Plas Coch and Llanrudd (*Burke's Landed Gentry*, 1852, I, p. 255).

[4] Mary Holland, née Davies (d. 1716; *Burke's Landed Gentry*, 1852, I, p. 256–7), daughter of Mutton Davies of Gwysaney (see p. 86, n. 2).

[5] Although the names are incorrect, this may refer to the cotton mill established at Mold by Peter Atherton in the 1780s/90s (Honeyman, *Origins of Enterprise*, p. 75).

[6] Lee made one sketch of Holywell at SJC, MS U.30 (6), ff. 43v–44r (see p. 315).

2. TOUR FROM HOLYWELL TO DUBLIN AND FERMOY

[SJC, MS U.30 (2)]
[ff. 1–5 *cut out*]

[f. 6r] ~~Tuesday~~ **(Friday) August 22**[1]
[*margin:* 1][2] Left Holywell ½ past 9. Passed through and examined Basingwerk Abbey.[3] A few fine round arches left and signs of its having been a fine ruin. But the chief parts of building are of sandstone which the people of Holywell pilfer to beat to dust to spread about their house. And thus by undermining and taking away the best stones it comes down and is yearly diminished. Some time ago a boy was killed by a mass falling. 20 years ago the Mostyn Family[4] resided in this very place. The Granary is still entire. No care of the place is taken and it will soon be a heap of rubbish. Went along the shore to Mostyn Rocks by the Rock house so called because of a large piece of rock in front[.] The Mostyn rocks present the most curious appearance[.] They appear of all forms and their nature is singular[.] There may have been some subterraneous fires which have burnt the whole of the rock and coal is found in the neighbouring parts. The rock is exactly like the remnants of a furnace extremely porous. In some places evidently it has been in a fused state. Red chiefly but blue brown and all the appearances of fire. When struck or beat off the stones of flint One may even fancy the pieces feel warm[.] Some parts appear glassy. Some pieces of the stratum are charged red as if by burning. The neighbouring rocks are externally blackish slaty chirt. Return to the small village of Mostyn and ascend through it. On the shore there are ~~several~~ (2) streams coming down of a very ochrous nature turning all the stones over which water passes red. Saw some of the oily particles floating on the surface. They come from the coal pits of Mostyn[.] A style [stile] takes into Sir Pierce [Piers] Mostyns grounds through [f. 7 *cut out*] [f. 8r] [*margin:* 2] Groves of trees and the path is very easy which leads to New market [Trelawnyd] untill it joins the road. A fine new gothic Lodge is building and walls on each side as appeared. The fields lead at length into the road. A field well irrigated by ~~ditches~~ (trenches) cut along it. A Lead Pit is sunk on the Path of the turnpike road and over the hedge several in a field. But how or by whose permission one is on the road I know not. Very wrong[.] There is a fine view from here[.] The Pharos according to Mr Pennant[5] or

---

[1] The last entry in the previous diary was for 16 Aug. – six days are unaccounted for.
[2] Lee began paginating this diary, but stopped doing so after just 4 folios. His page numbers are included here as marginal notes.
[3] 12th-century abbey near Holywell, Wales.
[4] In the late 16th century, William Mostyn (d. 1605) acquired the lands of Basingwerk Abbey by marriage to Anne, daughter of Henry ap Thomas ap Harry of Greenfield (Veysey, *Guide*, 54).
[5] Thomas Pennant (1726–98), Welsh naturalist, traveller and author. His *The History of the Parishes*, p. 112, describes and illustrates the Roman Pharos in detail.

the old farm houses on Top of hill is conspicuous. Sea fine[.] Pass a turnpike gate and take the R hand road. In the field on L is a tall stone stuck in ground with a round top and a [rouch?][1] ornament on it.[2] Why or for w*h*at nescio[3] did not go to it. Further on come to an ~~common~~ heath and at the End is a tall pointed hill called the Gop Hill with Newmarket at its base. The <u>Gloll hill</u>[4] on the Left. The Coon hills and parish ~~to the~~ between New*m*a*rke*t and them. *Hyoscyamus* [Henbane] in plenty and stinking finely. Go throu*g*h the village and come to where road has 3 points keep forward. Fine old handsome tree with four arms in a plat of grass in middle of the junction of roads. A little farther on a farm on the R out of the road[.] Turn up the lane to R and at the top of it road divides[.] L⎯⎯⎯
Go to the left. A little way on is an old Castle very much in ruins. (A scetch of it).[5] | lane
Farther on 4 roads cross ⎯⎯⎯|⎯R here[.] Take the left for Delargo [Talargoch] Mine[.][6]
But straight forw*ar*d is a |L little village and some fine trees and a large wall like a gent*lema*n's habitation but all cottage. We went up to it by mistake and were obliged to return. The Church is above the village on the hill. Upon asking soon after we had rejoined the right road if it went to the Mines. 'Yes sure' says a colleir [*sic*], 'you will soon be there or elsewhere.' The name of village sounded like Ciunescaur [Gwaenysgor]. Farther on a [f. 9r] [*margin:* 3] sketch of entrance of vale of Clwyd.[7] Upon leavi*n*g the lane and comi*n*g to the common, Go to the R between 2 hills and you soon see the pits and shafts. Go to them and all round the hill towa*r*ds the sea are shafts. Machines for working the water out of the lower p*ar*t of [the] pits up to the level of the sea where it runs off throu*g*h a level. The water is got fr*o*m [the] side of the hill as high as possible and conveyed in troughs to an over shot wheel w*h*ich turni*n*g round moves on its axis a bent strong iron on w*h*ich is fixed a long wooden line movi*n*g on rollers at proper dist*a*n*c*es. As the wheel goes round this long board is pulled forw*ar*d and backw*ar*d and thus motion is comm*un*icated into the well and pulls up the buckets with water fr*o*m bottom to the level[.][8]

The shaft has a square oblong centre up and down wh*ere* the ore is drawn and on the sides 4 Water engines can be worked if [there is] plenty of water. The middle has frames of wood round it and the men walk down by steppi*n*g on the cross bars at the corner. It is frequently the custom for the men to walk down the mines here using their arms and legs. The strata are 1st Gravel then sand. Then sometimes gravel. (Go such sometimes for 40 Yds) then rock of limestone then the vein of lead of differe*n*t thickness[.] They have fou*n*d 10 Yds of lead in thickness sometimes not 1. The level runs for [f. 10r] [*margin:* 4] abo*u*t 80 Yds[.] Calomine is fou*n*d in plenty in some pits. Went into a level fr*o*m side of rock, where plenty fou*n*d. Pit worked in all directions. Pits in some places and walk over boards. A considerable way in a wheel to draw up ore fr*o*m a lower part of the rock. Step over a very large break in the level by steppi*n*g first on left and then on R and soon after come to a large opening as man termed it a barn[.] Climb up it and get ½ way perhaps up.

---

[1] Rouch, meaning 'rich', possibly referring to the intricate design on the cross.
[2] The Maen Achwyfan, an early Christian slab-cross. Lee made a rough ink sketch of it in the margin of the folio, not reproduced here.
[3] A claim not to know (*OED*).
[4] The Glol at Tremostyn, property of Thomas Pennant (Pennant, *The History of the Parishes*, p. 114).
[5] This sketch is not found in Lee's extant sketchbooks.
[6] Talargoch lead mines, near Prestatyn, described by Lee below.
[7] This sketch is not found in Lee's extant sketchbooks.
[8] Lee sketched this apparatus in the middle of the page; not reproduced here.

A large high roof could ~~not~~ see the top. Spar in plenty the lower p*ar*t of level was limestone upper spar and top generally calamine. Under us was another level in a very inclined dist*ance*. The level is ab*ou*t 90 Yds in straight and you may go 100 Yds.[1] Curious story of the spar.

A workman had been accustomed to pains in bowels[.] Was recommended and did take the spar ground to a fine powder mixed ½ and ½ with white loafsugar.[2] He took it for many years and said it always did him good. And he *coul*d not rest with*ou*t it[.] At last the man died of – old age. Good specimens of lead and colored green ore[,] red lead ore and white lead f*ou*nd there. Bones were f*ou*nd in some of these mines at consid*era*ble depth below level of sea. Some in the solid rock some in the sand and at diff*eren*t depths and in xious[3] situations. Went round the Hill tow*ar*ds the remains of Deserth [Dyserth] castle[.][4] Nothing extraord*inary*. Ryddland [Rhuddlan] castle appears very fine[.] Path goes to village. Pass by Church and see at the side of a mill a curious cleft in rock all the way up [***] a fine cascade here.[5] Scene prodigious fine hollow bason and rock worn away in 3 or 4 Vast holes and then rock beyond them. The water is brought f*ro*m the top where there is a large natural Bason w*hi*ch is filled in winter and turns a mill but the extra water [f. 6v] [*margin:* 5] forms a water fall w*hi*ch is heard for a great dist*ance*[.] Ascended up to top and look down the waterfall. Fine bason of rock. Cave at end. Curious Lichen[.] The men at the level and the man at Diserth both affirmed the truth of the man eating spar. Just above mill, leave road and go over style w*hi*ch takes by fields to the Dean of St Asaphs house thro*ugh* a long row of firs. Plenty of rabbits. Going down avenue see Buckinsee farm on R[.] Deans house called Pot trethan. The path then goes f*ro*m the head of a lane just below his Gates across fields to a farm house go in front of it and in 1st field is a little Knowle [knoll] f*ro*m w*hi*ch [there is] a very pretty view of all the hills f*ro*m the sea up the vale. 2nd Hill is famous for a beautiful sort of reddish spar. Path goes by a mill and then gets into the high road[.] Got to St Asaph by 8 OClock[.]

Man at mine 1s[.] Man for ore 1:6[.]

Out 10½ hours.

Basingwerk abbey ½. Mostyn Rocks 1. 3 scetches 1½ = 3½ Miles[6]

Walking 7 hours or ab*ou*t 21 Miles[.]

[23 August] Saturday.
St Asaph Church. Town prettily situated[.] Bill for supper Breakfast. Sandwiches Bed 5s:2[.] Waiter [1][7] Writing Book 6d[.] Ch*amber* maid 1. String and [Hards?[8]] 6d[.]

Start at 10. Cross Bridges. Fine views all around as you ascend hill. Mr Jones ~~house~~ grounds fine views of vale Steward to Mr Hughes. Mr Hughes place delightful and noble called Kimbell.[9] Reach Abergelly [Abergele] 8 Miles by 2 OClock. Dined there[.] Bill 1:4

---

[1] Lee sketched the level in the middle of the page; not reproduced here.
[2] Sugar refined and moulded into a loaf or conical mass (*OED*).
[3] Various.
[4] A mid-13th century castle.
[5] Rhaeadr Dyserth waterfall. The illegible word may be Lee's attempt to record a place name.
[6] Lee may mean '3½ hours' rather than '3½ miles'.
[7] Cost is written in pencil on f. 8v, visible under Lee's ink overwriting.
[8] Possibly meaning pieces of hard board.
[9] Kinmel estate, purchased by Reverend Edward Hughes in 1786 (Habakkuk, *Marriage*, p. 471).

(for Porter 4. Veal cold Ham Pye cucumber shrimp.) Waiter 6[d]. Sign of the Bee. Started at ½ p*ast* 3. Views get much finer and more noble Orms [Ormes] heads shew to advantage. Sketches 3.[1] Sea very fine and grand the whole way. Road winds on Edge of hills by sea[.] [f. 8v] [*margin:* 6][2] At about 3 Miles f*rom* Conwy road leaves sea and goes between fine mountains rest of way. Water at Conwy begins to appear[.] F*rom* St Asaph to Dolgelly [Dolgellau] 8 Miles. To Conwy (Ferry) || path goes across the flat and cuts off a little. A few years ago this marsh was all heath but now drained and bears corn. Is sometimes over flowed. It was past 8 when got near Conwy. Moon shining bright thro*ugh* tremendous black clouds. Got to ferry house ½ p*ast* 8[.] No boat on this side and therefore resolved to sleep there[.] Views by moon light noble. A black deep shaded mountain at the foot of the castle. Could not see any parts but only the mass. Moon shining on water[.] A dark hue on all things. Heavy clouds. Raised tide. Light in Conwy. Lake up the river and hills shining by light. Very grand. Just see the tops of castle. Moon hid now and then by clouds, sombre and grand then cast a silver hue on the water[.] Met a sailor on the road. And said he was tired yet walked well. Very hungry and dry. Gave him a sandwich[.] He was Cap*tain* Williams and his vessel was at Rydland f*rom* whence he was com*ing*. He expected he wo*uld* sail on Friday[.] Loading with timber. Parted at Ferry[.] Fine pleasant fellow[.]

I was out 10½ [hours.]
4 Sketches 2 Abergelly 1½ [Lockros?][3] ½ = 4[4]
Walked 10½ [hours] = 19½ Miles accord*ing* to my calcul*ation*. And By road it is 19.
Went out of road once at a valley over a wall to see a very deep (narrow) valley and cave a little under road and walked down it[.] In all ab*out* a mile[.]

[f. 9v][5] Road leaves the sea and goes between fine M*ountains* and winds thro*ugh* them all [the] way. A path w*hich* conducts cross the flat – water very fine / past 8 and moon shin*ing* now and then thro*ugh* tremend*ous* black clouds[.] A very dark hue on all around[.] Come to ferry house at ½ p*ast* 8[.]

The Scenery. The oppo*site* black moun*tains* too dark to discern parts. Just see tops of Castle. Moon behind them now and then casts light on the dist*ances* and the water w*hich* [shined?] silver and they can be seen[.] 11 Good Miles[.]

Got to the Ferry at 9 OClock[.] Moonlight fine views. Old sailor tired[.] Got to the ferry house[.] The boat not on that side and ∴ staid there that night.

Sunday 23 [August][6]
Walked over the shore on both sides [of the] ferry house to see the views[.] At 2 OClock went over to Conwy. Bill 3. Maid 1[s]. Ferry 6[d]. Went to the Castle all prodigious fine. One tower ½ down. Rock of slate with small strata of marble and red dirt between high up. 1 Tor great [size?] 4 Towers on Each side. Island[.] Washing 9[d]. Woman said she wo*uld* have more [pay] for Sunday[.]

---

[1] These sketches have not been located in Lee's extant sketchbooks.
[2] This folio is written in ink, over pencil notes relating to Lee's walks of Friday 22 Aug. and Saturday 23 Aug..
[3] Possibly meaning Rhos-on-Sea or Llandrillo.
[4] These sketches have not been located in Lee's extant sketchbooks.
[5] This folio is a continuation of the pencil notes overwritten on f. 8v.
[6] Diarist error – Sunday was 24 Aug. This paragraph is written in badly faded pencil.

[f. 10v] Water all round[.] Extraord*inarily* thick walls[.] Good cement for pieces fallen whole. Chapel and arches towers and fireplaces. Walk both roads very fine[.] Fine old Gateway and [the walls?] all built on the slate rock[.] Charming C*hur*ch Yard[.]

Curious old House of Sir Tho*mas* Mostyn[.] Old windows Steps Entrance[.][1]

Methodist Meeting in Welsh. Language sounds fine and energetic. Old Drunken fid*d*ler[.]

[25 August] Monday Morn*ing*.

Cross water to Llandudno[.] [mussels?] along shore the whole way[.] Ferry 6ᵈ[.] Fine sands and bold hills. Coast of Anglesea. Flowers. Rose little and delicate and red leaves prickly. Pearl fishery.[2] A house at end of shore. [Turn?] to [pt?] across land. houses and ~~path~~ (road) where the pits [are.] Fine turf.[3]

Mine[4] produces ab*ou*t 4 pennywts to an ounce upon an average or 4½ cwt out of Ton[.] Shaft 70 Yds. Top Gravel Rock. Then vein levels[.] 800 Yds. Left my specimens and walked [f. 11r *blank*] [f. 11v] up to top of hill by ~~flagstaff~~ (signal post). Wind violently high and sound of cords[5] great at distance. C*oul*d not stand on the very top and was glad to run against the flagpost. Rain violent[.] Henbridge house. Went in house[.] Capt*ain* and Mrs Wright kind and hospitable. Dinner. [drest? Ham?] and Ladies who had been detained by rain at [***][.] They were sent for[.] Gr*ea*t Coach and horses came up. Mrs Rigby and daughters. Staid till rain over[.] Walked down home with them. Took my ferry[.] Man 1s. Ferry 6ᵈ. Hammer 1:3. Nail Bag 3ᵈ [pasteboard?] for Bonnets 6ᵈ[.] Paper 6ᵈ. Went down to water. Vessel had tried to go to Liverpool and sent back[.] Capt*ain* Williams brother [Hugh?][.]

Rain all day and night[.]

[26 August] Tuesday

Bill S14:10. Started at 8 for waterside[.] Wind w*oul*d not allow vessel to point of harbour therefore set out for Penman mair [Penmaenmawr] thro*ugh* fine old gateway. Fine hills, impatience to get to top of each hill one after the other to see views[.] Walls of fine hard sparry stone. Veins of spar and some quite spar. Suchnant [Pen-sychnant] Hill ½ mile long. Village of S—[6] turns up by the mouth by the brook wh*ich* runs over stones. Pass by cottages. Go in one. Girl spinning[.] Very neat brown bread, oat cake, buttermilk and butter[.] Fine girl. With*ou*t shoes. Go forward[.]

[f. 12r *blank*]

[f. 12v] Come to some turf heaps where road gets less plain (Sketch[7] of Orms heads and [Pen path?]) wind gently upw*ar*ds and fine views of Orms head. Go on and view of high

---

[1] Lee roughly sketched the front elevation of the house in the middle of the page; not reproduced here.

[2] Freshwater pearl mussel (*Margaritifera margaritifera*); see brief contemporary account of the pearl fishery on the River Conwy in Bingley, *North Wales*, I, pp. 108–10. These are likely the 'mussels' that Lee seems to refer to at the beginning of this day's entry.

[3] This paragraph is written in badly faded pencil.

[4] Great Orme copper mines.

[5] Lee was probably referring to the noise made by the cords, which were used to haul up signal flags, when they banged against the pole in the wind.

[6] Lee probably means Dwygyfylchi.

[7] This sketch is not found in Lee's extant sketchbooks.

hill Cottage with turf round it and (low) wall! Turf heaps[.] Go through gate. Broke some sparry stone and it had some appearance of chrystal [crystal] in it and found moisture about it. No taste. Several hills all taken for Pen*maen* Mawr. Ascend. Stone walls[.] Go on a short distance to next rising. Meet some sort of yellow ore found close by which men did not know what. Went directly to R to a new wall made by Mr Smith and follow it and round a corner descending very rapidly come to place. Very hard stone and [spar?] ore in small pieces could not get any [alluvial?] pyrites[.] Mile out of road. cut [along?] to the L[.] Pass some bogs[.] Water springs on hills sides[.]

Fine mostly soft walking. Fine mosses[.] Sheep walks [only?]. Wind stormy hardly stand[.]

[f. 13r *blank*]

[f. 13v] Very rugged part untill come to [top?] cottage. Ascend P*en*maen Mawr. Very rugged all stones. Top fine prospect. Spring [holes?] done round with stones pits. Stones all look regular placed and put in squares in some parts[.]

3 (double) Arches on which part of road is supported[.] Old road went much higher than the present and may be seen. Mr Smiths House. On fine day can see Isle of Man from road.

A well upon top of mountain in which is a treasure for any one who can find out the steps[.]

A man found the well and saw a treasure in it. Came down. Cut his stick into chips all [the] way fetched his friends and when they came he could not find the chips nor the well[.] They disappeared. Some men have got [some?] of the treasures found there[.] Vessels and old coin[.]

Mrs Williams over water lives at Tre Ganway [Deganwy.] Sir Thomas (Mostyn) Glorth [Gloddaeth].[1] Miss Mostyns live in the wood Bodscallen[.] Mr Lloyd at Marle [Marl][.] Return along high road. Village. Ascend hill ¾ mile long. Curious hole in rock where persons have been I believe. Man has seen goats formerly there[.] Once a goat leaped out[.]

[f. 14r] [*margin:* Bought of Mr F Sheriff of Worcester 2 Old Roman Rings for S31:6 which he bought 12 Months ago at the sale of Mr Bullocks Museum at Liverpool. They were found and brought from Herculaneum[.] From there Mr Bullock had a great many things. Mr Sheriff gave 25S for them][2]

[f. 14v] Cottage at first [mounting?] Penmanmair called Froyd yr Penman[.][3]

Cottage where Taylor lives called I believe Frith Nawydd[.][4]

Shoemaker 1:4.

Got to Conwy at 8 exactly –

Slipped only 1[5] about 70 Yds from bottom of Penmaen Mawr and tore one gaitor at ancle [ankle], little pain and broke gaitor buckle. Tailor 6ᵈ[.] Old woman for shewing me Mr Smiths ore 2ᵈ[.] Bread and butter at village 2ᵈ. Return at ½ past 8. Penmaen Mawr ~~limesto~~ sand stone[.]

---

[1] Gloddaeth Hall, Llandudno; a 16th-century hall with later additions (National Monuments Record of Wales online database).
[2] See SJC, MS U.30 (1), f. 28r (p. 52).
[3] Probably *Ffrwd y Penmaen*, 'stream of the promontory', but not found associated with any residence.
[4] Probably *Ffrith Newydd*, 'new pasture', but not found associated with any residence.
[5] Once.

[27 August] Wednesday.
Bill 4. Touched up drawings[.] Started at 1. Wind against vessel going out of harbour (laden with paving stone) ∴ gave up idea of going to Liverpool. Through Church Yard to South gate cross the moat and go through the lovely wood entirely oaks no underwood. Fern. Hills wind and [track?] fine. Views through the trees of water. Rumbling noise. Just a peep of opposite bank. You can imagine it. Keep about ½ way (up) on the hill. Wind round edge of hill along steep walks. Good road at bottom which fall into [Come Wagalen?][1] 2 roads both inviting and =ly beautiful[.] [Choose the] Upper because [it is] always easy to descend to [the] lower[.] [f. 15r *blank*] [f. 15v] Go along it and come to a charming house. Return to lower road at gate followed it. See on shore a Kiln which by clambering down an edge of the hill get at. Dont know for what use. Cockle shells about its top. Clambered up again (very difficult) to regain the wood in <u>preference to the shore</u> and about 20 Yds come to some cottages where walk ends[.] No opening. But find an outlet to the shore beside a [corner?] cottage when <u>obliged to go to shore</u>. Noble views of opposite hills. All the shore covered with trees to edges of slate rocks where strata lie there in all ways[.][2]

This wood the finest without exception I ever saw[.]

In some parts edges all fine little points where tide and air come. (Leave the wood behind) Go on and come to a lane strait[3] in direction of shore as nothing particular on shore. Followed it and go by Cottages. A gate and stone style with paths through field just beyond it to the R. A path cuts off a wind of river where nothing is. A fine bason of the river appears with all the Snow Range [Snowdon] (at least hill behind hill) and mountains around it draw up one behind another battle array. <u>Fine</u> indeed. Styles go to the shore. Sketch[.][4] Go on and come to fine slate rocks with fine oaks hanging over them. Points like needles. View at lowish tide taken.

A bason of the river[.] [f. 16r *blank*] [f. 16v] Slate rock worn by the tide into points[.] To a person without shoes it would be like walking on needles blunt. When the Road is not to be picked out good there is generally a track on the bank above which will be taken. We took it several times. The wild frith[5] growing on shore[.] Through some meadows[.] Several sorts of plantain[.] 2 unknown flower specimens. A bank which follow[,] sea fowl white. And black ducks with white Bills.[6] Follow Bank untill a gate here leave river in direction for Farmhouse way one long field and then skirt the new fields through a n° of nice gates[.][7] Come to a gors[8] bank, keep under it. View of wood opposite and piles and a good stone house over river. A little village and a summer house or gazebo. Hills behind fine[.] At corner of gorse cover fine rounded hills and a little farther round noble view of all the hills up the valley in terrible arrangement. Cliffs and through a gate and crossing some fields then come to the river again. Captain Forbes

---

[1] Not identified. 'Come' may be Lee's rendition of *cwm*, 'valley'.
[2] Lee roughly sketched the directions of the strata in pencil in the middle of the folio; not reproduced here.
[3] Lee means 'straight'.
[4] This sketch is not found in Lee's extant sketchbooks.
[5] Lee may mean sea thrift or sea pink (*Armeria maritima*).
[6] Possibly coots.
[7] Lee roughly sketched a gate here, in the middle of the text; not reproduced here.
[8] Presumably gorse.

white house Boednod.[1] Stopped at Taly cafn [Tal-y-Cafn] town on water side. Got some Dried Beef etc ale etc 1:4[.] Ferry 1^d[.] Cross the water [in] last boat. Wild fowl fine noble mountains. Keep the shore untill come to some steps wh*ich* take up to the high road[.]

[f. 17r *blank*]

[f. 17v] (Water at Taly Cefn fresh at low Tide and saltish at high[.]) Rocks in the river just above wh*ich* make water rough and noisy. Cairhyn [Caerhun] (Digging on river side) Mr Griffiths and village Church thro*ugh* the trees over water. Just beyond Llanbeder [Llanbedr-y-Cennin] village and a water~~fall~~ (course) thro*ugh* 2 mountains (or) Taly Bont [Tal-y-Bont] River. Farther on the Varhull. Moses Robert a farm house an old building down to road (all on other side of water)[.] First Birch trees on roadside and beyond hanging rocks of the mountain.

Farther on on R of river Porth Ilurd [Afon Porth-Ilwyd] river coming between the mountain. Doligarney river[2] beyond[.] Sketch[3] [made] during shower is sun setting behind clouds. Beautiful bend of river just beyond[.] Go on[.] A cottage on R side of road[.] Noisy 2nd waterfall[.] Road ascends up a hill side and a little way up when it comes to the corner go up the green path leaving the road for a few minutes[.] Have [the eyes?] ab*out* you. A cottage above and a stone wall[.] ~~get on it~~ (Go to it) and see the river winding *from* Conwy and [broken?] com*ing* all along the valley[.] Noble hills over it[.] Sides cultivated. See 3 Waterfalls[.] 2nd very fine[.] Observe river winding down to Llanrost [Llanrwst] and 6 diff*erent* dist*ance*s of hills down the vale[.] Noble bold edge wooded hill upon R look*ing* to Conwy. Evening tints on view. Noise of waterfalls when wind sets this way great [f. 18r *blank*] [f. 18v] precipices of oppo*site* mountains tremendous[.] Children specially afraid of strangers. Take up little infants and run away *from* them. Cottage on slate rock[.] Children come and peep when you are gone. Ascend another part of hill with cottage. 2 roads take the upper. Farther on bold noble bare tapering hills on L. Not a tree to be seen nor bush[.] 3rd waterfall opposite roaring away. 2 roads up higher is a cottage[.] Lower a gate. Go thro*ugh* it. Moon shines not clear and heavy thick black clouds[.]

Upper road[.]

Lord Gwidir house[.][4] Bridge very pretty. Fine bold woods. Road over vast masses of rock (some of wh*ich* each) which [*sic*] cover the road in sev*eral* places[.] Moon now and then shone a little but too dark to see any thing but masses[.] Got to Llanroost at 9 – sun set so very suddenly before was aware of it behind the hills. Got to Llanroost at 9[.]

[**28 August**] **Thursday** rained hard in night and all morn*ing* to 10[.] Set out for Gwidir [Gwydir][.] Glad of it as rain w*oul*d improve waterfalls[.] Bill 3:6[.] Water and Boats 1:2[.] Started at ½ 10 (summer house) 1597 (1⊠5 9⊠7) viewing antiquities[.]

[f. 19r] The Welsh for *Taurus* or Bull sounds like <u>*Torril*</u> and the word for window is like <u>*Fenestrum*</u>[.][5]

---

[1] Bodnant House, built by Colonel Forbes between 1770 and 1821 (National Monuments Record of Wales online database).
[2] Lee may mean the Afon Ddu, which flows through Dolgarrog.
[3] This sketch is not found in Lee's extant sketchbooks.
[4] Gwydir Castle, an early 16th-century manor house near Llanwrst.
[5] Lee repeats the note made at SJC, MS U.30 (1), f. 53v (p. 78).

Road through the finest woods of oak young birch. *Erica vulgaris* [heather] snapdragon [*Antirrhinum*]. Flower at Bastlow of which a hairy sort grows there tall and yellow[.] *Polygamia umbell[iferae]*. River just below road and hills beyond (through trees slaty coloured road[)]. Poured with rain. Beautiful bend in river. Several houses sited on opposite side of river with hanging woods between M[ountains?]. Come to a cottage and gate[.] Go through[.] View over water rather tamer. The woods on roadside still go on with a wall. Opposite hills cultivated nearly to the top. 2 or 3 very good houses on Edge of woods[.]

[f. 19v *blank*]

[f. 20r] The whole walk delightful[.] Come to a cottage at the turn of the road down which a stream comes in such a day as this roaring over the rocky course. Went up a little way to observe the [E]motions[1] of the water[.] Return to the road which makes a fine bend and from a rocky ridge of cliff over a style a most Enchanting view of the mountain along which I had come and valley and very bold handsome cliff in fine layers one above another and very ⊥^{r} towards the river which is as black as ink and winds along the valley. Flower the same as at Penmanmawr well.[2] Leaves like a *mesembyanthemum*[3] little red and white. Over the water a very good stone house [rented?] at foot of a bare tall craggy hill. Up the watery hills bare bold and barren. Downwards clothed with hedges and cultivated. Fine contrast. Above the trees along the road I came rocks covered with red[,] purple *erica* higher up. River broken by rocks and insulated masses and above a few cottages and waters roaring below them over no regular fall but rocks running in all directions. Hills uncommon sharp and bold edged; [crater?] appear ⊥^{r} but broken in thousands of pieces. Edges white other parts slate and fern between all[.] Sketch.[4] A curious effect all well sketched. Cottage ale and oatcake 8. Ponty pair [Pont-y-Pair] prodigious fine immense rocks and water foaming between them[.] Go on[.] Rain terrible. Turn to R for Penmachno. Come to a water course very fine and water from between 2 rock edges. Formed only by rain. A water course on each side of river (just beyond)[.] Farther bold rocks in valley with scattered trees[.] Immense rocks of mountain on R and in front a range of mountain cloud Capt and rain pouring so hard that all things look dim. No body could feel the situation untill exactly in similar one. Rapturous fine.

[f. 20v] Llanroost [Llanrwst] to Pontypair 3. To Mill[5] 3 or 4. To Rhydlan vair [Rhyd-Lanfair] Mountain 3 –

[f. 21r] Keep at Bridge. Most [effecting?] views. Most picturesque and romantic. The Hill beyond the bridge as before mentioned covered with shower hanging down from their tops ~~like~~ (with) chrystal edges.[6] Rain excessive[.] Charming rock over bridge by the hand post which go up to and examine. Then return over the bridge of 1 Arch but fine and new. Course of river through most striking rocks but not so bold as the Ponty Pair ones. Water black. And rocks black and foam ~~darkest~~ (dirty) white. Go on up river side. Little streams come down every part of the rocks where they can. River consists all the way of thousands of little cascades. Come to 2 Bridges where the other river joins the Conwy[.]

---

[1] This may be 'motions' or 'Emotions' – the original pencil text is smudged.
[2] Lee did not specify this plant in his entry for Penmaenmawr (see pp. 92–3).
[3] A genus of flowering plants not native to Europe, with daisy-like flowers.
[4] Not identified in Lee's extant sketchbooks.
[5] Possibly Pandy Mill on the River Machno.
[6] Lee seems to mean that the rain shower falling on the mountain top had the appearance of hanging crystal.

Cross the Bridge here[.] The foam and rocks are fine. Ascend for a long way up the Edge of a precipice[,] road winds round it and river just below roaring. Go on for some way. Scenes all fine and at last come to mill of Penmachno (raining terribly all the way[)]. Waterfall tremendous and sublime to look at and the part below as it winds thro*ugh* the rocks most picturesque and beautiful[.] White foam and smoking mists arise *from* the agitation of the torrent. Grand indeed. Hospitality of the good woman at the house. [seeing?] I was wet. Offered bread. cheese beer. and wine and upon refusing one, fetched out the others successively. Offered a handkerchief to put over head when she saw me put one on and said I sh*ou*ld come again tomorrow. Started for Rhydlanvair gave up all idea of Capel Cerig [Capel Curig] being quite wet and raining too hard and understand*ing* that there was a public house 1 Mile [and] ¼ off called Pont Rhydlanvair started for it. About [f. 21v] ¼ mile up a hand Post guiding to Penmachno village and to Voclas. W*hi*ch road follow. Here is a very fine water fall again but broken and water rushes with great impetuosity. A pretty Bridge[.] Go on[.] Ascend a hill, and beyond it as road narrow*ed* the streams *from* hill over flowed road. Got on a wall with umbrella up and holding End of rake w*hi*ch farmer guided got along to End of water. Curious Picture it w*ou*ld make. But as several places were over flowed, determined to walk thro*ugh* them and did[.] None deeper than middle of leg. Go on ascend*ing*. Cottage turn to L down a lane and see a bridge below hill in lane[.] 2 very fine water courses *from* the mount*ain* roaring terribly[.] Walk on and come to Hand post to Voclas and to Rydlanvair. Follow road to L and come to bridge[.] Water black and dirty[.] Another bridge on one side going to Mr Humphreys. Go on to Rhydlanvair Inn a capital house[.] 3 Elegant room*s* Bed rooms good and quite like a gentlemans house[.] The 2 Coaches to Holyhead Sleep there e*ve*ry night and dine. Got there at ½ p*a*st 4.

Good house.

[29 August] Friday
Bill 7:6[.] Maid and Waiter 2[.] Started in the Holyhead Coach from Pont Rhyd*lanvair* inn for road[.] Beautiful water courses all down the mountains go over 1[1] bridge by road of yesterday and see all the valley. This was the first bridge see the water fall at Pont y Pair and road *from* thence [f. 22r *blank*] [f. 22v] to Capel Cerig beautiful[.] P*air* Stockings 4. Boots 3[d]. Rocks bold. Birch trees. Bridges [torrents?] thro*ugh* most horrible rocks. Rain incessantly furious. Capel Cerig abused by Every body[.] Cruelty to an Officers wife. My friend on foots reception.[2] Wonderful rocks. Lake cottages here and there very picturesque. Several bold cascades but water com*ing from* the hills in all directions. Beyond the lake 2 waterfalls go in and form 1 on the R w*hi*ch goes thro*ugh* a fine Deep valley in most meandering streams, some times winding all in little streams then joining, the*n* rough and then quiet[.] Oh Fine. If one thing can excell another. This Excells the view beyond Llanroost[.]

Lord Penrys [Penrhyn][3] farm piggery and quarries. Railways. Hedges of slate twined with hazel [*Corylus*] twigs. Pretty railways cross the road and boxes loaded draw up empty

---

[1] First.
[2] Lee may mean that a person travelling on foot received a poor reception at the Capel Curig inn. For more on pedestrians, see the introduction to this volume (pp. 8–10).
[3] Richard Pennant, Baron Penrhyn, politician and owner of Penrhyn estate, Carnarvonshire (Lindsay, 'Pennant, Richard (*c.*1737–1808)').

Boxes. Stewards house pretty and Lord Penryns. Cottages sprinkled over the hills. Scene changes from the bare and picturesque to the plain and cultivated. Rain Bangor Village. Trunk sent to Holyhead and back 2S. Imposition. Go on to Ferry[.] Breakfast at 12. Cost 2S. The Harper 1^S. A very good one and plays and composes. The mountains covered with flowers and mist at the Lake[.] Could not see the ~~oppos~~ mountains beyond it. (Lake not but a pool) about a Mile and ½ long. Could not see tops of hills close to us for the clouds[.]

[ff. 23r, 23v *blank*]

[f. 24r] Altitude 2 feet. Inclined plane 25[.] 4 plane in a Circle[.][1]

[f. 26r] Beware of Capel Cerig inn the workers and chambermaids are very impudent.[2]

[f. 27v] NB. To draw the turnpike style at Holywell and to recollect that the machinery at Sutton Mill was worked by wheels with the leather band between each other.[3]

[f. 24v] Sailors [get] 18[,] Liquor (and a crown) and cabbin boy £10 besides what he gets by passenger[.] Wind N by E tolerable favourable[.] 2[OClock?] Weighed anchor Holyhead[.] Wind N by E.

Cross the Bangor ferry 1S. Pass through a bare bleak country such as one would wish to sleep through in travelling[.] Cleared up about this time and became a fine evening[.] Got to Holyhead at 5 and dined there[.] Bill for Dinner etc and provisions for voyage 8S. Waiter 1. Coach fare 1:8[.] Coach men and 2. Men at ferry 6^d[.] Boat 1. Porters 6^d[.]

The wind was against us[.] Tacked to get out of the Bay[.] Rain in sight and obliged to go below. Slept in a cot next the stairs. Very fine[.] The rocking and no bed so charming I was ever in. Slept from 11 to 7 or rather dosed [dozed.] A high swell in the night and the ship rolling and tacking. Many persons sick about me in the night yet never felt so untill the morning when a little about breakfast time but began fishing which quite cured me and caught a great many gurnets[4] indeed with a line, very long and baited with a bit of themselves. Had them dressed and made a hearty meal. No wind and did not go a knot an hour[.] Captain Fellows brother of Fellows of St Johns and the person who was shipwrecked on Island of Ice.[5] Like this [happy?] to sleep. In the morning [Saturday 30 August] rained but cleared up a little in the middle of the day but got foggy at the bay of Dublin and could not see the Bay of Dublin to advantage[.] Got to the Entrance at 4 oclock. Could not come across the bar[.] Saw Irelands Eye or the worlds wonder an Island.[6] Fare for vessel £1.1. Account of ship wreck 2s. Cook for [going?] into kitchen and man for Fishing Tackle 1S. Coming ashore beyond the Lighthouse to the Pidgeonhouse[7] 1:6.

---

[1] This note relates to Lee's account of the baths at Youghal. See p. 159, n. 1.

[2] This sentence has been moved from middle of Dublin narrative, where it appears as a marginal note.

[3] This sentence has been moved from middle of Dublin narrative, where it appears as a marginal note.

[4] 'One of the marine fishes of the genus *Trigla* or family *Triglidæ*, characterized by a large spiny head with mailed cheeks and three free pectoral rays' (*OED*).

[5] The packet-ship *Lady Hobart*, commanded by Captain William D. Fellowes and en route from Halifax to England in June 1803, struck an iceberg or 'island of ice', resulting in the crew and passengers floating for some days in the North Atlantic. The story was printed and reprinted in a number of magazines, including *The Chronicles of the Sea*, 17, 14 Apr. 1838, pp. 129–35. James Fellowes ran the *Loftus*, one of four 'King's Pacquets' between Dublin and Holyhead (*Wilson's Dublin Directory*, p. 4).

[6] The association of the name 'The World's Wonder' with Ireland's Eye is unclear.

[7] The Pigeon House at Ringsend, Dublin, named after John Pidgeon, who ran a storehouse and refreshments shop there in the mid-to-late 18th century.

[f. 25r *blank*]

[f. 25v] Got out of the Packet into the Mail Wherry and went round the Lighthouse to the Pidgeonhouse where our trunks were opened and just looked at and paid 2:6 for Each package of goods. Row with the Irish rascals of rowers. / 2:6 in carriage of 8 Wheels up to the *Custom* Office Tavern. Came to the Tavern in Kildare St at the recommendation of Mr Sayers.[1] Mc Evoys Hotel[2] Going into [*breaks off*.]

Book of Roads of Ireland[3] 12S English or 13 Irish[.] A Guinea English is of value 1:2.9 Irish. The pier is for the commerce which runs out into the sea 3 miles[.] Is built on sand ground. The foundation was laid on piles and wood. The Light house is at the End of it and the Pidgeon House where our trunks opened in the middle[.] It was 30 years Building and separates the harbour and keeps the sand out. Bay of Dublin one of the most dangerous places in the world[.] Sandshoals and a rough sea may by its blowing hard come on in 10 minutes.

Mr Sayers in the Rebellion[4] always locked up his front door as some in Dublin[.] Conspiracy of cook and groom to get the key. Overheard by a Swiss servant[.] Charged the cook with it who denied determinedly every thing. Went out and charged the man[.] He denied also but being told the cook had told he fell on his knees and confessed but being confronted with her knew by her looks she had not and then denied all again. Fellow ran away out of Dublin, was stopped by some rebels who [f. 26v] told him to go to such a place. Was in several engagements and at last was taken prisoner and wrote to Mr Sayer to say that unless he would give him a character he would be hanged[.] Got him off and the fellow told him how miserable he had been all the time. Raw meat etc[.] [f. 27r] He was afterwards sent into the army where he is now serving. Tired and fatigued went to bed early. The men who rowed us onshore were black rough hardy fellows and Captain Fellows says they will come out to the packet in the depth of winter.

Sunday September 1[5]

Got up at 9 and Breakfasted alone as Captain Jenkins went out. Afterwards went to Christ Church Cathedral which is situated in a very bad and narrow part of the Town above the Castle. Tis very narrow and much inferior to all the cathedrals I ever saw in England. It has its Bishop Deans etc[.] Several curious old monuments in it. Among the rest one of <u>Strongbow</u>[6] *vida* Guide. The Boxes are not portioned out to the different families but the Ladies all sit apart in pews separate from the men and none allowed to sit together. All the service chanted very badly. Some good voices spoilt in drawling out the Litany. The whole had a very bad effect[.] Worst chaunting I ever heard. Music tolerably good[.] After Church walked over the Castle, Stephens Green Merrion Square, and all that part of the Town. Dirty Lane [Bridgefoot St] up above the Church was the place where the late rebellion began under Emmet.[7] Went over the Bridges Essex and

---

[1] Richard Sayers of Greenwood, Malahide, Co. Dublin.
[2] William M'Evoy, 6 Kildare St (*Wilson's Dublin Directory*, p. 13).
[3] Most likely George Taylor and Andrew Skinner, *Maps of the Roads of Ireland, Surveyed 1777*, London, 1778.
[4] Probably the rebellion of 1798, rather than that of 1803.
[5] Diarist error – Sunday was 31 Aug.
[6] Richard de Clare, 2nd Earl of Pembroke (1130–76), also known as Strongbow, led the Anglo-Norman invasion of Ireland.
[7] Robert Emmet (1778–1803) led the failed rebellion of the United Irishmen in 1803 and was subsequently executed for treason.

Carlyle [O'Connell Bridge]. Dined with —. Mr Jenkins observation that the common people are filthy to an extraordinary degree and the lower people and beggars are objects of disgust and abhorrence from their dirt and rags worse than [I] ever saw in England. The Entrance from the Pidgeon House to Dublin is through a most foul and stinking region inhabited by beings as filthy and nauceous as the place in tattered clothes and those which are whole [f. 28r] are brown with dirt. The street also on the opposite side of the river to the Courts[1] and running parallel to river is a master piece of dirt and horrible muddy stinking puddles. No street or row to compare with Dame St and its construction. Oxford St[2] does now and will in future in a great degree yield to Lower Sackville St [O'Connell St] in every thing but length. Merion [Merrion] Square and the new Square[3] and Mountjoy Square will rival any in London. The shops are all very neat in the new Streets, and the advantage of Dublin over London is that all the Streets being lately planned are laid out with a regard to appearance and decency.[4]

Monday September 2.[5]
Breakfasted at Mr Jenkins who shewed us all over the Custom House.[6] All the different departments. Went up on the top. Very fine Irish stone. Hard[.] Will not work like the finer *stone* and therefore all the building is faced with Portland Stone which is much softer. The views from the top of the building are very fine and extensive and command the whole of the city of Dublin. Went up higher up to the circular room under the clock from whence more extensive prospects and finer still from above the clock all the river and harbour and the circumadjacent country at your feet. Wicklow hills [Wicklow Mountains] and Scarp. 2 Sugar Loafs.[7] On the opposite side all the country by Houth [Howth] and that way[.] River Liffey running into Harbour and ships drawn up in thick rows on each side of the shore. The Docks and slip and woods of masts in them. Fine prospects. Went over the Long Room where saw a sale of goods (which had been confiscated) by the inch of candle[.] As long as candle remains in bidding goes on and when out last bidder has the Lot. Commissioners apartments, the Commissioners [f. 28v *blank*] [f. 29r] Staircase called Holy Ground and hardly any but them go up and down that way. Went over the docks, Majestys Storehouses, fine drawbridge over dock where ships go in. Machine for pressing down tobacco when it has [stained?] the Boxes in which it is put. A common screw on a large scale does it. Saw the Hogsheads of Tobacco as they come over and saw the Tobacco taken out and weighed[.] In general about ~~180~~ lbs. Each tubful is worth with the duty about £150. Saw some which had been damaged and those parts cut away and carried close by the Custom House kiln[8] for fear of being sold. Docks filled

---

[1] The Four Courts, commenced by Thomas Cooley in 1776 and continued by James Gandon upon Cooley's death in 1784; completed in 1802 (Casey, *Buildings of Ireland: Dublin*, pp. 92–9).

[2] In London.

[3] Probably Fitzwilliam Square, first mentioned in 1791 (Goodbody, *IHTA no. 26 Dublin part III*, p. 22).

[4] In the second half of the 18th century and first half of the 19th, many Dublin streets were widened and new streets were laid out under the influence of the Wide Streets Commissioners, created by Act of Parliament in 1757 (Goodbody, *IHTA no. 26 Dublin part III*, p. 2).

[5] Diarist error – Monday was 1 Sept.

[6] Built by James Gandon in 1791 (Casey, *Buildings of Ireland: Dublin*, pp. 141, 144).

[7] Mountains known as the Great Sugar Loaf and Little Sugar Loaf.

[8] Original word order reversed here to clarify meaning ('kiln Custom House').

DIARY 2: TOUR FROM HOLYWELL TO DUBLIN AND FERMOY

with ships. Weighing machines all round the docks. The Custom House the finest building in Europe[.] Never saw one to = it or even to compare with it. Its front towards the sea most beautiful. Figure of St Andrew over the Clock. 4 figures in front of the building. Mercury Neptune, Ireland[1] and Plenty. Made of Portland Stone.

[f. 29v] [margin:] Peach 10ᵈ. Fee 1:1 Irish. Book of Ireland 13 Irish

[f. 29r] NB in Christ Church 3 horribly bad figures of James 2 and Charles done by some horrible bad Irish fellow[.][2] [*Line scored out.*]

Although the Liffey is very inferior to the Thames yet the former runs all up the middle of the City and there is a very fine broad street on the side of it and there will be more keys about the custom house and then you may walk along the riverside through fine beautiful streets. Each side of [the] river is paved. The bridges are very good and by the river being in the middle of the Town they are very fine ornaments to it. The Parliament house[3] is far superior [to] any of the buildings in London of the same standing[.] It is a *Chef D'Oeuvre*. The 4 Courts are also a most enchanting pile of buildings and also from the opposite side of river bid [defiance?] to any thing in London. The person who built the [f. 30r] Custom house Erected this also. The Alarum over the Custom House was never set off but 2ce[.][4] Once when part of the building was on fire and during the late rebellion[.] It makes a most terrible sound[.] The college from without and within appears a fine building but seems like more an appendage to the City than a noble royale university.[5] The walks and grounds are in dull negligence[.] Boys playing at cricket in the grounds nursing maids on the grass children women all about them. Probably they hang up linen there to dry. The Library is inferior in magnitude to the Public Library at Cambridge and inferior in magnificence to the Library of Trinity[6] and not to be compared to either. Carriages were in the courts of the college. We were told it was very loose in its discipline and of course it could not be productive of the same good effects as another university for the young men have so many incitements to idleness[.] Most have friends or relations in Town. NB some of the fellows are married although they do not bring their wifes in college. Yet this is winked at.[7] Castle a poor building.[8] The upper square is pretty good but upon the whole

---

[1] Should be 'Industry'.

[2] These statues, which were actually of Charles I and II, were completed by the Dutch sculptor William de Keysar in 1683–4. They were commissioned by Dublin's Lord Mayor, Sir Humphrey Jervis, to stand in the niches of the tholsel (guildhall) built on Nicholas St, close to the cathedral, by Thomas Graves in 1678. The tholsel fell into disrepair and was taken down in 1809, while the statues were removed to Christ Church Cathedral (Casey, *Buildings of Ireland: Dublin*, pp. 61, 336).

[3] The Parliament House, home to the Bank of Ireland since the Union of 1801, was commenced in 1729 by Sir Edward Lovett Pearce (1699?–1733), and completed successively by Arthur Dobbs (colonnade, 1739), James Gandon (additions, 1785), Edward Parke (additions, 1787) and Francis Johnson (remodelling for Bank of Ireland, 1804). See Casey, *Buildings of Ireland: Dublin*, pp. 380, 385.

[4] Twice.

[5] Trinity College, Dublin, was established in 1592. The ensemble represents the 'largest group of monumental C18 buildings in Ireland and is the most complete university campus of the period in these islands', occupying 40 acres in Dublin city centre (Casey, *Buildings of Ireland: Dublin*, p. 388).

[6] Lee means the library of Trinity College, Cambridge.

[7] Anne Plumptre notes the flouting of Trinity College's requirements of fellows upon marrying, until the introduction of a new oath in 1812 that fellows would notify the college within 15 days of marrying and vacate their fellowship (Plumptre, *Narrative*, pp. 22–3).

[8] Dublin Castle was the viceregal residence from 1560 to 1922 (Casey, *Buildings of Ireland: Dublin*, pp. 348–59).

it is very inferior to what one would expect the castle the residence of the Lord Lieutenant to be.[1] Mountjoy Square is very pretty and so is Rutland Square [Parnell Square]. Stephens Green is very dull although very extensive in size and bigger than any one Square in Ireland[.]

At 4 Mr Sayers sent his curricle for me and I drove over to Malahide about 8½ English [miles] from Dublin by the Custom house on that road through a very pretty part of the country. All gentlemens seats on each side of the road to his house. Got there about ½ past 5 and started at more than ½ past 4. Very [f. 30v blank] [f. 31r] fine and elegant place. House called Green Wood on the L hand side of the road. Walked around the grounds which are laid out in very great taste. He bought it of —[2] and this very estate belonged formerly to the famous Handel and in the pleasure grounds is a fine romantic (retired) pond over which above was a grotto where Handel composed his famous piece of music the Water piece and it was tried on this very water. He here composed most of his music but the Grotto is now down.[3]

Tuesday [September 2]

In the morning walked all over the Gardens which are surrounded with very noble fine walls[.] The first is a flower garden and in it is a most princely hothouse 306 feet long with 4 divisions so that the fruit of which it is full is in 4 different stages of forwardness[.] The garden beyond [is] fruit chiefly and the walks are loaded and the trees are almost bent treble with the weight of the produce[.] This land will instantly give the lie to any body who says land is better in England than in Ireland[.] Never in any English garden of double the size saw so much produce as this of Mr Sayers has in 4 Acres[.] Went all over the grounds and to —[4] hill where there is a windmill from whence saw all the Harbor at Malahide Colonel Talbots Castle and grounds Irelands Eye, Horth [Howth] and all the country round. Curious grant made to Colonel Talbots family as far back as the time of the Edwards of the liberty of importing into Malahide Port any goods whatever free of expence or suffering any body else to do so.[5] No person who takes refuge on his estate (manor) can be touched without his permission. He has all the wrecks for 20 miles on the coast[.] He is lord of the manor of a very great extent of land and his manor joins Mr Sayers[.] Government want to buy his right of Colonel Talbot[.] He [f. 32r] might if he exercised it make thousands of money[.] The estate has been in the family for many hundreds of years. Colonel Talbot [is] related to Lord Grenville and Buckingham[.][6] Mr Sayers Estate [is] about 420 Acres of land.

---

[1] In 1806–7, the office of viceroy was held by John Russell, 6th Duke of Bedford (Thompson, 'Russell, John, sixth duke of Bedford (1766–1839)').

[2] Greenwood was built by Sir William Montgomery, Bart. (Brewer, *Beauties of Ireland*, I, p. 249).

[3] Lee's information in relation to George Friedrich Handel is incorrect. In 1742, Handel stayed for two months with the Vernons of Clontarf Castle (Lennon, *That Field of Glory*, p. 161).

[4] Feltrim Hill.

[5] In 1476, Edward IV granted Thomas Talbot the customs of all goods coming through the port (*Burke's Peerage*, 1850, p. 966).

[6] George Nugent Temple Grenville (1753–1813), 3rd Earl Temple and 1st Marquess of Buckingham (Geoghegan, 'Grenville, George Nugent Temple').

DIARY 2: TOUR FROM HOLYWELL TO DUBLIN AND FERMOY

Returned to Dublin in Mr Sayers Curricle ab*ou*t 4 oclock and wrote to my uncle[1] and Mr Camden[.] P*a*ir Socks 2:6 English[.] Silk cover for hat 6:6 English[.] Mr Sayers *coa*chman 50 Pence Irish.

The Irish people seem astonished that you do not know the streets and places as well as they themselves and utter all sorts of exclamations of surprize at y*ou*r appealing to them and in general at the same time that they answer you interrogate you ab*ou*t y*ou*r business, y*ou*r plan, reasons, etc. It is an exclamation expressing their superiority very much[.]

[f. 31v] 'Pray in what part of this post office must I enquire for letters[?]' 'For what letters Sir[?]' 'For letters w*hic*h are here waiting for me.' 'And (pray) for how long since, Sir[?]' 'What business is that to you[?] Cannot you answer my questions[?]' 'Oh now I understand you Sir[.] At that window farther up to your left Sir[.]'

[f. 32r] **Wednesday 3 Sep*tembe*r**
Breakfasted and went to call on Mr Jenkins[.] After went to the Dublin Society house[.][2] Staid there 3 hours [and a] ½ just skimming over the arrangement. The house is in Hawkins St and you ascend a flight of stairs and go into the lecture room w*hic*h is filled up with benches etc *secundum artem*[3] and is a very good one. The Library and Laboratory are also well worth looking at although there are not a very great coll*ecti*on of books[.][4] Adjoining is a gallery filled with busts and all the best statues, Antony, Cicero Homer Demostho Cato, Canveallo like Sir Rusick Harvards, Rivergods L*o*rd Chesterfield, P*ri*nce of Wales, Geta, etc, Laocoon, <u>Sapho</u> Shelling and Niobe and sons and daughters.

[f. 32v] Beyond is a place where artists are allowed to come and sit and copy f*ro*m the statues. I saw several and stood over them as they were at work. A selection of artists are allowed every day between 7 and 9 to draw f*ro*m a living figure who is got to sit in diff*eren*t postures. Each posture has 4 mornings and the artists copy from life. 15 are the n° allowed to attend. The man who is the subject has a Guinea a week and the man who sat then was a soldier[.] No one is allowed to speak a word all the time[.][5] Saw the Laocoon and his 2 sons, Dancing faunas[,] Venus de Medici[,] Apollo Belvidere, Whistler, Listening slave and other statues.

A model in wood of curious Bridge in Switzerland given by the Earl of Bristol[.][6] Bridge now destroyed by the French[.] The museum for minerals is a most beautiful sight[.] The scientific arrangement begins with the precious stones and goes all throu*gh*[.] There is a gallery up stairs w*hic*h is ascended by a geometrical stair case w*hic*h is also filled with minerals. The next small room contains Books and a curious window of stained glass all (as we were told) of Irish workmanship. The coins are kept in a room across to this. Beyond is another great museum containing a most beautifully arranged coll*ecti*on of

---

[1] William Lee Antonie (see p. 341, n. 3); this letter has not been found among Lee's extant papers.
[2] The Dublin Society, founded in 1731, had its premises on Hawkins St until 1815 (Casey, *Buildings of Ireland: Dublin*, p. 52). It has been known as the Royal Dublin Society since 1820.
[3] 'according to the art'.
[4] See Clarke, 'The Library'.
[5] Despite Lee's impression, the school of life drawing was not administered with much regularity in the early 19th century. See Turpin, 'The Dublin Society's Figure Drawing School'.
[6] Carr recorded a model of the bridge of Schaffhausen over the Rhine (*Stranger in Ireland*, pp. 58–9). The original word order has been changed here for clarity.

shells. Also Birds and stuffed Insects of all sorts, Butterflies, and a great many natural curiosities in Spirits, Snakes, Scorpions etc etc[.] Around the room are hung a variety of curious natural productions Fossils, Monsters in every element, Seaweeds, Horns of all classes of animals etc[.] Above stairs is the museum [*Hibernicum?*] *minerale*[1] of all the minerals and ores fossils found in Ireland in the different counties and arranged by different counties.

Below stairs is a fine petrified tree found in a block of Portland stone and some pillars of various sorts from [the] Giants Causeway.

Piece of amber with a toad in it[.]

The department or case of the second room contained Roman curiosities found in Ireland.

But above all the liberality with which the whole is conducted is most gratifying to any person. For I was in there, with a [f. 33r] catalogue of some parts, and altogether for above 3 hours some times was locked in and at others not, without any one to plague one by accompanying or watching me and something might have easily have been stolen. For instance a few bottles of snakes or pieces of sea weed. From there went to see the College library[2] but it was beyond the hours but saw the Chapel[3] which is a neat building nothing extraordinary but good size. The Hall is plain and not particular. While standing at the Hall door just after the fellows had come out from dinner a sizar[4] from the Buttery threw a potatoe at me and hit the man close by me[.] As I was walking out to the (other) door another shot of something hard was fired but it missed me. He was in the Buttery and had his gown on, spoke to one of the fellows to know if this was the customary salutation which a stranger met with always[.] Very blackguard of them. Saw the room where the wax preparations are kept. Wax representations as large as life of 2 children joined together. Another one eyed figure of a woman the eye in the centre of the head. Another wax figure of a person with the 2 eyes close and the nose below both. Many most beautifully worked figures in wax and they look as if all alive. Such expression in the eyes and countenance. Saw the room where the preparations instruments etc and the anatomy Lectures were given[.] A very fine room much superior to any lecture room in Cambridge for the same. Skeleton of the Irish giant 8 feet 4 inches high.[5] Skeleton of a man ossified.[6] The 2 children joined together and a variety of anatomical preparations[.] Dined at Mr Jenkins. In the rebellion Mr Jenkins had information of a party who went out to sea in the bay to hold their meetings being so closely watched on shore, and he accordingly went and anchored alongside a lighthouse (on the custom house beach) and when the boat came out he made up to it and found them[.] With his ink and paper he took their names and habitations

---

[1] Carr named this as the Leskeanum mineral museum (*Stranger in Ireland*, p. 60), and Plumptre named it as the *Museum Hibernicum – Regnum Minerale* (*Narrative*, p. 25).

[2] The old library at Trinity College, Dublin, built in 1712–33 (Casey, *Buildings of Ireland: Dublin*, p. 400).

[3] The chapel at Trinity College, Dublin, built in 1778 (Casey, *Buildings of Ireland: Dublin*, p. 396).

[4] At the University of Cambridge and at Trinity College, Dublin, an undergraduate who received his 'sizes' (rations) for free, in return for performing serving duties (*OED*).

[5] The skeleton was that of one Magrath from Co. Cork, whose remains were dissected at Trinity College, Dublin after his death in May 1760; his skeleton is still on display in the Anatomy Museum (Kane, 'An Irish Giant', p. 98).

[6] The 'ossified man' is described in many late 18th- and 19th-century accounts of Ireland, including [Campbell], *Philosophical Survey*, pp. 188–9, where he is named as one Clark from Cork city.

down and Major Swan[1] went and examined their houses where were found sufficient evidence to convict them. Some were hanged and the others transported[.] 12 in all[.] Butchers and Baker and respectable shopkeepers in Dublin[.]

[f. 33v] With parties of his corps the Custom House volunteers he found many depots of arms which were buried and of pikes[.] Where pikes were found those persons they punished. In a garden close behind the storehouses of the custom house he found 2 pieces of canon[.] The people said they knew nothing about it. That was the general answer[.] He saw many persons hanged on Carlyle Bridge and all the great prisoners were given in care of his corps at first by the government as a great compliment to them. A cropt[2] head and [silk?] coloured handkerchief and brown coat was the dress of the rebels[.] When the conspiracy was found out many put on false tails to conceal them and powder and many of these tails were hung up on Carlyle Bridge.[3] On the Evening of Lord Kilwardens murder[4] his daughter just got to the castle in time to save it and gave the alarm, or else they would have had it in a few minutes. The rebellion began in Thomas Street and the great depot was in Dirty Lane where numbers of pikes etc were found. When they had taken the castle they were to have made signals by firing sky rockets to their friends who were to take the garrison at Pidgeon House. Mrs Jenkins was then with her family at her house close behind it and many persons observed that night what n^{os} of people were parading the streets and lanes and fields. They heard of the alarm and of the rebellion about 4 in the morning and were all women in the house without a man[.] Mr Jenkins was with his boat.

The people were all in crowds to storm the Pidgeon House had the castle been taken. About that time I believe Mr Jenkins received information of a vessel coming over which was bringing arms and people from France and was to land outside the Bay towards the rock[.] He went out in the Revenue Cutter and cruised about for 2 days and on the 3[5] saw a vessel of that description coming. Fired signals. Answered them. He bore up[.] She bore away. He fired[.] She kept sailing off and at last he kept firing at her. She took no notice and she went down in the dusk of the evening without a man saved within 2 miles of the shore. Fires were lit on the shore to give her notice of his being off there for her. If she was a rebellious crew he sunk her. If she [f. 34r] was not he did right as she would not come to. They could not make out who she was or what.

When the Ancient Britons[6] were defeated and drawn into a defile and obliged to fly Captain — his relation[7] was wounded and he went off to Bray to meet him. Just as he got there 2 fellows were taken up. Some soldiers charged them with having had

---

[1] Major William Bellingham Swan (1765?–1837) (Long, 'Swan, William Bellingham').

[2] Cropped, i.e., short-haired. Irish republicans and rebels adopted short hairstyles 'in the manner of the Jacobins and receiving the name "croppies"' (Gott, *Britain's Empire*, p. 130).

[3] Lee seems to refer to the common practice of cropping coat-tails to make a jacket, thought to have been understood as a uniform of sorts for United Irishmen (Reid, *Armies of the Irish Rebellion*, p. 45).

[4] Arthur Wolfe (1739–1803), 1st Viscount Kilwarden, politician and judge; 'he was driving from his country residence at Newlands Castle, Clondalkin, Co. Dublin, to Dublin Castle accompanied by his daughter and a nephew, Rev. Richard Straubenzie Wolfe (1779–1803). The carriage was stopped on Thomas St by rebels, and Kilwarden and his nephew were piked to death. When, dying, he heard a demand for the instant punishment of his killers, he insisted "let no man suffer for my death but by the laws of my country" ... His murder was widely regarded as the single most shocking event of the Emmet rising' (Johnston-Liik, 'Wolfe, Arthur').

[5] Third day.

[6] A Welsh cavalry regiment stationed at Newry during the 1798 rebellion (Gott, *Britain's Empire*, p. 490).

[7] A relation of Captain Jenkins.

correspondence in the country and as he was getting on his horse to proceed after watering him he saw them both hanging. So expeditious had they been.

When they took men up on suspicion, upon their denying any knowledge, they often flogged them with some 100 lashes w*hich* made them confess and thus they got a great deal [of] useful information f*ro*m them and f*o*und many arms and pikes[.]

[f. 34v] [*Start one page of rough pencil notes.*] At Killgobben [Kilgobbin] C*h*urch close by an old castle w*hich* was formerly called Sesson Castle abo*u*t 200 ye*a*rs ago all the property of Mr Vernon[.][1]

Wicklow a town without commerce manufactory or roads and a Bay with*ou*t fish[.] Mr [Gierson?] started for the hotel at 11 oclock and got no milk[.] [*Two lines erased here.*]

Some good houses about it. Cross bad barge over a worse river or brook. Some remarkably fine rats running an attacked [*sic*] along the river walk upon the hill. Drawing Book 4:6. Paper for D*itt*o 2:2. Compass 19:6. Watch mending 10:1¼[.] Shoes soling 3:9 ½. Bill 1:–

Washerwoman 1:8. Trunk at office to Carlow 3:5. P*ai*r Socks 2:8½. D*itt*o 2 pairs 5:5. Map of Dublin 2:8½. Man at College room 10[.]

Mountain of Wicklow cloud capt.[2] Rain all morning[.]

Not uncommon to see in Dublin women and children with bare feet and without hats, in caps only[.]

[f. 35r] [*Start one page of rough pencil notes.*] Ball in a sling on the Hill[.]

Kilgobben Church and small village a range of fires f*ro*m there to the Town[.]

[f. 35v] [*Start one page of rough pencil notes.*] A beggar said 'and pray be so good yo*u*r honour to hear 2 words' and walked on after this premium[.]

3 miles nearby is Torney [Taney] Church and the houses on the road are called Church Town[.] A little shabby 2 arch bridge over a puddle ditch[.]

Just beyond the continuation of scattered houses is called Dundrum.

Mr Mc Rayes (white) house not far f*ro*m 1st mountain[.]

Killgobben Castle, an archway thro*ugh* it, a square building small and nothing particular about it close by the road[.]

Fine view of the sea and Houth [Howth] Isle from the road side[.]

Come to the Scalp[3] wh*ich* is a very good road between 2 vast high great edges of rocks w*hich* obviously joined and below the road is undoubtedly masses of gr*ea*t rock for the water may in some p*ar*ts be heard trickling down[.] The craggy cliffs hang over in very large masses[.] The stone is fine stone it is not used for any thing although so near the road excessively hard. Go on and get a view of the 2 Sugarloafs and the Glen of the Downs in the distance.[4] Very good road about a mile or 2[.]

[ff. 36r, 36v, 37r *blank*]

[f. 37v] [*Start one page of rough pencil notes.*] Turn to R towa*rds* Old Connaught[.]

NB. Desiderata on Irish roads. A foot way[.] Evening charming fine[.] Cross a brook by stones laid across it[.] [*Three lines erased here.*]

---

[1] Kilgobbin Castle, Stepaside, Co. Dublin, was built in the 15th century (Irish Archaeology website). It is likely that the notes made here relate to Thursday 4 Sept., as Lee made no diary entry on that date.
[2] Capped.
[3] The surrounding scenery is sketched at SJC, MS U.30 (6), ff. 45r, 45v (p. 315), not reproduced here.
[4] Lee sketched this view at SJC, MS U.30 (6), ff. 46r, 46v (p. 315), not reproduced here.

Mr Greens house close by an old part of a fortification now in ruins and in stables and pigstyes[.] Turn down lane to R[.]

Widow Smiths house. From opposite gate sketch. Descend towards the Bay[.] Several fine houses in front[.]

Mr Wesbys House on the L through the Lodge gates. White surrounded with trees and plantations and the bare hills appear beyond it[.] Woods all to the water and the sea beyond them[.]

Road beautiful[.] Fine woods on all sides. Hills purple with the *Erica* on the distances and the sea in front over trees with ships on it and all the light of the picture on the sea[.] Come to the junction of another road from Dublin and the view along towards Bray most striking[.] Mr Hudsons house on the L.

On R an iron gate into a curious old ruin attracted my attention. Old small church in the most beautiful ruins I ever saw in my life[.][1] Walls all overgrown with ivy and some beautiful evergreens. In the centre of Church a grave ornamented with cut paper a garland and sticks with paper on[.][2]

Gravestones in all directions[.] The whole place in rubbish, surrounded with trees[.] Gravestones of *1*796 and 1801 thus yard used though not the church[.]

[f. 38r *blank*]

[f. 38v] Colonel Harwoods house[3] close by the burying place commands a fine view of the 2 Sugar Loafs[.]

[*One line erased.*]

Go along the road shaded on both sides with trees which meet at [the] top and come to a rising ground where there is a O^r opening[.] Trees around it[.] Then descend a little slope through trees as before. Very fine and comfortable in [*sic*] a hot day. Judge [Taileys?] house on the Left[.] He took it of Mr Hudson.[4]

Colonel Wingfields fine plan and Gates[5] on Turn to R[.]

Ledwigge a farmer and Keneddy a young man[.][6] Widow *K*ennedy's son taken without trial and hanged in the middle of the street. These were the 2 young men Mr Jenkins saw hung.[7] They were hung opposite (before) one of their own doors in the middle of the street. 2 others were shot on the common below the town. That very beautiful ruin of a church in Old Connaught is still used as a burial ground by the Catholics and only one Protestant has been known by Mr — the surgeon to be buried there for 10 years. In same manner he has known but of 1 Catholic buried in the Great Church of Bray in 10 years. Bray was not disturbed much by the rebels. They never came nearer than 6 miles of it except in small handfuls. Just after my arrival 2 Methodist wandering preachers came into the town in Black coats and fustier dark coloured Breeches, Coloured blue worsted

---

[1] Old Connaught church (ruins) and cemetery, sketched at SJC, MS U.30 (6), f. 47r, and reproduced at p. 108 (Figure 5).

[2] Lee roughly sketched this ornament in the page margin, not reproduced here.

[3] Lee probably means Colonel Howard; see p. 111, n. 4.

[4] Possibly Sir Robert Hudson; see p. 111, n. 5.

[5] Colonel Edward Wingfield (1772–1859) of Corke Abbey, Bray, Co. Wicklow, third son of the 3rd Viscount Powerscourt ('Introduction – Verner/Wingfield Papers').

[6] Evidently two locals with whom Lee spoke.

[7] Possibly referring to the story related by Jenkins on 3 Sept., but it contains no specific reference to the circumstances related here.

Figure 5. Sketch of ruined church and churchyard at Old Connaught, Co. Wicklow, as described in SJC, MS U.30 (2), f. 37v (p. 107). By John Lee, 3 September 1806 (SJC, MS U.30 (6), f. 47r). Reproduced by kind permission of the Master and Fellows of St John's College, Cambridge.

stock*ing*s jackboots and spurs well mounted and leav*ing* their horses first one mounted on a chair and prayed and then the other alternately gave a sermon of unconnected matter. And sang a psalm and then ended with a prayer[.]

[f. 39r] [*Two lines crossed out.*]

They travel the country and belong to some missionary society. One gave many quotations in Irish[.] The other spoke all English[.] They wore velvet caps close round their heads[.] Were very decent people to look at. Had many soldiers in their audience and praised the army. Ordered the children to be still. Story of the sweep who repented. Brought in several stories of people who had been brought over by them[.]

Friday [5 September]
Bray Castle a piece only remaining[.][1] The present occupier obliged to keep it in repair by his lease. Occupier Mr Donolan[.][2] *From* Bray cross the common and come to Fassar Row [Fassaroe] the residence of the ancient family of the Strongs.[3] A fine view fr*om* the top of the hill of the sea, Bray Bridge, Town Old Connaught[.] Woods on shore, bare hills in the rear and the Sugarloafs. The Strongs have had the farm for above 200 ye*ar*s[.] The land is Mr Tighes[4] who lets it for 3 lives or 31 years. [*One sentence erased.*] Come up by Col*onel* Crampton and below Mr Walkers house[.] NB You turn to the R to go to the farm of Strongs on top of hill[.] Old bit of castle there. Then go down the hill tow*ards* the Dargle. Cross a wooden bridge as a substitute for one w*hich* has been broken down[.] Come to a gate locked entrance, Lord Powerscourts domain[5] to Lovers Leap[6] then Lord Montroses Domain[7] is [the] castle [on the] other side of [the] water[.]

Go down to a part called the money holes[.]

[f. 39v] Scramble along the edges of the rocks w*hich* are very slippery[.] There had been rain in the night and the water from the bogs was as black as ink. Beautiful scenery[.] NB Turn short to the L down a path to the money holes. The river cannot be followed all the way[.] Climb up as well as you can to the top of the rock[.] There is one place w*hich* is called the flax holes. But go onto the Jackdaw holes[.] Go up to the moss house from the edge of the precipices. The oppo*site* rocks are superb. The whole is beautifully clothed with wood and the water below is delightful. Keep ascending fr*om* here to the Burnt Rock promontory[8] from whence you have a most overpowering and grand view of an ocean of wood forming a stupendous amphitheatre. Nothing can describe it[.] It is fine to descend down a little part of the promontory and then you have a more accurate idea of its height and sublimity[.]

---

[1] There were three medieval and late-medieval castles in Bray. It is likely that Lee refers here to Little Bray castle, built in 1459 (Davies, *IHTA no. 9 Bray*, p. 11).

[2] John Francis Donnellan of Bray Castle.

[3] Fassaroe Castle, built in 1535 (Stout, 'The Archaeology of County Wicklow', p. 131).

[4] William Tighe (1766–1816), politician, topographer, and landowner of Rossanagh, Co. Wicklow (McElroy, 'Tighe, William').

[5] Powerscourt Estate, Enniskerry, granted to Richard Wingfield in 1603 (Clavin, 'Wingfield, Sir Richard').

[6] A beauty spot on the River Dargle just south of Enniskerry, Co. Wicklow.

[7] Lee may mean the Monck Demesne. See p. 110, n. 6, on Charleville House.

[8] Next promontory on the River Dargle, to the east of Lover's Leap; sketched at SJC, MS U.30 (6), ff. 48r, 48v (p. 316), not reproduced here.

Lovers Leap a wonderful bold rock ⊥ʳ for an immense depth. Sugarloafs appear beyond those[.] Powerscourt House and Mr Grattons[.][1] The view[2] like the rest wonderful[.] There is a little close fence put up around [the] Edge[.]

Day cold and windy and no sun ∴ no humour to take opportunity of leaping. Next point is called the View Rock[.] Mr Grattons thatched house pretty on edge [of] opposite hill. A little father on [f. 40r blank] [f. 40v] there is a path which takes [you] below the Lovers Leap[.] Followed it but could not find the bottom of [the] cliff for I went close to the water and ∴ went round it a long way back by a path which seems as if only 6 people had ever been there before. The cliff does not go quite to the water and I got below between it and the water. Returned to the opening where the opposite rock is prodigious fine and below Mr Grattons house and then scrambled up into the road at [the] top of hill and following which brought me to my old place again where I set out. Soon after come to gate at end of the Dargle. Cottages close by from which descend [low?] alongside through trees and cross over 2 trees put across the water and ascend the opposite bank to the cottage, a most picturesque place at the edge of a precipice covered with woods[.] The walks through these sides opposite to those I came are quite if not more beautiful than the others for they seem to have been less cut. The Lovers Leap looks terrible from this side. Sketch of it[.][3] Return by same way to bridge. Follow the path through the trees and come out on a fine meadow surrounded with trees. Hay in it at the time. Get to the house grounds. Over the water is a +.[4] Mr Cannons above[.] The kitchen garden very pretty[.]

[f. 41r blank]

[f. 41v] The hills to the R of Sugarloafs called the Long Hills [Long Hill][.] Fine romantic bridge[.][5] The water above separates Lord Powerscourts land and Lord Monks.[6] Mr Grattons House looks well from [the] bridge and is close to it[.] Water runs through his pleasure ground. Lord Powerscourts lodge [is] opposite Mr Grattans[.] Go through grounds by water side for a long way[.] Road is very pretty[.] River close[.] After hopping from stones across river several stones and going through several gates we[7] came to an amphitheatre of mountain that on the ~~left~~ R [was] clothed with hay the others nothing particular but trees on them[.] Here we asked what was the way to the [Powerscourt] waterfall and was shewn what we had from some (minutes) time before seen and what appeared nothing but a small stream down [the] hill side[.] Extremely disappointed after a long walk but resolved to [walk] up to it. Some good picturesque trees on the way however almost repay one for the walk. Waterfall excessively tame and looks like [a] place where one could have said a gentleman has shewed his taste in making a waterfall more than a fine bold work of nature[.]

Wooden bridge. Summer house over it, upon a close inspection improves upon acquaintance. Fine bold rocks slaty colour. Water falls into a dark hole[.] It is a pretty delicate lady like waterfall and would make a pretty morning ride if one had nothing else

---

[1] Tinnehinch near Enniskerry, Co. Wicklow, the estate of the politician, Henry Grattan (1746–1820) (Kelly, 'Grattan, Henry').

[2] This view is sketched at SJC, MS U.30 (6), ff. 49r–51v (p. 316), not reproduced here.

[3] See SJC, MS U.30 (6), f. 51r–v (p. 316), not reproduced here.

[4] Cross.

[5] Possibly Tinnehinch Bridge on the Dargle.

[6] Charleville House, built in 1790–1800 (NIAH).

[7] Lee seems to have made parts of his tour in company with others, but these are not always identified.

to do. But *would* not have [stirred?] beyond [f. 42r *blank*] [f. 42v] Mr Grattans had I known what it was.

Returned part of the way back[.] Crossed the brook 3 times by stones put across it and about 2 miles back come to a beautiful cottage, on the side of *which* a road leads up towards the house[.] Up hill ascend for some way. Pass by a little one arch bridge on the L. About the house fine trees. Noble hall rather heavy double rows of pillars. Too low for its square length. The front next to the water very pretty a good lawn hanging down to the winding river. Fine woods of Lord Monk over the river. Go down the Beech avenue and come to the Lodge. Much out of order. It is a fine (turned) arch, but nothing else particular here[.][1] See the Scalp and the whole of the hills I had been under before sea and Bray in front. After walking [a] long way [the] road joins where I came into the Dargle and came [the] rest of the way back again. Benighted and *could* not find [the] track over Bray Common. Horrible lonely and gloomy lane to come down at night by water side[.]

NB. Stopped at 4 (Cabins) Cottages in going to the Waterfall and asked for a bit of bread[.] No such thing in any one[.] Got some potatoes on *which* I dined and a cup of milk[.] Set out at 10 and got back at 8 at night[.]

A Boy guided me over the common back. 'How old are you[?]'. 'I do not know.' 'Your father and mother know I suppose[?]' 'Yes they know.' 'But had you never the curiosity to ask them.' 'No they never told me.' 'Do you not know *your* birthday.' 'No I never asked. But I must be about [f. 43r][2] 11 or 12 years old or there abouts.' ~~Have you any~~ 'Do you never hurt your feet by running[?]' 'Often times when you run thorns in[.]' 'How do you get them out[?]' 'Let them stay[.] I have some shoes at home but do not like to wear them.'

Saturday [6 September].[3]

Co*lo*nel Howards[4] and up to Sir *Robert* Hudsons of Holybrook[.][5] Then top of Sugar Loaf. Glen of Downs. Mr Le Touches C*oun*t of Delgany.[6] Newtown M*oun*t Kennedy.

//

Dunran and then Luggalor [Luggala] and mountains adjacent and sleep in Roundwood[.]

//

7 Churches [Glendalough] and then to Newry [Rathnew] Bridge. Devils Glen[.]

//

1 Day to see neighbourhood of Newry Bridge[.]

//

Rathdrum[.]

To take Dunran Devils Glen Newry Bridge Mrs Tighes[7] in a day[.]

---

[1] Lee roughly sketched the arch in the page margin, not reproduced here.
[2] The paragraph order of f. 43r has been rearranged to appear chronologically.
[3] The first of two diary entries for 6 Sept. – the first is a brief summary, and the second is a fuller account.
[4] Castle Howard, seat of the brother of the Earl of Wicklow (Wright, *Wicklow*, p. 71); the Colonel Howard mentioned here is probably Colonel Hugh Howard (1761–1840).
[5] Sir Robert Hodson of Hollybrook, 1747–1809 (*Burke's Peerage*, 1832, I, p. 617).
[6] Peter Latouche of Bellevue, ?1775–1830 (History of Parliament Online).
[7] See p. 109, n. 4, for Tighe of Rossanagh.

Saturday. [6 September]

Started ¼ before 10. Bill 12:3[.] Waiter and Maid 3:4[.] Washing. Breeches Gaitors Waistcoat Cravat 1:1[.] Uncommon good accommodation at Mr Quinns house beds excellent.[1] Pass Mr Kirkwoods H*ouse*[2] on the L. 'And how far is it to Sir R Hudsons.' 'Sir Mr Hudsons Sir I declare and vow I don't know any such person Sir.' Little Sugar Loaf has 3 tops [when viewed] fr*om* this road[.]

[f. 43v] Upon enquiry find I had got the wrong road, but resolved not to go back to Bray and ∴ went down a lane on the R. NB ask your way fr*om* every Cabin or person you see and draw your own conclusion for its 1000:1 if you meet with 1 person who can direct you ½ a mile right or who knows so far about him as to give you a clear intelligent account of the road. Go across the fields to the R constantly and a path brings you on the right road ab*ou*t 1¼ M*iles* from Bray. Go on further pass Dr Sands H*ouse* and Lodge on L[.]

NB. On the L of the Scalp ab*ou*t a mile and ½ from road find a silver and lead mine wh*ic*h had been examined for 3 or 4 days specimens[.][3]

Sir Roberts house. Pond supplied with a river wh*ic*h carries fr*om* the Sugar Loaf and runs into the Dargle by the Bridge so the rock go*es* thro*ugh* the grounds thro*ugh* plantations and from it you see the Kilruddery E*arl* of Meath. The (hill) Head of Bray Bray Town, Part of land on wh*ic*h monument, Hill of Howth beyond. The hill where [there is the] mine, Scalp, Jous [Djouce] mountains where [there are] the waterfalls, Glan Cree [Glencree] mountains long strait ones where [there] was a camp in the rebellions, a wonderful fine great building for soldiers[.][4]

[f. 44r *blank*]

[f. 44v] Sir Robe*rt* [Hodson] was Lieut*enant* Colo*nel* of the Cavan militia[.] He had a corporals guard C*orps* and [20 men?] in house at [the] time of [the] rebellion, some of his reg*ime*nt [were] in Dublin, Some [were] in Arclow [Arklow] 12 miles bey*on*d Wicklow, some in Wicklow. Rebels never came nearer than Newtown M*oun*t Kennedy, nothing was disturbed here 'not a haputh'.[5]

'How old are you[?]' 'Indeed I don't know rightly[.]' (Ab*ou*t 16 years of age.) 'Dont you know y*ou*r birthday[?]' 'It was on the 1st Sunday of harvest[.]' He could not read or write well[.]

Fern with edge on leaves like saws[.]

'Where are we now[?]' ('Oh we are now quite convenient to the house [Hollybrook]') Evergreens are most beautiful. Cypresses. House quite gutted and building an addition to. About ½ mile on is a common with a fine ash on it close to road go to the R to go up the Sugarloaf. Beautiful Burial ground old Church in ruins no roof.[6] But tops cov*er*ed with trees of ivy, small, round door on 1 side and a pretty arch in the E end both perfect wh*ic*h forms a division in the middle[.] Gravestones all about in and round the ruin. In style

---

[1] 'Quin's famous hotel; his house is large, and kept with neatness, regularity, and elegance' (Wright, *Wicklow*, p. 8).

[2] James Kirkwood of Newcourt (Wilson, *Post-Chaise Companion*, p. 423).

[3] Probably meaning that people had searched there for precious metals during the Wicklow 'gold rush' described below, p. 139.

[4] Members of the United Irishmen hid in the Wicklow Mountains during and after the failed rebellion of 1798. The barracks at Glencree was built in 1806 (NIAH).

[5] 'not a halfpenny worth'.

[6] Probably the ruined 12th-century church at Kilmacanogue.

exactly like that at Old Connaught, but on a small scale and has a wall round it with no trees. Roman Catholic and Protestant buried there indiscriminately.

[f. 45r *blank*]

[f. 45v] Walk on to the entrance of the glen[.] The Sugar Loaf looks well from here. Most lovely cottage of Mr Latouches[1] and the room laid out in a pretty country style. Go through the pleasure grounds in the valley and looking up on the L see a house built as if for the prospect, cross the brook and make through the trees directly up to it. Mountain side, rough, stony steep and difficult[.] Great inconvenience from the young oaks which continually caught hold of my knap sack. Halted for breath many times and came out at the foot of the Prospect house from whence most extensive views beyond the Scalp and other side of the country and all round towards Wicklow. The mountain opposite beautifully wooded here and there a bare slaty appearance. Walk on to the R pass a pretty cottage and keep descending round the [hill?] and see all the sea to Wicklow head, Delgany Church[.] All about Newtown Mount Kennedy[.] Go to the [Turkish?] Stand.[2] Go back to the Old womans cottage[3] charming ('and I dare say you are as happy as a king[.]' 'Oh Glory to God very happy and I have the best master and mistress in the world[.]'). Curious seat made by Old Mr Latouche. Her neat cottage and bedroom[,] 2 beds[,] [for] her and [her] son. She laughed and [grinned?] and said she was 3 score and six. (and only pains in her legs and I should be [stout?]) 'My strength is going very fast.'

[f. 46r *blank*]

[f. 46v] The octagon has 5 windows[.][4] The tops fine stained glass and shutters of looking glass so that you may see all variety of views. Room upstairs kitchen and a little place for pantry 'where I keep some old potatoes because it is cool' and she laughed merrily[.] She was particular in shewing me how her son had made her a little garden on above rock and how nice her cabbages were growing. Dining room below[.] She saw the army going by but Glory be to God she never saw a man killed. Gave her 10d[.] 'I am most obliged to you Sir and if you had not given me a farthing you would be welcome.'

Go round other side of mountain[.] Ice house[.] Rocks on one side and among the trees is seen the whole range of county to the sea[.]

'Glory be to God I am the happiest old woman in the country[.] I have a good master and mistress and they no more say an angry word to me than you do and they do not trouble me but give me a fine house to live in and cloaths [clothes] etc[.]'

She got over a wall and offered and begged to take my hand and help me up[.]

3 Acres in the gardens in all, 16 men constantly at work and some times 20, 22.

2 large peach trees Orange house Grapery Greenhouse Pinery Cherry house all in a string[.] On each [f. 47r *blank*] [f. 47v] side of the Gardners house an early Peachhouse and a succession house for Pine Plants[.]

---

[1] Bellevue (see p. 111, n. 6).

[2] Possibly the 'pretty seat ... sheltered by trees, consisting of drapery and ornaments in the style of an eastern pavilion' in Bellevue Demesne (Wright, *Wicklow*, p. 36).

[3] This old woman's 'chief employments [were] the care of the octagon room, and to attend upon visiters [*sic*]' to Bellevue Demesne (Wright, *Wicklow*, p. 37).

[4] The 'Octagon Temple' or 'Octagon House' at Bellevue, 'a small building, raised upon a rock in an extremely exposed and elevated situation ... there is here a small but judicious selection of books, and some few shells and minerals', built in 1766 (Wright, *Wicklow*, pp. 34, 37).

In Sir Charles Hudsons Ground (mossy ground) *Anthericum ossifragum* [*Narthecium ossifragum*, bog asphodel] or *Adiantum capillus nigris*[.][1]

Just near the garden grows *Serapis helleborine*[.][2]

The hair [hare's] tail rush

Utricularia vulgaris [common bladderwort] grows in a bog near the house

Pinguicula vulgaris [butterwort] common about

Cochlearia officinalis [scurvy grass] close by at sea shore

Anthirhinum cymbellaris [*Antirrhinum cymbalaria*] from the South of Powerscourt on gravel

White digitalis

Circea lutetiana [enchanter's nightshade]

Aster montanus[3] on side of Glen of Downs

Serapis veredis [*Serapis veridis*] close by the house

Polypodeum cristum [*Polypodium cristatum* – a type of fern]

Alchemilla vulgaris [common lady's mantle], Statice (*Armeria*) common on the shore [*Fursulago*][4] (*officinalis*) common

Osmunda regalis [royal fern]. *Orobanche* [broomrape]

Asperula odorata [sweet woodruff]

176 yds of Glass in length straight. This passage is 64 yds long Mr Mannings taken from it[.] House very fine. The place is one of the finest I ever saw. More Glass houses I never saw[.][5]

[f. 48r *blank*]

[f. 48v] Getting out of the Gates of the Lodge the road to the L takes [you] to Delgenny [Delgany] Church, a fine beautiful building well worth the inspection of anyone. Was built by Mr Latouche.[6] The trees around *which* are fine. It is not far from [the] river or a bank. Several cabins very beautiful. One with rose trees, honey suckles etc growing round it[.]

Straw roofs and whitewashed white chimney and white edge on top[.][7]

Return back to lodge[.]

Very pretty village by a bridge[.][8]

Drommin [Drummin] Councillor Barringtons lodge on the L of the road and his house is seen[.]

'How far to Newtown*mountkennedy*[?]' 'Not far[.]'

Good white house on the R with a noble ash to see at the lodge gate.

On the R beyond is Lady Harriet Dalys *House*[9] [Bromley] one of the prettiest cottages I had seen in Ireland[.]

---

[1] Probably *Adiantum capillus-veneris*, the black maidenhair fern.
[2] A species of orchid.
[3] A genus of flowering plants, with daisy-like flowers.
[4] Possibly *Ferulago* (fennel).
[5] The conservatory at Bellevue, 264ft long, 'an object of much attraction to visiters [*sic*]' (Wright, *Wicklow*, p. 40), built by the politician and banker Peter Latouche (see p. 111, n. 6).
[6] Christ Church, Delgany, built in 1789 by the politician and banker Peter Latouche (see p. 111, n. 6).
[7] Lee roughly sketched the roof in the page margin, not reproduced here.
[8] Probably Delgany.
[9] Née Maxwell, m. Denis Daly, politician.

A house of Mr Bell on the L. NB all the houses have regular lodges to them. Just beyond a fine white house on oppos*ite* side of road. NB all the houses are white with fine slate tops. Never saw any part of England to = [the] County of Wicklow[.] So far it has all the hills of Wales. All the fertility of Liestershire [*sic*] and all the good houses in the neighbourhood of Cov*entry* ~~and all the~~ without the filth[.] All the fine scenery of the sea[.]

[f. 49r *blank*]

[f. 49v] Mr Guns place formerly the place of Lord Rusmore called M*ou*nt Kennedy.[1] Come to 3 roads meet with a noble ash. Go to the R. The grounds hereabout want rolling to improve them.

The road is very beautifully shaded by the trees of Mr Guns grounds all the way to Newtown M*ou*nt Kennedy[.] His place is called M*ou*nt Kennedy. All the houses of the place are very pretty white washed and roof of straw and they look as if quite new. Only 1 Cabin at the farthest end of the town was burnt down in the rebellion on the Newry Bridge road. The ancient Britons had been out the preceeding day scouring the mountains and had killed a great many men of them. They returned tired in the Evening and about 1 OClock when every body thought the neighbourhood looked empty of them they came in all directions in n° ab*ou*t 1500 with fire arms and pikes and des*cendi*ng on the town. Their chief force was fr*o*m Newry Bridge road and just in the narrow part of the street by the Market house was the grand struggle[.] There (were) 40 of the North Britons (about) 40 of the Antrim Militia, some few cavalry and some Band men as they were called from not having any regiments but only red bands in their hats and they had got their arms given them the preceding even*ing*[.] These were the forces in the town but not more than 40 were engaged, all the rest being in bed, some tired of the preceeding days work. The rebels tried to set the market house on fire but were prevented[.] The band men began the Engagement when the rebels were [got?] in the Town. Some piqucts[2] just gave a little notice of their approach and some of the North Britons were ready just opposite the market house[.] Capt*ain* Burganey[3] a young man on horseback was killed[.] His horse ran in among the enemy[.]

[f. 50r] Mr Armstrong a Tanner Brother in law to Mrs Archer of the inn and who was in Capt*ain* Gores Cavalry[4] at that time told me this how it is Capt*ain* Archers[5][*breaks off*]

Captain Gore was wounded and left for dead being kicked all over the belly but he recovered. Their sudden approach and numbers obliged the troops to retreat out of the town over the bridge as far as some tall elm trees which may be easily seen from the Inn[,] There being joined by a reinforcement of 15 (Cavalry I believe) from Mount Kennedy[.]

---

[1] George Gunn inherited Mount Kennedy after the death of his uncle, Lieutenant-General Robert Cunningham (d. 1801), Lord Rossmore of Monaghan (Atkinson, *The Irish Tourist*, p. 603).

[2] Pickets, i.e., small detachments (*OED*).

[3] Captain John Burganey, leading a company of Ancient Britons, died during the Battle of Newtown-mountkennedy on 30 May 1798 (O'Donnell, *Rebellion in Wicklow*, pp. 185–6).

[4] The mostly Protestant Newtownmountkennedy Cavalry, under Captain Robert Gore (O'Donnell, *Rebellion in Wicklow*, p. 129).

[5] Captain Thomas Archer succeeded Gore (see previous note) as commander of the Newtownmountkennedy Cavalry following Gore's injury at the Battle of Newtownmountkennedy (O'Donnell, *Rebellion in Wicklow*, p. 188).

They rallied and when they came up with the enemy below the market house they did charge them and broke them and were driving them all over the country until day break but [there were] only about 40 men in the actual engagement[.] Before this reinforcement the cavalry were ordered to charge which was impossible. They rode up within 6 yds of the rebels fired their pistols and then retired[.] Between the Bridge and the market place about 200 pikes were picked up which they had thrown away in the first beginning of their retreat. They had possession of the town for about 10 minutes. Only 1 man Captain Burganey was killed and of the Rebels about 80 bodies were found but many of the killed were secreted by the people of the place before the soldiers could find them. They were buried in holes and gravel pits any how. Got to the Inn at 7 OClock[.]

[f. 50v] **Sunday [7 September]**
Started at 3[.] Road from the 17 milestone on the L to the mountains[.] Pass Mr Hodkins house[1] on the side of the Hill. Cross a bridge and then begin to ascend the mountain side. On the road side on [the] L Mr Carthys House and at some short distance on R Mr Jessops (Hermitage)[.][2] Children without shoes or stockings or [hat?][.]

Higher up Mr Williams gate[.]

A man overtook me who in the rebellion 8 years ago, lived at a cabin on [the] roadside between Baltinglass and Blessington and was a labourer of Mr Hume.[3] He had 7 small children and ∴ was not a soldier. Mr Hume [was] a very good man and always told him never to go to the mountains for he would get shot and many were who did not follow his advice. They shot Mr Hume at the head of his army, for he was a colonel and was over the Cavalry and over the militia and over the infantry. He saw a power of soldiers go by the road and Thanks be to God none of the cars or carts and carriages ever ran over any of his children.[4] He now lives at Newtown and was then coming to pay for some peat which they brought him yesterday evening[.]

On top of mountain heaps of black peat heaped up all along[.]

'[The?] Master has married an English woman and she speaks very much like you Sir[.]'
//

Another man[:] 'How much is that bushel of peat worth[?]' '2:8½ Sir[.]' 'How many pieces are there[?]' 'Oh tis sold by admeasurement Sir.' 'How much does it measure[?]' '4 Beer Barrels full Sir.' 2 other men confirmed it who were drawing similar carts with baskets[.]

Cross a flat on the mountain and see very large peat digging[.] The whole flat from parts which remain must have been levelled about 2 feet and the low part is mostly wet and boggy. Cross a bridge of 3 plain arches [f. 51r *blank*] [f. 51v] and a very picturesque old cabin by it. Stream rapid[.] From the extraordinary greenness of the fir trees about it the land must be wonderfully rich. The turf is and all refitable soil for a great thickness[.] I did not see the depth of it. Road to the bridge turns to L[.] Rain all the day from 4 in the morning[.]

Scattered poor cabins all along the road[.]

[1] Possibly Hawkins (Wright, *Wicklow*, p. 49).
[2] Lee has erroneously recorded these two residences. The Hermitage was the property of General Carey; Jessop lived at Tinny Park (Wright, *Wicklow*, pp. 48–9).
[3] Captain William Hume (1747–98), Whig MP for Wicklow in the Irish parliament; killed in a skirmish in the 1798 rebellion (Burke, *Landed Gentry*, 1847, I, p. 616).
[4] This sentence is an example of Lee recording snippets of conversation with locals, and their colloquialisms.

DIARY 2: TOUR FROM HOLYWELL TO DUBLIN AND FERMOY

NB Mr Jessops house [Tinny Park] above ment*ione*d very advantageously situated. Woods behind it and the mountain above them and a noble view f*ro*m the front door on the hills ab*ou*t Newtown[.]
/

After asking the common questions for the road and receiving directions 'I Thank you.' 'You are welcome' is the usual reply. 'And a pleasant journey to you Sir[.]' The white *Polygala* [white milkwort] and 2 other curious plants just above the road ⊥^{r} to that *fro*m Dublin to M*ountain*s to the L. C̄ | C

Some fine handsome white goats all about here[.] I had seen them in diff*eren*t places before on the mountains[.]

From hence go over the mountain side to the R slanting a little forward and you cut off an L of the road and wh*ic*h turns to the R. You come into it again but cannot help admiring some of the most beautiful mosses wh*ic*h grow all about on the loose stones. At last after mounting a long steep hill you come to Mr La Touches Gate[1] wh*ic*h lead*s* you into his grounds and here you see a most beautiful view of noble mountains and a very fine glen with streams running down it in all directions[.] 2 streams *fro*m 2 diff*eren*t parts of the mountain [f. 52r] opposite join it ran down the valley to a lake beyond. The road winds on and at turning a point at the rock you see a lake [Lough Tay] of the blackest water at the foot of a ⊥^{r} mountain [Luggala] and the oppo*site* M*ountain* is cov*ere*d with young woods. I expected to see the house every minute[.] When turning another point you see before you the whole of the Glen and no house[.] The road seems to end at a wood, beyond wh*ic*h appears a fine luxuriant vale with greenest verdure and some trees among it. This seems to end it all but a town is not far off. Go thro*ugh* wood and in it have a noble point view of the opposite ⊥^{r} hill. Go thro*ugh* wood and come among the pleasure grounds and see the house close by a noisy roaring waterfall[.]

[The] Lower lake [is] not so wide as the upper but [is] longer by far and is 2 miles *fro*m the House[.] Lough Dan is its name. The upper lake is Called Luggila[2] Lake and is 85 Acres[.]

The Game Keeper there has lived with Mr Latouche 6 years 9th of last June. In the rebellion he was at Killala (near) where he was born at Kappa [Kappagh] Castle. All this country was quiet during the rebellion until the French landed at Killala Bay the 22 August.[3] Early in the morning saw some ship in the [offing?] and they hoisted French colours. 3 (very large) Frigates and a sloop like he believes 74 or 84S.[4] ~~When they~~ They hovered about in the bay and sailed tow*ards* Killibegs [Killybegs] in the county of Donnegal [Donegal] and the 3rd time they came round and cast anchor 1 by 1 in a line they then had out their long boats and the sloop and sent them back and forw*ards* to Kilkummen [Kilcummin] a point of land as if for fresh$_1$ water$_2$[5] but in reality were landing men and [f. 52v] ammunition. The boats ~~and rebels~~ wh*ic*h went out to these 2 Boats were of course detained one boat had some sea coast officers and some of the Prince of Wales

---

[1] Luggala Lodge, the hunting lodge of the La Touches of Bellevue, the house at which Lee will stay on this night.
[2] The mountain is Luggala; the lake at its base is Lough Tay.
[3] For more on the landing of the French force of around 1,030 men under General Humbert at Killala, Co. Mayo in 1798, see Murtagh, 'General Humbert's Futile Campaign'.
[4] A 74 or 84 gun ship of the line; warships were classified by the number of guns carried. Thanks to Dr Christopher Ware for information on this.
[5] Word order reversed here as indicated by Lee's subscript numbering.

fencibles[.] Kilcummen 4 or 5 miles from Killala. Then they came by Palmerston. Seat of Mr Brown[1] and by Castle Blake the seat of Major Knox.[2] Marched on forwards to Killala[.] His Brother was taken at Mr Knox['s house]. People were all day under arms but from the town they could not see them land nor did a soul know how things were going on for every body met was taken prisoner[.]

People were under arms but loitering about the town the first thing discovered them was when they [were] in the bottom of the town coming in to the street and they shot a man of the name (Henry) Rogers. He was a volunteer and being rather tipsey he went up to one of the French officers and asked him 'Where the spying rascals were going' for he took them for this. He was then shot. The next person shot was Hall Smith an apothecary who was also in his accoutrements[.] He fired 3 or 4 rounds at them and wounded some of them. They soon they got possession of the town and the few who could get out of the town and made the best of the way towards Ballena [Ballina]. About 8 or 9 oClock the next day every one was preparing. Picquets [Pickets] were stationed. But the French were busy landing their stores and securing themselves and did not come. The 2nd day Piquets fought and a Mr Fortescue.[3] The 3rd day about 12 OClock they came and had a battle, not above 3 or 4 killed and many of the French. Volunteers regulars etc not [f. 53r] above 400. The French had 800 besides all the rebels[.] They surrounded the town and Foxword [Foxford] Road they stopped but by road over the Bridge to Sligo many escaped. However they took him and about 20 men and made a prison of Colonel Kings house and put 2 centuries [sentries] over them. They laid down their arms and the French soldiers came up and said *Prisoner Englais* [*Prisonnier Anglais* – English prisoner]. Here they were kept 3 Weeks. They kept them well. They gave them bread meat salt Potatoes etc for 2 weeks during [the] time the French had them but when they only had a French guard to protect them and the place was in rebels hand they only [had] meat boiled. After 3 Week or on 23 of September their guards and rebels ran away[.] On going out they found the English coming into the Town. No battle what ever they knew nothing what was going on but could only guess by the signs and behaviour the days before that all was not right with them. The rebels visited but dare not beat the prisoners but through the windows called them all names[.] They could hear the rebels talk when they had gained any advantage over the English Army. Immediately on being let loose he joined the soldiers and marched with them to Killala the same day and retook Killala, he joined and fell in with the Prince of Wales fencibles. Nothing but a skirmish for the French were but guards then and a few others, their main body having been taken before. The chief battle was with the rebels there all [of] whom they shot. The French let the Rebels fight and they all went into the castle. There were not more than about 12 and [f. 53v] mostly officers for they were put over the rebels [whom?] they commanded. One other Brother was taken prisoner with him fighting. He had 2 other Brothers who fled to Sligo and who afterwards fought all the way to Killala and there all 5 Brothers met and their Father who had been all the time at Kappa Castle and an old man and ∴ not heeded by the French.

They say nothing is venemous in Ireland, but the little midge fly which is the smallest of the sort I ever saw and in vast quantities is 50 times more troublesome than any

---

[1] Palmerstown House, an 18th-century house with later adaptations (NIAH); John, 4th Earl of Mayo (1766–1849) (Debrett, *Peerage*, II, p. 955).

[2] John Knox of Castlereagh (1783–1861) (LED); Lee has recorded the seat wrongly.

[3] Rev. George Fortescue (1769–98), rector of Killala (Hogan, '1798 Remembered', p. 2).

venemous snakes *could* possibly be. For they will get to any part *which* is not covered and sting In the hair or any where.

The Church by Mr Latouches is a beautiful slated glass window at the R side of the *Church*. There is a fine mon*ument* of the late Mr Latouche and the present and his 2 Brothers and Mr Latouches former wife. The father is standing up and the 3 sons all sitting about at his feet. The lady is leaning and has her hand round the cornucopia[.][1]

[f. 54r] Farewell the scenes of joy and bliss
Where fancy loves to dwell
Farewell the groves and rocky springs
and Deep sequestered dell

Oft shall the mind by memory led
Oer thy wild Beauties stray
Each favourite haunt and cliff explore
In pensive extasy

For as soft music moves the soul
Past joys the thoughts beguile
Tho starts th' involuntary fear
The heart is seen to smile

For home shall for the throbbing breast
Th' assosiates dear erase
Who gave each wild fantastic scene
The matchless power to please

———————————

And with these scenes their virtuous lord
Our fond remembrance shares
Who to misfortune solace yields
and pining misery shields

———————————

Ici vient la Bonté qui désarme l'envie
Rend ses droits au malheur; l'équilibre à la vie
Corrige les saisons; laisse à l'infortuné
Quelques épis du champ par ses mains sillonné
Comble enfin par ses dons cette utile intervalle
Que met entre les rangs la fortune inégale[2]
Vous donnez ou qui de tel retraite la joye est etrangere
Faites y le bien (comme La Touche) et tout va vous pleine[3]

[1] The Latouche monument, Delgany Church, Co. Wicklow, erected in 1790 (Crookshank, *Irish Sculpture*, p. 29).

[2] An English translation of these lines from Jacques Delille's *l'Homme des Champs* (1800) is in Maunde, *The Rural Philosopher*, p. 23: 'Then should thy bounty cover envy's spite, / Give life its balance, and misfortune right; / Correct the seasons, and allow the poor / That field to glean his hands have furrow'd o'er; / Fill by its gifts the long, though useful, space, / That into different ranks divides our race.'

[3] The final two lines do not appear to be related to Delille's *l'Homme des Champs* (see previous note) and were most likely added by the sculptor. Translation: 'You give where joy is a stranger to those in this retreat, / Do good there (like La Touche) and much will come to you.'

[f. 54v] **Monday. [8 September]**
[*margin:* Mrs Cray 5:5]

Slept in a delightful room through whose window in the morning I saw the noble shepherd up hill with its sloping side and with the sun shining on its top. Walked out among the grounds go over two planks under which is the course of a noisy torrent which comes roaring down the hillside. Farther on the walk leads to another river which after winding through the hillside joins the other and they [*blank*]. The walks go down to the lakeside over a rustic bridge heaped up of old loose stones 2 arches then in an island. Large masses of marble rock lay about the bottom in irresistible beauty[.] Leave the house at ¼ past 11 cross the water all behind the house and ascend up a very steep hill from where is one of the finest views I ever saw[.] The lake, and cultivated meadow on this side almost ⊥ʳ mountain on 1 side of it and sloping ones on other and fine ones in the distance[.] A pretty river running through the meadow into the lake. The house just at the edge of the hill below me.

A large peat bog on the top of [the] mountain by turning along a road which leads to the turf bog instead of keeping on right forward I got on the bog and was obliged to cross it for about 400 yds and that was as much bog as I ever wish to go over. In some parts this vegetable soil [is] 6 feet thick and more but it was cut through so deep [f. 55r *blank*] [f. 55v] (NB it rained all yesterday) glad to get on the road. In every slope of Mountain runs down a torrent and crossed many of these which pass over the road. Step from stone to stone. Some you must walk through. Country (Mountains) I should think impassable unless well known. NB draw a Basket of turf in a cart. Wild and savage hills[.]

The sands all about here shine and the roads. They must be silver. Silver mines at Luggalor. Cross the Military Road[1] and dreary prospect. Not a town not a tree not a person in view[.]

Mr Rolands house[.] Story of rebels[.] Beef and milk[.]

While I was observing this I suddenly saw a party of soldiers making across the bogs from the opposite hill with 3 countrymen. Surprised to see them in that situation and coming directly to me, and stopped and when they got on the road, one [of] the sergeants asked me if it was the road to Blessing Town [Blessington], they had come across from Bray and the boors conducted me across the bogs. The sergeant was a very civil clever fellow[.] They belonged to the Wicklow militia and he was in all this country in the time of the rebellion. This road which I thought impassable he remembers many carts and cannon taken over it. Passed by an old building which I took at first for a church but examining it and seeing above a pool where had been a head of water concluded it was the remains of some factory. A little farther on saw some cottages in ruins where the rebels left a quantity of pots pans, and fires with the Beef boiling etc and plenty of milk in all sorts of vessels, and fled to the opposite mountain where their chief body was. All this was a scene of warfare and they had 21 companies of sharp shooters onto each side of the road. He pointed to where they had a camp[2]

---

[1] 200 soldiers were employed in the construction of the Military Road from Aug. 1800; by Apr. 1806, 30 miles of road had been completed, extending from Rathfarnham, Co. Dublin to Drumgoff barrack at Glenmalure, Co. Wicklow (Kerrigan, *Castles and Fortifications*, p. 180).

[2] The narrative continues at f. 56v.

DIARY 2: TOUR FROM HOLYWELL TO DUBLIN AND FERMOY

[f. 56r] [*Start one page rough pencil notes.*] Kippure[.] Mr Latouches shooting house[.] Water courses[.]

Major Welsh lives in the Marquis of Downshires lodge[.][1] He rents it[.] The house was burnt – [***]

Burgage cross and the near mountain Baltiboys River Liffey runs under it

[f. 56v] at one time and where at another. Their men *coul*d never come up to the rebels. They went with incredible speed over the *mountai*ns and always fled before them. From Blackamoor [Blackmore] hill near ~~Waterford~~ Blessington where the rebels had a camp they came in flights across to Wilp [Whelp] Rock and *from* there being pursued along that side and fled over the oppo*site* side of the river to the hills beyond the Ponsonbys shooting Box.[2]

Ab*ou*t a mile beyond this there are some miserable cottages and the valley is cultivated potatoes and corn and the river runs along the valley very tolerably, there were many watercourses to cross all the way but to my surprize we came to a place where it was necessary to ford the river itself. Accordingly all the soldiers took off their shoes and stockings and I foll*ow*ed their example[.] It was not higher than the knees but the stream was very strong [could] hardly stand and the stones were uncommonly pointed and sharp and se*ver*al after said they *woul*d not undergo such punishment again for any sum. Ascend a hill[3] and ab*ou*t 4 miles off is Balsington [Blessington] just seen but soon lost again. Farther on a sketch of Wilp Rocks.[4] Farther on some old mines appear and the place called I believe (the 3 castles)[.][5] Showers all the way some very bad. Pretty view of Bridge river hills and C*hur*ch and Town of Blessington[.] C*hur*ch very neat. Houses all new for the rebels burnt it down f*a*r as Blackamoor hill a fine [f. 57r *blank*] [f. 57v] place for their camp. There were thousands there and in Blessington not a soul who *coul*d walk there staid. Only children. Men women boys and girls went to their camp. Some shells were fired at the camp and when the rebels despersed [*sic*] 6 camps of cavalry charged up the hill[.] There were fo*un*d there 76 head of oxen, Material of all sorts tents all the Marquess of Downshires furniture.[6] His house near Blessingtown they burnt and it is now a skeleton and shot his deer and broke down the park walls[.][7] A Major Welsh now rents a lodge there[.]

Old Court [Oldcourt] is the village just before you come to Blessingtown[.]

On the left is a house at the foot of the M*ou*ntain called Baltiboys [Baltyboys] and the smaller mountain behind it goes by that name also. On the L not far off between Blessintown and Baltiboys is Burgage cross,[8] a cross erected *whi*ch may be seen *from* the road. The river Liffey runs all up this valley. On the L but nearer to the road is ~~Ballymore~~

---

[1] See n. 6 below.
[2] George Ponsonby (1755–1817), Lord Chancellor of Ireland and MP for Wicklow (Kelly, 'Ponsonby, George'), with estate lands at Goldenhill, Co. Wicklow.
[3] Possibly Black Hill.
[4] See SJC, MS U.30 (6), f. 54r (p. 317); reproduced at p. 122 (Figure 6).
[5] The townland of Three Castles.
[6] Arthur Hill, 2nd Marquess of Downshire (1753–1801) (Kelly, 'Hill, Wills').
[7] Blessington House, built by Archbishop Boyle in 1672 and destroyed by fire during the 1798 rebellion, as described by Lee here. See de Breffny, 'Building of the Mansion'.
[8] Possibly the cross base at Burgage, Blessington, said to have been about 14 feet (4.3 metres) in height (Lewis, *Topographical Dictionary*, I, p. 206).

Figure 6. 'View on the road within 3 miles of Blessingtown of the Welp [Whelp] rock from some cottages[.] At this spot the shower came on and while my companions the soldiers were sheltering themselves, this was scetched [*sic*]', as described in SJC, MS U.30 (2), f. 56v (p. 121). By John Lee, 8 September 1806 (SJC, MS U.30 (6), f. 54r). Reproduced by kind permission of the Master and Fellows of St John's College, Cambridge.

Rushborough Lord Miltowns House[.][1] There are some fine woods close by and in these woods the military used to have frequent skirmishes with the rebels who swarmed all over the neighbouring hills and would come so near, although the house was used as a barracks and always had many hundred soldiers in it. The sergeant of the Wicklow militia told me they used constantly to go out to clear the woods and that the men called it going cock shooting[.] There were 8 men of the Wicklow militia and we all came together to Blessingtown[.]

[f. 58r *blank*]

[f. 58v] The Inn was written on the side of a door in the town and glad I was to get to it for rather tired walking beyond my usual pace to keep up with the soldiers and it is a terrible long 12 Irish miles. However the Inn was nothing but an appendage to a grocers shop. A Grocer kept his shop and this house of call[2] also and I was obliged to go into the shop to get anybody to come to the door. Just saw the bedrooms and the order of the house and immediately resolved to march forward to Ballymore [Ballymore Eustace] 3½ further where the accommodations could not be worse and there I found them very good. Passed several gentlemans houses which were reduced to mere skeletons in the rebellion and still remained so. One on the R must have been a beautiful spot and had a noble view[.]

Got to Ballymore Eustace about six oclock. The sergeant who came to drink with me at Blessingtown told me that he and his men could not get (room billeted) accommodations there and that they had all resolved to go forward to Balting Glass [Baltinglass]. All this part of the country he shewed me where the enemy [was,] where and when our forces were encamped etc and said there was not a more wretched place than all this was[.] NB After crossing from Wilp Rock to the Mountains beyond Mr Ponsonbys shooting Box the rebels went toward Vinegar Hill. They were armed with musquets pistols swords pikes bludgeons hooks, scythes etc etc[.] Treated the soldiers with Porter, Bread and Butter 1:2½. We all came on together to Baltimore[3] and got there about 6 oclock[.]

[f. 59r] **Tuesday. [9 September]**
Walked up to the Church before Breakfast which is in ruins[.] All the roof is in pieces and the wood work still stands. In the church yard is a large stone pillar with a round (shaped) head and 2 circular rims round it in the middle as ambo[4] and one also but smaller in the pillar itself the date 1682 and some other writing is on the opposite part of the top but not legible.[5] The church I was told was destroyed by a troop of horse who made it

---

[1] Russborough House, built in 1741–8 (NIAH), commissioned by Joseph Leeson, 1st Earl of Milltown (*c.*1701–83). Lee refers here to Brice, 3rd Earl of Milltown (1735–1807) though he spells the name Miltown. (Beaumont, 'Leeson, Joseph').

[2] A 'house where journeymen of a particular trade assemble, where carriers call for commissions, or where a person may be heard of or contacted' (*OED*).

[3] Lee must mean Ballymore Eustace.

[4] A pulpit or reading-desk in early Christian churches (*OED*).

[5] The medieval Christian monastic remains in the Church of Ireland churchyard in Ballymore Eustace, with two surviving 'high crosses'; one, the 'northern cross', fits Lee's description, including an inscription recording its re-erection in 1689. See Manning, 'The Inscription', p. 112. Lee sketched this cross at SJC, MS U.30 (6), f. 3r (p. 309), not reproduced here.

their stable but instead of pulling off the roof one w*ou*ld have thought they w*ou*ld have wished it on.

No necessity for asking w*hic*h in a place in Ireland for only 1 in a place[.]

[f. 59v] Bill for Tea Bed Breakfast 3. Maid 10ᵈ[.]

Go to Lord Milltowns[.]

The highlanders[1] were stationed in Lord Milltowns house and the Durham fencibles and the Wicklow, a company of the Waterford Westmeath Leitrim militia[.] It was made a barracks[.][2]

The house consists of 2 fine wings in the front line from wh*ence* the house is retired by 2 circular arcades in the arches of wh*ich* are placed marble figures.[3] Beyond the wings and connected by walls are arches and beyond connected by walls [are] smaller wings. Gardens in ruins. Inside of house fine oak floors. Beautiful pictures[:] Sir Jos*hua* Reynolds,[4] Van Dyke[5] Guerchino[6] Rubens[7] Carlo Maratti[8] Gian Paolo Panini[9] [f. 60r][10] Dominichino,[11] Pompeo Batoni,[12] Teniers,[13] Gasparo,[14] Poussin,[15] Felice Reposto,[16] Luca Giordano,[17] Empoli,[18] Andrea del Sarto,[19] Wouwerman[20] Salvador Rosa[21] Rubens P.

---

[1] Highland Fencible Corps.

[2] In 1798, rebels took hold of Russborough House, to be shortly afterwards replaced by the British army, who occupied it until 1801 (Ryan, *Story of Russborough*, p. 13).

[3] The following 12 Classical figures: Jupiter, Ceres, Hercules, Bacchus, Venus, Saturn, Diana, a Faun, Tragedy, Comedy, Mercury and Apollo (Wright, *Wicklow*, p. 149).

[4] Sir Joshua Reynolds (1723–92), painter and art theorist. 'Three caricatures' (Wright, *Wicklow*, p. 150).

[5] Peter Vandyke (also Pieter Van Dyke) (1729–99), Dutch-born painter. Two portraits, one of Prince Rupert (Wright, *Wicklow*, p. 150); 'St Sebastian' (Neale, *Views of the Seats*, III, n.p.).

[6] Giovanni Francesco Barbieri, also Guercino (1591–1666), Italian painter (Zirpolo, *Historical Dictionary*, p. 258). 'Lot and his Daughters' (Wright, *Wicklow*, p. 150); 'Noon and Night' and 'St Agatha' (Neale, *Views of the Seats*, III, n.p.).

[7] Sir Peter Paul Rubens (1577–1640), Flemish baroque painter. 'Bacchanalians', 'Wild-Boar Hunt', 'Herodias, with John the Baptist's Head' and 'Judgment of Paris' (Wright, *Wicklow*, p. 150); 'Charity' (Neale, *Views of the Seats*, III, n.p.).

[8] Carlo Maratta (also Maratti) (1625–1713), 'Holy Family' (Neale, *Views of the Seats*, III, n.p.).

[9] Giovanni Paolo Panini (1691–1765), Italian painter. 'Two pictures, the Ruins of Rome' (Neale, *Views of the Seats*, III, n.p.).

[10] The paragraphs of f. 60r have been re-ordered for continuity.

[11] Domenichino (also Domenico Zampieri) (1581–1641), 'Adam and Eve' (Neale, *Views of the Seats*, III, n.p.).

[12] Pompeo Batoni (1708–87), Italian painter. 'Diana', 'Venus and Cupid', 'A Portrait', 'A Shepherdess', 'Portrait of Lord Milltown' and 'David with Goliath's Head' (Neale, *Views of the Seats*, III, n.p.).

[13] 'A Dutch Merriment' (Wright, *Wicklow*, p. 150). Possibly Cornelius Dusart, 'A Merry-Making' (1692) (Potterton, *Dutch Seventeenth and Eighteenth Century Paintings*, p. 40).

[14] Gasparo Lopez (1650–1732), Italian painter.

[15] Nicholas Poussin (1594–1665), French painter; a number of his works are listed in Neale, *Views of the Seats*, III, n.p.

[16] A number of his works are listed in Neale, *Views of the Seats*, III, n.p.

[17] Luca Giordano (1634–1705), Italian painter. 'Adam and Eve, with Cain and Abel' and 'St John preaching in the Wilderness' (Neale, *Views of the Seats*, III, n.p.).

[18] A number of his works are listed in Neale, *Views of the Seats*, III, n.p.

[19] Andrea del Sarto (1486–1530), Italian painter. 'Holy Family' (Neale, *Views of the Seats*, III, n.p.).

[20] Philips Wouwerman (1619–68); a number of his works and works after his style are part of the Milltown Gift to the National Gallery of Ireland, but it is unclear which pieces were part of the Russborough collection in 1806 (Potterton, *Dutch Seventeenth and Eighteenth Century Paintings*, pp. 179–82).

[21] Salvator Rosa (1615–73), Italian painter. 'Several fine landscapes' (Wright, *Wicklow*, p. 150).

DIARY 2: TOUR FROM HOLYWELL TO DUBLIN AND FERMOY

Veronese[1] Guido,[2] Furino[3] Cain and Abel by Guerchino, Benjamin and cup [by] Nicol Poussin[,] An Old Man [by] Titian[4] Bacchanalian [by] Rubens[,] [Sea?] [by] Van der Velde,[5] Reposto,[6] Corregio[7] Prince Rupert [by] Van Dyke[8] Rembrandt,[9] Teniers Concert[10] Claude Lorrain,[11] 3 Groups caricature [by] Sir *Joshua* Reynolds. Portrait E. Suffolk [by] H. Holbein.[12]

Stables grand with arched ceilings and cart horse stables below them.

[f. 59v] Fine marble inlaid tables. Beautiful Busts marble statues. Library handsome bronze figures. Scotch stole books destroyed all the parts of the house, all the privies and took up floors for firewood. Destroyed and gutted every part they were in. Not in the body of the house[.] Fine woods around[.] Fine view of river Liffey winding along the valley road to Waterfall [Poulaphouca] goes just above it. Cross a bridge[13] and beyond going to the water fall the river winds between 2 Rocky sides of a Glen[.]

'And Pray how far to Poll a Phuca [Poulaphouca]?' 'Not 40 Perches[.]' 'Do you think it is 30?' 'I dare swear it is[.]'

[f. 60v] Follow the river course and by tracking on the edge of the Bank which is all but [*word missing*] and in many places is ⊥[r] follow it untill you come to a walk over which getting one sees down the water fall from a pretty moss house which has a paved floor and 2 pretty rustic pillars in front. Some neat gravel walks lead gently along the edges or on farther from the water down the mountain side to another moss house which is extremely neat built.[14] Floor laid with pebbly pieces of rock and a table and benches in it and from here you command a fine view of [the] water fall of which the print is an accurate copy.[15] It consists of 3 parts and the 2 lower are very grand[.] The little one at top is discernible. The print seems to have been taken from the farther end of the strait path.

---

[1] Paolo Veronese (1528–88), Italian painter. 'Moses in the Rushes' and 'A Small Europa' (Neale, *Views of the Seats*, III, n.p.).

[2] Guido Reni (1575–1642), Italian painter. 'Cupid representing the Sciences' (Neale, *Views of the Seats*, III, n.p.)

[3] Probably Francesco Furini (1603–46); 'Two Academy Figures; a Magdalen and St Catherine' and 'A Bathing-Piece' (Neale, *Views of the Seats*, III, n.p.).

[4] 'Portrait of an Old Man' (Pietro Cardinal Bembo) by Titian (*c*.1488–1576).

[5] This could refer to Willem van de Velde the elder (1611–93) or the younger (1633–73), or Adriaen van de Velde (1636–72). 'A Sea-piece' (Neale, *Views of the Seats*, III, n.p.).

[6] 'Abraham offering his Son Isaac' (Neale, *Views of the Seats*, III, n.p.).

[7] Antonio da Correggio (1489–1534), Italian painter. 'Holy Family' and 'Nymphs Bathing' (Neale, *Views of the Seats*, III, n.p.).

[8] Anthony van Dyck (1599–1641), 'Prince Rupert von der Pfalz' (1631–2).

[9] Rembrandt Harmenszoon van Rijn (1606–69), Dutch painter and etcher. 'Two Old Men' (Neale, *Views of the Seats*, III, n.p.).

[10] Teniers, 'Musical Concert' (Neale, *Views of the Seats*, III, n.p.).

[11] Claude Lorrain (*c*.1600–1682), French painter and engraver; 'Campo Vaccini' (Neale, *Views of the Seats*, III, n.p.).

[12] Hans Holbein (1497/8–1543), German artist and printmaker. He painted Catherine, Duchess of Suffolk (1519–80), Henry Brandon, 2nd Duke of Suffolk (1535–51) and Charles Brandon, 3rd Duke of Suffolk (1537/8–51).

[13] Probably Horsepass Bridge (OS 1st edition, 6 inches to 1 mile, 1838).

[14] '[P]retty cottages, summer-houses, grottoes, banqueting-rooms, etc., are scattered through the hanging wood; seats, too, are placed in the most advantageous places for viewing each particular inclination in the waterfall' (Wright, *Wicklow*, p. 153).

[15] Lee evidently purchased a print of the scene; this is not identified.

Close at the back of the moss house are a small and great caves partly hewn out of the solid rock and when in they appear most noble the black slate rocks are fine[.] NB water comes down black rocks of slate[.] The tops of the precipices are clothed with green shrubs and young trees and ferns[.] The larger cave has a tiled floor and a rustic fire place the sides inlaid with pieces of spar and curious stones. From here it will much repay you for your trouble to go down to [the] waterside which may be easily done a little farther on and examine the curious forms and fine polished recesses which the water has made in the slate[.] The strata run ⊥^{r} and are intermixed with a few thin strata of marble[.] All the holes in the slate [f. 61r *blank*] [f. 61v] have water in them and fine sand which sparkles like gold dust. If the traveller is adventurous he may climb along the edge of the precipices and get to the Ball room which is situated on a point lower Down the stream. From here he has a fine view of the water fall and a near view of a pretty part of the river (sketch)[.][1] From hence mount the hill towards the cottage above and where a tent is fixed and where is a coach house for accommodation of visitors in coaches. From here wound down the river side which is over a rough ground up and down hill on the bank. Go on to Eustace Baltimore[2] and from thence to Russborough charming town. Lord Miltown, Mr Leeson Mrs Douglas[.]

Lord Milltown, old soldier served in Germany, West Indies etc. Lord George Sackville[3] commanded his regiment but just before he joined. Cowardice[.] Several Germans insulted Lord George Sackville but [he] took no notice[.] Charming marble Busts. Curious oak floors lain in O^r forms[.]

Descriptions of stay there[.]

Slept in a fine state bed upstairs[.]

[f. 62r] [*Start one page of rough pencil notes.*] 1500 soldiers in the house[.]

Soldiers there for 4 years.

Many rents for 3 lives at ½ Crown an Acre renewable for ever!!! But pay ½ years rent at death of a life[.]

[f. 62v *blank*]

[f. 63r] **Tuesday [10 September].**[4]

Came away at 10 OClock by other road by the river [Liffey] side. Bank on one side of it all [the] way. Other side meadow. Curious pillar on road side[.][5] Go on to Blessingtown[.] Pretty place[.] All new houses white and slate tops[.] Chimneys white and slate[.] Very neat 4 pointed spires[.]

No uncommon thing to see more smoke coming out of a black Irish cabin than up the chimney (if there is one).

Notwithstanding the miserable state of the Irish peasantry and the extream [*sic*] poverty which dwells among them and their food from years end to beginning, potatoes and buttermilk many no meat. Yet (some) they are the finest stout fellows in the world and plump and fat. Generally sallow from being smoke dried, many pay guineas for their cabins

---

[1] See SJC, MS U.30 (6), f. 55r–v (p. 317).

[2] Lee repeats his earlier error – he means Ballymore Eustace.

[3] Lord George Sackville (1716–85), soldier and MP; Viscount Sackville from 1782 (Bergin, 'Sackville, Lionel').

[4] Diarist error – 10 Sept. was a Wednesday.

[5] St Mark's Cross, near the castle ruins just south of Blessington, now on the bank of Pollaphuca reservoir. Lee roughly sketched it in the page margin with the caption, 'Boss in middle'; not reproduced here.

DIARY 2: TOUR FROM HOLYWELL TO DUBLIN AND FERMOY

4 3 and 2. And some only earn 9^d a day[.] Very sluggish and no idea of exertion[.] This arises solely from their depressed and hard slavery[.]

[f. 63v] 'How old are you[?]' 'Dont know[.]' 'When were you born[?]' 'At the cutting of the turf.'[1] 'Are you 6.' 'Yes[.]'

//

Cut off the corner of the road by crossing some fields with hay cocks and rocks like them in it. In front are some dilapidated farms. An old ruined castle and trees in the valley by the river and mountains with smooth circular edges on front. Behind back is the rebellions Blackamoor Hill which seems as if it was ready to burst from those bounds which nature has described for it, and to frown and grunt at being restrained at all[.]

Turf light and rough coated. Tattered like back[.][2]

//

Ireland not destitute of instances of female heroism[.] Women fought among the rebels and a Lady in the county of Wicklow not far from Russborough Mrs Sanders when her house was attacked in night loaded the fire arms as fast as she could for her husband and friends in the house. A woman of very great sensibility and delicate frame and fine taste and nerves[.] Fields or properly land at wall and around Wilps Rocks curiously diversified with hay cocks and rocks. Going down to the water side 8 children bowed and curtseyed and said 'Your servant Sir[.]'

'God save you Mister[.]' 'Godspeed you Sir[.]'

[f. 64r *blank*]

[f. 64v] The peat bogs are wonderful compositions and no malt liquor looks finer than the water. Even the cows on these mountains are astonished to see a stranger and wonder why this fool looks on them and stare at them with surprize. From the fording the river[3] only saw 2 boys riding 2 pigs 1 man mowing in the rushes or hay and 2 children pulling rushes[.]

There seem to be some most beautiful plants on these Mountains and are some fine lichens but one feels no desire to stop and dawdle when you see your neighbours the bogs and your road for miles before you[.]

NB The *Parnassia* [bog-stars] grows in a lush glory between Pull a Phuca and the lower waterfall[.] They sell the turf by the Irish = 4 Barrels. In general 3:9½ or 3:3 and some times 2:6 a Kish[.][4] (The turf about Luggalor has been dug 12 feet and bored with a turf pole 12 feet more[.])

NB Bread Butter wiskey at Blessingtown 7:

Got to Luggalor at 7 OClock[.][5]

~~Wednesday~~ (Thurs*day*) [11 September]

Boy for carrying knapsack to Kennedy [Newtownmountkennedy] 20^d. Started at 9 up the mountains for miles[.] They cut the turf in [the] mid*dle* of May[.]

---

[1] Cutting the turf, the harvesting of peat for use as fuel, begins in early summer. Lee notes this in the following day's entry.
[2] 'The thickest and best-tanned hides' (*OED*).
[3] Possibly at Aghavourk Ford over Cloghoge Brook, between Luggala (Lough Tay) and Lough Dan, Co. Wicklow. This may be the ford sketched at SJC, MS U.30 (6), f. 57r (p. 317), not reproduced here.
[4] Kish, a large wickerwork basket used for carrying turf (*OED*).
[5] Lee probably slept at Luggala Lodge again.

[f. 65r *blank*]
[f. 65v] When I had got to the top of the Mountain behind Luggelor all was in thick mist and quite cold although it appeared fine below[.] A bog of 12 feet is not considered very deep[.] A bleack [*sic*] cold foggy misty morning[.] The mountain looked fantastic and the mists and clouds hid all beyond the neighbouring mountains by hanging on their tops. The Watercourses have a porter like appearance[.]

Leaving the Military Road running just above on the Left and having a long walk to pass to get at it the temptation of saving a mile induced me contrary to my former vow, to cross the bogs to get at it at the expense of getting quite wet and black up to the middle of the leg and I made another vow never to cross any more whatever might be the inducements. From Luggalor to Military Road a good 2 mile. From thence to Blessingtown 10 Miles[.] To Barrymore[1] 3½[.] To Waterfall[2] 2[.]

From Military Road to Barracks 9 Miles[.]

The road winds very prettily along the sides of the mountain and is seen for miles before you. To be level seems to have been the object not straitness and I do not think it is 100 feet lower in 1 place than another all the way[.]

Come to a very stony rocky mountain from which a peep at a lake in the L distance is seen[.] I think it is the lake 2 miles from Luggalor. The masses of marble have curious veins running across each other in all directions. Capital road and as smooth as carpet[.]

[f. 66r *blank*]
[f. 66v] Many appearances of the stone on the road side having been blasted with powder. The stone seems to have been all got close to road side for there are places like holes dug for stone all the way to this place saw only 1 woman near Luggalor and 1 soldier and 2 country men on the Military Road. Not a cabin nor a tree. Nothing but Mountains stone and bog.

Beyond the rocky Mountain the road descends and you see more of it before you. You wonder where you are going next and fancy the 2 hills before you are the last of the chain. Walk on to explore[.]

Met a horseman[.] 'How far to Barracks[?]' 'Oh a long way yet perhaps 6 miles but I was never this way before.' 'How far to Dublin, 20[?]' said I making what I considered as an addition because I expected <u>my road</u> was much less[.]

Glinmuckanass [Glenmacnass] or Sporting Vale. A fine walk but all (in the heavy) rain[.] It is a pretty look down it[.]

Met the person who is forming the road. He told me that not a stone was in it, they pick them all carefully out. They lay sods on the bog and cover it all with gravel. The waterfall here [is] 150 feet deep.[3] They have cut through some spar in the rocks here with a sulphuric tinge in it[.] The road from here down the Glenside is all on hard stone[.]

[f. 67r *blank*]
[f. 67v] They were blasting the rock at the entrance of the Glen above the waterfall[.] Heard 8 or 9. All the way you see the parts of the blast bored some a foot deep. Masses of Irish granite have spar in them here and the shining flakes also[.] For the first time today

---

[1] Lee must mean Ballymore Eustace.
[2] Probably Pollaphuca.
[3] See description of Lee's sketch of the waterfall at SJC, MS U.30 (6), f. 60r (p. 318), not reproduced.

see cabins d*ow*n in the valley and along the road and some attempts at cultivation. The road is most beautifully made and as smooth as a carpet.

Come to the Barracks[.][1] Fine Build*in*g. Curious old Bridge there and the river [Glenmacnass] noisy w*hi*ch runs all down the road side. Several cabins close by it. W*illia*m Mahan, shop. Eggs and Bacon 1s:1^d. His advice to me ab*ou*t the Wicklow Girls. Proceed to the R tow*ar*ds the Churches[.][2]

The approach to the 7 Churches is extremely fine and the ruins and the fine pillar in the valley surrounded with bold awful mountains commands ones respect. One passes a ruin on the road side covered with ivy and you come to the river over w*hi*ch there are some famous stepping stones. You go thro*ugh* 2 round arches w*hi*ch are all of a building w*hi*ch are perfect and between 2 walls beyond them on the left are some pillars (and walls) ab*ou*t 5 foot high the fragments of a multisided room with a sort of a bow window tow*ar*ds the Pillar[.]

The Chief Church is in the middle[.] In the Chief *c*h*ur*ch on the L is a smaller one with a round tower steeple[.] Curious figures on the tomb stones[:] [f. 68r *blank*] [f. 68v] a saviour crucified, 2 figures on the side in arm*ou*r[.] Then pillars fluted and on 1 side a man on horseback and on the other a footman with a battle axe. IHS[3] at top of every inscription w*hi*ch end with Lord have mercy on their souls[.] [*Small, rough pencil sketch of cross in margin.*] In *c*h*ur*chyard a granite pillar[,] a curious old Holly [*ilex*] in *c*h*ur*ch yard where there seems to be new wood growing out of the trunk of the old tree[.][4] There is another close but quite dead[.]

The tower is [a] wonderful fine ruin. Heard many stories of men who c*oul*d throw stones over it and one young fellow thro over[.]

One man fixed his foot at the Base and threw over it. A man kicked a foot ball into the second window of this tower and he came with the funeral and I spoke to him and he said he did many years ago[.]

I waited to see the funeral[.] It was done with*ou*t ceremony[.] The childs grave was dug by its friends and they put it in while all the others were looking ab*ou*t the *c*h*ur*ch yard[.] No ceremony performed. Some were playing at hand ball against the wall and when the child was buried some time after all the women went to the alehouse at the bridge whilst the young men played for 1½ in the large yard at hand ball for 2Gs a side. 6 of them!!

[f. 69r *blank*]

[f. 69v] They then went to the alehouse of W*illia*m Mahon and thus the ceremony ended in giving the women some <u>drink to help them home</u> as a man told me[.] If it had been a man buried all the friends w*oul*d have joined in saying some prayers. That w*oul*d have been the only differ*e*nce[.]

The childs father had been the day before to tell W*illia*m Mahon to get some refreshments (ready) for the people for the funeral[.]

'Y*ou*r servant Sir' sa*i*d a ragged boy[.]

---

[1] Five barracks had been constructed along the Military Road by 1809; Lee is probably referring to Laragh Barracks, completed by 1802 (Kerrigan, *Castles and Fortifications*, p. 182).

[2] Glendalough early Christian monastic site, reputedly founded by St Kevin in the 6th century (Gwynn and Hadcock, *Medieval Religious Houses*, p. 81), and also known as 'the Seven Churches'.

[3] See p. 85, n. 1.

[4] See Lee's sketch of the scene, reproduced at p. 130 (Figure 7).

Figure 7. 'Curious holly at 7 Churches [Glendalough]', as described in SJC, MS U.30 (2), f. 68v (p. 129). By John Lee, 11 September 1806 (SJC, MS U.30 (6), f. 61r). Reproduced by kind permission of the Master and Fellows of St John's College, Cambridge.

DIARY 2: TOUR FROM HOLYWELL TO DUBLIN AND FERMOY

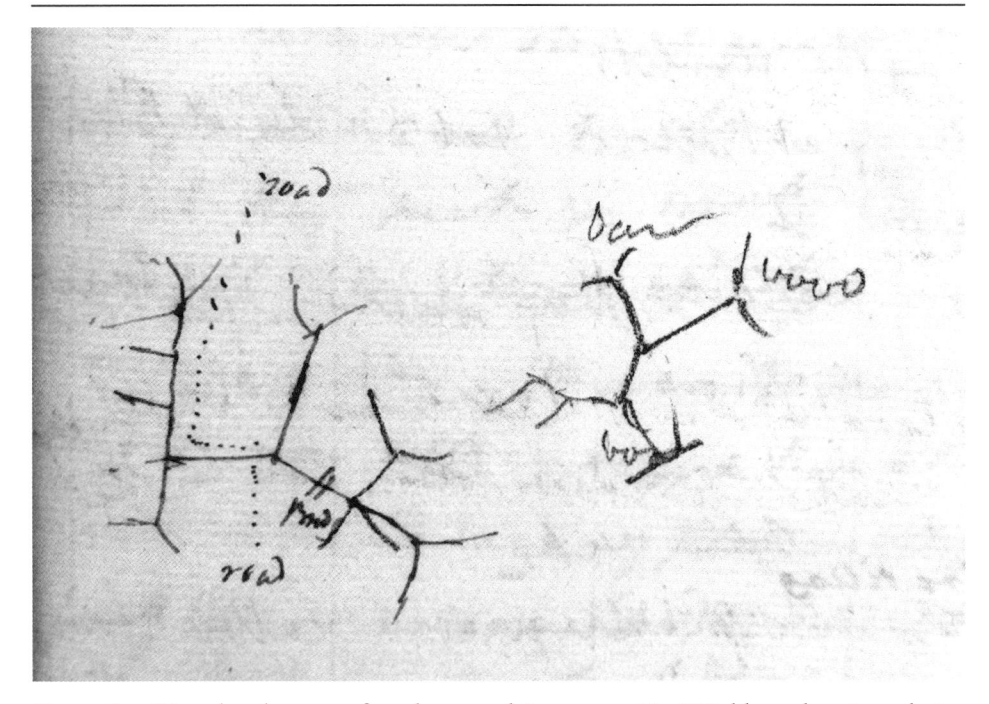

Figure 8. Two sketch maps of roads around Annamoe, Co. Wicklow, showing relative locations of Annamoe Bridge, Roundwood, and the nearby barracks, as described in SJC, MS U.30 (2), ff. 69v–70v (pp. 129, 131). The map on the right is a magnification of a section of the map on the left. By John Lee, 11 September 1806 (SJC, MS U.30 (2), f. 90r). Reproduced by kind permission of the Master and Fellows of St John's College, Cambridge.

No sooner was [the] child buried than the shovel with a long handle[1] was taken to splash some water out of a puddle on the fives ground and then went some turf to turn in its place[.]

The view from the Barracks is very fine[.] Noble M*ountai*ns in front[.] wh form into 3 vallies etc There are 2 vallies up by 7 Churches w*hi*ch come down and go in the other valley fr*om* [the] waterfall and all run down another. You may see 4 vallies at once fr*om* the left of the Barracks on the R Beside a pretty 4 arch bridge. It was too late to draw it[.] I wish I had[.]

Go on to Round Wood [Roundwood] on R or L of Barracks[.]

[f. 70r *blank*]

[f. 70v] Go up another vale side d*ow*n w*hi*ch runs river fr*om* Luggalor.[2] Annamore [Annamoe] a village 2 miles fr*om* Barracks with a pretty bridge. Go to L over bridge[.] Showers in day[.] Fine even*i*ng[.]

More cultiv*ate*d than in the mor*ni*ng[.] Woods and green fields[.]

Ascend a confounded steep hill. Best wind of river between high bank cov*e*red with wood and rock[.] Beautiful to the L.

[1] Lee roughly sketched it in the page margin, not reproduced here.
[2] Avonmore River, which actually runs from Lough Dan.

Mr Price[′s] white H*ouse* (and woods) and tucking mill[1] for cloth on the L. Very pretty[.]

Road very good but it began to get dark and I c*oul*d hardly see my way. Met 3 or 4 people all going to Roundwood. But a young man who was talking to a Boy on horse back seeing me go by wished me good night and came on and kept close to me and asked me questions[.] Did not much like my comrade, and kept at a good arms length from him but he kept close to me and I then kept my umbrella prepared for defence and my hand on the hammer[2] but upon com*ing* a little better acquainted with him he only wanted company as far as he was going and after a mile turned off to the L[.] 'How old are you? About 18 or 19 y*e*ars of age?' But he did not know rightly. Extremely dark when I began to descend f*ro*m tops of mountains into the valley and I 30 times resolved never to be out in the dark again as nothing to see and it may be dangerous. But knowing that a good bed was at Newtown*mountkennedy* and not much liking the appearance at Roundwood walked on and got there ab*out* ¼ before 9[.] F*ro*m Luggelor to Mil*itary* Road ab*out* 2½ [miles]. To the waterfall ab*out* 5½[.]

[f. 71r] To the Barracks 4. To 7 Churches and back again 2[.] To Roundwood 4. To Newtown 4. These are accord*ing* to the Irish guess but it must be more I think[.] No milestones on the roads. Desideratum[.]

NB Below the waterfall at bottom of hill is a very fine mineral spring. Ferruginous. Was going to drink and f*ou*nd it out to be so[.]

The people are said to drink after a funeral a drop of wiskey to drive (and drown) away sorrow[.]

[f. 71v] [12 September] Friday morn*ing*
Bill 3:9 = Waiter etc 1:10[.]

Started at ½ p*ast* 11. Fine day[.] Saw the sea and the shore wh*ic*h was very pleasing after some days mountain society[.]

'Pray Sir give me a ½ to buy a ½ of snuff' said an old woman. '½ of snuff? Why wo*ul*d you not spend it rather on bread.' 'Well give me ½ to buy ½ of bread.' 'Well I will if I have one. And wh*ic*h will you buy now[?]' 'Why Sir ½ of snuff for I cannot buy ½ of bread.' 'And how long will it last you[?]' 'To tomorrow morn*ing* ab*out* this time. God speed you and give you good luck on y*our* road.'

Farther on road barracks[.] Go to R and ascend*ing* still have a delightful view of Town and bay of Wicklow. A tower on the point. Mr Archers H*ouse* on the R.[3] Noble woods and rocks on the R of the road[.]

Go thro*ugh* a lodge gate and make for Dunran. Then ascend a steep hill thro*ugh* the woods and f*ro*m the top see the river [Vartry] winding below betw*ee*n the M*o*unta*i*ns. And the sea on one side and the bay of Wicklow on the other side of the oppo*site* Mounta*in*. Oppo*site* Mounta*in* bare and some (ever) greens[.] Go on up the summit of the hill. Here an ivy mantled tower close to the oppo*site* road and a burnt farm house at the End of [the] Ruin[.][4] Trees[.] Cross some fields and find y*our* way as well as you can to the High road for we missed ours but got to it by the village below[.]

[1] From tucking, the 'fulling and dressing of cloth' (*OED*).
[2] Lee's geologist's hammer.
[3] Probably Mount John, residence of Graves Chamney Archer (Lewis, *Topographical Dictionary*, I, p. 427).
[4] The ruined tower house at Dunran Demesne 'appear[s] to be a folly' (Grogan and Kilfeather, *Archaeological Inventory of County Wicklow*, p. 188).

Village Killiskey as many ruined cabins as stand*ing* ones[.] Little brook[.]

Old woman. 'In the name of God give me a ½ to buy a ½ of tobacco.' Asked a little boy the way and he ran away howling and afraid.

[f. 72r *blank*]

[f. 72v] The road is very pretty all along[.] Groves and plantations and Mr Tottenhams grounds on each side.[1] Farther on his Lodge. Fine plantations[.] Go on and come to a gate lead*ing* thro*ugh* a field. This brings you to the grounds of Mr —[2] and beyond is the entrance to the Devils Glen[.] The very entrance looks Devilish and infernal horrible looking mountain you pass under[.] There is no room at the bottom of the Glen for a road it is occupied by the river and if [it] floods [there is] hardly room for that. The road winds along the sides of the Glen just above the river. The M*ountai*ns are very bold (in) large fragments w*hi*ch project. Woods young and young trees are all in the bottom w*hi*ch form a good contrast with the above parts[.]

A bolder and more terror striking sight I never saw going on up the hill to the water fall. Just got to it and was preparing to make a drawing when I was attacked by a furious bull tearing up the sods and grumbling[.] At first I thought to frighten him away but glad to run back and get over the wall to the cottage and he after me[.] When I came there [a] child said 'Take care Sir for there is a very wicked Bull there who will pull you to pieces.' Thus my entertainment was spoilt and they never said a word to me going there. NB had left my umbrella and knapsack at entrance of the Glen[.]

To make this devilish place more infernal I *coul*d have thought of nothing more than planting Scotch firs there and Lo they have done so. Very [f. 73r *blank*] [f. 73v] proper for the scenery[.]

Wonderful rocks finest scenery in Wicklow[.] The views much finer com*ing* out than going in[.] One *woul*d say the rocks were put in the river on purpose in the most curious ways possible and so it seems until it strikes you nobody *coul*d do it[.] On some of the islands of rock grow the most fascinatingly picturesque oaks[.] At the entrance [*sic*] The rocks at [the] entrance are wonderfully bold, loose and projecting. Finest scenes in Wicklow or the world. Mr Sings [Synge's] new house [Glenmore Castle] looks very fine at the entrance. Built in the old gothic style[.]

Gave old man at Gate of Glen 5[d][.] He said he was put there to admit quality in and that there was a power of Q*uali*ty in now[.] Very fine curious house of Mr Sing[.] Gothic style[.] On the L Edge of the Entrance below is precipice and wood and the river[.]

Go in the road and at 2*nd* turning go to L. Follow road up a pretty hill to a fine old bridge and beyond it[.] No country the best cultivated can produce so beautiful a road and such lovely trees. Fine woods on the left and I never saw a road so ornamented any where[.] Its turns shew the fine trees so well[.]

[f. 74r *blank*]

[f. 74v] The road cannot lead to any place but Paradise and if it is on earth it must be the way[.]

Mr Tighe's Avenue[.][3]

---

[1] Woodstock, residence of Lord Robert Ponsonby Tottenham (1773–1850), Bishop of Clogher (Lewis, *Topographical Dictionary*, I, p. 427).

[2] Glenmore Castle, residence of Francis Synge (Carr, *Stranger in Ireland*, p. 91).

[3] Possibly Rossanagh, Co. Wicklow, residence of D. Tighe (Lewis, *Topographical Dictionary*, I, p. 506).

It would be wrong for any body to go to the Devils Glen merely to say he had been there. One should spend 3 or 4 hours there if the Bull will permit. If I had known the Bull belonged to a [jarvey?][1] at Dublin I should have wished him shot[.]

(Turn to the L[.])

Mr Hunts house on the way to Newry Bridge [Rathnew.][2]

Nothing can be more fine than this country. Land lets 3Gs an acre. Inn the best I ever saw[.][3] Got here at ½ past 6[.]

[13 September] Saturday

Bill Bed and Tea 3:3. Waiter 5^d[.] Started at 6 for Rathdrum[.] Go up to a village leaving the avenue to the R at top of village – turn to R and follow road up hill from where [is] a glorious view of the paradise of Newry Bridge and thereabouts[.]

It is impossible for any thing to be finer than the view from [the] top of the mountain. The most fertile vale that the imagination can conceive loaded with fine trees and some houses about it[.] The neighbouring hills finely and luxuriantly cultivated nearly to their tops which alone remind you of neighbouring [bassentes?][4] and the summits of the surly Wicklow Mountains above them [the] Sugar Loaf and Bray head. The Devils Glen just appears in the valley a large and a small lake and the sea beyond it taking up a fine bold part of the prospect many small vessels on it.

Some of the Mountains in distance cloud capt[.][5]

[f. 75r] Trees most luxuriant indeed[.]

[f. 75v] The little village below is Ramor[.][6] The Mountain on the R is Carney. Come to division of Road[.] Go to R and close by is another go to R. The other goes to Redcross[.]

Meet a car going to the woods[.] Get upon it and ride 2 mile[.] Very dirty and horrible road[.] Shaken to death. Horse began to stall and sat on the dung[.] All my Bag and Boots and Coat and Breeches dunged[.] Stopped under a bridge to clean myself. Lost more time than if I had walked on without riding[.] All these hills between 20 and 30 years ago covered with trees and wood[.] He[7] pays about 12 Shillings at the woods for the timber a load and the carriage to Wicklow is worth a crown[.]

Very rainy and wet to the Town of Rathdrum[.] When I got there thinking only a few miles to cover about to the Mines etc was told that to the Copper mines 3½ and to the Gold 8. What must I do? Got a boy to carry my knapsack and walked on[.] Breakfast 20^d[.] Boy 10^d[.] Fruit 6^d[.] Marquis Rockingham arms[.][8]

[f. 76r blank]

[f. 76v] Proceed on[.] Corbally Castle[.] Delightful view of the Avondale from it. Built by late Mr Hayes as ornament in imitation of old Guthrie[.][9]

---

[1] A hackney-coachman (*OED*).

[2] Lee sketched a view in the vicinity; see SJC, MS U.30 (6), f. 63r–v (p. 318), not reproduced.

[3] Lewis agreed: 'a superior family hotel, kept by Messrs Nolan, which has long been celebrated for the beauty of its situation and the excellence of its internal arrangements' (*Topographical Dictionary*, I, p. 506).

[4] Lee may mean 'basset', relating to strata cropping out at the surface (OED).

[5] Capped.

[6] Possibly Rathmore, Co. Wicklow.

[7] Presumably, the driver of the car.

[8] An inn on the summit of Rathdrum hill (Wright, *Wicklow*, p. 65).

[9] Lee may refer to Corballis, the home of Samuel Hayes (1743–95), politician, improving landlord, and amateur architect. When he inherited the Hayesville estate he renamed it Avondale and built a neo-classical house above the Avonmore River; it is likely that he was its architect (Donlan, 'Hayes, Samuel').

Lake at 7 Churches [is] Lock Nahanakin [Lough Nahanagan][.] The river comes down here. The Avonmore[.]

[Carrigmeel?] in [dist*ance?*] *from* view[.] Fine town[.] Pretty view in front of it[.]

Crawnbawn [Cronebane] hill the motly stone on the top.[1] Men pitched ½ into a hole on top where miners come on a Sunday to play at mott[.][2]

Fine view of the winding river *from* where the [turret?] formerly stood[.]

The Lovers Leap is the finest spot I ever saw[.]

That silent sweet river what a murmerly fine sound it has[.]

Views from the Old Battery[.][3]

Fine old hall hung with curious weapons[.] A gallery oppos*ite* the door[.] Curious looking weapons[.][4]

"Some deal trees as thick as a horses body and as tall and as straight as a whip[.]"

Saw a tree wh*ich* was *found* under the bog. They say they grow under the bog. All black thro*ugh* and thro*ugh* but sound. Many trees [are] *found* so. Big boughs go out of them.

Go thro*ugh* fine woods. River below[.] Come to Mr Parnels cottage[5] thro*ugh* an iron gate[.]

[f. 77r *blank*]

[f. 77v] Mr Parnels cottage the most beautiful that I ever saw[.] Quite in cottage style[.] River close to [the] window and noble rocks directly opposite running down to [the] water, partly cov*ered* with trees[.]

Path goes all along the edge of the river above it and come to a pretty white house, go on to R at a turn ~~towds~~ following the river, thro*ugh* fine wood and fine turf walk[.]

Thro*ugh* the wood see a most beautiful turn of the river before you the *Mo*unta*i*ns cov*ered* with trees[.]

Prodigious the fine noble river and woods, winds very much[.]

Go thro*ugh* a gate fastened with [an] iron bar into corn land[.] Capt*ain* Kings land[.][6]

A very pretty p*art* of the river with a gors [gorse] cover on the L[.] He has generally a couple of hogs for going errands or 2 English shillings.[7] 6[d] in silver is a white 6[d] in halfpence a black sixpence[.]

'There are a many ghosts all ab*out* this neighb*our*hood and th*a*ts why I'd be lothe to go back late. I never saw one but there's people in the town who have seen them[.] They are all ab*out* [the] neighb*our*hood[.]'[8]

When the army was here they saw many ab*out* [the] *church*yard. His father (on horseback) was followed cheek by jowl by one for many miles ~~until~~ they came to a running stream and it co*ul*d not pass it. There are a power of boys fairy struck in the neighb*our*hood who wo*ul*d bite any thing they co*ul*d[.]

[f. 78r *blank*]

---

[1] The Mottee Stone at Cronebane, Co. Wicklow. A granite boulder measuring 14.1ft × 10.5ft (4.3m × 3.2m) and the subject of local myths (Grogan and Kilfeather, *Archaeological Inventory of County Wicklow*, p. 34).

[2] Probably from mottie, 'a mark used in playing games' (Price, 'The Place-Names', p. 267).

[3] Lee's location is unclear.

[4] It is unclear to which house Lee is referring here.

[5] William Parnell Hayes (1780–1821), later MP for Wicklow; Avondale House (Wright, *Wicklow*, p. 69).

[6] Kingston, seat of Mills King (Wright, *Wicklow*, p. 70).

[7] 'Hog' is slang for a shilling (*OED*). Lee refers here to the fee usually collected by the boy he hired to carry his knapsack for the day.

[8] Lee relates words spoken, probably by the boy he hired to carry his knapsack for the day.

[f. 78v] Go over a pretty wooden bridge and see before it at top of hill a pretty white House, Mr Wavers[1] and [a] fine pretty tower at [the] top of [the] wood. Trimmed hedges. The river runs along in the valley. Delightful spot, woods [and] rocks above. Water and all that one can desire[.]

'The river so bad it will rain before night[.]'

The meeting of the waters is just below the wooden bridge. This is a beautiful delightful spot[.][2]

'The priest can cure any one he likes who is fairy struck[.]' (But then he must be paid for it[.])

Motting stone.[3] Ascend the hill [Cronebane][.]

The soldier at [sic] who lodged at their house saw a gost[.] It was like a big dog with a chain about its neck[.] The soldier was like to die with fear[.]

Go down by ladders 120 yds deep. 28 ladders down[.] Thickness of copper bed from 2 Inches to 4 foot[.] Sulphur ore about 11 foot wide the course is[.][4]

Go down 7 ladders[.] 1st quite ⊥r[.] 12 × [altogether?] then keep heading all [the] way down the holes where ore has been[.] North wall is quite rough and shaft quite smooth[.]

When down 15 ladders a Great large cavern[.] Immense river which was filled in[.] Much ore was in it very good. Now worked through. Then go down below it[.]

[f. 79r blank]

[f. 79v] When down 19 ladders you come to a hollow place and by the shaft and from there you go down down [sic] 13 ladders as the 7 first by the shaftside[.] Sulphur is got by powder and is the worst sort of copper[.] Black ore is got with pickaxe, or wedge and then is sent off[.] They do not know what becomes of it[.]

If 2 penny wt in Ounces it is very good[.]

Grey ore Best in general[.]

Black ore 3rd best[.]

Sulphur worst[.]

Yellow ore 2nd Best in general. Sometimes Best[.]

Spar and ore is broken and brought to dust[.]

The spar and ore is broken to pieces and is then powdered to dust and the good [dust] sinks when put in water in a machine and the bad swims[.]

The descent into the mine is by a n° of ladders which are placed at one end of the shaft on purpose to go up or down[.][5] This shaft is elliptical and not more than ⅓ is occupied by the range of ladders[.] The rest is open[.] In going down 1 ladder you come to a landing and from that you see another ladder head close at your feet[.] By taking hold of bars of wood you can easily step on to the first round then the descent is similar to the former[.] Going down 7 ladders of this sort you come [f. 80r blank] [f. 80v] to the bottom of this shaft and then you go along horizontal[6] and see the works in some places. but from thence

[1] As indicated by Lee's account of visiting a mine that follows shortly, this must be Mr Weavers, owner of Cronebane mine (Wright, *Wicklow*, pp. 73–4).

[2] A celebrated beauty spot said to have inspired Thomas Moore's 'The Meeting of the Waters' (Wright, *Wicklow*, pp. 70–71; Plumptre, *Narrative*, p. 183).

[3] The Motte Stone; see p. 135, n. 1.

[4] Here and in the following paragraphs, Lee describes a visit to Cronebane copper mine.

[5] Lee sketched the shaft in the page margin, not reproduced here.

[6] References in this section to the horizontal and the horizon are intended in the geological sense, that is, to refer to a stratigraphical position.

there are separate ladders at the bottom of each a landing of the rock as it happens to be and the descent is very easy but most wonderful untill you come in some places to large hollow caverns or passages leading out into different parts of the works which go to an amazing dist*ance*[.]

The copper runs in courses as it is called which are large strata leading at a very great Length to the horizon. B B[1] l represent different forms of the courses and their width is from 2 Inches to 4 feet or more. Sometimes large caverns fall Down these courses as they have been emptied are got deeper and deeper and they go thus down to the whole depth of the mine. At the foot of the ladders there are boards, pieces of timber fixed across the courses and on these they put the dirt and stone which in digging they meet with and which is not worth taking out. These are but sections of the courses as you go down but you might walk along at the foot of the ladder through any one of the passages for each has a different roof almost. C shews how the courses end in a point or else they break off in ribs so [f. 81r *Continuation of sketch of strata.*] [f. 81v] fine that they are not worth working[.] The whole mountain is cut in to these sort of courses of the ore and you may go down as I did about 19 of these ladders through the different floors or rooms and then you come to the shaft where the bucket goes down by a wimsey [whimsy shaft]. Here on one side of the shaft is a set of ladders as at the first and by going down them you come to the very bottom of the work where there are the same kind of chambers and courses as before[.] This shaft is about 70 fathoms deep[.] There are a great many passages through which you walk to the different parts of the mines[.] Went along one to see the place where they blast the sulphur. At the end or as far as I went we came to two small shafts down which men were going with their candles, but these were not more than 20 fathoms down Below our feet, but many below the surface. One cannot repeat a course but they go so that if you were to break away the boards (B B) on which generally a quantity of rubbish is laid then you would fall down the sides of the course[.]

All the water in these mines is very sulphuric and it is collected in a quantity at the bottom of the hill through which leach runs and drains the mountain into ponds like fish slews so that the (extra) water from one goes into the next and soon in these there are placed larger plates of iron and the [f. 82r *Rough ink sketch of strata.*] [f. 82v] water coming in contact with the iron leaves a crust of copper on it and these plates are well rubbed every morning and thus a quantity of native copper is obtained[.] [*Rest of page stained by spilled ink.*]

[f. 83r *blank*]

[f. 83v] There are a n° of these ponds also at the top of the hill. 4 in a line and 10 Rows so that the top ones feed the others[.] A great quantity of copper is obtained by this method. A man told me that not a <u>haporth</u>[2] of harm was done by the rebels at Rathdrum. He must have been a rebel[.] In coming down from the mines you come by a different route to that you go up and cross a light wooden bridge which is thrown over the river where the lower ponds are, from there go along the road and see the other mines a little farther on on the opposite side of the water to the others. Up this Mountain is the remains

---

[1] In this paragraph, the letters BB, A and C refer to Lee's illustrative sketch in the folio margin (not reproduced here).

[2] Halfpenny-worth.

of a very large melting furnace. Gave the boy who accompanied me this far 30^d. A little farther on met a lad who was willing to walk a little way with me[.] He went 2 miles and gave him 6^d. It was too late to proceed to the goldmines and a very thick fog came on so that I could not have found my way and besides the sole of my shoe came off here[.] ∴ made the best of way to Arklow. Having a load of specimens it was desirable to have one of my bundles carried by a boy. Here met another Boy who took my bag and thus made on with my 2 Boys at my side one carrying knapsack / other bag untill they would go no farther for it was very thick fog [f. 84r *blank*] [f. 84v] and they were afraid of going home in the dark and they said it would be night if they went any farther. Saw a woman driving home her goats and had a quart of milk 4^d. Gave another boy 2^d for carrying knapsack a little way[.] At last meeting a cart (load) of wood put bag in it and got to Arklow at ½ past 7. Found the place filled with soldiers of the North Down Militia and 14 Recruiting companies who were come to get the men from the militias for the Line, could have no room and therefore had my tea etc in a Bedchamber[.] The country I came through is very rich and well cultivated[.] The river runs all the way to the bridge beyond the Copper mines[.] The vales are very rich. Arklow is very pleasantly situated and the sea is very noble here and the shore consists of very fine sand hills[.]

[14 September] Sunday

Got my shoe mended by this morning[.] After breakfast walked down to the beach to see the fine shore[.] The sand is beautiful and fine and go for a great length along the shore[.] The river here runs close [f. 85r *blank*] [f. 85v] by the town and ships come close to the bridge which is [of] considerable length. The river [Avoca] below the bridge breaks off into 2 arms[.]

There is a barrack here capable of containing a few companies of soldiers[.] Behind the Barrack is an old bit of ruin[1] covered with ivy (on whose tower is erected a flagstaff)[.]

Had a dinner for the 2nd time in 8 days[.] Horrible bad dinner miserable mutton chop nothing but potatoes. Fowl quite tough no pie and no cheese in the house. Wine as hot as a spirit.

NB The Irish are not such imposing people as the English[.] They give you the legs wings head neck and very feathers on the head of a fowl But in English [England] they cheat you of the head and cut it off. NB the head of an Irish fowl the best part. The only part which is not tough[.]

Close by this town in a plain was fought a very hard battle between the rebels and the army in which the latter got the better with considerable loss on both sides[.][2] The Rebels were well posted as to situation.

Almost every fellow here was a rebel[.] They some confess it and say it is a frown[3] to deny it. 'Why were you rebels[?]' 'Dont know.' [f. 86r *blank*] [f. 86v] They followed the others.

The priests incited most of them to rebel and some say they will not be cajoled again[.]

---

[1] The remains of the 13th-century Ormonde Castle (Grogan and Kilfeather, *Archaeological Inventory of County Wicklow*, p. 181).

[2] The Battle of Arklow, 9 June 1798.

[3] In the sense of disapprobation (*OED*).

Monday 15 [September]

Paid for washing shirt waistcoat pair stockings socks cravat Gaitors Pocket Handkerchief 1:2[.]

Bill 15:2½. Quire paper 6ᵈ[.] Waiter and maid 20ᵈ. Wiskey for man 10ᵈ. Maid 10[.] Division of Roads L goes to Wicklow[.] R our road[.] See Lord Wicklows Monument which he built before he died[.][1] It is like a pyramid. His perchman[2] Mr Barley was buried outside of it[.] He had men from Dublin to build it[.] (It is in Kilbride Church yard[.]) [f. 87r] [*margin:* Although every body expected he would have been put inside with the late Lord.]

[f. 86v] Garden and house on other side of river[.]

John Kinsley went for 14 days and he got a very little gain[.] He got more loss than gain. His account of some people on mountains finding gold and buying cattle[.][3]

[f. 87r] [*margin:*] His account was that on the Mountains some of the poor folk got on well in the world. They bought cattle and hired land and other folks as poor as they were wanted to get on as well and it was a question how they got their money. They were often watched to the river side and observed examining the sand and then it got about among the neighbours and soon spread abroad and there were 1000s of people from Carlow and Kildare counties who came for many miles off to look for gold and they dug in all parts about. It was more crowded [f. 88r] than any fair was.]

[f. 86v] Mr Atkins house on the L a white house in a field[.] There is not better reared men nor better tempered in all the world than there is in the Kingdom of Ireland[.]

[f. 87v] Come through street (pretty) Powl a honey [Pollahoney] bridge and Earl Carysforts House[4] to the L and Lord Wicklows to opposite fine brook for trout. The honey hangs on the leaves all the [summer?][.]

The Hall meadow at Lord Wicklows is 20 Acres[.] The rebels came down in 1000s to attack the army in Arklow and there the Rebels were first beat[.]

Poulahoney [Pollahoney] woods[.]

He said 'I could give the best ½ Guinea I ever had to hear the song of the Gold mines and Patt Bridge and all the vales (and places) were composed in it.'

'It would open the eyes of one to hear the song [of] how the gold was got and every thing for the use of man was in the song which is found here[.]' ~~Army lost 190 men at battle at~~ Arklow and they only said there were 4.[5] For the worst must be made the best[.]

Deals and oak for Ballyarthur[6] and ash and yew for Shelton[.][7] These are the best places for them in this part of Ireland[.]

Birch he said would cover an acre of ground with their trees (a lie)[.]

Lovely country river runs through the vale of woody mountains[.]

---

[1] The Howard mausoleum, Kilbride, Co. Wicklow, erected by Ralph Howard (1726–86), 1st Viscount Wicklow in 1785 (NIAH).

[2] Possibly a coachman; a perch can mean the driver's high seat on a coach.

[3] In this and the following paragraph, Lee provides an account of the Wicklow 'gold rush' of 1775.

[4] Glenart Castle, seat of John Joshua Proby (1751–1828), 1st Earl of Carysfort (Geoghegan, 'Proby, John Joshua').

[5] The meaning of this remark is clarified below, at f. 88r (p. 140).

[6] Possibly Ballyarthur House, built in *c.*1670 and the seat of Michael Symes (?1762–1809) (History of Parliament online; NIAH).

[7] Shelton Abbey, built in 1770–75, the seat of the Earls of Wicklow (NIAH).

[f. 88r] The rebels came down to attack Arklow and set fire to it. They began about 11 oClock and at both ends of the town being ÷ into 2 parties. His[1] cabin was pulled down by order of the general to make room. He took his family down to a tradesmans House in the town, but going out in the evening to look at the place he was obliged to run into the Barracks and stand there all night. He saw many dead men lying in the streets and the army gave out that they had but 4 killed and he was at the burying of them but there were 190 killed but they would not suffer any body to say so[.] He saw a many who were buried privately in the Barrack yard and the <u>best is to be made</u> out of the worst that Men may <u>not be afraid</u>. He saw Rebels throw many of their company into the flames of the houses burning when they were killed. For when the breath is out of a mans body he is a poor bit of cold clay and what signifies what becomes of him. Besides they (Bodies) would have been hanged up in the town if found. When rebels got a place they first tapped all the drink and this made themselves unfit for battle and that was cause of many battles being lost[.]

[f. 88v] The separation of Lord Wicklow's [Shelton Abbey] and Colonel Simms estate is a valley. Lord Carysfort had a pretty cottage in the wood just above here in Powlahoney wood. Earl of Carysforts estate all the way[.]

Potatoes corn and hay all growing in a flat meadow where 3 or 4 years ago it was bushes and a wilderness of fir and faggots and the river ran on it until they got the means of keeping it off it by a bank. This is called the bottom of Kilcarrow [Kilcarra] or Kilcarrow holmes[.]

The fish all down the river are poisoned and they are often seen in it lying dead[.]

Account of the rebels throwing their dead companions into the fire to save them being hanged[.] What does it signify when the breath is out [of] a mans body[?]

Ballyarthur long walk nice gravel and laurel and rosy trees about the hall door. About ¾ mile long river at the bottom[.]

Perfumes and niceness of smells of every sort in the proper time of year.

'Ill shew you the river what runs through the hearts blood of the gold mine[.]'

[f. 89r] He praised ~~the~~ a famous song in which he said the gold mines and the Full of honey[2] woods and all the neighbouring houses and places and what ever was for the use of man was composed in it. His Daughter knew a few verses of it and he would have amost [sic] given ½ crown out of his own pocket for me to have heard it.

He had been drinking wiskey all the preceeding night and had taken 3 Glasses at home before he set out. He had 4 Glasses at the Inn and at the wooden bridge 4 more. He said he had drank 12 at a time but had known men who would drink a bottle at once. He said he could go better if he was to have a glass every 2 miles[.]

When we had got on the ½ way up the hill beyond the river which comes from [the] gold mine when he said if he had the money he was to have he would spend every farthing in wiskey[.]

[f. 89v] Claim of 10£ next cabin to the Barrack wall and many others[.] Pat Carthy and Pat Kelly and many others and the agent kept all the money and stopped above

---

[1] Possibly John Kinsley, one of Lee's local informants (see p. 139).
[2] Lee's corruption of the name Pollahoney (or Bollahoney), probably resulting from the application of the genitive case in Irish, resulting in lenition of the initial consonant 'p'. In the Irish language, 'ph' is pronounced 'f'.

DIARY 2· TOUR FROM HOLYWELL TO DUBLIN AND FERMOY

100 Claims in the Town of Arklow. He made him and his wife swear twice and kept it[.][1]

Agent[2] was Atkins[.]

The agent has about 1s a £ for receiving rents and a fat pig and a fat goose and fowls latter end of every year and they help him home with his hay and corn and turf and he is at little expense[.]

His father was a tailor and Grandfather and he had a pretty estate[.] But he was a drinking man and so was his father and they left him very little[.] He drank 4 Glasses more of wiskey at the house at the wooden bridge. The *Bridge* is stone but it was wood. He is a drunken beast[.] Cost 5^d[.]

Point of land just over Gold river from whence the 4 fine vallies all covered with wood[.] 2 other vallies bare[.]

From the road you may see at some times 6 or more vallies and most covered with fine wood. The rivers run down several[.]

[f. 90r *Two sketch maps*[3]]

[f. 90v] 'What Glen is this on the L of this *Mountain*[?]' 'The Rustigay [Rostygah] Glin[4] and if you was to take the river in your hand Sir you would go up to the Gold mines, but it would be inconvenient for you would have hedges and diches [*sic*] and cornfields to pass[.]'

Rustigay Hill we are upon[.]

Gold mine on Rar hin ruch[5] Hill[.]

Ancient Britons very wicked horrid murderers 95 of them killed in 1 day[.]

Ballinvalley [Ballinvally] (*Mountains*) in the R hand[.]

3 of them had 70 a year ago[.]

Level is gone in above (through) 200 yards all solid rock and nothing ever found in the level. Small quantitys in all the trials they ever made in the Brooks and places any where in the riverbeds[.]

At 3 miles off at Ballock and at 6 miles at Sheana[6] they have found it[.]

See the men riddle[7] it. They sometimes find 6 (or 8) oz a day formerly and now an 1 ounce or 2 ounces a day. Very poor some have more in 1 day than in a whole week[.]

Ballinasillog [Ballinasilloge]

Ballinasillog Hill go over called the Meen na Teig [Moneyteige] on opposite side. View of sea and Arklow[.]

[f. 91r] He held the Ancient Britons in detestation and said if an Irish man was to go among them in Wales they would soon have his bowels out[.]

At Bally Ellis [Ballyellis] near Curnew [Carnew] the *Ancient Britons* were going from Gorey to Curnew when the rebels who had lied in wait for them on all sides let them

---

[1] Lee relates details provided by local informants in Arklow on claims for damages to properties made by insurgents during the 1798 rebellion; Lee's informants accuse the local agent of intercepting and stealing their awards. For more on such claims in Co. Wicklow, see O'Donnell, *Aftermath*, p. 18.

[2] Agents or middlemen acted on behalf of absentee landlords. For more, see Reilly, *The Irish Land Agent*.

[3] Reproduced at p. 131 (Figure 8).

[4] Lee sometimes uses the spelling 'glin' for 'glen', presumably to reflect Irish pronunciation.

[5] Lee may mean Raheenleagh.

[6] Probably Croghan Kinshela mountain.

[7] To extract something by separation (*OED*).

come fairly into the middle of them and then they fired and piked almost all. They stopped up the road with cars and thus hemmed them in and hardly a man escaped[.]

At the Gold mine much dissapointed [sic][.] It is nothing but a brook[.] They take a little sand and dirt and mud up and put it on places so that the water runs on it and washes it[.] Below is another place into which the smaller stones and gravel runs and thus they separate it all and when washed they pick the small bits out.[1] Some times do not get ½ an ounce a day. There are 30 men at work now about a year ago had 80 men at work and tried many places in the neighbourhood for gold and found some little. All about it is found in small quantities. They have run a level in the rock about 250 yds but have never [f. 92r] found the least bit by it. So that it seems it is only on the surface[.] They sometimes (have) found 6 or 8 ounces in a day and at others very little[.] Last week found much[.] 2oz is more than the average. In 1 day sometimes find more than in several weeks[.][2] [*Rough pencil sketch of spade, captioned* 'Potatoe'.]

Gave the man who left me at the ford 3:8 he said he should go and drink a little and would probably stay at Annacurrough [Annacurragh] all night.

[f. 91v] See high road strait before us for Mountains[.] Kilpipe ford is at the bottom of the valley where the road crosses it and by which we go to the road to Tinahely[.]

We come down the sides of the Tomanern[3] river which rises in the mountains close by. Very clear and famous for trout[.]

A boy from Tomanern farm conducted me across the bogs to the ford. They searched for gold across those sides of the Mountains also[.]

Anacurrough where man left us[.]

Kilpipe Church in ruins on the R side of road and bogs along the bottom[.]

Go up. Immense peat bogs cut up and heaps all along the valley[.]

Curious flower on sea shore at Arklow and Conwy flowers like thistles and bluish and leaves like holly [sea holly, *Eryngium*][.]

It is curious to see the goats tied by a wisp of straw or twigs by the necks in pairs and at about 2 Yds length, and their a [sic] hind etc forepart tied ~~together~~ with hay. Very fine bog which I cross at about a mile from village of Tinahely. Cross a bridge at entrance and go to the Inn after having been there ½ hour [ff. 92v, 93r *blank*] [f. 93v] and got a room and a bed[.] The maid came up and said I could not have a bed then. (Master Rourke) Her mistress had told her so. Her mistress had got her sister and some friends in the house and she said the beds were to be engaged by her own family and she did not call it an inn and there was another house in the town, thus to make room for her friends I was turned out or perhaps not liking my appearance I was sent away but glad I was for I got very comfortable accommodation and civil treatment at the other house at Mr Barkers[.]

The rebels burnt all the place down and they encamped on Mount Pleasant close to the town[.] The inhabitants chiefly fled away and Mr Barker and his wife and 2 sons were absent about 3 months[.] They took what they could in a ~~moments~~ (hours) notice[.] They went to Haggetstown [Hacketstown] which place they left the day before the rebels took it and burnt it. The rebels sent word they would attack it and did. He gave in his

---

[1] Lee roughly sketched the apparatus in the page margin, not reproduced here.
[2] Lee made a sketch in the area at SJC, MS U.30 (6), f. 64r (p. 318), not reproduced.
[3] Tomanierin is a townland in Co. Wicklow. The river to which Lee refers is probably the Derry Water.

claim £86 and got it all. Lord Fitzwilliam[1] has built a new town and a very pretty market place and the houses are very neat. He rents about 83 Acres land and for most of it pays Guinea an acre[.]

The leases are mostly for 21 years and the life [f. 94r *blank*] [f. 94v] of any 1 person.

He had a few years ago on his ground a large mound with a deep fosse about it. There are a great many all over the country and from 1 you may generally see 3 or 4. This was all very rich land. It covered a great deal of land also and he resolved to level it[.] But the people look upon them as sacred ground and noone would do it for him. But at last several said if he would cut a few of the first sods they would do it for him but at the time they [fled?] off[.] They were afraid of the fairies. He however got hold of a harum scarum fellow who cared for nothing and he agreed if Mr Barker would cut the first sods and would take all the blame to himself to do it. Accordingly in the morning they came and Mr Barker cut up some sods and threw them down into the fosse and then addressed the fairies as if they were present and told them if they were offended not to hurt the man but to let the blame come on him[.] The man then set to work and in course of the work earned 3 Guineas[.] Everybody said he would suffer for it. They did not finish it that year. He planted and had a Good crop of Potatoes and the next summer as no harm had come of it he got plenty of persons to finish the job for him. He got a second very good crop of potatoes and this year a most excellent crop [f. 95r *blank*] [f. 95v] of wheat. When levelled it contained and he gained near 100 Square perches of land for before the cattle only could graze upon it[.] This year every body said the Fairies would come and take away his crop of wheat before he was going to reap it but none came and he has got it all safe without them[.] But this evening a man came and said he had heard the fairies had carried away a cart load and he wanted to know if it was true? Mr Barker of course only laughs at their nonsense[.]

From Arklow to Tinahely 12 Miles direct[.] My way not more than 14.

Started at 9 and got here about 5[.]

He with several others all went and buried their few valuables of silver etc so that if one was Kilt[2] the other might know where they were and thus may get them all again after the rebellion[.]

[f. 96r *blank*]

[f. 96v] **Tuesday [16 September]**
Start at 7[.] Breakfast Bed and Tea 32^d[.] Maid 6[.] Piece of flannel 5[.]

After going on the road a short way keep up the Mountain side on the Left by which leaving the road you cut off a winding of it[.] See on opposite mountain a road to Ochovanna[3] and to a Barrack there 8 miles off. A little farther on see the road to Carlow strait before you go over a style leaving the mountain road which leads to the L to Mr Leonards House above the Mountain. A river runs all along the valley[.] Perhaps this cut is hardly worthwhile making by itself[.] See 1 Mountain before us at the back of which is Hacketstown 6 miles from here[.]

---

[1] William Wentworth Fitzwilliam (1748–1833), 2nd Earl Fitzwilliam (British peerage) and 4th Earl Fitzwilliam (Irish peerage) (Kelly, 'Fitzwilliam, William Wentworth').
[2] Killed.
[3] Probably Knockananna.

Boy believes in fairies and said the man who levelled Mr Barkers mound fou*n*d some silver (and gold) candlesticks and many things and that he gave some to Cap*tain* Moretown[1] and some to Mr Barker. That Mr Barker has the curse of many people for it and of all the boys for stopping them fr*om* having a 5ˢ Alley[2] or Ball alley against the Marketplace[.] He says it is reported Mr B*a*rker is carried fr*om* bed and laid under the dresser every night by the fairies but he cannot say it is true. But Mr B*a*rker was near going mad some time ago for them (i.e. he was ill)[.] Boy thinks some harm will happen to him yet[.]

The White Rock is to the R of the road[.] Mr Morris lives there. On the R Mullens Mr Chamblay[.]

[f. 97r] NB at the Cross Bridge leave Hacketstown R*o*ad on the R[.]

[f. 97v] Just beyond the farm of 1 Simon Casle the road ÷, go to the left. Abo*u*t 30 yds on turn to the R and see for the 1*st* time in Ireland a flat plain country view i.e. Carlow. The road wh*i*ch goes to Tullow and Curnew[.]

Going down to Klenmore [Clonmore] pass a mound[3] like on Castle Hill wh*i*ch was told to be inhabited by fairies by George. Farther on ruins of the C*hur*ch on 1 side of the road and the C*hur*ch y*ar*d on the other[.][4]

C*hur*ch yard. Stones all with a cross on top and IHS[5] and all end with 'Lord have mercy on his soul'. Here is the remains of a large cross[.]

Just below the C*hur*ch is a perfect cross like that near Blessingtown but smaller[.][6]

Curious old castle[.][7] Remnants of a moat on side[.] [f. 98r] [*margin:* It stands they say on an acre of ground] [f. 97v] Stands on a square ground[.] 3 of the corner towers are partly standing. Round arches and narrow windows cov*e*red partly with ivy. Cabins and turf heaps in it[.]

But a greater curiosity is just on the rising ground on the road beyond a cabin with clear panes of glass in windows and <u>whitewashed</u>!! Go on for some way to Charlestown[8] a place of a few scattered vulgar cabins and nothing else but turf[.]

Fowls have a band of straw or hay across their backs to hinder them going into the oats[.]

[f. 98r] [*Top half of page contains a rough pencil sketch of a carter drawing turf.*]

[f. 98v] Several showers in Harlestown [Haroldstown.] C*hur*ch in ruins and cov*e*red with ivy[.]

½ a naggon[9] is 2 glasses[.]

Echorn [Acaun] Bridge is close by and built over the Slaney [Derreen] River wh*i*ch runs to Carlow they say[.]

---

[1] Possibly Captain James Moreton of the Tinahely Infantry (O'Donnell, *Rebellion in Wicklow*, p. 159).

[2] A fives alley; 'a game in which a ball is struck by the hand against the front wall of a three-sided court' (*OED*).

[3] Clonmore mote in the townland of Minvaude.

[4] The remains of a 6th-century Christian monastic site reputedly founded by St Maedoc of Ferns at Clonmore, Co. Carlow (Gwynn and Hadcock, *Medieval Religious Houses*, p. 377).

[5] See above, p. 85, n. 1.

[6] See Harbison, 'Early Christian Antiquities'.

[7] The remains of the 13th-century castle at Clonmore (Brindley and Kilfeather, *Archaeological Inventory of County Carlow*, p. 84).

[8] Probably Haroldstown, Co. Carlow.

[9] Noggin, a small quantity of alcohol, usually a quarter of a pint or 0.14 litres (*OED*).

‘George do you love wiskey[?]’ ‘Yes by God I do and theres many men in Tinahely who (dont) drink so much as I.’ He has taken 8 Glasses at a time and is only 16 years of age[.] Yet he thinks a good deal does one harm.

Close on the L hand side of Echorn Bridge is a curious heap of stones. Several are placed near each other and on the top is one large immense one placed on the top of them all.[1] A man told me it was very curious and that it was done in the time of the giants. Here George and I parted and I gave him 30^d and a naggin of wiskey = 2 Glasses[2] or 5^d and he returned. Some lime cars which were going to Carlow over took me and I got upon one of them and rode very comfortably 8 miles on a sack in which contained the hay for the horses.

I had rode in a stonecart a dung cart and wood cart but of all carriages none ever gave me so much pleasure as this did. For it did [not] shake very much and 2ndy[3] it saved my feet 8 mile. No Gentleman in his Chaise and 4 was ever so happy or comfortable as I. These cars came from Arklow that morning and were going to Carlow for <u>lime</u> which is sold there for 1^s:6^d a load and in Arklow for 10:6[.] It was to put on the land!!! Symptoms of enterprise in agriculture.

[f. 99r *blank*]

[f. 99v] It was worth their while to come 28 miles in this way they said on account of the difference of price although it would take them 2 days to go and get back[.]

Where we stopped to drink was called the Leathing house[.] Pass Rathmore Bridge, but no bridge there only the place so called. Within a mile of Carlow is a Place called Browns Walls from the walls of a Gentlemans house joining the road which is overshaded for about a mile nearly with trees and looks very pretty.[4]

The town of Carlow is tolerable good[.] It has some good houses in it and a tolerable street or two. There is a curious old Castle in it just above 1 side of the town[.][5]

A little boy came up to me in the streets and said ‘Pray Sir have charity on a poor scholar.’ He said he was a poor boy from the county of Tipperary who was travelling about for learning, that all the schoolmasters in every place give him instruction for nothing, that some of his school fellows give him now and then lodging and when they do not that he must pay for it, that he has to find himself in food and lodging and clothes and that he has instruction gratis. He was now learning Rule of three[6] and some other arithmetic and carried an arithmetic Book about under his shoulder with his sums in it. He could read and shewed me two books he had in his pocket. One an arithmetic Book, the other the 7 Champions of Christendom[.][7] [f. 100r *blank*] [f. 100v] He came last from Tullow and should stay here as long as the school master would allow him[.] He was a nice civil boy and seemed very well bred. He said many boys go about the country in the same manner.

---

[1] Dolmen, south-east of Acaun Bridge. Lee sketched it in the page margin, not reproduced here.
[2] Lee may have given the boy George half a noggin, rather than a full one, as he notes above that this quantity equals two glasses.
[3] Secondly.
[4] Browne's Hill House, Kernanstown, Co. Carlow, built in 1763 (NIAH).
[5] Carlow castle, built in the early 13th century (Brindley and Kilfeather, *Archaeological Inventory of County Carlow*, p. 84).
[6] A computation method.
[7] Richard Johnson, *The Famous Historie of the Seaven Champions of Christendom*, 1596/7, a chivalric romance widely read into the late 19th century.

He had been absent from home 2 years and should stay 2 more and when he was a good scholar he would go home and teach the others. Backing cloth 20. Packing needle 6. Book 10^d. Set out at 7 and got here at 3.[1]

Wednesday [17 September]
Quire letter paper 20^d. Stuff for gaitors 4S:½[.] Bill 8:4[.] Waiter and Maid 20^d
'Good dry lodging' written up on every board at every cellar in Carlow[.]
Washing for drawers shirt breeches and Pocket Handkerchief 12^d
[f. 101r] [*Rough pencil sketch, captioned*] View of tower in Lord Mount Cashels ground Sunday 28 September[2]
[f. 101v] On the (back) hill behind the street is a mound and an old castle on it.[3] It consists of 1 room about 18 by 9 paces[.] There are 2 fine round arches at the end in the middle and 4 on the sides 2 and 2 which are perfect,[4] but the building has been much mutilated and the inside is a terrible receptacle of filth and dung. At the N W end is a remnant of steps going up to the 1st floor above which are 2 perfectly arched windows, neither of them in the middle or proper proportionate distances from the sides. At the S end corresponding is but 1 Window in the middle and 2 small arched doors into the turrets. On 1 side are 2 windows and on the other 3. There seems to be no order observed. Above on the 2nd story are only one small peep out window at each end. In the three corners are passages leading to the round towers from the body and (in all of them) on the floor are 3 arched vaults on the 3 sides, 1 in front and 1 on each side. There are arches on the ground floor on 1 side and on the other (in the wall) on [the] E side a kind of <u>slant</u> vault going up to the 1st floor.

There are the bodies of 3 chimneys for the different floors going up to the top on the E side and they all join in 1 head which is standing. The walls are very thick as may be imagined by the slant passage[.]
[f. 102r *Plan, in ink, of Carlow castle*][5]
[f. 102v] There were wings to the N end about 12 years ago[.] Children will go up to the top and will run round notwithstanding it is very dangerous to go by the chimney. Go up the steps and in the tower you see a staircase standing over the other all up to the top and from there you may walk nearly all round with ease. There seems to be a walk round one of the towers. A man fell off from the chimney and only bruised himself. He is alive now[.] His name is Foley and is a smith. Children will run up to the top and hinder any from following them by rolling stones down the stair case. Story of its being taken on the stair case side and battered by cannon the other being cannon proof and harder than rock[.] Boys will stand on side and throw 10 stones on top [of] 12 in to the top of [the] chimney and they still come down[.] Cockfighting ball and all sorts of things were played here formerly and are now[.]

All seems built of fine blue hard stone slate[.]
[f. 103r] [*margin:* No cells in the bottom of the step and tower.]

---

[1] Lee refers to his journey from Tinahely to Carlow.
[2] See p. 171, n. 7.
[3] Carlow Castle; see p. 145, n. 5.
[4] Lee's plan of the castle clearly depicts these arches (Figure 9).
[5] Reproduced at p. 147 (Figure 9).

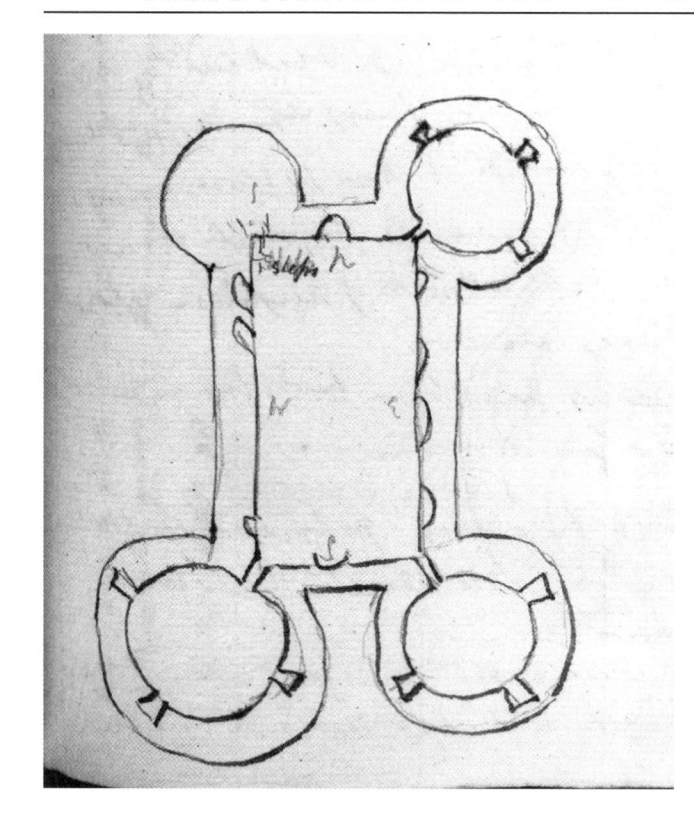

Figure 9. Plan of Carlow Castle. By John Lee, 17 September 1806 (SJC, MS U.30 (2), f. 102r). Reproduced by kind permission of the Master and Fellows of St John's College, Cambridge.

[f. 103r *Ink sketch, captioned*] View of a white rock and bridge over the river w*hic*h runs thro Lord M*oun*t Cashells grounds. The road to Fermoy from Kilworth Sep*tembe*r 28[1]

[f. 102v] Fine old bridge on the river. The tower of castle look well fr*o*m the road[.] Old Church Tower looks antique also[.]

There is a college in the town for Roman Priests and a Chapel to it but looks so so[.][2] A new [f. 103v] looking building just on one side of Tullow Street[.]

'Godspeed you now' s*ai*d the waiter on leaving the Inn[.]

'God save you y*ou*r servant Sir' said a man in a shop[.]

Pass by Cap*tain* Vigours pretty lodge. He is a County of Wicklow man[.][3]

The road goes along the side of the river over w*hic*h is a towing path for navigation. There is a fine range of hill all along beyond River[.] It is completely and elegantly cultivated and the hills go on a long way beyond the Bridge[.]

With the first dish at dinner in comes a large plate of potatoes with their skins on and you may eat them with every thing for seldom w*oul*d I get anything else when I had a dinner[.]

At Breakfast Waiter comes in and says 'Sir there is a gentleman who will be happy to breakfast with you' and down he puts the tea cup for him. Soon after he comes with

---

[1] Reproduced at p. 172 (Figure 11).
[2] St Patrick's College, Carlow, was founded in 1782.
[3] This may be Nicholas Aylward Vigors (1755–1828), father of the zoologist and MP (Carlow), Nicholas Aylward Vigors (Desmond, 'Vigors, Nicholas Aylward (1785/6–1840)').

the kettle and was going to fill it up[.] 'Dont put more water in' said I. 'But theres the gent*lem*an coming to breakfast with you.' 'Oh so there is' said I and he filled it up[.]

A Good way to save tea to club 2 gent*lem*en together who perhaps never ask each other but only on the waiters invitation[.] I waited a few minutes on to see if the Gent was coming and then began with*out* him and finished and never saw him at all[.]

[f. 104r] NB. The word hill now means itself. Before where ever used it means mount*ai*n[.]

[f. 104v] A very fine weir over the river and close by (some) new locks. Ab*out* ½ mile farther on Leighlin Bridge. Fine old Bridge, 8 arches, old bit of Tower at the foot of it[.][1] Go over Bridge[.] Ab*out* ½ mile bey*on*d Bridge curious old Stone by the roadside with ~~a coat of arms on it~~ (or writing on it) but much defaced. There is a hole in the middle ab*out* 5 Inches deep, and on the South side is some inscription but c*oul*d not stay to pore over it[.][2]

Fine black marble with diff*eren*t veins in it[.] Close by the Town of Royal Oak a pretty white washed house and an old desolated C*hur*ch opposite cov*ere*d with ivy as usual[.][3] Many new blue grave stones in it up to the present time.

Snack 2:2[.] Waiter 6[.]

Just beyond the Royal Oak are ruins on L side of the road[.]

Met a Chaise just going off f*ro*m Royal Oaks for Kilkenny and got carried for 40[d]: By wh*ich* I saved a day for noth*in*g to see on the road to that place[.] NB Started at 1 and got there at ½ p*as*t 7.

All the Clergy in Kilkenny on acc*oun*t of the visitation etc.[4] C*oul*d not get a bed at the Inn. Got accom*modatio*n at the Grocers shop[.]

[f. 105r] Mistress at Carlow, Mrs Coffy.

[*Rough pencil sketch of the stone described at f. 104v*]

One may see 7 lines of it and all are large letter*s*[5]

```
        ON
        NO
ANN       ARE
LEIGHLIN  BVR
ENSESCRVCEMH
  ERIFECERVNJ
ILLE
```

---

[1] The bridge at Leighlinbridge, defended by a tower house, was built in 1320 (but has since been replaced) (Brindley and Kilfeather, *Archaeological Inventory of County Carlow*, p. 97).

[2] Probably the 'base of cross' identified by the OS in 1840 (OS 1st edition, 6 inches to 1 mile, 1840).

[3] Possibly Killinane Church, Closutton, Co. Carlow.

[4] 'A visit by an ecclesiastical person (or body) to examine into the state of a diocese, parish, religious institution, etc.' (*OED*).

[5] Boundary stone, identified as 'base of cross' by the OS in 1840 (Archaeological Survey of Ireland; OS 1st edition, 6 inches to 1 mile, 1840). The inscription seems to have been completely eroded since Lee recorded it (Archaeological Survey of Ireland, National Monuments Service. Available at <http://webgis.archaeology.ie/historicenvironment/> [Accessed 1 Mar. 2018]). Lee roughly sketched the stone at the top of the page, not reproduced here.

[f. 105v][1] **[18 September] Thursday. Morni**ng
Candles and powder 10[d][.]
    Woman at cave 10[d]. Men 20[d]. Boy for car 35[d][.]
    Passage with market cross[.][2] Wonderful rocks in all directions[.]
    At the entrance of market cross a fine vaulted cave. ~~Cannot~~ [***] top like a buildi*n*g and all isicles[3] hang down[.]
    Market cross a fine pillar formed by droppings. The roof looks like [an] organ or pillar. Finely vaulted. See the light below *fr*om the market cross[.]
    Go into other cave and see a large lump cut off *fr*om a fine pillar.
    Many people take any out[.]
    480lbs was taken out to make curious things by [potterer?] Mr Shaw[.]
    [f. 106r] Walked about the diffe*ren*t parts of the Town. Saw the horse barrack w*hic*h are in one of the old Ruins by the river,[4] and went up to look at the outside of the Castle[.][5] It belongs to Lord Ormond.[6] On the top of one of the spires is a coronet and a crows nest is always there every year and the crow takes it down again. A gent*leman* at the Wheatsheaf Inn[7] said he had seen the nest one year.
    Mr Landlords name is Mr Comerford[.]
    Very good market. Quantities of women with their baskets of apples plums and pears[.] Breakfasted at the Inn for 1:7½[.]
    About 11 started with Mr Comerford who kindly offered to accompany me to the cave of Dunmore.[8] Went up by the Parkkeepers lodge at Dunmore and *fr*om thence across the fields and hedges [and] ditches a short way but w*hic*h was most fatiguing and altho*ugh* it was shorter still it was longer in time.
    Upon arrivi*n*g at some cabins close by, a woman went for 2 men, who normally go with strangers and who had got some torches and some candles on purpose w*hic*h were preferable to our supplies. She brought some fire to the entrance and lighting our torches we marched in[.]
    The entrance is very grand a large sort of square hole ab*ou*t 50 feet deep presents itself[.] The sides all but where you enter seeming ⊥[r] [f. 106v *blank*] [f. 107r] and fine masses of rocks appear[.] You go down the northside throu*gh* the young bushes d*ow*n a very slippery path and very steep just can walk down with help of bushes, and see the mouth of the cave on the left hand side of the square forming a prodigious fine natural arch ab*ou*t 10 feet high[.] Here the torches were alighted and clambering over some immense fragments or rather whole rocks keep descendi*n*g still lower for some small way[.] The rocks seem as if they must have tumbled down *fr*om the top but the top does not seem as if it ever owned them. Keep going to the Left and then begin ascendi*n*g over some immense masses

---

[1] This folio consists of rough notes relating to Lee's visit to Dunmore Cave on this day.
[2] A stalagmite pillar in Dunmore Cave, almost 19.7 feet (6 metres) in height.
[3] Icicles, that is, stalactites.
[4] The infantry barracks on part of the site of St John's Abbey in Kilkenny (founded 1211), and ceased use by 1818 (Bradley, *IHTA no. 10, Kilkenny*, pp. 13, 15).
[5] Kilkenny Castle, built *c.*1207–19, with later additions and renovations (Bradley, *IHTA no. 10, Kilkenny*, p. 14).
[6] Walter Butler, 1st Marquess of Ormonde (1770–1820) (Collen, *Debrett's Peerage*, p. 565).
[7] Located on Rose Inn St, Kilkenny, established in *c.*1700 (Bradley, *IHTA no. 10, Kilkenny*, p. 20).
[8] The limestone solutional cave of Dunmore, Co. Kilkenny, was a celebrated attraction; Campbell wrote in 1777 that he had 'heard a great deal' of it (*Philosophical Survey*, p. 106).

of stone heaped in all directions[.] Drops of water keep falling from the roof of the cave in many places and these coming on the rocks below petrify and form large and little knobs of innumerable sizes in different parts of the cave[.] The tops of the knobs are rather round and white where the water drops and without the aid of these knobs a stranger would be unable to climb up some parts of the cave[.] The roof all along forms a most wonderful appearance to see the numerous forms and figures which the water petrifying as it hangs down has made is wonderful. The sides are also remarkable[.] The trickling of the water down them has in its congelation formed a n° [f. 107v *blank*] [f. 108r] of hitherto unknown architectural ornaments and none inferior to those of art. Particularly on coming to the entrance at the market cross and all about it there appear fluted pillars about all the sides and the stories above are exquisitely ornamented with the variety of forms. New organ pillars, pipes, cones and all round and fluted figures appear. The market cross is also a wonderful thing[.] The continual dropping from the top has made in the course of time so large a round mass of petrefaction that it has reached to the top where it joins the ceiling and now forms a part and support to it[.] The water still trickling down its sides has variegated it with different fluted edges and it appears more like the most precious relique of antiquity than a work of nature. The petrefaction on being broken and pieces taken off are fine beautiful white marble and shine in the light[.]

    The cave does not glitter. I suppose it might formerly but the sides and top are mostly now black from the smoke of candles torches etc[.] From a spot close behind the market cross is seen down below through an opening some small glimpse of faint light which is about the beginning of the cave, for the cross is much higher than the entrance. You cannot get much farther in this cave than the cross. There is an end to it[.]

[f. 108v *blank*]

[f. 109r] The fluting of the sides and the isicles as they are called on the top are beautiful and from some great thing as this no doubt architecture took the hint. You return out of this cave the same way you go in. The knobs are very numerous and singularly ornamental and make very good footing. They are in some places very large and some centuries hence will form pillars like the market cross. The guides were apprehensive that the cave would soon be stopped up for the increasing of these knobs[.] In about 5000 years some such thing might some to pass!!! For they at the same time own that they do not grow much within their recollection[.] Upon getting back to the entrance of the cave you begin a new expedition up another cave now to the left. This is in the same manner at first ascending over large masses of rock through a spacious set of apartments. Pass by a large mass of the petrified marble which had been cut off from a very large mass which had formed and which in time would have made another pillar akin [to] the market cross but smaller. You see several very large ½ pillars at present but which will in time form a junction with the roof of the cave. At some distance in are rabbit boroughs [burrows] where there are plenty and on the R side among the rocks is a well where the water [f. 110r] may be seen through the rocks. Farther on is the place they call the well, which is a fine clear stream and what is very curious is that the bed of it which is not deep below the water consists of bones, which they say are all human, and many sculls and different bones leg and thigh bones are found there. Many persons take some away with them. How these came there one is at a loss to conjecture. Take up some of the small particles of the bottom and among it is a great quantity of bits of very small bones as if worn off from larger[.] I got several bones then. It could never have been worth any ones while to have taken them in there.[1] From thence we proceeded up the cave until it gets rather low and narrow and one is obliged to stoop very low to go on[.] The bottom here is smoother than any other part of the cave and the top comes nearer and nearer to the floor the farther you go. The ground is rather circular which makes the crawling more easy but at the farthest end it is flat again and here the top and bottom come so near that one cannot even stoop but one must crawl on all fours. I had heard that no one had ever ventured as far as one might go, then resolved to do so and accordingly crawling along and at last laying on my flat belly I pushed myself forward until I fairly stuck, then asking for a candle and holding it as far before me as I could I perceived that the roof and base were not 6 Inches asunder beyond and whither[,] notwithstanding this[,] people still affirm that there is another cave[.] I know not[.] They never will get to one unless the bottom is cut on purpose but I think the cave ends there. Getting out as well as I could [f. 110v *Ink sketch of interior of Dunmore cave with caption*, 'If the arch be represented as above the walk down is as much shelving as here shewn'; *ink sketch of water wheel at marble works*] [f. 111r] at the expense of having dirtied all my clothes I got back to the men and when able to stoop on account of the height put on my hat again and we returned the same way to the mouth of the cave. We fired several pistols in this cave but had not the least echo. In the market cross there was a little but not much[.]

In the entrance of the arched cavern the earth is not very far from the top and it shelves down just slanting enough to allow one to walk.[2] The whole beauty of the petrefactions makes it the finest cave I ever saw and it is a pity the smoke of the torches should have robbed it of its whiteness. We returned along the high road a good 5½ to Kilkenny, from passing by the Cottage in Dunmore grounds on the R where Lord — resides[.][3]

From the Town I then proceeded to the works down the river 2½ miles where the Famous Kilkenny marble is cut and polished[.][4] The machinery is very simple[.]

A water wheel turns a crank on its axis to which is fixed a beam which communicates to a frame containing ten saws[.][5] As the crank turns round this draws the frame backward and forward and thus cuts the blocks into planes[.] The frames are advanced by a machinery[.] The planes are then rubbed with some <u>Chester grit</u> which smooths them a little and then with a brush, after which they are put on [f. 111v *Ink sketch of apparatus*] [f. 112r] on [*sic*] a frame consisting of five which will admit 5 slabs at once. There is a crank below on the other side of the waterwheel which turns a long bar to which a frame of 5 bars is fixed and on each of these is a rubber made of rags, as these bars go backward and forward by the crank the slabs are rubbed and receive their last polish. A little emery is constantly dabbed on. The machinery will saw at a farthing an inch a boy told me and before it came the work was done by the hand[.] It cost 5 or 6 shillings[.] Crossed the river and walked back towards the town by the marble quarries in which the layers of

---

[1] The *Annals of the Four Masters* records a massacre of 1,000 people in 928 CE, that may have occurred in Dunmore cave (*Annála Ríoghachta Éireann*, 2, p. 623).

[2] Lee sketched the effect at f. 110v above.

[3] Dunmore Cottage, built *c.*1775, formerly in use as a summer house by the Ormondes of Kilkenny Castle (NIAH).

[4] Probably Colles's marble works at Highrath and Maddoxtown on the bank of the River Nore, just south of Kilkenny city, established in 1730 and closed in the 1920s. At the time of Lee's visit the proprietor was Richard Colles (1774?–1849) (Woods, 'Colles, William').

[5] Lee sketched the apparatus at the marble works at ff. 110v, 111v above.

stone from their tiers differently marked have different names. The silver bed is so called because the marble in it is all covered with little white spots. The shell bed because many large shells appear in the polishing and the ½ moon bed and the black bed from the marble being quite black. Beyond nearer the town is a fine pleasant walk all up the river side through trees. But the road leads along through 2 rows of trees and brings you out by the castle and down the road to the Wheatsheaf Inn.

[f. 109v] Note sent to Mr (R) Collins [Colles] at the Stone mills

Having been informed that a very great variety of beautiful marble is obtained from your extensive quarries and being willing to take back with me to England as many different specimens of the natural curiosities of this country as I can attain, I should be extremely obliged to you for small specimens of all the different marked marble which are found there. The beauty of the specimens which I have in my possession has induced me to make this bold request and had my time allowed me I should certainly have accepted your kind invitation and have walked down a second time to see your works and the quarries which the lateness of the evening prevented me from examining[.] Any small parcel directed to Mr Fiott at Mr Comerfords Grocer, Parade, Kilkenny would be taken care of, and would be forwarded in the course of 10 or 12 days to Dublin for me etc[.]

[f. 112v] **[19 September] Friday.**
Walked to see the Church and the pillar in the Church yard[.][1] Bishops house an arch way across the lane from his House to the Church.[2] Church in bad situation surrounded with huts[.] Saw a funeral going down (the street) and over the bridge to a Church yard beyond. No Ch[3] then many people and old women in the train. Going up the street saw another coming down about ½ past 8 in [the] morning. First 3 Roman priests then corpse and a great number of females and men following them all on foot[.]

Fine market this morning[.] A great quantity of fish.

8 Cobblers in a row in the street ready for employ and women without shoes or stockings sitting on some straw on the flags by their baskets of apples etc[.]

Started at 20 before 11[.]

[f. 113r] Today saw a great deal of fine fish in the market[.] No poor laws in Ireland and ∴ all the poor people go wandering about and get a penny where they can[.][4] At every Inn door you are sure to see N^{os} and at every place where a chaise stops they come about it. Poor people sometimes die on the road side[.]

[f. 112v] Met a woman who told me the account of Father Caryl at Callen [Callan] who being excommunicated married any couples who went to him for 2^s:2 in a few minutes. She said she would have no more obligation going with me than to the potatoe ground if I had asked her and [*breaks off*]

All along the road where there are materials for [mending?][.] It is fine black marble and a great quantity of shells of various sizes in it. Loitered very much in looking for them

---

[1] St Canice's Cathedral, 'adopted as cathedral in 1111', and round tower (c.1111) (Bradley, *IHTA no. 10 Kilkenny*, p. 13).

[2] Built by 1360 (Bradley, *IHTA no. 10, Kilkenny*, p. 25).

[3] Probably coach.

[4] The poor law was passed in Ireland in 1837. See Crossman, *Politics, Pauperism and Power*.

DIARY 2. TOUR FROM HOLYWELL TO DUBLIN AND FERMOY

and got to Callen at 3 where on the entrance of the town is a fine ruin of a church[1] and an [*sic*] a mill and brook and then bridge AS[2] rocks then 20ᵈ go on. A boy on the road told [f. 113v] me on my asking what sort of a man was Father Caryl that he was a drunkard and here they thought him a blackguard[.] He was turned out of the priesthood. He can marry but not say a mass and all he gets he spends in drink[.]

'What book is that in your hand.' 'My reading book[.]' 'What is it[?]' 'A very good one.' It was the last Passion and death of Jesus and his cousin bought it for him who is now ordained to be a priest. It cost 13ᵈ[.] His father paid the price[.] His cousin is a learned man and can read Latin[.]

Pass a church yard with a noble handsome ash (tree) in it. Saw several during the walk[.] Several showers and rain between Kilkenny and Callen. Boys with shoes and stockings and hat throwing stones at each other between a hedge.

2 Children up to their (naked) middle in mud and water gathering blackberries.

Asked for a glass of water and had some given me in which I could see the little animals all swimming about and [the] woman said she never observed them before until I shewed them [to] her and they were wont to drink it always so perhaps [*breaks off*]

A child ran out of the cabin crossed the road went up to the hedge side in my sight and did [f. 114r *blank*] [f. 114v] its affairs before a stranger – O! [oudor?[3]]!! Within in [*sic*] a mile of 9 Mile house [Ninemilehouse] the road going between 2 mountains ends[.] On the R is Shleiv na Man or the womans mountain[4] where is good fowling and airing and my Lord goes there often[,] Lord Ormond[.]

Get to the 9 mile house and there get carried in a post chaise 12 Miles to Clonmel along the new road at 13ᵈ a mile. 13ᵈ for 1 Turnpike. Paid ½ or 8:4ᵈ[.] In the Rebellion the Irish had 3 oaths which were administered to the people. One commands secrecy another, something very little short of murder etc[.] They had also 2 acrostics which pains were taken to make out. They were Eliphismatis and Eliasmantle and the 1ˢᵗ was discovered by 1 man only the other they could not get at.[5] It is wonderful how secret they were for each other and how well they behaved. The only way by which the greatest secrets were discovered were by whipping and that means most things were found out[.] A Sir Edward Fitzpatric[6] in this neighbourhood discovered more things that way than anybody. He flogged a great many and did a great deal by it. He flogged an Inn Keeper at — and an apothecary at — and got a great deal from them, it is a bad way!! After the rebellion he raised a regiment of these fellows every one of whom he knew to have been rebels and told them twas the best thing that could become of them. He was their colonel. They went to Gibraltar to Malta and behaved very well and were called the Ancient Irish. He wanted them to volunteer to Egypt and they refused to go. Upon which he told them that by God they should volunteer but that if there was any one who would come out and would box with him and beat him that he should be the colonel of the regiment. To joke

---

[1] The mid-15th century Augustinian friary (Gwynn and Hadcock, *Medieval Religious Houses*, p. 297).
[2] The meaning of this abbreviation is unclear.
[3] Possible misspelling of 'odour'.
[4] Slievenamon or *Sliabh na mBan* (Ir.), 'the women's mountain'.
[5] The acrostic 'Eliphismatis' and the associated oath has been traced back to the *Freeman's Journal*, 2 Apr. 1796 (Curtin, 'The Transformation', p. 479). Some historians doubt its authenticity (see Wilson, *United Irishmen*, pp. 47–8). See also below, p. 154, for the meaning of the oath.
[6] Lee means Sir Thomas Judkin-Fitzgerald; see SJC, MS U.30 (5), p. 267, n. 3.

with an Irishman [f. 115v] goes a great way. They did volunteer and behaved very well and at the peace they were disbanded and many of them now make very good inhabitants. Sir *Edward* Fitzgerald[1] got a dispensation from the pope when abroad and liberty to say masses although a protestant, upon his return here he did go and perform a mass and now the people here although he flogged and persecuted them and his soldiers so often would probably sooner follow him than do him harm.

[f. 115r]
Every   E L
Loyal
Irish   Eliphismatis
Protestant Eliasmantle
Heretic
I
Shall
Murder
And
This
I
Swear

[f. 115v] Many fellows will confess freely that they were rebels[.] 'Blood and ons [ounds] Sir were not every body so and how could I help it!!!' say they. Most of the poor people were sworn to secrecy although they did nothing and if they had not they would have been all shot and their cabins burnt[.]

[20 September] Saturday.

Walked about the town went over the Church and yard. All the church yard walls built in marble and there is a parapet on the top of most parts. Saw the corner house in which Mr Sterne[2] was born[.] Walked down to the river [Suir] which is very fine here but at the town its course is diverted into different parts to turn mills etc. Saw a great butter house from which they pack it up and send it in casks to London and different places. They send off on an average of 500 Barrels each Saturday in the week and each is worth about 9½ Guineas = 5:2:4½ or about £2500 a week or £25,5200 = $\frac{520000}{4}$ = 130000£ in a year.

A little farther on is a very extensive piggery where they buy pigs every day and by any n° at a time[.] They keep them for about a week and then kill them [f. 116r] salt and cure them and send them to all parts of England for store for Bacon. The Offal heads etc they sell on the spot to the people here. The fat also. On an average every pig is bought for about 4£ (all prices between 3 and 5Gs) and they kill about 100 a day. The season for killing begins about this time. Last week was the commencement and it lasts till May or June[.] I saw about 40 Pigs hanging up in the long store house which had been killed in the morning. And fine fat fellows they were. There was one room quite filled with salt for curing them[.] Saw the styes for them and the underground cellar a

---

[1] Lee means Sir Thomas Judkin-Fitzgerald; see SJC, MS U.30 (5), p. 267, n. 3. Lord Edward Fitzgerald (1763–98) was arrested for his role in the proscribed Society of United Irishmen and died in prison in Mar. 1798, before the rebellion took place.

[2] Laurence Sterne (1713–68), novelist and clergyman (Ross, 'Sterne, Laurence').

fine long vaulted room under a store house in which the pigs are put in summer for preserving them the better.

100 × 4 = 400Gs a day × 6 = 2400 a week
24 × 3200 = 2 × 62400 = 124800£ a year

The Landlord generally leaves his estate to the care of his agent. The agent lets it out, perhaps in 10 different parts to different persons who are called <u>Middle men</u> and who neither till it themselves nor do their sons work[.] They are perhaps all young fellows who hunt etc and consider them selves as all gentlemen. These let it out again to perhaps each 10 different other people and these cultivate the land perhaps. They have it only by the year and if their rent is not paid up to the day – then the middle men will take all their cattle and drive and sell it for what it will fetch and thus these poor fellows are thrown on the streets [f. 116v *blank*] [f. 117r] and ruined. For as the landlord generally lives in England and he writes to the agent for remittances. He presses the middlemen and they in turn the lower people. Thus the lower suffer and then they go and kill the cattle of the middle men and commit murders etc etc[.]

Thus whenever land is out, it is put up to be let at the highest price and if one fellow bids higher than what is usually paid for the other land, he soon receives notice from a great many offices that if he does not leave the country he will be killed. If he stays he is generally killed. For the poor people unite into clubs and have a fund to hinder the rising of the price of land and they will not allow any one to live in peace who does give a higher price.[1] The leader of a large gang in this neighbourhood was some time ago taken and a poor man who had been persecuted by him and swore against him[.] He was committed and the poor person bound over in a penalty – to prosecute him[.] This man had great sums offered him by the club not to do it his penalty would have been paid by them and he would never have been hurt by them any more but the offers of the Government and Mr Jephson[2] who took up the fellow were better and the Chief was hanged at Clonmel[.] He was a young man about 28 years and he died with the utmost composure and as calm as possible[.][3] Mr Jephson heard that they had elected another chief soon after.

[f. 117v *blank*]

[f. 118r] Reverend Mr Douglas says that many of the poor people in the cabins who have had land for many years of which some have notwithstanding their extreme filth and their appearance yet on account of the great depreciation of money and that high increase in the value of land that there are many who could lend you 100£. Unlike the English peasantry they have no idea of laying out on their own comforts[.] They have by habit got settled in filth and dirt and smoke. They sometimes spend a good deal in whiskey but never in increasing their comforts.

Dined with the Officers of the 66th at their mess in the new Barracks[.][4]

---

[1] Agrarian secret societies protested against enclosure, the payment of tithes to the established church and conacre rents. See Smyth, *Men of No Property*, pp. 33–51.
[2] Probably Denham Jephson (?1748–1813) of Mallow Castle, MP for Mallow in the Irish parliament and at Westminster (1802–12) (History of Parliament Online).
[3] Maria Luddy records a number of similar instances in 'Whiteboy Support in Co. Tipperary'.
[4] Kickham Barracks, built in 1805 (NIAH).

[21 September, Sunday]
Breakfasted with Mr Doughlas and Cap*tain* Elmor.[1] Went to *Ch*ur*ch* wh*ich* is a very neat fine elegantly fitted up [building], 2 good galleries, and the E and W windows are very elegant and neat, in the Gothic style. Very good congregation[.] Mr Douhglas [*sic*] preached with*out* Book and is a very fine orator. His figure remarkably fine and handsome[.] His language action voice and style very commanding[.] The finest public speaker I ever heard, any where. Elegant choice of words[.] Dined at Col*onel* [*left blank*][2] Ab*out* 2 miles *from* the town. Very fine lodge. Land luxuriant. The Trees and the foliage of land in Ireland more deep green than in England. There are some of the largest ashes I ever saw, and very immense bodied poplars[.]

[f. 118v] The River Suire [Suir] runs close at the Back of the H*ouse* and is very fine. Col*onel* Bagwell built the H*ouse* himself. Very fine rooms, spacious. Offices well concealed in the wings. In 1 wing is a Green House in the other a Good library[.] Just over the river some *Moun*tains rise suddenly and boldly wh*ich* are planted and will soon be a great addition to the place[.]

Drove round by Mr Moores place. His farm wh*ich* is a fine large house and excellent land a lake in front of H*ouse* and some noble woods beyond it. Trees most flourishing and strong.

Excellent land. All worth 6Gs an Acre[.] In Clonmel Mr Bagwell lets his land at 1½ Guineas a foot in the front and it goes 150 feet or more behind the front[.]

[f. 119r *blank*]

[f. 119v] Gaitors mak*ing* 3:3[.]

[f. 120r] Mr Elmor going *from* Clonmel to Capoquin [Cappoquin] met once ab*out* 5000 men armed with axes, pitchforks, some guns knives scythes etc. He addressed them 'And well my Boys where are you going' etc and *fou*nd out that this was the case[:]

Some men who took turf *from* Newcastle to a place in Nicholas Town, a place ab*out* 4 or 5 miles *from* Clonmel in a particular barony[3] and they were insulted and one desperately wounded ∴ the whole barony arose and were going to meet the opposite barony ~~in the and as~~[.] He recommended them to go back and said that the army woul*d* be obliged to be called out at Clonmel and much disorder woul*d* ensue. We will go for revenge is sweet and let wh*at* will happen we will have it and thus he left them. They said they did not wish to hurt them and woul*d* not. The next day coming back he met them again and understood that something had happened and all had been settled amicably, or the 2 class woul*d* have fought and much bloodshed woul*d* have ensued[.]

[f. 120v *blank*]

[f. 121r *Ink sketch, captioned*] 'Tower in Lord Mo*un*t Cashel grounds near Fermoy Sept*ember* 28'.[4]

---

[1] This unidentified person is mentioned again on 22 Sept. (see p. 158), 25 Sept. (see p. 163) and 19 Jan. (see p. 265). Lee spells his name inconsistently as Almer, Aylmour, Elmor and Elmour.

[2] Colonel John Bagwell (1752–1816) of Marlfield, landowner and MP (in 1792–1800) (Quinn, 'Bagwell, John').

[3] Barony of Iffa and Offa West.

[4] Reproduced at p. 173 (Figure 12).

DIARY 2: TOUR FROM HOLYWELL TO DUBLIN AND FERMOY

[f. 121v] **[Monday 22 September]**
Monday leave Clonmel and go to Capoquin over the mountains. Along the side of the River Suire, very beautiful. Go through Lord Dunoughmores grounds[1] and pass through Newcastle village where is an old bridge (and) a fine ruins of the church[.] Ascend the Mountains pass by Knock Meldown [Knockmealdown] mountain and come to the village of Capoquin, a good village on the fine Black water [Blackwater] river[.] Start at ¼ past 5 to go down the river in a boat. See some fine views[.] Just down the river is a nice limestone quarry. The mountain Knockmil down looks fine from here. On the top of it was buried Major Eeles and his dog.[2] He was a great shooter and often there[.] Saw a great many cranes. He left a sum of money to have his dog and guns buried there. See a pretty ruin on the R shore.

See Mr Musgraves house and store house[.] Tide rises 14 feet at Capoquin and vessels of 260 tons can come there. Islands[.]

Mariners call the Knock mel down Mountains The high lands of Dungarvan[.]

Come to the rock of Dromana and on top of it a House of some Park Keeper or person on Lord Grandisons manor. [f. 122r] [*margin:* (Lord Grandison dead and now the estate in family of Stuarts)[3]] [f. 121v] Whole rock in summer covered with wallflowers[.] House of Sir Richard Musgrave[4] on the R. Very old House and fine ruins of a Castle joining the house Fine woods Dairy of Dromana on the L[.]

[f. 122r] Bill: £1:1:6
Boy for errands. 10^d 2nd Washing 3^d
Mending shoes S5:5^d
½ Chaise from 9 Mile House to Clonmel 8^s:4
Post horse to Capoquin 10(S):6 Dinner there 3:5
½ Boat to Youghal 5:3

[f. 122v] Weirs for catching salmon. Lay nets and a weir of platted hurdles at the end of the river which is narrow is a net and he catches the fish by judging when they are in[.]

Dromana house is the finest situation I ever saw. Sir William Homand[5] lives there[.] He is agent to the Stewart family. House on a ⊥^{r} point of land over the water. Fine woods on each side[.]

Below the house a place like a fortification[.] 2 bastions above each other Boatmans house close by. 3 arches below the bastions[.] All the building of rough stone[.]

Lord Grandisons other Daughter was not married[.] She died <u>out of reason</u> said a man[.]

Look up the river the view of Dromana House and the mountain is wonderfully fine[.]

House of Mr Usher on the R side. Mr Huson lives there now. Mr Usher married Mr H sister[.]

---

[1] Richard Hely-Hutchinson (1756–1825) of Knocklofty, Co. Tipperary, 1st Earl Donoughmore and MP (Hourican, 'Hutchinson, Richard Hely-').

[2] Henry Eeles (1702–81), writer and man of science; the appellation 'major' was not a formal title but a name by which he was known locally (Flood, 'Henry Eeles').

[3] George, Earl of Grandison died in 1800, leaving Dromana to his daughter, Gertrude Amelia, and her husband, Lord Henry Stuart (*Burke's Peerage*, 1850, p. 552).

[4] Sir Richard Musgrave, 1st Baronet (1746?–1818), political writer (Woods, 'Musgrave, Sir Richard'); Camphire House was rebuilt *c.*1840 (LED).

[5] William Jackson Homan was created a baronet in 1801 and acted as agent on the Dromana estate (LED).

Gent said it was the finest river but the Delaware in America. Deep red sunset and moonlight also[.] Suns red finely reflected on 1 side and on the other moon reflected[.]

Villiers town [Villierstown] on the L about a mile from water where later Lord Grandison had a factory. Opposite is Mr Smiths House of Headborough[.][1]

[f. 123r *Ink sketch, a view of a river, probably the Blackwater, and distant hill.*]

[f. 123v] River Bride[2] goes up to Mr Smiths house[.]

A vessel sank of 200 tons laden with cullum [*margin:* Cullum] a sort of fine coal and at low water there is 16 feet water over her main deck. 2 barges hired to raise her but could not, this time 3 years.

Vessels come from Whitehaven, Workington[,] Whitehaven and Swansea here[.]

8 or 10 pairs of boats fishing for salmon[.] There are 2 men in each boat one minds the end of the rope the other the boat[.] When a fish gets in the net the men feel it and the boats row together and draw the net out[.]

A man said his Father paid 48Gs for the fishing of the water for 5 Months. His time begins 10 of August. Space between Capoquin and 3 Miles up Lismore. (Mr Welsh and Mr Kiff) hires the whole fishery of Mr Musgrave for 900£[.] They sell fish for 3^d a lb[.] [*margin:* (5^d a lb in Lent)[3]]

No rebellion hereabouts but a man in the parish of Capoquin taken out and flogged[.]

Average his father catches 85 one night. Once 3 fish from 20 to 30 lb a piece. Catch about 15 on average a night of fish, sometimes 40 or 20[.] Weir costs 30 or 40£ and any body who buys a piece of land may build one[.]

[f. 124r *blank*]

[f. 124v] Weirs made of common Irish timber or oak or red deal[.]

Stran Coles Castle an old fortress[.][4]

Mr Powers, Clashmore House[.][5]

The Bay of Clashmore[.]

Ballinatray [Ballynatray] the House of Mr Smith [Smyth] on the R lower down the river fine woods round it.

Come to the fine bay at Entrance[.] Got ashore [*margin:* at Youghall] but got off again and got here at 9[.]

[f. 125r *blank*]

[f. 125v] A boy would run from here to Cork 24 Miles and come back next day for a dollar[.]

Captain Elmor had a boy (man) to go from Clonmel to Limerick distance 42 Miles with a letter and he came back the next night for ½ a Guinea[.]

[f. 126r *blank*]

[f. 126v] **[23 September] Tuesday.**
Walked out to see the Baths, the neatness and elegance of which are extremely well worth seeing[.] Six of them in a row nice neat small apartments with carpets, fireplaces, and in

---

[1] Headborough House, still privately owned and occupied.
[2] A tributary of the Blackwater.
[3] Marginal note moved from original position for clarity.
[4] Strancally castle, a tower house built *c.*1571 (Moore, *Archaeological Inventory of County Waterford*, p. 229).
[5] Probably Richard Power (1775?–1834) of Clashmore House, Co. Waterford, MP (History of Parliament Online).

DIARY 2: TOUR FROM HOLYWELL TO DUBLIN AND FERMOY

the front is a bath by w*hi*ch water can in 3 minutes be admitted and fill them[.] They are round and can be filled with hot or cold water. They face the sea and have a neat colonade in ~~front~~ the back. In the yard is a swing on Merlins plan.[1] Price of a cold Bath 10^d a hot one 2:6. The plan on w*hi*ch they are filled deserves attention. At one end is a buildi*ng* at the top of one part of w*hi*ch is a large reservoir 8 feet square by 5½ w*hi*ch is filled with fresh water *fr*om the sea every morni*ng* by means of a pump above, and *fr*om this the cold water is supp*li*ed to a large boiler close by w*hi*ch heats the water. There is a large Quant*it*y of water kept hot all night and day, by fires underneath in w*hi*ch a layer of cullum and a large of lime (stone) are alternately placed and thus the water is kept boiled.

There are pipes w*hi*ch go out below the low water mark into the sea and these are brought to the bottom of the pump. The water is lifted up ab*out* 24 feet *fr*om the bottom of the pump to reservoir. The pump is worked by pretty machinery.[2] The handle is a long rod and is a lever havi*ng* 2 arms of = length *fr*om a fulcrum w*hi*ch is in a wall. Then is a system of 8 Inclined planes, 4 up and 4 down w*hi*ch are [f. 127v] turned round by a horse acting below. Thus when the horse goes round the floor over w*hi*ch turns the machinery once round and the end of the pump is forced up one inclined plane and goes d*ow*n the other[.] The altitude of the planes is 2 foot 1 Inch and the incli*ne* ab*out* 25° and thus as this end of the pump moves thro*ugh* 25 Inches the piston at the other end does the same, and as the Drawi*ng* of the pump is 6 Inches thus the area occupied by the water pumped up every rise and fall of the handle is [K*now*n?] as a horse will go round ab*out* 4 or 5 times in a minute. There are 4 × 4 or 4 × 5 barrels full of water pumped every minute[.] [*Bottom half of page is an ink sketch of the mechanism.*]

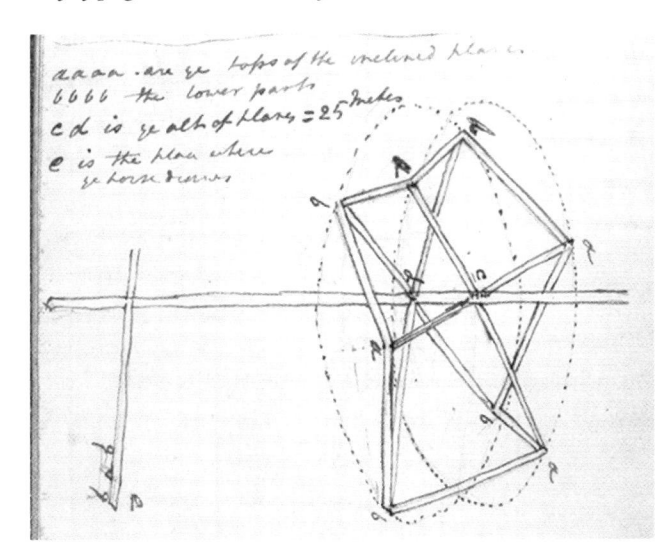

Figure 10. Sketch of water pump mechanism in Youghal baths, as described in SJC, MS U.30 (2), ff. 126v–127v (pp. 158–60). By John Lee, 23 September 1806 (SJC, MS U.30 (2), f. 127v). Reproduced by kind permission of the Master and Fellows of St John's College, Cambridge.

aaaa are the tops of the inclined plane.
bbbb the lower parts
[f. 128r *Another ink sketch of mechanism.*]

cd is the alt*itu*de of planes = 25 Inches
e is the place where the horse draws

---

[1] Invented by John Joseph Merlin (1735–1803), a mechanical swing thought to have health benefits and a feature of a number of public baths; see [Greater London Council], *John Joseph Merlin*, pp. 57–8.
[2] Lee's sketch of the mechanism, originally at SJC, MS U.30 (2), f. 127v, is reproduced above (Figure 10).

[f. 128v] At the end of the arm of pump is a weight w*hich* makes the end descend by its weight d*ow*n the inclined planes thus the horse has only to raise it up.

[f. 127r] [*Start one page of rough pencil notes.*]

Pillar.

Inclined plane. 2 feet ⊥ʳ and ab*ou*t incline of 25°[.] 4 plates in a Circle, all turned by a horse[.] A horse will go round 5 times in a minute or 20 times in a minute. ~~Lever~~ (Dist*ance*) w*hich* horse sits f*ro*m Centre is. Arms of pump = and D*iamete*r of pump 6 Inches and 2 feet 1 Inch the Depth this the q*uantit*y of water will be fo*u*nd in 1 turn and ∴ in a minute Water is elevated by the pump 24 feet. There are pipes w*hich* go out to the low watermark[.] 8 feet square by 5½ the cold reservoir and there arm one 8 feet oval. Then is heated by limestone and cullum[.]

[f. 128v] Man who keeps these baths and has built them is an Englishman. The place is delightful. Walked along the shore round the point and see the fine sea noble red rocks, beautiful studies for pictures. There is a fine bay [Youghal Bay] round the point of land on the R of the town. Fine spot of sands for a horse race. Pretty to see all the women com*ing* along the shore ro*a*d [of] the bay to market in diff*erent* parties. Picked up a great many pretty shells and pebbles and returned along the shore am*ong* the noble rocks. The entrance to the Harbour (Bay) here is very dangerous at low tides. There being a bar at the mouth and sometimes there is not above 2 feet [of] water on the bar. (at low water of the spring) tides (there is not at) here ab*ou*t 2 feet.[1] The Gaol a most elegant building in the middle of the street and a fine arch under it. A great many gentlemens H*o*uses all ab*ou*t the town and in it and it resembles an English town more than any I had seen, however in many parts there are cabins with dung heaps in front and a kennel for the pigs to live in. Saw many pigs go d*ow*n to the shore to eat either seaweed or else the shellfish and shrimps. Shoals of fish in the harbour jumping about all small and many diff*erent* sorts of sea fowl within shot fishing for them[.] Cormorants, Shags [*Phalacrocorax aristotelis*] etc[.]

Crossed the ferry and f*ro*m the oppos*ite* side the town [f. 129r] w*hich* is situated at the foot of a hill looks divine. The fine keys [quays] are noble and the warehouses and the white buildings look very well[.] It is a large long town[.] The mouth of the Bay is very narrow and a long tongue of ~~land~~ sand forms it. Walked along the shore to the point to see the town in its diff*erent* points of view. Most charming sands – very fine. Several small ridges of rock w*hich* correspond exactly with those on the opposite side of the mouth, some white and others red.

Crossed again and saw all the boats return home fr*o*m fishing and come and moor near the quay. Immense q*uantit*y of fish. Saw all the women buy their fish dog cheap and then resell it again. The finest immense large turbot I ever saw might have had for 3½ Crowns and perhaps for less. Hake in large quantities immensely long ab*ou*t 6 or 8 lb each were sold by the stalls for 6ᵈ each. Large ling or lyng w*hich* they called the Beef of the sea might have bought for an English shilling each, and some perhaps 10 or 12 lbs each and more[.] There were plenty of live herrings to be sold for 6ᵈ a doz*en* and these were the prices of the fish women, when one might have bought them [cheaper] off the boats. Sprats in myriads and plenty of the largest pla*i*ce and sole. Fine sight.

[f. 129v] Saw one of the Gunboats. It had a large 36 pounder in the head. Each balot is commanded by a midshipman and the whole by a Lieut*enant* who has a guinea a day. Each costs [the] Gov*ernmen*t ab*ou*t 54Gs a month or 648 in a year[.]

---

[1] This confusing sentence seems intended to qualify the previous sentence.

4 Gun Boats. They are of no use whatever they land these under pretense of defending the harbour and any little French privateers could blow them to pieces[.]

Down from the extreme narrowness of the harbour a 2 Gun Battery at the Entrance of the harbour could be of infinitely more service and it might be built for the one years expense of a boat. Or a martello tower would do very well and it would be only the first expense[.] A Battery on each side would guard from any thing, but these boats are useless and cost about 3000 a year[.] In the boat are fixed 4 or 6 small guns which are capable of being turned round in any direction and useful for close action. The accommodations are horrible and bad, and the ballast was large stones on each side piled loose up, a sign the vessel never goes to sea[.]

The Assembly rooms are admirably situated on the waterside and in front is a fine promenade[.] The room upstairs is very fine has 3 fine lustres[1] and plenty of Glasses and lights.[2] There is a Ball once a week. 12 Balls for ½ Guinea. As [in general?] gentleman pays 2:8½ and a lady 1:7½[.] Among the rules I observed that the Stewards are not obliged to find Partners for any Gentleman[.] 'That noone be admitted in Boots or Pantaloons[.]' That 2 Gentleman or 2 Ladies do not dance together.

They begin at 8 and end ½ past 12.

Below is a news room and a court room for I suppose justices.

[f. 130r]

Dinner at Capoquin for	2. – 6ˢ:
Water	:10
	s.6:10
Boat and 4 Oars…	11:4½
	S.18:2½
Play house at Youghall	6:3ᵈ
Powder and shot 1lb and 7 lbs 4 / 3:7ᵈ =	(S)7:7
Flints 2ᵈ. Ferry 3ᵈ.	:5
Men 2 days for shells. 20:15ᵈ	2:11
Sailors to Gunboat	1:1
Fruit	1:10

[f. 130v] [**24 September**] **Wednesday.**
Went a Bathing on the shore. Undressed in a fine [neat?] cave which is nearly at the point and from there walk on a fine sand in to water. Charming[.]

Saw a great many nets drawing on shore with different draughts of fish. The nets are 200 fathoms long and a rope at each end the same. A boat goes out from shore and compasses a large portion of water and then brings the rope round again to the shore and the ends are brought together when the net is nearly coming to the shore that it may touch it they take a smaller mesh net and Draw round the large ones at a short distance for the sprats (or ~~small~~ herrings I forget which) as soon as they feel the net touch ground then dart

---

[1] Chandeliers (*OED*).
[2] The Assembly Rooms at Youghal opened in 1789, at a cost of almost £2,000 and with seating for 200 (Dickson, *Old World Colony*, p. 423).

thro*ugh* it and try to get away but the small net holds them.[1] They go before it untill it does[.]

2 John Doreys immense size sold for 2:6. All sorts of fish dog cheap. Went out in the Harbour in a small boat belonging to the Gunboat to shoot seafowl killed some. Cap*tain* McGuire[2] sent me the boat, a friend of Cap*tain* O[.]

Mr Barrets pretty house over the water[.]

Dined with the Cap*tain* McGuire and then in the Eve*ning* went to the Play and saw the tragedy of *Hamlet* and the farce of the *Rehearsal*.[3] All miserably murdered indeed. Except a Mr Talbot in *Hamlet* and Puff[.]

[f. 131r] A horse Bill at Youghall
Sept*em*be*r*
23 To 2 Horses and	2 feeds	4:4
24 To 2 D*itto*	and 6 D*itto*.	6:6
25 To ——	2 D*itto*	1:1
		11:11

Inn Keepers names Howard.
The York Hotel Tavern.
//
Servants Bill
Sept*em*ber
23 Tea	1:1
24 Breakfast............	1:4
Dinner and Porter........	1:7½
Break*f*ast..............	1:4
	5:4½

22 Tea for 2.............	3:3	
23 Breakfast.............	3:3	
Cash..............	2:2	P*ai*d Boatmen
Dinner for 2.............	4:4	Sole, etc etc
Porter a Bottle............	:6	
Claret............	6–	
Tea for 2.............	3:3	
24 Breakfast.............	3:3	
Cash...............	5:5	Hired Beds wh*ich* they paid for
D*itto*............	–:2	
25 Breakfast ——	3:3	

[1] Lee drew two arcs in the page margin to illustrate the effect created by the ropes; not reproduced here.

[2] Captain Maguire RN oversaw the erection of signal posts on the Cork coastline from Dec. 1800 (Tuckey, *Cork Remembrancer*, p. 207).

[3] Probably Henry Fielding, *The Rehearsal*, London, 1753.

```
                    1:14:10½
                       5:4½
                      11:11
                      ─────
                    2:12:2
                      4:8½
Waiter
Chamber Maid ──      3-
                    ─────
```

[f. 131v] Orchestra consisted of 2 fiddles. Worst theatre I ever saw not more than 4£ in the Boxes at 3S. each person on the Benefit of the best actor. However they make up in Time for what they lose in good acting and keep us there till ½ past 12.

This place was the quietest place in world before [the] rebellion. Terrible during it and quiet now[.] Several murders committed here. Very horrible indeed.

While the yeomanry were going to the funeral of a Brother officer, a murder was actually committing as they passed through the street (as was afterwards found out)[.] The men were tried and on clear evidence proved guilty and 3 were hung ~~before~~ by 4 oclock that same evening[.]

A man, his wife maidservant cat and dog were all cruelly murdered close at a farm near the town[.] He had been marked and threatened because he refused to lower the price of his milk[.]

This day was devoted to shooting[.]

[25 September] Thursday.

Terrible bad rainy day, foggy, and misty[.] I had agreed to come up to Lismore with a man in a boat but they would not go and Lieutenant Sparks was going up with Mr Talbot the actor in his own boat and offered to take us with him, which we accepted [f. 132r *blank*] [f. 132v] and got carried up to Capoquin amidst the rain and fog, which just gave us room to see the shores as we passed along. Amazing difficulty to get silver in the country towns and they constantly pester you with a quantity of nasty 5 Shillings and six Shilling notes and ½ Guinea notes of the little Bankers at the different places. Hardly any person will take a note of the Bank of Ireland from you without your putting your name on the back and many people prefer the notes of the neighbourhood Banks to those of the Bank of Ireland[.][1]

Wonderfully nasty the Irish are in their 4 [Courts?]. The doors are frequently open and people feel no delicacy in going there. They seldom shut the door if any vacant place remains in the [Court?]. Never saw but one which was comfortable and convenient and that was at Carlow[.] It was only for 2 at a time. I have frequently seen men sitting with the door open.[2] We had a fair wind up the river and the tide in our favour also and run up to Capoquin very quick. Dined there in a very pleasant party of ourselves[.] Dinner 4:4 including a Bottle of port and several of cyder. Captain Almer and Mr Talbot went off for

---

[1] The Bank of Ireland was established in 1783, but by 1801 there was still no bank with the means to regulate currency across the island; in 1797–1804, note circulation trebled for a number of reasons (Ó Gráda, 'Industry and Communications', pp. 150–51).

[2] Lee describes a public latrine. See also note on sketch in SJC, MS U.30 (8), f. 70r (p. 339, n. 3).

Clonmel and I for Lismore up the river side where I got in the eve*ni*ng when it was dark and in the fog. I was asking Lieut*enant* Sparks ab*out* the duel w*hi*ch he had a few days before been fighting with Mr — the parsons son and he told me how it originated at the theatre. He said it was wonderful that ever since he had been at sea he had never had a quarrel but that since he had been at Youghal with the —[1] Irish he had been [f. 133v] engaged in 3. <u>In the last</u> duel he shot the Gent in the Guts but he is getting better[.]

[f. 133r *Two small ink sketch plans of public latrine, one scored out.*]

[f. 133v] On the Tuesday Capt*ain* Elmour and myself were stand*i*ng on the Quay when an old woman came up and said to me 'God bless you my young master I know you and so does my husband the old soldier with one leg we have paid rent to your Lord Duke[2] yo*u*r father these 40 years and I heard that you was come here to see this place fr*o*m England with that other Gent but did not wish to be known but I know you well enough for all that —.' Surprised at being thus raised to the peerage, we thought the woman was mad, and asked several persons who said no, she was only a talkative old woman and of course wished to know my new title and asked her w*hi*ch Lord Duke son she thought I was. 'Oh we know that you are the Great Dukes son who lives ~~far~~ (some way off) *fr*om here and you are come God bless you to Youghal *fr*om England to see this country' and then a shoal of praises and blessings fell to my share. There were several people who were all about during this convers*atio*n and who were laughing also. However I met her again in the street in the course of the day and accosted her asking her how she was, for w*hi*ch condescension I rec*eive*d a thousand blessings. The next day Wednesday several times in the day was called 'the young Duke' by the people at market and old women and on Thursday mor*ni*ng when I was at the Mayors office on the Quay waiting for Capt*ain* Elmor thereabouts sever*a*l old women gathered about me and were very anxious to get me to stop and speak to them and they called me the young Duke, 'look at the young Duke' and pointed me out, and when a man [f. 134r *blank*] [f. 134v] was sent by the mayor to Lieut*enant* Sparks to request him to take us with him to Youghal, this fellow had got hold of the story. For Lieut*enant* said that a man brought him a message saying that the Duke of Bedfords son requested him to be so good as to take him up in ~~the~~ (his) boat and he was surprised at it as well as Mr Talbot.

A sailor who carried my knapsack for me *fr*om Capoquin to Lismore told me that a sailor of the *Glory*[3] had informed him that my friend and me were come to have the Gunboats and the Fencibles out and that they were to go out of harbour and that we were come *fr*om England and were going all over the country. Upon his being not credulous the other swore it was true and that we had been on board the *Glory* <u>just to examine her</u> w*hi*ch was true for our curiosity led us there[.]

The Pay of the Lieut*enant* is not more than 8S a day. Capt*ain* McGuire has a Guinea a day[.]

---

[1] This dash may represent a swear word used by Sparks in conversation.

[2] Youghal was part of the extensive Devonshire estates in Ireland, and because the family invested so heavily in the first two decades of the 19th century, in improving Youghal and other towns on their lands, 'the sixth duke was fêted like royalty on his visits' (Dickson, *Old World Colony*, p. 436) – which explains the old woman's enthusiasm for the young man she supposed to be the duke's heir, William Cavendish (1790–1858), 6th Duke of Devonshire.

[3] HMS *Gloire*, a French 40-gun frigate captured by the British in 1803, added to the Royal Navy, and broken up in 1812 (Royal Museums Greenwich collections website).

Thus the old woman made me a Duke and *from* that became a Duke of Bedfords son and *from* that an inspecting officer and all this series is easily traced *from* the garrulous old woman spreading her report about but how she came to find out the true part and to add the false is beyond our comprehension[.] We *coul*d not learn *from* anyone. She said her husband knew me better than she did.

The Irish are confounded prying and they will if possible sift out who you are where you are going and *from* whence you came and it is extraordinary how they will get at it. You never can get a direct answer *from* an Irish man. They always begin a humbugging cursed round about way of telling you something very dis*tant from* the question [f. 135r] and almost always leave you in an uncertainty. I never heard a clear satisfactory answer given. They will also extort *from* you if possible.

'How much will you take us *from* here [Lismore] to Youghal for.' 'Why Sir we have had some gent*lemen* who have been down and who have given us 16 or 18 Shillings and they were very well satisfied for that and said we had not too much for our trouble,' etc etc etc. Then if you cut them short 'Hold *your damned* round about tongue Sir cant you tell me in plain words. Will you go for 10S.' 'Why Sir we *coul*d not so as to pay us for our trouble and to pay the men also and to sup*por*t them' and then a long story. 'I will not give a farthing more.' 'Why Sir if you *would* give me a ½ Guinea and our allowance of drink to oblige you we will try to get my men to go.'

Such was part of a bargain w*hic*h took place and they are all of this sort[.] They however went for the 10S at last, and even on the way the fellow produced only 3 men and said he *coul*d not get another, and upon our then enquiring he *woul*d not go at all with*out* a fourth and kicking up a row the other man who had been laying by in reserve in case he *shoul*d be wanted came for*wa*rd.

[f. 135v] **[26 September] Friday.**
Went out immed*iately* after Breakfast and intended to go the greatest dist*ance* first w*hic*h was to be ab*out* 3 mile on the Road[.]

Go over bridge up the Glen. Oun ne sheard Glin [Owennashad glen]. The Hills called so too[.]

A little on the R is a pretty (little) Glen called Gloun Taun [Glentaun]. It goes to a village called Murnana tour [Monalour.]

Below a sort of waterfall are some very narrow deep holes w*hic*h are quiet water and are called the ponds of the Glin of Ouneshead. There are some very ancient stones above this part of the river. It is said that they are the washing places of a great giant, Foun Mal Coul.[1] He was*hed* himself every morning in them. He put one foot on each side had his towel laying on the neighb*our*ing rock and then stooped down his head and took up the water in his hands[.] He lived on the rock just below w*hic*h is called Carnegaen or the Giants rocks and is a very fine bold rock[.] Entrance below it is a little cascade coming down its side in such a wet day as this[.]

Drahed nen our Bridge[.][2]

All the glins here have the same name. Very pretty road all along it is cut thro*ugh* the side of rocks all the way and very fine slate appears in many places[.] Just below the bridge

---

[1] Fionn MacCumhaill is a central figure in Irish mythology, leader of a group called the Fianna.
[2] Possibly Drohidcaman, a bridge over the Glenaknockaun River. In this and the next paragraph Lee gives only vague indications of his location as he roams around the Knockmealdown mountains.

165

a fine glen runs up to the L[.][1] Some fine trees are left standing on the one part of the South M*ountai*n[2] and many are laying about stripped [f. 136r *blank*] [f. 136v] of their bark. Probably all will soon share the same fate[.] The river here divides, one runs up each Glen[.] The road to the R goes to Clogheen ab*ou*t 10 miles. Go along it and ascending the M*ountai*n for a mile and then turn back to the bridge[.] Cross the water by stepping stones at the meetings of the rivers and go up the other glen where wood [has been] cut down. Go up the Glen and see the finest scenery my eyes ever beheld there is a greater collection of beautiful and boldest rocks, some of the finest old fantastic timber oaks. The rocks are the finest I ever saw[.] The points of M*ountai*n come one behind another in the boldest manner and in most immense masses. The river runs over larger rock than can imagine. There is no (regular) path but by clambering up and down you get on cliffs ⊥ʳ on the river below[.]

Charming[.] Go far some way up and then return[.] Little Irish boys curiosity who accompanied me afraid of me at first, my Glass. At last picked my pocket and eat my bread and laughed [at] every thing he took[.] He jumped about[.]

[f. 137r] There was a little boy met me at the meeting of the waters who was at first afraid of me and jabbered Irish as fast as he c*oul*d[.] He followed me and kept chattering and at last was not afraid but laughed at my not understanding him. We could not make each other out and the endeavour was curious[.] When I stopped to draw he came close up and at last ventured to touch my dress chattering all the time[.] He took hold of my spy glass and looked thro*ugh* it as he saw me do. He then felt the outside of my bag and then ventured laughing to put his hand in looking to see if I liked his so doing. He then felt something and pulling it out, uttered exclamations on getting a bit of bread w*hi*ch the rogue immediately began eating[.] I made signs for a bit w*hi*ch he broke off and held to my mouth and I snatched up and bit his fingers w*hi*ch amazed him and surprised [him]. He then felt for some thing else and on pulling it out fo*un*d it was a bit of slate. Expressing some words of surprise he put that in again, and tried for some thing else. The next thing was another bit of bread for w*hi*ch I begged for a share and he w*oul*d not put that in to my mouth but laid it on my portfolio.

On taking another view, he got out a ½[3] with w*hi*ch he was wonderfully delighted and then for the first time spoke English and said 'An ½ penny' and soon after 'give me one more ½ penny' and feeling some ventured to get at them but I hindered him[.] He then got my spectacle can out and was astonished to see it red, and upon opening it and seeing the silver and the same glass as my spy glass he ran away with it and seemed ½ inclined to be off. I thought the joke carried too far and was afraid and ran after him a short way but he w*oul*d have beat me hollow ∴ I stopped and pretending to laugh heartily went back to the place I was sitting drawing at and began to pretend to draw in an easy humour, not caring about him, but took out my compass [and] began to look at it, trying to coax him to me [f. 138r] to see it. He came very near, and asking him for the glasses he w*oul*d not give me them but began a bargain, How many ½ pence I w*oul*d give him, and then took out a bottle and pretended to drink wiskey w*hi*ch brought him still nearer but he kept on his guard, all the time. Then going on sham drawing, I got ready and made a dart after him

---

[1] Possibly along the Glenaknockaun River.
[2] Possibly Knockaungarriff.
[3] Halfpenny.

when his eyes were not on their guard and did catch him but he gave the glasses up reluctantly. I then gave him another ½ and as I came out of the glen he said all the way, 'give me one ½' and at my not doing so when we came to the meeting of the water he was very indignant and stamped as if to threaten me and on his stopping there he I suppose abused me all the way.

Thus he w*ou*ld have gone on and asked for another if I had given him that.

The Inn at Lismore called the New Inn[.] It is kept by an apothecary, Mr Fitzgerald. He has 5 five [*sic*] daughters, Mary, Jenny, Nancy, Judy.[1]

On Monday next the whole house and many beds in the town are bespoken. 4 Packs of Foxhounds are coming then and above 40 Gentlemen to hunt the country. Mr F*itz*gerald was gone to Cork today in provisions. They stay a fortnight and the barn is converted into a kennel[.] Not a bit of his hay or corn is got in yet for had it the dogs w*ou*ld have spoilt it and on their ac*coun*t it was left out[.]

[f. 139r] The old man at the Slate quarry is reckoned the greatest ancient historian in the country round. He knows all the stories of the giants who ever lived and has them d*ow*n in writing. He is a great scholar. He c*ou*ld not read English print, but c*ou*ld read Irish and English in writing and in Irish characters[.] He said he had got stores of Irish stories in writing for he was always fond of reading and writing, and c*ou*ld never be tired of it but he got nothing by it and was obliged to earn his bread[.]

There are 2 sorts of slate in the quarry. Top layer is stone, then light coloured slate in wh*ich* vast quantities of small lumps of an ore looking stuff is fo*un*d, I believe brimstone. Below is the dark coloured slate and now is fo*un*d in it [*blank*][.] Slates sold for the 1000, 3:3, 4:4 or 5:5 a 1000[.]

The Ridge [*breaks off*]

[f. 137v] Very long ridges of slate about the Giants Rock[.] They are very deep. There is a pretty water fall just above them[.] Came down other side of river oppo*site* road amo*ng* the rocks. F*ou*nd the *Osmunda Regalis* [royal fern] growing near the farm cottage where trees are being felled and several other plants[.]

In the river are some pieces of spar and very fine chrystals in it indeed and some layers of d*ifferen*t sorts. Crossed the river hopping over the stones and ascending the road just at foot of Giants Rock[.]

The approach to the town of Lismore is wonderfully fine down the glen and when you just get a view of the castle stop and consider what you see and hear[.] A noble foreground of bold slaty M*oun*tain cov*ered* with trees a river running at y*our* feet over a stark slaty course fine shady wood over it and a waterfall close at y*our* feet a 2[2] distance, not so bold and more bare at the end. Dist*ant* red rocks quite bare, just over wh*ich* the tower of the castle, the noble trees and town appear. A dist*ant* range of m*oun*tain behind bare fine contrast with fine ground[.] The river runs strai*ght* before you Down the mi*ddl*e of the picture. The wood consists of oak ash Mountain ash with their red berries and the leaves all have a tinge[.]

[f. 138v] It began to rain. I had not got my umbrella, and upon recoll*ectio*n left it when taking a sketch[.] Ran back [and] met some carmen[.] Had they seen it[?] 'Yes Sir it is laying by [the] roadside farther on[.]' (Honesty). Rained all the way back to the Bridge

---

[1] Lee lists only four of the five daughters here.
[2] Second.

where I turned to the R to go see the Deans House[1] which is very pleasantly situated not far from the riverside. Fine trees all around it and beautiful grounds[.]

~~There are 2~~ The Bridge is very pretty and the arches are very fine[.] One of great expanse[.]

There is a very large salmon weir by the Deans House[.] There is a very fine colonade of trees from the high street leading to the church[.] At the end is a fine old gateway with 2 small doors on the sides, and a fine body of trees inside. The Church is at some short distance behind the gate and fine rows of trees on each side [of] the path. There are very fine trees all round the church yard[.] 4 Good monuments of marble in the Church[.] It is very elegantly fitted up and the neatest in Ireland I saw[.] Curious old windows. Stalls of old seats etc[.] Pillars under the organ gallery. Curious old windows at E end[.] Outside are three most cumbrous and many arches abutments on the South side. There is also a small arch from it to the others[.]

Beautiful gate and entrance[.]

There is also a fine but inferior row of trees leading to the castle. At End is an old gateway round arch and 1 square tower on each side[.]

[f. 139v] Then there is a long passage with a high wall on 1 side and an immense row of large firs on it on the other side a wall. The road leads to another gate[.]

Over the 2nd Gate which is a fine round arch is a coat of arms with 4 fleur de lis on 1 side, a helmet and a crest of some animal on it. There are 2 supporters and underneath is written in capital letters GODS PROVIDENCE IS OUR INHERITANCE 1615[.][2]

Through this gateway you come into a fine large court, irregular on the R side a fine (ruins) and over covered with ivy. The entrance to the House is continued through the middle of the Court to a modern Gate and Portico. There is the ruins of the chapel and several large rooms. Could not see the hall[.] The cursed boy who should have had the key could not find it[.]

From the garden is a beautiful view of the river and country around below the bridge the stream dividing and forms an irregular island[.]

The murdering Hall is said to be the tower in the garden is hollow and goes down near to the waters depth a boy told me. The key of it was also lost. Mr Lowe lives in the Castle and takes care of it. A bath in the garden. They are nothing extraordinary.

Several parts of the grounds you are told are not worth seeing which are the best eg, the bowling green a fine lofty mound on the top of which is an extensive flat and the sides planted round with noble and tall ash trees. From the edge of the bank the river is seen through the most delightful grove winding in a multiplicity of forms and creating the finest river scene I ever saw[.]

[f. 140r] [*Two small pencil sketches of coats of arms*] From Capoquin to Lismore 3 Miles

[f. 140v] 'And is not everybody delighted with these grounds which you call the wilderness, and which you call the wilderness [*sic*] and which you said were not worth seeing.' 'I dont believe any body ever (asked to) see them before Sir[.]'

By going also to see the wilderness, you see a fine part of the old house in ruins which they say belonged to Sir Walter Raleigh. It is behind the chapel[.]

---

[1] Lismore deanery, built c.1790 (NIAH) and located on the bank of the River Blackwater.
[2] Lismore castle, built by King John in 1185 and remodelled by Sir Richard Boyle in 1621 (who purchased the castle and grounds from Sir Walter Raleigh); Lee saw the castle in a neglected state, as rebuilding did not begin until 1814 (Moore, *Archaeological Inventory of County Waterford*, p. 214). Lee cites the Boyle family motto here.

[27 September] Saturday
Bill: 13:9
 Start for Castle Richards[.][1] Go through the wilderness and made towards the river side. Go opposite Dean Scots house[2] which is pretty on river side. Fine meadows opposite and the wilderness. Woods extending all in front on high banks.
 Go on through meadow, and see the river winding gently but you may be above 2 mile up it noble woods bounding it the whole way and woods in the distance and beyond all Mountains cultivated.
 Paddy Hogan Son of Tom Hogan is going for 13 Years[.]
 On the opposite side of the river is South Park a House in the trees S of Mr Northesk. There is a fine old great gate in front and a noble rocky glin just behind the house on the R. The banks opposite are bare[.] Higher up is Fortwilliam a plain looking House but pleasantly situated, belonging to Counsellor Grumbleton[.] From some parts of the river you may see up and down it for 2 miles. People gathering in their hay from the meadows.
 [f. 141r] NB To draw the plan of a weir[.]
 [f. 141v] Path beautiful above the Counsellors House. Noble groves on the banks bounding the meadows[.]
 You have to climb over mud banks which separate the fields and sometimes a gate or a wall with steps met but path very good all the way. The foliage of the ash trees uncommon deep green[.]
 A little higher up the path goes by an amazing fine bed of rock which evinces what the whole bank is and shows on what the fertile trees grow[.]
 Castle Richards the House of Captain Grumbleton[3] is about a mile from his brothers similarly situated on the bank and hemmed in with trees all behind and to the river side and fine woods all down the banks to his brothers House. By the rock we enter a fine rich meadow which goes up to the foot of the House. I Go up to the Captain's House and nothing can compare [to] the view down the river from it. The noble woods hanging over the river all decked with the autumnal tints[.] The view down the vale woods in the distance and fine lofty mountains in the farthest of the picture barely peceptible. It is a fine spot if situation could give happiness this would. Charming situations for any 2 Brothers. Only 2 miles from Lismore the boy said which is 5. Strike straight across the Park over the road to a wood leaving the House just to the R and go through the wood and come ⊥^{r} on the High Road[.]
 [f. 142r *blank*]
 [f. 142v] 'I did not think Paddy Hogan would tell me such a lie as to say it was more than 5 mile and it is but 2.' 'Faith no more he would Sir and it is 5 Miles. And the man knows nothing about it for he lives at Tullough and not at Lismore and I would not have come at all if I thought you would not have paid me for 5.'
 There is a glen opposite the Captains House which runs up the mountains[.] The sides are covered with wood[.] The river Blackwater runs through 2 ranges of Mountains[.]

---

[1] Castle Richards was the residence of Richard Gumbleton (d. 1819), son of Richard Gumbleton and Elizabeth Connor. The Gumbletons held extensive estates around Ireland (LED).
[2] Rev John Scott, Dean of Lismore, 1796–1828.
[3] Castle Richards was the residence of Captain Henry Connor Gumbleton's elder brother, Richard; see n. 1, above. Captain Gumbleton (d. 1834) of the 13th Dragoons resided at Curraglass (LED).

There are some fine deep glens up the other side of the water[.] The M*ountai*ns are some cultivated to the tops, others nearly so[.] Here and there a range of wood[.]

Pass some neat cottages built under 1 plan close by road side by Geo*rge* Gumbleton.[1] Road very pretty[.]

Just over the river is a fine neat white H*ou*se of Mr Drews and very pretty grounds, trees and plantations. A ruin of a fine old castle joins the house[.][2] Behind is [a] fine glen with some wood on its sides. On this side of the river is the neatest farm house I had seen in this p*ar*t of the country[.] It was white outside and inside and Kept in very neat order. The man rented ab*ou*t 150 A*cre*s of M*ou*nta*i*ns[.] St George[.]

See on the road many beautiful white goats with 2 legs tied with hay and a stick connecting them by 2 w*hic*h is fastened round their necks, like Bullocks in harness[.] Women in general in a blue surtout and in caps[.] Most no hats. All bare foot. I have seen a pig in an apothecarys shop a cow ½ in a cabin and horses go to their stable thro*ugh* a cabin[.] In Clonmel the only entrance for pigs boys girls fowl etc was the same[.]

[f. 143r *blank*]

[f. 143v] I offered a Boy a 10^d bit (and then a shilling) to take my knapsack to Fermoy 2 Miles[.] He began grumbl*ing* and when I offered the 2nd Piece he said it was not enough. They are a set of imposing blackguards[.]

I heard a blackguard fellow ask 20 Shillings to carry some trunks to Clonmel f*rom* Capoquin 18 Miles or a common car a return postchaise (to Cahir) wo*u*ld ~~not~~ have taken them for 16S. At last another car was got for 12.

You may make a return chaise carry you for ½ price.
//

All up the river Blackw*ate*r the cultivation is beyond idea fine and luxuriant. Deep green pastures[.] River extraordinary straight for miles[.]

Coming along the road within a mile of the Town of Fermoy a gentleman*'s* horse was startled by my *tout ensemble*[.] Wh*en* recovering I asked w*hich* was the best inn in the place etc[.] Some conversation ensued[.] He got an insight into my plan and told me he had walked thro*ugh* England and pointing to a house over the river said it was his and his name was Dr Drew[3] and asked me to dinner w*hich* invitation I accepted and went there and was pleasantly entertained enough[.] His wife and a Mr [*blank*] an apothecary at Fermoy and at Cork were the party.[4] In the Even*ing* a lawyer came in who lives just beyond, and who married an East Indian lady of fortune and from him I learnt that Mr Anderson a great Cork Merchant bought not quite 1500 Acres of land all about the place for ab*ou*t 20000 some years ago[.][5]

[f. 144r *blank*]

---

[1] Possibly Rev. George Gumbleton, vicar of Affane, Co. Cork and father of the horticulturalist William Edward Gumbleton (1840–1911) (LED).

[2] Mocollop Castle, Co. Waterford, probably inhabited at that time by John Drew, eldest son of Dr Francis Drew (d. 1787) (LED).

[3] Dr P. P. Drew of Fermoy, Co. Cork, who published on obstetrics.

[4] While it cannot be certain that it was he who dined with Lee and Dr Drew, one George Barrett is listed as apothecary at Fermoy in 1806 (*Return of Persons*, p. 99).

[5] John Anderson (1747–1820) was a Scottish merchant and stagecoach operator who purchased land in Fermoy in 1791, rejuvenating the stagnating town by gifting land to the crown for the building of a British military barracks in 1797 (Cooper, 'Anderson, John (1747–1820)'.

[f. 144v] That at that time there were but a few wretched cabins here and that the place has been wholly built new within these last 10 years. His income from this place alone is now 7800 per an*num*. Its chief support is the barrack. When some gent*leman* was asking a very high price for the rent of some ground, Mr A*nderson* told the persons engaged that he knew a gent who w*ould* give them some ground for nothing, and brought them to his estate at Fermoy. When a good situation being chosen a Barrack was built and afterwards a permanent one has continued. This has been the making of the town. This Mr Anderson was the Gent who first established the 4 or 5 Mail Coaches through different parts of the Kingdom and he is a man of very great enterprise[.]

All about this part of the country there are a great n° of old Castles and Danish Mounts[1] and from Dr Drews house you may see 5 or 6 old Castles. Thus it is finely situated on the edge of a rock comm*anding* a fine view up and do*w*n the river. There is also the danish mound close behind his house. There is an old round tower on the other side of [the] river nearer to Fermoy.

[f. 145r *blank*]

[f. 145v] [28 September] Sunday

Went up to the barracks w*hich* are the noblest buildings I ever saw and form 3 sides of a magnificent parallelog*ram*[.] There is a small draw bridge at the Entrance[.] [*Small rough pencil sketch of drawbridge in folio margin.*] They will contain 3000 men and behind are barracks for 2 troops of horse, a set of stables at each end. In each stable is for 14 horses 7 on a side double stables, 2 Comp*anies* of the 23 L*ight* Dragoons. Singular manner of meeting with Foljambe.[2] He gave 5S for his goat[.]

Strike across the fields for an old tower in Lord Mount Cashels grounds[.][3] Pass through large fields of potatoes and at length come opposite the castle wh*ich* stands on a rock over a fine parling[4] stream or river. The Bank is all the way up planted with firs etc different trees. Higher up the river in a meadow is a large white rock,[5] w*hich* seems as if it had been once fortified[.] Close by it is a most lovely bridge[6] of 5 or 6 arches w*hich* joins it and a fine winding stream or river up between two Banks w*hich* contain it and a meadow. Go over bridge and along the road and come down into the park tow*a*rds the high tower,[7] which is an oblong round tower like a parallelogram with its corners rounded very thick

---

[1] These *ráth* or ringforts are a common feature in the Irish landscape and their origins were the subject of antiquarian debate in the late 18th and early 19th century; Carr, *Stranger in Ireland*, contains some general observations (pp. 178–9). The designation of archaeological remains (both earthen and stone) as 'Danish' was not uncommon, and the provenance of 'ringforts' and other remains was a matter of some debate. For more on this complex topic, see Ní Cheallaigh, 'Going Astray'; Stout, *The Irish Ringfort*.

[2] The Foljambes of Derby are mentioned in Lee's personal correspondence, appearing to be friends of a friend of Lee's (SJC, Box 1a, Doc. 18, Letter of T. F. Twigge to John Lee, 27 Feb. 1806). The man mentioned here is probably Major George Foljambe (d. 1821); thanks to Erica Fay of the Waterford Archaeological and Historical Society for this information.

[3] Moorepark, near Fermoy, seat of the Mount Cashell family. The tower to which Lee refers is Cloghleagh Castle, an Anglo-Norman fortification built by the Condon family. Lee's sketch of it is reproduced at p. 173 (Figure 12).

[4] This word could have a similar meaning to 'murmuring' – in *OED* the adjective refers to 'persuasive conversation'; the noun refers to 'the action of speaking or talking' (*OED*).

[5] Lee's sketch of this view, originally at SJC, MS U.30 (2), f. 103r, is reproduced at p. 172 (Figure 11).

[6] Downing Bridge, River Funshion.

[7] Cloghleagh Castle, Moorepark, Co. Cork.

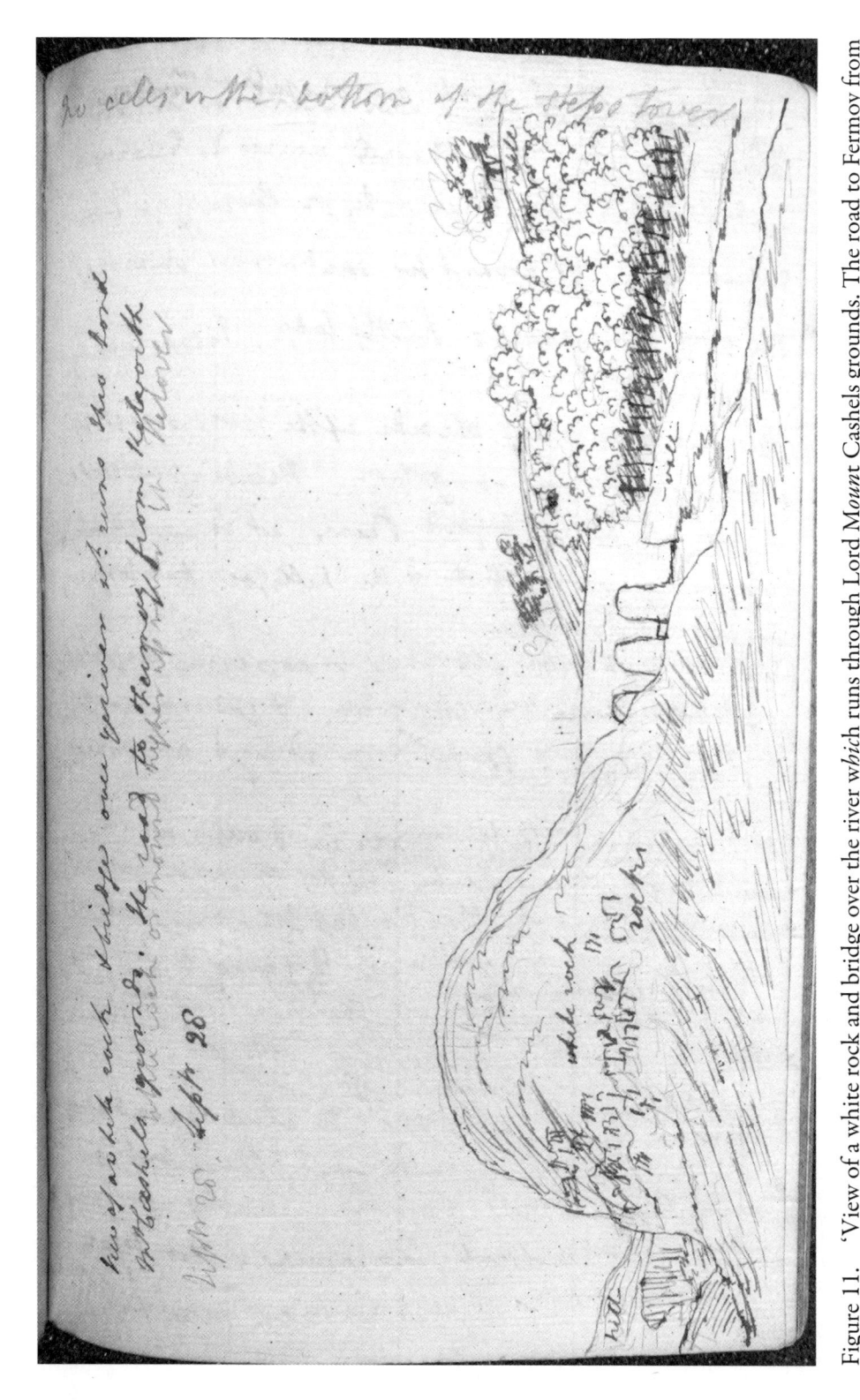

Figure 11. 'View of a white rock and bridge over the river which runs through Lord Mount Cashels grounds. The road to Fermoy from Kilworth September 28'. The scene is described in SJC, MS U.30 (2), f. 145v (p. 171). By John Lee, 28 September 1806 (SJC, MS U.30 (2), f. 103r). Reproduced by kind permission of the Master and Fellows of St John's College, Cambridge.

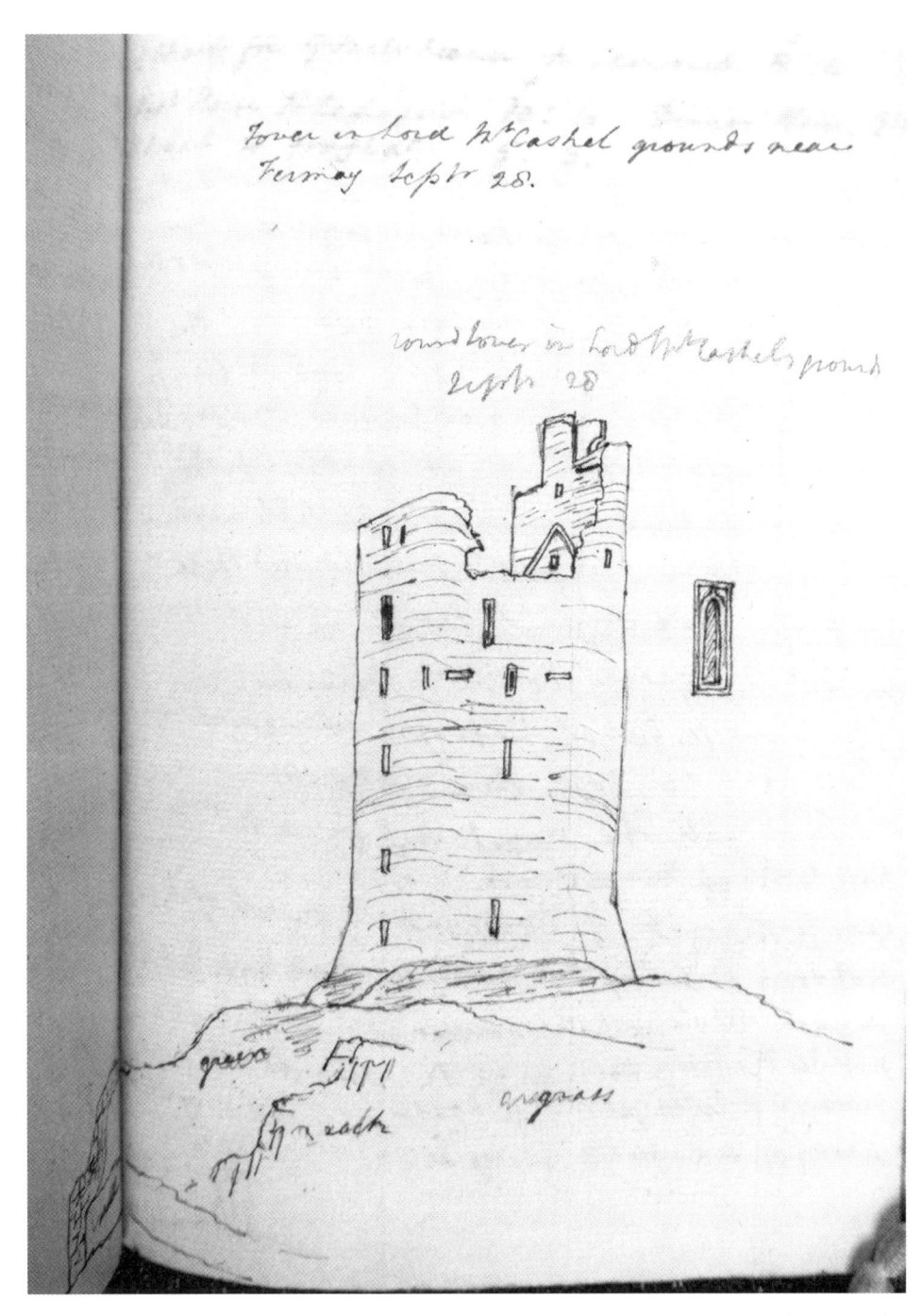

Figure 12. 'Tower in Lord M*ou*nt Cashel grounds near Fermoy Sept*embe*r 28'. The scene is described in SJC, MS U.30 (2), f. 145v (pp. 171, 174). By John Lee, 28 September 1806 (SJC, MS U.30 (2), f. 121r). Reproduced by kind permission of the Master and Fellows of St John's College, Cambridge.

and raised on the edge of the rocks[.] A commanding situation[.] There seem to have been other works about it and a piece of a wall remains on the W side. The river is named Fenshun [Funshion] and the curious cave is called Tagnaphalys hole per as a robber who lived there many years ago. The place is called Moore Park. Wonderful crops of grain in the meadow and the grounds are most beautiful[.]

[f. 146r] Went round the grounds and returned to the House from whence the view of the grounds which are finely [taken?] is very fine[.] The distant Mountains by Fermoy striking. Returned through Kilworth a very large village and down by the bridge again the river from whence cannot be too much admired, and also that from the top of the rock close by it. Came round the road and saw a Hurling match[.][1] The people from 1 village challenge those of the town of Fermoy[.] They sometimes play for a quantity of porter or 1:8½ each man. The sides are sometimes of 12 and sometimes 24 or 18 according to the n^{os} they can get. The play is exactly similar to Hockey, but the Ball is almost as large as ones head, and the sticks are large and broad, but varying a little according to the taste of the men[.] These sticks they call worlies[.][2]

It is more dexterous than Hockey and to see a fellow catch the ball from [the] ground by his worly and strike it up is very pleasing[.]

They all come to play in their Sunday clothes and take off their shoes and stockings and borrow a bad hat from their friends. They take off their coat and waistcoat and put on white jackets like cricket. Some men would not play because they had no white jackets. There were hundreds of women men and boys etc all come to see them and there is generally a market every Sunday which generally end in battles broken heads skin etc if not prevented[.]

Dined at the — Men of the 23rd

[f. 146v] **[29 September] Monday.**
Charming Bridge. Noble view of the Town from the Barracks. They are very elegant[.] The front is in general 4 windows between 2 doors or 2 Windows and a door. There are 47 windows in the middle$_1$ row$_2$.[3] The wings which are ⊥^{r} are a door and 3 windows but the space between the windows is much larger than in the front. There are 30 in each wing so that it is probably a square. In the front and middle are a few coloms [columns] and a railing in the centre part too. The horse barracks are behind the middle and got at by 2 arches. There are 2 Hospitals at the behind corners, on each side a forage yard which lies between them. Every convenience, Blacksmith shop etc. Saw 2 regiments of infantry and the 2 companies of horse in a Barrack parade, and went through the common routine. All marched around in 20 companies. After their knapsacks were all laid out and examined. Very pretty sight to see the order and cleanness[.]

Brushes. 2 Shirts 2 pair shoes etc Combs etc.

Saw a man flogged for striking a sergeant 500 lashes. Lieutenant Corporal gave him 25 and the man counted each stroke before it was given. He cried out lustily[.] There were about perhaps 1500 men in all on parade and a fine day[.]

---

[1] The Gaelic field game of hurling is played with a hurley or *camán* (a stick with a curved end) and a small ball or *sliotar*. Lee roughly sketched a hurley stick in the page margin, not reproduced here.
[2] Hurleys.
[3] Word order has been changed following Lee's subscript numerals. Lee sketched the front elevation of the barracks at the top of f. 147r, not reproduced here.

After the parade was over rode with Foljambe and Captain Drake and Captain [Kolmer?] to see the holy well.[1] It being Michaelmas day and out in the Mountains was a well which was celebrated for its water and said to cure all sorts of disorders. The Roman Catholics give a great deal of credit to it[.] The priests recommend their flocks to go to it I suppose and keep up the farce. We rode along below the Barracks on road by Dr Drews, beyond Lord Mount Cashels park and then go on [f. 147r] for a long way, crossing the mountain on horrible roads or rather lanes and cuts along the mountains over stones and turf. It would be impossible for any thing like a carriage to go there[.] An Irish car might for they are the Devils Carriage. See great n^{os} of people who were coming away and with bottles of the water under their arms. People come from all parts of the country to the well on this day and some come and stay there for 1 or 2 days before. It is said to heal the lame and man said it restores sight. Asked many people if it had done any cures this year. 'Oh, many.' 'Do you know any it has cured[?]' 'I wont go for to tell you a lie Sir. Indeed I do not' said one man 'but theres many people who do.'

'Do you believe in the power of the water?' and after some time fellow confessed he did. ('Do you ever hear of any people being cured.' 'Yes numbers Sir[.]') 'Do you know which disorders it cures[?]' 'All disorders.' 'Do you know anybody ever cured.' 'Not I but many others do.' Thus every body confessed he never knew it do good but threw it on others and nothing but general answers could one get. After riding along the Mountains for some distance in the bottom where 3 small little glens on the top of the Mountain meet and down which there are small streams. We saw a vast concourse of people in the hollow and all sorts of noise going forward. There were a great n° [of] very ordinary Booths erected like long gipsey huts and hundreds of people there[.] With difficulty we could get through the crowds on our horses and ride up the bottom of the hollow along the course of the sacred water which streams over the rocky stony bit of a brook and close by the little stream on the South side is a well which was crouded [sic] thick round by old women etc. We tasted the water which is certainly very fine and clear and pleasant, very cold but could perceive no other qualities. They say the drinking of it assists propagation and makes people become fathers and mothers more easily and .·. all the women and girls were drinking away. We did not see the priests there at the well. They were [f. 147v] rather in the booths getting drink or had gone home but there are always some in the early part of the day praying etc there. The Blind and lame crawl along about the well 3 times but we were too late to see this. Also numbers had been doing so we were told in the morning. Some begin their operations at sunrise. There were many drinking and some walking around the well. The plan is this. One walks round 3 times and then rests and says 5 pater nosters. Then walk 3 times more round and say 5 more paternosters. Then walk 3 times more round and Ditto and then that person has done his business. Of course all who come there[,] for many attend it all religiously inclined[,] Do so whether ill or not and it may keep them from harms way. It had all the appearance of a fair only it was held in such a horrible place and on the bare mountain in a hollow where a small stream comes down. There were persons amusing themselves at the games usual at fairs. Knocking the bread off from sticks etc etc. Almost all the Booths were for selling wiskey and spirits and at about 8 or 9 oClock there is generally a deal of fighting and all sorts of things going forward for the people generally get drunk[.] The scenes which follow are not of a very

---

[1] Tobernahulla or St Michael's well, a natural spring in Tobernahulla townland, Co. Waterford.

religious kind. They are forgotten by that time. We did not stay long but going home saw a woman and 2 childer[1] in a car. I was told that one of the children had for a long time (many months) been very ill and could not eat, that it had been ill for 1½ year nearly and that when she had drunk the water it was very much better (4 hours ago) and could eat now pretty well. People are obliged to come 3 years successively before they are quite cured if it all. (This is good latitude) A Boy was there last year who was blind and then he could see a little after drinking the water. This year he came for the 3rd time and although not cured yet he could see now better than ever. A man confessed that the evening preceeding the priest had after prayers told them in church that it would do them good to go. Another fellow said he had said nothing about it and [others?] who was at [f. 148r] the same Chapel with them said the Priest dissuaded them to go to the well. The People lie confoundedly and they have such habits of it that they dont mind it now[.] Came back through Kilworth and round by the Bridge I so much admire. Dined as before. Heard 2 Harpers Mr Obrien a very famous Irish harper play very well indeed and something like music[.]

How the deuce people could have found out the well I dont know for tis in a most out of the way place. It required some ingenuity to find out the well. Many of the people would stay there as long as money and wiskey could be found for several days, but several told us that many people would sooner drink that water than wiskey for the time[.]

Woman at the holy well	10^d
apple man ———	10
Stuff for greatcoat…	4: 8½
Trunk to Fermoy	2: 4
Booking it to Cork	: 2
Bill at Fermoy ———	15: 4[2]

[f. 148v] **[30 September] Tuesday.**
'Are there any letters for etc.' 'No Sir but I believe you are of the 20th Light Dragoons and one of your men come Down every morning so you will be sure to get them if there are any.'[3] NB I had nine altogether and riding for 2 last days with the Officers[.] This shews the Irish are an observant people.

Started at 9, for Mallow. Crossed the bridge from the road by Castle Hyde[.][4] The town Bridge and vicinity of Fermoy looks beautiful. Distant Mountains on the Dublin road very fine. Fermoy would furnish many good pictures and the Mountains around it make [a] glorious back ground[.] At 4½ mile Mr Hyde and 2 Miles Colonel Stewarts Gate to House[.]

A person who was acknowledged to be the best judge of the country directed me as the most beautiful way to go was along the road on R of the water, but trying this for a mile, found I could see nothing on foot and ∴ struck down to the waters edge along which you may easily go and through beautiful rich meadow and come to the delightful village of Ballyhooly[.]

---

[1] The colloquial form of 'children'.
[2] This list has been moved from its original position at the top of the folio.
[3] Quotation marks added.
[4] Castlehyde, a late 18th-century house and residence of the Hyde family (LED).

There are the small ruins of a large old Castle[1] situated on rock hanging over the river and commanding 2 fine windings of the river[.] There are several abutments in the castle and a well like hole going on to one below where are rooms also you may go up 1 story there is the remnant of 2 old round towers 1 close adjoining the castle the other close by[.] Women at the river washing clothes. They beat them with a piece of wood then rinse and [soap?]. There is the ruin of an old Church close by the Castle – and a stone quarry at the front of it and a new Church beyond the castle[.]

[f. 149r *blank*]

[f. 149v] As I was drawing Bally hooly Castle a man said 'and is it any offence to ask you why you are taking the drawing of this place Sir.'[2]

Bally hooly Bridge most elegant. The white rock on which the new Church is built is truly grand and picturesque. Some majestic rocks indeed which have caves in them. Obliged to get over them some how or another and wind round. This forms a point in the river and look admirable from the either side there are caves on both sides[.]

Conway Moor [Convamore] House. Lord Lismore house is the one I drew and there is a fine rock directly opposite which I would advise noone to go round but keep above it for it is very difficult to get over it.

A boy and his father killed 19 Salmon once cross fishing.[3] Mr Wallis House, higher up and Reverend Mr Barclay above it. He kills his salmon 3 4 or 5lb. and catches fish of 9 to 20lb[.] Go over Carreg Gir veoch Rock famous formerly for Fox earths. A fine rock also on which Mr Wallis House is built called Carreg [Ringee?] and a fine well at the bottom Springs from under it, round and deep, elegant water[.] See some yellow and some black rabbits over the river[.] Charming well. Come to the junction of the [f. 150r *blank*] [f. 150v] Obeg [Awbeg] and Blackwater. I defy the whole world to shew finer scenery than all about here[.] Climb up a ⊥ʳ rock. Fine ruin of castle here.[4] Sketch of it[.][5] Fine view up the Obeg river and the pretty bridge and a glimpse at the rocks above[.]

Come to Farm House, civil good milk[.] Cross a brook and regain the river side. Brook called Baladague [Ballydague] and farther on cross Baladur[.][6] Farther on a pretty glen at the end of the road having trees on each side. There is [a] pretty bridge at [which?] a brook and wood all round it[.] Brook called Carreg a hunor [Carrigacunna]. Colonel Foots land all about.[7] Over the (Black) water is a House of Mr Martens called Ballinaraugh. NB to describe the small glen as if the wood down it was standing for it is just cut down and not my fault that I am just too late to see it[.]

Carrigacunnor Castle now forms part of a farm house it is over the river.

Over the river is Monanemy Castle[8] and fine woods all on the river side and very noble rocks all the way up. Higher up over water is a Keilvillar [Killavullen] Mill for wheat[.]

---

[1] The medieval tower house at Ballyhooly.
[2] This sketch has not been located in Lee's extant sketchbooks.
[3] Fishing 'with a line with many hooks attached extending across a stream' (*OED*).
[4] Possibly the Priory of St Mary at Bridgetown, a 13th-century Augustinian priory on the bank of the Blackwater (Gwynn and Hadcock, *Medieval Religious Houses*, p. 161).
[5] This sketch has not been located in Lee's extant sketchbooks.
[6] Possibly Ballyduff.
[7] Carrigacunna tower house, possibly built in the mid-16th century (Power et al., *Archaeological Inventory of County Cork*, 4: North Cork, pt 2, pp. 525–6), and the attached 18th-century house of the Footes (NIAH).
[8] Monanimy tower house; an earlier house fortified in the 17th century (Power et al., *Archaeological Inventory of County Cork*, 4: North Cork, pt 2, pp. 536–7).

Potatoes a Barrel = 33 to 36 stone. 21 or 33 lb for 12 (Shillings) 21 lb for 3 3½ or 4. Land sells at 3 3½ or 4 Guineas[.] Mutton 3½ or 4^d lb according to the quality. Milk 1^d a quart skim milk [f. 151r *blank*] [f. 151v] 2^d new milk[.] NB A Child began howling and running away every time I put up my glass to my eye[.] The cabins all let for at least 3Gs each, but if you build one your self you pay 1 Guinea per an*num*[.] Asked for some bread at the 2 Shops and they had none[.] The village of Killuvillin[.]

Bread a man sold me was <u>damnation scarce</u>. Apple orchards in plenty in the village. They sell from 12 to 20 a 1^d according to goodness[.]

All this country between the Mountains called the Roches country[1] for 4 Brothers who had it in <u>Mr Cromwells time</u>.[2] Beyond the Mountains on the L it is called Barrys Country[.]

Noble Mountains all around in the distance[.]

Being tired of climbing Rocks and getting shaken about follow the Road from village of Killavillin which is very pretty in some places large orchard of crabs and apples[.] Pass seat of Sir — Cotter.[3] Road here fine cultivation on each side of it and just on coming out of them had a most noble view of the setting sun before me. In the bottom is a new Church and all before me is fine cultivated ground. A rich gold sun set and [in?] blue sky[.]

Come to Ballymahooly [Ballymagooly] a village said to be only 2 mile from last place!!! Just below is Ballygarret Brook with a little bridge over it,[4] 2 miles from Mallow. It was too dark to see the Town got there at 7 oclock. People at the Inn pay 2^d a guest for new milk[.]

[f. 152r] NB – one of the necessaries of human life[.]

Coming to an Inn, cold and chilly ordering a fire to be lit, walk round the room while it is doing and when it gets up and begins to cast some heat draw your chair near the fire and begin to feel your self comfortable. Have a good dish of tea and then find that the bottoms of the chairs are damp and cast a chill and feel wet and forbidding to ones posterior[.]

This was my case at Mallow[.]

[ff. 152v–153v *blank, and several folios cut out.*]

[*Back cover*]   1:2:9
            11
            ———
            11:8

---

[1] The Roches held lands in Munster from the 13th century, but Cromwell's forces captured the family home in Castletown Roche from Maurice Roche (1597–1670), 3rd Viscount Fermoy, in 1649 (Ó Siochrú, 'Roche, Maurice'). See also p. 250, n. 4.

[2] Oliver Cromwell (1599–1658) led a military expedition to Ireland in 1649–50 (Morrill, John, 'Cromwell, Oliver, (1599–1658)').

[3] Sir James Laurence Cotter, 2nd Baronet (1748–1829), politician, of Rockforest, Co. Cork (O'Hart, *Irish Landed Gentry*, p. 614).

[4] Possibly Yellow Bridge.

3. MALLOW TO BANTRY

[SJC, MS U.30 (3)][1]
[f. 1r] A man offered to make me a coat such as I have on for 4 Guineas. 5 Yds stuff at 2:6. Lining 2 Yds at 2S. = 12:6 + 4 = 16:6. Molds[2] First etc 10 17:4 + making 3 but by rights he ought to have a crown.
//

Wednesday ~~September~~ **Oct*ober* 1:**
Visit the famous well[3] here which is a spot which might be made very pretty if Mr Jephson was a man of taste[.][4] The water boils up in the middle and to feel it it is quite hot. It runs in a stream down towards the town and alongside of another stream which comes from a pretty glen at the back of Mr Jephsons domain. In his grounds is a noble ruin of a castle or dwelling house in high preservation[.][5] It is said that Mr Jephson receives 4 or 500 per acre as long as a stone of that castle remains on another. The stone casements of the windows are still perfect[.] It is finely situated on a rocky foundation, commands a fine view of the Bridge of Mallow which is also extremely pretty with its coned arches and [parted?] pillars, and behind and round it are fine noble woods and a pretty deer park along the riverside, only a fine meadow between. The grounds are nothing extraordinary, there are long walks on the banks which separate the fields from each other and which serve as hedges, and indeed all hedges on each side between the noble trees all along the middle of them. At the end of the farthest is a mound from which you obtain a more[6]

[f. 1v] Wed*nesday* Oct*ober* 1 Fine day sun shine
Th*ursday* 2 Rain all night and the morning. Small rain. Cleared up at 4 –
[Friday] 3 Stormy all morn*ing* windy. Boisterous and rain all even*ing*.
[Saturday] 4. Fine enough for com*mon* weather
[Sunday] 5. Fine day

---

[1] This is the shortest of Lee's diaries, but the most problematic. The quality of the pencil handwriting and of the paper is poor, rendering some of the text difficult to read or, in places, illegible.

[2] A fitting mold, or mould, is a part-finished form of a custom-made garment, used to try the fit before finishing.

[3] The oldest recorded hot spring in Ireland, Lady's Well in Mallow was a fashionable spa in the early-to-mid 18th century (Kelly, "'Drinking the Waters'", pp. 99–146).

[4] See SJC, MS U.30 (2), p. 155, n. 2.

[5] Mallow Castle, known as 'Short Castle' or 'Castle Gar', destroyed in 1642 (Power et al., *Archaeological Inventory of County Cork*, 4: North Cork, pt 2, pp. 512–13). The remaining buildings were extended by the Jephsons in the 18th century (LED).

[6] Sentence continued on the next page in the original manuscript.

[Monday] 6 Fine ⎫
[Tuesday] 7 Fine ⎬ and cool
Wednesday 8 Fine
Thursday 9 Fine and cloudy
[Friday] 10 Fine, cloudy.[1]
Caen leshin tegshin[2] whose house is that

[f. 2r] [*word missing*] view down the river about Sir Cotters Estate[3] and woods and close below on the riverside rises a fine rock from the top of which is made a lovers leap and the view on both sides from here is very fine up and down. Mr Jephsons woods and Mr Hares grounds like 2 mirrors reflect beauty on each other across the water. Return all up the riverside and at the Bridge through the rich meadows and crossing the bridge go to Mr Hares lodge the man sat still on my asking him to let me in and said there is no liberty for any person but Gentlemen to go in Sir, but by speaking sternly to him he had the door opened[.] Walk down to the riverside and get into grounds where are some fine rocks with a walk formed below them[.]

The Irish Gentlemen evince infinitely more taste in laying out Grounds, you never hardly see any [one thing?] which puts you in mind of the Citizen who rack their eyes so much in England they all seem naturally to have a true knowledge of the picturesque and a proper idea of it. Mr Jephsons grounds are laid out very stiff and formal and the only one I ever saw so[.] Mr Hares are modern and very elegant[.] He has made the most of his rocks indeed. Some fine red rocks are among the trees. Mr Jephsons (white) rocks look very well over the river just below. There are several seats placed in the [surroundings?] very advantageously. The grounds are small but much is made of them. The view from the castle[,] round wood [hut in?] the top of the rock is as beautiful as any thing can be. Return over the bridge which consists of 11 Arches and 2 land ones but [they are] little. I had got to the Inn of Mr Lynch and — and [*sic*] a very bad inn it is, no locks on the doors, no comfort what ever every thing dirty. They [f. 2v] keep a linendrapers [house?] also and there is no silver to be got anywhere you are pestered with six shilling Banknotes, and 9S and ½ G^s and even 13^d notes[.]

The other inn is for the best I should suppose and the landlord has made money some how for he has built a temporary barrack for which government pay him £500 per annum and many of these then are in the town, when one would imagine that the whole building would not cost more than double that sum and many inhabitants say that is the case. It seems general in Ireland that the poor pay for their cabins for rent what they are worth almost and ∴ it is perhaps not wonderful that government does so and that they should follow its example[.] Shameful expenditure of public money.

Visited the old castle again and the well. Walked about the town[.] Saw the Barrack[.]

I did not taste the water at the Spa for I saw on a stone cut out Ladies 2 Sh. and Gentlemans footings 2:6[.] Pay now and trust tomorrow[.]

---

[1] Lee omitted to write a full entry for Friday 10 Oct., but made a brief retrospective note in SJC, MS U.30 (4), f. 3r (p. 181).

[2] Lee's rendition of the Gaelic, '*Cé leis an teach sin?*', 'whose house is that?'.

[3] Sir James Laurence Cotter; see p. 178, n. 3.

[2 October] Thursday[.]

Started at 7 ~~for~~[.] Rained all the way. Pass [filthy?] dirty village of Ballynamona on the farthest side of which are some very extensive ruins[1] close by the road side[.] In this place I saw a woman up to her knees in dung which [heaping?] it up [she heap?] it on to the side of the house.[2]

[f. 3r] Ballyclough[3]
9.0. Bearer one shilling and 1 Penny
£0 1:1   Signed

Six Shillings Cork Bank

Charleville Bank. 9S.

Cork Bank. Nine Shillings

Bill for Tayloring 9:5. Mercer 16:8

Pencil 12^d. 2 Books 2:2 and 2:8½ 2 Knives 1:4^d
3 more pencils 14^d.

Bill at Mallow 13:9

Got to the halfway house on Bottle Hill [Bottlehill] which was a residence of Mr Gordon. The place called 6 Mile Water [Sixmilewater]. The nasty dirtiest road I ever travelled no such a thing as going without getting dirty and wet up to [the] ancles [ankles]. Got a boy from Bottle Hill to go with me over to Mr McCarthys at Carrignavar[4] and he asked whether I would go the shortcut, upon saying yes he took me a short way over the Glen ditch and bog, and got horribly dirty and foul, I rowed him for not telling me of this before, and every time he said 'O now you are over Sir and we shall [go] all the way through elegant fields as ever you saw' and so it was until the next bad place[.] His father rents 20 Acres 10 potatoe and oat field for 8 Gs but he just [takes?] of the common Mountain[.][5] He [pays boarding?] 1G for his cabin he built new 3 years ago. His name Jack Colon[.]

[f. 3v] Mr McCarthys a very pretty place a small pleasant one but fine woods and trees behind it[.] A pretty glen in front which goes all the way down serpenting to Cork nearby. A brook which rises in the [mountains?] above runs down it and the opposite

---

[1] Probably the early 13th-century Mourne preceptory of the Knights Hospitallers (Gwynn and Hadcock, *Medieval Religious Houses*, p. 358).

[2] The narrative continues after the following financial notes.

[3] Ballyclough, Co. Cork, is just to the north of Mallow and therefore not on Lee's route from Mallow to Cork city – but is en route to Charleville, Co. Cork, where he visited a bank. This appears to represent a deviation from his southbound route to Cork city.

[4] The castle of Carrignavar was seat of the McCarthys from the mid-17th century; it is possible that the McCarthy referred to here and again later may be Justin McCarthy (LED).

[5] Lee probably refers to land on the mountain held in common.

bank covered with trees. Fine cultivation all over the mountains about here. Roads quite red[.]

Gave boy for coming the 4 Miles 12ᵈ. It is 4 mile to Cork. The Boy asked me what I would give him to carry my knapsack to Cork[.] I said 10ᵈ. He said it was too little and asked 12 and so we parted. This 2ᵈ he considered as enough to make him refuse to go. The road is the dirtiest I ever travelled in Ireland and the observations which came within my line when on foot, were that although the peep from the top of the hill on Cork below [was] so very pretty yet a more filthy stinking, foul infernal place I never saw, the streets actually are filled with mud and if a person wishes to walk in them he had better not go in well blacked shoes it is throwing blacking away. You are seen to get dirty to the ancles and the people splash you without hurting themselves for they do not wear shoes or stockings. On crossing the 1 [first] Bridge all down the street on the other side of the water untill you come to the other Bridge you see and pass through as rich a scene of horrible nastiness and filth as ever the warmest fancy could have pourtrayed in the most glaring colours[.] I saw a silly woman sitting down on the pavement side, ½ covered but many parts of [f. 4r] her body to be seen. People walking in the mud barefooted is too common to mention again[.] Upon crossing the second Bridge back again to the l side of the water and passing through the arches of the building at the foot of it the streets are as bad untill you come to the Grand Parade which is a very fine street and at the middle is an equestrian brown not whitewashed statue of George 2[.][1] at the bottom Go to the Mail Coach Office and get there at 5 OClock. Go out after dressing and visit the streets. St Patricks Street is also a good one because it is modern and clean and because it resembles one in England[.] At the bottom of the Grand Parade is the river or a canal [River Lee] and here a fine street also runs || to St Patricks called the South Mall which is I believe nearly E and West. At the End of this there are seen the masts of vessels and on going down it at the farthest end you have a good view on part of the river. This quay is called Sir J.B. Warners quay[.][2] Go up it and along the street in which is the Play House[3] it seems to be a small insignificant one. Post office in Caroline Street. Go and get my dinner at Blakes Hotel.[4] Dinner 2:2. Spruce Beer 6½ Negus[5] 10 – Coming into the Town a soldier [f. 4v] met me and I for conversation sake asked him what regiment he belonged to, the 50 I believe. 'Do you know if you have a Captain Colman' said I for fun. 'No Sir we have a Captain Coote I suppose you mean him[.]' 'Oh yes I do I mistook the name.' 'I suppose' said he 'you Sir are an officer also',[6] Upon which he (I) said nothing but smiled and he offered to carry my knapsack to the Inn which I let him do. His name was Corporal Champion a good name for a soldier and was at the Barracks.

---

[1] George II (1683–1760). The statue, which stood on Grand Parade at the intersection of Tuckey's Street and George's St (now Oliver Plunkett St), was commissioned by Cork Corporation to the Dutch sculptor, Van Nost, in 1760, and was unveiled in 1761 (Archiseek).

[2] Lee may mean Warren's Place (now Parnell Place) (Draft of work in progress from Ní Laoi, 'Cork', p. 45).

[3] Possibly the Theatre Royal, located on George's St in 1801 (Beauford, *A Plan of the City*).

[4] Edward Blake is listed as a hotel and tavern keeper on George's Street, Cork, in *Holden's Annual London and Country Directory ... 1811*, II.

[5] A drink made from wine (usually port or sherry) mixed with hot water, sweetened with sugar and sometimes flavoured (*OED*).

[6] Quotation marks added.

[3 October] Friday

Go down the Channel and pass by Laps [Lapp] Island for it was Lap[1] who lived there formerly[.] The whole of the best part of Cork the most genteel part is built on this island[.]

Pass Mr [~~Tates?~~] ~~house~~ Penroses[2] H*ouse* from whence Sir H Hayes[3] [ruins?] are against mess*rs* Pike[.]

Pass down very beautiful river all the Banks covered with houses and trees and quarries of stone. Spike Island[4] has been levelled nearly 8 feet [a marl?] [***] and is about 100 Acres many hundred [men at work?]. Many hundred Barrels of gun powder spent in blasting[.]

Black rock tower where the corporation come down sometimes and have their drop of good thing[.][5]

[f. 5r] Glandmeir [Glanmire] channel beautiful on the L side which runs up a pretty fine Glen for some miles. Vessels may go up of small size. Land about here is valued more or less for 10Gs an Acre[.] Pass ~~Mr~~ The Little Island which is all the property of Mr Bury[6] who is the poorest man on it and any of his servants could buy him from the gallows. Mr [*breaks off*]

The little island is about 3 Miles long[.]

~~Olivers frolic~~. A tenant and [*sic*] Mr Smith Barry is a tenant who died the other day and was worth 38000 per annum and Mr Jackson [allowed?] him a fine large house. Olivers frolic a continuation of the house which cost 800 or 900.

Mr Barry has set leases for ever to these Gentlemen[.]

Mr Marten a tenant also he lives lower down, and he could afford a [guinea?] as well as the best of them[.]

On the R is Hop Island so called because a dancing master lives there but was called the Red Island before. Mr Edwards is the dancing master[.]

Had a fine breeze and went down at a great rate[.]

See many boats heading for oysters[.]

All this proper river down to the Horsehead[7] is called Loch Mahon[8] and this is the only part which people fear on the river[.] On the L a long way up the R channel is Bellvelley [Belvelly] Castle[9] which ~~goes~~ is on the Cove and the R channel just runs round it. Small craft go round this way but no vessels. They are building a bridge over the narrow part of the channel.[10] The channel is all narrow.

---

[1] A Counsellor Lapp was listed as living at Patrick Street, Cork, in *Holden's Annual London and Country Directory ... 1811*, II.

[2] Cooper Penrose (1736–1815), Quaker and merchant, whose house at Woodhill, Co. Cork was an important centre for the arts (Geoghegan, 'Penrose, Cooper').

[3] Sir Henry Brown Hayes (1762–1832); see SJC, MS U.30 (5), p. 261, n. 7.

[4] Construction began of a hexagonal bastioned fort on Spike Island in Cork Harbour in 1805, and was completed only by around 1860 (Kerrigan, *Castles and Fortifications*, pp. 226, 257).

[5] Blackrock Castle at Mahon, Co. Cork, built *c*.1582 for defence of Cork city, and used by Cork Corporation in the 18th and 19th centuries for 'entertaining and functions' (Power et al., *Archaeological Inventory of County Cork*, 2: East and South Cork, pp. 229–30).

[6] Phineas Bury of Wallinstown (Lewis, *Topographical Dictionary*, I, p. 290).

[7] A point of land at the southern end of Lough Mahon.

[8] Not a lake, but part of Cork Harbour.

[9] A 15th-century tower house (Power et al., *Archaeological Inventory of County Cork*, 2: East and South Cork, pp. 222–3).

[10] Belvelly Bridge, built in 1800–1805 to connect Cobh to Fota Island (NIAH).

Below the Horsehead is Passage Point [Passage West], all rocks 15 fathoms here at High water and the same at low Water at St Johns Stairs lower down[.]

[f. 5v] Pass Blackpoint on the L and Mr Roches House[1] just below and the white Rocks called White Point from the colour of the rocks.

Pass Arbolin [Haulbowline] Island on the R a fine bed of Rocks high above the water, some stores on the top. It is a little island. Cow Island [Rock Island] is 5 Miles long and 2 across and it all belongs to 3 gentlemen[.] Lord Middleton[2] has built a fine wharf on the shore and a market house for the good of his island[.]

Town of Cove [Cobh], mostly new houses. There is a barrack there which is occupied by some of the 4th Regiment of [***] some are [***] [about here?]. The town is irregular and built all along the front of the rock but a quay in front there is a rock mountain running all along the back of the town[.] Cross the water to Spike Island and see the works there an old garrison built in 1790 by General Valencey,[3] horrible bad plan they say. They are now making a new one[4] under the direction of Sir J Haliday who was in Egypt and knows Dr Clark[5] who brought one of his curiosities from his House. There are to be six ravines and the whole island in the works is now being levelled 8 or 10 or 16 yds in different places. There will be accommodation for 3000 Men when finished. It has [f. 6r] been two years at work and not 2 ravines are finished[.] This part of the island around will form a slope to the batterys. The whole Island is stone on 1 side to the R is fine limestone quarries proper for building and on the otherside it is all small slaty pieces as if broken by some compression of nature. The times of blasting the quarries are at 9 (AM) at 3 and at 6 PM. There are in the whole works about 600 men employed. These works will go through the old one and will be one of the finest things in the Kingdoms. Between the 2 Ravines is a covered way. Came down from Cork to Cove in 1¼ hour[.] Wind N W and many squalls. Wind being high and stormy all day and almost unpleasant <u>even to me</u>[.][6]

Was delayed nearly from 3 to 4 at Spike Island before I could get a ferry over. Consequently the Boat I came down in was gone and I was obliged to walk up[,] the wind wavering[,] boisterous[,] etc[,] just getting more so and I had hardly landed at Cove and started out of the town when it began to rain. With great difficulty I could keep up my umbrella so as to be of any use to me[.] However I walked the 2 long miles to the ferry as quick as possible and lo there I saw the ferry boat going over. It was now 5 OClock and I ought to be up at Cork at 6 to dinner, but now nothing but patience could be of use. Waited for a long while and hailed the boat it did not come. The wind and waves strong[.]

---

[1] Probably John Roche Esquire, magistrate (West, *A Directory, and Picture, of Cork*, p. 8).

[2] George Brodrick, 4th Viscount Midleton (1754–1836), whose improvement works on his estates included works at Cobh harbour (Dictionary of Irish Architects online).

[3] Charles Vallancey (1725?–1812), soldier and antiquary (Nevin, 'Vallancey, Charles'). Vallancey designed a new, 'small irregular' fort to replace the older star fort in 1791, but his plans were extended (Power et al., *Archaeological Inventory of County Cork*, 2: East and South Cork, p. 290).

[4] A fort constructed at the eastern end of Spike Island in Cork Harbour during the American War of Independence (Kerrigan, *Castles and Fortifications*, p. 13).

[5] Probably Edward Daniel Clarke, antiquary and mineralogist, who travelled in Scandinavia, Russia, the Levant, Greece, and Egypt as tutor to a wealthy young man, John Marten Cripps (McConnell, 'Clarke, Edward Daniel (1769–1822)'). Lee and Clarke were acquainted, and Clarke cited Lee's Scandinavian diaries in his *Travels in Various Countries of Europe, Asia and Africa*, 6 vols, London, 1810–23.

[6] While crossing the Irish Sea, Lee prided himself on his immunity to seasickness (see SJC, MS U.30 (2), p. 98).

At last it came over and when I wished to go over with 2 of us it would not but said the Mail Boy would be there soon and they must wait for him but ½ an hour passed before he arrived [f. 6v] and when he did in about ¼ hour we set off. The waves went a little into our boat[.] On landing it was sink dark and the road in some places was close to sea side[.]

The tide was rising and the wind down the river ∴ the sea was so rough that it came in froth on the shore. The roads execrably dirty and obliged to [track?] them as they came. In short what with dirty road, with the rain directly over the right shoulder and sometimes in front, I could not have thought that the tempests which would have rented a king Lear could have all conspired to such a great pitch of animosity as to attack with such inveterate spite a poor harmless traveller as I.

Ferry 1^d.

[Saturday 4 October]

Visited the Dyke, and the rivers which join at the top. Saw the beautiful views from thence vented. The Exchange (poor building),[1] the Bank the Commercial Rooms (very good) the Markets which are very fine. Fish and Fowl market and noble Butchers Ditto, 73 Stalls all in rows each man pays 7:6 or 6 for a weeks rent and ∴ one part always has better meat than another. Turkeys selling for 3:3 : 2:8½ very fine. Meat Beef and Mutton 5:4½ 6½ a lb. The corporation are said to make £2000 [f. 7r] a year by these Buildings. A fellow I met at Cove the day before came out of a Wiskey shop and asked me how I did and wanted me to come and drink[.] Visited Mr Newsons Stores, which cost above £3000 3 years ago building. He rents the land for ever and pays 2Gs a foot for the front or £400 a year. Very fine buildings. Curious ~~pots~~ kiln for drying corn before shipping it.

Went from here along the shore to Glanmire and up that most lovely of Glens the hanging woods and the river at [the] bottom [and] the view of the beautiful Church at the end. The fine bridge and woods all around[.] Go up the hill towards Youghal and view the lovely trees and glens and a view of the country beyond and then come back[.] This is as pretty a thing as any I had seen in Ireland.

[Sunday 5 October]

On Sunday go up to Sundays Well[2] a fine spring and breakfast with the Shandy Club young fellows who have breakfast every Sunday morning, fine fun and quiz[3] each other. From that || the Ugly club also breakfast who are older men in general[.] This has been established 30 years. One rule of the Shandy Club carried by a majority of 1, was that every member give 3 weeks notice if they intended marriage with name and age [of] the lady or forfeit a dinner. All very fine clever gentlemen. 1 Black bean [f. 7v] excludes.[4] 26S ½ yearly subscription and every member forfeits 3d when not there at 9. The president wears a whistle over his neck which is [laced?] on the teapot. Returned down the Dyke. Went to Church and heard Mr Quarry[5] very good an extempore preacher fine Church

---

[1] The Exchange, built in 1710 at the junction of Castle St and South Main St (Draft of work in progress from Ní Laoi, 'Cork', p. 79).

[2] A 'pretty hamlet' and a spring well (Smith, *Cork*, I, p. 356).

[3] To make fun of, mock or tease (*OED*).

[4] Lee seems to describe a process of 'blackballing'.

[5] Probably John Quarry (*fl.* 1810), author of *A Letter Addressed to ... Thomas ... Lord Bishop of Cork and Ross*, Cork, 1810; and *The Rule of Faith, and the Right of Private Judgment Considered. A Discourse*, Cork, 1830.

good pews. Dined at Dr Newsoms[1] and spent even*ing* at Mr [Avershews?] Board*ing* School. 2 ferrys and 3 Bridges[2] [***] [vessels?] go by at high tide.

[6 October] Monday.

Set out and visit Blarney Mr Jefferies H*ouse* where are beaut*iful* grounds a fine old castle.[3] Go to top of it[.] Story of Blarney Castle and the stone on the top that any one who kisses it is allowed to tell his [story]. Fine walks all thro*ugh* the grounds, lake very pretty. Go *from* thence to Woodside Mr Carletons[4] and saw Mr Sullivans at Beech Mo*unt*[.][5] In the valley is a branch of the river Lee wh*ich* turns a*n* iron mill and a paper mill and *from* thence runs down a lovely vale to the other branch. On the top of [the] hill above Mr Sullivans the remains of an old house belon*ging* to the McCarthys where many a bottle of claret and round of beef have welcomed a stranger or guest[.][6] Go along the far corner to counsellor Fittens[7] wh*ich* is a lovely spot 2 branches of the river, one winding finely and they meet below a gothic bridge in front beyond, a dist*ant* view of Cork and river and ~~the well~~. Close by ruins of an old C*hurch*[8] ivy covered fine rocks on the South branch of [the] river. Pass Powdermills[9] belon*ging* to Governm*ent*[.] Above is Iniscarrow [Iniscarra] Bridge 12 arches Gothic cross it and join riverside and pass the Beaut*iful* situat*ion* of the C*hurch* at the turn of the river and Mr Beresfords Glebe house up the Glen. Go up the Bridge to the Ovens H*ouse*. Nice dog kennel pretty C*hurch*[.]

[f. 8r] Extraordinary well horses are broke in. They lead (ride) them over all sorts of walls and ugly places and go any where[.] I never saw any thing like it in England. Neat kennel at Ovens ab*out* 30 [couples?] there, hounds light and then close at [the] front of [the] kennels the river and the Chusest[10] Hounds fed on potatoes and meat and mixed with gravies, wh*ich* is the dregs of chandler fat this makes them not get along bad in my opinion. Seldom give them meat until they get a dead horse. It wo*uld* be too expensive.

Sat do*w*n to a fine jolly dinner with 14 foxhunters[,] conversat*ion* ab*out* hound*s* horses leaps foxes ditches etc etc bawdy and and [*sic*] beastly. Tom Hawkins with his [bruised?] leg hopping[.] Bets. Parted at 9 tolerably steady for ev*ery* one co*uld* walk[.] King C*harles* and glorious me*mory*.[11] Fox hunts all bumper toasts and Nelson also. Last Monday they were very drunk and when well <u>up to it</u> they do not give glorious mem*ory* untill late in [the] even*ing*[.]

---

[1] Possibly the same as the Mr Newsham mentioned in SJC, MS U.30 (5), p. 258.

[2] Lee may be referring to the number of bridges and ferries serving Cork city.

[3] A castle was built at Blarney *c*.1480, with later additions into the early 18th century; the castle and estates were purchased by Sir James Jeffereys *c*.1703 (Samuel and Hamlyn, *Blarney Castle*).

[4] Ino. Carleton (West, *A Directory, and Picture, of Cork*, p. 83).

[5] Beechmount House, built *c*.1740 (NIAH).

[6] See p. 181, n. 4.

[7] Richard Fitton Esquire, of Gosworth (West, *A Directory, and Picture, of Cork*, p. 30).

[8] Inishcarra church, reputedly built by St Senán (*fl*. 6th/7th cent.) (Gwynn and Hadcock, *Medieval Religious Houses*, p. 386; Breen, 'Senán').

[9] The first gunpowder mills at Ballincollig were opened by Charles Henry Leslie in 1793, but a state monopoly on the product after 1798 led to the purchase of the mills by the Royal Ordnance in 1804; Lee saw the mills shortly after the building of a new canal and eight new powdermills in 1805 (Bielenberg, *Cork's Industrial Revolution*, pp. 88–91).

[10] Probably meaning best or preferred.

[11] A toast, described in the next paragraph.

DIARY 3: MALLOW TO BANTRY

It is drunk with a bumper standing and 3 cheers, then a bumper on knees 3 Cheers then a bumper all on table 3 cheers thus it was on last Monday. Every body dead drunk[.] Dr Newsom swore he was sober and would go home[.] He got on his horse and was running about in the river for some time and knows not how he got out but his horse an old stager[1] knew he was drunk as well as he could and took him safe to his own door. Plenty of oaths. 'Gods blood' 'Blood and ouns [ounds]', 'by the Body of Christ', 'by the h[2] of God' 'by the blessed Jesus', 'by the Holy Ghost.' 'Damned it Damn [***].' 'Damn your eyes to hell.' Ditto Blood etc etc[.][3]

[f. 8v] At Bandon untill within these 5 or 6 years they would let no Papist live there nor suffer a papist to be in the town, they would have torn one to pieces for they say that King James marched in to the town to the tune of the pipe.[4] But lately all the lands have been newly set and Papists have taken them[.][5]

Every gentleman of much fortune hunts and most of 500£ keep hounds. By the time we got merry every one was eager to invite me to see his part of the country except one Mr [blank] who had been in England a shy but clever fellow[.]

[f. 9r] **[Tuesday 7 October]**
Tuesday at 7 oclock went in to the Ovens[6] and staid there 2 hours. They differ from any other cave in being so many vaults. Tops are either gothic arches or else like Keels of ships and all formed of petrified water[.] Many of them are separated by thin partitions of this petrefaction, which is white and like chrystal[.] Went to the end of several and had got a good way in one which they say goes to Cork when a fellow was seized with a panic and because he had never been farther and would go no farther. I desired him to stay where he was untill we 3 went on he was afraid to stay by himself in short he began gabbering Irish and frightened the other fellow who begged me to go no farther, as he was never there before. The little boy was of no use they would not let him go and I was ∴ obliged to turn back[.] I had got a very long way in very easy walking indeed and dry[,] many side passages and we came out by a different one to the entrance. Explored several to the end, one very curious one which goes 3 sides of a parallelogram and so on but did not go to end[.] Very low at 1 place crawl under, fine tenacious clay and [in rows?] it hades[7] farther in. One passage comes out close by the church. Any body might[,] I should think[,] follow the passages with ease to the end from which I saw the fellows on getting out to [sic] near the entrance made crosses on the ground for safe delivery. I sent one [f. 9v] away for fear of his frightening the others and made several excursions with him and the little boy. Many [passages] seem to communicate in all directions and most go off or bend in [part?]

---

[1] Experienced, or, formerly a stage-coach horse (*OED*).
[2] Possibly hook.
[3] Quotation marks have been added throughout this paragraph.
[4] James II and VII, king of England, Scotland and Ireland (Speck, 'James II and VII (1633–1701)'). This is a reference to the capture of Bandon, with its Protestant majority population, by Jacobite forces in 1689.
[5] Following the 1798 rebellion and the Union of 1801, sectarianism in Munster increased. Upper and middle-class tendencies towards religious harmony reversed, with some 'small, well-publicised' instances of sectarian behaviour and activities around Bandon in *c*.1798–1810. Despite this, by 1831, Bandon had 'a firmly Catholic majority' as a result of the collapse of its economy and the emigration of a large portion of its Methodist population (Dickson, *Old World Colony*, pp. 474–96).
[6] The Ovens: caves, near Cork city.
[7] Inclines or slopes (*OED*).

Ls.[1] Pillars in some places and some places like the end of [the] cave near Kilkenny[2] [have] foxes earths in them and bones of fowls. Man afraid to go in many places and I told him to stay with [the] boy till I returned[.] [He was] afraid to do that and [I] blew out his candle and [he] came running to me to light it. Bill at towers Inn 19:8[.] Guide 20ᵈ Boy 5. Whiskey for the Schoolmaster 5. I had a man sent to me who keeps a public house and [he is] a drunken sot but [was] born at Killarney and [is] a scholar. He wrote a Latin letter for me to his father and talked Latin very well, all the classics and Virgil, Horace, Juvenal. A drunkard.

Visit the Kilcray [Kilcrea] Abbey[3] about 2 miles from Ovens house[.] Beautiful and extensive ruin[,] finely ivy hung, a fine tower in [the] middle and a great nº of apartments filled with gravestones, pieces of wood lying about in all directions, bones sculls [skulls], vaults partly open and coffins seen in them. Fine round pillars supporting gothic arches. Many tombs new and new graves [f. 10r] lately made[.]

Near the burial place of Edward Connellan is under a small arch a staircase which takes you up a short way[.] A dreadful picture of mortality, probably the pieces of wood are pieces of old coffins[.] Upon examination many were. Some tops and sideboards. Place for holy water[.] Ivy filled with bees. [Wandering find the oratory?]. Very perfect arches. Under the tower 2 fine round arches[.] The entrance is through a good gothic arch and over it another, then a row of [green rock?] on the sides of which are heapt (2 rows of) bones regularly piled up and many blanched skulls.

Take a view from the bridge. Close by is the remnant of an an [sic] old castle. Common people spinning and thrashing their oats in the middle of the road[.]

Hardly any people in Cork could tell me any thing about the Ovens or had heard of them only 1 person had been in a little way. The fox hunters although their kennel is close by know [it] not, only Mr William Hawks[.][4] 'Is there a short cut to Mr William Hawks[?]' 'Oh yes Sir a big short cut. Go over those fields then etc etc then etc etc and then across the bog.' 'Oh thank you my friend'[5] said I and away I went on my road. He was directing me to another Mr Hawks beside as I afterwards understood[.]

[f. 10v] In Ireland you may make a big shortcut of ½ a mile when you may go the high road of 2 miles in ½ the time, for the footpath is generally across hedges ditches common and frequently bog, as in the present case. NB Never lose time and go the short cut unless you can see every inch of the road to be good in your own opinion. Kilcray is situated in the flat which by good cultivation all the way up might be made the richest land in the world. Fine flat vale river running up it[.]

Came to Mr Hawks House[6] and rode from thence across the Lee at Cronodey [Cronody] up to Shandy Mr Cross, then along to Mr Lindseys of Peak[7] and saw the bog Coolacullig which supplies the whole county with turf[.] (river) Delahegna [Delehinagh] runs through it and falls into the Dripsey at Dripsey Castle.[8] Cross the valley and go down

---

[1] L-shapes.
[2] Dunmore cave, Co. Kilkenny, visited by Lee on 18 Sept. 1806. See SJC, MS U.30 (2), pp. 149–51.
[3] The mid-15th-century Franciscan friary of Kilcrea (Gwynn and Hadcock, *Medieval Religious Houses*, p. 251).
[4] Possibly William Hawkes of Grange, Athnowen, Co. Cork (LED).
[5] Quotation marks added.
[6] See description of sketch at SJC, MS U.30 (7), f. 2r (p. 319), not reproduced.
[7] The Lindsays of Peake House, Aghabulloge (LED).
[8] The rivers meet at Clonmoyle, a short distance to the west.

to the paper mills worked by the Dripsey river then come to its junction with the Lee cross the Lee lower down and come thro*ugh* Clasheneure [Clashanure] and went to the great view to the to [*sic*] top of Mulloughroe [Mullaghroe] and see all round the country Cork city Lough Mahon and up the country as far Clearough [Clearagh] or Kilmurry[.]

At Kilmurry in the Bason[1] of Muskerry County of Cork is a famous spring,[2] to w*hich* all the papists resort on the 10 July and on that day they say it cures it [*sic*] all sorts of diseases and if they are cured they promise to say a n° of prayers w*hich* they call the rounds. This last year when [f. 11r *blank*] [f. 11v] the well was dry on the proper day was with*out* a drop of water upon w*hich* the people went for buckets of water and poured it in to the well and began washing and tasting the water w*hich* they conceived to have the same efficacy as the original water as soon as it had touched the sides of the wall[.]

We met a man walking the lane[.] That fellow is as clever a fellow as any in Ireland, he swore to a false oath in court for 4½ hours to save a rebels life and never prevaricated once but he did not save him and 11 were hanged before the rebellion for robberies.

At Bandon the people were always old protestants w*hich* set of people are called <u>Millations</u>. They are also called Black Mondays bec*ause* they were summoned every Monday by King James to give up the town and they refused and they were relieved by King William while defend*ing* the town[.]

If you meet a Bandonman he will often say to you come my friend let us <u>spat</u> over the bridge, W*hich* arises fr*om* the idea that a man who will come and put his arms on the bridge and spit over it is independant [*sic*][.]

Mr Will Hawkes a very pleasant man, famous sportsman, fisherman, makes his own flies and rods, bit of botanical, flute player great farmer and every thing[.] He was brought up to study the law. Famous shot has killed 22 brace snipes in a day plenty wild fowl woodcocks etc[.]

[f. 12r] **Wednèsday [8 October]**[3]
Started at ten OClock and see ab*out* 2 miles on [roadside?] Mr Wardleys[.] Beyond is the Glen of Aglish and a little bridge over the brook and beyond a Forest a fine woody Demesne [cant see?] H*ouse*. Fine rocks all ab*out*. Come to Bridge of Carrickarudrig [Carrigadrohid] over the Lee. Fine rocky bed and rocks on sides on the W side of the Bridge is built in the middle of the river and join*ing* the B*ridge* a fine old Castle in ruins ivy covered and the water runs round it never saw one like it before.[4] About a mile on enter a beautiful glen Coum [Caum], finely wooded and the ground all rough and craggy [with] fine turf in [the] bottom. Woods look delightful. I wo*uld* not have lost sight of it for 1000Gs[.] Any man of a drop of spirit must fall in love with it. The Banks of [the] river Lee are very high all the way and fr*om* Cork to its source no land or any river side (in Ireland) is ½ so bad. Get to Macroom w*hich* is pleasantly situated up the river w*hich* joins

---

[1] The basin of the River Lee.
[2] A well dedicated to the Virgin Mary (Smith, *Cork*, I, p. 200).
[3] Lee sketched three views during his walk on this date at SJC, MS U.30 (7), ff. 3r, 4r, 5v–6r (p. 319), not reproduced. It is unclear where he slept on the preceding night, but it was possibly at Hawks of Athnowen, about 4.3 miles (7km) from Clashnure. Lee's imprecision makes identification of places mentioned in this entry difficult.
[4] The 15th-century Carrigadrohid tower house (Power et al., *Archaeological Inventory of County Cork*, 3: Mid Cork, p. 361).

another just below the town at a pretty bridge[.] Stream on the N wind*ing* away very elegantly[.] The River Silaan [Sullane] comes up to the town and the river Laney runs away to N. River Lee is to the S of the town over the M*ou*ntai*n*. Go thro*ugh* Mr Hedges.[1] An old castle repaired ab*ou*t 2 years ago.[2] Fine avenue of trees.

NB. the river Silan joins [the] Lee lower down at Ballyglasheen [Bealahglashin] Bridge[.]

Go all up to where M*ou*nt Pleasant is see the most beautiful view of dist*ant* country and woods, all the town and the bridge and fr*o*m above Mr Hedges a wonderful [f. 12v] extent of rocky country. Ab*ou*t 2 Miles [off] is Ashgrove[,] Mr Ash[.][3] The river runs close by it and an old castle[.] Pass by Castle — on the left of the road.[4] Immense M*ou*ntai*n*s one over another for miles and bare rocks on most even d*ow*n in the vallies [valleys][.]

Bog Anahaly [Annahala] runs for miles up the country[.] Wonderful view fr*o*m ab*ou*t a mile fr*o*m [the] road[.] See straight before you the 2 M*ou*ntai*n*s between wh*ich* the road runs[.]

Road goes all along the side of the M*ou*ntai*n*s sometimes over bare rock. Below is the river winding in separate courses among the wood and the bogs beyond it. On the side of [the] river stands an old ruin of a church down below.[5]

Cross a long narrow bridge over the Lee and bogs and march forw*ar*d thro*ugh* the vale with bogs and woods beyond, on the R is all bog and most barbarously craggy M*ou*ntai*n*[.] Ascend a Hill a good way on and fr*o*m it have a short command*ing* view all around the neighb*our*ing and dist*ant* M*ou*ntai*n*s wh*ich* although full of rocks and large masses of Stones yet are cultivated to the tops[.]

A great deal of timber [and] firs f*ou*nd in the Bogs about here near the lake of Gogon Barry [Gougane Barra]. Mr Barry[6] once in 1798 dug up a large fir ab*ou*t 6 feet below [the] surface, 60 feet long and squared in centre 3½ and in some parts 12 feet in circumfer*ence*. Now a great deal of fir wh*ich* was dug out of the bogs. They say all the country fr*o*m Macroom to [Bantry?] was formerly so thick with wood that you might go by [f. 13r] the boughs fr*o*m 1 tree to the other[.] A piece of turf in general [is] 9 Inches in thickness[.]

Mr Barry has now marked but not raised out of the bog as much timber as wo*ul*d cost in Cork 100Gs. He is going to build a new house next year.

A man came in and said a person was ill and bad in his inside with worms and asked for some gunpowder[.] He thought that wo*ul*d cure them. Worm powder[.] Plenty of all sorts of game hereabouts.

In the lake of Gougane Barra are char and plenty of salmon and trout and the best fishing in the land[.] It is reported that this lake and that in Cumberland[,] the only places where char are f*ou*nd[,] are both in the possession of a Mr [*blank*] who lives on this side of Cork near the bridge on the 2 rivers[.]

Go over the bog [Barry's Bog] on where was an old castle close by Mr James Barry's H*ou*se, [Kilbarry] hard cement made of river gravel. Vast quantity of wood, boughs, roots

---

[1] Henry Hedges of Mount Hedges welcomed Latocnaye in 1797 (Latocnaye, *A Frenchman's Walk*, p. 87).
[2] Possibly the 'old castle' serving as a garrison in 1797 (Latocnaye, *A Frenchman's Walk*, p. 87).
[3] At Templeniery, Co. Cork (LED).
[4] Probably Carrigaphoora castle ruins. The name is indicated by a dash.
[5] Possibly Macloneigh church ruins, Co. Cork.
[6] James Redmond Barry, Viscount Buttevant, an enterprising landowner in west Cork (Dickson, *Old World Colony*, p. 435).

etc [are] found in all depths of the bog. [The] Bog [is] 16 sods or more deep in many places. Hazel and the very nuts are found in good preservation but being exposed to the air they fall to pieces. Saw some pieces of timber and hazel in the bog. The people here will not believe that meadow land can be formed from bog[.] Mr J. Barry last year dug up about 4 acres [of] bog[,] (cut) drains, put 80 barrels of lime on an acre, sowed oats and wheat on 2 parts [f. 13v] of it and a great quantity of grass seeds. He has got very fine crops of oats and wheat and there is now an amazing thick and strong crop of grass on the stubble[.][1] Next year he will get above 4 for an acre of hay[,] value at least 4G^s a ton[.]

Hay in general [is] 4G^s a ton[.] Straw [is] always much dearer than hay[.] It has been 8Gs a ton when hay is 3Gs[.] 7Gs and 6Gs for straw is [the] common price[.]

He has about 5000 Acres in his demesne here and it goes on to the long bridge over the bog and river Lee. He has an estate near Bandon and some land near the bridge where [the] castle is on it. He is a plain farmer but allows everybody to come to his House[.] Every poor person[.] Travellers may sleep and have a breakfast there. My bedfellow told me he has been there when there has been so much company as to sleep 2 [to] a bed[.]

No necessary[2] in the Garden[.]

He is a man of great hospitality and his father was so[.]

The approach to Inchegela [Inchigeelagh] [is] very pretty[,] large masses of rock all along the road for foreground. The river in the valley winding [in] the ~~bog~~ middle of the picture 16 or 18 different distances all rock and fern and red heath[,] the old tower of Inchegela[3] in front and [the] bold distance[.]

[f. 14r] **Thursday 9th [October]**
Start at 11 OClock[.]

Mountains in the rear[,] nothing but the tower seen[,] trees hide the town. Pass this old tower which is on the river and a new House[4] close by it and about 1 Mile on is Inchegela[,] a place of about 12 poor cabins scattered. Go through it straight[,] crossing the brook by stepping stones and go along the worst road that ever was created[,] enough to make hair stand at an end. Go forward and come to Kealmore [Kilmore] over the most frightful rocky road. Got a young girl there to conduct me across the mountains[,] Peggey — and a more horrible frightful road [I] never saw in my life[,] up rock and down others[,] scenery nothing but stony Mountains all the way and across boggy hills. Get to Mr James [*blank*][5] a common farmer[,] dined on potatoes milk and butter in company with 16 fellows around a table loaded with potatoes[,] each had a wooden platter of milk before him. I had a bason and sat at a table with my host Mr James Cronins and his Brother. Soon after in came a parcel of boys and girls and set to the potatoes[.] He has a great deal of land about and pays rent 85£ a year, 4½ Acres of potatoes[.] After dining with my

---

[1] 'A field that has been reaped, and not yet ploughed again' (*OED*).
[2] Privy (*OED*).
[3] Carrignacurra tower house, built in the late 16th century (Power et al., *Archaeological Inventory of County Cork*, 3: Mid Cork, p. 362). Lee sketched a view of the tower at SJC, MS U.30 (7), ff. 7v–8r (p. 319), not reproduced.
[4] Probably Castlemasters, owned by Captain Pyne in 1814 (Leet, *A Directory*, p. 100).
[5] Cronin, named below. The farmhouse was likely in the neighbourhood of Ballingeary; the Cronins were historically stewards of the church at Gougane Barra.

company Cronin put on his Sunday coat and waistcoat[,] dressed himself and we took a walk towards the Lake which is 2 mile from his Cabin across the Mountain side and over dreadful stones[,] rocks, bog brooks etc[.] There [f. 14v] is in contemplation to make a road along here and a dreadful job it will be. The Mountains are very bold and one cannot see the lake untill one comes upon it.[1] The Guagane Rocks on the R of the Lake are beautiful bold and almost so very high, saw 30 or 40 goats some on top and some on the sides[,] how the Devil they could get there is wonderful. At the foot of the Mountains are a few Cabins where about 70 years ago one Ensign Brown who had received a hurt and returned from the army retired and [lived?][.] He became acquainted with one Bishop Brown[2] an English Bishop who lived 2 miles from Cork and he came over to visit him in his carriage, but the carriage was carried on the backs of men from Inchigela there about 7 miles and it would be totally impossible for the carriage to go any other way[.] The lake looks beautiful and the river here runs out at the end of it over large Rocks and through different masses in a very elegant manner[.] Below formerly was a sort of bridge erected by a priest who lived about 100 years ago on the island[.] Get round to the S side of [the] island and see an old arch of loose stones which was they say a church and in it are a n° of pieces of wood which look as if they had been little thin pillars curved. One says they were parts of the church which fell down[.] Others say they are brought by people who are cured and left there. They are all similar and look as if belonging to some building all round. They say the priest who lived on the island was buried in the Church and the Church [was] locked and the key thrown into the lake. Just before the remnant [of] the Chapel are some steps of stone where all the people who come begin the round. Close to the Church side is a burial [f. 15r] ground and they shew the place where a tomb was found in it. They say on the tomb in the Church was writing but the roof all having fallen in you cannot see any thing of it.

James Calanan a peasant about 50 years ago had caught a little grey filley on the S side of the lake and only had a halter on it. He came to the waters edge and the filley began to drink and put down its head as if for that purpose, when going in a step too far it plunged in and darting forward began swimming across. He had no power over it with a halter and only stuck fast, somewhere in the middle it rested on a piece of wood or something under water and then darted forward again and carried him safe over. Mr Cronin has heard him tell it 100 times. His son now lives at Guogane where his father did live. Close by the Church are rows of stones in all directions over a great deal of ground[,] all forming narrow parallelograms[.] These are the places where there are tents and cabins erected for the 24 of June[,] the great day.[3] From the sides of the lake the island looks beautifully [sic] as it is a small acre covered with ash trees and very fine ones too and they had different tints on them. There has been made from the south side a narrow passage in it and just at the entrance of this passage down 4 or 5 steps is the famous well for bathing which cures all sorts of diseases. There is a fine ash by it. Going into the island you go up steps and then get down into a square area[.] On each side are 2 arched chapels [cells], plain arches like

---

[1] In the following paragraphs, Lee describes a visit to Gougane Barra Lake and church ruins, near Ballinageary, Co. Cork. The site of the 6th-century hermitage of St Finbarr was a site of 'pattern days', described here by Lee as occasions of pilgrimage and prayer.

[2] Peter Brown, Bishop of Cork and Ross in 1710–35 (Goldberg, *Jonathan Swift*, p. 37).

[3] The annual day of pilgrimage at Gougane Barra.

those of a bridge but called chapels, round at [the] top. There is a walk on the [f. 15v][1] top up then around. [an old?] lonely [***] picturesque trees [***] in the middle is a [square?] [***] of [steps?] [***] top of which is a pole for a cross and no [***] on it. The whole appearance of the place is [resplendent?] [***] on the E side is another Chapel separate and long and the whole floor is covered with small stones. Near it is the remnants of a building and a chimney and they shew a place which was an oven[.] About 100 years ago a priest Father Denis Mahony lived on the island and this was [his] house, and he took particular care of the whole place and kept it in fine order. He had an orchard and it was a fine place [***]. On the 24 June all the people in thousands flock to this [place?] to the well. It is considered that all ill people who come will be cured of all diseases.

They begin their rounds by praying on the steps by the old church[.] Then they go in the island and take 40 stones in their pockets and in the 1 [first] Chapel of the 8[2] on the S W corner they say 5 prayers taking 5 stones into their hands by which they count them[.] At the next they take out of pocket 10 stones and so on 25, 20 and saying 15, 20, 25, 30 prayers in the different chapels in order. Then they go and pray in the 9th Great Chapel and leave all the stones there. At the S end in an arch left and at [the] N End are 2 ash trees from which the bark is all taken off and carried home by different people [to cure any?] people [who use?] it as a charm. Here is a place which is considered as a [home?] of some priest. The ash are very fine and are preserved by the credulity of the people [f. 16r] for they think they are [*** *rest of line illegible*] [*** from credulity?] order and they told me [***] that formerly all the wood on the island was sold with [oak?] which was cut down and the bark sent to [***] tanyard where Mr Orpen lives they belonged to the [abbey?]. One man of the name of — who was cutting wood down was [drowned soon?] after and all the things which were tanned by the bark rotted and no good came by it, and every man who had a hand in it died within [***][.] Mr Orpen has offered his tenants the wood [***] but they would not accept of it nor cut a bit down [***] he must get somebody else to cut it down for they would not[.]

They say if a child is brought there [***] and bathed in the water it is immediately killed or cured. Cronin has known many instances of all sorts of cures done by it. *James Cronin* himself had [a bad hand?] and when the time came he went his rounds and every time he patted it it got better very quick although it had been bad for a year. They say that all mad dogs run in all directions to the well and if they are not killed before they get there [that they should?] drink and are cured immediately and it will do men good too. Many dogs have been cured. Just over the Lake on the R side they [climb?] on a rock on the top pointing to the east. From this a [priest?] once leaped down on the shore just below and they shew [***] the marks of his feet on the bottom.[3] He [often jumped and was?] safe[.] Farther on on the high cliffs is the eagles nest and boys will climb up from the lake to it and take the egg or the young one. An Eagle lays but 1 egg for 4 years each [f. 16v] and the 5*th* year 2 eggs. It is wonderful for boys to climb it[.] Up above the lake the river[4] runs

---

[1] The rest of this paragraph, and the next paragraph, occur on pages badly smudged by pencil rubbing, rendering much of the text illegible.

[2] Eight circular cells.

[3] Possibly 'Cloghbarra' stone at Inchimore, with reputed imprints of the hands and feet of St Finbarr. See FitzPatrick, *Royal Inauguration*, p. 236; Power et al., *Archaeological Inventory of County Cork*, 3: Mid Cork, p. 351.

[4] Probably the Owennashrone River, Co. Cork.

to the [*Eagle's* Nest?] and then takes a turn to the R round a M*ountai*n and rises farther up at the foot of a M*ountai*n like a well mouth. The Glin ends there also[.] Had a bad walk in the sunset back the same way[,] but [for that] I co*ul*d not have fo*un*d my way. The passing of the river out of the lake is very fine. The M*ountai*ns here are finer than any I have seen any where. In the Eve*ni*ng all the men washed their feet and sat round the fire, boys and all talking and laughing and the potatoe pot was put on the fire late[,] abo*ut* 8 OClock potatoes were boiled[,] had supper butter honey and milk then went to bed at 9. Slept with Denny Cronin[,] a great fellow of 18[.] Along side was the bed on [*sic*] Mr and Mrs Cronin and 2 children[,] beyond bed of 3 young ones. When we were all bedded a ladder was drawn and the rest of the family mounted it and got on the boards over our heads and there slept, but sleep had not the eyes of *John* F*iott*[.] About 12 the cock began to crow and order to morning in the house. I was taken short and went out of doors in my shirt, for no pot[1] was there. A Kettle was placed under my bed[.] The young ones were [raining?] nature in the night in Mr and Mrs *Cronin's* bed[.][2] Abo*ut* 5 I was glad to get up but my bedfellow snored and slept soundly and was as hot as a toast.

Friday [10 October]
Started at 6[.] Go down the M*ountai*n side[,] cross the Lee and proceed all the way up it to a very beautiful waterfall, narrow but fine[.][3] It winds serpentining thro*ugh* a bed of black rocks and from a Rock stop below it is seen to great advantage[.] M*ountai*ns called [Isochsheneen?][4] – cross the Vale and ascend the sides of Duhill [Doughill.]

Bantry Bay is seen fr*om* the top [of] the M*ountai*n Duhill, but to get to [the] top you have a long tedious walk far over M*ountai*n Rocks[,] small bogs[,] up and down[.] Very fatiguing[.] There is a very deep narrow rocky glen runs alongside of you wonderfully rugged and bare[.]

[f. 17r] From top of M*ountai*n see the Bay, Whiddy Island, Bear ~~Island~~ (Haven) [Berehaven] Rabbit Island and Horse Island and all the M*ountai*ns in the county round[.] See dark M*ountai*ns just north of us[.] It was too thick to see before us at a great dist*ance*[,] horrible walking or rather jumping and jolting. Get down the immense m*ountai*n to the vale below [and] get to a fine house called Insheroe [Inchiroe]. We passed Insheroe just opposite Cronins. Farther on near the road[,] crossing to get to it another small brook[,] is Gortlocara [Gortloughra River] and village of Dous[.] Beyond Dous [Douce] M*ountai*n is Gortlocara M*ountai*n[.]

Never was a poor mariner more rejoiced at seeing the shore than I was in rejoining the high road and I swore I never wo*ul*d leave it again[.] F*rom* Gortlocara M*ountai*n you may see all the sea round the coast. Mr Cronin pays his servants or those men whom he finds, cabin turf and feeds 4^d a day for their labour and others who work for wh*ich* they can get 6½[.] The road hardly deserves the name of a High road but to me it was more acceptable than a sight of the gold mines of Peru[.] Potatoes ab*out* here go to sell for 4^d a weight =

---

[1] The remaining three lines of this entry appear in the middle of the following day's entry; they have been moved to here for clarity.
[2] Lee describes the provision of toilet facilities – the 'pot' underneath his bed – and the bedwetting of the Cronin children.
[3] Possibly the waterfall at Garrynapeaka, on the River Lee.
[4] Lee must mean the Sheehy Mountains.

14lbs[.] They do not think them dear untill they come to 12^d, 14^d[.] They have been known at 2^s:2^d and in the famine 6 years ago last March[1] they cost 3:3[.] Mrs Cronin said if they had known of my coming they would have killed a sheep and had some meat. After supper the wiskey bottle was produced and they were surprised that I would not touch a glass. Cross a single arch bridge over Caermontean River,[2] just above it is a noisy waterfall. But not worth going far to see[.] Every person from the proudest peer to the poorest peasant's son is naturally fond of dancing[.] A woman at Insheroe where I got a draught of raw milk had 10 children and her sons were at school at Kealkill learning their Books and dancing and sure enough when I went by Kealkill I saw 2 schools where a fiddle and a pipe were going and some were writing[.] Dreadful road[,] in many places quite green except a few rocks in it. Symptom of [f. 17v] little traffic. All along the noble Mountains of Dous and on the Mountains are the leading fisheries in the area. Come suddenly on the little pretty and pleasant Lough of Droumeneasting[3] [Dromanassa] by which the road runs[.] This is about 3½ miles from Bantry across Mountain to High road 4 Miles and up the top more. 9 Miles from road to Bantry. From the lake you begin to get peeps at the Bay and they always improve upon you as you go on. The approach to the town is nothing extraordinary and you pass down a long street of most filthy miserable looking cabins which would be best set on fire. The town seems a wretched hole and the inn is as bad as in any town in Ireland and the sight of the petty grocers shop seems to point out that it is but poor[.]

---

[1] A 'partial potato failure' occurred in 1800, following a severe winter (Wilde, 'Tables of Deaths', pp. 159, 362).

[2] Owngan River in Cahermoanteen townland.

[3] Cappanaboul Lough in Dromanassa townland.

4. BANTRY TO CASTLEMAIN

[SJC, MS U.30 (4)]
[f. 1 *cut out*]

[f. 2r] **Tuesday [October 14]**[1]
Started from Mr Simon Whites House[2] at 12. Went along the head of the Bay. Road [is] very wild and see at [a] distance Hungary Mountains [Hungry Hill] and the Sugar Loaf[.] See a cascade[3] falling down [the] Mountain[,] the largest and highest in Ireland after much rain. Pass the head of the Bay[,] [a] fine river [flows] under the bridge like [the] Pont y Pair river.[4] Curious freshwater lake [lies] close to the sea, a great quantity of timber and trees at the bottom of it. Nets cannot draw it on that account, [it is] very deep. Road goes along winding [round?] the bay[.] At 6 Miles from Bantry is a fine brook and bridge and then the road goes to the R direct up the vale and around the long Mountain called the Priest Leap[5] for several miles up a most wild Glen which is alongside and below. At the End [the] road winds up to the middle at [the] head of [the] Glen and from hence they say a priest leaped to near the head of Bantry lake[,] 5 or 6 miles[,] and they shew the marks of his feet. Clever and a wise fellow[,] for by so doing he escaped a miserable stony boggy road[.] Views all along of Bantry are beautiful for the heights near the road have a noble view all around both ways[,] by Bantry and towards Kenmare[.] All the latter were in tops of [the] Mountains[.] It was quite clear and sunshine where I stood here at first suddenly it got thick, clouds and rain came on and in ¼ hour the tops were all in clouds it became dark, could not see the vallies. 2 or 3 pretty bridges over streams[,] as wild and fine as any in Wales. Only no wood[.]

[f. 2v] The first[6] is very fine if the traveller is so lucky to travel in or after rain. Uncommon wild and dirty road. Met people all the way going to Bantry fair which is tomorrow[.] Could have bought plenty horses for 5 and 6 Guineas but not enough cash with me. Saw 2 eagles in the air hovering over my head (when on the top of the Mountain), also [saw] one from the window of Mr Whites House. Come to a narrow passage through the Mountain which is called the Gap and it is very narrow, nothing but

---

[1] This entry is out of sequence, coming before those of 11, 12 and 13 Oct. Entries for those dates may, therefore, be retrospective, but this cannot be certain due to Lee's irregular pagination.

[2] Simon White (1768–1838), brother of Richard White, 1st Earl of Bantry (see below, p. 197, n. 2). Simon White also welcomed Latocnaye in 1797 (Latocnaye, *A Frenchman's Walk*, p. 95).

[3] The waterfall on Hungry Hill is also described in Smith, *Cork*, I, pp. 286–7.

[4] See 28 Aug. 1806 (SJC, MS U.30 (2), p. 96).

[5] According to local tradition as received by Latocnaye in 1797, a priest leapt from the spot to ensure the administering of the last rites to a sick parishioner (*A Frenchman's Walk*, p. 97). Lee sketched a scene nearby; see SJC, MS U.30 (7), f. 9r (p. 320), not reproduced.

[6] Lee may mean the first stream over which the traveller passes on this walk.

Mountains before me[.] Go on along a straight road, come to 4 cross roads and was at a loss how to proceed[,] whether forward or to the L[,] but seeing the water which appeared to be the head of the Bay on the L[,] I went down that way and [had walked] for some way when I found that it was the wrong road. It was now getting dark and being very much confused [I] was very uncomfortable. Repaced my steps and went along the proper road and for a very long way. It got quite dark and after walking for a long time [I] came to the Bridge over [the] Kenmare River, heard the murmuring on the distant Mountains of waterfalls which is the Mountain roar of the rock, also the waves breaking on the coast made it very awful[.] Crossed the Bridge and went up to the 4 [cross] roads[,] go to the West and come to Mr Spreads House about 7 OClock, about a mile from town[.] 14 Mile from Bantry.[1] The Priest Leap not ½ way[.]

[f. 3r] NB. On ~~Saturday~~ (Friday) 10 October met 2 Gentlemen about 8 Miles from Bantry, who were going a shooting. Asked them how far to Bantry etc[.] Conversation ensued. What oclock etc[.] They asked me to come <u>next</u> morning and breakfast with them, and we parted[.]

[11 October] Saturday

Saturday morning went and breakfasted with Mr Simon White. Afterwards went on the water and rowed up to Glangarriff [Glengarriff] with 8 Boatmen, fine rowers best I ever saw. Lord Bantrys[2] pinnace. Went up to Mr White's new house which is situated on Glangarriff Bay in a lovely situation. It will be soon finished. Pass by Whiddy and several islands on the way, and by an island on which [the] government have built a new fort and a martello tower at [the] entrance of Glangarriff Bay. Rode about Mr White's grounds[,] fine subjects for the pencil. [A] Bold round Mountain [lies] opposite his House over the Bay. Beyond it is a Mountain called [the] Sugar Loaf from its high point[.] Beyond his House on the road to Bearhaven and Lord Bantrys cottage is a fine Glen with a bridge of 2 arches and a fine cascade up it a little way. Beyond is another glen and a bridge also. The rocks are very noble and grand and well wooded about here. Return from here by water to Mr White's House near Bantry[.]

[f. 3v] Sunday [12 October]

Immediately after my coming from Bantry and breakfast we started on the water and went out at low tide to Chapel Island, to see the oyster Beds and saw on the shore of it Oysters in shoals all sticking to the rocks and laying in streams on the shore, below the water, but men venture up to their knees and with hammers and pickaxes broke them up. I knocked a great many off the rocks and eat them on the spot. In the Bay a great quantity of coral is found and dragged on shore by the people for manure[.] It is got in great quantities by boats dragging for it and it is put on the land in a state of sand and makes the best possible manure. [I] Never [before] saw coral sands used so. Picked some pieces out of it[,] tolerably large. Went up to the ground which Mr White reclaimed from the sea. A large tract of about 19 Acres[,] it now produces excellent corn and grain[.] He built a wall around it and at High Water its surface is considerably below the level of the sea. When

---
[1] Lee means that he had travelled 14 miles to get to Bantry from his point of origin earlier that day.
[2] Richard White (1767–1851), 1st Earl of Bantry (Geoghegan, 'White, Richard').

the French were in the Bay[1] by some unaccountable accident the wall broke and it was all covered with water[.] Boats went over it and fish were taken in it. Went on shore on Whyddy [Whiddy] Island and saw the middle battery. On top of the ditch there are about 20 24 pounders all round it[.] The fort is built at [the] top of a part of [the] island which runs to a point and their guns command the whole circle. The men who work there are covered [f. 4r] up to the middle[.] There is an immense fosse[,] a considerable draw bridge on a lever[,] the banks around it slope off to the sea. Whyddy Island [is] very uneven[.] There are 2 rises of land on it which make it very singular[.] The land is uncommon fine[.] There is a battery building at [the] E and W ends of the island. There is a stone quarry near the middle one from which it was built[,] and [a] very remarkable thing is that in the middle of the island are a fresh water and a salt water lake close to each other[.] Not far from [hence?] on the S side is a Deer park and some red Deer in it. There is an immense no. of hares in the island. Go up to the house which Mr White formerly lived in and which [the] government now rents for 200 per annum for stores[.] Beyond this on the shore is found an immense no. of sandstones of metal[2] which Mr White says in the storms are in great n° about then[.] The sea dashes against the rocks and bats large stones up and these fall down again and thus he thinks this ore is beaten out of the rocks or sea[,] they are washed up by the water from the Bottom[.] He could get [a] cart road up it a long time to Lord Bantry slate quarry one may get some very fine chrystals[,] hexagonal[.][3] Soon board again and row by Lord Bantrys house and [on] to the town and go home. See a very great [f. 4v] variety of shells and of fish, and a great deal of coral bits but none very great. In all the islands in this Bay at low water and on the rocks the seals[,][4] a very large beast[,] are seen laying asleep on the rocks or else in the sea rolling about and you may some times get a shot at them, but when you fire a stone all the rest drop in the water and disappear. Sea gulls [*laridae,*] Cormorants [*Phalacrocorax carbo*], diver[,][5] rabbits [common rabbit, *Oryctolagus cuniculus*] etc in plenty. Saw some wild swans [mute swan, *Cygnus olor*] which look very fine.

Monday [October] 13.
Rode on the Bearhaven road along the Mountains to Glangarriff[.] See the improvements Mr White has made in the new parts of the road, his new road avoids all the great high hills. Went his new road and rode for 2 miles on ground new made over bog swamp and which shook under our horses feet[.] He has reclaimed all the land about his house by 1st planting it with potatoes then laying it down, and picking off the stones and blasting the rocks[.] [A] Charming spot [is] Glangarriff for a few 100 Sketches with its variety of wood[,] water, bogs[,] bays[,] Mountains and rocks. Go on towards Lord Bantrys shooting lodge[.] Road wonderfully wild and picturesque[.] The rocks are magnificently

---

[1] In Dec. 1796, the French, accompanied by United Irishman Theobald Wolfe Tone (1763–98), attempted but failed to land a fleet of 43 ships and 15,000 troops at Bantry Bay (Foster, *Modern Ireland*, p. 278). This resulted in the construction of three batteries on Whiddy Island in 1806/7 (NIAH), with a further four Martello towers on nearby Bere Island.
[2] A combination of shale and sandstone (*OED*).
[3] Lee seems to mean that Lord Bantry's slate quarry was some distance away, so a cart would be useful for the transportation of the crystals to be found there.
[4] Possibly the grey seal (*Halichoerus grypus*), the larger of the two seal species found in Ireland.
[5] A family of water birds.

bold[,] particularly near the bridge where the road [diverges] to Killarney and to Bearhaven, [the] finest rocks I ever saw. Go through fine woods and a little way to the R [is] a path through the wood to a high rock from which [is] a noble view just out of the trees [f. 5r] all around and see the Cottage[.] Return to the road and go on through the woods to the lodge which is in a spot on a fine brook and surrounded with rock and Mountains[.] In the distance see the Eagle's Nest and some eagles flying about. Saw a bridge made of the mast of the *Surveillant* ship[,] French[,] which sank in the harbour.[1] Behaviour of Lord Bantry and Mr White when the French came there.[2] Saw several rocks out of which were growing 6[,] 7 or 8 different trees and [numerous?] herbs or flowers. Oak, Birch[,] Beech[,] Ash[,] Arbutus[3] [nut?] etc etc[.] Return by the Arbutus grove and in it [are] some of an immense size. Get on the road and I on a fine poney [all the day?] yet rode back in the storm and over the bad old road over the high Mountains[,] 12 miles in 80 Minutes[.]

Saw the spot near Whyddy Island where the French ships lay. Mr White and Lord Bantry [were] very active in the rebellion.[4] It never raged there[.] A party of 12 [United Irishmen] came down from Dublin to swear in the people. They swore [in] 1 man who came to Lord Bantry and asked what he should do. He took the fellow up and Mr White took the other 11 and sent them all abroad. They took up a D^{os}[5] OConnor and Mr OConnor steward of Connorville [f. 5v] without any ceremony having proof against them and sent them out of the country. For 17 Days when the French came on the coast they were up night and day with their corps and when the French boats with men a gun and matches lighted went about making soundings in the harbor, they were sometimes up to the horses middle in the water to oppose the landing if they [the French] had attempted[.]

Mr and Mrs Newenham[6]

Wednesday. [15 October]

Went on the water Kenmare up to the island where Mr Harboard[7] who owns Muckruss has built a little cottage. He pays no tithes or taxes as the Island is in no parish or county[.] Went from thence ~~up~~ down the river towards the place where the river Blackwater joins the Bay and a more beautiful spot I never beheld[.] The river is narrow but [there are] fine rocks on each side and it winds along and at the top you see one arch of a lovely bridge and then (the) ~~an~~other which are round and below the river comes down in a grand cascade[.] The arches are very high and the pillar between them is built on a rock. Water in high tides or floods comes through the R hand arch also[.] Go up to the bridge[,] [stand] on the top and then under it[,] and it looks excessively grand and sublime[.] I never saw any spot so <u>romantic in</u> Wales[,] positively not[.] Came back all along the Left shore, through the islands and go up the river [f. 6r] Kenmare to the place called the sound

---

[1] *La Surveillante*, a French frigate sunk in Bantry Bay in 1796 (Bourke, *Shipwrecks*, I, p. 145).

[2] Lee refers to a story expanded upon in the next paragraph.

[3] A genus of flowering shrub.

[4] Richard White, 1st Earl of Bantry (see above, p. 197, n. 2) was prominent in the defence of Bantry Bay during the threatened French invasion in Dec. 1796 (Geoghegan, 'White, Richard').

[5] Full name not known.

[6] Possibly a reference to the parents of Sarah Newenham, wife of Simon White from 1801 (see above, p. 196, n. 2) (Debrett, *Peerage*, II, p. 1030).

[7] Charles John Herbert (1785–1823), landowner (Hourican, 'Herbert, Henry Arthur').

and [f. 6v] through it, which is a very narrow passage indeed of the river which soon after widens as far as ever and someway up on the R is a little bay etc[,] [a] noble waterfall[1] into the sea[,] a fine body of rocks through which the water falls[.] A cottage on the R hand[,] a pretty Bridge[2] above the water and a noble high rough Mountain behind.[3] [A] Fine subject for a picture. Go on shore to the Boat house. See n[os] of seals, redshanks [*Tringa totanus,*] cormorants, etc[.] There are sharks in this river.[4] We went down about 8 miles to the Blackwater River,[5] but could not see down the Bay which extends 11 or 12 Miles further[.] It is very fine but not quite as broad as Bantry. The mountain scenery here is most grand and wonderful. Mountains of all sorts and sizes and forms and features. The house in which Counsellor Spread[6] lives is the mansion to Lord Henry Pettys[7] Estate here which extends all along each side of the river for many miles[.] It is in some parts 40 Miles long and he has more land in all than any man in Ireland, but much of it [is] not worth 1 penny an acre. Leases [are] let for 3 lives, or 20 Years and a life. There are many leases for ever on some parts. The annual value is about 8 or 9000 per an*num*. The town of Kenmare is very insignificant[.] [f. 7r] There is a Company of soldiers in it. They are now building a new town hall[,] (hotel) etc in 1 mass[.] Going in fm (on) the river you see several old ruined Churches on the sides but on the point there is one[.]

Thursday 16. [October]
(Started at 7.) Rained all the night very hard and on starting at 7 it was misty but fine. On ascending the hill, had a fine and curious view. The town, L Hand [side,] R Hand [side] and grounds and all were in a mist which at first looks like a noble river, this mist was all in the valley but on a narrow inspection you see through it and the river[.] Sun just appearing through mist. Opposite Mountains all in a mass, the parts between them filled with mist like lakes[.] On standing still you hear a regular murmuring on all sides from the water courses being all filled and flowing with water[.] It is literally and correctly the Poetic Mountain roar.[8] See the fine waterfall over the river by the farm.

NB on Tuesday Evening observed a fine effect[.] It was thick, about 5 OClock at night, darkish and the sun had just got down behind some Mountains[,] all in red about that part[.] [The] Mountains to the East were all in shade except just their ridges which were quite red and a rainbow was behind one of them[,] still a rainy thickness was a medium through which it was seen[.] [f. 7v] It was all shade except these Mountain tops for I was surrounded with Mountains and below me there were streams turning and roaring and the <u>Mountain roar</u> was going and I was walking by the river side on this side [of] the Gap coming towards Kenmare. This effect did not last 5 minutes.

---

[1] Poulgorm falls at Sheen Bridge.
[2] Probably Sheen Bridge.
[3] This could be any one of a number of mountains in the vicinity.
[4] Probably the basking shark (*Cetorhinus maximus*); by 'river' Lee may mean 'estuary'.
[5] Not to be confused with the much larger Blackwater which flows through Kerry, Cork and Waterford.
[6] Charles Spread was agent of the Lansdowne estate from 1801 (see next note) (O'Loughlin, *Families of Co. Kerry*, p. 117).
[7] Henry Petty-Fitzmaurice, 3rd Marquess of Lansdowne, known as Lord Henry Petty until 1809 (Wright, 'Fitzmaurice, Henry Petty- (1780–1863)').
[8] Not an uncommon image in 18th and 19th-century poetry. Williams outlines the soundscape of the sublime and appreciation for the sound of thundering waters in *Creating Irish Tourism*, pp. 79–80.

DIARY 4: BANTRY TO CASTLEMAIN

Pass over a most excellent bog on the top of the 1st *Mountain* belonging to *Lord Henry Petty* which he allows all his tenants to cut for themselves. A man who chose to buy it [turf] in the town of Kenmare instead of fetching it, pays 3^d and in winter 4^d for 2 panniers full. (So a fellow who was selling some told me[.]) Some of the *Mountains* elegantly cloud capt[.][1] The bog might all be made excellent meadow for there is a fine fall on both sides of it[.]

NB. At the Priests Leap U[2] pass out of the County of Cork into Kerry[.]

//

On leaving the romantic Blackwater yesterday, and getting some way up the river coasting it, because [the] Wind [was] on [the] E: [The] Tide [was] flowing and ∴ [it was] very rough[,] [so] that the waves sprayed over us. Mr Spread handed the Brandy bottle and a Glass to the 8 Rowers[.]

Bowman 2 and 3 (and 4) helped themselves, [the] 5th or 3rd on [the] L side passed it on to the next without taking any. Why? He had made a vow at Michaelmas last not to take a drop untill that time next year and as yet had kept it. He is quite mad when drunk but as quiet and steady a man when sober as any [f. 8r] one living. 'But Ned have you not left St Patricks Day out of your vow.' 'No Sir.' 'Nor any day at all.' 'Yes Christmas Eve and Christmas day Sir[.]'[3] The fellow could not resist saving them for himself and he will get 10 times more drunk then than he would have done had he not made an oath. Also when his time is expired (if he does not forfeit the oath – he will and begin [drinking again] before the time) he will get drunk for a month together to make up for lost time[.]

Little boy with his books under his arm[.]

'God save you boy.' 'Your servant kindly Sir,' 'Where are u going[?]' 'Home Sir.' 'Where is that.' '~~Out there Sir~~ (to the) west Sir.' 'What is the name of the place.' A devil of a name[.][4] 'What Book is that under your arm[?]' 'Ovid Sir.' 'Have you Brothers[?]' 'Yes Sir.' 'How many.' '2 Sir.' 'Are they better scholars than yourself.' 'Yes Sir they are older[.]'[5]

//

Upon coming to the top of the road between the 2 *Mountains* from whence you loose [sic] sight of the side of the country around Kenmare[,] You get a most wild view among the *Mountains* towards Killarney. This is a sort of gap where U stand U [sic] in the road winding in several opposite directions and at first it struck me that there were several roads and I began to think of my late mistake at night[6] and was doubting which road to go untill advancing I saw my mistake[.] You see where you are to go by the bits of road for several miles[,] perhaps 4, for the view is not more extensive than 6 miles but so diversified with *Mountain*[.]

[f. 8v] Obliged to take off my shoes to walk through several [water] courses which were swollen by the rain in the night. You hear water roaring on all sides and on the R at [the] top of the ridge between the 2 *Mountains*[,] next to where I came through[,] is a very

---

[1] Capped.
[2] You, an abbreviation repeated later.
[3] Quotation marks added.
[4] Lee indicates his inability to spell an unfamiliar Irish place name.
[5] Quotation marks added.
[6] See 10 Oct. (p. 194), where Lee was lost after dark.

pretty dist*an*t waterfall[.] Some scattered trees increase the wildness of the scene and many parts of the rocks look uncommon white[,] like marble[,] fr*o*m being overgrown in bits by a moss [lichen]. Some of the tops of the M*o*unt*ai*ns are cove*re*d with clouds, a mist still remains in the valley and [in the] cracks between the M*o*unt*ai*ns and by seeing here and there a stream of blue smoke[,] you may be able to find out by tracing it the cottages here and there fr*o*m whence it comes[.] Otherwise I sh*ou*ld not have seen them. As I descend into the valley I see streams rolling in the bogs and become more and more aware of the height of the M*o*unt*ai*n on wh*i*ch I lately beat my way and had under my feet. Tried in this wild sequestered place to walk barefoot[,] and did for a long way with ease[,] but it delayed me too long to continue so. I have no idea of not being able to do wh*a*t the common people do every day, [f. 9r] and wh*a*t Adam did before me. As I go forward I hear a loud roaring (in the Glen) on the R and am anxious to get forward to see wh*i*ch water course it is, I suppose it comes fr*o*m the waterfall of wh*i*ch I see a bit on the top of that M*o*unt*ai*n on the R[.] The road winds here very steep under a rock, and I see it going away under my feet. How can it possibly communicate with [that] upon [which] I stand. The noisy water course alongside of me, hinders me from thinking how it can go down, but advancing I see the elegant winds it takes. Very steep[.] On the Bases of each M*o*unt*ai*n side are a few scattered trees wh*i*ch are sufficiently close to produce a very fine romantic effect with their various particolored leaves[.]

Oh the autumnal tints! what diff*eren*t colours do I not see!! Wh*a*t part of the best M*o*unt*ai*n scenery is not before me. But I must ~~cross~~ (wade) this brawling water course before my feet and tarry no longer[.] Going on get a view of the most elegant torrent rushing down the glen only see that part near the road wh*i*ch is picturesque to a max*imu*m. Fine white and dark rocks[,] trees[,] oak, birch and holly intermixed [and] thinly scattered so that you see the rocks between them and [the] noble M*o*unt*ai*ns all around[.]

[f. 9v] The road is here very steep thro*ugh* the rocks and winds well, ~~rocks~~ (stream) forms cascades all down the road side very violently, and further on I have to cross it and a very strong rapid course it is[,] up to near my knees, [so I] walk barefoot[.] Farther on is another little stream[,] just above wh*i*ch on [the] road are some fine rocks[,] woods beyond them and the rough tops of the m*o*unt*ai*ns above this on the R, but the views are of this description all the way [and it is] no use to draw, one on R. Fine slate rocks all about here, they c*ou*ld be very valuable near a town.

// (At the <u>great</u> waterfall, this was omitted[.])[1] At [the] R [are] fine stags [*cervidae*], are they disturbed by my step or by the noise of the course of water fr*o*m wh*i*ch they fly and cross the road[?] Surely it is the magnificence of the latter[,] for they c*ou*ld hardly hear my feet for the [noisy and bouming?] torrents[.] // They disappeared among the rocks and when I come to the spot where they crossed and got among the rocks I cannot get another view of them[.] //

[f. 10r] Fine cool day, every thing smells and looks fresh after the rain. This [is] more awful and grand than if the sun shone out[.]

Go on and look around, (turn about and) look at the road I have just left[,] and the M*o*unt*ai*ns around and the one I came down, the fine torrent on the R with the scattered rocks, the cottages thatched at the bottom, turn about and look at the view before me

---

[1] This sentence was inserted later, with Lee noting that he had earlier omitted to mention the content within the slashed lines.

DIARY 4: BANTRY TO CASTLEMAIN

and the road I am to go[,] and go up part of the glen and then let every body cry out and say, What can be more grand, more magnificent[,] more sublime[,] more surpassing all the powers of description or narration. Look at the jumble of rocks and the fine green and white faces they shew, look at the bodies of the trees, covered with ivy or else white (as the birch) and see how they all swear that nothing can surpass their beauty and how jealous they w*ou*ld be if they thought you admired any thing more than they[.] Surely this is too fine an approach to the Lakes of K*ill*arney. It must be the entrance to ~~a~~ paradise, for it is divine [f. 10v] and the higher I go the more I am confirmed in my opinion. Oh may the sensations I now feel never leave me. May this delusion never end!! A companion here w*ou*ld spoil one to this, for no person c*ou*ld share time to speak the mind[,] and [the] soul is so wrapt up in itself and so full of the sensations w*hi*ch the surround*ing* objects excite[.]

// Of the spot just farther on I can only say that it is indescribable. On the R you see a fine bold M*o*untai*n* ~~its base~~ (ragged) and bare[,] its base set with fine ~~dist~~ trees and a noble wild cascade coming down[.] You may judge of its size for I walked thro*ugh* the water on the road up to my knees for ab*ou*t 20 Yards in the deepest part. On the left you see from the brink of the waterfall a little of it[,] but it is so ⊥^{r} and so divided by rocks and hid by trees that you cannot see any of it but close at y*our* feet 2 edg*es* of mountains [are] close below you and are cov*er*ed with wood[.] The water fall goes d*ow*n between them but is not seen a bit. Then ridges of m*ou*ntai*n*[,] all standing down in the middle[,] fill up the centre and in the dist*ance* is a long range of [f. 11r] bare M*o*untai*n* tops in clouds and at the foot you just see a bit of a lake, you can see the rocks and trees and every tree almost separate by its color and shades[.] Road keeps ascending untill you come to [the] top of [the] M*o*untai*n*[,] fr*om* whence you loose sight of the M*o*untai*n*[.] Near Kenmare it [is] yet extremely wild, [and] windy between rugged uncouth cliffs running suddenly out of the ground[.] Come to a very narrow pass with high rocks on each side and trees growing on them[,] water running down below the roadside, see a waterfall forward and the road winding for a long way over a M*o*untai*n* Side[.]

[The] Road [is] very steep d*ow*n here[.]

Rain had been collecting on the hills ab*ou*t Killarney and now it began to fall close to the pretty elegant waterfall below[.] The water comes pouring over and among [the] rocks and forms a little round pool in front w*hi*ch runs over on the farthest Right hand corner and twists and twirls with froths and foam in a very extraordinary serpentine manner. You must either get over among the rocks of the waterfall or wade it below as I did[.] By its direction I imagine it runs into Upper Lake[.]

[f. 11v] Troublesome little rain and I only got to the beautiful waterfall [opening?] at the Lake at 12 OClock.[1] About 6 Miles in 5 hours[.] Every thing had wet charm[.] // The whole scenery is wonderfully grand[,] one cannot describe it[.] See just before me 2 M*o*untai*n*s w*hi*ch just have room for a stream to run between them. [The] One on the R is quite to a point, on coming up to them find a stream broken all to pieces running down between ridges of M*o*untai*n*s and the road on the L hand side M*o*untai*n* [is] cut along its side, [the] M*o*untai*n*s [are] wonderfully ragged and and [*sic*] loose stones appear hanging over the tops as if ready to fall. I must leave off and go on or they

---

[1] Possibly the waterfall on the Owenreagh River at Looscaunagh, Co. Kerry (OS 1st edition, 6 inches to 1 mile, 1838–42).

will certainly come down on me[.] // The rocks are very white with the moss on them, some parts in the valley of the stones look like the foam of the water w*hich* goes between them, since I came in this glen the Clouds have hid the R handside fr*om* me and I cannot see the M*o*unt*ai*n tops for them[,] altho*ugh* they are close alongside. Pass do*w*n the Glen and come to a 2 arch bridge.[1] The M*o*unt*ai*ns here appear to be limestone, but there seems to be slate at [the] top also. The view now seems as if one was coming to an open and less hilly country[.]

[f. 12r] Just at the Bridge get a peep at the lake and see some smoke as [if] fr*om* a town beyond it, but a country flat and smooth [lies] beyond the town, the view by no means gave me any pleasure[.] It surprised me[,] not expecting to see Killarney in such a place. The M*o*unt*ai*ns I (just) came thro*ugh* are wonderful and the one on my R goes quite to a point.

By degrees you get a more full view of the ~~river~~ (Lake) [Lough Leane] on w*hich* the town is situated and after having been at the magnificent Bantry Bay, and seen some of the few Beauties of it, after hav*ing* visited a bit of Glangarrif Bay and the surround*ing* scenery, after hav*ing* been sailing on it and on Kenmares noble river and seeing [the] Blackwater and beautiful scenery on the road all today, to hop fr*om* 2 noble mountain*s* on [to] a little bit of a petty lake dotted with spots of land and beyond it a flat open bare country, is very provoking and disappointing[.] The wood ab*ou*t the place sets it off a little and[,] to my eye accustomed to see water on a grand and noble scale, The whole place ab*ou*t here looks like a gentlemans park tolerably wooded with a pond in it. The road fr*om* here to Muckruss and into Killarney is very pretty, [with] some fine trees on the road side and pass Mr Harboards [Herbert's] Walls [f. 12v] and Grounds. // NB Gave Counsellor Spreads servant 2:6 // Cross a fine river and get to the town about 4 OClock. NB the greater of the water courses where I waded up to my knees and where the water fall*s* in to the valleys is called Galway River, the people say that all the rivers I crossed and that [one] in particular <u>are very treacherous</u>, because you may go over them one hour and the next owing to showers or storms they may be impassable almost, other time*s* some of them may be nearly dry. Such are the advantages of seeing this mount*ainou*s country as I did a day after heavy rains.

Friday 17: [October]
2 Balls [of] string 8ᵈ. Shoestrings 10ᵈ. Sealing wax 8ᵈ. Packing Cloth 2 Yds 2:8ᵈ

Walked out after Breakfast into Lord Kenmares[2] grounds and saw his house and gardens, the latter are all gone to ruins and the greenhouse and hothouse are all fallen to pieces for want of the presence of the master. Went down the grounds behind the house, in the grounds near the house is a wonderful large <u>sallow tree</u>,[3] of 4 ~~branches~~ bodies[.] There was another but it was broken by the winds. Go thro*ugh* his grounds and get on the road to Ross Island[.][4]

---

[1] Possibly Galway's Bridge over the Galway River.
[2] Valentine Browne (1754–1812), 5th Viscount and 1st Earl of Kenmare, Catholic activist and landlord of Castlerosse, Killarney, and created Earl of Kenmare in 1801 (Dunlop, 'Lawless, Valentine Browne (1773–1853)'; Quinn, 'Browne, Valentine').
[3] Trees from the genus *Salix,* willow.
[4] In the following paragraphs, Lee makes observations on the copper mines at Ross Island, Co. Kerry.

[f. 13r][1] Wheel 16 feet Draw 6 feet breast. Charcoal brings well [water] 5½ on wheel and takes wheel 2 feet below breast. Depth of mine 66. 4 pumps[.] 300 Gallons in a minute the mine makes in water[.]
Native copper
Ore in 20 penny wts Richest produce 7 in No.
ore poorest (new directions) 3. Richest at Cronebaun 2½
ore mixed lowest price 35:10 to 41:1d
£8000

A little stream of about 10 Inches (deep) is conducted along the road side and carried to the copper works[,] which water turns the wheel there. It goes for about 2 miles. The wheel which it turns is 16 feet Diameter and 6 feet the breast. The water channel brings the water only 5½ feet on the wheel and takes the wheel 2 feet below the breast. This is all owing to bad management and the ignorance of the person who made the channel about the pressure of [the] water[,] for he made the channel so slight that it burst its sides in many places and has cost them altogether 7000.[2] The wheel turns very slowly and to the ends of its oars on each side are cranks which[,] turning, draw backwards and forwards 2 very long wooden beams, at the ends of which are pumps in the shafts and this gives motion to [f. 13v] the pump heads which draw up the water, beyond 1 pump and to its head is fixed another ~~pump~~ (beam) which goes onto another pump and thus any no. of pumps might be continued at pleasure in ::n[3] to the power. The mines is [sic] supposed to make 300 Gallons of water in a minute in general upon an average[,] but in wet weather as all the rain which falls on the island of course drains down in to the mines and to the lowest parts[,] they are then plagued confoundedly with it. The deepest parts of the mine are 66 feet. The ore which is dug is very rich and moreso than in any part of the kingdom. There is native copper there and some of all colors and no mine abounds with a greater variety of specimens[:] green[,] blue[,] white, red, purple, grey is the best[,] and a blackish grey. In some of it they find[,] upon trying it in the assaying house[,] as much as 7dwts in 20. The poorest is 3 penny wts in 20 and the best I believe at Cronebawn is about 2½ in 20 p~wts. Although there is ore of different values yet they have generally sold it all mixed and it fetches at the lowest price £35:10 a ton. Some has fetched £41:15. The ore lies between beds of blue limestone filled with numerous [f. 14r] veins of spar in all directions, or else it is in the spar entirely. This mine was worked by the Danes and there is a large place which has been excavated and where the copper came up to the surface of the ground.

Ross Castle at the entrance of the island is a poor old insignificant thing and a barrack is built out of it (there are 2 or 3 rusty old cannon on one side of it).[4] Came home and then went and saw the Roman Catholic Chapel which consists of a long body[,] 2 aisles, and 2 galleries over them and one at the W End. It is very neat and well built. Saw the altar and the tabernacle and the boxes in which the people hear the confessions. Saw the incense Box

---

[1] These rough notes on mining are expanded upon in the following paragraphs.
[2] The figure '7000' is written over the original '8000'. This may relate to the '£8000' cited in Lee's rough notes at the top of the folio.
[3] Proportion.
[4] Ross Castle, a 15th-century tower house with later additions, on the bank of Lough Leane, Killarney.

and the 3 chains to it and the chain to the top going thro*ugh* a ring.[1] The Bishops house is a very neat and elegant one and on [sic] the chapel is a neat monument erected to the late Bishop[2] who was a Dr of Sorbonne[3] and had many good qualities[.]

Proceed and see the sessions house on the L hand side of the way, and go on and see the nunnery, a neat plain building on the R hand side of the same street[.] Went in and saw the Chapel wh*ich* was very [f. 14v] neat, flowers well placed on the altar and round the tabernacle[,] crucifixes etc about, and pictures hung up around the chapel of the crucifixion. Saw one nun above the door in the gallery praying but she did not look up and I could not see her face. Lower down the street is a chalibeate [chalybeate] spring, on the R hand [side] and a neat plain well top made to it. On the surface of the water is a thick skin but the water below is a fine and clear and strong taste[.] All I co*ul*d learn of its good qualities are that it wo*ul*d cure internal complaints and that many persons drank it.

A notable good spring[,] in faith[,] to do such universal good. Gave the old woman there [a] 5[d] bit. Went from thence into Lord Kenmares domain[,] over the bridge on the river Dannigh [Deenagh] wh*ich* runs into the lake, and proceed to the mount from the top of wh*ich* you have a compleat view of the whole of the Lower Lake and the town and the neighbouring country all round[.] It is a beautiful spot and fit for many views[.] The top of the mo*un*ta*i*n is a long ridge and you see very well all around [f. 15r] from it. Come home about 4 OClock[.]

Saturday 17.[4] [October]
Started at 8 and went down to the copper mines and breakfasted there with Cap*tain* White[5] and Counsellor Lapp.[6] Mr W*hite* has 16 shares and Mr Lapp [has] 10. The whole mine is ÷ into 64 shares. They have a lease of the mines and may dig anywhere on Lord Kenmares estate for 31 Years except on one island and on the demesne[.] The company have already expended ab*out* £20000 and have raised £8000 of copper, and this year ab*out* £3000. They are now sinking a new shaft of a very great width wh*ich* is to contain 4 pumps and it is close to the great wheel and will ∴ save all the force wh*ich* is at present lost in hav*ing* the pumps so far f*rom* the wheel. They have got 56 feet deep and pay £14 a ton to the fellows who are sinking the shaft. ~~They ha~~ The miners who take diffe*ren*t parts of the mines have f*rom* 3[£] to 6£ a ton according to the difficulty of working and for this they are obliged to break it to pieces and to [f. 15v] free it f*rom* the limestone and to prepare

---

[1] Lee sketched it in the page margin, not reproduced here.
[2] Monument to Bishop Gerald Teahan (d. 1797) in the RC Chapel on New St, Killarney; the epitaph was printed in Carr, *Stranger in Ireland*, pp. 225–6: 'Entombed / near this Monument, lie the remains / of the Right Reverend GERALD TRAHAN, [sic] / Doctor of the Sorbonne, and R. C. Bishop of Kerry. / His doctrine and his life reflected credit on each other. / In him were blended / the easy politeness of a gentleman / with the purest principles of a Christian. / Given to hospitality, gentle, sober, just, holy, continent, / his charity was diffusive and exemplary; / the patron and protector of honourable merit. / He was learned without ostentation, / and religious without intolerance: / his affable manners and instructive conversation / charmed every ear, and vanquished every heart. / To perpetuate the memory of so beloved a character, / his mourning friends have erected this monument, / a frail memorial of their veneration for his virtues, / and a faint testimony of their grief for a misfortune, / alas! indelibly engraved on their hearts.'
[3] University of Paris, known as Sorbonne.
[4] Diarist error – Saturday was 18 Oct.
[5] Brother of Richard White, 1st Earl of Bantry (see p. 197, n. 2).
[6] Not identified; Lee met Lapp on several subsequent occasions.

DIARY 4: BANTRY TO CASTLEMAIN

it ready for being shipped off. After breakfast went down into the mine with Mr Lapp[,] having previously put on a p*ai*r [of] trowsers and [a] jacket[,] and we were 2½ hours underground, the entrance is very easy down an opening w*hi*ch comes up to day [light], down this you go by steps and then along passages winding about in all directions[.] Sometimes they are very narrow and difficult and at others very easy and you must stoop very low. Saw all the diff*eren*t pumps at work[.] They are placed in the parts where the mine <u>hades</u> and are inclined in them. Saw 3 or 4 [pumps] together[.] They are worked by men[,] w*hi*ch brings the water up out of the lower parts of the mine, and then it is drawn up from these places by buckets or by pumps w*hi*ch are worked by the machinery[.] In some parts of the works there are places where old mines have been worked and they can and have got into places w*hi*ch have been stopped up [f. 16r] by old rubbish w*hi*ch they had left. In some parts of the old mine and all the neighbourhood they find a kind of very hard stone with[,] in general[,] a small hollow cut all round the middle[.] These stones are very hard and very smooth and they call them the Danes hammers[,] with w*hi*ch they say they formerly worked these very mines but th*ese* parts of the mines seem of later work than the Danes time and quere [query] whether the Danes were ever here to work them at all.[1] Most parts of the mines are let out to a set of miners 3[,] 4[,] 5 or 6 who hire certain walks for 2 months and who raise it at so much per ton[,] from 3[£] to 6£ according to the difficulty of getting and of clearing it. These men have under them 5[,] 8 or 10 or more labourers who work by the day or week and have 9:9^d per week ~~or 14d a day~~ perhaps[.] The miners get as much as they chose to raise and clean. The company take out the water at their own expense and the men at the pumps have 14^d a day[.]

[f. 16v] Before these mines were worked none of these fellows c*ou*ld get at their com*mon* occupation more than 8^d a day[,] so that they like the work very much. Each set of miners works 8 hours at a time and then another set go down. If any one of the miners does not go to his work in his turn or within 3 or 4 hours of the beginning of it, he is fined 5 Shillings for he not only loses his own time but the company are working their pumps and no good is doing. If any man has done any thing sufficient to make him a marked man, the Gent*leme*n post him on the outside of the Blacksmith shop and mention his case and then the miners can see whether they dare employ him. They blast a great deal[.] The miners find every thing for themselves[,] candles and powder[.] It is considered a good time spent to make 3 blasts for one man in 8 hours. They put in generally 2 inches of powder at the bottom and they drive [f. 17r] on a little turf to prevent the action of the powder and the rock when hammered down fr*o*m taking fire[,] and over the powder they put in a little more turf (small quantity)[.] The matches are not made of touch paper[,] but a bit of brown paper tallowed over and dried is lighted and this sets fire to the train, it does not burn so expeditiously as touch paper and gives them more time[.] I saw several blasts while in the mine[,] one I saw w*hi*ch flew out a very great way and some of the pieces knocked a bucket over and over. On the west mine they find ore and spar mixed with lead but the lead they do not think worth their while to work and throw it aside. The ore is f*ou*nd chiefly between 2 beds of blue limestone mixed with a great deal of spar and this is the hardest of all to get at[.] The very richer [*sic*], and the richest ores are dug out with the pickaxe without any trouble of blasting[.] There are specimens of grey

---

[1] The copper mines at Ross Island are arguably the oldest in Europe, dating to *c*.2400–2000 BCE (O'Brien, 'Ross Island').

blacking[,] grey red, blue [and] green ores and a white sort of chrystallized ore called cap tooth [f. 17v] ore. There is a native ore found here which is also as rich as possible and when washed will produce 20 dwts – as it ought and [ore] such as this is worth whatever the value of copper is worth[.] Got a great no. of specimens. A share in the works would now cost about £500[.] They are constantly repairing the canal and covering it up with coats of clay and endeavouring to make it more secure. Such was the unparalleled ignorance of the man who first undertook it that he made it go more than 800 Yards outside the course it might have gone. He estimated it at [£]1100 making and it has cost [£]8000 or more and he was so ignorant of hydrostatics that he took it a round about way because there was an old ditch which he made high ⊥ʳ banks to and thought it would keep in the water[,] when as soon as it was filled the pressure burst the sides of course and got under them and blew them up[.]

[f. 18r] As the company may have enemies there are watchmen stationed along the Banks all night for 14ᵈ a night and they see that no malicious person does any harm. A man asked Mr White whether or no he must keep in the watch house all night, 'Yes surely and you must walk along the bank side (about 300 yds) and meet the other man and then turn back and keep doing so', he began at this to make excuses and at last as Mr White removed them all, he confessed that he should be afraid to go so far by himself in the night and would not agree to do it. This was a man. He was afraid that if he should be by himself that he should see the devil[.] Mr White said they were obliged to keep 2 watchmen at the head of the water from where the supply comes for one man would be afraid to stay there by himself[.] They fancy that Ross Castle and all about there is haunted and Mr White said that when he slept in it for about 6 weeks last summer that no one would have come up even to his room [f. 18v] to put out a candle for 100 Guineas or would have gone up stairs alone, so cowardly are the people in the night[.]

Sunday. [19 October]

NB. At Kenmare on the river[,] higher up than the boat house and nearer to the waterfall[,] is a holy well on the sea shore[.][1] It is an excellent spring[,] fresh water[,] yet so close to the sea that it some times overflows it. On the top of the brickwork over this is a stone laying there which the people who come there to pray place on their heads and then put it down again[.] It is said that praying there and drinking the water cures all sorts of cases[.]
//

Mr Coffy[2] once saw a gentleman go on the lake from Ross Castle. He had hired a boat and got a supply of things for dinner and every usual thing prepared and when he had got about 80 Yards out he ordered the men to pull to shore again. Astonished at this they obeyed and he went on shore and did not pursue his days party. What was the use of going [f. 19r] on the water any farther? He had been on the lake of Killarney.

Went to the Chapel (at 8) and saw all the mass[.] After Breakfast went around the grounds of Muckruss and visited the old Abbey[3] which is held in such esteem by the

[1] St Finian's Well in Kenmare parish, Co. Kerry, traditionally resorted to for the cure of a variety of ailments (Logan, *Holy Wells*, p. 58).
[2] Coffy (or Coffey) owned inns at Killarney, Co. Kerry, and at Ten Mile House, Co. Cork, as reported in ['An American Gentleman'], 'Tour', pp. 828–9.
[3] The Franciscan friary of Irrelagh at Muckross, founded in the mid-15th century (Gwynn and Hadcock, *Medieval Religious Houses*, p. 256).

people and country round that it is a very much frequented burial place and people come from all parts to it. It is the most perfect ruin I ever saw, and there are some very large trees[,] ash etc all about it. In one square room of the abbey is an immense high yew growing in the middle and its branches spread all around and hang over all these walls[.] The di*ff*e*ren*t parts are very perfect[.] You may go up to the first floor. There are cloisters all around one square. On the outside and in di*ff*e*ren*t parts of the abby are large heaps of bones and skulls, for the *church* y*ar*d is so filled that when anyone is buried there they take up a great many bones and skulls and heap them together[.][1] In some places all the recesses or arches are made the receptacle of these remains. There are new tomb stones erected [f. 19v] of very late dates and belonging to very respectable families. These spots are considered quite sacred by the people and no one w*oul*d dare to bring away a stone or a piece of wood. From thence walked on thr*ough* the beautiful demesne up to the house w*hich* is very plain and poor and go forward by some very fine masses of blue rocks with trees about them[.] They are limestone, in them is a very pretty cave w*hich* goes thr*ough* the mass of rocks and appears to have been made on purpose for there are the marks of its having been blasted on the side[.] It is not more than perhaps 20 Yards thr*ough* but very good walking and very dry[.] Go on up to the west quay where there is a beautiful marble mixed with the limestone and w*hich* w*oul*d well be worth working I sh*oul*d think, it is of a reddish tint, with veins in all directions. Beyond is a place where some copper mines were formerly worked but Col*onel* Herbert does not now continue them for it w*oul*d be under the necessity of having all the men constantly [f. 20r] going thr*ough* his demesne and by his H*o*use w*hich* w*oul*d be very inconvenient. Returned by [Mns?] Domain and come back to the Town over the fine bridge w*hich* crosses the river —[2] w*hich* runs into the Lake[.]

Dined with Counsellor Lapp, Col*onel* Hall and Cap*tain* White[,] the chief proprietors of the mines[.]

Monday Oct*ober* 20

Mending ~~gaitors~~ umbrella 20[d]: Gave man for shewing me Muckruss cave 10[d][.] Intended to go off on the water to the Upper Lake but it rained quite hard in the morni*n*g[,] contrary to expectation. Rode out on Mr Coffy's poney along the road to [the] Bridge at the ~~W end~~ end of the lake and from thence went to the river beyond Dunloe Castle[3] over w*hich* is a bridge w*hich* leads on tow*ar*ds the famous Gap of Dunloe. The view of the mountains fr*om* here beggars all description[.] It is impossible to describe them[.] Their grand and awful forms almost frighten one and they rise suddenly and so steep. One great beauty of Killarney is that the variety is endless[.] On one side [of] the lake is a flat range of country[,] on the other Mo*un*tains begin ⊥[r][.] The road to the top of Dunloe begins to be [f. 20v] striking as soon as you pass Dunloe Castle and you soon come to the little lake at the entrance[.] At the head of this there is a very pretty 1 arch bridge [Loe Bridge] w*hich* looks admirable amidst the surrounding scenery[.] // I ought not to omit that there is a very pretty waterfall at the end of this lake w*hich* runs down am*ong* rocks in front of the road[.] // Beyond this Bridge is another largest [*sic*] lake and it is built just over the

---

[1] Latocnaye reported that local traditions and beliefs forbade the touching or removal of remains scattered by the gravedigger's spade (*A Frenchman's Walk*, p. 101).
[2] River Flesk.
[3] Tower house built in 1213 (Coleman, 'Castles and Abbeys', p. 155).

little space w*hi*ch separates them and has the stream beneath it[.] The road then winds all along at the edge of the lake and at the foot of the ~~far~~ noble M*ou*ntains at the Left hand[,] on the top of w*hi*ch are streams of small stones and turf mixed. The road is wonderfully wild and in some places you seem to be quite under the cliffs and expect them to fall on you every step you go. In one place there are some of the largest pieces of rock thro*ugh* w*hi*ch the road has been made that I ever saw, and as you come more and more near to the narrow pass it looks more horrible [and] more dreadful[.] Although I have been under many cliffs [f. 21r] and on many passes of the sort yet I never before was afraid, here I was certainly and when thro*ugh* [I] wo*u*ld have given any thing to have got safe back[.] Oh how dreadful do these black masses hang and threaten me with destruction for ~~coming~~ (daring) to come[,] such a little insignificant puny fellow as I am[,] amongst them. So much uncomfortable was I that I tried to think of something else [other] than them as I came back and then[,] when out of them[,] wo*u*ld have almost consented to have been at the bottom of them even at the time of their falling and to be dashed to pieces!! merely for the sight of them rolling and dashing on the steep[.] Beyond the pass is another little lake with a Rock standing in it and from this you cannot see the stream w*hi*ch runs to the second [lake] for it goes down the narrow pass w*hi*ch is all at the bottom filled with logs[,] vast enormous masses of rock and some overgrown with turf or sod [so] that you only hear it run down. On all sides of these M*ou*ntains there were streams and little [f. 21v] waterfalls com*ing* down, in some places, a pretty stream came over the middle of a large inclined rock w*hi*ch looked black with the wet. Another was very pretty[,] water com*ing* suddenly over a ⊥ʳ rock and pitched ⊥ʳ on a slab and then dashed about[.]

Got home again safe[,] tho*ugh* very much pleased with my terror. Passed an orchard, where they aspired to make 20 Hogsheads of Cyder this year and for each 1½ Guinea. The best apples in the country grow there[.] I bought 100 for 2:2ᵈ. It is ab*ou*t 2 Miles fr*om* town. The road I went today is a new one they are going to make across the M*ou*ntains. The string of lakes is called Cummeen Tomeen Lakes[1] and a wilder scene I never saw[.]

Tuesday. (21 Oct*ober*)
It was a very rainy morning but as the sun shone and as the mount*ai*ns seemed clear at [the] top I resolved to go up the water and see the Upper Lake. Accordingly having laid in a [f. 22r] stock of beef and some porter we set off down to Ross Island where a Boat and four men were ready to take us[,] for it is usual to feed the men ~~and to~~ to dine at one of the islands[,] as they call it[,] 12 Miles up to the Cottage in the Upper Lake.[2] The boat was a very large thing and never meant for a party in n° less than 8 or 12 and such bad poor sticks of oars I never saw. ~~Crossed from Ross Isle and~~ (As we) were waiting at the West point of Ross Isle for the bark to come around we saw a dog pursuing a sheep on the rocks at a very out of the way place. He dogged it backwards and forwards am*ong* the rocks and at last tired it very much and bit it several times[,] when the sheep darted into the water and the dog after it and they were swimming[,] pursuing and pursued[,] about for sometime in some very rough water[,] the dog snapping and catching hold of the sheep every now and then[.] At last the sheep got a good way out from land and the dog

[1] This name has not been found in use. Lee may have corrupted the Irish name for the Gap of Dunloe, *Bearna an Choimín*.
[2] Knight of Kerry's Cottage, Upper Lake, Killarney (OS 1st edition, 6 inches to 1 mile, 1838–42).

returned back to shore and stood there looking at what he had done[.] Immediately [I] ran back into the Island to the *House* of the man[,] Mr Plunkett[,] whose sheep it was and told his son who went to the point. They would not lend me a gun [f. 22v] to shoot the dog[,] at least did not seem much anxious about it and luckily our boat coming round it saw and picked up the sheep and brought it to shore but the young man did not seem to care about it. The sheep was a very good one and worth perhaps 12 Shillings as they told me. Several boys and fellows saw it, but stood looking on and made no exertions or wish to do any thing but looked quietly at the dog and wondered if the sheep was drowned or how it swam so far[.]

Crossed over and passed by a cluster of islands. Pidgeon Islands, O Donnahues [O'Donoghoe's] Table, Coarse island,[1] besides several others which take (and vary) their names[,] probably from the fancy and disposition of the different boatmen, but they were today named Cior[2] Islands[,] Hen and Chickens[3] and from there cross the long bed of the lake and come up to the cottage which is situated at the foot of Glenaa [Glena] *Mountain* and called from thence Glenaa *Mountain*[.][4] All this *Mountain* was formerly[,] as every body said and sighed as it was told, very fine and beautiful untill the whole wood was cut down by Lord Kenmare[5] and many thousands [of] £ of timber [were] cut out of it[.]

[f. 23r] At present there is nothing but the young shoots of 2 Years old to adorn it and I was told the rest [of the wood] all up to the Upper Lake is coming down. This cottage is very pretty and commands an extensive view down the lower lake, the town etc and behind it are fine woods and the *Mountain* rising ⊥ʳ[.] Just here the gut to the Upper Lake begins which is a long winding stream like a river, the passage goes about a very pretty Island called Dinis [Dinish] and here is the narrow pass into Muckruss Lake[.] These 2 passages form the island[.] Around it are fine pleasant walks and it is a lovely spot. From hence the passage gets narrow and just above is a very strong stream for about 100 Yds which comes under the old weir bridge which is a picture. Here they are obliged to tow the boat up[,] it is so strong[,] and to land the passengers on the R shore[.] The course winds about backwards and forwards round rocks and at the foot of the *Mountain* pass a pretty little bit of an island called Miss — (Plummers) Island because on a party once a young lady of that name being taken sick[,] she was landed there untill the whole party [f. 23v] went up and came down again. Upon coming to the foot of the Eagles Nest,[6] the horns are generally landed and the boat goes round the point there, when yet [*sic*] hear the most delightful echoe from the music you even conceive a strong clear repetition of the sound take place quick, then there are more delicate music seeming to come out of the Eagles Nest and then all the whole *Mountain* seems as if it had [an] ecclesiastical choir sitting about its top and that they were all joining in music together[.] Most enchanting[,] most ravishing sounds[.] One fancies one is listening to the music of angels and one's soul is ready to melt with extacy [*sic*] at the sounds which warble and trill through the veins.

---

[1] Probably Rough Island.
[2] Possibly Lamb Island; Lee may have corrupted the Irish word for 'sheep', *caorach*.
[3] The Hen and Chickens is a collection of rocks (OS 1st edition, 6 inches to 1 mile, 1838–42).
[4] Lee means Glena Cottage, a cottage orné built by Mary Browne (née Aylmer), Lady Kenmare for the entertainment of visitors to the lakes (Archiseek; Ó Ciardha, 'Browne, Sir Valentine').
[5] See p. 204, n. 2.
[6] An elevated spot celebrated for its beauty and the unusual quality of its echo, described in a number of travel accounts, including Young, *Tour in Ireland*, I, pp. 448–9, and Latocnaye, *A Frenchman's Walk*, p. 103.

This is the effect of the horns. If a Bugle is then played and some of the strong and clear trills sound[,] they are wonderfully [and] finely repeated and you hear a great many repetitions but in 3 divisions. ~~They~~ (3 or 4) come very quick together, then 3 or 4 more for 3 times but the first echo is close to gone and these seem to ascend and come from around the other sides of the Mountains. [f. 24r] 3rdly. The sound of a paterara[1] or of a common musquet is again different and perhaps more astonishing than those because more unexpected. As soon as it is fired you hear a confused noise as if the whole neighbourhood was filled with noise and smoke and thick with sound[.] This soon goes off, then you hear a singular series of noises which go rattling around the Mountains and exactly from the beginning to the end like a rolling clap of thunder[,] all is silence and admiration and you are all ready to begin talking together and to burst out in exclamations of surprise and astonishment when you hear it again from the Mountains just higher up the lake, exactly rumbling as before but not so loud. Then a third takes place after a pause and if you attend and listen you may hear it broken into small sounds at last and ending in a hum[.]

The first and finest come from opposite the Eagles Nest. But in several places up the river there are similar echos [f. 24v] from near Dinis Island. The Glenaa Mountains give a very delicate return, and then higher up, at the Eagles Nest you have it and from in fact almost every rock[.] Just by the Eagles Nest they shew you about its way up the Mountain and just above the trees a bit of ivy and close above that, a part of the rock which they say looks like a bird with stretched wings[.] In this is a hollow where an eagles nest is. The Mountain is very astonishing fine and it rises most $\perp^r$ from the water side to a point, the lower part finely clothed with trees and although it is not so high as some few of the parts of the Mountain yet its grandeur and very surprising form and situation make it as great a wonder when seen from its base as any thing there. The river is wider just round this Mountain and higher up for some way are some very fine large pieces of rock which from their situation and size and appearances have got different names[.] There is one called the man of war from its form being like the hulk of a man of war and one may fancy some resemblance as also to the cannon rock which is not unlike an immense cannon with its mouth ½ in the water as [f. 25r] it lies slanting. There is also here a rock called the Knight of Kerrys Rock[.] The side of the Mountain on the R is called the Long Range and this is the straightest part of the channel. Higher up you come to a very great turn and pass through a very narrow passage between rocks which they call Colemans Eye and this is considered as the Entrance to the Upper Lake. On the West side of this narrow gut they shew you ~~the~~ (some) marks in the rock which look like footsteps deep sunk in and they tell you that Colman leaped over from the other side to this place[,] without his shoes on[,] at a standing leap. A little above are the marks as they appear of feet bare and you are shown the toes etc[.] Here they say he was accustomed to leap over at a running jump from the opposite rock and that he took off his shoes to do it. This Colman was a giant who lived at this Upper Lake and who was accustomed to pull up large trees as big as [they were] long and use them as hunting staffs. He had a wife as big as himself[.]

[f. 25v] Higher up in the side of the rocks is the Bellows Rock [so named] from its similarity to a Blacksmiths Bellows and higher on is the Arbutus Island[,] a most beautiful one with fine trees completely covering it and its fine rocky sides are smooth [from] being

---

[1] From the Spanish *pedrero*, ordnance used to fire salutes.

washed with the water. Opposite this is a rock standing straight up which they call the Black Boy and they show you many things of this sort but you must have a strong imagination to make many of them out. The Rump of Beef is a large round rock of the same sort. McCarthys Island and the Eagles Island and several others are very beautiful and form pictures in themselves[,] even without the circumscribing scenery. At Ronayns Island is a most elegant cottage on the edge of the lake[,] well backed with trees and rock[,] and forming a most beautiful object. These cottages Lord Kenmare has built for the accommodation of strangers who frequent the lakes and you may dine and sleep there as long as you please[,] bringing your own accommodations. At Ronayns Island a gentleman of that name lived for 6 months [a year] for many years there. The shooting and fishing is excellent [f. 26r] on many of the islands[.] 6[,] 8[,] 10 or more brace of cocks have often been killed and the sides of the Lake are as plentifully stocked. You may go on the lake and catch trout[,][1] perch[2] or salmon [Atlantic salmon, *salmo salar*] in 5 minutes of all sizes and the latter are killed weighing from 12 to 20lbs[.] In the season the latter are killed drawn in nets constantly and numbers taken. The scenery of the Upper Lake is wonderfully fine and as it had been wet weather just before, there were a few waterfalls coming down the sides of the different Mountains but [they were] too far off to be striking. The Galway river cascade is the finest. The day was clear and [there was] fine sunshine but [it was] excessively stormy ∴ we could see when it was going to rain and as the storms came on they hid the different parts of the Mountains from our view which[,] when over[,] returned again to our sight. The effect of the light and shade on the pictures was beautiful. Every now and then the we had a beautiful and most perfect rainbow coming from the water across the very mountains down to the water's edge again, entirely whole from [the] water's edge on both ends and a second [f. 26v] now as fine as a common one; the effect of the rain or the showers shewed us the lakes in every beauty for the sky was very clear and the cloud capt reeks[3] appearing and disappearing and the Derricunighe [Derrycunihy] Mountains looked fine[.] Sometimes the distant Mountains appeared a complete blue mass of shade[,] at others you could clearly distinguish every part of them[.] Returning down again, we had a fine view of the Entrance of the Upper Lake[.] The Mountains are[,] although not so high as the Wicklow[,] yet sufficient to be sublime and when in the lake you may imagine yourself as shut out by the Mountains on all sides from the rest of the world. It is wonderful how superstitious the people are and they tell 1000 of stories of O Donnahue. One man in the boat[,] an old fellow[,] said that he had actually seen Donnohue about 10 years ago[.] He was coming with a party out early in the morning from Ross and going on the lake and they saw him walking across from Darbys Island to Bensons Point[.] He had got a red suit of cloaths on and a [f. 27r] gold laced cocked hat, and many gentlemen in the boat saw him also. This Odonnohue revisits this country it seems every 7 years and he has now been absent 6 of them and ∴ somebody will see him next year[.] Like other Irish nonsensical superstitions every body almost tells you that <u>many</u> people have seen him but each individual cannot say he ever did. He is seen sometimes riding on a great white horse and they say that if he was to be pointed at with a gun that he would cause the gun to fire out at the butt end and the ball would blow out your own brains. We dined at Gleana [Glena]

---

[1] Probably the brown trout (*Salmo trutta*).
[2] Perch is a name commonly given to many fish, so Lee may not be referring specifically to the family *Percidae*.
[3] Irish English word for hills or mountains.

Cottage[.] Dinis Island is a pretty spot and they are now building a new cottage on it. The boats are very bad[,] there is no one smaller than is big enough for a party of 10 and ∴ one cannot go out with less than 4 oars[.] The accom*modati*ons are very bad, bad [coursers?][1] and impudent[,] and shameful bad tackle and besides[,] you pay a high price of 5S for the loan of a bad boat of Lord Kenmares when you wo*ul*d give a guinea for any other and smaller[,] and although the expense is but small for a large party [f. 27v] yet ~~you~~ (an individual) cannot go on in any way for less than 2 Guineas, for the men will have or expect a bottle of wiskey each w*hich* is 2:6 or now 3ˢ a Bottle[.]

Their Bill was

5 Men at 2:2	———————	10:10
Boat	———————	5:5
Horn	———————	5:5
1lb of powder	———————	4:4
		1: 6:

The 5 men were also fed all the day and I only gave them 2 Bottles of wiskey and a large store bottle of Porter. One Bott*le* of wiskey they emptied before they set out and on asking them why they did not reserve it, they said it was for them and they might do as they pleased with it and that it was their own loss if they had it at once and did not save it. In short the impositions are very great and the 5 for the boat is an imposition[.]

Returned home by moon light and had the horn playing the Echo and ~~th~~ what [f. 28r] effect and the fine deep dark shade of the M*ountai*ns on the water was delightful.

Wednesday. [22 October]

Started for Philadown [Foiladuane]. Went near to the Bri*dg*e over the Flesk river and turned up the road to the L and [went] thro*ugh* a most elegant wood of oaks w*hich* goes close to the riverside, This is a noble spot and puts one in mind of forest scenery or of some of the ~~mis~~ Shakespeare prints[2] or descriptions of Jaques.[3]

Ballycasheen woods[,] these extend all the way to the turnpike from whence there is a new road now making and which I followed very comfortably for a long way untill[,] to my surprise[,] I f*ou*nd it end in a bog very suddenly[.] It is not finished. Obliged to return and strike up a lane[,] happy to get to the old road w*hich* is very bad[.] There is nothing very remarkable for some miles but dist*ant* views of the M*ountai*ns[.] The river Flesk runs all up on the R. Come to a new bridge over it.[4] On the side of the river I had left is Brusterfield [Brewsterfield] House Mr Murphys [f. 28v] w*hich* is in a barbarously rough neighb*ourhoo*d but not in a bad situation[.] Opposite to it are the ruins of Killaha Church[,][5] not a bad object [when seen] f*rom* hence. There are some scattered houses all

---

[1] Possibly meaning the locals engaged to show visitors the local hunting grounds.

[2] The Boydell Shakespeare Gallery, which in 1786 commissioned scenes from Shakespeare's works for exhibition in Pall Mall, London, and a series of engravings for a new edition of Shakespeare's works in 1802 (Stevens, ed., *The Dramatic Works of Shakespeare Revised*). See Ritchie and Sabor, eds, *Shakespeare in the Eighteenth Century*, p. 417.

[3] Jacques d'Arthois (1613–86), who specialized in wooded landscape paintings (Myers, *Encyclopedia*, V, p. 234).

[4] Probably Flesk Bridge near Brewsterfield.

[5] The ruins of the 13th-century Augustinian priory at Killaha or Killagh (Gwynn and Hadcock, *Medieval Religious Houses*, p. 182).

along this infernal road and a little chapel farther on[,] Glanflesk chapel. There is a ridge of Mountains[1] on the L whose edge you now begin to see as you advance and [a] vale begins to appear, so you get the edge of these Mountains between the eye and the sky[.] They look very rough and ragged and they are in fact the hidden entrance to the Mountains.

The Country goes close up to the mountains[,] all about here [is] very flat and you come into them every where very suddenly as in this case and again at Turk [Torc] pass and at the entrance by Dunloe Castle, the river winds very prettily all up this Entrance and on the R you have the Mountains close above you and you go at the foot of them[.] As you gradually advance[,] the road winds about with the valley and you lose sight of the [f. 29r] flat country of Killarney and then get[,] in a quarter of an hour after coming to the entrance, completely shut in on both sides by 2 ridges of Mountains which are as rough and as naked [as] can make them[.] The river winds very beautifully up the vale and just at the foot of the noble ~~Glen~~ Philadown near Devils Clift Rocks it has a most beautiful winding course. These rocks you come suddenly close under on the R and the road not only winds at the foot but also winds in and out around their base[.] They rise very suddenly and abrupt and are quite disrupted, they hade very much but appear to be very much broken into very large regular square or R*igh*t ⊥^{r} masses and in many parts large crags actually hang over in the recesses of the rocks[.] The scattered trees are growing out most elegantly and most picturesque, Birch and ash ~~and oak~~ they are thinly scattered but quite sufficient to give a most ravishing character to the whole scenery[.]

[f. 29v] Close under some of the cliffs are two or 3 cottages and one snug farm house[,] very neat[,] *a langlais*[,][2] is a lovely picture close to this[.] It is under the immense cliffs set in a corner and they are all around it and trees growing out of the rocks above it and some are on the ground around it. Close to this farm and about 200 yds from the road up in the Cliff is a curious cave called Laubig-Owen [Labig Owen] or the bed of Owen. He was a famous pirate who lived there not more than 30 years ago and who used to rob and plunder the whole of the road near him and stop every body who went by. The place is very well hid in the rocks and the trees about conseal [*sic*] it completely, you go to it and getting close up to it ascend a ladder about 14 yards up and then come into a small space like a room in the rock and in the far end of this is a narrow part of the cave where he used to sleep. There are the appearances of his having had [f. 30r] his fires but the smoke never detected him. People knew he lived somewhere in the rocks but were afraid to go and look. He used to pull up and let down this ladder whenever he went in or out and nobody could catch him. He was watched frequently but never taken[.] He used to come out in the night[.] From the mouth of the cave (or door) you can see all the road, though you are not seen in it[.] At last he was shot by persons set to watch him and then the people were not afraid to look for his cave[.] The ladder was found and this discovered the cave near it, and in it they say was great treasure. They talk of many bones of the people he killed being in it, but they are perhaps those of sheep or things he stole.

Just beyond the cottage the road goes close under some rocks which do actually hang over it and below the bridge which is built is the river which winds close below. It cannot be called a bridge but a pass built up over the river to carry the road by it[.]

---

[1] Probably Killeen Mountain.
[2] 'In the English style'.

[f. 30v] Probably this rock will be more blasted away when the road gets more frequented. Beyond this the scenery is not so bold nor precipitous[.] The valley widens but it is very wild and farther on you pass through the most elegant scenery in the world, fine noble beautiful woods of Birch, holly, hazel and oak fill up the valley, and the Mountain sides[,] and the road goes through them most elegantly[.] There are a n° [of] streams and water which you pass the whole way and on the left is a large morass and bog but mixed in some state with the trees and copses all the way. At the end of the scene the vale separates into 2 parts and the road goes on to Kenmare through scenery not altogether so fine as at Philadown rocks but very beautiful and the Glen on the right is also a wild charming thing[.] There is a waterfall just at the entrance of this R hand Glen and this is the stream which comes from the head of the Flesk river which gives [its] name [f. 31r] to the whole Glen. No scenery can be more wild or romantic than this and the cock shooting is very fine here[.] Dozens are seen every day by those who choose to go for them. Very bad rainy stormy day. Wind violently high[.] Here are studies for any 100 painters for a year[.]

Mem. eagles build about Philadown[.]

Thursday. [23 October]

Being a fine clear and frosty morning[,] started for the Devils Punch Bowl.[1] Rode Mr Coffys horse to Muckruss and just beyond the stream which crosses the road [I] turned up the lane by a copse of wood and follow a tract which I was told to have been formerly the road to Kenmare, it winds very much and the ascent to the ground above the (new) road is very gradual and from hence you have a noble view of the Turk[,] Glenaw [Glena] and the whole extent of the lower lake and of Turk Lake[,] also the town of Killarney and the Mountains of Tralee and the Castlemain river[.]

[f. 31v] The ascent to the Punchbowl is long[,] tedious and troublesome over very ~~bad~~ good slant but nothing adventurous in it and many ladies have rode up to it. The views get more grand (extensive) as you ascend and I was surprised to see on the Left a fine pretty lake of Lough Kathane [Guitane] which has a small rock in it and an arbutus tree growing on it. A Major Bland a great fisherman had a small boat on it and caught trout [of] 30lbs weight and under, in it[.] The finest fish in the county are there. It empties itself in to the Flesk.[2] Besides this[,] on this side [of] the range of Mountains I went [by] yesterday is a peep at a smaller lake between me and Lough Kathane, its name is lough a'Garreghe [Garagarry, *Garaigre* (Ir.)] or the short lake. Then [it] struck me not knowing that I was close any one but the punchbowl. At last I got up to the L end of the punch bowl where the stream runs out down and walked all along the East side, through the great stones and bits of rock which lie above the bog and also over parts of [f. 32r] the bog and on coming to the passage which separates it from the other lake, the Punch bowl is on the top of the Mountain Mangerton and is of an oblong form, the [Bowl?] is in a hollow bason of the Mountain[.] The E side is not very steep but the W end is quite steep and very high above the level of the water and (the) rocks are very ⊥ʳ, but from the S end you suddenly look down upon a more extraordinary and wonderful lake than the Punchbowl itself[.] You stand on this narrow separation which rises as [it] at first appears high above the Punch Bowl but the depth of the

---

[1] A small pool near the summit of Mangerton, west side.
[2] Via the Finow River.

other lake is infinitely *great*er and so ⊥ʳ that you can but just look d*ow*n and see some parts of its edge just below you[.] The West side is also wonderfully steep and deep down, the lake looks buried almost in the earth as you look at it and the rocks are quite naked and ⊥ʳ[.] This is the most frightful place to stand and look down on, we went up to the pass and creeped up to the high cliff over this lake and walked round [f. 32v] the west side and from hence you see another lake beyond it and others in a string. The name of the 1ˢᵗ is something like Lough <u>Herer</u>, [Erhogh] the second is called Lough Mannough [Managh] or middle lake and the 3ʳᵈ Lough a Garrighe.¹ The view of this is far more wonderful than the *P*unch B*owl* itself[.] We returned along the Edge of this and then crept along the edge of the *Punch Bowl* wh*ich* seemed nothing to look down [on] after it[.] The walking was extremely bad and slippery and the whole bog was frozen 1½ Inch thick and [there was] a great quantity of ice in the little streams of the water although it was 12 and the sun [was] fine and shining[,] yet it was very cold. Here I observed a beautiful effect of nature[.] The Bog turf was very fine and breaking up some of the ice, it had penetrated thro*ugh* the bog like the thin fine fibre of trees[.] It looked like the cells of honey infinitely diminished in thickness and the fine needle like threads looked beautiful. The day was clear and we walked all over the top of the M*ou*ntai*n* [f. 33r] wh*ich* is complete bog except here and there where [there] are stones. I saw all over tow*ar*ds the Western ocean. Kenmare River is a picture of itself and lies or seems to lie close at y*ou*r feet[.] It is said to be 40 miles long d*ow*n to the Bull Cow and Calf[,] some rocks at the Head of it [Kenmare River]. Bantry Bay we partially saw[,] and all the mass of M*ou*ntai*n* tops and tow*ar*ds Castlemain Bay and the Tralee M*ou*ntai*n*s. We fancied we c*oul*d see some parts of the Shannon and of the County of Clare. The M*ou*ntai*n*s between me and the Cas*t*lemain Bay[,] all the Reeks and [*sic*] look like the tops of some sugarloaf and on the M*ou*ntai*n*s between me and Kenmare there are some lakes and many pools of water. At the End of the 1 [first] Lake [Erhogh] and just where it joins the second [Lough Managh] is quite up in the bend of the Cliff [there] is a large slanting flag[,] on wh*ich* the water from the parts of Cliff by it comes upon it and runs down it and into the mid*dle* lake, it is black [in] colour owing to the water and this flag is called <u>Corok</u>₁-<u>Knock</u>₂ or the black.₂²

---

*Powl*₁ *an affrin*.₂ hole.₁ Bottom₂ of hell.³ The Irish name for Punchbowl

[f. 33v] coffin,₁ and they say that this is opened 1 in 7 years and that under it is a fine large rooms [*sic*] and that when it is opened [a] thunder like noise is heard fr*om* the cave and is one of O Donoughhue's palaces and that he comes there but, he⁴ never saw him but many have. Lower down is a large place in the rocks where people come in summer and live who feed their cattle and look after them[.]⁵ They call it something in Irish[,] the

---

¹ Lee illustrated the relative positions of the lakes in a rough ink sketch map in the margin of f. 32r; not reproduced here.
² The word order has been reversed here, as indicated by Lee's subscript numbering. The narrative continues at f. 33v, two lines below.
³ *Poll Ifrinn* (Ir.), literally, 'hell's hole'. Here and in the 'black coffin', subscript numerals indicate Lee's attempt to understand Irish language place names.
⁴ Lee's local guide.
⁵ Lee seems to describe transhumance, known in Ireland as booleying – the transfer of livestock to upland pasture in summer months.

English of it is Kerrys Castle. They are obliged to water their cattle and sheep for otherwise they will get on the very cliffs and fall down and get dashed to pieces in the lake[.] I was told of a dog who pursued a foal and caught hold of it and both fell from the top of the cliffs into N°. 1 Lake [Erhogh] and [were] killed and a cow lately fell from the cliff in to [the] *Devils Punch Bowl* –

NB. All these stories are probably not general among the people, but they perhaps fabricate them on the spot to tell strangers who ask questions for they never are at a loss for an answer[.] However they may help to shew how [f. 34r] fertile the people are in invention and what superstitious ideas they have. I could see Killarney Castle just below me and a great deal of the road I traversed yesterday on the Philadown and saw Kilgarvan[,] [a] little village and Glanflesk [Glenflesk] from the part of the Mountain above N° 1 Lake [Erhogh]. The whole of the Mountains which embosom N° 1 Lake and the parts which form the cone in whose vertex it is placed is called Courn n cappel [Horse's Glen, *Corn na gCapall* (Ir.)] or the clift [cleft] of the horse[.] They say the *Devils Punch Bowl* was never fathomed[1] although it has been tried. The N end is very shallow for some way in. There are 2 points from whence they say Charles Fox swam across and many to be as great men as he[,] do the same now and then, It is now done by some every year, and ~~the only~~ It must be done merely <u>to say one had done so</u> for it is not very broad and no proof of good swimming. They say the water is very cold, it probably may be so without giving any miraculous power to it for it is on high land. The only credit is due to the first person who did it and that is in wondering what could induce him [f. 34v] to do it, but in an imitator that vanishes[.] Returned down the strait side of the Mountain over the bogs[,] hopping from one lump to another nearly the whole way which was more far going than coming up the singular line. Sometimes got a little better accommodation down a brook course which was harder. This short way was much the most tiresome and troublesome as most of the Irish <u>great short cuts</u> are. It is certainly a great short cut down the Mountain but not a short cut home[,] for it brings one on the Kenmare road beyond the Gap between the Mangerton and Turk and about 4 or 5 Miles from Killarney where I had my horse waiting and from whence I rode home[2] as much delighted as with anything I had seen since I had been here. The Reeks however are higher ground than where I was.

2 Boys[,] gave [them] 3^d –

Friday. [24 October]
Rode out to Lord Kenmares Park[3] and saw the grounds there which are nothing particular, the park is a very ordinary one and there is a very fine commanding view of the whole of [f. 35r] [the] lakes from the rising ground in it, and it looks very well for, at ones feet is a long range of timber wood which [shows?] the second distance very well. There is a very pretty little glen in the park[,] well worth going to see if one is in the the [*sic*] park but by no means such a wonder as the people tell you[,] nor is it to be compared to the Dargle[,][4] as I was told it was like it. The people think it a wonder and a shew but it is not worth going on purpose to see[.] It is a brook running down between 2 banks and the hollow is

---

[1] To ascertain the depth of (*OED*).
[2] To Coffy's inn, Killarney.
[3] See p. 204, n. 2.
[4] See 5 September 1806 (SJC, MS U.30 (2), pp. 109–10).

filled with nut trees. The course of the brook is in some places open long banks of rock. At the lower end is an out of the way ugly bridge thrown across, not [just] the brook but the land also. It is a very tame view. Returned to the town and was going to see Muckruss again but at Flesk Bridge met with a sailor who was going a fishing and I went and saw him catch trout[.] A fine comfortable pleasant fellow[,] he had been for 18 ye*a*rs on board HMS and was at the battle of Trafalgar, [was] a native of this place [f. 35v] but had been out of the service (and had got prize money) for 2 months w*hi*ch he had spent here shooting and fishing and had a boat on the water[.] After this went down to the Mines and staid there seeing the blasting and saw one fellow nearly killed by the pieces w*hi*ch flew fr*o*m the blast, being rather too curious to peep at it, they came out and flew all ab*ou*t him but did not hit him[.] Fine clear day[.]

Saturday. [25 October]

Rained all day and could not stir out at all. A most heavy violent hurricane, for 48 hours rain and wind[.] Saw a funeral go by, it was a plain coffin carried on 2 long poles with 3 cross sticks for it to rest upon and the people who carried it and who went with it were howling and crying out as it passed thro*ugh* the streets. ~~I have heard~~ It was going to the burial place of the poor persons family. I have heard of several bloody battles having frequently been fought when the coffin is carrying to the Ground. If the ~~come~~ relations are [f. 36r] not settled whether it shall be buried at the C*hur*ch where the Mens Relations or Womans are buried[,] if they come to a cross road w*hi*ch leads to either[,] they do sometimes actually lay d*ow*n the coffin and fight on the spot, for all the relations make a point of going with the corpse. It is still a custom here ~~for~~ when a person is dead, to have the body laid out on a table[,] wrapped in linen and the friends and relations all come and wake it[.] That is[,] they all meet and mourn and howl[1] over it and according to the abilities of the relations the whole party are regaled with punch and potatoes, wiskey etc etc and they have pipes [and] tobacco and the women take snuff and every now and then they howl[.] This is kept up for 2 nights and days and then they take it to the burial place of the family. When a corpse is passing[,] old women frequently begin howling and ask ~~for who~~ [who] it is going by[.] This many persons told me they had seen done[.]

// A*n* English gentleman steady, good servant was going with him in a post chaise fr*o*m ~~Mallow~~ Fermoy to Cork and was very much surprised with the accom*modatio*ns they met [f. 36v] with being so much inferior to those in Eng*la*nd and he began asking the driver why he did not buy himself better clothes and why he did not get a pair of boots. The fellow turned around and with a look w*hi*ch seemed to shew a great deal of surprise at the question and even contempt for the man who ~~asked~~ (advised) him about spending his money in so silly a way, And pray if I was to buy Boots what should I do for wiskey said he?!!!

Washing Bill 2:9[.]

Sunday [26 October]

Rained all day and was not able to stir out of this house. Wrote letters[.]

---

[1] Keening, the Irish tradition of lamentation for the dead; from *caoine* (Ir.).

Monday 27. [October]
Rained almost all day but went out with my gun. It was a fine day for fishing and ∴ all the fellows in the town were down at Flesk river a fishing with rod and many caught a vast n° of 2[,] 3 or 4 do*zen* of trout. Everybody here is a fisherman and you see fellows with their leather aprons on who can afford to spend a day fishing[,] so much do all the people prefer their pleasure and idleness to their trade. Coming home with my Gun [I] saw a funeral going by Lord Kenmares to Muckruss and then[1]

[f. 37r] Mr Fiott
– Laurence King takes your Portmanteau w*hich* he promises to deliver in good order[.] Mr Farrel is his security –
  for Joseph Garde[2]
  11 Oct*ober* 1806   Richard Carey
  Bearer is not yet Paid
  R Carey

O Sullivan Moore and O Donnohue Glen
If I had my money once more I wo*ul*d not trust ye again[3]

---

laid down my gun and followed it, ~~it was~~ the corpse was taken on a carriage with wheels and had a canopy over it supported by four (thin) pillars. 2 women were sitting on the coffin, leading it with a pony and thus it proceeded thro*ugh* the street. A great concourse of people went on[,] all howling and shouting and crying, although many did not know the person at all who was dead, but they very frequently follow a corpse when they meet one and it is thought indecent not to follow one, if you meet it any where. They howled all the way to Muckruss and then the whole procession walked once round the abbey and the corpse was then buried[,] but while this was performing, many were the [f. 37v] people who ran to the dif*feren*t graves of their families and friends and wept and howled over them untill[,] the corpse being deposited in the ground[,] the whole procession came away again[.] In the Evening I went to see a wake[.] A man had died in the course of the day and he was laid out and covered with white linen and laid on a bed in a room (opposite the chapel) on a temporary bed, his hands had gloves on and the upper part of his body had a trimming in rows on like a waistcoat with [a] wide red border but probably there was a cross worked on it, his head was laid on a pillow and his feet raised to a table at the end of the bed, on w*hic*h were burning 12 candles, [and] over his head on the bed hung a crucifix. The room was filled with women and men, who were all sitting silently together and upon asking why they were so silent, [I] was told that there wo*ul*d be not much crying for he was an old man and they wo*ul*d not so much lament him as if he was a young one and had died in the bloom of life. But in general they begin howling every hour or so, this wake is kept up for 24 or more hours all night [f. 38r] [with] persons going out and others coming in at pleasure[,] but every one makes a point

---

[1] Narrative continues after the third solid line, below.
[2] Joseph Garde (d. 1835) of South Mall, Cork, was sheriff of the city from 1813 and mayor from 1830 (Bickersteth, 'Query', facing p. 201). Lee refers to this person on a number of occasions throughout the remainder of his diaries, with variations in the spelling (Garde, Gaard, Guard).
[3] See Lee's explanation of this phrase below, p. 223.

of going to the wake. In the Evening there is wiskey handed about[,] Pipes and Snuff and tobacco[.]

NB. On [the] day I went to [the] *Devils* Punch Bowl, on the old road just beyond the *Punch* Bowl is a heap of stones, some man once travel*li*ng that road in winter was frozen to death and died there and every body who goes and has gone by has thrown a stone on it and thus it has arisen to a heap[.][1]

Tuesday – (28) [October]
Being tolerably fine[,] [I] went on the Lake with Counsellor Cullen and Mr —[2] 6 Oars went up under Dinis Bridge[3] w*hi*ch is a most beautiful effect[.] The single gothic arch and the fine noble Turk M*ount*ai*n* looked majestic. Go on and come to Dinis Island and land there and walk round it and come to the new cottage w*hi*ch is building there and w*hi*ch seems to be situated as tho*ugh* on the highest ground yet on the very worst spot[.] There is one very large room[,] arched on top[,] one very large window, church like w*hi*ch looks quite up the Turk[4] lake but there is nothing beyond it but tame [f. 38v] ground. The M*ount*ai*n*s are not seen[.] It is a poor thing altogether and only fit to have a dance and to see wh*at* is inside of it[.] It seems built to shew, that even in a most beautiful central situation on water and gallant M*ount*ai*n* that a cottage can be built f*ro*m w*hi*ch you shall see none of them. Disappointed with the window view you fly to the door and anxiously looking out find y*ou*rself shut up in trees there also. However it is not a bad plan to have a bad cottage am*on*g the good on*e*s to set them off the better. There had been such incessant rain that the water was 4 or 5 feet higher than [on] Tuesday last and it was with the greatest difficulty that the boat c*oul*d be dragged by main force up thro*ugh* the bridge[.] The men all took off their Breeches shoes and stock*ing*s[,] waistcoats etc (who had them on) and dragged f*ro*m rock to rock and got her thro*ugh* with the greatest diffi*cul*ty. The stream was very impetuous through [f. 39r] the bridge. Went on up to the Upper Lake, the Rump of Beef, Cannon Rocks and Bellows, the Colemans Eye were all under water. We had a great many showers all the way up and sunshine between[.] M[5] fired a ½lb paterara at the ~~Eagles Nest (and Turk Mn~~) (Drooping M*ount*ai*n*) and had 1 sudden tremendous echo f*ro*m it the Eagles Nest and a long peal of thunder f*ro*m the Turk and one f*ro*m Droo*pi*ng M*ount*ai*n* and a murmur f*ro*m the Dist*ant* M*ount*ai*n* also[.] Dined at the enchanting Ronayns Island and returned d*ow*n to the *E*agles Nest where Mr Coffy and his party fired their paterare and we fired ours several times. Guns also. ~~Trumpets~~ (Horns) sounded f*ro*m one Boat to [the] other. Fine echos came thro*ugh* the bridge like lightning after the other boat, very fine[.] Went round by the Bridge again and thro*ugh* Turk Lake and over to the shore[.] ~~In the Eveng~~. One man on the boat had also seen Donohue on the lake riding a fine black gelding[.] He [f. 39v] went f*ro*m Bensons Point walking and then trotted fast and then galloped over to —[6] Island. He had on a fine black suit of 6 leathers with silver buckles. The story is that Odonnohue was formerly

---

[1] This paragraph has been moved from its original position at the top of the folio, for continuity.
[2] Name not known.
[3] Probably Bricin Bridge, at the meeting of the three lakes of Killarney.
[4] Lee probably means Muckross Lake, which lies near the slope of Torc Mountain.
[5] Possibly the 'Mr —' mentioned at the beginning of this day's entry.
[6] Name not known, represented by dash.

a Resident of the Castle of Ross. He had a most beautiful wife and he was a fine man[.] She was jealous of him and shut him up in the chamber upstairs from which in a fit of despair he leaped out of the window into the lake and was never seen afterwards, he is now considered as to be the Genius of the lake and the Boatmen say that he is their very good friend, and they say that none of them ever was hurt by him, (or drowned) but a Gentlemans boat was sunk and he drounded[1] some time ago and this they think was partly owing to ODonnohue[.][2]

In the Evening walking about the town [I] heard a howling upstairs in a room and after listening [for] some [f. 40r] time, ventured up, ~~it was~~ a child had just died and the poor relations were stamping about the room, beating their heads with their hands and ~~tearing as~~ taking hold of their hair near with closed fists and leaning against the door posts all howling. The child was laying on the floor and was not yet laid out, and they were then in the first emotions of grief[.]

// In general they howl at wakes the most for young people and the stated times are more frequent, because they think it is so dreadful for persons to be cut away as it were before their time[.] // But there is a very great degree of regularity and method in their weeping and [at] funerals and at the Church Yards they run away from the corpse they follow to the graves of their own departed friends and weep over and howl [over them] and then return and perhaps they are laughing in 5 minutes[.] //

Bill for the Boat, for luncheon, for dinner and for the Breakfast and whole day was ⅓ of the whole expense[3] = £1:8:0

[ff. 40v–41r][4] **Wednesday [29 October]** was employed in packing up my specimens, and in getting my Box made for them which cost 5:5[.] Also bought lb of ([handkerchiefs?] 4 and a Quire of Paper) = 10^d.

1 Pair of straps for my knapsack cost 1:9. Rope for Box cost 10^d[.] This day was literally spent in packing up and making preparations for my departure[.]

Thursday (30) [October]

Clear in the Morning. Breakfasted and started at 11 with Mr Garrick and Coffy for Dingle[5] [*Daingean Uí Chúis* (Ir.)] and got there at 5 – Walk along a plain road as straight as an arrow and leave the Lake and Mountains behind us but from the Mountain which you pass over it looks very well. These Mountains are called Shlamish [Slieve Mish] Mountains (Slaighmish Mountains or bog) and are a red soil and the water on the bogs looks quite red, have a most fascinating view of the highly cultivated vale of Tralee, the pretty town the bay and the Distant tops of the Mountains which are alone not cultivated, fine green meadows and new looking farm houses scattered about. Getting dark and a sombre view on all sides. A noble fine bog on the top of the Mountains on both sides[.]

Tralee is a neat town, although the street entrance from Killarney is most despicable, there are some very good houses in it quite modern. There is a fine new playhouse just

---

[1] Lee uses the colloquial form of 'drowned'.
[2] Latocnaye also reported local tradition respecting the ghost of O'Donoghue on horseback crossing the lake on certain days of the year (*A Frenchman's Walk*, p. 100).
[3] Meaning one-third of his total bill at Killarney; see the total on 30 Oct. (p. 223).
[4] From this point, Lee writes across both folios.
[5] Lee means Tralee.

fitting up which is made out of an old Church[.] This is rather a singular use to turn an old Church to. In [the] County of Kerry there are said to be 999 dozen princes for every pothouse, farm or cabin is inhabited by people who trace themselves from old families. The Mr Odonnohue who lives near Killarney is the only one of that family now left, but his father lived in a great style[,] kept open house and squandered away all the estate[.] Nearly [ff. 41v–42r] all the Glens at Philadown belonged to him and he was prince of all the Glens and all the people considered him as such. There are families of the OSullivan Moores[,] etc etc[,] OSullivan this and that[.] About 50 years ago even these fellows travelled about in great old coaches and cocked hat[,] tweed and lace cloathes and never thought of paying for any thing at an accommodation house, this gave rise to the 2 lines above mentioned[:][1] 'OSullivan Moore and ODonnohue Glen If I had my money once more I would not trust you again.'[2] And any fellow would suffer for it who would apply for his right to them[.] At Kenmare a widow, who has a son and daughters there[,] is as high as any princess and the fool of an ignorant lout her son would no more take your horse to the stable as he would fly. Mr ODonnohue married a rich merchant's daughter of Cork who has in a great measure nursed his estate and will bring it about for him but all the poor beggarly noble princes are damnably irritated at a prince of such noble blood degrading himself so far as to marry a merchants Daughter. The late ODonnohue kept open house and after dinner had the door sometimes locked and would let no guest go out but always left them drunk with himself under the table. Bill at Coffys £10:6:9. NB Found out a young lad who had a natural taste for drawing and was at school[,] of the name of Reily, and got some of his drawings[.] Gave him 5S to buy colors. Very fine taste. Tolerably fine day[,] only 2 showers all the way we were going[,] but it rained all the night[.]

Friday (31). [October]
It was our intention to starting [*sic*] at 7 and we ordered the waiter to call us at 6 OClock as we had to go 22 Miles to Dingle but she came to my room and said the day was breaking! Up I rose and called up the others[,] dressed and got ready and just as we were putting on the knapsacks, it struck 5!! She had called us up at four. I [was] pleased with this and delighted at being an hour sooner than expected, we went to the door and opening it [hie?]! to our surprise it rained! We never thought of knowing what sort [f. 42v–43r] of a day it was before we got up. What could be done. Impossible to start, held a consultation and determined to wait till after breakfast and see how it was. Coffy went to Bed again[.] We sat by the Kitchen fire and went to sleep and about six we took off our shoes and went up stairs and throw ourselves on bed, and about 8 up comes the waiter and says it is a fine morning. It had rained all night and was so [a fine morning]. Breakfasted, all in high spirits. Agreed to walk to some cottages [that lie] ½ way [to Dingle]. Set out at 10[.] Bill 20:2[,] paid at Night. Breakfast. Bill next morning 6:11. It was a glorious morning[,] sun clear, sky blue, walked on to the pretty bridge which is a picture of itself, on the head of the bay and over it [lie] a few houses and [a] fine body of Mountain [lies] behind. We were so much enchanted by the Morning that we now agreed to walk on all the evening and night by moonlight to Dingle and to stay ½ way and get a snack there, walked brisk and then slow at pleasure[.] Passed through the village of Derrymore (5

---

[1] These lines were noted earlier, on 27 Oct. (p. 220).
[2] Quotation marks added.

Miles), A man met us who was travelling the same road. We learnt from him that the road divided farther on our way[.] Went into the Mountains and you see nothing but bare Mountain untill within a Mile of Dingle, the other way was along the shore. Not much longer than the other. Agreed to go this [way] of course to keep the sea view and walk along Tralee Bay shore. There are houses or villages the whole way, Killelton village is a mile farther on. At Derrymore is an elegant watercourse and a picturesque mill close to the Bridge. Beyond Tralee Bay is a round broad but ~~very~~ (not) deep in length bay called Ballyheigue Bay[.] Beyond this the land runs out to a point called Derry Head. 7 Miles on is Runnour Village and just beyond [is] Kilgobbin Church and Parsonage 7½ Miles[,] Reverend Mr Stewards. Beyond is Capel Clough [Cappaclough] South. The Mountains we had come round the foot of now looked delightfully [sic][.] The fine courses made by the water in it were very elegant and characterizing[.] The Mountain was very fine and [the] houses [ff. 43v–44r] and villages round the Base of it. Going on about 12 Miles, come suddenly to a very pretty white house of only one floor and thatched and 2 Wings forming 3 sides of a square, its neatness and respectability and comfortable looks[.] Stopped and asked anybody to look at it and out came Captain Rowan[1] its possessor and civilly inviting us in, telling us that we should not meet with any accommodation on the road and that we could never get to Tralee[2] that night[.] (NB (we) had now given up all idea of going there today but wanted to get to the foot of Brandon Mountain and to see the Mountain and the view from it next morning.) We went in and had some wine and cold Beef[.] He then made us put up the rest the of Beef and brought out 2 Bottles of wine and asked us to take it with us, the Beef we did, but not the wine. From his House is a noble view of Tralee Bay, and Muckloch [Mucklock] Rocks and and [sic] Kerry Head and the Mouth of the Shannon and of the Loop Head Point and he [Rowan] could see the Light House with his eyes[.] I could not without my glass. See the Point of land and the Macheree [Magharee] Islands. Pretty Place[.] Left his House and went on. A mile farther or 13M[3] is Castle Gregory[,] a village[,] and beyond it some way on is the village of Killaney [Killiney], in which is a most elegant ruin of a Church and behind it is a chapel with its top covered with moss and green verdure which form a very fine contrast[,] and the Mountains close behind on the L and the sea on the R[.]

We go along the strand and hear an universal murmur from the waves and surge dashing on the shore[,] which noise is augmented by the Echos of the Mountains. Stradbally 16 Miles. In several places we were obliged to walk across the streams which go into the sea and along the whole road we had passed over 8 or 10 brooks[,] so well is the country watered. The tide was not high and [so] we could walk the sand and only here and there had to walk over the water courses. Our fellow [ff. 44v–45r] traveller left us at Liscarney, from whence, a man took us along the road which was now almost invisible from the dark and we were now and then obstructed by and got into bad parts of the road which were boggy and[,] when within ½ a mile of Clahan [Cloghane, An Clochán (Ir.)] where we were told we could sleep at a wiskey house[,] the fellow told us there was a part of the road which we could not pass if it was high water without a boat and that he would go in and see if it was high water. Never hearing of this before[,] we were astonished at being

[1] Probably John Rowan of Castlegregory.
[2] Lee must mean Dingle.
[3] Lee means 13 miles from the commencement of that day's walk.

DIARY 4: BANTRY TO CASTLEMAIN

thus stopped within ½ mile of our journey's end and found that it was high W*ater* and that we must stop till 12[.] We then tried to get a boat and a man went for one, but soon after a man passing by said it was not high water and that we *cou*ld go over easily[.] Accordingly went to it and *fou*nd it a little insignificant brook w*hic*h we easily got over stepping on the stones and the tide was not ~~quite up~~ (up so as) to hinder us. Got to Clahan and to Pat Fitzgeralds House[,] where we expected to rest our wearied limbs. He was not at home but gone a fishing[,] and the man who answered for him gave us a cold reception[,] probably *fr*om being afraid of 3 strangers or [from] surprize[,] and when we asked him whether he intended to turn 3 strangers out. [He said] 'Oh no.' Such a thing was never done in that p*ar*t of the country[1] but as he did not seem to be quite at home himself we set out a mile for Maurice Fitzgeralds[,][2] a farm house[,] over abominable bad road[,] stepping *fr*om stone to stone and soft [in] between and getting in [to water] now and then[,] and just as we came near the H*o*use [we] saw the moon rising out of the sea[,] a most glorious sight, it was red, the size much magnified. It was cold and frosty[.] We expected a fine charming morning to ascend the Brandon Hill [*Cnoc Bréanainn* (Ir.)] and had already in imagination seen the extensive view *fr*om the top when we got to the cottage. Mr F*i*tzgerald was not at home but his wife welcomed us and gave us some salmon and potatoes and new milk for supper. 1[,] 2[,] 3 and 4 pitchers of milk were emptied and we drank as if we sh*ou*ld drink up the Cow herself[.] When we were told the Bed was ready, each wanted [ff. 45v–46r] to stay by the fire, but no. At last all went in together!!! 3 of us. It was a very good bed indeed for it was not damp but too short and too narrow for 3. We *cou*ld not put d*ow*n our legs far enough and we were obliged to Right Face and Left Face to leave room but never lay broad[.] It was impossible. Bed not soft for it was straw and stuffed. However <u>we passed</u> the night warm and better off than we might have have [*sic*] been and got up <u>early</u> in the morning, and willing to start. Lo all our expectations of the preceeding [*sic*] Even*in*g were blasted. No Brandon hill views for us[.] It rained *fr*om 1 OClock and still poured all the time. We breakfasted and were told that by Brandon M*o*unta*i*n the road was 7 miles but it was no use to go up for the view[.] We gave all ideas of it up and resolved when clear to go the short way by Connor Hill [*Barr Conarach* (Ir.)]. Mr Maurice Fitzgeralds cabin or farm is situated close under a very high M*o*unta*i*n which has a most rocky cliffy side and *fr*om the cabin door[,] if the smoke does not prevent you[,] you may see all the pretty little bay of Clahan w*hic*h comes broad up to the End and looks like 3 sides of an oblong. It is a little bay in the large bay round whose shores we walked the Even*in*g before. They resolved to stop till 12 and then[,] [whether] raining harder or not[,] to dash forward and get to Dingle[.] But I resolved [to] go forward at once and not to take the chance of the change of the day[,] and accordingly set out at 10 in the middle of the rain. Got down to the Bayside where this tremendous little rivulet w*hic*h stopped the preceed*i*ng [*sic*] even*in*g was[,] and *fou*nd it not over my shoes and a man said you edge over it at any time high or low water. It rained prodigiously hard and the wind was intolerable and with the greatest diffic*u*lty I c*ou*ld get along. Clahan is ab*o*ut 22 Miles or more the way we went *fr*om Tralee and then we had to walk a mile to our lodging house, where we got at 8 oclock in the even*in*g. ~~This~~ We were told it was 5 Miles thence to Dingle but it is at least 6 or 7. The rain was [the] most severe as I ever recollect and the

---

[1] Quotation marks added; Lee paraphrases his conversation with the man.
[2] Lee sketched the cottage at SJC, MS U.30 (7), f. 12r (p. 320), not reproduced.

mist [ff. 46v–47r] hid everything from view. Crossed a little bridge by some cabins[,] retracing the former road[,] and then took a road not much frequented towards the Mountains. This was above a mile long[.] When getting into the great road which takes one up towards the Mountains[,] the fog began to disperse and when at the foot of Cunnur [Connor] Hill it was quite clear and free from rain, and I could see all around me, and thankful was I to the weather as it gave me a sight of the precipitous Mountains around me[,] for before me was a hollow range of Mountain from which there seemed to be no escaping[,] nor could I see an outlet anywhere, the road winding round the East side of this Bason of Mountain or this semi crater of Mountain at length brought me to the middle of it and then it winded back and forward directly up the ⊥ʳ Middle of the Mountain and the view as you arise gets bolder and bolder, and your astonishment increases at every turn[.] You see the ground ⊥ʳ below your feet and this curious winding staircase road has 13 winds in it as I counted[,] but there are certainly not less and probably more[.] The view at each turn attracted my attention and amused me to stop and gaze [at] the four lakes below[1] (at your feet) and the bowl in the distant Mountain like the Devils Punch Bowl (all are fine features)[.] Several cascades to the Left are observable, and an immense bog seems to fill up all the space below[.] Before [you] also is a large quantity of pieces of rock covered with white moss which are scattered about like plumbs [plums] in a pudding and evidently have fallen from the ⊥ʳ cliffs of the range of Mountain under whose side the road winds. The passage is very narrow and down it winds a little stream[,] for it seems to have been originally a watercourse which has been widened and made a road. Horses go up it but men always walk up by their sides. No car could go up. There was a stream running down all the way. A gleam of (sun) light just gave me a fine prospect of all the bay and part of the sea, to the Right from whence I came [ff. 47v–48r] and just as I got to the top and had one moments glance over the country towards Dingle and could just see the bay and the wide Atlantic, a thick cold mist came on and hid every thing from me and I could not see five yards before me. Had I been 5 minutes sooner I could have surveyed and studied the whole but as it was I only got a glimpse. There was no use in stopping and the road down the other side was tolerably good. Had 2 very rapid watercourses to walk through on my way down the hill and passed a very large heap of stones several yards long and about 8 feet high where some person[,] as I was told[,] was formerly murdered. This Cannur [Connor] Hill has another name in Irish signifying the (Bulls Mountain) for they say a large wild bull lived there formerly[,] with iron hoofs[,] which noone could catch and that he made that road down the hill[.] Dingle is about 2 Good Miles from here and as this thick mist ended in a very severe storm of rain[,] after it the sun came out and the day was delightful and I had a fine view of Dingle and the Bay and the Harbour as I went down the Mountain side. The town is much better than I expected[.] It is situated in the bottom of 3 Mountains and a long street extends up 2 hillsides with a brook at the bottom. Went to see the pier which runs into the Harbour[,] which is plain and neat[.] The mouth of the harbour is deep enough for vessels of 800 tons but none of more than 100 can come farther in the harbour [as] the mouth from the Bay is very narrow. Around it opposite the town is a fine Mountain[,] a good object [for a picture]. There is a street which runs ⊥ʳ up the brook which is the Entrance [by which]

---

[1] Lee made a rough ink sketch map in the page margin, of the relative positions of the four lakes; not reproduced here.

I came. Beef [costs] 2½ a lb in the market on a Saturday but prime [ff. 48v–49r] meat is 3½ a lb[.]

Sunday (2). [November]
It rained very hard all the preceding night and all this day very hard and all night also for 48 hours. Could not stir out of the house all day. Went to mass, at 9 – Wrote letters[.]

Monday 3. [November]
Rained untill 12 and then it cleared. Set out on the road to Ventry [*Ceann Trá* (Ir.)] and have a fine view of the harbour of ~~Ventry~~ Dingle harbour and the narrow mouth. See Lord Ventry's house on the opposite side without a tree near it. His house is called Ballingolin or Burnham House[1] the English name. There is a 2 arched Bridge over which you go to his house, at high water the waters come up above the bridge[.] The road to Ventry commands very fine views of the Mountains to the R and of the Harbour of Dingle and the distant Mountains of Iwragh [Iveragh][2] and upon coming over the rising ground you come suddenly on the fine Bay of Ventry[3] and at the foot of it are the paltry cabins which are called Ventry village[,] about 100 of them. There is a plain covered (*Roman Catholic*) chapel there. The bay is a fine round shape and the most beautiful strand that can be seen anywhere, along which we walked. On these strands the Gentlemen frequently make up horse races in the summer. We waded through 2 water courses[,] our only interruption on them. The sand is fine and smooth and yet hard and we walked close to [the] sea shore for a long way[,] then turned suddenly to the R about the middle of [the] Bay and follow a very excellent road which you see straight up the Mountains before you. Singular enough that this part of [the] road should be so much better than that between Dingle and Ventry. The fine Mount Eagle [*Binn an Choma* (Ir.)] a range of Mountains[,] is on the Left and there are several villages all at the base of it. NB. A village is from 5 to 14 [cabins] or more hereabouts[,] with or without a chapel[.] They add very much to the general Mountain scenery and form specks on its base and serve [ff. 49v–50r] as marks to shew the height up the Mountain[.] On the R about ½ way up the Mountain is a R fine view of Smerwick Harbour and the valley between the Sugar Loaf Mountain and the one [with] a round top. Several scattered sets of cabins are in the hollow. The noble Mountain in the rear of Brandon and that neighbourhood and of Connor look magnanimous. It is a most fine Mountain scene, ascend the road and at the top get a view of the Atlantic and of the great object of our search the Blasquet [Blasket Islands, *Na Blascaodaí* (Ir.)].[4] We stopped to breathe and to look around, and to satisfy or to glut our eyes with the view and then begin to descend, this is[,] it seems[,] not far off but [you] have [a] continual, long descent and coming to a stream got on a wall as it was fine and clear and made a repast there on our cold meat and wiskey and water from the stream[.] Thus enjoying ourselves we enjoyed

---

[1] Burnham House, Dingle, built in 1790 by Thomas Mullins, 1st Baron Ventry (1736–1824) (LED). The area was formerly called Ballingolin (Barrington, *Discovering Kerry*, p. 242).
[2] Lee sketched this view at SJC, MS U.30 (7), ff. 13v–14r (p. 320), not reproduced.
[3] Lee sketched this view at SJC, MS U.30 (7), f. 15r (p. 320), not reproduced.
[4] Lee's sketch of the scene is at SJC, MS U.30 (7), ff. 16v–17r (p. 321), not reproduced. Lee's visit to the Blasket Islands was probably motivated by his local travelling companion, Coffy. It is not likely to have been inspired by any published work, as no other pre-20th-century non-Irish visitor to the islands has been found (Woods, *Travellers' Accounts*; see also Introduction, p. 13, and Byrne, 'Dashing Waves').

the fine scenery of the highly cultivated M*o*untains and the scattered cabins[,] the sea[,] the islands and the white waves dashing over the reef of rock[.] After wa*r*ds proceeded on and were directed by young Morearty to Mr Neagles farm on the Left of the road. Here we were very hospitably entertained for the evening and the next day young Mr Neagle took us out and lent us guns and we went along the cliffs shoot*in*g fowl. Our walk was to Dunmore point [Dunmore Head, *An Dún Mór* (Ir.)] the the [*sic*] most westerly point of land that we c*ou*ld go to, walking over the M*o*untain we came down to the farthest edge and laying d*ow*n our guns we scrambled over the rocks for a very great way, and proceed*in*g with caution we at length got to the very extremity of the rocks and stood on the edges of them, the Rocks w*hi*ch are beyond are called <u>Leur Rocks</u> [*Liúir* (Ir.)] and these we c*ou*ld not get to[,] but in spring tides and fine weather and at low water you may get on them by help of a long stick, however we went as far as mortal c*ou*ld go. The rocks are very easy and safe to walk over being all eaten into such very fine holes and points and edges by the waves. There is one p*ar*t of the rocks w*hi*ch are remarkably separated fr*o*m the rest by a very singular chasm not more than 1 yard wide in some parts but laying down and on peeping down it you see the sea [streaming?] all up it[.] It completely separates the whole rock fr*o*m the rest. At the extremes of this rock There are little ones w*hi*ch seem as if it was easy to get at fr*o*m a small dist*an*ce but they are not to be got on, only in the cave above [the] M*o*untain. One of the Leur Rocks is [ff. 50v–51r] very fine and completely bare and pointed and all [the] edges over it [are] worn by the waves. All the whole shore is very dangerous and bad and in stormy weather it is impossible to land there, even where there is any surf. We c*ou*ld not get over to the Blasquets this morning[,] it was too rough. The cliffs are very high and bold and ⊥ʳ and there is no strand all round. We staid here for above 2 hours am*o*ng the rocks while it rained and [there] was fine shooting and looking at views. The Blasquets and the Skelig [Skellig] Rocks are all in the view and the Bray Head land and Valentia Island.[1] Sometimes it rained and then [was] fine and thus with sunshine and clouds we saw the views in all the forms and appearances of the weather. The sea was very high and the surf beat over some parts of the rocks. The Cliffs at Dunquin [*Dún Chaoin* (Ir.)] where the boats are kept w*hi*ch go over to the islands[,] are actually ⊥ʳ and the one at the landing place is 25 fathoms high, for formerly there was a rope and by pullies they pulled up the sea weed here for [fertilizing] the land before the winding passage was made d*ow*n to the shore. Down the Cliff now is a sort of winding road made and horses can go down part of the way. They bring up the weed on their backs the first part of the way and then carry it up to the land in baskets to the land [*sic*] and spread it thickly over and then dig it in. There are Cliffs to the Northwa*r*d much highere [*sic*] and so there are to the S of Dunmore point but not quite so ⊥ʳ. Shooting and looking around we went to the S of Dunmore Head and round to the other bay beyond the village[2] where is a little sand strand, shooting at the red shanks. The whole of Dunmore point is a fine strong turf and most excellent bite for sheep and cattle as I ever saw. Cormorants and seagulls etc in plenty and jackdaws and wild pidgeons. Several very hard showers came on in the course of the day but fine in the intermediate time. Went back to Mr Neagles and were again hospitably entertained[.] Sent over to Dingle for wiskey w*hi*ch came not before 12 at night on Monday, and sat up drinking and singing till past 3 and all ill fr*o*m

---

[1] Lee sketched this scene at SJC, MS U.30 (7), ff. 24v–25r (pp. 321–2), not reproduced.
[2] Probably Coumeenole.

it. Mr Trant an old Blind Gentleman[.] Mr Neagle somehow beat me at Backgammon. He was a man of some prospects when young and getting through it was obliged to go abroad and enter into the King of France's service where he staid for 6 years and then was in the Prussian Service for 4 years and he [ff. 51v–52r] spent his time in the Army and has been back these 40 years or more, But he was a man who had seen a great deal of the world and told us a great many stories. Mr Neagle had also been in France thus we met in an [absurd?] farm in Dunquin 2 men who had been abroad and one an old <u>gentleman</u>.

Wednesday 5. [November]
Rain all night, But calm and clear in the Morning. After Breakfast set out for the Dunquin Cliff and had a great deal of trouble to get the boat launched, which was drawn up on the slanting side of the path down the cliff to be out of the reach of the sea. The cliff looks most dreadful from below and seems to threaten instant destruction on any one who dares to look up at it[.] When the sailors had got our boat, still there was the utmost difficulty to get on board[.] The boat was brought to the edge of a rock and every now and then an opportunity with the tide offered for one to jump in and thus one by one we got on board it, it was a small row boat open, and in all we were 13 men[,] as several labourers wanted to go to the island. 2 men to each oar pulled us over about a league to the nearest Blasquet [Beiginis] although from the high cliffs it looks not a mile[.] We landed at the nearest of the Blasquets which is also as difficult to get at and here we were obliged to jump 1 by 1 onshore on the rock[.] It is a low flat Island and very fertile and a fine turf. Keeps a great many cattle[.] Cliffs all round and rocks[,] plenty of rabbits[,] but [as the] day [was] bad[,] saw only a few. Shot some cormorants at sniping etc[,] then walked all round it[.] Went off to the big Island [Great Blasket Island, *An Blascaod Mór* (Ir.)]. There is one House on the flat one but not inhabited. The big one is of very large extent and is very difficult to get at and [boats] only can land at certain times on account of the surf. It was even hard to get on shore for the wind got higher than when we set out. On the E side under the side of the Mountain are a few scattered cabins done remarkably neat, well thatched and bands of straw or hay going directly over these from 1 side to the other and each end of the bands had a large stone tied to it, and across in [slanting?] directions was a long band crossed and recrossed to make all fast. The Mountain rises very steep indeed from the cliffs and on the south side [it rises] the most[.] It is very high and on the middle of the island is a new watchhouse just built[,] to which we went up and had a fine and noble view of the sea and the few islands beyond, but there is another large high Mountain of the island beyond and a Deep valley between it and that on which stands the tower.[1] At the farthest end of the island are some immense rocks[,] cliffs[,] etc[,] 3 times as high as the Dunquin ones[,] but it was too precarious weather to stay all night on the island and as the wind was swelling we were obliged to hasten back to the shore and to the cabin where after making our dinner on potatoes, milk[,] wiskey and a certain kind of fowl, we were glad to get into the boat again which we did with great difficulty 1 by 1 and at intervals, as the surf was rough. The birds they dressed for us were called in Irish *fahirs*[2] which are the young ones before they leave the nests[.] The Old ones are called *Canoques*[3] and have black backs[,]

---

[1] Lee sketched the view from this tower at SJC, MS U.30 (7), ff. 25v–26r (p. 322), not reproduced.
[2] *Foracha* (Ir.), guillemot.
[3] *Cánóg* (Ir.), the Manx shearwater (*Puffinus puffinus*).

black bills and black legs and white on the breast, the young ones are greyish [in] color and they catch them by tying a long string round ferrets and then pull them out by them. They are quite lumps of fat and very high[1] and you cannot hardly eat them when [they are] fresh. They salt them and are obliged to send some down every year to their landlord. They were put into a pan with*ou*t a drop of water and broiled over the fire and even then although killed, yet abounded in fat and made a great quantity of sauce[,] very rich. The birds are not puffins, but were red and very fat and eat deliciously high. The people on this island live better than any in Kerry[.] They have plenty of fish, turbot [*Scophthalmus maximus*] hake [Atlantic hake, *phycidae*] etc in the season. Rabbits [are] in plenty on the island, and they pay their rent with their skins w*hic*h is 200 Guineas a year for the island[.] Fowl of all sorts and a few sheep now and then. There are 5 or 6 of the cabins who pay the rent between them[.]

[ff. 52v–53r] We met with a hearty welcome and on our return we had a very stormy rough surf to pass over[.] Wind enabled us to sail or we cou*l*d not have got over[.] Mr Neagle has been several times wind bound there [on the Blasket Islands]. He was once for 12 days and at Christmas time. We got safe back but it was very wet and uncomfortable fr*o*m the high sea w*hic*h nearly beat over our boat, and we had very great diffi*cul*ty to get ashore again. The length of the big Blasquet [is] 3 miles, and the North Island [Inishtooskert, *Inis Tuaisceart* (Ir.)] [is] 1½ Mile or thereabouts[.] There are 2 families and one family on the western island Ennis vi Killan [*Inis Mhic Aoibhleain* (Ir.)]. On the end of the Northern Isle is a remarkable shaped ridge of rocks w*hic*h rise much higher than the rest of the land by them. The big island runs W and E. There are a great many rocks all about there and the flat Is*land* is surrounded with them. It is beautiful to see the cormorants sitting on the rocks and flapping their wings. There is a very large rock of an island [Tearaght Island, *An Tiaracht* (Ir.)] w*hic*h is to the West of the big island and w*hic*h rises to a point very rough and high and no boats can get to it but in very calm weather[.] It looks like a soldiers cap. This is a very dangerous coast and ships are frequently lost on it[.] There was a part of a wreck fo*un*d last week[,] piece of a cabin and doors, and on the shore at [the] Big Is*land* was laying a piece of Mahogany 16½ long and 20 Inches squar*e*[.] Ships f*ro*m Limerick and the North pass betw*ee*n Dunmore p*oin*t and Big Is*land*[.] There is a rock close to the shore over w*hic*h the sea Dashes and discovers itself by the white foam and in the middle there are 2 sunk rocks not very near each other w*hic*h makes the sound very dangerous. Ships go close to the island. The name of the high pointed rock between the Bugnes [Beiginis] and big Is*land* in w*hic*h 5 Cormorants were sitting is called Binnagh [Barnagh] rock and is like the dis*tan*t island[.]

[ff. 53v–54r] Upon coming on shore at 5 OClock we went to take leave of Mr Neagle and Mr Trant and then set out for Dingle and on the M*ou*nt*ai*n were caught in a most violent storm of wind and rain, w*hic*h quite robbed us of the little light that remained and thus we came d*ow*n to the Ventry shore when it cleared up a little[,] but in this fine gloom we passed for the 4 Miles f*ro*m Dunquin to Ventry and got back by 8 to Dingle.

The village ~~near~~ over the M*ou*nt*ai*n where Mr Neagle lives is called Trevorey[2] f*ro*m a House where formerly lived a very hospitable widow of the name of Moore and then it was

---

[1] Rich.
[2] Lee sketched the scene at SJC, MS U.30 (7), ff. 18v–19r (p. 321), not reproduced here. 'Ty-Vorney Geerane, or Mary Geerane's House' is mentioned in many contemporary travels in Ireland, including Smith, *Kerry*, p. 182.

the only house of the village and in Irish house is *Tre*,[1] and thence the name of the place *Tre Moore*[,] *Tre voore*[,][2] *Trevorny*, and they shew the house now as a curiosity to strangers as the place where much hospitality was[,] but it is now nothing but a place cut in and close under the foot of the Mountain[.]

[f. 53v] **Thursday. [6 November]**[3]
Upon settling our Bill with Mr Moriarty we found that we had not sufficient money to pay the Total, what was to be done. For some in doubt Mr Moriarty and his son looked Black[4] and although we had spent our money like jolly fellows yet still he thought it odd and hummed and smiled. At last Coffy agreed to pay the Amount of the Bill into a persons hands in Killarney and although he was clear that his money was safe still he [Moriarty] thought it was devilish strange[.] All[5]

[f. 54r] Ballymullen Brewery
    Due to Bearer
sixpence Halfpenny
    Chule and Crumps
[*margin*: Chule and Crump, *written vertically along folio edges*][6]

Edward Fitzgerald Dingle
Received from Bearer
    Threepence
    Edward Fitzgerald

[ff. 54v–55r][7] together the whole of the people in Dingle thought us odd fellows. Some thought we were people sent down by [the] government, others thought we were much worse, and although no thing unpleasant occurred yet surmises were all on float[.] Even old Moriarty did not divest himself of this idea and he said to Coffy, 'Why do you follow these Gentlemen. Are you going from amusement also?' and afterwards said with a significant nod and gestures 'Ah I will be bound that you ~~are not~~ are well paid for this trip'[8] (meaning by Government), and nothing Coffy could say would make him believe the contrary[.] Their seeing my writing notes confirmed them and every one in the House was endeavouring to sift out what they could.

    I wished to get some seal skins but could not get any at that time. About a year ago a vessel was found out at sea with out a man on board[.] She was brought to Dingle and sold to Mr Hixon [Hickson] for [£]300 and on board were above 100 Dozen seal skins which

---

[1] *Teach* (Ir.). *Tigh* (dative case) is used colloquially.
[2] Lee notes the application of the genitive case in Irish, resulting in lenition of the initial consonant 'm'. An initial 'mh' in Irish is pronounced 'v'.
[3] Lee returns to writing on a single folio here.
[4] Angry or threatening (*OED*).
[5] Sentence continued below, at ff. 54v–55r.
[6] This note and the one following appear to relate to the incident related in the preceding diary entry, i.e., the writing of a promissory note to cover the cost of their stay at Moriarty's inn in Dingle. Ballymullen Brewery was located about 1.2 miles (2km) to the south of Tralee, on the River Lee.
[7] Here, Lee resumes writing across the verso of one folio, and the recto of the next.
[8] Quotation marks added.

were thrown overboard into the sea. Any one who chose might get any n[os] and many took some. But they were washed on shore and there they rotted on the shore and made such a stench as to hinder any person going down near it. Many loads of lime were thrown on them. There was no great demand here for them and ∴ they were lost. The people hereabouts are very anxious for wrecks and many are the instances of persons being murdered to get at the wreck. We started out when it was fine for Castlemain and were annoyed the whole of the 7 Miles to Ballinclare by James McCarty alias Quality[,] Mr Ray Bailiff of Derrymore Esqu*ire*[,] and were obliged to take him down to Justice Agar[1] of Ardrinan [Ardrianne] a Mile or more from Ballinclare who took charge of him. The road is all along the M*ountai*ns and commands an indiffe*re*nt view of the Bay on the R[.] The M*ountai*ns are fine on the Left. Down on the shore not far fr*om* ~~Derr~~ Ballinclare is Minard Castle[2] a most romantic spot. Staid at Ballinclare all night[.]

[Friday 7 November]
In the morning it rained and all day wind tempestuous[,] no possibility of getting out. Went to the Blacksmiths shop and saw an Irish shovel made for digging potatoes, they cost 3:3 each[.] Making is 13[d] if iron and metals are brought to the smiths, the shop was nothing but a poor old cabin thatched over but being a rainy day it was the resort of all [ff. 55v–56r] the fellows in the village. A Cabin family like Mr Hamiltons furnishes itself with almost everything. From the meat the fat is made into tallow[.] They make their own candles. The wool of their sheep is dyed with brambleberries and then sent to be made worsted. They make it into skeins and have it woven and the whole expence costs them a few pence. It is then sent to a friezing mill and then ready for wear. They make their own flannel also[.] Their sheepskins they also get turned into leather at a very moderate price.

In the Evening sent for a fidler[.] He came and we had a continual Irish Jigg. When either is tired they hold out their hands and round and then the gent*leman* has the liberty of asking for a kiss[.] The other then bows or curtsies to an other and so it goes on. The lower class of Irish are wonderfully fond of dancing and there are frequently two dancing masters in a small village of 10 Cabins. Many play on the fiddle and children are frequently hopping about and will dance before you for 1[d]. A young tailor danced uncom*monly* well indeed and kept time remarkably well with his feet[.]

Saturday 8 [November]
Started at 7 for Castlemain and ascend the great M*ountai*n just beyond Ballyclair [Ballinclare][.] See the lake in the M*ountai*n on the R and on getting to the top of the M*ountai*n have a fine noble view of Castlemain Bay. From hence the road goes all along the shore to Castlemain but we had a great many (near 20) streams and floods to pass thro*ugh* on the road. Road not very interesting. M*ountai*ns over Ivragh [Iveragh] look respectable and the ridge of M*ountai*ns run the whole way on the L at a dist*ance fr*om the road and are of one unifo*rm* height and even appearance[.] Road as straight as an arrow. Castlemain is a poor dismal hole and consists of a few wretched cabins, but here we saw a few trees for the first time since leaving Killarney and Mil*l*town[,] crossing the bridge[,]

---

[1] John Eagar, Justice of the Peace, and husband of Sarah Blennerhasset (d. 1826) of Blennerville, Co. Kerry.
[2] Minard Castle on Dingle Bay, blown up in 1641 (Coleman, 'Castles and Abbeys', pp. 156–7).

looks like a respectable place am*on*g the trees, it is wonderful how fine they app*ear* to the eye after a long vacancy *from* them[.] Saw Sir — Demesne and house (very poor)[.][1] The town is nothing remarkable[.] The Inn is kept by Dr Sidmarsh and a poor place it is, Happy is the man who does not sleep there[.] Bought a seal skin and goat D*itt*o[.]

[f. 56v] **Sunday 9. [November]**[2]
Rained all night and all the day
breakfast and walked to Killarney and not
way. / NB. Miss Hamilton gave me some
fo*u*nd in a rock and plenty more not for
make a chapel /

Monday 10 [November]
Staid indoors all day to rest.

[ff. 57r–59v *cut out*]

[*Back cover*]
James McCarty or <u>called</u> Quality
Bailiff of Mr Ray, Derrymore
Receipt for 75£ *from* Mr Hickson
Mr Hamilton of Ballinclare
Mr Agar of Ardrinan the justice Judge Day –

---

[1] Probably Kilcolman Demesne, Milltown, Co. Kerry, property of Sir John Godfrey.
[2] Half of today's entry is missing, as the recto folio facing this verso has been cut out.

5. KILLARNEY TO DUBLIN

[SJC, MS U.30 (5)]
[f. 1 *cut out*]

[f. 2r] **[Friday] November 13.**[1]
Started from Killarney for Tralee and got there without a drop of rain, proceeded on towards Ardfert across the bare grounds untill you come to the place where you are immediately struck with the appearance of the venerable ruins of the Cathedral[.] At the East End [of the cathedral] is a remarkable fine handsome and plain window, the W end is a plain wall except at the N W corner where are 2 small round and one large arches[.] The great E window is 5 long narrow divisions[.] It is of considerable length and within it and all around it are the burial places of the different families whose forefathers lie there. In the middle of the Cathedral under foot and partly erased is a stone figure of some bishop with the cap on his head and the crook in his left hand. There are the ruins of several smaller chapels on the N and west ends of the Cathedral.[2]

Lord Glendowens[3] domain is approached by a lodge whose portals are opened wide and it is close to the end of the street[.] The domain is pretty enough but of all beauties none can vie with the fine old ruined abbey[4] close to the mansion, here are the fine ivy mantled arches[,] the round pillars and the fine cloysters in all their perfection[.] There are 2 sides of a [f. 2v] cloistered square in perfection. The venerable ivy grown S window is as fine as any I ever saw. The sacred ruins[,] the mouldering tombs, the monuments of human frailty[,] skulls[,] bones and coffins pieces[,] all raise a mournful melancholy train of ideas in the mind. The whole of the ruins are surrounded with trees and some very fine ones are growing out of the middle of them[.] Lord Glendowr's gardens are celebrated for their size and goodness but not extraordinary[.] The House is what in England would be called a good seat, The Abbey is one of the most beautiful in preservation. The fine gothic windows of 5 arches are all covered with ivy and the top is all completely ivy mantled[.] Around the sides of the long chapel part are tombs in some Degrees of preservation and the sculls and bones of its ancestry and (passers on) still are placed in heaps or in the nitches of the walls. There are several stones with memorial inscriptions on them and the figures on them[.] On the West side are some large fine round arches next to the tower end and [on the] opposite side are cloisters of 3 small arches in one and there are 2 sides of a cloistered square still

---

[1] Diarist error – Friday was 14 Nov. Four days at Killarney are unaccounted for, since 10 Nov.
[2] These ruins of a 13th-century cathedral at Ardfert, and the two small churches in its vicinity, are described in Leask, *Irish Churches*, pp. 124, 156–7.
[3] John Crosbie (1753–1815), landowner, MP, and 2nd Earl of Glandore. He resided at Ardfert Abbey, Co. Kerry (Geoghegan, 'Crosbie, John').
[4] Ardfert friary, founded by the Franciscans *c*.1253 (Gwynn and Hadcock, *Medieval Religious Houses*, p. 242).

DIARY 5: KILLARNEY TO DUBLIN

existing[.][1] The tower at the N W end is still preserved[.] There is an inscription on the side of one of the western Pillars of 3 lines, but much obliterated[.] The first line is said to be partly [f. 3r] [*blank*] and the third is *Orate Pro* etc the date of the year[,] but it is not clear that it is the date[.] There are some letters after *Orate pro*. Dr Pococke could not read it.[2] A French man[3] made out (the steward said) all that was ever made out but it did not seem to me to be right as he unravelled it. Its obscurity has given it a name but it is not worth the trouble of making out. The park is very pretty and there are some noble trees all around the house. There is a fine avenue of beech in the park[.] Its size is about 100 Acres English[.] The gardens are laid out in the old ~~dutch~~ style[,] pastures and fortification like *a la Potzdam*. The ancient name and fame of the place and the reliques of the buildings fill the mind with many pleasing reflections. Besides[,] these are heightened by its being so near not only the sea but the wide and vast Atlantic[,] and the trees and foliage on that account are so much the more endearing and valuable[.] Perhaps no park has such flourishing appearance [so far] to the west as this is[.] We were at the H*ouse* of Mr Dooly[,] Lord H[4] Steward[,] who keeps a house of entertainment there[.]

[*margin:* November 13. Went from Killarney to Tralee. November 14 To Ardfert]

[ff. 3v–4r][5] **Saturday November 15.**

NB. From this time keep a journal of the weather of the preceeding [*sic*] day in the commencement of the next.

// Morning clear and bright. One shower. Rain all night. Much wind all the 24 hours and clear in the morning again[.] //

Started for Ballyhighe [Ballyheige] along the side of the Bay, the road very dirty and low[.] Pass through several small villages whose names I did not even inquire. Five miles off at the corner of the Bay is Ballyhighe a small village, few cabins[.] Just above it is Colonel Crosbies House.[6] The whole view [is] interesting[,] for Kerry head lands rise directly behind the village and in front is the bay formed by the head which winds out to sea and is a rocky shore. One glance is enough to bestow on the place, and from thence took a guide to go to see Ballengary [Ballingarry Island] which is directly across the promontory about 2 Miles[.][7] There we were much dissapointed [*sic*] as our expectations had been wonderfully raised But it is a singular place. A large part of the land is completely separated by a prodigious chasm which the rough and boisterous Atlantic has worn through the rock[.] It is in some places not more than 6 feet wide or less but the water rolling a strong current all round this insulated rocky spot. They call it the entrance to the Shannon but it by no means deserves the name from Kerry Head[.][8]

---

[1] Lee sketched the arches in the page margin; not reproduced here.

[2] Lee seems to borrow here from Wilson, *Post-Chaise Companion*, p. 182, who writes of the same inscription: 'Dr. Pococke … could not make it out'. A partial inscription was published in Hitchcock, 'Gleanings', pp. 128, 131–2. *Orate pro* means 'pray for'.

[3] This could be a reference to Chevalier de Latocnaye, who visited Ireland in 1796 and 1797, but his account does not mention the inscription (Latocnaye, *A Frenchman's Walk*, pp. 108–12).

[4] It is unclear to whom Lee is referring.

[5] From this point, Lee writes across both folios.

[6] Colonel James Crosbie (*c*.1760–1836) of Ballyheigue Castle, MP (History of Parliament Online).

[7] Lee sketched the view from the spot at SJC, MS U.30 (7), ff. 26v–27r (p. 322), not reproduced.

[8] The mouth of the River Shannon lies between Kerry Head, Co. Kerry, and Loop Head, Co. Clare. Lee seems to suggest that the appellation is not justified.

Formerly there was a castle on this spot and there are the marks of the foundation and the ground floor is partly visible[.][1] It was formerly only accessible by a draw bridge but now the Bank has given way and by sinking in has made a sloping easy entrance. The place where the draw bridge was still remains and it is not more than 6 or 7 feet wide and in appearance not so much, a man in liquor once jumped across here[.] Mr Crosbie saw him[.] It is no very great jump but the scenery and the ideas which an immense chasm and a roaring sea below produce might frighten many [sic] one. Upon the whole the fine view of the sea and Shannon are well worth seeing but the cave etc and the roaring of the sea and this very [ff. 4v–5r] wonderful spot may be worth an Irishmans while to go and see but a bolder shore and finer (sentiments) caverns and a more tremendous scene the Englishman may [see one?] much finer in the neighbourhood of Bristol and in Wales[.] From there went along the shore towards the Tower on the Kerry Head[2] and its situation is wonderfully fine and romantic as being surrounded with the tide and boisterous Atlantic and Cliffs[,] many of them 100 feet high[,] and hardly anywhere to get down[,] the sea dashing over them in. Down the high cliffs I was surprised to hear that very frequently women tie rope under their arms and are swung down the cliffs to go and pick up (some sorts of) seaweed which they boil and sell[.] Men are also often let down by ropes to go and fish among the rocks and by this means they often in August and September get down and kill and catch the young seals which are in the caverns of the rocks below here[.] Here are caves where the Kerry stone is often found and there was formerly a quarry worked by some of the Glendore family and some amethysts of great value found in a quarry here.[3] A great deal of fluor spar[4] is found. Lieutenant Fodour of the Tower was very polite. In the tower lived his Midshipmen and 2 Men and a corporals guard[,] or 1 Corporal and 3 men[.]

Sunday 16 November
Clear at 9 and cloudy all the morning[,] a fine light shower. Very sharp air, cold and windy all day. In the Evening at 5 very heavy rain and for most part of the night[.]

Started and went to Breakfast with the Lieutenant of the tower. I must not omit that at 9 the preceeding [sic] night we left his tower and crossed the bog to a well about a mile off where we slept.[5] We had 2 Guides who each carried a piece of turf lighted and the wind blowing kept it alight untill it was all burnt out[.] We then had not far to go but sent one boy to fetch another bit from his fathers and he returned and met us and took us safe only [f. 5v][6] quite wet through with the bog. Effect of the (turf) bog lights curious enough. Before Breakfast went down to see a farmhouse called Keilmicud daw where a family whose name is Coryton tenants of Mr Crosbie boast of having lived these 1200 years and there is the outside wall of an old dilapidated chapel[.] [There is a] Chapel close to the Cabin where they say all their ancestors lie buried and they will allow none but their own

---

[1] Ballingarry Island is a promontory with ruins of draw bridge and dwellings; the castle site was nearby on the mainland (OS 1st edition, 6 inches to 1 mile, 1838–42).

[2] In 1804–6, a chain of 81 signal towers were erected around the Irish coast, with accommodation for crew and guards (O'Sullivan and Downey, 'Martello and Signal Towers', pp. 46–9). The signal tower at Kerry Head was 'ready for occupation in October 1804' (Kerrigan, *Castles and Fortifications*, p. 160).

[3] This area is referred to as 'Amethyst Cliffs' in Smith, *Kerry*, flyleaf map.

[4] Fluorite, the mineral form of calcium fluoride.

[5] Possibly St Macadaw's Well, Kerry Head.

[6] At this point, Lee returns to writing on one folio at a time, rather than across facing verso and recto folios.

family to be buried in it.[1] There are[,] as in most other old burial places, skulls[,] thigh bones etc laying about the place[.] It is a very small place and the stones are placed on each other only. We were told that the bones were of an enormous size but they are nothing extraordin*ary* and some of the largest might have belonged to men 6 foot high even in our own days. The shore is not remarkably bold as we expected to find it. Further to Kerry Head is[,] near the shore[,] the remains of some old fortress and there is a most singular subterraneous set of cells[.][2] You go down by a narrow passage slanting and come into a small room[.] Beyond this is another of larger size and thus there are four w*hich* commun*icate* with each other, beyond is a passage w*hich* some say goes to the cliff [f. 6r] but it is too narrow to be pursued. In the second is a little stream of water and the people say these were made by the Danes.[3] We had no candles to explore it. In Col*onel* Crosbies Garden were also some subterraneous caverns also and to the West of his house[,] not very far[,] are some more w*hich* are in many apartments[.] Over on the opposite side of Kerry Head[,] to the North[,] are above 30 apartments or courts all under ground close to the sea shore, and these are not infrequent about this part of the country[.][4] Who formerly made them nescio,[5] probably they were used by the smugglers and that one we were in[,] a man told us[,] was in Irish called the <u>Fortress of the Cats</u>. Returned to Ballyheig and took a snack at Col*onel Crosbies* H*ouse* and went on along the shore to Ardfert[.] Very fine strand indeed most noble and by crossing 2 streams w*hich* run into the sea you may continue on to Tralee or at least to Blennerville close by it. It is reckoned 5 Miles f*rom* Tower[6] to Ballyheig and 5 *from* thence to Ardfert and D*itto* to Tralee. Dined at Lord Glendores[.]

[f. 6v] **Monday 17 No*vember*.**
Last day at 9 it was cloudy and threatened rain. Rained most of the morning, but intervals of sunshine. From 12 rain and boisterous wind and rain in great showers, and rain regularly all the night.

// Walked again over the abbey and endeavoured to make out the meaning of the writing on the wall.[7] Walked from Ardfert to Tralee and saw the Chairing of the 2 New Members [of Parliament,] Mr Herbert[8] and the Knight of Kerry.[9] Chairs very delicately made and it was not unlikely that they might have had a fall. On the backs of the chair each ~~man~~ (had his) coat of arms and the crest on the sides. The ribbons etc looked not unlike a May garland. The Electioneering spirit of the people sudden and flighty [*sic*] for

---

[1] The farmhouse took its name from the church of Kilmalkedar (*Cill Mhic a' Deaghaidh*, also Kilmacida or Kilmacdaw) at Glenderry on Kerry Head, which was used for Corridan family burials (O'Donovan, *Letters ... Kerry*, p. 129).

[2] Ballingarry Castle ruins, Kerry Head; see p. 236, n. 1.

[3] See p. 171, n. 1, for general context on 'Danish' archaeological remains in the Irish landscape.

[4] The Ordnance Survey identified a number of caves in the vicinity of Ballyheige and Kerry Head (OS 1st edition, 6 inches to 1 mile, 1838–42).

[5] A claim not to know (*OED*); lit. Latin, 'I do not know'.

[6] Lee may mean the signal tower referred to above.

[7] See Lee's remarks at Ardfert, p. 235.

[8] Henry Arthur Herbert (1756–1821), landowner and MP for Kerry in 1806–13 (History of Parliament Online).

[9] Maurice Fitzgerald (1772–1849), 18th knight of Kerry and MP for Kerry in 1801–31 (Geoghegan, 'Fitzgerald, Maurice').

the moment but an hour after all was quiet and still, not carried to that pitch wh*i*ch [it is] in England. No 2399266 or 42163. The Knight went to Killarney and Mr H*er*bert to Dublin directly after. In the Even*i*ng went to the Play wh*i*ch was badly and most inanimately performed[,] notwithstanding the Carlow regim*en*t performed as band on the occasion. The Gallery was most vociferous in their joy or sorrow necsis,[1] and they made a most tremendous roar all the time. House well filled and better than when it was a church[2] (A 1517 446 612236649) A 1517 442 the 835516920 15186 55333453 34696. There was a clap for Mr Sagisson[,] the defender of his country[.][3]

[f. 7r] **Tuesday 18 Nov*em*ber.**
Monday. Clear all the morn*i*ng. A shower or two in the day. But very heavy severe rain fr*o*m 6 in the Even*i*ng and all night. Boisterous wind and sharp cold morning on Tuesday[.]

// Started at 11 for Listhowel [Listowel] passing thro*ugh* Abbeydorney [after] 4 Miles, Ballinagarath [Ballynageragh] [after] 8 Miles. In all 14 Miles. The road is very dull and dirty. At Abbey dorney on the L are some ruins of an old Abbey.[4] Country [is] quite bare[.] Pass by the monument of the Grand Father to the present Lord Lord Kerry.[5] About 3 miles fr*o*m the road appears a tall round tower and near it are some ruins of some abbeys.[6] Listhowel is a small (not) insignificant place[.] There is the remnant of an old castle there[.][7] The Bridge over the river is very handsome and has a number of fine bold arches[.] The river itself is very grand. Here was a wake in one of the houses or cabins and they were howling as I went by. The town is mostly one large square with the houses round it[.]

Wednesday, 19 Nov*em*ber
Tuesday at 9 rain showers heavy[,] but clear at 11. Showers all day and just as I got to Listhowel at 5 it began and continued to pour with rain all night most furiously untill day break. Then showers till 9.

Started p*a*st 10 for Newtown Sands[8] 5 Miles and then to Glyn [Glin] 5 more [miles] and got there at 3 –

See nothing on the road remarkable[.]

[f. 7v] **Thursday 20 Nov*em*ber**
From 9 it rained untill 12[.] Cleared up for intervals then poured again from 2[.] It rained hard all the Even*i*ng and hail in the night as I heard it against my window. At day break cleared up till 9.

// Started from Glyn at 10[.] Walked 2 long miles to Loghill where there is a very pretty bay on the Shannon. Road all the way on the riverside. There is a ferry here wh*i*ch plies

---

[1] Possibly meaning 'as necessary or appropriate'.
[2] The theatre was housed in a former church, as Lee noted on 30 Oct. 1806 (SJC, MS U.30 (4), pp. 222–3).
[3] A character in the unidentified play Lee attended.
[4] A mid-12th century Cistercian monastery (Gwynn and Hadcock, *Medieval Religious Houses*, p. 123).
[5] The Kerry Monument, Kilbinane Hill, near Lixnaw, Co. Kerry, built *c*.1690 (NIAH).
[6] Probably Rattoo round tower.
[7] The remains of a 15th-century tower house (Bennett, 'The Archaeology of Co. Kerry', p. 49).
[8] Newtown Sandes is now known as Moyvane.

from both shores[,] or 2 boats[,] every day at high water[.] [It is] about 1 Mile over or more and it is a horse ferry. Just at the Head of the town by the Bridge 2 brooks[1] join which come down 2 deep glens which run E and west from the bridge[.] They join at the bridge and the whole river falls lower down into the Shannon. The road is all along the rising ground which just looks over the water and for many miles it continues so untill you come to a place called Barryowen [Barrigone] well. The high grounds on this stage give the most beautiful river scenery imaginable and the part of the river up towards Ennis and the islands there are very fine.[2] At Barryowen well is a great short cut of at least a mile but unless the traveller is fortunate in his [hits?] and has plenty of light and happens to meet one or two persons on it, it is 10 to 1 he gets [it] wrong[.] I did not fortunately. Passed by Cappa [Cappagh] Counsellor Rices[3] on the riverside and (it has some trees about it!!!) Got to Askeyton [Askeaton] about 4 and went with Mr Ware the Town Clerk who shewed me the abbey[4] which is a most remarkable perfect building. The Cloisters are the most perfect and best finished I ever saw[.] They are a complete square and all of limestone[.]

[f. 8r] These are regularly all a round. 4 pillars on each stone. There is at one angle the figure of a man, or as I was told of the founder of the Abbey, cut out in the pillar and on the other side is a fine high polished slab which is so clear that you may see yourself in it and this they say served him as a looking glass before which he always shaved himself[.] The building is remarkably fine[.] There are in different parts some most elegant arches of all different rocks. Chapel with 3 Altars and one remarkable monument at the farther end belonging to some family. Opposite this high up is a little stone figure most beautiful arches of different sorts, pillars round square, squares[5] with corners cut off etc[.] From a high ground beyond the abbey is seen the Shannon. In one part of the building they shew where the friars had nets fixed across the (small) river which runs close to the abbey and when any fish were in the nets they by struggling rang some bells which were on the net strings and thus were then drawn out. The rapid river —[6] which falls into the Shannon runs close to the abbey walls. In the town is a most picturesque Bridge over the rapid river — and just over the bridge is the Old Castle which was destroyed in Cromwells time. He battered it to pieces[.] The Castle is built on a rock and separate from it is a fine large building which was formerly the dining Hall[.] It is a noble apartment and shews grandeur in its present form[.]

[f. 8v] Under it are 4 fine large arched vaults, and they all appear to have been formed by layers[,] a circular body of hurdles and building over them[,] for the marks of the hurdles are apparent in the arched form, the river forms into drains just above the castle and they join just below it at the bridge so that the castle is quite an island. Part of it is turned into a Barrack for a few soldiers. Just above the town on the river —[7] is a fine

---

[1] Glashanagark River and White River.
[2] Lee sketched three views on this day's walk, at SJC, MS U.30 (7), ff. 30v–31r, 33v–34r, 35v–36r (pp. 322–3), not reproduced.
[3] Stephen Edward Rice (d. 1831) of Mount Trenchard House, Foynes, Co. Limerick (History of Parliament Online).
[4] The Franciscan friary, founded in the late 14th or early 15th century (Gwynn and Hadcock, *Medieval Religious Houses*, p. 242).
[5] Corrected from 'suqares' in original MS.
[6] River Deel. The name is represented by a dash here and in the following sentence.
[7] River Deel. The name is represented by a dash.

waterfall near a mill, the water rushes with great impetuosity down and the channel is between rocks and over them. On one of the steps going up to the top of the abbey is a little small ruler fixed into the stone, of ivory and on it are the inches ½ and every division. It is very short[,] not more than 4 Inches[,] and they say that by this rule the whole abbey was built. There are 2 pillars in the cloisters w*hich* are deficient and these they say were taken away in a vessel to France a long time ago. They tell the story how this abbey came to be built thus, A friar had committed some offence in France and all the monks were to punish him[.] The Father abbot whose name was OConnor told him that his punishment was to be that he was to go over to Ireland and at —[1] he was to build an abbey. 'Where is it?' 'You must go and travel Ireland over untill you find out the place where it is.' Well off he set fr*om* France and came over and travelled about but no such a place co*ul*d he find untill after wandering about for many years he came to a herdmans cottage near Askeyton. Here [f. 9r] he went in. The herdsman was at his dinner and received him hospitably and set before him potatoes ~~milk~~ and sheepsmilk and bacon. After he had well eaten he said that and he was rather pressed hard by his walk that he sh*oul*d like to rest himself and take a little sleep. 'Well' *said* the herdsman pointing to a spot close by 'There are bulrushes and fine good (clean) green green grass and and [*sic*] posies lay down y*our*self there and take yo*ur* rest.' He laid down and some short time after says the herdsman to the young boy, 'Boy go and drive the sheep out to feed at — [.]'[2] Hearing the well k*now*n sounds [of the place name] up starts the friar and begs to accomp*any* the boy[.] He did so find out the place and build there the abbey.

To call the Shannon a river is to disgrace it with an inferior title, it ought at least to be considered as a channel for its size is worthy of the name and there are large streams w*hich* well deserve the names of river w*hich* fall into it, such as that at Listhowel and at Askeyton, its form size and majestic appearance well ranks it the prince of streams and Limerick well deserves to be the metropolis of the United Kingdom. What a noble river for it!! People at Askeyton have their turf brought 2½ [miles] fr*om* the town. A horse will go backwa*rds* and forwa*rds* 4 times and has for each kish he brings 13^d or 4:4 a day. Michael Nash the postman has ab*out* 48 Kale[3] = 96 Kishes of turf this season for his own use, besides this porterage people pay £5:10 or £15 per annum for the bog accord*ing* to the [f. 9v] goodness of the parts of it fr*om* w*hich* the turf is cut!! So that upon the whole it costs them ab*out* 2:8½ each kish and a poor person will burn 3 kish in a month sparingly. Land lets for 21S[,] £2[,] £3 [or] £4 an acre about the town of Askeyton[.] The whole of that part of the County of Limerick I went thro*ugh* to Adair [Adare] was very dull and uninteresting, very rocky and stony, very much in waves,[4] not a tree to be seen, castles in ruins here and there, and old forts and abbeys at distances all about[.]

---

[1] The place name is represented by a dash here and later in this paragraph.
[2] Quotation marks have been added to all dialogue in this paragraph.
[3] The meaning of 'Kale' here is unclear, but it may be Lee's rendition of a variant of the Irish word *caol*, meaning an osier or twig used in basket-weaving. Alternatively, it may be a misspelling of the word 'creel', a 'large wicker basket; formerly applied to the large deep baskets, coupled in pairs across the backs of horses, for the transport of goods' (*OED*).
[4] 'A long convex strip of land between two long broad hollows; one of a series of such strips' (*OED*).

Friday 21 No*vem*ber.
At 9 it rained but at 10 [it was] Clear. A few hailstorms, several showers and intervals of sunshine and fine rainbows all day till eve*nin*g. From 6 constant rain or hail all the night and D*itt*o in the morning[.] At 7 started in a violent hailstorm, then fine till 9[.]

// Started at 7 from Askeyton, and in a severe shower of hail, pass by Mr Hunts House[1] to the Left and down his avenue, then plain road, pass the bog and very good road up and down gentle risings the whole way to Adair. Pass Curragh[2] then at [*sic*] a Lady Hunt[3] and here the eye is regaled with the sight of ~~a few~~ trees again, there are large woods about the house. What makes them more valuable is that they [f. 10r] are the first one see*s* after passing the whole way fr*om* Ardfert. At Adair there is plenty of occupation for any person for some days and a more beautiful village I never saw. The park and grounds are well worthy [of] inspection. Fine noble trees[,] ivy covered. The House[4] commands a pleasant if not an extensive view and it is a snug white but not large building. The winding canal looks stiff enough close by and alongside the river [River Maigue]. But the abbeys[5] are the ornament of this place. In the village is one w*hic*h in any other place wo*ul*d be considered as a very fine old building and so it is, the tower and the several apartments are still plain and perfect no roofs, there are no cloisters here, but all the ground work is plain.[6] Behind it at a short distance is a curious round building with a low little door,[7] and on entering it you are in a round room with the roof w*hic*h slopes in gently and forms a circular opening in the middle, thro*ugh* w*hic*h hard green grass etc enters in the most picturesque manner. On the outside[,] from the edge w*hic*h forms the roof[,] the top is overgrown with grass and weeds, it appears to be a very old building[.] The whole road ~~from~~ thro*ugh* the village and around it is on both sides well wooded and there are woods all about the place w*hic*h give it quite a divine appearance after seeing the places I had left lately. Nearer to Limerick in a meadow on the river side on the left at the bridge is the white Abbey[8] and this is the most beautiful [f. 10v] and as perfect as any can possibly be[.] The outside walls are completely covered with ivy w*hic*h hangs in festoons all around the windows, within 6 or 8 feet of the ground all the arched windows are perfect in form. The East window of the Chapel is a noble arch and hung round with ivy. The whole stands on a~~n immense~~ (great) space of ground and is bounded by a small river on the N Side. Within[,] the separate apartments are perfect and the altars in the chapels are remaining. Even there is the painted paper under the belfry w*hic*h still remains. The tower is also ivy covered and is the grandest and most venerable I know. The cloisters are all perfect and

---

[1] Probably Inchirourke More House, Askeaton, Co. Limerick (LED).

[2] Possibly Curragh Bridge House, Adare, Co. Limerick.

[3] Eleanor (d. 1820), wife of Sir Vere Hunt, first baronet (d. 1818) ([Anon.], 'Vere, Sir Aubrey de (1788–1846)') and their mid-18th-century house, Curragh Chase, Co. Limerick (LED).

[4] Probably Adare Manor; the 18th-century manor house that Lee saw was demolished and rebuilt in 1832–50 (NIAH).

[5] Adare was home to a number of early and medieval Christian foundations. The Trinitarian monastery was established by 1226; the Augustinian or 'Black' abbey was founded in 1317; and the Franciscan church of St Michael Archangel of the Friars Minor was dedicated in 1464 (Gwynn and Hadcock, *Medieval Religious Houses*, pp. 217, 295, 242).

[6] The Trinitarian abbey (see previous note).

[7] This round building is depicted but not named on the OS 1st edition, 6 inches to 1 mile, 1838–42; it may have been a dovecote. Lee sketched this building at SJC, MS U.30 (7), f. 37r (p. 323), not reproduced.

[8] The Franciscan abbey (see n. 5 above).

not so fine worked as at Askeyton. There are chambers above which are also all perfect but [for] the roofs. You are shewn the Kitchen, cellars etc[.] Some of the arched vaults here also appear as if they had been made by an arch of faggots heaped up and the building done over them. The Bridge[1] is even an object well worthy of notice in itself and above it on the waterside is another beautiful ruin of an abbey[2] which is also very perfect, and farther off is a fourth,[3] besides several pieces of old buildings adjacent which are partly overgrown with boughs and ivy. At Askeyton[,] its abbey,[4] the rolling and furious river which falls into the Shannon near it and the bridge and the Castle and [f. 11r] waterfall are all together beautiful but quite different from Adair and no comparing it[.] Then there is a bare wide open country. The other is retired and surrounded with trees and sheltered and retired. Walked on to Limerick over 8 of the worst miles I had passed in all Ireland. Roads literally a sea of mud and very deep in some places. What is very provoking is that you get no view what ever of Limerick before you are in it, you may guess where it is, but you must be in the subburbs [sic] before you fairly see it and they are if possible more filthy and dirty than Cork. Got to Swinburnes Hotel[5] at 4 OClock.

Saturday 22 November
Fine at 9, but showers all the morning and some very heavy, sunshine between them. Very heavy rains in the middle of the day, showers all the Evening. Whole day sharp and cold. Visited the several parts of the town, Newtown Perry [Newtown Pery] is the modern part, and the streets are very well built and houses are like London ones[.] Delivered my letter from Lord Glendore to Captain Launcelot Hill,[6] whose house when he built it 20 Years ago was in the country and [there was] only one beyond it and within the 20 years it has been here all the houses [became] inhabited opposite to it.[7] The whole of the land about Newtown Perry belonged to the late Lord Perry and now to Lord Limerick.[8] The Newtown is separated from the old by the small river [Abbey River] at the end of it, over which into [f. 11v] the old town within these 20 years the Bridge has been built.[9] Before this the only communication between the old town and the new town was by the old bridge [Baal's Bridge] on which are built a row of about 6 houses and which turn their backs down on the other bridge below. This old bridge with a row of houses on the W side of it is very ancient and it is a pity but that the next high wind hurricane and storm would rid the town of the houses or if not them alone, of the houses and bridge together for they and it are a public nuisance and a better is either wanted

---

[1] Adare Bridge, originally built c.1390–1410; rebuilt in 1837 (NIAH).
[2] The ruins of the medieval St Nicholas' Church.
[3] Probably the Augustinian abbey.
[4] The Franciscan friary; see p. 241, n. 5.
[5] On Sarsfield St (O'Flaherty, *IHTA no. 21 Limerick*, p. 38).
[6] Hill was a brother-in-law of Edmond Sexten Pery, see n. 8 below (*The Hibernian Magazine*, June 1774, p. 366). For Lord Glandore, see above, p. 234, n. 3.
[7] By 1752, the area within Limerick's old city walls was 'densely occupied', and in 1760, the walls were demolished. New streets, squares, bridges and quays were laid out and, by 1769, a new suburb, Newtown Pery, was planned (O'Flaherty, *IHTA no. 21 Limerick*, p. 8).
[8] Edmond Henry Pery (1758–1845) was created 1st Earl of Limerick in 1802. He was heir to his uncle, Edmond Sexten Pery (1719–1806), 1st Viscount Pery and Speaker of the Irish house of commons (Geoghegan, 'Pery, Edmond Henry' and 'Pery, Edmond Sexten').
[9] Mathew Bridge, built in 1762 (O'Flaherty, *IHTA no. 21 Limerick*, p. 44).

or it would not be a bad plan to cut off the old and new town from each other for the former is a disgrace to the latter. The old town was formerly fortified and had a wall and forts round it[.] It is surrounded by a small branch of the Shannon which runs only by the custom house and joins the river again above the town. Went into the Market near the old barbarous bridge with houses on it[.] Turkey 2:8½ or 2:2 each[,] mutton 5ᵈ a lb. There is a great part of the old fortification still remaining on the Shannon side where the Military Barrack[1] now is and over the river just above is a remarkable curious and old bridge thrown over in the time of King John.[2] It is quite flat on the top and every 2 arches are different from each other, it has a very fine appearance and the distant range [f. 12r] of Mountain looks to advantage from the Custom house quay. The Custom house is a fine good substantial building.[3] Nothing extraordinary. Situated just at the End of the Newtown Perry. The Old town is again nominally ½dᴅ[4] into the English part which is the most ancient and is nearest to the river and the Irish part which is more in towards the land. It is singular that the only communication with the County of Clare should be the Old narrow Bridge built in King Johns time. That side would be much more advantageous for houses and for the town as the channel of the river runs nearest to it and it is on the north side and the houses would have a south aspect over the river, but I understand the owners of Newtown Perry side were very averse to such a proposition as [it] would diminish the value of their land if the other could be easily come at. NB the houses on the old bridge are the property of Lord Cork[.][5] It would be well worth his lordships while[,] if [he were] a man of taste[,] to pull it down. The part of the bridge on the Clare side has been lately widened and 3 new arches built. The Shannon looks prodigious fine from the centre of the bridge.

It is very inconvenient to a stranger passing through all the little petty towns and villages to be pestered with the endless variety of small notes which he meets with. If he offers a Cork or a Dublin Guinea note for any thing he is sure to have his change presented in 3, 9½, 6ᵈ½, 2[,] 8½ etc Notes but he should [f. 12v] not take them, he must probably be kept ½ an hour while they pretend to send for change having before told you they had none in the house[.] You are then offered a note or 2 to the next place you are going to and a few 10ᵈ pieces with some English shillings, probably light weight and ∴ly[6] at the next place if they are not full weight, if they have any marks or letters beat in them, and unless they have some symptoms of a head on them they will not take them from you[.] Perhaps also you are given dollars for 5:5 Each and the next place are told that they do not go for more than 4:10½ or 5. A tradesman in Killarney gave me a dollar for 5:5 and about a week after refused to take one for more than 4:10½. They tell you that they will not take them for more than 4:10½ and that they will not fetch more at Killarney and etc but confess at the same time that they go for 5:5 in Cork[,] Limerick etc and what is worse [is] they will not give you one for <u>less</u> than 5:5 as they make a profit by them. Consequently in travelling

---

[1] Lee seems to describe King John's Castle, built c.1212 and converted to Castle Barracks in 1751 (O'Flaherty, *IHTA no. 21 Limerick*, p. 26).

[2] Thomond Bridge, built by 1199 (O'Flaherty, *IHTA no. 21 Limerick*, p. 44).

[3] Built in 1765 on Custom House Quay (O'Flaherty, *IHTA no. 21 Limerick*, p. 27).

[4] Halved or divided.

[5] The earls of Cork and Orrery had extensive holdings in Limerick as well as other southern counties of Ireland (LED).

[6] Consequently.

much you loose no trifling sum of money by these nasty notes [f. 13r] and shews that very money which is good in England and in the great towns is refused to pass. It would be well worth while for some speculators such as there are in England to come over and gather up all these vile bits of paper and prosecute the persons who spread them to the discredit of HMS coin,[1] or it is a pity government do not interfere. ~~Even~~

Even in the noblest and most hospitable circles people have often given out their indirect suspicion that the reason of my travelling on foot was to save expense (little thinking that it was as expensive as going on horseback by such questions as this) 'Oh but it would not cost you much more to travel on a poney', 'You might buy a poney for a trifle' etc. 'You would be able to travel much faster on a poney and see more for near the same expense',[2] Never considering the independance [sic] of my method of travelling. Gentlemen have frequently been surprised and astonished at my declining to take ½ in[3] or to accept a place in their postchaise for a stage, and at my preferring to walk and have my thoughts and body free instead of being parked up in a cage and travelling like a dead body in a hearse, While I have frequently been pleased and by no means surprised to get to the end of the stage sooner [f. 13v] or soon after the Chaise by setting out <u>when it is ordered</u>. I have frequently started when gentlemen were ordering a chaise and got to the destined place before it[,] with 2 horses and even with 4[,] for so much time is lost in saddling, putting to, waiting for the drivers etc and in fact 4 horses travel very little faster than 2 Except on those roads where 2 cannot go[.][4]

// With regard to the Brogue[,] it is in England considered as general subject of merriment to hear an Irishman speak English[.] He is immediately known and has brasing[5] questions put to him, and is quizzed about his manner of speaking over the water[.] This mark of incivility is natural to the English, they never learnt it from any other nation, nor do they reflect how much other nations have them in their power for their rough clumsy way of pronouncing all other languages. At least Ireland has her revenge in her sight. The English pronounce the Latin in their own selfish way quite different from other nations of Europe and there are many poor peasants [f. 14r] in Ireland who in this point would put their best scholars right not only in the pronunciation but in speaking the language itself[.] For my opinion[,] I do not think the Brogue[,] as it is called[,] is so ludicrous or laughable as a rough country brute says it is[.] ~~and particularly from~~ In Ireland you hear English spoken in all the towns more pure and without dialect than [in] any parts of England itself and the brogue from the mouth of a lovely Irish lady[,] as all of them generally are[,] has a degree of interest and livelyness and sweetness attached to it which you never feel in hearing it drawled out of the mouth and between the teeth chewed from a serious stiff Englishwoman. At least it is much better to hear it with this interesting pronunciation[,] English spoken which is good and grammatical, than to have from a fine London lady a set of phrases in which noun pronoun verb and substantive and all grammar are heaped in a mass together and in which all grammar is confounded and murdered[.]

---

[1] His Majesty's coin.
[2] Quotation marks added.
[3] To share their postchaise.
[4] For more on innkeepers' perceptions of pedestrians, see the introduction to this volume (p. 8).
[5] Brazen (brasin, *OED*).

[f. 14v] **Sunday No*vem*ber 23**
Sat*urday* at 9. Dull and showery all day, dismal and foggy, latterly rain in the Even*in*g and rain all night[.]

The People in Limerick say they never knew such a wet winter as this has been for many years indeed. Although this season is generally wet yet this is incomparable[.] In Ireland the winters are in general more mild than in England and it is very seldom that there are 2 days in the year when the ice is thick enough for skating. Mr Hill says that he has many winters known at Limerick that there has not been snow enough for a Boy to make a snow ball, But their severest winter*s* are in general furnished with snow and not ice[.]

How wonderfully the commerce of this place has increased within these last 6 years. Some 8 (or) 10 years ago many of the Houses about the End of St Patrick St were in the country and at least commanded a fine view of the river[.] Now they are all shut out by stores and new quays have been built the whole way on the river side. The corn stores are the most numerous[.] All the county of Clare[,] Kerry and Limerick bring their corn in boats up to Limerick, where it is dried[,] cleaned and prepared for market and sent off to Dublin or exported. A country boat brings corn [f. 15r] *fr*om Tarbert[1] to Limerick for ¼ a stone[2] and the same for any other distance between thence. Much traffic is now beginning to be carried on with Dublin by means of the Canal w*hic*h is now open and the Locks of the river.[3] Visited Mr Rocks extensive provision stores and saw the Pigs wheeled in and cut up and rubbed with salt packed (loose) and then sent to be pickled.[4] Then tasted and then packed for good and hammered down. The method of trying whether the meat is fresh by the smell or taste is curious and must require a fine judgement. Curious method of saluting a stranger on entering the works. The fellows make a rattling against their cleavers with their knives and hold out their cleavers flat for money. Immense pile of salt in the salt room w*hic*h is dug and sifted like gravel and then sent out in casks and thrown on the dressers[5] wholesale[.] NB (All) This was seen on Monday[.]

Went to the Cathedral.[6] Curious old inscriptions in the vestry explained in Ferrars List of Limerick.[7] Curious old Monum*en*t. Great improvem*en*ts going to be made in Cathedral. Also Organ removed back.

Visited the Fever Hospital[.][8] It is curious that this was the first that was ever set up in the [*sic*] Great Britain ab*ou*t 20 year*s* ago, now they are more common but in [f. 15v] all other places Fever or infectious cases were never admitted. In all the late plagues and pestilences Limerick, when all the country round it has been much infested, has in general

---

[1] Tarbert, Co. Kerry, on the south bank of the River Shannon.
[2] A farthing per stone weight transported.
[3] Grand Canal, commenced in 1757 and completed *c.*1760 (O'Flaherty, *IHTA no. 21 Limerick*, p. 45).
[4] Possibly John Roch's stores on Bridge St (O'Flaherty, *IHTA no. 21 Limerick*, p. 38).
[5] Those who prepare the meat for sale and/or consumption.
[6] St Mary's Cathedral (Church of Ireland), built in the late 12th century (O'Flaherty, *IHTA no. 21 Limerick*, p. 22).
[7] Ferrar, *An History of the City*, pp. 80–81.
[8] St John's Hospital, which functioned as a fever and lock hospital from 1780 (O'Flaherty, *IHTA no. 21 Limerick*, p. 47).

been healthy.[1] The situation [is] a very good one on high ground and it was formerly a gate of the old fortifications and now there are the vestiges of it rem*ain*ing. Curious and noble arched vaults in the house w*hi*ch are laid on hurdles.[2]

The Square is a poor place but it is curious that when first built all the Fashion flocked to that quarter as they do now to Newtown Perry[.] Mr Hill[3] recollects when the fashionable walk for the beaux and belles was along the tops of the old fortified walls and all about ~~the~~ where the fever Hospital is now built[.]

Assembly rooms very poor[.][4]

Ditto Play House[.][5]

[f. 16r] **Monday Nov*ember* 24:**
/ Sunday rain*in*g[,] thick[,] cold [and] foggy the whole of the day and rain all the Eve*ni*ng and night. Place ½ flooded[.]

Most of the things seen today were ment*ione*d in yesterdays journal[.]

// <u>The Militia of this country is on a most</u> trifling footing. In general the whole regiment is but the Electioneering Party of its colonel. The Col*onel*[6] or his brother and [*sic*] is a member of Parliament and as all the Commissions are in his gift they are upon every opportunity bestowed on his friends or given to Farmers sons to make interest or to Young boys[,] sons of Gentlemen of Property[,] to get them f*ro*m their homes to keep them for a short time f*ro*m the stables and kennel of their Father[.] Conseq*uent*ly [there is] no discipline for [the] Col*onel* dare not Enforce it for fear of offending his friends and those who are his friends get to the best quarters and can easier obtain leave of absence for 3 or 4 Months per ann*um*. An offic*er* told me he had 3 times had 4 months leave and that he c*ou*ld get off a long time[,] for a few weeks or so. At Glyn I met 4 Officers of the Kerry [Regiment] who had got leave of A*bsence* under pretence of going to vote at the Election for the County[,] alth*ough* at the time [the election was] starting they knew it was over!! but the general did not. They were boasting how long they sh*ou*ld stay away[.] One was getting away to recruit in Cork but said he sh*ou*ld be at home all [f. 16v] the time[.] Cap*tain* 4̄1̄3̄4̄9̄0̄ was one of 8̄3̄5̄5̄1̄6̄9̄2̄0̄. Besides[,] said they[,] 'Gove*rnmen*t wink at our goings on for they know well enough that the officers have generally farms or homes w*hi*ch they must go every now and then to look after[.]'[7]

At Killarney I saw some of the Carlow Regiment and the officers on parade did not even know wh*at* they were to do in the ranks. A sergeant went up to one and put his sword right for him[.] The officer said he did not know how to give the word of command

---

[1] Lee is imprecise here, but he may be referring to the 'two years of scarcity which followed the rebellion of 1798 ... This century opened, as the former closed, with unusual severity of weather, and great distress among the people, owing to the high price of provisions and two successive but partial Potato Failures, contemporaneous with which appeared Fever, Dysentry, Scarlatina, Ophthalmia, and Influenza' (Wilde, 'Tables of Deaths', p. 159).

[2] The citadel at Limerick, built *c*.1653, was converted to St John's Hospital in 1780 (O'Flaherty, *IHTA no. 21 Limerick*, p. 27).

[3] Probably Launcelot Hill (see p. 242, n. 6).

[4] Built by 1768 on Charlotte's Quay (O'Flaherty, *IHTA no. 21 Limerick*, p. 51).

[5] Probably the theatre on Little Gerald Griffin St, built in 1770 and in ruins by 1840 (O'Flaherty, *IHTA no. 21 Limerick*, p. 51).

[6] Charles Vereker (1768–1842), 2nd Viscount Gort and naval and militia officer, was MP for Limerick in 1802–17. He lost his militia command due to his opposition to the Act of Union (Long, 'Vereker, Charles').

[7] Quotation marks added.

and the Adjutant was the only one who knew any thing and he had no power[.] Many were boys and rough country farmers sons who only got drunk and paraded about the streets, when they wo*ul*d have been doing infinitely more service to their selves[,] King and country and friends if they had been at the plough tail. There are of course exceptions to these[.]

Tuesday, November 25
Mond*ay* raini*ng* all day and stormy. Rain all even*ing* and night[.] Staid indoors all day. Tempest in the night[.]

[f. 17r] Wednesday Nov*em*ber 26
Glimpses of sunshine and then thick heavy weather, showers and thin misty rain all the hours of day. Clear Moonshine night at 11 and till 12[.]

Thursday Nov*em*ber 27
(Limerick) Tolerably clear but showers all the day, and in the Even*ing* misty rain. Dreadful storm in the night and thunder and lightening [*sic*.] Visited the Old Bridge again and went over to the mill[1] wh*ich* is built on the river and w*hich* can only work 6 hours each tide as the water goes down[,] or 12 hours in the 24. For at high water the water is ⅔ over the wheels wh*ich* are under the mill[,] in this case 2 Wheels. Tide rises 12 feet there at spring tides. Visited the House of industry.[2] Which on acc*ount* of its very great poverty is not kept so well as it ought to be[.]

NB. The inside is the ground floor, the outside the upper floor[3]

1. Stewards Room	9 —
2 Kitchen	10 Most respectable women sleep*ing* room
3.3 A long room where women spin etc	11 Lower order D*itt*o room
4. Old men weaving etc	12 Bridewell
5 —	13⎫ Lunatics ⎧Women
6 Dining Hall	14⎭ ⎩Men
7 Room where men old ~~work and~~ sleep	15 Hospital
8 —	

[f. 17v] Every body who can work does something and their labor is sold and part of the profit they have[,] and the rest goes to the fund. If the house was only for the Town it wo*ul*d be suffi*cient* to supp*ort* them excellently but persons *from* all the neighbo*uring* counties are admitted and it is over full. The servants are of the charity and the rooms etc are cleaned and all kept in order by those who can be of service[.] Ab*ou*t 150 persons or more when I saw it[.]

Friday November 28
Thur*sday* [a] bad[,] foggy[,] misty day, rain in showers and in the Even*ing* stormy and windy.

[1] This could be any one of a number of mills operating in Limerick at the time.
[2] Built in 1774, the house of industry served Limerick's destitute poor until the opening of the workhouse in 1842; it was established with funds from the County and City Grand Juries of Limerick following a 1772 Act of the Irish House of Commons to establish poor houses in every county. See Lysaght, 'The House of Industry'.
[3] The following list is a key to Lee's small sketch plan of the House of Industry, not reproduced here.

Started at 6 OClock for Doneraile and passed through a country well cultivated and looking extremely rich[.] Immense prospects [are visible] from the heights. The whole country waved and affording extensive views[,] very rich and the land all paying rents of 2: to 3:10 or 4£ an acre[.] In many parts the land lets at 6 Gs an acre. Passed by many old Castles and got to Doneraile at 2 OClock. Went over with Mr Arundel Hill[1] to Cloghen [Clogheen] his House[,] 2 miles from Doneraile[.]

[f. 18r] **Saturday November 29**
Friday [a] Cold Morning and thick and threatening rain, About ten and 11 some mistly showers[.] but In the Evening some showers[,] wind arose and rain in the Evening[.]

Rode over from Cloghen to Doneraile which is a remarkable fine situation for a town on the side of a gentle₁ hill₂,[2] the river Obeg [Awbeg] which falls into the Blackwater at Castle Town Roche, runs through the lower part of the town, a handsome bridge over it. But Lord Doneraile[3] does not encourage the prosperity of the town and would be glad to get rid of it[,] thinking it no ornament to and too near his desmesne [sic] which is one of the handsomest In Ireland[.] Grounds [are] laid out in the modern style[,] river runs through it[.] Well wooded fine park walled in. Curious trees all feathering down[,] chestnut or limes[,] I forget which. Well stocked [with] Leister [Leicester] sheep and Devonshire cows. Ground all waving up and down. Pleasure grounds near the house [with] 3 fine ponds. Beautiful woods. There are several spots in the neighbourhood from which the town and Demesne look wonderful and the distant hills and mountains admirable[,] particularly one over the road to Fermoy on the n in a close on the side of a road on the hill. Connexion of the demesne by passage under the road to Fermoy – The Doneraile and Goalty [Galtee] Mountains [are] fine bounds to the scene[.]

[f. 18v] Beautiful hill on the Demesne etc to form is most lovely[,] tapering off on all sides elegantly into the plains and finely wooded and all [the] land [is] down in grass and so productive that it keeps an endless quantity of stock. I never saw so much grass in any demesne (in summer) in England as there was seen [here] notwithstanding its being well stocked, but in fact the ground is so productive that they cannot keep it down[.] I never saw a spot better situated for a town than this is and it might be made any thing[.]

Sunday November 30
Saturday rainy and wind blowing it about all day[.] Very uncomfortable to be out. Rain in drifts most of the day and when we were out [it rained] all the time. Never clear from misty rain. Rain all night with wind[.]

Went over to Doneraile and to Church[.][4] The Church is elegantly situated on the opposite slope of the river to the town, surrounded with trees and as neat and pretty and plain as any I have seen. A gallery on the N and W ends. P. Pulpit[.][5] In the Church yard is a monument erected to the memory of a former Steward[,] an Englishman who was brought over by Lord Doneraile's Father to improve his grounds. He left the parish some

---

[1] Of Clogheen, near Buttevant, Co. Cork; Lieutenant Colonel in the South Cork militia (*Burke's Landed Gentry*, 1852, I, p. 574).
[2] Word order reversed here as indicated by Lee's subscript numbering.
[3] Hayes St Leger (1755–1819), 2nd Viscount Doneraile (*Burke's Landed Gentry*, 1852, I, p. 314).
[4] Doneraile Church of Ireland, first built in 1633 (Gaughan, *Doneraile*, p. 23).
[5] P. refers to the location of the pulpit in a small sketch plan in the page margin, not reproduced here.

money and [f. 19r] they have erected it to his mem*o*ry[.] It has a curious brick cover erected to it[.] Charming domain. So very elegantly paved and wooded. In one of the woods [is] a petrifying spring w*hi*ch makes a great noise there[.] The people are astonished at it[.][1]

D*o*neraile is finely seated on the side of a sloping hill, at the foot of w*hi*ch under an Elegant Bridge runs the Obeg into the demesne w*hi*ch bounds the town on the E. The street is good. Situation admirably adapted for a great Market town. Mail to Limerick runs thro*ugh* every other day and the other *fr*om Cork [runs on] the intermediate ones. The Houses are all very bad[,] slovenly [and] dirty, thatched and in fact far *fr*om giving it the encouragement w*hi*ch wo*ul*d make it a city[.] Lord D*o*neraile wishes it to sink to decay[,] thinking it an eyesore to his demesne. [It is] A Pity that his interest is not consulted better[.] There is a Chapel at the S End of the town in a fine grove of trees.

D*o*neraile is the best wooded and most elegant place for an inland Town I have [*breaks off*]

[f. 19v] Monday 1 [December]. 1806

Day so bad that we c*oul*d hardly get over *fr*om Cloghen to D*o*neraile witho*ut* being wet thro*ugh*. Rained all day. Could only get out for ½ hour[.] Rain all Even*ing* and night. Rained at 8 on going home and all night.

Only rode over to Doneraile. Dined yesterday with Mr Hill*'s* Father in Don*e*raile[.] Returned home to dejuner [*déjeuner*, luncheon].

Dec*em*ber 2 Tuesday[.]

Day raining but a clear interval now and then, but in the afternoon [the] rain [was] very bad[.] Wind arose to a hurricane and contin*ue*d howling all night. ~~Their~~ I seldom knew it so high, immense rough storms of hail early in Tues*day* Morn*ing* and violent ab*out* 8. Many trees blown up in the demesne. Took a ride in the mid*dl*e of the day out to the West by the 2 Pot House [Twopothouse] and saw several pretty boxes scattered about the country. Went to Buttevant[,] one of the family seats of the old Family of the Berrys.[2] There is the Shell of the old castle still remaining.[3] Round Building[.] This estate with 2 others [were] all bought by Mr Anderson[4] who is now going to let it as the leases are out and to make a new town w*hi*ch will probably ruin Doneraile as it is on the true high road to Limerick but the Mail goes thro*ugh* D*o*neraile. ~~for~~ Swap the town[.]

[f. 20r] Mr A*n*derson has fitted up the rooms in the ruin and made several floors and roofed it in. Noble view *fr*om the top of it. Not far off is the celebrated abbey of Buttevant w*hi*ch is in high preservation.[5] Curious walls of bones heaped up, a few bushes growing out among them. Many curious pieces of stone workmanship and very old Irish inscriptions in several places. Some old tombs of the Barry family[,] one or 2 above 200 Y*ea*rs old, but the place is in utter decay and will wear away in time for it wo*ul*d be considered a sin to touch a sod by the people[.] Curious vaults all under the abbey w*hi*ch

---

[1] Croaghnacree chalybeate spring (Smith, *Cork*, II, p. 272).

[2] In *c*.1177 Philip de Barry was granted land in north Cork, including the manor at Buttevant (Cotter, 'Archaeological and Environmental Heritage', p. i).

[3] Tower house and bawn, Castlelands, Co. Cork, built on site of earlier castle in the late 16th century (Power, et al., *Archaeological Inventory of County Cork*, IV: *North Cork*, pt 2, p. 527).

[4] See p. 170, n. 5.

[5] The 12th-century Franciscan friary (Gwynn and Hadcock, *Medieval Religious Houses*, p. 243).

you may get in [to] from the East ~~side~~ (end) of the Abby. The river [Awbeg] runs close to this end. The whole abbey is built on ~~very~~ ground[(1)] sloping[(2)] down to the river.[1] In these vaults it is said the conspiracies of the Rebels were carried on. This place was the very soul of rebellion[.] Its phosphoric flames burst (from here) and were here in great fury. The common people cannot bear the idea that the old place and estates should part from the old family and be bought by a foreigner as Anderson is thought to be. Although he will make its fortune and improve its value. On the road near the turnpike begins the famous Ballybeg glin which runs for many miles and is the [f. 20v] admiration of all fox hunters as a famous reservoir for them, it is nothing in a picturesque point of view. Several very fine points of ground about here for gentlemens houses and there are several scattered about. The clergyman of Buttevant was the only loyal man in it and the only protestant in the rebellion but he was not molested[,] being a quiet peaceable man and not disturbing or interfering with any magistrate's business[.] Besides he was married to a Catholic[.]

It is said that Mr Anderson in bying [sic] the 3 Estates of Lord Barrymore and selling 2 cleared Buttevant by the Bargain.[2] The Curious old vault in the Castle which was the roof probably to the kitchen if one may judge by the fire place in it, is thrown on hurdles as all the arched buildings have been. Returned to Clogheen after riding a circuit of about 9 Miles. Saw Mr Bensons fox hounds running merrily across the country near Buttivant[.]

[f. 21r] **Wednesday December 3.**
Morning wet and rainy. Wind boisterous[.] Rode out in the rain. Wind high and a hurricane at night. Thunder in the night, and raining all the night.

After a most violent night it was [a] tolerably fine morning[.] Went to *Doneraile* from thence all through the demesne and to the East of the County[,] a most beautiful ride, saw a great deal of very excellent land which has been lately reclaimed from the heath and which is in a most excellent train of cultivation. Method of its cultivation. F.P1.[3]

Rode along the Sides of the Obeg all the way down to Castletown Roche and there are some views which would make most exquisite drawings and which I shall never forget, particularly about Castle *Town Roche*. The winding river[,] the high cliffs[,] the bridge[,] the Mill [and] the Old Castle[4] are too finely contrasted to be soon forgotten[.] The Castle itself is a curiosity[.] Many of the works remain. Gardens curious[.] It is situated on a high rock and is 2 sides surrounded by the Obeg which winds round it at the Base of the rock and a little below the castle it makes another sudden wind[.] Rock nearly ⊥^{r} in some places. The tower is very perfect. There is a very curious passage down 105 or 107 steps cut through the rock in some places and only covered in on others. It winds down in all twisting directions and the only light is conveyed in this one hole at the end of each bend, you go down this [f. 21v] long tedious passage in the dark to the bottom where is a well which was the supply of the castle in former times when it was a fortress and even now a

---

[1] Word order reversed here, as indicated by Lee's superscript numbering.

[2] Lee may mean that Anderson cleared the cost of buying Buttevant lands by selling two of his own estates. Alternatively, this may be an obtuse reference to Anderson's re-routing of the Main Street of the town, which involved housing clearances (White, *Historical and Topographical Notes*, p. 364).

[3] The meaning of this abbreviation is unclear, but it may refer in some way to one of Lee's sketchbooks. A similar abbreviation appears at the end of the next paragraph.

[4] Castlewidenham tower house and bawn, Castletownroche, Co. Cork; forfeited by the Roches after the Cromwellian wars (Power, et al., *Archaeological Inventory of County Cork*, IV: North Cork, pt 2, pp. 530–31).

great deal of water is ~~drawn~~ taken up by it. A tiresome job to go down and up. Returned to *Doneraile* and in the rain for the whole way, But stopped to look over Mr Hills farm. Cottages very neat. F.P.3.

The ride today was thro*ugh* as rich a country as the King has in his dominions[.] Dined with Mr — Hill[1] in *Doneraile* and slept at the Old Gentlemans[.]

Thursday Dec*embe*r 4
Day clear at 9 and untill 2 fine then began to darken and to promise rain wh*ich* came on about 3 drisly [drizzly] and continued untill 12 OClock at night at least[.]

Started this morning at 8 OClock on Mr A*rund*el Hills horse to Mallow, got there[,] breakfasted and hired a hack to ride to Mill Street and went thro*ugh* as fine a country as I could have imagined[.] The vale all up is agreeably fine and the river is ~~wonderf~~ extremely ornamental. The first 8 Miles is thro*ugh* a very rich cultivated country[,] the latter 8 are not so good and the Mountains begin wh*ich* continue all the way to Millstreet, the country is more open. Mill S*treet* is a poor[,] dirty [f. 22r] nasty place[,] not a good house or building in it, happy is the man who gets out of it the quickest[.] Not being able to get a hack here[,] walked on 15 Miles to Killarney and got there about seven. The road is fortunately most strait and impossible for a person to miss but my walking was thro*ugh* the dark for the three last hours, and it was drisly and foggy besides, the 6 Mile Bridge was broken down and fortunately 2 Gent*lemen* on horses came riding up at it who carried me behind one of them over[,] otherwise I must have walked thro*ugh*. It was too dark to see the country about for I co*ul*d not see the appearance of the road 20 Yds before me, road dull[,] a wild bog and rough M*ountai*n all the way. A good days journey f*ro*m the time of the Glen 6 + 17 + 15 = 38 Miles Irish[.]

Friday December 5.
Fine clear morning. Continued clear all day. At 4 it began to be drisly and rained slightly and was mistly the whole of the Even*ing*[.]

Staid in doors and wrote letters. Rather fagged[.]

Saturday December 6
Day tolerably clear in the morning. Rain in heavy showers and then sunshine and D*itt*o D*itt*o all day. Rain in the Even*ing*.

Did nothing particular but write.

[f. 22v] Sunday Dec*embe*r 7
Day sunshine and heavy showers as usual interspersed[.]

Monday Dec*embe*r 8
Clear from 9 to 12. Then some heavy showers and hard rain[.] Cleared up but was a doubtful[,] foul[,] dirty day. Wind high. A little frost in the morning[.]

Met Cap*tai*n Ferris[2] who is appointed over the Fencibles at Tralee //

---

[1] Arundel Hill; see p. 248, n. 1.
[2] Captain William Ferris RN (1783–1822) of Battle, East Sussex, appointed to the sea-fencibles at Tralee in 1804–9 (*The Gentleman's Magazine*, June 1822, pp. 567–9).

Tuesday December 9
Showery[,] nasty day[.] Clear at 12, and fine for a couple of hours, frost in the morning[.]

Set out at 8 in a post Chaise for Millstreet. The morning was clear and sunshine and never did Killarney look to such perfection. The whole chain of mountains from the Paps to Mangerton[,] Glenaa and even to Milltown were in [a] majestic state this morning and their tops as clear as day. This is certainly the most enchanting entrance to Killarney for coming from Millstreet across a dreary strait road with a ridge of Mountain on [f. 23r] one side, upon coming within a few miles of Killarney the contrast is enough of itself to please a dunce in picturesque and sublime scenery. If I had entered this way I should certainly have admired it 10 times more than I do for the first impressions would have then been in its favour which mine were not. The frosty coldness of the air and the sunshine gave the scenery a most delicious tint and never shall I forget the effect which this scenery has made on my mind. Got to Millstreet. Breakfasted and started at 2 for the 10 Mile House across a most diabolical mountainous road and walked a great deal of the way up the steep parts[.] The whole 5 or 6 miles from Millstreet is steep ascent and a little sudden descents but from thence it is gradual descent but over horrible road. We were fortunate to get safe to the 10 Mile House at 8 OClock without breaking any of our bones[.]

Wednesday December 10
Morning frosty[,] Clear. Sunshine bright, but masses of fine cloud. Clear till mid day when it began to rain and was showery or drisly all the day and Evening. Wind high[.] Walked over Mr Gibbs Demesne[1] which is considered as a very fine one but is nothing but a mere common Gentleman's House with a few trees about it, but as there are very [f. 23v] few trees in general, they make this a wonder and in fact they are the first you meet with in coming from Killarney.

Thursday December 11
Rainy[,] bad[,] thick day and foggy. Drisly showers[,] bad day went out even in the rain. Showers heavy at nightfall[.] Thunder in the [*breaks off*]

Went out a shooting[.] Day tolerably clear but frequent showers in the day[.] Saw a great quantity of snipes[.]

Friday December 12
Morning not very fowl [*sic*], showers very frequent and cold wind. Rain all the Evening. Thunder rolling in the midday[.]

Started at 8 and went across the Country by Dripsey to Mr Hawks[2] by crossing a Bridge over the river Lee which is a fine ornament to the country. Staid and dined with him. Garrick broke down and obliged to get a horse to ride[.][3]

Saturday December 13.
Morning Showery at 7. Clear at 8 and fine till ½ past 9[,] then it began to rain and continued so all the day. Poured very hard in the evening and all the night[.]

---

[1] At Derry, Co. Cork (LED).
[2] See SJC, MS U.30 (3), p. 188, n. 4.
[3] Lee seems to mean that his companion, Garrick, was too tired to walk. Garrick is not identified. He is mentioned again on 13, 16 and 23 Dec. 1806, and on 12 Jan. 1807.

[f. 24r] Started after Breakfast and walked to the Ovens and just went in to shew their nature to Garrick[.] From thence we walked on to Cork and kept on the side where the powder mills are and sh*oul*d never recommend any one to go on this side of the river[.] It was horribly bad. Great want of a foot path[.] Got in about four and dined at a Beefsteak house[,] the Hole in the Wall[.]

Took Lodgings in the Grand Parade at a hatters,[1] just opposite the end of Georges Street [Oliver Plunkett St.]

Sunday Dec*embe*r 14:
Morning clear, but we had not been long out when very severe storms came on and then clear again and sunshine and thus it contin*ue*d all the day, storm every ½ hour at most. Wind too high to allow the benefit of an umbrella.

Did not stir out far. Walked to Mr Gaards.[2] Not at home. Dined at Mr Fitzpatricks[,] the music seller S Mall[,] and heard some music on the piano and Violins[.] Very pleasant even*ing*[.]

Monday Dec*embe*r 15.
Day showery but fine on the whole, weather warm[.] Got a fiddle f*ro*m Fitzpatricks. Domesticated[3] myself[.]

[f. 24v] **Tuesday Dec*embe*r 16**
Day dark and foggy. Thin sheets of rain, but not very wet. Dull day. Showers in the Even*ing*[.]

Staid in Doors all day. Began to practice singing with Garrick, Mr Bowden[4] coming every day at 9 to 11[.] Terms 8 lessons for a Guinea[.]

Wednesday Dec*embe*r 17
Day clear in the morning and continued so till noon, then the preparations being made, a coat of thick Clouds being put on and the showers being prepared it rained from 5 till the Even*ing* and was rain*ing* this Morn*ing* at 7 OClock and Weather excessively mild. I have frequently complained of being too rain [*sic*]

Walked merely about the town. Writing all day and settling accounts[.]

Thursday Dec*embe*r 18
Day raining and thick and foggy and continued so the whole day[.] No possibility of keeping dry if out. Weather very warm indeed. Close and misty and foggy[.]

Domesticated. At ten in Even*ing* went with Garde to the Catch and Glee Club, Supper of oysters[,] Porter[,] fowls etc very plain, and after supper nothing but punch allowed[.] Go [as] soon as supper [is] over[.] Grace was the Canon of *Non nobis Domini*.[5]

---

[1] Mr Nugent's, as indicated in SJC, MS U.30 (7), p. 319.

[2] Either Joseph Garde (see p. 220, n. 2) or John Garde (d. 1832) of Ballinacurra (Bickersteth, 'Query', facing p. 200).

[3] 'To make to be or to feel "at home"; to familiarize' (*OED*).

[4] John Bowden (d. 1829), composer, violinist and teacher; cellist at the Theatre Royal, Crow St, Dublin; left Dublin for Cork in 1806 (Hogan, *Anglo-Irish Music*, pp. 208–9).

[5] *Non nobis Domine*, composed by W. Bird in 1590.

Unfortunately all the best voices were absent and heard nothing but catches and Glees of 3 voices but they were very good and well sung. Mr Galespi[1] a Bonvoice a teacher of the piano in Cork [has] an excellent voice. Got home at one very much [f. 25r] delighted with the evening[.]

Friday [December 19]
Rainy all day[.]
  Domesticated[.]

Saturday December 20
Tolerably clear but not fine till 12 then begun raining a little and continued increasing and in the even*in*g[.] A most violent tremendous continuation of hail like rain all night and into the morn*in*g[.] Also Called and had a visit to $\overline{4}\overline{1}\overline{8}\overline{2}\overline{6}\overline{6}\overline{3}\overline{2}$ $\overline{2}\overline{3}$ $\overline{4}\overline{1}\overline{1}\overline{1}\overline{6}\overline{3}\overline{0}$[.]

Sunday December 21
Rain all day. Foggy all the morning, dirty[,] filthy and foul at twelve OClock[.] Went to the nunnery Chapel,[2] to hear High Mass[.] Upon looking around, the Altar was beautifully decorated, the Chapel hung with pictures of Our Saviour and the Virgin etc etc.

On one side[,] I believe West[,] was a pulpit. On the other and the whole breadth of the part of the chapel in rails, a grate with a curtain drawn over the lower part of it and within this part of the chapel I supposed the nuns to be who were excluded from sight. By judging *fr*om the roof *whi*ch c*ou*ld be seen over the curtain, the room was large. The priest came in from the door by [the] altar and kneeling down before [f. 25v] it[,] judge of my surprise to hear an organ strike up within the grating and all the female voices sung the service. The Effect of so many female voices struck me with astonishment and rapture and I never felt such affecting sensations before from music in my life. Its unexpected appearance on the organs was a most affecting thing and $\overline{4}\overline{2}\overline{5}\overline{3}\overline{1}\overline{6}$ $\overline{3}\overline{4}$ $\overline{5}\overline{5}\overline{1}\overline{6}$ $\overline{9}\overline{2}\overline{1}\overline{6}\overline{5}\overline{0}$ $\overline{7}\overline{5}\overline{6}\overline{6}\overline{3}\overline{3}\overline{9}\overline{2}$ $\overline{3}\overline{9}\overline{3}\overline{4}$ $\overline{3}\overline{2}\overline{1}\overline{6}\overline{6}$[.]

The singing was very pathetic[,][3] solemn and affecting. In the middle of the service the Curtain was withdrawn for a short time and I c*ou*ld see a great part of the place within the cage like separation. But not the organ. Saw some black veiled figures. The Mass was over in ¾ hour and together with the burning of the incense the whole is a service *whi*ch strikes the ~~eyes ears and~~ senses very forcibly. It is a very fine striking service[.]

Dined with Mr Garde at Mrs $\overline{4}\overline{1}y\overline{1}\overline{6}\overline{2}\overline{1}\overline{6}$ and spent a most pleasant and agreeable evening. *Sat verbum sapienti*[.][4]

[f. 26r] Monday December 22.
Morning Foggy[,] misty, clearer at 12[.] Began raining at 5 and continued so all the Even*in*g and night. Rained at 1 OClock this morn*in*g and also at 7[.]

---

[1] William Gillespie (*fl.* 1806–20), piano teacher and, later, concert pianist based in Cork (Hogan, *Anglo-Irish Music*, p. 210).

[2] Possibly the South Presentation convent, at the junction of Douglas St and Evergreen St (Draft of work in progress from Ní Laoi, 'Cork'). Lee made a small sketch plan of the chapel at the bottom of the page, not reproduced here.

[3] Moving, stirring (*OED*).

[4] *Verbum sat sapienti* (*est*), 'a word to the wise is enough'.

Mr Daly the Bookseller[1] happ*eni*ng accidentally to say that he knew a grocer who understood Irish very well and who read[,] wrote and had a many Irish Books[,] called on him and f*ou*nd him to be a most excellent Scholar, acquainted with all the Irish History[,] Knew French and Latin and all his knowledge he picked up at his leisure hours, in his shop. He has got some most ancient MS. Irish and a collection of Irish Books. Introd*uce*d me to a schoolmaster Mr John Mullen who is going to write out for me some Irish MS. A very clever fellow[,] he composes Irish and does not understand Latin. Saw some of his compositions, and [they are] very good. He lives in a nasty mud cabin ~~with a~~ and his school table runs all along the middle. Dark and dingy and quite in a nasty stinking end of the Town. Agreed to go up to him and take a few lessons in Irish writing of him. The Grocer Mr OFlyn.[2] Grocer lives [at] Nº 2 Shandon St and has an immense deal of Business although his (little) shop is in a nasty[,] [f. 26v] small[,] close[,] confined place. I was obliged to stand by a treacle barrel for ¾ hour seeing 12 or 16 people coming (and going) constantly before he c*oul*d get away to conduct me to the School Master and his shop had been so all the day and for many days. 'You see Sir I have not much time to spare for my reading[,] I wish I had but we must attend to Business first as our Grand object[.]'

Dr Crea[,] Miss Man[3] 26192 4366 419 Mr 1157263. Mr Guard and Dr Mans[4] nephew[.]

Tuesday. Dec*ember* 23 Sund*ay*.
Morning clear at 9 and till 12[,] then little thin rain and drisly till noon and Eveni*ng*. D*itt*o at 8. Rain till 10 or 11. Clear at One[,] foggy at 7 and D*itt*o 8 and 9[.]

Called on and set the school m*aste*r to work in copying some Irish poems of — which it is said form the groundwork of McPhersons works.[5] Agreed to go and be a scholar and to learn Irish. Terms a Guinea a Quarter. In the Eveni*ng* went with Garrick and Mr Bowman[6] to the Instrumental Music Club. Heard some very good music[.] Great many good performers[.] Mr Scott the president plays the flute admirably fine bold style, noble execution. Mr Bowman first fiddle. 1 and 8 Concerto of Corillin[7] were played admirably. Flute concerto.

---

[1] Possibly Eugene Daly, 'bookseller and stationer' on Paul St in 1787 (Lucas, 'The Cork Directory', p. 141).

[2] Dennis Flinn or Flynn, grocer on Shandon St (West, *A Directory*, p. 110). Lee obtained at least two Gaelic manuscripts from Flynn: 'Keen on Maurice Fitzgerald, Knight of Kerry' and 'Keen on John Fitzgerald, Esq. Son of the Knight of Glin'. These were published in English translation in Croker, *The Keen of the South of Ireland*, pp. 12–35, 43–52. The following note, from Lee to Croker, was published alongside the 'Keen on John Fitzgerald': 'John Lee, Colworth. These poems were written for me from old MSS. during the winter of 1806 and 1807, at Cork, by the favor and assistance of Mr. Flyn, a learned grocer of that town, who introduced me to an old schoolmaster well skilled in ancient Irish history and mythology' (p. 43).

[3] Probably a daughter of Dr Mann (see next note).

[4] Probably Dr Anthony Mann on George's Quay (West, *A Directory*, p. 96).

[5] James Macpherson (1736–96), Scottish author of: *Fragments of Ancient Poetry Collected in the Highlands of Scotland* (1760), *Fingal, an Ancient Epic Poem composed by Ossian, the Son of Fingal, Translated from the Gaelic Language* (1761/2), *Temora* (1763) and *The Works of Ossian* (1765). These were hugely popular and internationally influential, but their authenticity remains in question. See Curley, *Samuel Johnson*.

[6] Lee may mean the cellist John Bowden (see p. 253, n. 4).

[7] Turlough Carolan (Toirdhealbhach Ó Cearbhalláin) (1670–1738), Irish harper and composer (White, 'Carolan, Turlough').

[f. 27r] Swindhels[1] 4 Overture and several others[,] 3 or 4 Violins[,] 2 Flutes. 2 Violincello players[,] 2 Base horns etc etc. Began at 8 and Ended ½ pa*s*t 10. Then a cold supper of Oysters and <u>Boiled fowls</u>. The Society is the oldest in Ireland has been in existence more than 40 Ye*a*rs without intermission. Members pay 1:6 Each night for expenses whether there or no. In all there are about 50 Members[.]

Wednesday Dece*mbe*r 24

Thick morning, dull in the day[,] rain in the Eveni*n*g as usual[.] In the morning at ½ 8 went up to the School M*a*ste*r* accordi*n*g to agreement and when sat down and ready to begin, says the Old Boy, it is better that we (do not) begin today for the 2 next days are both Holidays!!! (The very reason I wished for a long lesson[.]) This is the common plan with Irishmen[,] they never tell you wh*a*t their plans or wishes or wills are untill they are obliged and flatter or deceive you up to the very moment.

Had a Call from Mr Lapp.[2]

Dear Ally Croaker[3] is an Irish Tune. D*itt*o Shepherds I have Lost my Love[,][4] D*itt*o The Soldiers Say. D*itt*o Langolee[.][5]

[f. 27v] Thursday Dece*mbe*r 25

Wet[,] rainy day[.]

Dined at Mr Fitzpatricks.[6] Went to the Convent again and heard the whole of the High Mass. All the boarders dressed very elegantly[,] Van Dyke Clokes[7] and pretty white caps close to the head and poking in front like 4166̄14̄4̄4̄0̄, Exactly the same ceremony as the last[.]

Friday Dece*mbe*r 26

Christmas day very thick[,] foggy, and disagreeable. Rain in the morning at 8[,] 9 and 10 then clearer[.]

Went to dine out at Dr Bennets[.][8]

4366 4̄17̄166̄1̄ 1̄29̄92̄3̄ 24̄9̄47̄19̄ 41̄1̄163̄0̄.26 1̄9̄2 336 1̄64̄33̄26 12̄9̄92̄3, 21̄66318̄

Saturday Dece*mbe*r 27

This day passed without rain!! but it was thick. All the Evenings are most beautiful moon light nights. No frost symptoms whatever[.]

When going up this morni*n*g to Mr Mullins the schoolmaster, to begin a regular lesson he was out and gone to prayers, devilish provoking, had to walk back again. He had not begun the poems of Lister and St Patrick yet[.]

---

[1] Friedrich Schwindl (1737–86), Dutch composer (Wellesz and Sternfeld, *New Oxford History of Music*, p. 429).

[2] See SJC, MS U.30 (4), 17 Oct. 1806 (p. 206).

[3] 'Ally Croker', composed in 1725 by Lawrence Grogan (1701–?30), was popular into the 19th century (O'Neill, *Irish Minstrels*, p. 42).

[4] A popular air, referred to as both Irish and Scottish in contemporary compilations.

[5] Possibly George Thomson's 'New Langloee', published in 1775 (White, *Music and the Irish Literary Imagination*, p. 74).

[6] Probably the music seller with whom Lee dined on 14 Dec. (see p. 253).

[7] This probably means that the cloak had been furnished with 'vandykes or deep-cut points, after the manner represented in Van Dyck's paintings; to cut or shape with deep angular indentations' (*OED*).

[8] Possibly William Bennet, bishop of Cloyne and antiquary (Courtney, 'Bennet, William (1746–1820)').

[f. 28r] He asked me if I *could* lend him a bit of money as <u>he was out</u> of it and he wanted a bit to do him good[.] Gave a 10ᵈ bit and it was sent out to buy wiskey immediately!!!

Sunday December 28
Rain[,] foggy and miserable day[.]

Went to see Mr Calverts[1] drawings and sketches, of w*hich* he has many 100dreds, mostly pencil and in chalk, some put into water colors. He never uses but 3 colors[,] indigo[,] red and raw sienna – *from* w*hich* he makes everything he wants. Has been drawing all over Scotland and Ireland. Lodges at Purcels Booksellers[,] end of Fishamble Lane [Liberty St.]

It is singular that all the soldiers who come or go across the Drawbridge in Cork pay a ½ each time of going or coming *from* the Barracks and so does every body, but one *would* think that they ought to be excused, in general[.] Probably they are not supposed to have any business in the town and so they must pay like com*mon* men if they do want to go down. If soldiers are on guard or [f. 28v] are sent on orders by the others, then they must bring a ticket with them w*hich* excuses them. Drank Tea with Mr Flyn and supped and played at Chess. Curious conversation after supper and elucidation of his opinions —

Monday December 29
Day clear in morning, But sudden rain at 2 OClock w*hich* continued all the Eve*ni*ng to twelve at night and later[.]

Dined at the Bush Tavern, Oysters 2S a dozen!!! Bill for 6 Dozen 12[S]. Veal cutlets 4:4 and Porter 17S:5!!! A complete take in[.]

Writing and reading all day[.]

Tuesday December 30[2]
Day as usual[,] abominably thick and foggy and although the sun shone you *could* not see around. Rain in the Eve*ni*ng[.]

Reading and writing. Dined at Miss F—. Mds[3] and 2 Miss Fawlkeners.[4] Delightful Music on (Harp and Piano)[.]

Wednesday 31 [December]
Day D*itto* – D*itto* –[5]

Saw all the drawings of Mr Grogan[6] the master in this town. Sketches very good and also his fancy drawings[.]

---

[1] Frederick Calvert (*fl.* 1807–30), landscape painter at Cork in the early 19th century (Strickland, *A Dictionary of Irish Artists*, I, p. 150).

[2] Lee's sketchbook indicates that he took a walk that day; see SJC, MS U.30 (7), ff. 37v–38r, 39r (p. 323), not reproduced.

[3] Mesdames, i.e., more than one Mrs Falkiner.

[4] Possibly members of the Falkiner family of Cork bankers and landowners (LED).

[5] Meaning that the weather on Tuesday was the same as it had been on Monday.

[6] Probably Nathaniel Grogan (*c.*1740–1807), Cork-born painter (Minch, 'Grogan, Nathaniel'). His sons Nathaniel and Joseph were known for making copies of their father's work and had a studio on Mardyke St, Cork in 1810 (West, *A Directory*, p. 112).

[f. 29r] Thursday January 1: 1807

Moderately dry but thick fog all day. Sunshine but rain in thin coats now and then[.]

Went as usual to Mr Mullan the writing Master in the morning and after to Mr Field the reading master in Irish. Dined with Mr Guard, Dr Bennet and Mr B—[,] Dr Mann, a Mr McGrath, Mr Newsham, Mr Ned Bennet who sung a medley etc etc[.] In the Evening at 10 went to the Catch and Glee Club, present about 22 Members and after supper heard a great n° of very fine catches and Glees sung by 4[,] 5 or 6 voices[,] or 7 or 8[.] Finest harmony I ever saw. Where the Bee Sucks,[1] [***] Club etc "Non nobis domine", "Poculum, quam bonum in visceribus meis"[,][2] Peace to the souls of the heroes[3] etc etc. Came away at ½ past one.

Friday January 2: 1807

Very fine day[,] no rain for a wonder, but thick mists flying about[.] In the Evening went to the theatre to see the *Cure for the Heart Ache*[4] performed by the Gentlemen of the Apollo Society,[5] it went off very well. The young Rapid. Old Vortex which was by a Dr of the — Regiment, and old Rapid were the only good Characters[.]

[f. 29v] The farce was *The Upholsterer*[6] in which the best characters were its only support[.] Tolken the Jeweller on the Grand Parade did young Rapid. The performance was for establishing a fund, to enable them to pursue their charitable purposes. The old Vortex was the only one of the set who had got his part correct[,] the rest were not often out but altered it materially[.] The Irish in General have a wonderful passion for theatricals. There is (to be) or has been a play performed for charitable purposes (as I was yesterday told) at Tralee by the Gentry of this neighbourhood. Lady Glendore[,][7] Mrs Verelst and Mrs Sanders were to perform.

The females on the Cork stage were hired for the purpose and a Mrs Johnson was the only one that was Genteel to say the best of her. She had a good velvet spencer[8] on and Miss Vortex *en deshabille* and a very elegant vandyke cloak as the same in full dress[.]

Saturday January 3 1807

As usual. Foggy[.]

In the Evening spent a most pleasant evening at Dr Manns. Galespi the Piano forte Player. Bowden. A Mr St Leger a Gent ~~plays~~ Singer and a Mr [f. 30r] Smith a violin performer and a Mr Morton a connoisseur. We had a great many quartets most excellently performed. Some concertos on the Piano with a Violin and Violincello by Miss Mann, who plays most elegantly. The best performance for a Lady I ever heard. Miss Mann and

---

[1] 'Where the Bee Sucks' is a song from Shakespeare's *The Tempest*, adapted for performance and published by composers like Thomas Arne (1710–78) in the late 18th and early 19th centuries.

[2] Lee may mean '*Poculum Elevatum*', a glee for 5 voices by Thomas Arne (Fryer, *The Poetry of Various Glees*, p. 89).

[3] A glee for 3 voices by John Wall Callcott (1766–1821) (Fryer, *The Poetry of Various Glees*, p. 63).

[4] Thomas Morton, *A Cure for the Heart-Ache, a Comedy, in Five Acts*, Cork, 1797.

[5] The Apollo Club or Society had a theatre on Academy St in the 19th century (Day, 'Art Catalogue', p. 309).

[6] Arthur Murphy, *The Upholsterer*, Glasgow, 1758.

[7] Diana Sackville (1756–1814), daughter of George, 1st Viscount Sackville, and wife of John Crosbie (1753–1815) (see p. 234, n. 3).

[8] 'A kind of close-fitting jacket or bodice commonly worn by women and children early in the 19th century' (*OED*).

Galespi played some of Von Eches concertos together addmirably [*sic*]. Altogether with singing, music and drinking punch we did not break up till ½ past two. Dr Man*n* imitated the west country fellows and danced a most admirable set of Irish jigs[.]

Sunday 4: January
Fine clear sunshine day[.]

Monday 5 Jan*uary*
As in general. No rain[.]
 I forget how Monday passed (Jan*uary* 10)[1]

Tuesday Jan*uary* 6
Spent the Eve*ni*ng most delightfully and musically with 3̄3̄2̄\. 4̄1̄7̄2̄6̄6̄3̄2̄ 7̄1̄6̄3̄0̄[.]

[f. 30v] **Wednesday January 7 /**
Finer than usual, but nothing to Boast of[.]
 Breakfasted with Garde over Mr (Chapels) stores nothing beyond the common run of such places / One man who weighs the pieces of beef etc[,] takes them and throws them on a block according to the weight of the whole, another man immediately chops it up into pieces (each I believe weighing 6lbs apiece) with astonishing correctness[.]
 From there went to Mr Wises distillery[2] w*hi*ch is the largest I ever saw[.] He has one room of an amazing fine size and length and seven large vessels all kept as neat and elegant as possible[.] Each is 19 yds Diam*ete*r and 20 [yds] High and capable of containing 2000 Gall*on*s each[.] There were about 5000 G*a*ll*on*s of spirits in them when we were there. They can all be regulated any one stopped or all filled equally at pleasure. The very cocks cost above 20 and 30 £ each. 4 Men are kept constantly filling up the fires with coal and burying it. They pay £2000 a Week Duty regularly and work or not ~~and as much~~[.] Their large tubs whence the liquor and malt etc are put is astonishing size. I counted 14 men and there are more probably [f. 31r] at diff*eren*t times who are stirring it about. They had long immense sticks as rep*resente*d here [*by a rough sketch in page margin.*]

Thursday Jan*ua*ry 8
Sallied on to Westrop and saw his fine collection of prints, drawings[,] I mean saw a few of them. He has got one very fine picture by Guerchino[3] of a holy family exquisitely done, and bought it in London for 14Gs at an auction. He has four of the Shakespeare pictures f*ro*m w*hi*ch the prints were taken,[4] and a very pretty oil colored painting of a cottage and 2 fine trees in front by Morland[.]

Friday Jan*ua*ry 9 /
Fine day[.]
 Spent the Eve*ni*ng 1̄3̄ 4̄1̄7̄2̄6̄6̄

---

[1] Lee indicates that he made this note later, on 10 Jan.
[2] On North Mall (West, *A Directory*, p. 136).
[3] See p. 124, n. 6.
[4] See p. 214, n. 2.

259

Saturday January 10 /
Fine day[.]
Dined at 13 4 17 26 6 and went in the Eve*ni*ng to Dr Mans where there was a charming concert, Trios, Quartetts [*sic*], Duett [*sic*] on Piano, Duets on Piano [f. 31v] accomp*any*ing. A Glee of 3 Voices. Concerto on Piano (by Galespi), D*itt*o Violin by Bowden, and aplenty of all the most celebrated glees and a few catches. From 9 to 12 contin*u*ed there a large party of Ladies and Gents to partake of it[.]

Bowden ran for a wager from the Playhouse in Georges Street round the Lock and back again in 22 Minutes[,] 3 Miles and had 2 tumbles[,] one in a ditch and the other over a car and lost his hat. He has engaged to do it again in 18 minutes as a man did a short time ago[.][1]

Sunday January 10[2] **/**
Fine day[.]
Went over to the Ten Mile H*ouse* to meet Coffy.[3] He was not there[.] Saw Mr Lapps and Counsellor Spread. Set out at ½ past 7 and got there in 3½ hours!!! Returned by Blarney. Dined with Mr Garde and drank tea out[.]

Monday January 11[4] **/**
Morning at 7 as thick and cold a fog as possible, cleared up and was clear and fine at 10 and to 2 and then came on a thick dreadful fog again[.]
Nothing particular[.]

[f. 32r] **Tuesday January 12**[5]**/**
Very fine day[.]
Walked out with Garrick[,] Guarde and McCarty[6] to see Mr Penroses house and grounds w*hic*h are most elegantly sit*uat*ed 2 Miles below Cork[.][7] Very fine picture Gallery[.] Fine picture of Schedoni by himself[8] and very beautiful [Lace?] girl by Morillio[9] and a fine highly finished head by Raphael.[10] A Good Dutch group of a man probing anothers wound and a fine figure leaning over his shoulder. A fine picture by — of a Band of Banditti and Spanish soldiers engaged in a skirmish.[11] Leading f*ro*m the Gallery a passage takes [you] into a most elegant suite of 3 rooms w*hic*h he is fitting up for Busts and statues and w*hic*h will be open for any artists or young people who chuse to go there and draw ~~or~~. The style is most simple and chaste and far exceeds in taste any thing I ever saw like

---

[1] This paragraph has been moved from the middle of the preceding one, from which it was separated by horizontal lines in the original manuscript.

[2] Diarist error – Sunday was 11 Jan.

[3] See SJC, MS U.30 (4), p. 208, n. 2.

[4] Diarist error – Monday was 12 Jan.

[5] Diarist error – Tuesday was 13 Jan.

[6] See SJC, MS U.30 (4), p. 181, n. 4.

[7] Woodhill; see SJC, MS U.30 (3), p. 183, n. 2. Lee may have sketched a view from nearby the house; see SJC, MS U.30 (7), ff. 44v–45r (p. 324), not reproduced.

[8] Bartolomeo Schedoni (1578–1615), Italian painter (Zirpolo, *Historical Dictionary*, p. 479).

[9] Bartolomé Esteban Murillo (1617–82), Spanish painter (Zirpolo, *Historical Dictionary*, p. 377).

[10] Raphael (1483–1520), Italian painter and architect (Zirpolo, *Historical Dictionary*, p. 124).

[11] Not identified; Lee represented the artist's name by a dash.

it before. There is also a drawing room or study ~~to~~ which communicates with the other statue rooms. The plan Mr G[1] says exceeds any thing he ever saw anywhere but in Italy[.] The Print room contains all the celebrated Berrys works who was a native of Cork[.][2]

1 Printroom
2 Gallery pictures
3 Passage
4[,] 5[,] 6 Models and busts
7 Study[3]

[f. 32v] From there went to Mr Barters and there saw besides some fine grounds the most elegant and wonderful shellwork I ever heard off [sic].[4] The part of a great house is separated and made a grotto and the work is immense[.] It was all done in 3 summers[.] The variety of shells [is] prodigious. Together with ores, Kerry stones and Coral and other curiosities. The shellwork in the tower is nothing but a daub compared to this as Mr Garde and Garrick confess, it is a most wonderful and convincing proof what perseverance can do. It is impossible to say any any more about it. Where the materials could have been collected from is wonderful in itself. The [sic] must have made a compact with Neptune to Monopolize all his treasures and he must have to work all his Nymphs to sweep the seas for his grotto. Calypsos was not to be compared to it, if the Eveque gives a true account of it.[5] — The materials as they consist of curiosities[,] shells, ores, coral, pebbles etc etc are extremely valuable and would sell for many hundreds.

Add to this the spot and [the] houses are on the most ravishing situation and command a fine view down the river by Loch Mahon and Passage and up to Cork the other way.[6] Saw here a [bit?] of a curious spar inlaid with silver which was found in the Bog of Allen[.]

From thence went to see Mr Spere and here[,] besides the most ravishing view [f. 33r] up and down the river[,] is a collection of the finest evergreens I ever beheld. There is a row of cypress which is impossible to be equalled and an avenue of evergreen immense large — such as I can never expect to see again. Besides a vast profusion of hollies and some garden evergreens and some immense arbutus trees[.] Beautiful Lodge and entrance[.]

I understand he has sold this estate and is going to live over the water. He has been a great deal in [the] W Indies and married a Lady there. He has a fine Daughter.

/ From this place can be easily seen Sir I. Hayes seat to which from this Mr Penroses House he ran away with Miss Pike.[7] Just above Miss Bailees[8] is Mr Newenhams[,][9] the

---

[1] This could refer to either Garrick or Garde.
[2] Cooper Penrose was patron to Cork-born history painter, James Barry (1741–1806) (Murray, 'The Cooper Penrose Collection', p. 121).
[3] This list refers to Lee's sketch plan of Penrose's gallery, not reproduced here.
[4] Belleview, house of the 'Miss Barters', with a 'very curious collection of shell-work, and a beautiful myrtle-garden' (West, A Directory, p. 22).
[5] A reference to The Adventures of Telemachus (1699) by the French Roman Catholic bishop, theologian and writer, François Fénelon (1651–1715).
[6] The sketch at SJC, MS U.30 (7), ff. 42v–43r (p. 324), not reproduced, may have been made during this walk.
[7] Mary Pike (1776–1832), Quaker heiress, went to reside with her relatives the Penroses at Woodhill on the death of her father. On 22 July 1797 Sir Henry Brown Hayes (1762–1832) abducted Pike from Woodhill; he was sentenced to transportation to Botany Bay for his crime (O'Riordan, 'Pike, Mary').
[8] Possibly the Baileys of Ballinaboy (LED).
[9] The Newenhams of Coolmore, Cork, but with other holdings in the county (LED). Lee most likely refers either to the politician Sir Edward Newenham (1734–1814), or his nephew the economist and politician Thomas Newenham (1762–1831) (Geoghegan and Quinn, 'Newenham, Sir Edward'; Geoghegan, 'Newenham, Thomas').

Barkers[1] and not far from it Mr — a Quaker who had a most beautiful set of China very valuable, and as he thought that to keep such a thing by him was only encouraging the idle vanity of this world, He therefore prudently taketh resolution and breaketh the whole collection (This Guard affirmed to have been a fact)[.][2]

Wednesday. January 14 /
Clear fine day. Sunshine[.]
    Called on Dr Westrop and settled nothing of the business I had with him. Called on Dr Man who gave me a picture of his daughters doing. Called on Mr Flyn, Dr Bennet and Mr Guarde and Miss Tavesers and drank Tea there.

[f. 33v] **Thursday January 15 /**
Dull[,] rainy[,] thick[,] foggy day and all the Evening[.]
    Started at 8 in the Coach or mail for Youghall and got here at 5[.][3] Came through the most beautiful Glanmire and along to Middleton. Saw Castle Martyr, Canal, Woods, the house,[4] and old Abbey and Lodge. Town very pretty[,] better than Middleton[.] Fine flat land beyond Castle Martyr and to Youghall on the Right and so for immense distance[.] The first 12 Miles are beautiful all down by Cove.
    Curious party in the Coach. 1 English Gentleman, 1 Painted Widow[,] a young married fisherwoman and a lively gentleman[.]

Friday January 16 /
Fine warm day, a misty sky but not so as to be troublesome[,] no rain, no wind[.]
    Set out from Youghall about 9, and walked on to Clashmore[,] a very pretty village 4 Miles on the road, then crossed the mountains for 6 Miles[5] and come within two miles of Dungarvan, which is on the flat below, from the top of the Mountains see all over the Country towards Clonmel and Waterford and on the other side towards Youghall of which the entrance of the Bay is observed[.][6] At Dungarvan the Innkeeper's son 20 Years [of] age plays the fiddle flute and Piano[,] very extraordinary taste for music[.]

[f. 34r] **Saturday January 17 /**
Cloudy but fine day, windy, a few ½ hours of drisly rain about one OClock[.]
    Set out from Dungarvan at 8 as the bell was ringing for the workmen[.][7] Crossed the ferry and came along untill seeing a curious chasm in the Mountain side[.][8] Went up to

[1] The 'Miss Barters' of Belleview (West, *A Directory*, p. 22).
[2] Possibly Joshua Beale (West, *A Directory*, p. 22); the Beales had property at Myrtle Hill (Windele, *Historical and Descriptive Notices*, p. 89), which Lee would have passed if he walked along the Owenboy River from Ballinaboy.
[3] Lee sketched the view from the ferry across the River Blackwater before he commenced his walk to Clashmore and Dungarvan; see SJC, MS U.30 (7), ff. 45v–46r (p. 324).
[4] Lee probably means Capella Castlemartyr House, Castlemartyr, Co. Cork, a two-storey 25-bay country house built c.1730 by Henry Boyle, 1st Earl of Shannon (NIAH).
[5] Lee made one sketch on this route, at Aglish, Co. Waterford; see SJC, MS U.30 (7), ff. 47v–48r (p. 324), not reproduced.
[6] Lee sketched the scene at SJC, MS U.30 (7), f. 50r and ff. 50v–51r (p. 325), not reproduced.
[7] See description of Lee's sketch of Dungarvan ferry and quay at SJC, MS U.30 (7), f. 49v (p. 325), not reproduced.
[8] See descriptions of sketches at SJC, MS U.30 (7), ff. 21v–22r, f. 48v and ff. 51v–52r (pp. 321, 324, 325), not reproduced.

it and found it a beautiful little Glen with a fine brook running down through it,[1] the corresponding craggs of the Mountains were very ⊥ʳ and hanging over. View of Dungarvan very fine from the Centre of the Glen.[2] Go on up a steep hill || to this Glen and then over immense Mountains for many miles[,] ~~and see~~ [there is] still fine Mountain on the left Untill [you] arrive at Kilmac Thomas[,] a singular village on the edges of a steep valley which has a bridge of one large arch over the bottom at which runs a small rivulet.[3] Kilmac Thomas is quite in a hole and farther on is the Newtown Inn and the village so called[4] where I stopped[.] The Host can talk Irish and write it and to my astonishment was quoting and saying by heart pieces of the beginning of Horace and Virgil which he learnt at school 30 Years ago at Dungarvan. Many Gentlemen could not do the same. He holds a farm of about 300 Acres for 300Gs a year and has about 14 Years more out of 40 to run[,] when [he] says that he shall be turned out for he would then give 400 a Year for it but it will let for more!!! It belonged some time [f. 34v] ago to Mr Musgrave the father of the present Sir W Musgrave[5] who gave him his lease. Mr Musgrave sold about 1000 Acres here[.] Kilmac Thomas belonged to the Marquis of Waterford[.]

Sunday January 18 /
Fine charming Morning at sunrise and continued so all the Morning[,] clouds blowing over, sun clear, wind brisk from the westward. About one a sharp shower from the west and then fine again[.]

Slept at the Newtown Inn where the accommodations are not gay but they may be made tolerably comfortable, set out at 10 for Waterford and had a fine Walk, but over a very uninteresting country. The view of the amazing cordon of Mountains [Comeragh Mountains] which I walked alongside of yesterday was certainly most grand, majestic, sublime, their heights were as it seemed tattered and torn by the winds and weather and the edges and points and craggs were all white rock. The Mountains seemed as if all together they had been shaken and melted together for their roughness and multiform [f. 35r] figures looked like a heap of Mountains instead of one Massy one. There were in appearance ½ some conical craters like those at Killarney. The white cliffs and edges when the sun shone partially on them was very fine, but I never had a fair view of the whole Mountain for the clouds which rested on them,[6] although the rest of the Sky was a perfect Dutch Blue. The part of the Heavens near the horizon was rather white and misty. Glorious sight[.] The whole road to Waterford [is] uninteresting untill within a few miles [of the town,] when white houses appear scattered about and peeps at the Suire [Suir] assist to enliven the landscape. Get into town about three OClock[.]

---

[1] Possibly sketched at SJC, MS U.30 (7), ff. 51v–52r (p. 325), not reproduced.
[2] Possibly sketched at SJC, MS U.30 (7), ff. 52v–53r or f. 54r (p. 325), not reproduced.
[3] Sketched at SJC, MS U.30 (7), f. 56r (p. 326), not reproduced.
[4] Newtown, Co. Waterford.
[5] Sir Richard Musgrave (1746?–1818), 1st baronet, political writer, 'was the first of the three sons of Christopher Musgrave (d. 1787) of Tourin, near Cappoquin, local agent to the Duke of Devonshire' (Woods, 'Musgrave, Sir Richard'). The family had extensive holdings around Co. Waterford.
[6] See description of sketch at SJC, MS U.30 (7), ff. 57v–58r (p. 326), not reproduced.

Monday January 19 /
Day very fine, cerulean sky, very fine clouds, Very heavy wind all night, and still more blustering in the Morning. Very sharp and as if inclined to freeze and snow[.]

Mr J. Scott of Liverpool was my *compagnon de voyage* from Cork to Youghal. Meeting him again at Waterford. He told me that he was mentioning to Mr Green of Youghal that he had travelled with a Gentleman of my description. 'Ah' said Mr Green 'that person was here about 2 months or more ago and was taking observations, views and drawings of this place and we did not know what the devil to make of him[.]'

[f. 35v] It was so bad a day that one a person [*sic*] could hardly stir out of doors and ∴ I did not venture out but for a short time.[1] The Quay is of very great extent but not an English mile[.] It [Waterford] is a most beautiful town and the wooden bridge is a wonderful thing[.] There is a fine draw bridge at the S side of it and on the shore a turnpike at which chaises pay both going and coming 1Sh. Every thing is of wood[,] the arches or piles are very close to each other, the [floor?] for carriages and for foot passengers[,] of which there is one on each side[,] are of wood. On the N Side there is an immense rock or line of shell or stone which has been hewn out ⊥ʳ to the water side to make a road along its base.[2] The whole is very curious[.] The upper part of the bridge is all painted white[,] as much as is above the footway[.] It is a most elegant structure and does high honour to its builder[.] The river [Suir] is very fine at Waterford and ships are laying all along the Quays, Opposite the East end of the Quay is a most curious looking shore and such a piece of hill as is seldom seen, the whole is a heap of stones or rocks in profusion / bravery[3] of it. The Cathedral is a very neat[,] plain[,] modern Building[.][4] The steeple is a very heavy piece of [f. 36r] workmanship, square and ⊥ʳ in some parts rounded off above and the ornaments are very heavy and dull. At the East End are 2 very curious old tombstones at the corners of the cathedral. In rail ways on one are 4 figures of stone carved on Each side and 3 at Each end besides other smaller ones, and there are 2 [pillars?] of stone lying one on each side [of] the tomb[.] There are 2 inscriptions around the slab but very much erased[.][5] The place is not kept in any repair. On the other side is another curious old tomb with family arms on it etc etc and a deal of carved work in stone.

In the Evening went to the Fancy Ball or Masquerade given in honour of His Majestys Birthday. The greatest part of the company were in masks[.] There was a very good Magician with a goats beard and wand and Italian Book under his ~~hand~~ arm, A Good pedagogue talking Latin[,] 2 good clowns, a most excellent man man [*sic*] maidservant seeking a place, an incomparable Tinker, an old Jew, A noisy Foxhunter. A devilish clumsy[,] awkward[,] neatly dressed Harlequin without one trick, a Good Giant, A parcel of crasy [crazy] Girls, a stiff Quaker etc etc. A most elegant supper was prepared indeed and the room near as Elegant as possible, 2 rows of 4 pillars down the room divided it in some measure into 3 parts, of which the middle between the pillars was as wide again as

---

[1] See description of sketch at SJC, MS U.30 (7), ff. 59v–60r (p. 326), not reproduced.
[2] Sketched at SJC, MS U.30 (7), f. 61r (p. 327), not reproduced.
[3] In the sense of 'ostentatious' (*OED*).
[4] The cathedral of the Holy Trinity or Christ Church Cathedral, possibly a pre-Norman foundation but replaced by a new building in 1779 (Moore, *Archaeological Inventory of County Waterford*, pp. 189–90).
[5] Probably the tomb of James Rice, mayor of Waterford *c.* 1469. The inscription on the tomb is transcribed in Smith, *Waterford*, p. 174.

the other side [*small sketch plan in margin*], there was a most Elegant supper [f. 36v] prepared for ab*ou*t 200[,] the n° of people there nearly, Dancing very little or 2 Dances before supper and a great deal after. The Masquerade was done much better than I expected. A great n° of fine girls. There were 3 fine rooms on a floor and the rooms are as fine as any I ever saw for a set of four. Met Cap*tain* Aylmour[1] there and his Lady[.]

Got to bed ab*out* ½ p*ast* 2 at N*ig*ht[.]

Tuesday Jan*uary* 20 /
Day raining all the morn*ing* and even*ing* windy[.]

I started for Carrig [Carrick-on-Suir] in a post Chaise with Mr Scott[2] at 8 OClock and came thro*ugh* a most beautiful country, villages very neat[,] fine woods on the S side of the river and some also on the R, many Gent*lemens* seats all up the river, several fine old ruins in sight, The whole has the appearance of a fine rich flour*ishing* country. See the river constantly winding along. Fine old Castle[3] at Carrig[.] Foljambe[4] not there, set out on foot for Clonmel at ½ p*ast* 12 and came up the river side by [the] towing path. Scenery the most beautiful I had any where seen. A Gr*eat* n° of fine old ruins and the M*ountain*s on the S [were] all cov*ere*d [f. 37r] with wood, [the] dist*ant* M*ountain*s were very high and their tops were cov*ere*d with snow w*hich* had a very fine contrast with the surround*ing* scenery w*hich* was quite fresh and green. This walk is as fine as any on the Black Water and is well worth a persons while walking down the river to Carrig to see[.] I loitered so much and was gazing with such pleasure that it began to grow rather darker by the time I had not got 6 Miles on my way and ∴ [I was] obliged to tear myself away f*ro*m the enchanting scenery. There is ample room for a painter to exert his pencil on this river and the M*ountain*s and tower and ruins on it.[5] River very rapid indeed, saw many barges going merrily down. It due West ward every where appears very fertile. Saw persons plowing as late as 4 OClock in the Even*ing*!! A lone barge w*hich* was towing up the river[,] [there] were 13 men a hauling her along!! The M*ountain*s on the S side w*hich* run all along the river side are all cov*ere*d with woods and timber, and then and there a dist*ant* range of M*ountain*s peep in cov*ere*d with snow (very fine)[.]

A post Boy in Carrig offered to carry [for] me, I gave him my knapsack and asked [that] he s*houl*d set out in an hour[,] I said I w*oul*d walk on, I did, he never overtook me although I took 5 sketches on my way[.][6]

[f. 37v] Wednesday Jan*uary* 21 /
Morning raining, clear at 9 and all day, Wind very violent and due West[.]

'Waiter where is my [Chaise?][,] What the devil are you so long about, am I to be kept here all day.' 'Oh dont be in a hurry noble Cap*tai*n the horses are getting ready and we will

---

[1] Not identified. This person was previously mentioned on 21 Sept. (see p. 156), 22 Sept. (see p. 158) and 25 Sept. (see pp. 163–4). His name is inconsistently spelt as Almer, Aylmour, Elmor and Elmour.

[2] The man from Liverpool with whom Lee travelled from Cork to Youghal and met again in Waterford. See SJC, MS U.30 (2), p. 264.

[3] Ormond Castle, Carrick-on-Suir, Co. Tipperary, built *c.*1565 (NIAH). The castle and its surroundings are sketched at SJC, MS U.30 (7), f. 62r (p. 327), not reproduced.

[4] See SJC, MS U.30 (2), p. 171, n. 2.

[5] See descriptions of sketches at SJC, MS U.30 (7), ff. 62v–63r, 64r (p. 327), not reproduced.

[6] See descriptions of sketches at SJC, MS U.30 (7), ff. 62r, 62v–63r, 64r, 65r and possibly 65v (pp. 327–8), not reproduced.

send you off like a general —'¹ Who can help laughing at the quick repartees with which the Irish abound, If you are in a passion they will make you laugh in spite of yourself.

One of the views on the river Suire yesterday was very fine. River in front, 2 of the Mountains meet each other and at their hollow [there is] an old ruin in the distance and an immense high range of Mountain covered nearly with snow behind it, only marks left here and there by which you could tell it was a Mountain range (My sketch of it)[.]²

After calling on Mr Watsons Bank[,] set out about eleven for Cashel. Mr Carter keeps the mail Coach Office [in] Clonmel. Pass by Mr Sparrows fine white House and grounds[.]³ He was formerly a Quaker I am told. Farther on is Mr Moores House⁴ on the Right where Mr Douglas⁵ took me[.] Grounds very fine and elegant[,] fine sheet of water in the front of his house, very rich pastures. The Mountains near Clogheen and Ardfinnan form [a] most noble back ground to this scenery and were snow capt[.]

[f. 38r] My curiosity to see the Rock of Cashel was very great[,] but my surprise was also great at not getting a sight of it untill you come close on the town. This Gibraltar of Ireland[,] this wonder of Nature[,] is nothing extraordinary, there are many as sudden and rocky mounds of land in that part as that of Cashel, there are 2 risings or waves of land close by it which are higher and more commanding than it. The wonder of this place arises from the singularity of their building on that high rocky point more than on any other, the Ruins of the Abbey are the wonder, they are curious and interesting and there is some fine sculpture but nothing very extraordinary. On the Monumental arch near the cathedral is a base and body of an old statue which they say is that of St Patrick.⁶ There is as much chance of its being his as any body elses[,] if it ever was a likeness of a human being. The round tower is a strong but not handsome building, it is considerably wider at [the] bottom than at [the] top. There are a great n° of curious old tombstones etc [and] inscriptions in the Cathedral which are all going to ruin from neglect. This Cathedral was 40 years ago roofed in and it was taken down by one of the Archbishops who the people say died 6 days after it. Town is said to be one of the cleanest in Ireland[.] It may [be] but I saw dozens of heaps of dung all before the doors and in the streets.

Cashel is said to abound more in milk than in <u>water</u> and some archbishop sometime ago brought water in [from] a source 2 mile off to the town which ran down through the street, but it had only been [running] a week when a Mr Pennefether[,] having some disagreement with the Archbishop[,] stopped it from running through his grounds although he owened [sic] most of [f. 38v] Cashel. It is a disgrace to Cashel also that the late ArchBishop sent an architect down to examine about making a water course and it would have with the act of parliament have cost about 800£ of which the ArchBishop

---

¹ Quotation marks added.
² See description of sketch at SJC, MS U.30 (7), f. 62r (p. 327), not reproduced. The sketch clearly depicts the two mountains meeting, with a ruin at the base and the river in the foreground.
³ The Sparrow family were located at Clonmel from 1667 until the early 19th century (LED). Oaklands house was built c.1770 (NIAH).
⁴ Probably Barn House, seat of the Mount Cashells from the 18th to 20th century (LED).
⁵ Possibly the Rev. Douglas mentioned in SJC, MS U.30 (2), p. 155.
⁶ The Rock of Cashel began as an early medieval fort and has had religious associations since the 7th century; a cathedral and round tower were constructed in the early 12th century, and a Cistercian abbey was established in the 13th century; while extensive repairs were made to the buildings in the early 18th century, Lee would have seen the buildings in a state of decay that was not addressed until the mid-19th century (Manning, *Rock of Cashel*).

offered to subscribe 300[,] but the Gent*lemen* and the people of and about Cashel had not spirit enough to do it. Blackguards and fools[.]

Dined with an officer of the 97 Who was recruiting at Cashel, and 2 other men, very curious conversation all the Even*ing*. This Officer had been formerly in the 17 Dragoons and among his Egotisms he was telling that when at Nottingham he and another fought and licked 3 of the stoutest fellows there. Lord Paget[1] hearing of the fray came out to know w*ha*t was going on and being told, said 'the 17 Drag*oo*ns are always doing something of this sort.' 'You lie[,] <u>my lord</u>[,]'[2] said he[,] and kicked him out of the room!!!

[Thursday] Jan*ua*ry 22 /

Fine and sunshine till 10 then rain till 12 then fine but very windy and terribly cold and sharp freezing[.]

Went over to Sir Tho*ma*s Judkin Fitzgeralds,[3] and staid within all day. Lady F.[4] Capt*ain* and Mrs Sadler[5] and Miss Hare.[6] Sir Tho*ma*s this day fortnight was com*ing* home ab*ou*t 2 OClock in the morn*ing* fr*om* Thomastown (Lord Landoffs)[7] and getting out of the coach he mistook the step and fell down and dislocated his ancle and broke one of the small bones and has been confined to his bed ever since but is now getting better every day. The most extraordin*ary* man I ever saw. His beard off. He is of an amazing size and the strongest man [f. 39r] in the world. The most gentle and mild tempered but most violent on occasions[,] the most intrepid in all the action of his [life here?]. Owing to his wonderful native exertions the whole county of Tipperary was preserved and the rebellion being checked there[,] this was the reason of its not spreading over Cork and the south[.] He was so active and so dreaded that the rebels offered £700 to any body who w*oul*d kill him and he knew this very well[.] He had such good information of their all [*sic*] proceedings that he w*oul*d send to the chiefs of the rebel party to be at such a chapel with their whole force on such a day and w*oul*d make them deliver up their arms. In the county of Tipperary there were between 70 and 80000 men and women and under 5 Generals[,] 3 of whom Sir Tho*ma*s had at one time in custody. At some times he w*oul*d order parties to appear at certain places and order them to deliver up their arms, and w*oul*d say when they were all collected Capt*ain* — (calling him by his name) call out your comp*any* (Sergeant — (search out draw out the 20 or 30 men[)] and thus shew them that he knew all their plans[,] by wh*ich* they were so cowed as to submit and give up their arms and

---

[1] Henry William Paget (formerly Bayly), 1st Marquess of Anglesey, army officer and politician (Anglesey, 'Paget, Henry William (1768–1854)').

[2] Quotation marks added.

[3] Sir Thomas Judkin-Fitzgerald of Lisheen (1754–1810), high sheriff for Co. Tipperary in 1798. He earned the alias 'Flogging Fitzgerald' for his activities during the rebellion, torturing and persecuting suspected rebels (Long, 'Fitzgerald, Sir Thomas Judkin'; Betham, *Baronetage of England*, V, p. 480).

[4] Elizabeth, second daughter and co-heir of Joseph Capel, Cloghroe House, Co. Cork, married Thomas Judkin-Fitzgerald (see previous note) in Jan. 1785 (Long, 'Fitzgerald, Sir Thomas Judkin').

[5] Likely the Sadliers of Holycross, given that Lee and Captain Sadlier rode to Holycross the following day.

[6] Possibly Barbara Hemphill (née Hare) (d. 1858), novelist; her father, Patrick Hare, was rector of Golden, Co. Tipperary, and vicar general of the diocese of Cashel.

[7] Thomastown Castle was the seat of the earls of Landaff, a title created in the Peerage of Ireland in 1797 for Francis Mathew, 1st Viscount Landaff (1738–1806). He was succeeded in 1806 by his son, Francis-James Mathew, 2nd Earl of Landaff (1797–1833) (Burke, *A Genealogical History of the Dormant ... Peerages*, 1866, p. 361).

[were] glad to depart in peace[.] He would frequently harrangue [sic] the rebels[,] 'this [man see?]' and get on a wall or a table to be more conspicuous[,] Captain Sadler saw and was with him when he has got on a table and after abusing the fellows for their plots he has called up a captain among them by his name and ordered him to get up by him 'and now you rebellious rascals look here, here is one [f. 39v] of your own captains[,] a poor small trembling fellow who is afraid to look me in the face[.] Look at him and is this the captain to whom you obey, and look now at me[,] look at the Kings Captain, I am not afraid if all of you set to get to me[.] I hear that you have offered £200 for my head then and why do you not some of you come forward and kill me at once, you cowardly rascals, there are 100s of you to my small force (about 40) you dastardly cowards, By the holy Jesus if any one of you dared to pick me I would have every man (of you extirpated) to all of you murdered, by the on the spot'[1] and then he would kick the posteriors of the Captain and take him by the cape and throw him Down out some distance off. At one time he made the people give up to the nº of 40000 pike heads which he had in his house and 30000 stand of musquets. They were afraid and in dread of Sir Thomas.

January Friday 23 /
Day most tempestuous and stormy[.] Wind due W[.] It blew a hurricane and one could hardly walk against it. It blew down a house in Cashel and many tiles off other houses. Very cold and a hard frost in the Evening[.]

Walked out with Mr Walter about Sir Thomas' grounds and saw within 400 Yds of [f. 40r] the house many rabbits[,] a wood copse, 3½ couple snipe, a covey of partridges. Game is wonderfully common in that country. Went all round Sir Thomas' farm of Bally Griffin[.] His grounds are very well laid out and [on] very rich land[.] The river Suire borders them very elegantly. Fine rich land. Noble field of Swedish Turnips[,] land of it as rich as Garden mold. Kerry bullocks feeding and fattening on hay and these turnips[.] They can be bought for 4Gs a piece and in 4 Months will sell for 10 or 12Gs apiece. Sir Thomas brought once a nº of Shorthorned Cows of the best sort from England and calves they furnished him with bulls and young cows and 10 of them altogether cost him at first £1000 in buying and bringing over for he keeps all her bull calves and lets them for 3 or 4Gs to his neighbours of good land on condition of their being well kept, only then when they are returned to him he keeps them up and gets them fat and sells them for — Guineas which is clear profit all but for the time it is fattening. And his yews [ewes] are very fine, he gets the largest sheep possibly [sic] over from the county of Galway and puts the English rams to them and their lambs for the next [as well?] are his breed yews, after this time he buys fresh yews for they degenerate very fast and thus he always keeps a good fine sheep — by this mixture. Land is all about here very [f. 40v] rich and would let for 3 or most of it 4Gs an acre. There are many pieces of land near to Cashel which let for 9Gs an Acre and Sir Thomas has land there which he lets for 14Gs an acre, but the general price of land is 3Gs or 3½[.]

After returning from the farm rode with Captain Sadler to Holycross[2] from Lisheen and went all over that curious ruin and here is the finest piece of black marble I ever saw,

---

[1] Quotation marks added.
[2] The abbey at Holycross, Co. Tipperary, founded by Cistercians in 1180 and among four abbeys founded by Domnall Mór Ua Briain (d. 1194), king of Thomond, in 1170–95, who was 'conscious of their political value'; extensive reconstruction took place at the site from 1431 (Ní Mhaonaigh, 'Ua Briain, Domnall Mór'; Stalley, *Cistercian Monasteries*, pp. 14, 239, 245–6).

Dermot OBriens Tomb and the work is exquisite and would do honor to 3 centuries after us although it is of very old date. The sum of all the Arches is exquisite and there are some and numerous marks of taste and judgement in architecture unknown in the present day. I never saw such fine reliques all going to ruin and oblivion so shamefully[.] In one part of the abbey a fine old tomb with pillars of exquisite workmanship has been destroyed to make way for a plain tomb of 30 years ago. Went all over it and from the top of the abbey can be seen 26 or more ruined castles or abbeys around, here this part of the country swarms with them. The Arches are beautiful and the finished work of the stone marble wonderful. It is quite the spot for a painter and an antiquarian. Nº of old inscriptions on old stones [f. 41r] laying about in neglect. But the tomb of Dermot is the most beautiful thing[,] sombre and the work wonderful. Up on the first floor the plan of one of the chimneys was curious, (see sketch in one of my books).[1]

[f. 41v *Ink sketch of bridge and surroundings, captioned*] View of 6 Mile bridge broken down. Taken from *P*ost Chaise in the middle of the river[.]

[f. 42r] At the bridge of Holy Cross is a curious inscription. There are 2 coats of arms of one of the better family and his wife and under neath on another stone a Latin inscription (which see in my Book).[2] On the *B*ridge Cap*t*ain Sadler saw a rebel killed[.] He was riding and not being able to avoid a party of yeomanry coming down on him he leaped over the side and fought there, and then leapt into the river where he was shot. Returned along the E side of the Suire and pass by a curious spot where a river arises out of some rocks on the road side[.] There are a great nº of springs all running together[.] They immediately form a good stream called [in] the Irish words the golden river. Close by this are some rocks and points of land where the rebels once made a stand to give battle to Sir Thomas Fitzgerald[.] They were about 1000 strong and had occupied advantageously the [swards?] of the [wood?] and behind them was the river. He came on with about 40 men, They fired a few shots and immediately set off all a scampering and did not await for their return. The leader and captain was on a grey horse and he set off the first towards Holy Cross. Several of the rebels were killed. Being asked some time after why he did not make better defence the Cap*t*ain told Mr Sadler (in whose company in Sir Thomas' regiment he was) that in the morning there were some discontents in his [f. 42v] forces and he was afraid they would not stand the battle and when they saw Sir Thomas coming with so few men they gave themselves up for lost and thought they were surrounded for that [surely?] Sir Thomas would not advance by himself with as few men and ∴ he took to his heels not being able to trust in his own men. (In going to Holy Cross pass by a chapel not far from Cap*t*ain Longs[3] where Sir Thomas had about 1500 collected at his order and made them deliver up their arms.) at a little Chapel with a [still?] his Church not far from it on the other side of the road[.] Coming on pass by Armaile [Ardmayle] a celebrated place formerly the castle of the Butlers.[4] At this place was formerly a celebrated pass over the Suire and here it is said the circumstance took place between the Earl of Desmond (Ormond). (The Fitzgeralds) and one of the Butlers in a battle Earl Desmond knocked down. Carried away by a Butler. On the bridge Butler said 'Where is

---

[1] This sketch has not been located in Lee's extant sketchbooks.
[2] This sketch has not been located in Lee's extant sketchbooks.
[3] Possibly the Longs of Fort Edward and Longfield, Cashel (LED).
[4] The medieval castle at Moyaliff, Co. Tipperary (Farrelly and O'Brien, *Archaeological Inventory of County Tipperary*, I, pp. 311–12).

the great Earl of Desmond now.' *Ormond* recovering from his swoon said 'where he should be on the neck of a Butler[.]'¹ The latter so enraged threw him off over the Bridge and the other swam back safe to his friends[.]

[f. 43r] Cap*tain* Longs is a beautiful place and he made it all when he came of age[.] His father sold all their estates and paid off all their Debts, the money remaining was £280 Gs. Cap*tain* Long took 80Gs[,] left his father the rest[,] volunteered in the army[,] went abroad to India, and having friends though no money he soon got on and being up the country he made a deal of money (many say 1̇0 3̇46632̇421̇96, 3̇463̇562 1̇22546̇. etc)[.] He came home with 100000 and bought his place[,] built there etc[.] He built the factory at the bridge and brought a canal 2 Mile along river side to turn it[.] People [were] surprised at the water channel being obliged to be cut when [the] river water [was] so near. Channel through Blue coat school[.] Estate Factory built out of part of old Castle. Did not succeed[,] the Men brought from England cheated him and he lost 10 (10000) or more by it. He is now out of his mind and they say that in his fits he runs about and creeps under the bed and gets in corners. 16̇01̇92 "3̇32̇242̇" etc Reason not very clear[.]

Saturday 24 Jan*uary* /
Day very hard frost, wind sharp. Beautiful clear sunshine and moon light night. Not a cloud, no snow but like it[,] very cold and freezing[.]

[f. 43v] NB many people abuse the Mines at Ross Island. As ugly and the ruin of that scenery[.] I differ. It makes the scenery more beautiful[,] increases the contrast and variety for which Kerry [is] celebrated. Like Stygian² Lake. Wheel going round only wants a size put on it. Princes of Kerry condemned for their livelihood to work there. Ghosts walking the lake. Elysian fields are Muckruss or Upper Lake[.] Bones and bodies in the Abbey. Inisfallen Is*land* etc etc[.]

Sir Tho*mas* F*i*tzgerald is one of the boldest farmers in the country whose grounds I saw. His sheep are the best about there. Saw a great many bits of land which have not been broken up in the memory of man and as fine and flourishing as possible and as much grass as in many English fields in summer. The land fattens cattle immediately. The places where his cattle are now fattening were formerly the stables of Lord Clanwilliam's³ hunters!!! and the best field on the Bally griffin farm where they were exercised is now filled with sheep and so rich that it is worth 15Gs an acre to him!!! Through his farm runs a covered⁴ dead hedge and an old bank which formerly divided the Estates of the ~~Butlers and~~ Ormonds and the — families[.]

[f. 44r] Rode out this morning to see Golden which is a small town of no consequence and about 1 Mile down river are the ruins of an extensive Abbey.⁵ Rathassel, bare walls remaining. Pass by several Danish Mounds of which this Country abounds. Sir Tho*mas* has several on his estate. Sir Tho*mas* levelled one many years ago and the people think the fairy caused his bad leg[.] 'And How is Sir Tho*mas* today' said a peasant to Dr Evans Jun*io*r of Cashel one morning soon after [the] accident. 'His leg is very bad and quite

---

¹ Quotation marks added.
² A possible reference to the River Styx of classical myth, meaning 'dark'.
³ Sir John Meade (1744–1800), 2nd Earl of Clanwilliam, of Co. Tipperary (Gibney, 'Meade, Sir John').
⁴ 'Thickly clothed with some vegetative growth' (*OED*).
⁵ The priory of St Edmund at Athassel, built *c.*1200 (Gwynn and Hadcock, *Medieval Religious Houses*, p. 157).

black', 'Well and Pray Dr how long will it be before he comes am*ong*st us again[?]' 'He will not be able to walk for some time.' 'Well now I can tell you w*ha*t will cure him immediately.' 'What.' 'Let him only shovel up the mound (again) and the fairy will then be satisfied and cure his honours leg[.]'[1]

A person had a son born who was tongue tied and ∴ dumb and the people all laid it to the fathers fault for hav*ing* levelled some years ago the mound and told him the fairy wou*l*d be up to him but unfortunately the ~~Dr~~ (person) who dressed Sir T*hom*as' leg cut the string[2] and the boy spoke well. Inshort [sic] whether ~~ys~~ any accident happens to the person who disturbs these fairy grounds or his sons or relations the fairys are said to punish them for it sooner or later and you cou*l*d not beat it out of the people that it was not so. The reason why another gent*leman* who levelled one never was <u>hurted</u> was that he did lay it down with grass and planted fine trees and flowers [f. 44v] and made it a pleasant retreat for the fairies and ∴ they forgave him[.] This Sir Th*om*as said a man told him. The crime is not so great if you plant fruit trees and flowers for the fairies like that and <u>do come in the night and eat them</u>. But it is horrible to pass a plough over it or to sow corn //

The person mentioned an extraordinary case in w*hic*h he was cutting the string w*hic*h caused a boy to be dumb and no sooner was it cut than the first words he ever spoke were "Devil damn you mother take me out of this place[.]"

Rode on to Thomas Town the seat of Lord Landaff, where there is a domain having 2200 A*cre*s in closed in walls. There are fine trees, and the land is reckoned the richest in all Ireland. The deer park is a fine turf but there is not one spot w*hic*h a painter wou*l*d call fine or picturesque[.] The hedges and cabins are miserable and the whole has the appearance of shameful neglect[.] There are not probably any deer in the park, for the gates are broken and in pieces and they cou*l*d easily get out. No place seems more neglected[.] There are some very fine trees and the limes are curious being quite bushy and thick in the middle but they are inferior to Doneraile.

[f. 45r] The land is certainly fine in appearance and rich but I saw some miserable cattle and sheep on it. House plain. Some pieces of water in front and a stiff waterfall[,] some people may think it pretty. It looks as if it was forced to flow against its will[.] Went from thence to Dundrum where nature has been wonderfully assisted by taste and elegance[.] The grounds are here laid out in a most elegant manner and they possess that fine uneveness w*hic*h Burke says constitutes the Beautiful,[3] the waving of the ground w*hic*h is all (turf) meadow and the judicious plantations and woods form a most interesting <u>English</u> Demesne[.] There is a rising behind the house near a sunk fence and from whence the grounds are Elegant and the Gualty [Galtee] M*ou*ntains rising at the extrem*i*ty of the <u>demesne horizon</u> w*hic*h is scattered with woods and trees make a most beautiful painters studies [sic]. The house is a modern structure[,] form and grace[,] fine out build*ing*s and offices in an Elegant design. There is a small river seen meandering thro*ugh* the demesne and at one side over the road a most picturesque Bridge (from some points of view) at the Entrance of a wood very judiciously and tastily arranged. This spot or demesne if second

---

[1] Quotation marks added.

[2] A ligament or tendon, or the fraenum of the tongue (*OED*).

[3] Edmund Burke, Dublin-born politician and author (Langford, 'Burke, Edmund (1729/30–1797)'), and author of *A Philosophical Enquiry into the Origin of our Ideas of the Sublime and Beautiful* (1757).

to any it is Doneraile. It is the property of Lord Haywarden[1] but nobody lives there and [the] house has been shut up 10 years or more. In the offices is the head of an Elk with a pair of beautiful firm branching horns in most excellent preservation w*hi*ch was dug up with others in the bogs adjoining the place. I am told [f. 45v] there are some at Lord Landoff, and Mr Lloyd of Tipperary[2] told me that he fo*u*nd in a bog several larger than this but it was too decayed for preservation[.] The other bones were there also. Near the factory at Armaile [Ardmayle] Mr Long[3] dug up a fine old Helmet of great size and he has it now.[4] Returning to Lisheen come by a Gent*leman*s House on the Left where is close by [the] skeleton of an old castle[,] 4 fine round towers at the corners.[5] It is a very curious build*i*ng. On the left may be seen the celebrated bog part of w*hi*ch moved and flowed do*w*n the river Suire in 1786.[6] It is of very large size. The people never knew (observed) that it kept rising and rising untill it broke out and flowed all down the flat grounds towards Bally griffin and on to Golden where it joined the Suire, and flowed do*w*n to Clonmel where Mrs [*blank*] said she saw some of it going do*w*n river and it went down to Carrig and I believe people in Waterford had turf for some time. All the fish were killed. It is of ~~immense~~ (large) extent and owing to the water w*hi*ch probably was choaked up the bog arose and when of a suffi*cien*t height it being of a soft pulpy nature run over, thick lava[.] It covered all the fine flat lands and now a great deal of them are bog w*hi*ch before were profitable and rich. There is a bog at Golden w*hi*ch was [f. 46r] made in this manner. Quere [Query] might not bogs have been originally propagated in some degree in this way? Many are at tops of M*o*u*nta*ins and on high ground[.] C*ou*ld not these have formed others when the passages by w*hi*ch a certain quantity of water usually flowed out was stopped?

/ Quere [Query]. May we not argue that men were formerly not much larger than at present for in the old Abbeys, the windows [and] staircases are so small that no man of moderate size at the present day can go up many of them? At Cashel and Holy Cross w*hi*ch are very ancient they are small and at Holy Cross is a retired place up one flight of turret steps w*hi*ch a fat man c*ou*ld not go up and then when up if his occasions required him to retire f*ro*m the rest of mankind for a few minutes he *could* not get in at the door? Or were the small narrow stair cases [and] little doors made for (the) smaller part of the commonalty alone? // Sir Th*oma*s saw the bog moving and now its centre is so much sunk that places can be seen across it where their tops were only visible before. It has spoilt a great deal of good land.

// Sir Tho*ma*s F*itzgerald* had a law suit with a Gent*leman* of the name of — which went on for many years and ∴ they were not friends[.] He had a natural Brother who was also a fine stout man and every body was afraid of him. He was called [f. 46v] the

---

[1] Cornwallis Maude, 3rd Viscount Hawarden of Haywarden, Co. Tipperary (1780–1856) (Lodge, *The Peerage and Baronetage*, p. 288).

[2] Possibly the Lloyds of Lisheen, Co. Tipperary (LED).

[3] Possibly Captain Long; see p. 269, n. 3.

[4] It was later suggested that this helmet may have belonged to a soldier slain there as Strongbow's forces retreated from Cashel in 1174 (Lewis, *Topographical Dictionary*, I, p. 53).

[5] Remains of a small castle at Lisheen were described in the early 19th century, beside a 19th-century castle (Farrelly and O'Brien, *Archaeological Inventory of County Tipperary*, I, pp. 325–6).

[6] This bog burst was described by another writer: 'At the bridge of Ballygriffen the moving bog that broke out in the year 1786 joined the river Suir. This bog covers almost three hundred acres, all of which are rendered totally useless to the proprietor' (Sleater, *Introductory Essay*, p. 121).

Undaunted Buck of the Glen. The other I believe was called the Brown Buck (for I have forgotten the ~~first~~ accuracy of this first part of the story as Cap*tain* Sadler told it to me with regard to names)[.] However one of them, the stoutest and dread of the country said it was useless always going in so slow in law and that he w*oul*d settle soon w*hic*h had taken up the lawyers so many years to do and he would shoot Sir Tho*ma*s the very first time he met him and this he boasted in every company so that Sir Tho*ma*s was not long before the friend of both parties told it him and what does he do but says[,] 'Very well let him if he dare' and so it happens that one day as Sir Tho*ma*s was out riding and that very day of all others he had not any body with him nor a servant neither nor any body with him but a stick when upon coming to a sharp turn of the road such as my gentle reader and I have often met with in our walks and of w*hic*h he can fancy twenty in a moment when there meets Sir Tho*ma*s with this Buck who no sooner espies Sir Tho*ma*s than out he pulls a pistol and fires it at him and misses him but not on purpose and then he took out another and kept it steadily aimed at Sir Tho*ma*s who now dismounted and goes and takes up the pistol that the other had thrown away and getting his horse out of the way [f. 47r] he stood boldly, holding the unloaded P*i*stol in his hand saying[,] 'Fire and bedamn you cowardly Rascal there. Why dont you fire you villain. You cant hit me you are so cowardly villain. Fine and I will smash your brains out immediately[.]' All the while the other kept his pistol fairly levelled at Sir Tho*ma*s Who is a man of the largest size I ever saw and as broad and lusty as any. How long this went on I know not. However the Buck was so intimidated or sunk into a panic that he gave up the pistol and surrendered himself prisoner. (Had he fired he must inevitably have shot Sir Thomas for he was close to him[.]) Sir Tho*ma*s tied his hands behind him[,] mounted his Horse and[,] holding the loaded pistol in the hand[,] he thus marched the Undaunted Buck into Clonmel Town and lodged him in Gaol. The people w*oul*d at any other time have risqued him but such was the panic on seeing the dreaded Buck marched in this way that every body was thunderstruck and c*oul*d not believe that it w*oul*d have been possible for Sir Tho*ma*s to have got him in that state. At the Trial One of the Lawyers began browbeating Sir Tho*ma*s (who [was] a lawyer himself I believe formerly)[.] 'Well Mr Fitzgerald' (He was Baroneted since the rebellion for his services) 'and can you safely swear that this gentleman did present the pistol at you and ought (not) you at the time be so afraid and confused that you ~~might~~ (thought) it was at you when in fact it was only at a blackbird in [f. 47v] the hedge. Can you positively swear that you was not so frightened I mean to say flurried as to be in doubt why the pistol was fired.' To Mr Lawyer s*ai*d Mr Fitz*geral*d[,] 'I can safely swear and here take my oath that the pistol was fairly levelled at my body and as to my being afraid Mr Lawyer it was not the case for I here swear by this holy court in wh*ic*h I now stand and by the most solemn word of honour that never in the whole course of my life was I placed in any trials [or] circumstances as to know what fear was.'[1]

This is not correct as to the words Cap*tain* Sadler used, and I believe it most strictly[.]
/ Although a most violent man and ∴ dangerous when any one offered to offend or affront him yet ~~when in~~ after a bottle *from* that time any thing said or done cannot make him in a passion or angry. Wh*ic*h is a fortunate circumstance[.]

An instance of his wonderful command of temper. A servant who had letters and papers [bringing?] to him from some neighbouring place ~~out to~~ was out several hours

---

[1] Quotation marks added to all dialogue in this paragraph and the one following.

later than he ought to have been. Sir Thomas was uncomfortable till his arrival[.] When he did come [he said] 'Damn you you rascal why was you not home before.' 'And damn you' said the fellow, 'Who are that you dare call a better man than your self a rascal.' Every body thought it was all over with the fellow and [f. 48r] that Sir Thomas would have immediately pulled him in pieces. When after about 2 minutes deep silence[,] 'Here —' calling his butler by the name[,] 'take that drunken fellow away and see him put to bed', Said he in as mild and gentle a voice as ever man spoke. (Captain Sadler [was] present at the time[.])

Sir Thomas has a Brother[,] Colonel Fitzgerald[,][1] who lives at Cork by an Island below Cove near Carlisle Battery. Colonel of the S Cork Militia, he is an excellent good character also. He represented the county for 2 parliaments, or else Cork itself but declined this time being too aged to stir about. There might be other reasons[.] Sir Thomas said he would shew what could be done with the Irish and when the rebellion was subsiding he raised a corps of yeomanry[,] 400 of the very fellows who had been in the rebel ranks[,] and sometime after raised a complete regiment of them and took them to Waterford from whence they went abroad to Minorca [Menorca] where he left them[.] He always walked though Colonel and thus no one could complain. They afterwards volunteered and went to Egypt[2] and behaved gloriously, Captain Sadler was there with them. 600 in all were afterward recruited with 500 more and at the peace they were disbanded[.] Many went into the line[,] 300 I believe[.] About 100 died at Minorca of illness etc etc but about 150 came home and many are scattered about in the country now[.] They were fine[,] hardy[,] good soldiers [f. 48v] and were very faithful to their officers, for though Sir Thomas had[,] in the rebellion[,] flogged many of them[,] yet they liked him upon the whole, for say they he never killed any body except in the battles with rebels[.]

Hogs are a great article all over [the] South. Every cabin has one or two and Sir Thomas says he thinks they sell for 2000000 annually. A poor person gives them what they can get and potatoes and they are well kept and they can get 4Gs a piece for them which helps towards paying their rent. The pig factory at Clonmel has been of great use to the country and people stick up on the chapel doors that on such a day persons will come round to buy pigs etc etc[.]

/ Captain Sadler said he was witness to the following, that [the] sheriff was going to hang a rebel who stood in a car and was tied up. The priest spoke thus to him[,] 'Christ died innocent[,] so do you[.] Christ died for the good of his fellow creatures[,] so do you' — (and another sentence the exact words I forget)[.] The man was just going to speak[,] possibly to confess[,] and had just said 'Mr Sheriff' when the priest took up his stick[,] hit the horse and drove off the car from under [f. 49r] him. The man was cut down immediately but it was too late[.] Yet the priest was done [sic] nothing too. He might have heard the mans confession[.][3]

// Another fine[,] stout[,] good looking young man was going to be hanged and his wife who stood by and also had 6 young children by him said 'Thady you thief, on your honor dont spake [speak] a word' (and he was hung)[.]

---

[1] Robert Uniacke-Fitzgerald of Lisquinlan and Corkbeg, MP for Co. Cork (1797–1806) (Long, 'Fitzgerald, Sir Thomas Judkin').

[2] In 1798, Napoleon invaded Egypt; the invasion ended in defeat by the British at Alexandria in 1801.

[3] Quotation marks added to all dialogue in this paragraph and the one following.

// Sir Thomas fought many duels. He had one with Colonel — of the Tipperary Militia and notwithstanding being a very large corpulent man yet he always stood broad and with his arms up. Colonel — was standing on one side and diminishing his size as much as possible. Sir Thomas laughing and joking in a cool manner. 'Damn it Jack or Tom dont be so shy[,] stand fair man', and firing soon after hit him through the hat, 'By James[,] Jack you did right for had you been any other size I should have knocked the life out of you.'[1] This duel was for politicks. He generally spake joking or abusing his antagonist in these cases and was as cool as in his own room[.]

In Thomastown beauty is having the Gualty Mountains so near it[,] but I think they do not look so well as from Dundrum. They are too near the former and you see them too close for a picture[.]

[f. 49v] **Sunday January 25 /**
Day very hard frost. Fine[,] clear[,] Bright sky[,] sunshine.

Set out at 7 and rode to Tipperary through very fine good meadow country. Saw a great many Danish Mounds[.] The country swarms with them[.] There are many about Tipperary[.] The Danish forts are all round, the Roman oblong and there is an old British Fort near Tipperary which is square. None of the land possessors live near Tipperary[,] all [are] in England[,] and Mr Lloyd says above 10000 goes from thence out of the neighbourhood every year. Tipperary [is] famous for Butter [and] sends it all to Limerick and fat oxen. Did not go into the town [of Tipperary], Went off past to Pallis [Pallas] through delightful country indeed. Most of it pasture, finely waved, rich line of valley all the way on the Right and a low range of Mountains beyond. Scattered white houses [are] every where. Fine Lough or Loughs running in the bottom all along the vale and round beyond Pallis Mountain[.] Many Gentlemens seats to Pallis and beyond[.] Several very fine[,] comfortable ones and very much improved ones, with trees and plantations. Road in general [is] very bad, broken and stony and deep and narrow. Up and down all the way. Fences are chiefly stone walls or Mud walls lined with stone or topped with it[,] Or stone walls with rodded tops, very [f. 50r] few trees and hedges but some. Rich country. The hills frequently end abruptly and run in banks and are ended like the sea shore in ridges often[,] as if they had been formed by the washing of a tide. They run after out thus into a fine flat. None of them are very large. All this country admits very extensive prospects from these risings like boats on an ocean. Get to Limerick about 5 OClock[.]

Monday January 26. /
Day frosty at 6 and 7. Went off as sun rose, fine clear and cheering day, growing day, mellowing the land. Sunshine all day. No rain, but heavy[,] wet looking showers after 12 OClock. Wind rather active and alive[.]

Called on Mr Hill[.]

A great deal of land is now let on lease of 30 Shillings and some 18S In County Tipperary and yet many of the farmers live in cabins of mud walls and are poor in appearance. Mr Sadler told me he has a farm for which he pays (3 or) 4Gs an acre (I forget) at 100 Acres pasture. He has just taken it[.] Dined at Mr Launcelot Hills.

[1] Quotation marks added.

[f. 50v] Tuesday January 27 /
Moderate day, drisly, thick in the forenoon, then clear and fine. Mild[,] no frost[.]

Set out at 8 from Swinburnes Hotel[.]

He [Swinburne] was formerly a servant to a gentleman who went abroad. They parted at Waterford[.] He had at first a pot house [tavern] in Limerick which he did not like and lost about 40£ by when the Hotel was offered him about 3 years ago. He took it, a friend lent him £100 to fit it up[.] For 3 Months got no custom[,] was afraid he would not have money to pay his rent. Then on a sudden money came in and has continued to do so. Built [a] set of stables and paid in the course of 9 Months 300[£] or 500£ for them. Has fitted up the house in great style. Several Beds cost him 60 Each and several 40[.] I saw them. Rooms all neat and elegant[.] Prints in the house cost £150 for ornament!! A short time ago Mr Leach a gentlemans servant joined him with 450[£] and they have taken the next House which is at [the] corner and made in both into one. Mr Leach was also to furnish it in that manner and his expense at starting will be £1000 [f. 51r] But every thing pays and soon they will collect fortunes. The two houses are now already too small for the company.

Came along the Dublin road to Anacotty. Cross a good river there [Mulkear River.] Pretty Estate of Colonel Gorfs,[1] and over the road is the extensive estate of Lady Clare[2] whose walls I follow for a devil of a way. Very pretty all around[.] See the falls of the Shannon [Falls of Doonass] in Lord Masseys Demesne,[3] and opposite is a Captain Masseys. River very pretty[,] pleasure grounds to the waters edge and plantations and fine woods trees. At Castle Connel river [is] very fine ground and well laid out. Passing woods. Curious rock in the village on top of which was a fort, some walls now standing, and many ruins are laying down about the foot of the rock.[4] It is as great a curiosity as Cashel but smaller[.] The rock is a great natural curiosity. Go over an immense bog to Obriens Bridge[5] which might easily be drained and cultivated, fine slope to river, some edges of it [mown?] little pieces cultivated[.]

Noble (old) bridge[6] at Obriens, and from thence go along the towing path all up to [f. 51v] Killaloe. Flood on [the] river and [there is] water on each side of [the] path frequently. Fine sublime views of the County Clare Mountains and Tipperary all the way.[7] Come to a double Lock and Canal. Fine Chamber in the Lock, finished last year[.] Boats pay 2d a ton per mile. River not navigable from here to Killaloe[,] [the] river [is] so swift and over rocks whole way. [The] Canal [is] 19 feet above [the] river[.] Fine bridge of 17

---

[1] Possibly Woodsdown, Annacotty, home of the Gough family in the late 18th and early 19th centuries (LED). Sleater mentions Gough of 'Gran' near Annacotty (*Introductory Essay*, p. 130).

[2] The 'celebrated beauty' Anne Whaley (d. 1844) married the lawyer and politician John FitzGibbon, 1st Earl of Clare (see p. 288, n. 3) in 1786; their principal residence was Mount Shannon (Johnston-Liik and Quinn, 'FitzGibbon, John').

[3] Possibly Nathaniel William Massey, 2nd Baron Clarina and army officer (Murphy, 'Massey, Eyre').

[4] The ruins of the medieval castle of the O'Briens. See description of sketch at SJC, MS U.30 (8), ff. 1v–2r (p. 329), not reproduced.

[5] Lee sketched his first view of the spot; see description of sketch at SJC, MS U.30 (8), f. 3r (p. 329), not reproduced.

[6] Lee sketched this bridge; see description of sketch at SJC, MS U.30 (8), ff. 3v–4r (p. 329), not reproduced.

[7] Lee sketched two of these views; see description of sketch at SJC, MS U.30 (8), ff. 4v–5r, 6r (p. 330), not reproduced.

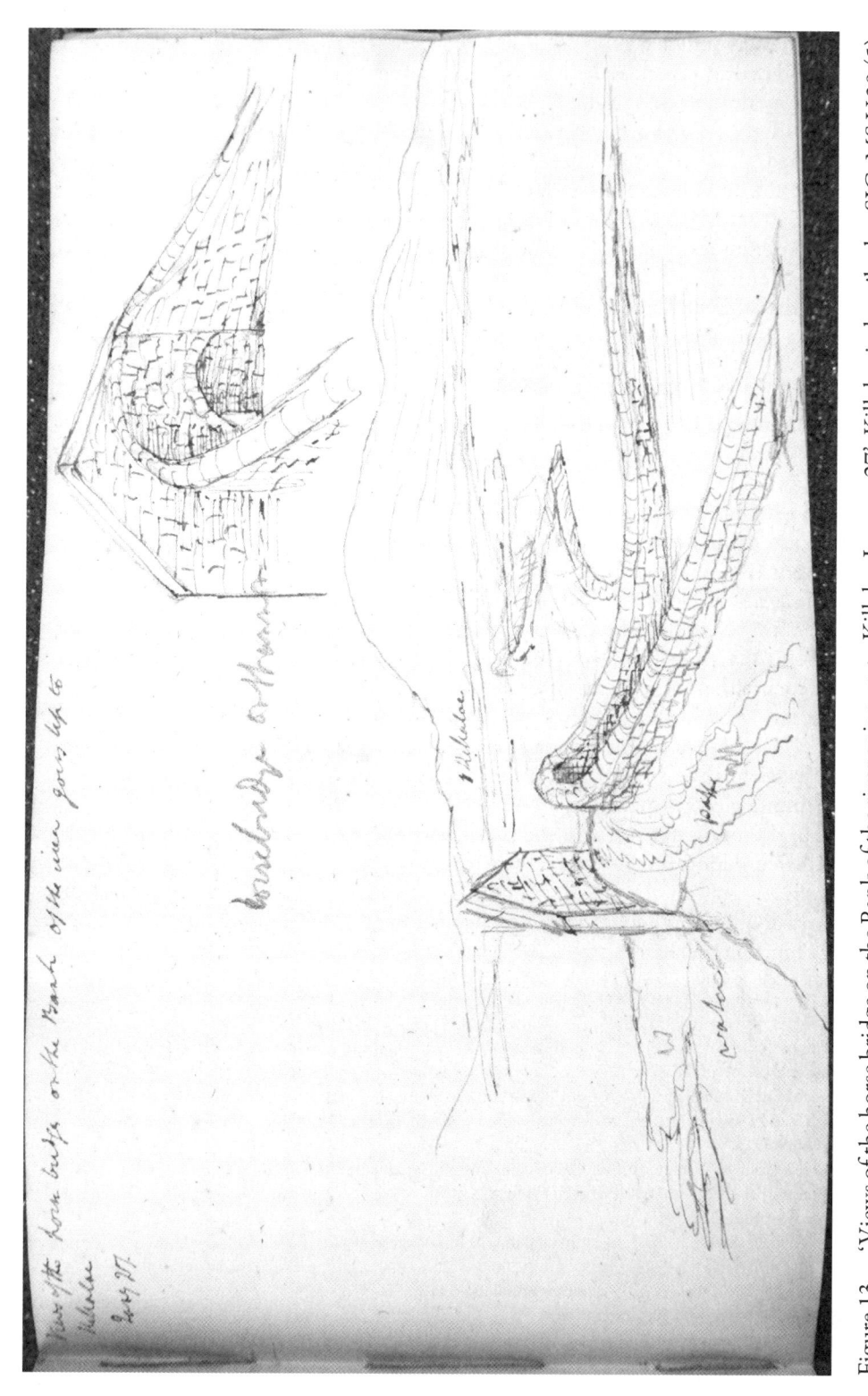

Figure 13. 'Views of the horse bridge on the Bank of the river going up to Killaloe January 27'. Killaloe is described at SJC, MS U.30 (5), f. 51v (pp. 276, 278). By John Lee, 27 January 1807 (SJC, MS U.30 (8), ff. 6v–7r). Reproduced by kind permission of the Master and Fellows of St John's College, Cambridge.

Arches[.][1] 2 were cut away to make [the] canal. Ruin on a little island [Ballina Castle] above [the] Bridge, [a] fine cathedral.[2] Curious oratory[3] in the C*h*ur*c*h Yard[,] the 2 doors perfect as modern work. Cath*edral* [is in the] form of a long cross. Steeple sup*port*ed by 4 gothic arches. All the ornam*en*ts inside [are] gothic[,] very neat. Most beautiful and neat Cathed*ral* and kept well. Curious old Gateway or arch of Brian Borimhe inside [the] *c*hur*c*h[4] and with most wonderful gothic ornament[.]

[f. 52r] **Wednesday January 28** /
Day beautiful[,] Clear, Sunshine. Wind very cold[.] Set out at ½ p*a*st 8 But there was so thick a fog that I c*ou*ld not see 20 Yds and it was intensely cold[.] Went over the Bridge and into a cabin, where I staid ½ hour, and [the] fog getting thinner [I] went on and had one tolerably clear view of Derry[5] and the Shannon w*hic*h is very wide there. The fog was all gone but in the deep valley where[,] to my surprise[,] it came on again and then I c*ou*ld not see about me. Curious effect [of] having the front ground clear[,] the tops of the M*ou*nt*ai*ns clear and as bright that every part c*ou*ld be seen but the bases and river all in fog[.][6] I c*ou*ld see some parts of road and not others. On com*ing* to [the] top of one M*ou*nt*ai*n I c*ou*ld see the tops of the surround*ing* one*s* very plain and a little before me but valley entirely filled with fog and when the Lough [Lough Derg] is seen to greatest advantage.[7] I c*ou*ld see within 2 yards where the fog began and curious the Entrance into it. All the [packets?] going indirectly down to the valley and when emerging on oppo*site* M*ou*nt*ai*n they were going downw*ar*ds in contrary to the others. On coming about ½ way the fog then dim*inish*ed and the distances c*ou*ld be seen tolerably clear[.]

Pass over [the] most beautiful first 6 Miles [of] river running at [the] foot of [the] Clare [f. 52v] M*ou*nt*ai*ns [Slieve Bernagh] and the road high up on [the] oppo*site* side[.] Derry [is a] beaut*iful* place. Fine plantations and woods and ground finely and advantageously waved. [The] Last ½ [of the] way [the] country [is] open and not very interesting, the hopes of a good dinner made it so and a comfortable inn, when after having been in a room for a short time and just warming myself and being glad at being well off, on ordering dinner, [the] waiter came in and said All their Beds were bespoke, I perceived it was a lie but wh*at* c*ou*ld I do, [I was] obliged to turn out and go to another and worse inn, [a] room with*out* [a] fire, no lock on [the] door, w*h*ich constantly flew ½ open[.] Horrible[,] uncomfortable. The H*ou*se where I was turned out was Mr Canterell[8]

---

[1] Lee's error – the bridge, built *c.*1770, had 13 arches (NIAH). The error is repeated at SJC, MS U.30 (8), ff. 10v–11r (p. 330).

[2] St Flannan's Cathedral, Killaloe, established by the early 13th century on the site of an earlier church (Gwynn and Hadcock, *Medieval Religious Houses*, p. 86). Lee sketched the cathedral and its surroundings; see descriptions of sketches at SJC, MS U.30 (8), ff. 8v–9r, ff. 10v–11r, f. 12r and f. 13v (pp. 330–31), not reproduced.

[3] The Oratory of St Molana, sketched at SJC, MS U.30 (8), ff. 14r, 15r, not reproduced; see descriptions of sketches at p. 331.

[4] The site has a connection to Brian Bórama, high-king of Ireland (see p. 288, n. 11). 'It was the policy of Brian Boruma [*sic*] ... to make Killaloe the principal church of his Dalcassian kingdom in Clare' (Gwynn and Hadcock, *Medieval Religious Houses*, p. 86).

[5] Derry Castle, near Killaloe, Co. Tipperary, owned by the Head family (LED).

[6] Lee sketched this effect; see descriptions of the sketches at SJC, MS U.30 (8), ff. 16v–17r, ff. 18v–19r, ff. 20v–21r and ff. 23v–24r (pp. 331–2), not reproduced.

[7] Lee sketched this view; see description at SJC, MS U.30 (8), ff. 25v–26r (p. 332), not reproduced.

[8] Isaac Cantrell demised to William Considine in 1804 a carriage house, stable and inn on Castle St, Nenagh (*Nenagh Guardian*, 26 May 1945). The establishment must have retained the name of Cantrell's at least into 1807.

((or such n*ame*)) at the sign of the Red Lion Saltant rampant[1] and I since understand that the reason of all the beds being bespoken was that they are rich people and not liking the appearance of a traveller with*ou*t a horse refused me thus. They do not look (*said* a man to me) upon any worth attending to unless they have horses and carriages and are great folks and it is [f. 53r] a common trick with people at many Inns to do so and w*ou*ld sooner refuse to behave civilly <u>than do so</u> and have their beds oc*cu*pied than that they sh*ou*ld be used by a person whose shew [appearance] they dont like.

At Cashel[,][2] on going to the Inn there[,] I was told the Beds were all bespoken, they will let me have some dinner and I was shewed into a room where I dined with some others and sent a boy off with a letter <u>to Sir *Thomas* J*u*dkin Fitzgerald</u> in sight of the people[.] The waiter in the Even*ing* overheard me and told me (on asking him to look out for a bed for me) that I must say nothing and he w*ou*ld give me another mans Room who had a promise of one but that he did not know wh*at* would become of himself (making a merit of the service he was going to render me)[.] I had a most excellent doublebedded room to myself[.]

Here I do not believe my humble appearance was the cause of the negative answ*er*, for their beds might be all engaged as the assize was going on[.]

// Lord Cornwallis[3] requested that when ever Sir *Thomas* J*u*dkin Fitzgerald came up to Dublin he w*ou*ld call on him. Sir Tho*mas* did so. 'Well Sir Tho*mas*' after complementing him on his very spirited exertions, 'how could you possibly escape so many hair breadth [f. 53v] scrapes and any other person w*ou*ld have been afraid to act so resolutely and boldly as you did.' 'My Lord' *said* Sir Tho*mas*[,] 'I always had envied y*our* lord ships conduct and with y*our* Lord*ships* example before me I never was afraid to act as I have done[.] There are no two persons who have smelt more powder than Lord Cornw*allis* and Lord Hood[4] and yet they are now both aged men and have never been injured although their valor has exposed them so much. With 2 such examples before me I sh*ou*ld have ventured my life more than I did[.]'[5]

This anecdote was the substance of it was told me thus incorrectly by *Captain Sadler*[.]

Thursday Jan*ua*ry 29. /
Day cold, frosty and a very thick fog, wh*ich* cont*inu*ed til 10 when [the] sun began to disperse it, Came on again in ½ hour and cont*inu*ed till 11[,] then clear[,] then thick again and ab*ou*t one ~~saw~~ it got very thin but never all day abandoned the deep vales and rivers. Very hot on [the] M*ou*nt*ai*n tops and very cold in [the] fog[.] Sun shines all day. No view[.]

[f. 54r] On a new bridge built between Killaloe and Nenagh are the miles thus accurately marked down

7 Miles 1 Quarter 29 Perches to Nenagh } 1801
4 *Miles* 1 *Quarte*r 11 P*erches* to Killaloe
and a rough hewn fish on the endstone[.]

---

[1] Saltant or rampant; leaping, jumping or dancing (*OED*).

[2] Lee refers back to his visit to Cashel in Jan. 1807 (see above, pp. 266–7).

[3] Charles Cornwallis, 1st Marquess Cornwallis, Governor General of India and Lord-lieutenant of Ireland (Bayly and Prior, 'Cornwallis, Charles (1738–1805)').

[4] Samuel Hood, 1st Viscount Hood, naval officer (Baugh and Duffy, 'Hood, Samuel (1724–1816)').

[5] Quotation marks added to all dialogue in this paragraph.

Mr Heads Slate quarry[1] near Derry is very large and seems to have been worked for many years[.] Very fine slate. It sells for 13S a 1000 and the larger bits for 2Gs a ton[.]

In add*itio*n to my reception yesterday on com*ing* to the 2*nd* Inn, and asking for a bed and a room[,] the 2*nd* Waiter said to the first[,] 'and Why ~~did~~ (do) not you let the Gent*leman* have them at y*our* H*ouse* [Cantrell's inn].' 'Our Beds were all engaged' s*ai*d he with a signifi*cant* look, holding my bundle in his hands, the chamber m*ai*d was com*ing* do*w*n when she said, 'Faith and I do believe all our Beds are engaged ~~likewise~~ (also), An [*sic*] Major of the Queens County Militia', then slipped up and told me this was a com*mon* trick am*ong* them and then upon enquiry and mak*ing* a little bustle, a Bed they said was not engaged and a room was given me, but my treatment was not that [f. 54v] of a Gent*leman* com*ing* in a C*oach* and 4. Mr Fitzpatricks Inn[,] I am told[,] is the most civil / Upon asking whether ~~there~~ was (the next R*oom* was) a Coffy [coffee] room, 'yes But you must not go into it for none but Subscribers are admitted', 'Are no strangers[?]' 'Sometimes but very seldom.' It appears gentlemen strangers may go in. 'But' said the Waiter[,] 'when all the Comp*any* are gone out I will bring you a paper although there is a fine for taking papers out[.]'[2]

// In [the] morning walked ab*out* [the] town. A very high (square) steeple wh*ich* I took for an old round tower at [a] dist*ance* attracted my notice. Went to it. 'What is that[?]' 'The steeple of the Ch*urch*[.]' Where is the Ch*urch*[?]' 'That is it' (a small build*ing* behind at some small dist*ance*.) 'What[,] are they thus separate[?]' 'Yes but the Ch*urch* is only begun and they are going to build some more of it and then they will be joined together!!!' Curious old ruin of a fort[.][3]

Pig market. All pigs [are] tied by [the] leg with a bandage of straw. Market small. Pigs dear[.] Asked prices of many, large and small. Some little [f. 55r] ones as low as 24S, some 3Gs, 3½, 4½ the com*mon* price. There was one as large a pig as I ever saw for 5½Gs.

Upon paying the waiter the Bill and not forgetting him in the account (a 6^d extraord*inary* [tip] to show him I was a gent*leman*), I took the liberty of giving him a lecture and told him never to refuse any hospitality to a person who travels on foot wh*at* ever may be his external appearance. I was not refused but <u>it might have been</u> so[.] He blamed the people at the other H*ouse* [and] told me he knew me for a gent*leman* by my appearance more than if I had 50 Horses etc and we parted friends[.]

Medio Tutissiumus Ibis.[4] Is sometimes false. Going to necess*ary* place [privy] the *pars pro toto*[5] met with a bad reception fr*om* the middle seat of wh*ich* there were 3. In many places and in all the new Inns they lock up these retreats and right they are for so doing for otherwise the people in the whole town wo*u*ld come to them[.][6]

---

[1] There were a number of quarries on Head's estate, described in Donnell, 'An Account of Certain Slate Districts', pp. 171–2.

[2] Quotation marks added to all dialogue in this paragraph and the one following.

[3] Nenagh castle, built in 1200–1220 and seat of the Butler family until the second half of the 14th century (Farrelly and O'Brien, *Archaeological Inventory of County Tipperary*, I, p. 312).

[4] 'You will go most safely by the middle course'.

[5] 'a part (taken) for the whole'.

[6] Lee seems to describe taking the middle of three seats in a privy in the inn, in the hope of deterring other users from entering at the same time as he, but to no avail. See description of his sketch of such an 'accommodation' at SJC, MS U.30 (8), f. 70r (p. 339, n. 3), not reproduced.

Get on the top of the Coach and with the Guard came along passing Toomavara [Toomyvara],[1] Moneygall etc etc[.] At Dunkerrin the church yard is all built on arches and these are niches in which a person could get into[.] It is said they were made for pedlars at fairs[.][2] [*At bottom of page, small ink sketch of four arches.*]

[f. 55v] Country all very rich and delightful all the way and a great deal in fine order. See the Mountains which run to Limerick[,] very plain[,] and the Mountain called the Devils Bit but not very far from the road[.][3] It is a curious hole in the Mountain which they say the devil going up once was tired and bit a piece of it and laid it on the side and sure enough there was a piece on one side which would exactly fit it. There is a bridle road and [one] for passengers I am told up through it[.] Roscrea is a good town, large[.] It was market day, curious to see all the pigs in baskets, etc etc[.] There is the door of the Church which is a most curious piece of old architecture with ornaments cut in the stone. Close by is a very fine high round tower with a light top supported by wooden pillars.[4] There are floors put all up it and garrets made in it communicating by ladders I am told. It is a beautiful tower. There is a very curious old Castle in the town and a part of a round fort[5] in the spot and some other parts of the ruin are a persons (timber) deal yards. A most amazing bog laying here[,] Bog of Mowla[6] up [to the] R of [the] road and for an immense extent and depth[.] Farther on is a great deal of it on the L and from which [it] appears most of it might be reclaimed for that which is [reclaimed], is land of wonderful fine appearance. Some most beautiful meadows.

[f. 56r] Rush Hall[,] the now ruins of the Earl of Mountrath[,] are on an amazing fine spot for they command a most extensive prospect on all sides, the view on the N is bounded only by the Slieve Bloom Mountains at some distance but which run the whole extent of horizon[.] The land between them is very fine and there is an immense bog / all parts of the Bog of Allen.[7] The view to the S[,] E and W is unlimited in many parts[.]

I am no farmer but could not help observing some turnip fields where the turnips had been gathered by the hand and buried in earth keeps like potatoes. The tops had been cut off and were laying about the fields and as the gard [guard] told me were left to rot[.] This surprised me. Next (to) [the] village of Castle town[,] about ½ mile on this side[,] the land of Mr Pirce would strike any body[.] I never saw better sheep or better pasture land and kept in neater order. Then for the first time I saw [a] neat sheep fold, Land on both sides of [the] road shews it is in the hands of a good master. Farther on [are] very neat

---

[1] Lee made a sketch at Toomyvara, described at SJC, MS U.30 (8), f. 27v (p. 332), not reproduced.

[2] Wilson states that the 20 niches were 'recesses for pedlars wares during the fair' (*Post Chaise Companion*, p. 220).

[3] Lee sketched this view, described at SJC, MS U.30 (8), ff. 29v–30r, f. 31r and f. 31v (p. 332), not reproduced.

[4] Remains of the monastery reputedly founded by St Cronan in the 7th century (Gwynn and Hadcock, *Medieval Religious Houses*, p. 96). Lee sketched the tower and nearby cabins at SJC, MS U.30 (8), ff. 32v–33r (reproduced at p. 282 as Figure 14) and f. 34r (p. 333).

[5] The stone castle at Roscrea replaced the earlier, 13th-century timber castle and moat in 1278–80 (Farrelly and O'Brien, *Archaeological Inventory of County Tipperary*, I, pp. 314–15).

[6] The bog of Monaincha, Co. Tipperary, a branch of the Bog of Allen (see n. 7 below) and formerly known as Monela.

[7] The Bog of Allen is a major topographical feature of the Irish midlands, and one of the most extensive raised bogs in the world. Following centuries of industrial peat extraction and agricultural reclamation, in the late 20th century the bog comprised 444.3 sq. miles (115,080 ha) extending into the counties Galway, Kildare, Laois, Longford, Meath, Offaly, Roscommon, Tipperary and Westmeath, but with the core of the bog lying in Kildare and Offaly (340.6 sq. miles, or 88,210 ha). See Hurley, *Bog of Allen*, pp. 3, 6.

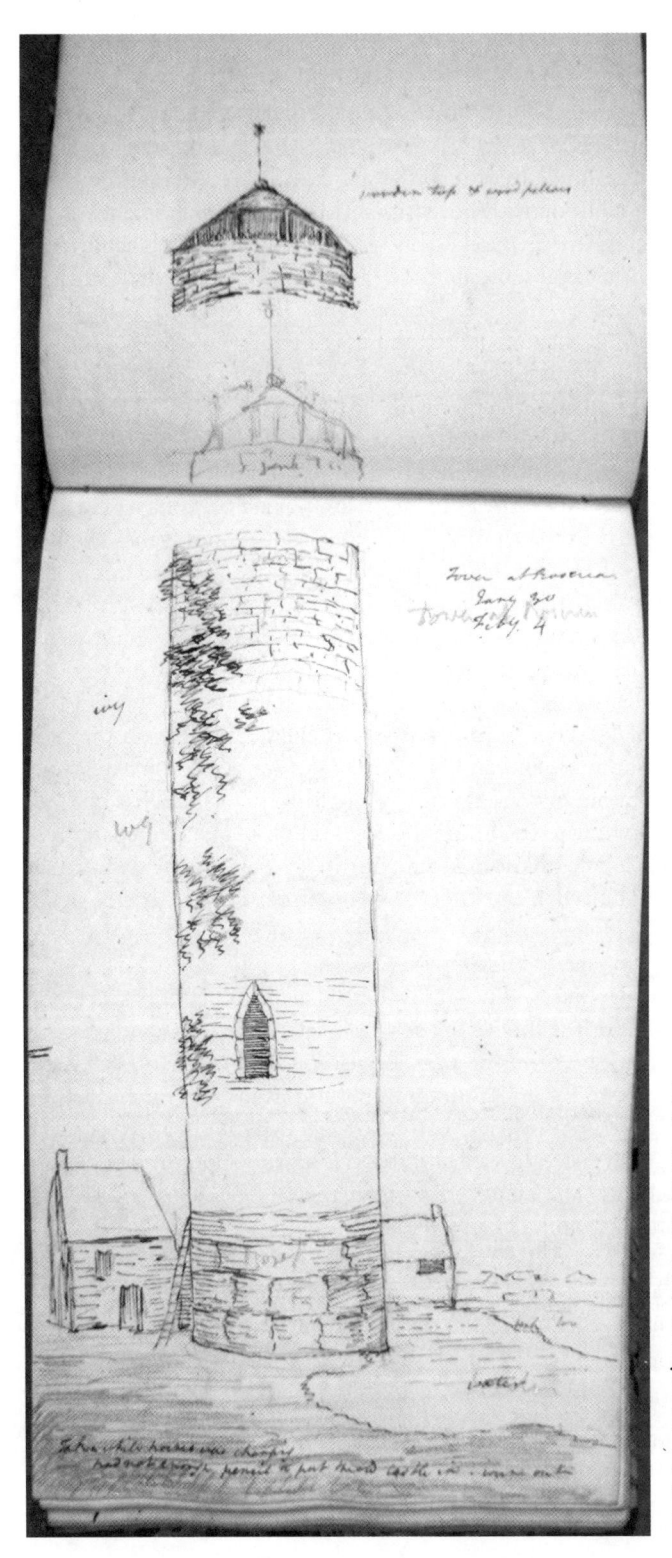

Figure 14. Sketch, 'Tower at Roscrea Jan*uary* 30 Febr*uary* 4', described in SJC, MS U.30 (5), f. 55v (p. 281). The date of the sketch is more likely 29 January 1807, as recorded in Lee's diary. By John Lee (SJC, MS U.30 (8), ff. 32v–33r). Reproduced by kind permission of the Master and Fellows of St John's College, Cambridge.

hedges of clipt furze which make a neat and excellent fence. The village of Castletown is a picture and the prettiest thing I had seen for some time[.] All [the] houses [are] neat and clean and with windows and chimneys and whitewashed. A small Δ flat of grass in the centre of [the] village. It does credit to its owner. There is [f. 56v] a curious old castle,[1] a very venerable bridge and picturesque mill on the L side — Garde[2] told me that in the rebellion he has seen 100 fires all lit on the Slieve Bloom Mountains and as many on the other side of [the] road. [He was] Never attacked but once when 1800 rebels came [and] stopped [the] coach[,] made every body get out, took [the] Mail Bags, set [the] coach on fire and did not rob or hurt one passenger. They said they only wanted government intelligence. There were many gentlemen among them and many were on horse back, others were with pikes, forks, spades, and with pieces of meat[,] pork etc sticking on the Ends, and many quite to rakes. A priest of the name of Murphy was one of the chiefs. One poor looking fellow ½ naked begged Guard 'for the love of God'[3] to give him an old coat which he did. Some fellows were going to take some of his clothes but the officers rode up and made them desist. They made [the] coachman bring fire and set it to the Coach. // He says that the Coach setting out from Limerick at 6 OClock is the signal for people going to work and that not a man would stir till it was off, it is as good as a Bell to call in to work, and if [it] was to be delayed they would not go.

On coming to Maryborough [Portlaoise] he gathered up all the hay on which we put our feet and the straw on which we sat and threw it down to a female[,] one of his family[,] at the entrance of the town. Economy!!

[f. 57r] He has been garde 15 Years and was 14 Years before that in the 5 Light dragoons which never went out of Ireland and consisted all of Irishmen, Colonel would not take a Connaught man, reasons why, he had an antipathy to them[.]

Garde said that the people who are reclaiming the lands in Mowla bog were said to be dying every day[.] 'Why[,] is it unwholesome.' 'No, but they say it is wrong to use the land which belonged to [the] Church.'[4]

Friday January 30 /
Very fine[,] bright[,] sunshine day, hardly any wind, but air sharp[.] Bluish sky which gave a fine tint to all the scenery[.]

Set out at about ~~11 by the mail which from there being only one guard (other ill) got me a place~~. 7 Exactly. Often rowed for doing things impetuously and in a hurry. Insisted on being called at six. 'What is the use Sir[,] ½ after [6] will do?' 'No[,] it wont[,] call me', 'Very well Sir[.]' Up I got at six[,] dressed and stood idle at the door of [the] Inn at ½ after. Office man said one Gentleman had spoke before me for [the] outside place and he knew all inside [was] full from Limerick[.] Coach came at 7 to a moment. Only one outside place [was] vacant. Where was [the] Gentleman who spoke before me? [He] Did not come, [I] paid my fare (as he had done before) [and] Up I jumped and about 400 Yds on we met him running to meet us. Too late. So that hurry does good some times and at 1 in 100 times it is useful to me[.]

---

[1] The tower house known as 'Cody's Castle', Castletown, Co. Laois (Sweetman, Alcock and Moran, *Archaeological Inventory of County Laois*, p. 111).
[2] Likely reference to the guard of the post-chaise, rather than Lee's sometime travelling companion.
[3] Quotation marks added.
[4] Quotation marks added.

See the rock of Dunamass [Dunamase] on the R[,] ruins of some building on it[.][1]

Rail Castlecoote S house[2] on the Left[.] [f. 57v] On the left farther on is Seat of Earl of Portarlington,[3] tolerable good house[.]

The Neighbourhood of Monasterevin is very pretty and the grounds of ~~Lord~~ Marquis Drogheda[4] are beautiful, finely wooded. River [Nore] runs at the base of the hills to the R of the road and [the] Canal [lies] between it and road. The Abbey[5] is situated in a most unfortunate place close to the town and in a hollow when there are very fine spots where it would have looked to advantage. Ruin [is] very good[,] [a] respectable size and very pretty here. All the plan is a good one and very respectable. Very good houses in the town and neat.

I must not forget to say that the chief inn at Maryboro is a capital one for comfort. Charges cheap enough. Fine groves and woods of Marquis Drogheda[.] Kildare is a very small place but there is a beautiful round tower[6] there which while the Coach was stopping I ran to look at and [there are] some ruins there but they are surrounded with I believe a high octagon wall and I could not get in time enough. Tower [is] much overgrown with moss. About a mile on this side [of] the town is a rising ground on one side close to the road on which Sir J. Duff[7] planted 2 pieces of cannon and was going to batter the town down that was in the hands of the rebels but they left it in time and he pursued and had a battle with them on the Curragh[8] where many were killed. On the entrance to the Curragh on the [f. 58r] R is a *rath*[9] or round mound of Earth where they entrenched themselves and fought from and here it was that one of the officers of the yeomanrys horse ran away with him out of the line and went into the very Ranks of the Enemy. One fellow fired 3 times at him and missed[,] another was going to pike him but the pike head came off[.] He then took the but end and hit him with that and broke some of his ribs[.] The Uncle of the yeoman told me the circumstance on the top of the coach[.] His nephew got his horse away and saved his life. A County of Clare Gentleman was in the Coach when it was once stopped and robbed by the rebels and he pretended to be a priest. His name [is] Molony. 'Arragh and ~~you~~ will you rob me[?] Dont ye know me[,] Father Molony of the County of Clare.'[10] They took his money[,] coat and Clothes from him

---

[1] Ruins of a 'large Anglo-Norman fortress founded on a rock eminence' by 1215 (Sweetman, Alcock and Moran, *Archaeological Inventory of County Laois*, p. 109).

[2] Probably Ballyfin Demesne, Co. Laois, owned by the Coote family. Castlecoote, another of their properties, is in Co. Roscommon.

[3] Emo Court, Co. Laois, begun in 1790 (NIAH).

[4] Field Marshal Charles Moore, 1st Marquess of Drogheda, army officer and politician, of Moore Abbey, Monasterevin (Dunlop, 'Moore, Charles (1730–1822)').

[5] The Cistercian abbey at Monasterevin was founded between 1177 and 1181 (Gwynn and Hadcock, *Medieval Religious Houses*, p. 142).

[6] In Kildare cathedral churchyard, probably built in the 12th century (Andrews, *IHTA no. 1 Kildare*, p. 9). Lee sketched the tower while the horses were being watered; see description of the sketch at SJC, MS U.30 (8), f. 36r (p. 333), not reproduced.

[7] Sir James Duff, army officer; Lee refers in the following lines to Duff's capture of Kildare during the 1798 rebellion, during which attack his men killed about 200 rebels on the Curragh (Stephens, 'Duff, Sir James (1753–1839)').

[8] An open plain of commonage in Co. Kildare, used as military grounds and for horseracing.

[9] 'Chiefly in Ireland: an enclosure of roughly circular form made with a strong earthen wall, and originally serving as a fort and place of residence; an earthen ring fort' (*OED*).

[10] Quotation marks added to all dialogue in this paragraph and the one following.

nevertheless. A Gent*leme*n fr*om* near Nenagh[,] my fellow traveller[,] told me that his Uncle was on the coach once when it was stopped[.] They robbed him of his purse and some guineas and asked him on his honor if he had more money, [he said] no. He then to amuse them and turn their attention [he] told a fellow that he was welcome to the money but wo*ul*d be much obliged to him if he wo*ul*d take it all out and give him back his purse for he had a great fondness for it as it was made him a present a by Lady. 'Who was she' said the rebel, 'Oh she is a very fine girl and I should [a] person for whom I have a very particular esteem.' 'Then give my love [f. 58v] to her' (sa*i*d he) 'and I will keep it for her sake' putting it in his pocket[.] He had at the time ab*ou*t 100Gs in Bank paper. The Cork Coach and 2 post Chaises were at the time with the mail and all robbed and the 12 horses all taken away[.] The C*o*ach man who drove was a passenger another time when Mr Blood[1] was killed by a random shot and the mail attacked and he shewed us the spot, nothing very particular in it. The rebels had Kildare in their possession for above a week and the reason of Sir James Duff marching for Limerick up the road was that he got no despatch fr*om* Dublin[.]

The Curragh is a most beautiful Course and contains above 500 Acres of land as smooth as a lawn and covered with sheep to such n[os] that hence the proverb 'as poor as a Curragh Kildare Sheep'. There are 1000s of them on it. I am told there are 3 M*i*les long and 7 or 8 long. It is a beautiful plot of ground far exceed*in*g Newmarket[2] and the stand is very advantageously situated. I co*ul*d not see the course for all the posts are taken up in winter[.] It is a pleasant thing to see all the bogs on the roadsides are begun to be cultivated. They find the advantage of turning that land to some use, they often after paring[3] and burning it for turnips or in Aug*us*t a crop of rape [f. 59r] wh*i*ch in the follo*win*g Aug*us*t will produce as much as that the n° of barrels of rape shall be worth 30 an Acre. Saw a great deal of fresh reclaimed bog sown with rape. Kildare is a great corn country, and saw a great deal of wheat and most luxuriant crops indeed. The lands are in general very narrow and look like long English asparagus beds not wider nor many so wide. Whole country [is] very well wooded and very fine looking. Much of the bog beyond on this side [of] Kildare might easily be finely cult*ivat*ed. There is a gravelly soil not very deep below [the] surface[.] Hon P. Moores[4] H*o*use on D*ublin* side of Curragh [is a] very nice place, new house, fine woods around it[.]

Jigginstown House[5] is a most singular ruin, it is an extensive ruin all built or faced with very fine dutch Brick (I am told)[.] The extent is now clear, the vaults or cellars seem all built on fine arches but how the devil anyone co*ul*d think of fixing on such a spot for the residence of the Lord Lieut*enan*t I cannot imagine, it is close to the public road wh*i*ch wo*ul*d be a nuisance. The situation is bad, [there is] no view from it and [it is] quite confined.

[f. 59v] Naas is a town built on a rising spot. On the top of the Gaol is now suspended on a pole the head or rather scull of Dr —[6] who had an officer of some regiment to dine

---

[1] On 15 Apr. 1801 a Mr Blood of Gardiner St, Dublin, was killed during a robbery of the Limerick mail (*Walker's Hibernian Magazine*, Apr. 1801, p. 255).

[2] Newmarket racecourse, Suffolk.

[3] Removing turf from the surface of the soil before burning.

[4] Ponsonby Moore of Moorfield House, Co. Kildare.

[5] Built *c.* 1637 by Thomas Wentworth, Earl of Strafford, near Naas, Co. Kildare (Manning, 'Ditches', p. 227).

[6] Name not provided, but represented by a dash.

with him and who was telling him that in the neighbouring village how weak his force was only himself and — men, After parting the same night the Dr at the head of a rebel party went and overpowering the party murdered them all. [The] Dr was a man of fortune and well related. This happened close to Naas and I was shewn the Drs House on the Left.[1] A Danish fort is now turned into a fort[2] on which are cannon mounted and a company of soldiers[.] Bishops Court on the L [is] the seat of Mr Ponsonby,[3] who seems to be draining properly a deal of good ground. It is a pretty place and [there is] room for improvement[.] On the top of the next hill is a round tower[,] not very high[,] and [the] Church of Oughterard[.][4] Nothing very particular in it at 1 [first] view. Church in ruins[.]

Newlands seat of Lord Kilvarden [is] on the R[,] from whence he was going into Dublin when he was massacred and his son and Daughter was in the [f. 60r] carriage who run into the castle yard out of her senses.[5] A gentleman on top of [the] coach said he saw lord Kilwarden a few days before his death. Knew him well and that his last words were, that the men who had committed the act might be tried by the laws of their country!!!

On the L is Clondalkin village and the round tower[6] there which looks very well from the road. [The] Grand Canal[7] is a fine object and the trees down each side are a great ornament to it, on each side is a road for foot and horsemen. Many locks on it[.] We cross it twice[.]

January 31. Saturday /
Raining at 6 and till 8[.] Clearer and more clear after[.] Fog dissappeared [sic]. // Fine all day. Frosty at night[.]
    Called on [blank]

February 1. Sunday. /
Dirty. Foggy till noon. Sunshine, but cold in the shade and Frosty. Called on Mr Sayers. Dined there. Mo [breaks off]

February 2 Monday /
Hard frost in Morning and frost all day[,] sunshine. Frost at night and till 12[,] then not so not all morning[.]

---

[1] Lee appears to relate a rather garbled version of the story of Dr John Esmonde (1760?–98), physician and United Irishman of Osberstown, Naas, who was convicted and condemned by court martial for directing an attack on the barracks at Prosperous on 24 May 1798; he was hanged on Carlisle (now O'Connell) Bridge in Dublin on 14 June 1798 (Woods, 'Esmonde, John').

[2] The *dún* or fort of Naas, built *c.*277 CE, was chief residence of the kings of Leinster until 904 CE; a 'small barracks' was erected on the site in the 18th century and it functioned as an 'outpost' in 1798 (Gibson, 'North and South Moats', pp. 49–50).

[3] William Brabazon Ponsonby (1744–1806), 1st Baron Ponsonby, politician, of Bishop's Court, Co. Kildare (Murphy, 'Ponsonby, William Brabazon').

[4] Church and round tower, 6th–7th century (Gwynn and Hadcock, *Medieval Religious Houses*, p. 400).

[5] Arthur Wolfe (1739–1803); see SJC, MS U.30 (2), p. 105, n. 4.

[6] An 8th-century round tower (Archiseek).

[7] The Grand Canal extended from the River Shannon to the River Liffey at Grand Canal Docks in 1785 (Casey, *Buildings of Ireland: Dublin*, p. 456).

DIARY 5: KILLARNEY TO DUBLIN

[f. 60v] **February 3. Tuesday** /
Thaw. Dirty[,] Dismal[,] Dreary[,] Foggy[,] Damp day[.] Sunshine and fine at noon. Snow in the Evening[.]

February 4: Wednesday /
Foggy and Misty. Dirty and Cold[.]
Went to the Dublin Society[1] and saw the whole departments which are arranged in a most elegant manner. Saw a specimen of the Wicklow Gold and a model of the large piece which was found some years ago[.]
Went to see the Calf with six legs[.] It has four as is common and two growing out of the back near the shoulders[.] That on the Near side or one [sic] the left shoulder is the longest and about 9 Inches long[,] the other about six[.] They lay down and you would not perceive them as you look at the Calf. They are made like legs[,] have bends and hoof on them. The shoulder of [the] animal [is] very high above [its] back. [The] Mother respects [the] Calf like a common one. [It will be one] Year old next March. [It was] Born at Naas at the Carriers Inn (County Kildare) and was brought up to Dublin where the owner [f. 61r] bought him for 8 Guineas. [It is a] Heifer. Large for the age. Eats well etc[.] Paid 13^d[.]

February 5. Thursday /
Foggy and bad day[.]
Went to the 4 Courts[2] and heard [the] Chancellor Mr Ponsonby[3] and Mr Curran Master of Rolls[4] — Beautiful design and building and wonderful Dome[.] Walked up to the Phenix Park, through [the] grounds by Phenix[,] round by [the] Mound and fortification[5] and over Island Bridge. Up <u>Bow Lane</u> and through [the] <u>Liberties</u> [and] home[.] Account of all this hereafter[.] Dined with Mr Guard[.]

Friday February 6. /
Cold wind, thick day[,] nothing particular, fog and rain a little in Evening[.]
Went over the ~~Library~~ College [Trinity College] with Mr Fitzgerald,[6] saw the Printing Office[7] (Paltry)[,] [the] Chapel[8] which exceeds any building of the sort in both our Universities.[9] Fine Organ[,] 5 Seats on Each side. Very wide. Pulpit in middle[,] seats all

---

[1] This was Lee's second visit; see SJC, MS U.30 (2), 3 Sept. 1806 (pp. 103–4).

[2] See SJC, MS U.30 (2), p. 100, n. 1.

[3] See p. 121, n. 2

[4] John Philpot Curran (1750–1817), politician and lawyer with a reputation as an 'outspoken Whig', and who defended Robert Emmet in his trial for high treason in 1803 (see SJC, MS U.30 (2), p. 99, n. 7) (Geoghegan, 'Curran, John Philpot').

[5] The Phoenix Park was created in 1662 as a royal deerpark; the magazine fort was built in 1738 (Casey, *Buildings of Ireland: Dublin*, pp. 287, 305).

[6] This could be Rev. Gerald Fitzgerald, Vice Provost and Auditor, and Lecturer in Oriental Languages (*Gentleman's and Citizen's Almanack*, pp. 121–2), or he could be a local guide, the 'old man' referred to below.

[7] The Printing House, built c.1735 (Lennon, *IHTA no. 19 Dublin part II, 1610 to 1756*, p. 35).

[8] The original chapel of 1629 was rebuilt in 1787–9 (Goodbody, *IHTA no. 26 Dublin part III, 1756 to 1847*, p. 95).

[9] The universities of Oxford and Cambridge.

of dark oak or [***] mahog*a*ny. Beaut*iful* ceiling. Nothing to compare to it. Saw the Great Bell in the Corner of Botany Bay Court[.][1]

[f. 61v] Went over the Examin*atio*n Hall w*hic*h is also a beaut*iful* Chamber and on the side correspond*ing* to the Chapel. Noble Statue or group of 3 fig*ure*s in it[,] Old Provost and Angel and some other female fig*ure*.[2] The 2 fig*ure*s are out of one block of marble and the angel [is from] a separate one. (It may be so). Done by an Irishman of Co. Tipperary (but done in Italy)[,] Cost 8000. This is the old mans story[,] it may be true. The figures are excellent and the Angel is beautifully light, <u>very thin body</u>. Around the Chambers are ab*ou*t 6 pictures on each side[,] large size. One of Queen Bess [Elizabeth I] seems to be the best. A very good one of Lord Clare[3] and of Burke.[4] One of Dean Swift[5] *fr*om w*hic*h my print in *British Classicks*[6] is taken. Benches etc for exam*inatio*n and circular Seats where exam*ination*s for fellowships are held at [the] upper end of [the] room. Very elegant room and good size and well suited to the Coll*ege*, but inferior to our Senate House.[7] Museum is a paltry thing and contains a heterogenous [*sic*] mixture of Birds[,] Beasts, Fishes[,] Shells, Fleas[,] Butterflies [and] fossils[,] all in admirable confusion. A true Pidcockian[8] room [f. 62r] Of a little bird in the air and the fishes in the sea etc it reminds one of that old Boys play.[9] There is one very good and valuable Chap[10] w*hic*h is that where all the Irish antiquities are placed, that have been fo*un*d. Brian Borimhe's Harp,[11] His spears[,] His Broaches. Curious old Broaches[,] spears, Crosiers, swords [and] A Druids Box like an Inkstand[.] A piece of butter fo*un*d <u>at some depth</u> in a bog!!! A curious Antiquity[.] It is a disgrace to a learned society to have a Museum in such [order?] and puts one in mind of the heterogenous [*sic*] coll*ectio*n of an old tailor of Worcester who was collecting <u>curiosities</u>[.][12] / There is a great variety of Indian Instruments[,] fishing hooks[,] lines[,] nets[,] cloth of Masts of trees and some complete dresses w*hic*h are very superb and curious[,] a funeral dress[,] a Naval commanders dress etc and besides all sorts of things exquisitely worked with bones and (or) shells and (or) feathers etc and Hammers and other instruments of stones etc and wood –[13]

---

[1] One of the two early 19th-century residential quadrangles, the other being New Square (Casey, *Buildings of Ireland: Dublin*, p. 403).

[2] The marble 'Baldwin Monument' of provost Dr Richard Baldwin (d. 1758), erected in 1781, with the figures of 'Science' and an angel (Casey, *Buildings of Ireland: Dublin*, p. 397).

[3] John FitzGibbon (1748–1802), 1st Earl of Clare, lawyer and politician, and graduate of Trinity College, Dublin (Johnston-Liik and Quinn, 'FitzGibbon, John').

[4] See p. 271, n. 3.

[5] Jonathan Swift (1667–1745), writer and clergyman (McMinn, 'Swift, Jonathan').

[6] Probably a volume in the *Harrison's British Classicks* series, published from 1785 onwards.

[7] Senate House of the University of Cambridge, built in 1722–30 and designed by James Gibbs (Friedman, 'Gibbs, James (1682–1754)').

[8] Reference to Gilbert Pidcock, menagerist and showman (Sorrell, 'Pidcock, Gilbert (d. 1810)').

[9] Not identified.

[10] Lee may mean 'chapter', in the sense of 'category' (*OED*).

[11] Brian Bórama (Bóruma, Boru) (d. 1014), high-king of Ireland (Ní Mhaonaigh, 'Brian Bórama (Bóruma, Boru)'). While the harp, still held at Trinity College Dublin, has long been associated with him, it is now known to date from the 14th century.

[12] A reference to Mr Sheriff, a former tailor and 'curiosity monger' Lee visited at Worcester; see SJC, MS U.30 (1), pp. 51–2.

[13] Lee's description of what he saw in the university museum is characteristically imprecise. He may have seen some of the Polynesian artefacts donated to the museum in 1777 by James Patten, surgeon on the HMS *Resolution* during James Cook's second voyage (1772–5) (Hooper, *Pacific Encounters*, p. 273).

A curious model of the Giants Causeway in wood also[.][1]

A curious plaster [of] paris model of a vessel or canoe below [f. 62v] stairs. A few monkies. A little of a hortus siccus. Some Elk bones[.] Inshort what is there not there a little of. There only wants the curiosities which are mentioned in the farce of —[2] to make it complete. A Chinese junk[.]

The fossils and minerals are arranged in better order than the rest[.] Quere [Query] Is there not a person in the College who can put this room to rights[.] If not it will be fortunate when the rest of the birds and beasts <u>are also</u> rotten and obliged to be thrown away[.]

I am told all the fellows are married but that if it *could* be proved that they were so they *would* be turned out of their fellowships. Who is to do it and if it *could* be proved are they to accuse themselves[?] The Servants and Porters all wear Huntsmans Caps. [O prop Deus atq: Homn?][3] etc. Can it be expected that the young men can read when they see these symptoms of a fox chase every hour before [f. 63r] their eyes. It is very proper that one of these caps is in the ante room of or on the staircase of the Museum[.] I should be too putting it in the Glass case with Brian Borihme Harp as a curiosity. This cap does not shew the dignity of the Collegiate. In the University printing office upon going up to some work that was printing, it appeared to be a very neat and probably a learned edition of Juvenal and Persius[4] and by some learned Doctor as I was told and the next work was the Terms of Mrs — Boarding School!![5] Admittance etc Boarding. Young Ladies taught H — etc and so gratis!! A fine amusement for a Coll*ege* Press, to press the Ladies boarding school!! But probably the Lady had interest in College as she might be teaching young Ladies while her husband might be Lecturing young men *Hic pares*[6] etc etc[.] A petticoat University!! Thus the com*mon* opinion that fellows marry*ing* does harm may be wrong. The Int*ire* of the college may be recruited by it. These opinions of married fellows are in every [f. 63v] persons mouths. I do not vouch for the truth of it, [nil despran?][7] as they are com*mon* that they can give no one umbrage.

Went to see Mrs Linwoods collection of Worsted Pictures[8] Price 2:2[.]

No 1. Admirably done, on close exam*ina*tion one can see the worsted rather rough in some parts. One of the 4 Best. Majestic[.]

2. Wood very stiff and coarse. Badly done. Design hideous, but the picture is high up and one cannot see too much of it.

3. Nothing particular [in] any way, rather below the standard of mediocrity but it *would* be well done for a connoisseur. I disapprove of the subject[.]

---

[1] Anne Plumptre notes that this model was taken from the section of causeway at Pleaskin, not at the the Giant's Causeway itself (Plumptre, *Narrative*, p. 21).

[2] This play is not identified. It is possibly the same 'old boys play' as mentioned at p. 288, n. 9.

[3] The Latin is unclear here, and appears to be abbreviated, but this may mean 'O appease the gods and man'.

[4] Roman poets, *fl.* 1st and 2nd centuries CE.

[5] Just one of a number of female boarding schools in Dublin at the time (Goodbody, *IHTA no. 26 Dublin part III, 1756 to 1847*, pp. 90–96).

[6] 'This equals'.

[7] This may be *nil desperandum*, 'never despair'.

[8] Mary Linwood, English artist in needlework, whose exhibition toured Britain in 1804–9 and whose work was exhibited in London for over 40 years (Myrone, 'Linwood, Mary (1755–1845)').

4. Woods well done. Some thing unpleasing in the Design. Fox head awkward [in] places and poked forward. Picture stiff. Probably it is her own design[.]

5. Excellently done. Jeptha rather too savage phyz[1] which he by no means would put on in such a case. Girl lovely and interesting[,] man holding her hands good[.] The group does a Opie credit for its composition[.][2]

6. Pretty. No particular marks of genius either in the design or in [f. 64r] the work. My grandmother did one, from Sir J. Reynolds[3] picture[.]

7. Figure of David. Fine and comely[.] Face too broad and strong for a boy of his age. Miss L*inwood* has done her part well[.][4]

8. Horse shews[.] Blood and dog well done.

9 —

10 Hare hanging well by the leg. Subject for Moses Haughton.[5] Well done[.]

11 Grapes by Jackson[.]

12. Ass and Children[,] Gainsborough.[6] Admirably done. Subject also interesting[.] Good picture[.] Ass Head incomparably shaped[.]

13. Mou*n*t Vesuvius[,] Wright.[7] Very accurately copied indeed and quite W*right's* style whi*ch* I admire[.] He is a man of fire[.]

14 Head of Lear, Reynolds. Hair too stiff and countenance not (very) striking but probably it is not her fault[.]

15 Madonna della Sedia.[8] Inimitably done[.] Female accurate beyond expectation[.] Boy Well done but bad legs. 3 [third] figure's face [is] too coarse and red and old if for a youth or too young for a sage. Very like the Painting at Lord Limericks[.] When I meet such a Woman [I] Will marry her whoever she be[.]

[f. 64v] 16 Dogs at Play Moreland[.][9] All Morelands are well executed and you may know that they are his[.]

17 Cottage girl and Sheaf[,] Russel.[10] Interesting[.]

18 Virgils tomb by Moon light[.] Good effect[.] Clouds rather too woolly[.] Design not bad. Some good[,] sombre touches[.]

19 Pigs by Moreland —

20 Portrait of Mr Lambert, Singleton.[11] Accurate even to the Chaw[12] and a living resemblance[.]

21. Setters by Moreland[.]

---

[1] Phiz; face or facial expression (*OED*).
[2] 'Jephtha's Rash Vow', after John Opie (*Miss Linwood's Gallery*, p. 3).
[3] See p. 124, n. 4.
[4] 'David with His Sling', after Carlo Dolci (1616–86) (*Miss Linwood's Gallery*, p. 10).
[5] 'Hare', after Moses Haughton (*Miss Linwood's Gallery*, p. 17); probably Moses Haughton the elder (bap. 1735, d. 1804), portrait and still-life painter (Weinglass, 'Haughton, Moses, the younger (1773–1849)').
[6] 'Ass and Children', after Thomas Gainsborough (Belsey, 'Gainsborough, Thomas (1727–1788)'; *Miss Linwood's Gallery*, p. 17).
[7] 'Vesuvius in Eruption', after Joseph Wright (Egerton, 'Wright, Joseph (1734–1797)').
[8] After Raphael (1483–1520).
[9] 'Dogs at Play', after George Morland, landscape and genre painter whose subjects included country and farming scenes (Perkins, 'Morland, George (1763–1804)'; *Miss Linwood's Gallery*, p. 16).
[10] 'Harvest Girl', John Russell (Walker, 'Russell, John (1745–1806)').
[11] Henry Singleton (Cust, 'Singleton, Henry (1766–1839)').
[12] Jaw or chaps (*OED*).

22. Pomeranian Dog, D Catton[.][1]

23. Gloomy landscape, Cozens.[2] Very dull indeed. I do not like the effect of these gloomy ~~cotton~~ (worsted) colors, nor is the composition of the subject to my liking[.]

24 American Owl[,] Reignale. This is not one of her first rate performances nor does it approach the original so near as some others[.]

[f. 65r] 25. Lady Jane Grey, visited by the Abbot and Keeper of Tower, Singleton.[3] This picture all the town runs to see and produces her ⅔ of the receipts. The figure[,] The subject is interesting, composition well executed and the ideas expressed (in picture) and which it excites are pleasing yet serious. I never saw the picture before and it does Singleton infinite credit[.] The Abbot is rather too handsome and rather of a masquerade look than of a grave[,] dry, serious minded man. The Keeper admirable and sternly looking[.]

Miss Linwoods performance in the Countenances is exquisite, Lady Grey full[4] is admirably worked and stiffened. The old Boys Head and attitude and whole figure well done but his grey Breeches or cloak or [pelisse?] is also too heavy by far and would suit a Woman who keeps a Sunday school better. This heaviness in the Gown and Mans dress is the only fault I can find with the picture. The shades are admirable, the Gown is the only part which shews that work to be of worsteds[.]

26. Portrait — Hohner[.]

[f. 65v] 27. Lodona[,] Maria Causeway.[5] This picture is a beautiful composition and I admire in it Maria Cosways Taste and ideas. Scenery delicious, and romantic[.] Dress and attitude easy[.] Most beautiful Hair. I should like to be near the original. Miss Linwoods admirable. One of my favourite pictures[.]

28 Woodcocks and King fisher[.]

29 Dogs Watching[,] Moreland[.]

30 Partridges[,] Moses Haughton[.]

33 Landscape effect of Moon light near head of Lake Albaro. The subject is nothing particular nor is there a leading feature in it. The front ground too heavy[,] dull and framelike.

31 Landscape a fishing party — Dull and uninteresting in the subject and the work moderate.

32. Goldfinch starved to Death in Cage[,] Russell. Bird well done. Girl moderate[.] The old idea of hiding the face was not necessary here. The gold finch may be the leading feature of this picture?

34 Sea piece. Brisk Gale[,] Ruysdale.[6] Well done and colors not dull[.]

[f. 66r] 35 Laughing girl } Sir J. Reynolds[.] Both very dull, you must examine to
44 Sleeping girl } see whether the one is crying or laughing and the other is in an awkward position for sleep. They seem to be well

---

[1] The artist is likely Charles Catton the younger, landscape painter and book illustrator (Baker, 'Catton, Charles, the younger (1756–1819)').

[2] This could be a piece by either of the landscape painters John Robert Cozens or Alexander Cozens (Sloan, 'Cozens, Alexander (1717–1786)'; Sloan, 'Cozens, John Robert (1752–1797)').

[3] This may be 'The Offer of the Crown to Lady Jane Grey' by John Singleton Copley (1738–1815), portrait and history painter.

[4] Possibly meaning 'as a whole'.

[5] 'Lodona' by Maria, Baroness Cosway in the nobility of the Austrian empire, history painter and educationist (Lloyd, 'Cosway, Maria Louisa (1760–1838)').

[6] Jacob van Ruisdael, 17th-century Dutch landscape painter; painting not identified.

copied but if the originals are finished paintings, I sh*ould* think they were subjects below the thrust of a great master and they do not convey any grand marks of Genius to me[.]

36 Gleaner[,] Westal.[1] Pretty subject and tastily performed by Master and copyist[.] The Ears of corn seem too large and the stems in the fields also.

37 Landscape, Cozens[.]

38 Carp[,] J. Miller. Good[.]

39. Lobster and Crab[,] F Place Esq*uire*[.][2]

40 Farmers Stable, G. Moreland.[3] Quite excellent. Subject good[.] First Horse grey and rather thin[,] ribs well done. Collar and [worsted?] ornaments admirable[.] Poney capital and seems to be the copy of a poney every individual can call to his recollection. 2 [second] Horse good. Lantern, Barrow, Tools, etc [are] well placed[.] Straw and man gathering it up not to be excelled. The only fault I can with exception find is that as the coloring is very high, [it is] Useless to put red roses and flowers in [the] cartmans Hat. A bit of corn or a turnpike receipt w*ould* have been more in character and of a better color. Best picture of all and best done[.]

[f. 66v] 41. Oysters. Moses Naughton[.] Excellently done[.]

42. Eloisa. A Nun Sophie[.] Too serious and dismal[.]

43. Kennel of Dogs[,] G Moreland. Like the rest. excellent. Dog at window Best[.]

44 Sleeping Girl —

45 Shepherds Boy in Storm. — Storm and landscape well done, particularly the first[.] Would a boy be sitting d*own* in a storm in such a careless Manner, witho*ut* hat and staring at it? His face is unmeaning and as flat as a deal board and the sheep is too familiarly placid by him and seems as unconcerned and as stupid as its master. I do not like the Subject and its parts, but work good[.]

46. Cottage in flames, Wright. This and the M*oun*t Vesuvius are the only good landscapes in the Colle*ctio*n and the landscape is an inferior conside*ratio*n in each. Well done and exactly Wrights style. Moon locked up in the tree and [would have been] better been snuffed out or with leave eclipsed[.]

47 Boys angling on Banks of Ice. Unmeaning and bad[.]

48 Head of St Peter, Guido[.] Not very striking[,] Too Learish. Beard [f. 67r] too stiff and *a la* Charles 2. Probably not well copied or the original not a good one.

49. Waterfall, Ruysdail. Like very few plays or novels. There are too many incidents and circumstances to produce the effect. Too many trees and bushes and all together etc[.] Not grand but pretty and triflingly picturesque[.]

50 Landscape[,] Cozens[.]

51 Woodman[,] Barker.[4] The scenery is all in Snow. But there are no marks of the feet of Dog or man. Every thing excellent wh*at* is done[.]

---

[1] Richard Westall, painter and illustrator (Westall, 'Westall, Richard (1765–1836)'); painting not identified.

[2] Francis Place, printmaker and potter who etched several sets of birds and animals (Nurse, 'Place, Francis (1647–1728)'); print not identified.

[3] 'Horses in a Stable' (1791, Victoria and Albert Museum) by George Morland.

[4] Thomas Barker, painter and lithographer (Sloman, 'Barker, Thomas (1767–1847)'); 'Woodman in a Storm' (1789).

| 52 Lions and Lioness | } Stubbs[1] very good } | The scenery around them does Miss |
| 53 Tygress | | Linwood. credit[.] It is well conceived and happily arranged. |

54 Woodsman in storm[,] Gainsboro Excellent} The spectators are all in the dark and the lights are conveyed on the picture *from* above[.]

These observations are made mostly on the Subjects, not on M*iss* L*inwoods* work wh*ich* is beyond criticism and defies it[.]

[f. 67v] In the Eve*ni*ng went to the play. Saw *Adrian and Orilla*.[2] Dancing by Mr St Pierre[3] and 4 Miss Adams[4] very good. Farce *Of Age to Morrow*.[5]

Mr Frederick Jones[6] in Frederick is inimitable except in the Gentlemans part wh*ich* is stiff. He was the only character that was above mediocrity[.] Mrs Stewarts Maria very lively and girlish[.]

House very good size.[7] Not much smaller than Drury Lane [London]. Mr H Johnstons[8] Adrian was easy, elegant but too affectedly modest and his down cast eyes were too sheepishly done[.] A great attitudinarian. The Critique on the several performers in the Plays is accurately drawn in N° 1 *Cyclopaedian Magazine*[.][9]

Pit very bare but £40 in it and Perhaps £100 in all. Very moderate performance and it wou*l*d have been hissed in many [a] country Town in England. The [***] performed better than the Actors here this night. Mr Johns[10] Michael Disgusting, quite a scaramouch. The Gallery certainly laughed at him. I cou*l*d have cried with vexation[.]

Febru*ary* 7. Saturday /
Day as usual[,] dull and Dirty. Rain in evening and frost in the Night[.] Staid in doors the greatest part of the Day. Dined at Mr Sneyds[.][11]

---

[1] George Stubbs, painter, engraver, and anatomist; there are several versions of 'Lion and Lioness' (Egerton, 'Stubbs, George (1724–1806)').

[2] William Dimond, *Adrian and Orilla, or, A Mother's Vengeance: A Play, in Five Acts ... As Now Performing at the Theatre Royal, Covent Garden, with Universal Applause*, London, 1806.

[3] A celebrated dancer from King's Theatre who was the principal male dancer at the Theatre Royal, Crow St, from Dec. 1803 onwards (Greene, *Theatre in Dublin*, II, pp. 468–9).

[4] Popular dancers and singers, the four Adams sisters (only recorded in playbills by their initials – A[nna]., H., E. and S.) were the principal dancers at the Theatre Royal, Crow St, in the 1806–7 season, when Lee saw them perform (Highfill, Burnim and Langhans, *Biographical Dictionary*, I, p. 32; Greene, *Theatre in Dublin*, II, pp. 466–7, 470).

[5] Thomas Dibdin, *Of Age Tomorrow: a Musical Entertainment in Two Acts*, Dublin, 1801.

[6] Either Frederick Edward Jones (1759–1834), theatre manager, or his son of the same name (dates unknown) (Geoghegan, 'Jones, Frederick Edward'; Greene, *Theatre in Dublin*, II, pp. 296–327).

[7] The Theatre Royal, Crow St, managed by Frederick Edward Jones (see previous note), the principal theatre in Dublin at the time and attended by Lee on many subsequent evenings.

[8] Probably Scottish-born Henry Erskine Johnston (1777–1845), actor-manager, who performed in Dublin regularly for seasonal engagements, including the 1806–7 season, when Lee saw him perform (Greene, *Theatre in Dublin*, I, pp. 291–2, 296).

[9] *Cyclopaedian Magazine*, 1, Jan. 1807, pp. 48–53. The frontispiece of this issue of the magazine is a colour plate of 'Mr H. Johnstone, in the character of Rugantino'.

[10] An abbreviation of Johnston (see n. 8, above). Johnston played the role of Michael (*Cyclopaedian Magazine*, 1, Jan. 1807, p. 49).

[11] Possibly Nathaniel Sneyd (*c.*1767–1833), wine merchant, politician and governor of the Bank of Ireland (Geoghegan, 'Sneyd, Nathaniel').

Bad wine sent from Dublin to Jersey and Guernsey to gain the drawback and take chance of selling it[.]

February 8 Sunday /
Day as usual[,] Cool, foggy and frosty at night and wet in the following Morning till 9[.]
 [f. 68r] Breakfasted with Mr Fitzgerald[1] and went to Chapel. Service like other colleges But Singers all up in the Organ[,] [the] best in front. 2[2] is the pulpit[,] 2 [is] the stand where the Sermons are read. 4 [is the] Organ and this part up to the organ left where are seats for ladies in front[,] Boxes for Strangers [are] behind them. The whole chapel is fitted up in a most chaste[,] modern manner. Architecture elegant[.] 2 Pillars between Every window. Fine red Curtains Elegantly hung. 3 Neat Chandeliers suspended from roof are directly over No. 3. Singers [are] good and more decent than ours[.] Sir S Stevenson[3] was there among them and a Mr —.[4] It is more like a room for regal dignity and for a kings levee than a Chapel[.] Very elegant (slightly) arched roof and very high[.]
 Five rows of seats on each side and a case of wood in front not like our places where the men sit with their legs in the middle of chapel, to trip up an incautious person coming in. Organ not particular. Singing not extraordinary. Young men wear Bands[.][5]
 [f. 68v] Went to St Patricks Cathedral[.][6] Turret and steeple venerable. Curious old turret close to the high steeple. Building venerable and much battered by storms and tempests. Large but the *tout ensemble* is a collection of patch work and of all sizes. Monuments of Swift and of Stella[7] in the W Aisle[,] (both) very plain and Swifts forms a fine contrast with the long marble, lettered and sitted Monument of one Bishop Narcissus Marsh,[8] with Latin enumerating the time of his taking every step in the Church. Opposite is a monument to Archbishop Arthur Smyth.[9] The inside of the Cathedral where [the] service [is] performed [is] very striking and venerable. Curious old organ. Old Black oak seats, (I believe) and some of the most curious Monuments I ever beheld. On the ~~Right~~ L of the Communion is a mass of Monument[.] A wonderful thing if it is all one Monument, but there seem to be story upon story like a house and a great n° of figures, it is of an amazing height[,] nearly as high as the Cathedral inside[,] at least as high as it could conveniently go[.] There are heroes and female figures in the different departments of it and at the bottom female and men figures Kneeling with [all lifted?] hands etc[.][10] There was such a crowd about it that I did not thrust myself up to examine or read the inscriptions. All of stone.

---

[1] Possibly Rev. Gerald Fitzgerald; see p. 287, n. 6.
[2] The numbers in the following sentences refer to a sketch plan in the page margin, not reproduced here.
[3] Sir John Andrew Stevenson (1762–1833), Irish composer and chorister at Christ Church and St Patrick's Cathedrals, Dublin (Geoghegan, 'Stevenson, Sir John Andrew').
[4] Name represented by dash.
[5] 'The development of a falling collar into a pair of strips (now called *bands*) hanging down in front, as part of a conventional dress, clerical, legal, or academical' (*OED*).
[6] St Patrick's Cathedral, Dublin, founded in the 13th century (Casey, *Buildings of Ireland: Dublin*, p. 602).
[7] Jonathan Swift and his beloved friend, Esther Johnson (1681–1728) (Carpenter, 'Johnson, Esther'; McMinn, 'Swift, Jonathan').
[8] (1638–1713), archbishop of Cashel, Dublin and Armagh (McCarthy, 'Marsh, Narcissus').
[9] (1706–71), Church of Ireland archbishop of Dublin (Beaumont, 'Smyth, Arthur').
[10] Monument dedicated to Lady Katherine Boyle (d. 1630), wife of Sir Richard Boyle, 1st Earl of Cork; completed in 1632 (Casey, *Buildings of Ireland: Dublin*, pp. 621–2).

A very fine monument to one Lady Doneraile with a Bust.[1] Very well executed[.]

[f. 69r] A fine old monument on the R of the Communion with a figure of some abbot etc kneeling down,[2] and several other smaller ones —

The Helmets of the Knights of St Patrick are all hung round the Cathedral from 2 Seats opposite each other which are probably for the Lord Lieutenant and suite[.] They begin at these forming a circular row by the organ. The swords are all suspended between and over the Helmets[.] Erected high are the banners of each over his helmet. Very good singing but rather too catch like and I understand the service here is called the Irish Opera.[3]

There is one thing which a stranger going to St Patricks cannot but observe[.] Going up Nicholas St and St Patrick St and in several other places he sees the shops as usual open. Wiskey houses in full request while the very bells for service are ~~going on~~ (ringing). Butchers stalls in numbers with meat for sale. Cabbages etc and garden stalls[.] Inshort every thing which can be wanted to be bought and sold within 200 Yards of St Patricks Cathedral and I at first felt pleasure at seeing such n^{os} of people going and coming that way[,] thinking it was for Church[,] but no such thing[.]

[f. 69v] Was it not for the horrible stench of the streets and lanes there and the filth ancle deep of the streets you might say every article of the *Utile et Dulce*[4] is to be bought round St Patrick's on a Sunday[.] I am surprised they do not erect their stalls against its walls.

February 9: Monday /
Day bad[,] rainy[.]

Went to see Madame Tussauds Cabinet of figures[5] which are admirably done and was extremely delighted[.]

In Evening went to [the] Play (Holmans Benefit)[.][6] Saw the *Heiress*[7] and *Rugantino*,[8] Benefit Mr Holman[.] House overflowing. Talbots[9] Lord Gayville was below my expectation. Holmans Clifford perfectly genteel and fashionable. Mr Putnams Mr Blandish horribly gauky[,] a poor stick.[10] Mr Foots[11] Rightly bad, he acted Duke of Venice

---

[1] Monument to Elizabeth, Viscountess Doneraile (d. 1761), with a bust of her husband, Hayes St Leger (Casey, *Buildings of Ireland: Dublin*, pp. 620–21).

[2] Monument to Thomas Jones, Archbishop of Dublin (d. 1619) and Roger Jones, Viscount Ranelagh (d. 1620) (Casey, *Buildings of Ireland: Dublin*, p. 622).

[3] Lee's meaning here is unclear, but the term seems to relate to his previous criticism of the standard of singing.

[4] 'Useful and pleasant'.

[5] Anna Maria Tussaud, known as Madame Tussaud, founded a waxwork exhibition that toured Britain and Ireland for three decades from 1802. The exhibition was in Ireland in 1804–8 (Concannon, 'Tussaud, Anna Maria (bap. 1761, d. 1850)'; Pilbeam, *Madame Tussaud*, pp. 65–95).

[6] Joseph George Holman (1764–1817), English actor, theatre manager and playwright who frequently visited Dublin (Knight, 'Holman, Joseph George (1764–1817)'; Greene, *Theatre in Dublin*, I, p. 301).

[7] [Anon.] *The Heiress: a Comedy in Five Acts. As Performed at the Theatre-Royal Drury Lane*, Dublin, [1786].

[8] Matthew Lewis, *Rugantino, or the Bravo of Venice*, London, 1805; an 'extremely popular' play (Greene, *Theatre in Dublin*, I, p. 176).

[9] Montague Talbot, a 'popular actor' (Greene, *Theatre in Dublin*, I, p. 150).

[10] Stick, a "wooden" person; one lacking in capacity for his work, or in geniality of manner; *Theatr.* an indifferent actor' (*OED*).

[11] 'Fat' Foote, actor (Greene, *Theatre in Dublin*, I, p. 46).

much better, and was decent in it or properly bearable. Miss Walstein[1] is an elegant fig*ure* and suits modest characters admirably. Mrs H Johnsons[2] Alscrip was very good and she seems suited to such characters. A fine fashionable [f. 70r] figure but walks badly, seems as if she knocks her knees. Seems to be very tall and very thin. ~~Mrs McCullough~~ Mrs Williams Blandish [was] very fair[.] Females are very good[.] Mrs Edwins[3] L*ady* E*mily* Gayville [was] of course pleasing and attractive. Mr Williams[4] in Sir Clement Flint, bearable[,] but he stares and rolls his horrid eyes most ludicrously[.]

Bravo of Venice[5] was got up wonderfully well and superbly performed. H Johnson [Johnston] did the part of *Rugantino* extremely well, and his fine figure suits it. Mr Putnams Contrarino [was] not bad, I mean not too good but his own acting is hid in the fine dress[.] Mr Williams Memmo suits the stage and the Gallery must have such a character in every performance[.] But it is not Lewis Memmo,[6] quite the contrary, how w*oul*d any conspirators ever have admitted such a buffoon ever as a tool in to their plot, but the Gallery must be amused and he *outres* the character very well to suit them[.] Rigantinos [Rugantino's] sev*er*al characters are well supported and charged and he manages his voice well[.] Dresses all excellent. [Rugantino is] Very expeditious in his changing dress. Scene with the conspirator well supported <u>by him</u>, Memmos quaint sayings d*itt*o here but they w*oul*d not bear translating into Italian. But he is the gallery hero and ∴ like a king cannot do wrong[.] [f. 70v] Scene with the Duke well maintained throughout. Scene where he is an old man and kills the conspirator [is] well supported but not clear, unless one had read the Novel a person c*oul*d not tell what takes place for you do not know that the fellow is going to kill Rosabella and when A[7] says he has saved her life, we feel surprised.

In his last change into Milans Duke, he is a most elegant figure, but why? or how does he become Duke, I attended to the words as much as possible but from the play do not see how he makes himself out so. There are too many fine scenes and too much shew wh*ic*h confuses the meaning or else the play has been so much curtailed to make room for pageantry that it is become unintelligible, *Brevis esse laboro, obscurus fio*,[8] but any body can excuse it for the *tout ensemble* is quite eye captivating[.] He is an elegant figure as Duke and the tight pantaloons do not hinder his legs and thighs from being well remarked. He is a fine [f. 71r] manly figure, and very handsome beside being a good actor.

---

[1] Elizabeth Walstein, a 'beautiful and talented' actress, referred to in *Faulkener's Dublin Journal* in 1818 as 'one of the most accomplished actresses, and the greatest favourite that ever appeared before a Dublin audience' (Greene, *Theatre in Dublin*, I, pp. 309, 314n.).

[2] Nannette Johnston (née Parker), actress and dancer, was a daughter of William Parker, proprietor of Edinburgh Circus. She made her debut at the Theatre Royal, Crow St in Feb. 1797 and was 'active' in the 1806–7 season, when Lee saw her perform (Greene, *Theatre in Dublin*, I, pp. 291–2).

[3] Elizabeth Rebecca Edwin (Richards) (1771?–1854), actress and singer (Clarke, 'Edwin (Richards), Elizabeth Rebecca').

[4] Possibly Edward Williams, actor (Greene, *Theatre in Dublin*, II, p. 706). He is mentioned again in the following paragraph.

[5] The subtitle of *Rugantino* (see p. 295, n. 8).

[6] Lee means that the part of Memmo was not performed in the way that he thought the play's author, Matthew Lewis, intended.

[7] Possibly the character of Andreas, Duke of Venice.

[8] 'When I labor to be brief, I become obscure' (Horace).

Rosabella is an enchanting girl and performed well, danced well and did every thing well. Very pretty shape and light and airy. I admire her much[.] Camilla[,] Mrs Culloch[,] is a character the fellow to Memmo[,][1] made to please the Gallery. Very *outre* and ridiculous, and it has its effect, but they both take off from the delusion in a great degree. Masque as well got up as on a London stage. Dresses excellent and processions also. I do not like to see the Dukes Daughter dancing in public before all the Venetians like a hired dancer but would not have it as it sh*oul*d be (and loose [*sic*] her dancing) for all the world. The D*uke* of Milan, late A[2] believed to be etc etc yet on a sudden very intimate with the D*uke* and shews he is an equal for he chats, talks[,] laughs etc cutting jokes and wispering all the time of the Masque and leaning on his knee with [his] Elbow, as 2 old friends might do[.]

I admired the performance but wished and thought the other evening's *Performance* ought to have been damned[.]

[f. 71v] **Tuesday Jan***uary*[3] **10 /**
Rain in straight showers; Foggy[.]

Had an audience with the Lord Lieutenant.[4] Went to the play. *Provoked Husband*[.][5] Mrs Edwins Lady Townly in the last scene was uncommon pathetic. Mrs Hitchcocks[6] Lady Wronghead [was] extremely good[.] Squire Richard[,] Mr Johnson[,] [was] very fair and Mrs Stewarts Miss Jenny D*itto*. Holmans Lord Townly, Boisterous and [stout?][.] I do not admire Mr Holman much. The rest were empty headed characters.

Mr St Pierre excelled himself in his Dancing and he ought to have done for it was his Benefit. Miss Adams[7] has quite captured me. Pleasing night to see the four [sisters] all dancing together. The other 3 all [have] thick legs. My Miss Adams [is] very much [in] the style of Parisot[8] but not quite so finished[,] not confident of her abilities[.] If she were she w*oul*d dance better.

Uncommon good *Minuet de la Cour* between Pierre and Miss A*dams* and served as a good contrast for one in the farce *High Life below Stairs*[.][9]

Talbots Lord D.[10] does not exactly suit me, he is too affected and forces the character. His laugh [is] unmeaning, ie neither ludicrous nor absurd, not satirical, but very loud and squeaking.

---

[1] See his comments on the character of Memmo on p. 296.
[2] Possibly Andreas.
[3] Lee's error – the month was February.
[4] John Russell, 6th Duke of Bedford (1766–1839), Lord-lieutenant of Ireland for a brief period in 1806-7 (Thompson, 'Russell, John, sixth Duke of Bedford (1766–1839)'). William Lee Antonie sent a letter of introduction to Russell on his nephew's behalf, and instructed him to leave his calling card at Dublin Castle at the 'first opportunity' (SJC, Box 1a, Doc. 22, William Lee Antonie to John Lee, 28 Dec. 1806; see Appendix 2).
[5] The manuscript of *The Provoked Husband* by Sir John Vanbrugh (1664–1726) was found among his papers after his death; the writer, actor and theatre manager Colley Cibber (1671–1757) adapted and completed it, and it premiered at Drury Lane in 1728 (Downes, 'Vanbrugh, Sir John (1664–1726)').
[6] Sarah Hitchcock, née Webb (d. 1810) was 'very popular on the Dublin stage', where she acted from 1781 until her death (Geoghegan, 'Hitchcock, Robert').
[7] It is not clear which one of the four Adams sisters Lee is referring to.
[8] Mademoiselle Parisot was a scandalous French dancer on the early 19th-century London stage.
[9] *High Life Below Stairs: a Farce of Two Acts* by James Townley (1714–78), playwright and Church of England clergyman, was published in 1759 (Eckersley, 'Townley, James (1714–1778)').
[10] The character of the Lord Duke in *High Life Below Stairs*.

They say that to act a good clown one ought to be an excellent harlequin ~~to~~.

[f. 72r] By parity of reasoning to be a good Lord D's domestic one ought to be a perfect [***][.][1] Talbot is not but sets it[.]

Mr Moore in the Gentleman Freeman[2] is a blackguard and bad as needs be, but in the disguise of the Yorkshire tout he does extremely well and gave me great pleasure[.] He is so perfectly at home in it and easy and agreeable and truly comic and laughable[.] Mr Johnson in Lovel has as much title to the character of a gentleman on the stage, as he would affect it, It is a lobbly[3] gentleman he represents.

Mr N Jones Phillip is not so good as he can act I am told, I am heartily glad to hear it[.] Mr R Jones[4] [acts] Sir Harry tolerably well[.] Miss Walsteins Kitty [is] poor[,] she does not interest one nor is she[,] when she goes off, anxiously looked for on her return. Mrs Radcliffs L. Charlotte [is] a good representative of a fat[,] full dressed maid of the Chamber[.][5]

The rest were not good enough to notice nor bad enough to (be worth) criticising[.]

[f. 72v] **Wednesday February 11 –**
Forget. February 14[,] Dined at Mr Burghs[.][6]

Thursday February 12 / 1[7]
Went with Mr Burgh over the whole of the Parliament House,[8] About 400 by 200 feet and he explained the whole to me and shewed me the new alterations and their use. It is singular that some of the pillars on the side of Entrance near College (when the populase [sic] set a great deal of the timber for alterations on fire) was so burnt as to be completely made lime and became dangerous and they have been new patched and very cleverly mended. Old House of Lords [is] a noble room indeed[,] fine black oak. [There is a] Beautiful model of the whole building upstairs. Immense pile of building. Went all over it and out on the top. Curious to see how well every part is finishing and how bold and what good work. It is inshort a wonder of Ireland.

Went over the Hawkins St Museum[9] again and then to the new round church[10] which for plainness and neatness of execution[,] for chastness [sic] of style yet grand effect[,] surpasses any thing intended for a public building I ever saw before. [The] Oval pulpit and [the] Organ over it [is] in the Extremity of Main Axis. In [the] Centre, [is] the Bason of fine Italian marble for christening. Seats rise to the side and a [there is a] small passage round in which [is] a circular gallery round upstairs. [The] Neatness of work [is] beautiful[,] all Oak – [f. 73r] [the] seats [are] all plain and similar except the 2 at opposite extremity of [the] Main Axis[.] These are only trivially different.

---

[1] The last word of this sentence is squeezed into a corner of the folio, obscuring it.
[2] A character in *High Life Below Stairs*.
[3] Possibly intended in the sense of a 'lob', 'a country bumpkin: a clown, lout' (*OED*).
[4] Richard Jones, actor (Greene, *Theatre in Dublin*, I, p. 302).
[5] Philip, Sir Harry, Kitty and Lady Charlotte are all characters in *High Life Below Stairs*.
[6] Thomas Burgh (1744–1810), MP and administrator with residences at Sackville St (now O'Connell St), Dublin, and Chapelizod, Co. Dublin (Quinn, 'Burgh, Thomas'). This diary entry is retrospective.
[7] The meaning of the number '1' here is unclear.
[8] See SJC, MS U.30 (2), p. 101, n. 3.
[9] Museum of the Dublin Society; see his earlier visits on 3 Sept. (pp. 103–4) and 4 Feb. (p. 287).
[10] The late 17th-century St Andrew's Church, Suffolk St, was rebuilt in 1793–1807 (Goodbody, *IHTA no. 26 Dublin part III, 1756 to 1847*, p. 45).

Passage round the Extremity of the ☉[1]

A the Door. In C*entre* Slab and a spare around it.

B. Pulpit elevated and Clerks seat below.

All the — are passages between each row of seats to the Middle but not so many as here represented[.]

The seats in the rings of course form ☉ in themselves, and each exterior row is a few inches higher than the interior.

Gallery upstairs in same plan but of course is narrow[.]

AB the 2 doors into it w*hic*h come up from C in the lower part of C*hur*ch.

It does the owner of the design infinite credit and it would be a good plan for any Building whatever[,] for public speaking or Business – DD are 2 galleries ascended into from below and not so high as the gallery, for singing Boys and girls. There will be a very high steeple behind[,] 150 feet higher than the top of the Chapel itself[.]

[f. 73r] Attended the Chemical Lecture delivered by Mr Higgins.[2]

[The] Subject [was] Attraction. [The] Laboratory [is] confined and close, very crowded with all sorts Ladies and Gent*leme*n[.]

Friday Feb*ruary* 13 /
Went out with Mr Burgh[,] riding all up the Terrace thro*ugh* [the] Park[3] along the river side and a most beautiful thing it is, the river runs meandering thro*ugh* [the] banks like those of the Obeg at Castle Townsend[4] and its shew of beauty [is] like the Blackwater betw*ee*n Cappoquin and Mallow[.] Fine ruins and Hanging woods. Extraordin*ar*y that it should be so beautiful near the Metropolis and while there are so many mills, manufactories etc all going in within a stones thro (nearly) of each other. Strawberry Beds[5] are com*mon* on the very steep sides of terrace and very numerous, open witho*ut* hedges. No one wo*ul*d rob them bec*ause* they belong to poor people!!! This a fact. Set in long rows of 4 roots in each and where no farming c*oul*d be carried on[,] all a Bed of Limestone[.] [*Small, rough sketch of layout in page margin.*] Mr Whites demesne and grounds[6] defy description. It is situated on the side of the Terrace over the river wh*ic*h is very picturesque and bending that it has [f. 74r] glens in itself with the most beautiful rocky, woody scenery, waterfalls in pitts [pits] and above or out of the glens above a noble strait of water running thro*ugh* a grand demesne of fine rich lawn with wood and every thing in high modern taste. Very grand Bridge over the sheet of water w*hi*ch is wider than the river[.] House is a big one like an old castle, turrets etc[.] Oh it cannot be described neither inside nor outside. The view from the parlor of the very extensive lawn (I admire very much) backed by the Wicklow M*ou*nt*ai*ns by all means go to the extremity of the demesne up the river[.] Island on the point of land wh*ic*h hangs over the river on [the] rock side of you[,] 2 cabins and [the] river winding below and [the] land opposite

---

[1] The following symbols and letters refer to two small, annotated sketch plans he made of the church in the page margin, not reproduced here.

[2] William Higgins (*c.*1762/3–1825), chemist, who ran a popular series of lecture courses in chemistry in Dublin from 1797 until the 1820s (Byrne, 'Higgins, William'). See Grossman, 'William Higgins'.

[3] Through the Phoenix Park along the River Liffey.

[4] Castle Townsend is not on the Awbeg; Lee may mean Castletownroche.

[5] The Strawberry Beds run along the north bank of the River Liffey, to the west of Phoenix Park.

[6] Luke White (*c.*1740–1824), bookseller and politician, of Woodlands, Co. Dublin (Hourican, 'White, Luke').

Elegantly farmed, and 2 fine seats and [the] W*icklow* M*o*unt*ai*ns in the dist*ance*. Returned along the High ground by the School,[1] so as to see the College Observatory[2] at a dist*ance* and thro*ugh* [Phoenix] Park and round by the front of [the] L*ord* Lieut*enant*s lodge[3] then by [the] Water head and con*tinu*ed over new Canal[4] and under the Aqueduct[5] wh*i*ch is thrown over [the] road. A useless work and might easily [have] been avoided[.]

[f. 74v] **Saturday February 14** /
Day very fine but high wind[.]

Sunday February 15 /
~~Went~~ Went with Mr Grade[6] to the Canal[.] Noble work[.] Walked down it to the Basons[.] Camden Bridge[.][7] Noble stretch of water. Went to Rings End. [The] Bridge there [is] broken down fr*o*m I think [the] found*ati*ons giving way. [The] Second Bason [is] very grand and Enough. Saw there [the] dry Dock for refitting shipping[.] Went up Sir John Rogersons Quay[8] wh*i*ch is very grand and when finished will be the finest thing heard of[.] It will extend 2½ Mile up thro*ugh* the whole town[.] Ships lying all along the sides and a Quay on the opposite side of the river to correspond. Custom H*o*use looks very grand fr*o*m this side[.]
    Dined at Mr Gards[.]

Monday February 16 /
Attended Mr Higgins lecture on Attraction[.][9]

[f. 75r] **Tuesday February 17.**
Called on Mr Sneyd.[10] Went to Miss Adams[11] Benefit. [The] Play [was] *Mountaineers*[12] and *Paul and Virginia*[.][13]

---

[1] The Hibernian Military school in the Phoenix Park, established in 1766 (Casey, *Buildings of Ireland: Dublin*, p. 302).

[2] Dunsink Observatory, the observatory of Trinity College, Dublin, established in 1785 (Wayman, *Dunsink Observatory*).

[3] The mid-18th century Viceregal Lodge (from 1782) in the Phoenix Park (Casey, *Buildings of Ireland: Dublin*, pp. 292–5).

[4] Grand Canal, commenced in 1765 and completed by 1792 (Goodbody, *IHTA no. 26 Dublin part III, 1756 to 1847*, p. 85).

[5] The Royal Canal opened in 1796 (Goodbody, *IHTA no. 26 Dublin part III, 1756 to 1847*, p. 87). The Foster Aqueduct (*c*.1800) carried the Royal Canal across Broadstone to Royal Canal Harbour (Casey, *Buildings of Ireland: Dublin*, p. 282).

[6] Possibly the Mr Garde, Gaard or Guarde previously mentioned (see p. 220, n. 2).

[7] Grand Canal Dock, completed in 1785, and Camden Lock, opened in 1796 (Goodbody, *IHTA no. 26 Dublin part III, 1756 to 1847*, pp. 85–6).

[8] First built in 1716 (Lennon, *IHTA no. 19 Dublin part II, 1610 to 1756*, p. 32).

[9] For William Higgins, see p. 299, n. 2; the lecture on 'attraction' related to his atomic theory.

[10] Possibly Nathaniel Sneyd (*c*.1767–1833), see above, p. 293, n. 11.

[11] It is not known which one of the four Adams sisters Lee is referring to.

[12] *The Mountaineers, a Play in Three Acts* (1793), by George Colman the younger (Burling, 'Colman, George, the younger (1762–1836)').

[13] *Paul and Virginia: a Musical Drama* [Adapted by J. Cobb from *Paul et Virginie* by J. H. B. de Saint-Pierre], Dublin, 1801.

Wednesday February 18 /
Day rainy, snowy, and bad. In [the] middle [of the day was] rain and in [the] Evening [the] Hail [was] severe[.]

Set out at 8 in (Coach long) for Drogheda and got there[,] 23 Mile[,] at ½ past 3!!! Very pleasant party ten inside. A sailor[,] an attorney[,] a washerwoman, an ironfounder man, a Cattle driver etc etc nescio.[1] – Exports from Cumberland are Coals and Ironware[,] pots[,] kettles etc etc very little bar iron.[2] Imports nothing actually, few Cows[,] horses, sheep. Attorney told a variety of excellent law jokes (Curran[3] telling man he would give him a good roasting[,] then 'If you do I will afterwards give you a good basting' and such like[)]. Upon arriving at Drogheda[,] walked out to Old Bridge town to see the Obelisk Erected in Memory of [the] Battle of [the] Boyne.[4] Road [goes] all up riverside[.] See plainly on [the] S side of [the] River where [King] James Forces were and on the opposite Hill he is said to have stood and looked on and a good point (it is) to retreat[,] as he did[,] from to Dublin. Descend into the hollow where there is a flat meadow [f. 75v] and where [there is] a ford at [the] river, and all along here his troops marched down and forded over. Drawings N° 1 and 2 may be considered as one,[5] The river runs all along under the front ground (field) at [the] back of [the] Cabin and Close by [the] Obelisk and at [the] foot of ([the] steep bank). Between. [sic] Between [the] Bank and [the] Cabin his army came down and crossed, and ⊗ signifies the Situation of the Glen shewn in the following Scetch down which his army came. Lord Cunningham's House[6] and grounds and woods are in the distance.

N° 3[7] After descending the ground in [the] last [sketch] (N° 2) by [the] cabin and turning to the Left to get to the river side, [we] come to [the] ford. We are now in the flat behind the last cabin and can see how the (steep bank) which is the same as in [the] last [sketch] surrounds[.] The Course of the ford where a <u>horseman</u> would go [is] marked out, but they would not be so particular. I believe there was no hard fighting on this side but only firing over [the] river, as disputing the pass[.]

[f. 76r] On the opposite side [is] a grove of trees and [there are] many scattered all about and under their boles are seen bits of houses and barns etc (where it is marked)[.] The rest is a fine flat meadow with trees scattered over it, the river goes round the obelisk and then makes a great turn to the right of [the] picture as shewn in the following. The Glen is here seen[,] down which King William's army marched coming from the North[.] King James's was chiefly on [the] opposite side. It is very narrow and rough and [the] sides [are] very steep as are those of [the] bank skirting the river although a road runs at the foot of it all the way. The 2 lines mark where the army <u>is said</u> to have crossed (for all I here mention I had from hear say)[.]

---

[1] 'Nescio', a claim not to know, may refer in this context to the assortment of ten people with whom he was travelling, in the sense of 'I know not who else'.

[2] This information must have been related to Lee by the iron founder.

[3] See p. 287, n. 4. Lee did not meet Curran but notes here a story related by another lawyer in whose company he travelled to Drogheda.

[4] The Boyne Obelisk, 'erected in 1736 supposedly at the point where William of Orange led his army across the river to rout the Jacobite army' (Howley, *Follies and Garden Buildings*, p. 15).

[5] Lee refers to sketch in SJC, MS U.30 (8), f. 39v and f. 40r (pp. 333–4), not reproduced.

[6] Henry Conyngham (1766–1832), 1st Marquess Conyngham of Slane, Co. Meath (Quinn, 'Conyngham, Henry').

[7] Lee refers to sketch in SJC, MS U.30 (8), ff. 41v–42r (p. 334), not reproduced.

[Sketch] Nº 4[1] shews the opposite side of [the] river where [there] is a bridge (over a canal) and over which the people say King William's army marched, It is False[.] The Bridge could not have been there at that time nor the Canal either.[2] This shews how cautious in believing vulgar reports a person must be[.]

[Sketch] Nº 5[3] is a near view of the Obelisk[.] I stand on the spot marked Ⓥin [sketch] Nº 3 and am [f. 76v] only separated from it by about 20 Yards[.]

[Sketch] Nº 6.[4] View of the ground above [the] pillar. Taken from ⑨ and [the] scenery [is] very beautiful[.] 3 fine bends of the river[,] meadow on R[,] green and with scattered trees. Fine distant woods evidently on banks like that on the left which is bare. ② is not many yards from the Entrance of the Glen where this steep bank is broken. The whole of the bank from [the] top to the road slopes[.] You do not see the flat Ground on the top[,] it is very much like the side of a regular made fosse. The rough ground on the left and the scenery between are the next view which shews

[Sketch] Nº 7.[5] The Glen itself and a sort of road running down it, below which at the bottom winds a little stream which from its steep descent is a continued series of waterfalls untill it comes to the Bridge, where the 3 roads meet[.] ~~and it goes in front of~~ That to Drogheda goes in front of the Cabin near [the] bridge and in rear of the Hoggat but is not seen.

A wall is built round the point where the bank makes a sharp angle[.]

[f. 77r] Williams army is said to have come all down this glen, and that he had his cannon etc all on the tops to cover it (But it is very narrow for an army[)][.] Quere [Query] How long must they have been in marching down? They could have come very well over the bank sides but not in such good order[.] Probably some came down but nearly all did not march in defile that They must have then spread and come in all directions over the front ground where I now stand and gone to the river behind my back[.] The peep at the distance is magnified in a separate place[.]

[Sketch] Nº 8.[6] is the base of the pillar to shew the rock, between it and where I now stand is a steep hollow which looks as if it had been made by art rather than nature[.] This spot is nearer to the pillar than Ⓥin [sketch] Nº 3[.]

[Sketch] Nº 9.[7] A view nearer still and close to the edge of the front ground[.]

[f. 77v] In [the] Evening invited William Cair a blind Harper[8] to come and take some punch[.] We had a great conversation on Irish music. He had bad eyes when young and began learning music when about 12 years old, "thinking it might be of some service to him as well as amusement" (ie he was afraid he should go blind and ∴ learnt to play the harp)[.] He was always fond of it. He had some instructions from Arthur O Neil[9] and

---

[1] Lee refers to sketch in SJC, MS U.30 (8), f. 43r (p. 334), not reproduced.

[2] The Boyne Navigation, begun in 1748, bypasses the worst rapids on the River Boyne (Ellison, *The Waters of the Boyne*).

[3] Lee refers to sketch in SJC, MS U.30 (8), f. 44r (p. 334), not reproduced.

[4] Lee refers to sketch in SJC, MS U.30 (8), ff. 45v–46r (p. 335), not reproduced.

[5] Lee refers to sketch in SJC, MS U.30 (8), f. 47r (p. 335), not reproduced.

[6] Lee refers to sketch in SJC, MS U.30 (8), f. 48r (p. 336), not reproduced.

[7] Lee refers to sketch in SJC, MS U.30 (8), f. 49r (p. 336), not reproduced.

[8] William Carr (b. 1777) (Yeats, *The Harp*, p. 60). Lee sketched Carr and his harp at SJC, MS U.30 (8), ff. 50r, 51r, 52r (p. 336), not reproduced.

[9] Arthur O'Neill (1735/6–1816), harper (McCabe, 'O'Neill, Arthur').

DIARY 5: KILLARNEY TO DUBLIN

also from from Patric Quin[1] of the Co. of Armagh, as well as himself – In [the] year before [the] rebellion he was at the Belfast Musical Meeting[2] and although but a young hand yet they encouraged him to play. Quin his master lent him his Harp[.] He recollects that there were 11 Harpers and believes these were all[:]

// Charles Fanning[,][3] Co Cavan (got 1st Prize, 10Gs. Was best player by much)
Patric Quin[,] Co Armagh (5Gs 2nd Prize)
Arthur O Neil[,] Co Tyrone
[f. 78r] — Williams a Welsh man[4] (played very well on a Welsh Harp. They were in doubt whether to admit him, but on his playing all Irish tunes they did[.] 5Gs.
Hugh Higgins from Connaught (P*layed* very well and had an Elegant harp) (Dead)[5]
Daniel Black (dead since)[6]
Charlie O Byrn *from* Leitrim[7] (played worst)[.] He was originally but the servant to a harper and always carried his Masters Harp ~~but he~~ and he only took a fancy to learning as well as he *coul*d, never well Educated for it[.]
Rose Moony from West Meath[8] (a woman played very well and better than some[)]
William Cair of Portadown Co Armagh. He rec*eive*d 2Gs. He was but a beginner and they gave him[,] he says[,] this to encourage him[.]
Dennis Hampton[,] Co Derry.[9] Man men*tione*d by Miss Owenson,[10] he did not play so very well as some and was then very old.
James Duncan[,] Co Down[,][11] played very Moderately (since Dead)

Cair only knows of one more harper in the Kingdom than the survivors of these and he is an infirm old man and was sick at that time[.] His name [f. 78v] is Patrick Lynder [from] Co Armagh and he could not attend. He thinks there are no more respectable ones in Ireland or he sh*oul*d have heard of them. His harp was an old thing made accor*din*g to his own directions by a carpenter, he chalked out the plan for him, He gave 2Gs for it when done but the head piece being too straight he was obliged to have another made wh*ich* cost him ½ more as he now was obliged to be [buy] a new piece. [A] Harp has 32 Strings and they are wires but the Welsh harp are cords w*hich* makes a great diff*eren*ce in the sound[.]

Thursday February 19 /
Day cold[,] Snowy but Clear at intervals and sunshine[.] Wind high. Snow *from* 3 to 5[.]

---

[1] Patrick Quinn (b. *c.*1745), teacher at the Irish Harp Society from 1809 (Yeats, *The Harp*, p. 69).
[2] The Belfast Harpers' Festival took place in July 1792 – not in 1797 as Lee suggests. See Yeats, *The Harp*.
[3] Charles Fanning (*c.*1736–*c.*1800) was from Co. Leitrim (Yeats, *The Harp*, p. 62).
[4] Known only as 'Williams the Welshman', he was the only non-Irish harpist to perform at the Belfast festival (Yeats, *The Harp*, p. 69).
[5] (1737–96), from Co. Mayo (Yeats, *The Harp*, p. 65).
[6] (*c.*1716–96), from Co. Antrim (Yeats, *The Harp*, p. 60).
[7] Charles Byrne (*c.*1712–*c.*1810), who in his youth travelled as a guide to his harpist uncle (Yeats, *The Harp*, p. 60).
[8] Rose Mooney (1740–*c.*1798), from Co. Meath; one of only two female professional harpists in Ireland at the time (Yeats, *The Harp*, p. 66).
[9] Denis Hempson (1695?–1807), from Co. Derry (Yeats, *The Harp*, pp. 62–5).
[10] Sydney Owenson, Lady Morgan (*c.*1783–1859), novelist, literary celebrity and compiler of *Twelve Original Hibernian Melodies*, published in 1805 (Leerssen, 'Owenson, Sydney (Lady Morgan)').
[11] 1747–*c.*1800 (Yeats, *The Harp*, p. 62).

Walked all over the town [Drogheda] which I like the next to Cork and Limerick. Situation [f. 79r] uncommonly striking on [the] steep banks of [the] Boyne[,] the wood at [the] upper end of [the] town sets it off to great advantage, [the] Town in some parts [lies] much above tops of the houses below.[1] [The] River runs up all [the] way between steep banks. There is a curious old tower of a large Church or Abbey still standing and the traces of the building may be followed among the Cabins and through the dunghills around. [Its] Foundations go to great extent[.] [The] Steeple is very fine and [is] the only part which remains, [with a] fine Gothic arch through the middle at [the] bottom. [It is] Exactly like the tower in all old Abbeys. Windows [are] very perfect and complete. The Old East Gate[2] still remains entire and part of the walls are also standing. Small tower in the walls.[3] *vide* Scetch[4]

Came off to Dublin in the Evening.[5]

On this side of Balruddery [Balrothery] is a reservoir of water, I asked the Coach man which pool it was he told me, 'A ship carpenter belonging to Cork, as he was going with me up to Dublin' (says the Coach man), 'asked me about 3 years ago the same Question. Why says I[,] did you ever hear of the River Thames. Aye havent I said the Carpenter, and believe and is that it, well I never saw it before[.] Well then you see it now' said Coachy. He assured me on his honor that this happened and he is certainly a wag.

[f. 79v] **Friday February 20**[6] /
Fine day[,] very cold. Wind high[.]

Went over Mr Sneyds extensive wine vaults,[7] a great nº of long cellars, on each side [it is] 2 Bins deep. In the first [cellar] I counted 120 Bins[.] Each had a pipe[8] of Porter it in Bottle. There were many other vaults running || to this. Claret Vaults with Hogsheads packed in each. 7 × 7 in front and 6 deep or about 24 Dozen in each bin. About 618 Bins in all and Mr French[9] said that frequently there was £100000 of wine in those cellars[.]

I was impressed to see with what nicety the different wines were preserved[.] The Madeira Cellar [is] kept warm and with a flue round them. White wines [are] in cool cellars etc etc. Bottles are infinite [in] No. Mr French said they often buy £200 worth a month. Neat manner of packing up the wine sent into the Country – Corks [are] obliged

---

[1] See descriptions of Lee's sketches of the town at SJC, MS U.30 (8), ff. 60v–61r, 62v–63r (p. 338), not reproduced.

[2] See descriptions of Lee's sketches of the East Gate at SJC, MS U.30 (8), ff. 53v–54r, 54v–55r, 56r (p. 337), not reproduced.

[3] Drogheda has its foundation in a medieval walled town (perhaps late 13th-century) that was furnished with ten gateways and a number of mural towers (Buckley and Sweetman, *Archaeological Survey of County Louth*, pp. 352–3). The uncertainty surrounding the number and locations of the towers makes it difficult to identify with certainty those Lee describes.

[4] Lee refers to his sketch at SJC, MS U.30 (8), f. 57r (p. 337), not reproduced.

[5] Lee's sketchbook tells us that he stopped in Swords on the way, where he sketched the round tower and a nearby cabin. See descriptions of sketches at SJC, MS U.30 (8), ff. 38r, 68r, 69r (pp. 333, 338), not reproduced.

[6] Lee has now returned to Dublin from Drogheda.

[7] Nathaniel Sneyd (see p. 299, n. 2) succeeded his father in 1781 as partner in the wine firm Sneyd, French and Barton (Geoghegan, 'Sneyd, Nathaniel').

[8] 'Typically equal to two hogsheads or 63 wine gallons (105 imperial gallons, approx. 477 litres), but varying with the substance' (*OED*).

[9] Possibly one of the partners in the wine firm of Sneyd, French and Barton (see n. 7 above).

to be aired to get rid of the [f. 80r] new smell w*h*ich corks the wine[.] I always thought that defect arose fr*o*m the Cork being rotten, and not fr*o*m its smell when new. French corks are best and of the best wood.

Dined at Mr Trails. Fine large party and elegant dinner and an evening party assembled many ladies and Gent*leme*n[.]

Went to the Chymical Lecture. Saw the prettiest Girl there I have seen since I have been in Ireland[.] Who c*oul*d she be?

Saturday Febr*uary* 21 /
Day wet, rainy. Wind high. Very severe shower ab*out* 4.

Went over the Linen Hall, a most extensive Fabric, it was built by a Board at Gove*rnmen*t Expense as an Encourageme*n*t to the trade, saw [the] store full of flax, yarn. Stuffs of all values and the linens to an immense amount. The Building is built on parallell [*sic*] open[,] narrow and 3 floors high[,] and all occupied with goods.[1]

[f. 80v] I was informed that I saw goods to the value of [£]3000000. Nothing shews the pitch to w*h*ich this art is brought so much as the Tablecloths w*h*ich are worked with patterns in them. Saw a set of table Cloths and napkins for [the] *Prince* of Wales wh*i*ch w*oul*d Cost ab*ou*t 100Gs. Most beautiful fineness and wonderful patterns of flowers and his arms in middle and crests[,] feathers etc. Pretty pattern of napkins. Battle of Trafalgar[,] a set with table Cloths for 12Gs. They can work any pattern you send them on a drawing and will make a set of napkins and tablecloths with your arms on them for ab*out* 14Gs[.]

Messrs Coulson Stores[2] and their works are at his bus*i*ness in the North[.] Their elegant Coffee Room [is] as neat as any in London[.]

[f. 81r] Dined at the Castle[.][3] A very large party[,] 22 in tot*al*. Those who I c*oul*d make out where [*sic*]

1. J. Fiott
2 Lord W. Russel[4]

[*Fragment of sketch of seating plan visible. Rest of page cut off.*]

[f. 81v] [*Most of page cut off.*] Went over the College library[,][5] very similar to Trinity C*a*mbridge. C in shape[.] Gallery [is] something like that in [the] Senatehouse when up in it, but this is only library I have seen w*h*ich has a gallery over the Bookstands and [is] supported by them. A room at the End filled with Books. Librarian (Dr Usher[6]) Fellow said there were about 60000 B*o*oks in *toto* [total].

[f. 82r] Very convenient readers room close by it[.] This library is only opened on certain days. There are so many holidays kept wh*i*ch <u>ought</u> in such case as this to be abolished for these holidays inconvenience persons who wish to study. View fr*o*m [the] fellows Gardens [is] very good and [the] College looks well fr*o*m here[.] Saw the debating Rooms[,] admirably fitted up[,] and [the] plan of the institute [is] excellent[.] They have ab*ou*t 1700 Books[.]

---

[1] The Linen Hall, King St, built *c*.1725 (Goodbody, *IHTA no. 26 Dublin part III, 1756 to 1847*, p. 75).
[2] John Coulson, linen factor, 55 Bolton St and William Coulson, merchant, 8 Linen Hall St (*Wilson's Dublin Directory*, p. 30).
[3] See SJC, MS U.30 (2), p. 101, n. 8.
[4] Lord William Russell (1767–1840), Whig politician (History of Parliament Online).
[5] See SJC, MS U.30 (2), p. 104, n. 2.
[6] Possibly Rev. Henry Usher (*Gentleman's and Citizen's Almanack*, p. 122).

Tuesday February 24 /
Breakfasted with Mr Franklin in the college. Went at one with Fitzgerald[1] and Simkins to the Rotunda[2] to hear the Debate and [the] resolution passed by the Catholics about sending up their petition to Parliament.[3] A Mr Keough[4] informed us that the Catholics are between 4 and 6 Million persons[.][5] Mr Burke[6] a young man[,] very officious. Counsellor O Gorman[7] made an empty speech. Mr O Connel[8] and Mr O Connor.[9] Began about 1 and lasted till near four[.]

[f. 82v] **Wednesday February 25**
Went to see St Georges C*hur*ch[10] w*hic*h is now building and[,] when finished[,] w*hic*h will be ~~one of~~ the largest in Dublin. Plan does not strike me as good. Called on Mr Gregory.[11] Dined at Mr Sneyds. [*Small sketch plan of St George's Church in page margin.*]

Thursday February 26 /
Met McCarty on his return f*ro*m England. Went with Mr Sneyd to the Castle to (332)26398 11525̲2

Friday 27 [February]
Dined at Mrs Latouches[12]

---

[1] Possibly Rev. Gerald Fitzgerald; see p. 287, n. 6.

[2] The Rotunda or assembly room adjoining the Lying-In Hospital, Parnell St, built in 1764 (Casey, *Buildings of Ireland: Dublin*, pp. 162–3).

[3] While 'penal' legislation banning catholic schools and restricting property ownership had been lifted in a series of acts passed in 1772–93, catholic emancipation remained 'the single most important issue in the politics of early nineteenth-century Ireland', as catholics remained excluded from senior office and from parliament. Lee was in Dublin at a time of crisis, as in Jan. 1807 a series of catholic meetings had taken place in the city and a petition supported by catholic gentry was presented to parliament; on 4 Mar. 1807 the catholic militia bill was introduced, opening all army and naval commissions without religious restriction (Connolly, 'The Catholic Question', pp. 26, 33–4).

[4] Probably John Keogh (1740–1817), silk merchant and catholic politician (Woods, 'Keogh, John'), and 'veteran leader of the 1790s' (Connolly, 'The Catholic Question', p. 31).

[5] Before the 1821 Census, population figures were necessarily tentative, but the total population of Ireland was around 5 million in 1800 (Houston, *Population History*, p. 18).

[6] Possibly John Burke (1789–1845), priest and political activist for catholic emancipation and repeal of the union (Murphy, 'Burke, John'); he was aged 18 in 1807.

[7] Nicholas Purcell O'Gorman (1777/8–1857), barrister and secretary to the Catholic Association (Woods, 'O'Gorman, James').

[8] Daniel O'Connell (1775–1847), barrister, politician and nationalist leader (Ó Tuathaigh, 'O'Connell, Daniel').

[9] Not identified. It is unlikely that this is the politician, revolutionary and writer on economics, Arthur O'Connor (1763–1852), as he was in exile in France following the 1798 rebellion (Kelly, 'O'Connor, Arthur').

[10] St George's Church (Church of Ireland), Hardwick Place, built in 1802–13 (Casey, *Buildings of Ireland: Dublin*, p. 120).

[11] Possibly William Gregory (1762–1840), public servant, who had been secretary to the board of inland navigation since 1800 (Geoghegan, 'Gregory, William').

[12] Identification is difficult due to Lee's imprecision, but possibly either Elizabeth La Touche (née Marlay), wife of David III La Touche (1729–1817), banker, or their daughter-in-law, Anne Caroline La Touche (née Tottenham), wife of John David La Touche (1732–1810), banker (Beaumont, 'La Touche, John David').

Saturday 28 [February]
Dined at Mr Guards

[f. 83r] **Monday 2 March**
Went to the Levee
[*Rest of page cut out.*]
[f. 83v *cut out*]

[f. 84r] **Wednesday 4 March**
Went with Mr Burgh to see the Farmers Society,[1] which is a company who make all sorts of farming Utensils and sell them to the public. Their show was very good[.] Great number [of] fine cows[,] Fine pigs, one black boar the fattest I ever saw, no neck, fed on Tipperary [*blank*] Weight 5 Cwt and 5 lbs. Man asked £10 for it[.] Small size Show Sheep. Several Bulls. Great N° of new invented machines[.] Evening party at Dr Stewarts[.]

[f. 84v] **Thursday 5 March**
Mrs Trails party was attended by an immense party of fashion – Did not leave it till ½ past 3[.]

Friday March 6
Went with Dr Stewart to see the Bluecoat Hospital.[2] School room. Dinner Room. Meat 3 [times] a week. Soup broth always bread – Milk and stirabout. Good variety but no <u>vegetables or potatoes</u>. Bread every day[.]
   3 Dormitories of 10, 40 and 20 Beds. 2 Boys to a Bed. Good Blankets and sheets. Plain but clean.
   [f. 85r] Chapel very neat and elegant. A picture of Christ rising from the tomb done by a Boy who was in Hospital. They send a certain n° to the Dublin Society to draw.
   Many eminent men have been educated there. No Boy [is] allowed to go out of the Grounds without a Pass – [the] Board Room [is a] very good size. All the offices [are] excellent. Front and Back[,] [it is a] very fine building [and has] a Chaplain regular. [The] Endowment [is] very good – [the] Plan [is] similar to London's Blue Coat Hospital[.]
   Went to the Female Orphan School. Only established 16 Years last January. Dean Kirwan once collected £1015 at a Charity sermon.[3] [It is] Supported by Contribution. [The] Land [is an] Acre and fraction on which [are the] House and Garden. Pay 30 per annum. 11 Acres of land for Cultivation[,] potatoes and Vegetables at 11 per Acre [rent]. This is Lord Palmerstons[4] property. The House stands on Lord Monks [*blank*][5]

---

[1] The Farming Society of Ireland (est. 1800), meeting at 34 New Sackville St; Thomas Burgh (see p. 298, n. 6) was a member (*Gentleman's and Citizen's Almanack*, p. 133).

[2] The Blue Coat School on Blackhall Place was established in 1671, and rebuilt in 1773–80 (Casey, *Buildings of Ireland: Dublin*, p. 252).

[3] Walter Blake Kirwan (1754–1805), a clergyman well known for his sermons, which raised large sums for Dublin charities; 'Speaking on behalf of the house for the support of orphaned girls established on the North Circular Road in 1793 and named after him, he raised a total of £8,608 between 1790 and 1800.' (McCabe, 'Kirwan, Walter Blake').

[4] Henry John Temple, 3rd Viscount Palmerston (1784–1865) (Steele, 'Temple, Henry John (1784–1865)').

[5] Henry Stanley Monck, 1st Earl of Rathdowne and 2nd Viscount Monck (1785–1843) of Charleville (*Burke's Peerage*, 1852, p. 692).

[f. 85v] Rooms very neat, whitewashed. Girls very neat and even elegantly (neat) dressed. 140 in all. [They] Do all sorts of needle work. 2 Dormitories[,] Beds very neat. Beds of Hair[,] Boys [beds] were of straw. Rooms much neater than the Boys.

This is one of the numerous charities supported by voluntary [*sic*] subscription and it is singular that when any charity is once set on foot in Dublin it <u>never</u> fails. *Vires acquirit eundo*[1] notwithstanding the N° of new ones the old keep their ground.

[ff. 86r–86v *blank*]
[ff. 87–88 *cut out*]

[*Back cover*] First Class
July 28th 1806
Thomas Minton[2]

---

[1] 'She gathers strength as she goes'.
[2] Possibly the Stoke-on-Trent engraver and pottery manufacturer (1765–1836) (Jones, 'Minton, Herbert (1793–1858)').

APPENDIX 1

Sketchbooks of Lee's Tour in Ireland, England and Wales

Lee's annotations to his sketches often appear on the verso side of the folio. Where this is the case, the sketch titles and/or descriptions are not separated by a paragraph space. Lee normally uses the spelling 'scetch' for his sketches. Page references to this edition are in brackets following the MSS references.

6. SKETCHBOOK, 1806

[SJC, MS U.30 (6)]

[Flyleaf *and* f. 1r *are stained by a pressed leaf which had been covered in aphids.*][1]

[f. 1v *blank*]

[f. 2r *Ink sketches of Severn salmon punts, captioned*][2] Boats on the Severn at Worcester

[f. 2v *blank*]

[f. 3r *Two pencil sketches of a woman, front and side profile, in an elaborate hat,*[3] *and ink sketch of a high cross, captioned*]
Stone Pillar in Ballymore Eustace C*hur*ch[4]
2 Circular rims are rep*resente*d by 2 lines and a Boss ½ way up and in the middle. On the knob on this side is   16
                                       82

[ff. 3v, 4r, 4v *blank*]

[f. 5r *Pencil and ink sketch of five-arched bridge, captioned*] Bit of Worcester Bridge

---

[1] See SJC, MS U.30 (1), f. 30r (p. 54).
[2] See SJC, MS U.30 (1), f. 16r (p. 43).
[3] See SJC, MS U.30 (1), ff. 19v, 20r (pp. 46, 47).
[4] See SJC, MS U.30 (2), f. 59r (p. 213).

[f. 5v *blank*]

[f. 6r *Three ink sketches of engine parts, annotated*]
1. A cylinder
2. The Hollow Tubes join*in*g at End
Head of N° 2. 28 holes around the circumference[1]

[f. 6v *blank*]

[f. 7r *Ink view of bridge and surrounding buildings, river, quay and turnpike; captioned, annotated*] Bridge at Gloucester

[f. 7v *blank*]

[f. 8r *Ink and pencil landscape with house, captioned, annotated*] View of — Top of house slate blue House white Shrubs in front of house
[f. 8v] View of Hallow Park.[2] The house in front w*hich* one window[,] 4 windows in Each side and 2 on the other sides of it. Flowers in front hide the barn. A Grain house on the L. Behind on the R fine dark woods hanging over. On the L dark woods. In the 3rd Ground on the L is a lawn with a road across it w*hich* is partly hid by trees. Ground 2 is a wood and the front a Green meadow with the towing path in it. On the R *Ground* 2. is field. *Ground* 1. bank. *Ground* 3 Wood and *Ground* 4 dark wood

[f. 9r *Ink and pencil landscape with houses, captioned, annotated*] Opposite the point is a small open*in*g on the rock of red rock[,] The rest is completely cove*red* with trees. A gate for the track
[f. 9v] View of Mr Evans Brick Kiln[3] opposite the point is a wood with one opening of red rock in the middle. The path winds along the left bank in the front is a hedge and gate and beyond the River is another wood and over the water a field. Beyond the wood on the R are fields and a few trees

[f. 10r *Ink and pencil landscape with river and boat, captioned, annotated*] View about 2 miles above Holt[4]
Path along a bend of the river on the right fields and trees on left
High banks and dark woods with bits of ~~green~~ (red) in between
[f. 10v] View about 2 Miles above Holt. On the R side of the Scetch is a woody bank, a meadow, woods a few fields and woods beyond them. A wood at the head of the river. On the left are meadows with the path running thro*ugh* them trees in hedgerows and a piece of dis*tan*t country beyond. A vessel is on the river

---

[1] This sketch relates to one of the manufacturing sites Lee visited, possibly Williams' distillery in Worcester, described at SJC, MS U.30 (1), f. 26r–v (pp. 50–51).
[2] See SJC, MS U.30 (1), f. 29r (p. 52).
[3] See SJC, MS U.30 (1), ff. 30r, 31r (pp. 53, 54).
[4] The area is described at SJC, MS U.30 (1), ff. 33r–34r (p. 55).

[f. 11r *Ink and pencil riverbank scene, annotated, captioned*] 7 Miles and a little [Yards?] from Bewdley
Over the river is a tri cornered field two banks of wood and in the middle is a distant view of a hill covered with wood. Pollards on the left and trimmed the river runs in the front with its bank covered with flowers[.] The field was a light yellow green just mowed
[f. 11v] View 7 Miles and a little beyond Bewdley. River has fine wooded banks. A 3 cornered field. Wood on the Right is nearer than that on the Left. A little peep at a distant wood. River side covered with flowers. Field had a light green yellow tint

[f. 12r *Ink drawing of a bridge, river and boats; annotated*]
[f. 12v] Bridgenorth or Bewdley Bridge. Iron. In floods water runs through the small arches

[f. 13r *Three ink sketches of stile, captioned*] Curious stile above Stourport
[f. 13v] Curious style above Newport. The first figure is as it appears in its proper state the 2nd is with one bar [pressed?] down and the 3rd with them all down[.] It is convenient for horses going along the tow path. It is a lever of which the Middle post contains the fulcra of each bar

[f. 14r *Ink and pencil river scene, captioned*] View about a mile from Bewdley down the river from the Gate leading to Mr — House
[f. 14v] View about a mile below Bewdley from Mr Prattlesons of Repsford [Ribbesford] Gate.[1] The range of hill on the R winds along and terminates in a great head[,] the top of which is barren. On the right a field then Hedge near the road path and river[.] Above the opposite bank which is partly covered with bushes and partly red rock are fields and hedges above a hill then a barren one

[f. 15r *Ink and pencil river scene, annotated*]
[f. 15v] View of the Tickley Hill from on board the Wherry.[2] In the front a (red) rock covered with trees. On the right a cottage peeps through the trees[.] At the bottom of the wood appear several stumps of the trees[.] On the left above the bank is a green field and a tree in the front ground the corner of a wood is just beyond another field just appears

[f. 16r *Red and black ink landscape with church; drawn within oval frame; annotated, captioned*] View of Quatford Church from the Barge[.] Bushes and shrubs all up the river side[3]
[f. 16v] View of Quatford Church from the Barge

[f. 17r *Rough, unfinished, outline pencil sketch of a ruin, not identified*]

[f. 17v *blank*]

---

[1] See SJC, MS U.30 (1), f. 34v (p. 56).
[2] See SJC, MS U.30 (1), f. 37r (p. 57).
[3] See SJC, MS U.30 (1), f. 39v (p. 61).

[f. 18r *Red and black ink landscape, annotated, captioned*] View down the river from the Barge. View taken just below Quatford Church. In front distant green fields and hills to the L. Green Bushes and flowers on the R Bank and quite conceal it.

[f. 18v *blank*]

[f. 19r *Red and black ink landscape; drawn within oval frame; annotated, captioned*] The Tumbling Sailors about 1½ Mile below Bridge North. View up the river[.] Rock red and white

[f. 19v *blank*]

[f. 20r *Ink view of rocky landscape, annotated, captioned*] View just above Bridge North of a rock on the N Side of the river. Rock called the Tailors Rock[1]

[f. 20v *blank*]

[f. 21r *Rough pencil outline sketch, captioned*] View down the river of Tailors Rock

[f. 21v *blank*]

[f. 22r *Ink outline diagram, captioned*] Iron Rail way Cross.

[f. 22v *blank*]

[f. 23r *Rough pencil outline sketch, annotated, captioned*] View below Iron Bridge at 8 at Night[.][2] The smoke and mist so thick that the hills are hardly to be seen and appear as masses here and there[.] The side of a house is clear from the fire

[f. 23v *blank*]

[f. 24r *Rough pencil outline sketch drawn within oval frame, annotated; location not identified*]

[f. 24v *blank*]

[f. 25r *Rough pencil outline sketch of church and surroundings, annotated; not identified*]

[f. 25v *blank*]

[f. 26r *Rough pencil outline sketch of church and surroundings, annotated*] View near Church of Atcham[3]

---

[1] Lee records local folklore about a tailor falling from this rock at SJC, MS U.30 (1), f. 38v (p. 60).
[2] See SJC, MS U.30 (1), f. 41r (pp. 60–61).
[3] See SJC, MS U.30 (1), ff. 46v, 47r (p. 69).

[f. 26v *blank*]

[f. 27r *Rough pencil outline landscape; location not identified*]

[f. 27v *blank*]

[f. 28r *Two rough pencil outline sketches of interior of house; not identified*]

[f. 28v *blank*]

[f. 29r *Ink and pencil landscape, annotated, captioned*] View about 1 Mile above Llangollen. Rocks in the river. (house white with slate. a road)[1]
[f. 29v] View about a mile up the river from Llangollen. The river comes round a turn by a rock. On the Bank is a white house with slate roof and a road before it. Behind is a hill the middle covered with trees. The boles appearing here and there the top is bare. The 2*nd* Hill is rather rocky and partly covered with furze[.] 3rd Hill Bare[,] 4*th* Ditto and 5*th* (green) furze all about the middle. 6*th* Bare. The rocks in the bed of the river cause the water to run briskly and it is much disturbed. To the L of the picture the water is shallow and pebbles. Rocks are of slate

[f. 30r *Ink and pencil landscape, annotated, captioned*] View just above the other from a tree through which you get over a hedge and it has steps cut in it.
Trees on this bank through which the river is seen and the opposite rocky bank is covered with trees through which a mountain meadow appears
[f. 30v] View just above the other from the foot of a tree through which you get. It has steps on the one side cut on purpose and is in the middle to a hedgerow. On the Left is the Canal and road and a wood about it. The front is a meadow[.] The river appears between the trees great rocks of slate in the middle form a little waterfall on the opposite bank which is seen through the trees are woods and in the back ground bare mountains. The course of the river is rough and shallow

[f. 31r *Rough pencil and ink landscape with river and hills, annotated, captioned*] View near the tannery[.] 2 winds of the river[2]
[f. 31v] View of 2 Winds of the river from near the Tannery below Llandsilio [Llantysilio]. The front hill is covered with wood variously broken. The front of the wood has several large trees in it[.] The vales on the sides have first hills with wood and then bare hills beyond. The top of the front hill has a wood at top the other is bare

[f. 32r *Rough outline ink and pencil landscape, annotated*]
[f. 32v] View from the Side of [Hardicks?] Hill just above the Beautiful Birch trees. 1[3] Is the top of the Hill 2 The Birch with the river rock here and there through the trees. 3 the Hill opposite with the Holyhead road winding along it. Some fields below 4 Castel Dinas

---

[1] Lee describes a similar scene at SJC, MS U.30 (1), f. 58v (p. 81).
[2] Lee describes a similar scene at SJC, MS U.30 (1), f. 55v (p. 79).
[3] Numbers 1–7 refer to points in the illustration.

Bran Hill. 5 Cefn Uchan. 6 Eglwsig Rocks all Limestone in strata appearing as if it was was [*sic*] fortified 7 Is the head of another Hill which just peeps in[1]

[f. 33r *Rough outline ink and pencil landscape, annotated, captioned*] Valle Crucis Abbey[,] Bron Vawr
[f. 33v] Valle Crucis Abbey[2] from the Side of the Hill on the path from Llansilio Birches. 1 is the B hill. 2 is rocky and bold, green patches of the fern are on the hill. 3 Is a hedge End and the path winds down it. 4 is Bron Vawr the summits of w*hi*ch are bare to the middle greenish with fern in patches and the bottom woody with trees and bushes. Just a glimpse of the West Window is seen am*on*g the trees and the top of the farm house. In the bottom are fields of corn and pasture.

[f. 34r *Ink and pencil sketch of ruin surrounded by trees, annotated, captioned*] Valle Crucis
[f. 34v] View of the E Window of Valle Crucis Abbey f*ro*m the meadow. 1 is a ~~brook~~ (stream) w*hi*ch falls into the murmuring stream in the wood behind where the view is taken. 2 is a fine meadow bounded by a hedge wh*i*ch goes to the base of the Abbey 3. Is a Grove of fine trees under whose boles bits of the river are seen and beyond are scattered trees and hedges[.] 4 is a side of a bare hill[.] 5 is a hill with wood at the base and bare at top – 6. Bare hill. Scattered trees and bushes hide the bases of 5 and 4.

[f. 35r *Rough pencil sketch of an unidentified bridge, annotated*]

[f. 35v *blank*]

[f. 36r *Rough pencil outline sketch of a forest, annotated*]
[f. 36v] View ab*ou*t 50 Yds f*ro*m Bridge among trees in the grove. The water flowing at the foot of the trees is seen thro*ugh* them here and there as is the parts of the bridge. View taken f*ro*m Path sitting down at foot of tree stones at foot of path

[f. 37r *Rough pencil outline sketch of bridge, annotated*] rail along tops of Bridge[3]

[f. 37v *blank*]

[f. 38r *Rough pencil outline sketch; drawn within oval frame; annotated, captioned*] View in Wynnstay Walk or brook

[f. 38v *blank*]

[f. 39r *Pencil and ink sketch of memorial in garden, annotated*][4]

[f. 39v *blank*]

[1] Possibly the scene described at SJC, MS U.30 (1), f. 55v (p. 79).
[2] The Cistercian abbey of Valle Crucis, Denbighshire, founded in 1200/01 and in ruins since the mid-to-late 16th century (Burton and Stöber, *Abbeys and Priories*).
[3] The sketches at ff. 35r, 36r, 36v, 37r may be the scene described at SJC, MS U.30 (1), f. 60v (pp. 81–2).
[4] See SJC, MS U.30 (1), f. 62v (p. 82).

[f. 40r *Pencil sketch of small building in garden, annotated*][1]

[f. 40v *blank*]

[f. 41r *Rough pencil outline sketch of unidentified village and surrounding hills, annotated*]

[f. 41v *blank*]

[f. 42r *Rough pencil outline sketch of river and nearby unidentified village, annotated, captioned*] View from Bridge beyond[2]

[f. 42v *blank*]

[f. 43r *Pencil sketch of castle and grounds, annotated*][3]

[ff. 43v–44r *Rough outline landscape sketch, pencil, captioned*] View from Holywell[4]

[f. 44v *blank*]

[f. 45r *Rough outline pencil landscape, annotated, captioned*] Scalp entrance about 8 Miles from Dublin[5]
[f. 45v] View of the Entrance of the Scalp [Mountain] from the road. The Sugar Loaf appears through the 2 sides of the Scalp

[f. 46r *Rough outline pencil landscape, annotated*][6]
5 Glyn of Downs
6 The Dargle
View from Scalp
Bold large masses of rock on edge and all about
Rock and confused stone
[f. 46v] View from the Scalp between the 2 parts of it. N°s 1 and 2 are bold edged rocks and stone[.] 3 is a ridge of the mountain but green the road winds at its base[.] 4 is a bold rocky part of the mountain. 5 the distance is bare barren mountain. 6 is lower ground but bare on the bosom appear a line of wood which is the Dargle. 7 the Sugar loaf. 8 the lesser Sugar loaf at whose base is the Glen of the Downs[.]

[f. 47r *Well-finished pencil and ink sketch of ruin among trees, captioned*] View of an old ruin of a church[7]

---

[1] Probably in the garden of Wynnstay Park, described at SJC, MS U.30 (1), f. 62v (p. 82).
[2] Possibly the bridge mentioned at SJC, MS U.30 (1), f. 66v (p. 85), on the way to Caergwrle.
[3] Caergwrle castle, described at SJC, MS U.30 (1), f. 66v (p. 85).
[4] See SJC, MS U.30 (1), f. 68r (p. 87).
[5] See SJC, MS U.30 (2), f. 35v (p. 106).
[6] See SJC, MS U.30 (2), f. 35v (p. 106).
[7] Reproduced at p. 108 (Figure 5).

[f. 47v] View of an old ruin of a church in Old Connaught[.] In the front is an old ~~gateway~~ (arch) through which inside is a confusion of rubbish and some graves. One could be seen ornamented with a garland of cut paper and several pieces of wood covered with the same. The ivy grows all over the tops of the ruin and seems to form a covering to it. At the W end is a very fine tree which hangs in beautiful masses and grows in a luxuriant state[,] at the E end is the same. The middle is a lighter foliage of I believe lime. The shades were on all the picture but the lime on which the sun shone. Gravestones lying about in confusion and every thing suffered to decay. Trees all around the Church yard

[f. 48r *Ink and pencil outline landscape of hills and trees, annotated*][1]
[f. 48v] View from the Burnt Rock point taken a little below its summit down the side. The front ground No. 1 is rock of a reddish hue all in fragments. On its edges grow small oaks which fringe it very handsomely, ~~with~~ mixed with fern. No. 2 is a fine edge all completely covered with wood in mossy shades. No. 3 is the other edge of the Burnt rock on the left with trees also skirting it. No. 4 is a vast amphitheatre of magnificent wood the green turf is just seen at the bottom but not the water.

[f. 49r *Caption only, no sketch*] View from the Lovers Leap[2] which is a great rock projecting itself from the mountain which is on all sides covered with trees[,] its sides are $\perp^r$ and in the front is a small defence built up of stones. The path and few of the trees about it are in the front ground. Beyond is a vast range of fine wood with the hills above Bray and the 2 Sugar Loafs just appearing[.] This view is down the valley
[f. 49v *Rough pencil landscape, unfinished, annotated, captioned*] View from Lovers Leap

[f. 50r *Rough pencil landscape, annotated*]
[f. 50v] View from the ~~Sugar Loaf~~ Lovers Leap within a yard of the other [sketch]. But up the valley the front ground is the rock. No. 2 is a fine woody Edge and No. 3 is the same But the bottom of the valley is not seen[.] The Sugar Loaf and some hills to the R just appear over the trees and in the Edge of the wood on No. 3 is Mr Grattans cottage Lord Powerscourt house and woods about it are on the middle of a distant hill and beyond this another hill just appears[3]

[f. 51r *Ink woodland scene*]
[f. 51v] View of the Lovers Leap from the opposite side of the river. in Mr Grattans ground it is just seen between the trees and the edge of the hill on which it is situated in the bottom between the trees. see the river rolling over a rocky bed. A great many trees are in the front ground. The view is taken about ⅓ down the precipice

[f. 52r *Rough pencil landscape, unfinished, annotated, captioned*] View from the bridge at Entrance of Glen
[f. 52v] View from the Bridge at the Entrance of Glen of Downs. In the front is the road and the corner of a wood with a brook under it and some dead trees laying across it and

[1] See SJC, MS U.30 (2), f. 39v (p. 109).
[2] See SJC, MS U.30 (2), ff. 39v, 40v (p. 110).
[3] See SJC, MS U.30 (2), f. 41v (p. 110).

a wall marks the bound*ar*y of the wood. The 2 distance is a meadow, and a pretty cottage in it and the Sugar Loaf is in the distance

[f. 53r *Very rough pencil outline sketch, unidentified location*]

[f. 53v *blank*]

[f. 54r *Ink and pencil landscape with thatched cottages in foreground, annotated, captioned*] View on the road within 3 miles of Blessingtown of the Welp Rock from some cottages[1] At this spot the shower came on and while my companions the soldiers were sheltering themselves, this was scetched

[f. 54v *blank*]

[f. 55r *Rough pencil view of waterfall, annotated*][2]
[f. 55v] View in the Grounds of Pulla Phuca waterfall from ~~near the Moss house and the Hermitage~~ (the Extremity of a wall w*hich*) goes down to the Edge of the precipice

[f. 56r *Ink and pencil landscape with cross, tower and bridge, annotated*] View abo*u*t a mile *fro*m Russborough Going to Blessingtown by the lower road

[f. 56v *blank*]

[f. 57r *Rough pencil and ink landscape, annotated, captioned*] View from the edge of the hill w*hich* goes down to the river Liffey where the ford is going to Luggila f*ro*m Blessingtown[3]

[f. 57v *blank*]

[f. 58r *Pencil and ink landscape, annotated, captioned*] View abo*u*t 3 Mile f*ro*m the military road going f*ro*m Blessingtown. The Military road runs along in the edge of the di*stan*t hills near their surface. It goes on this side No. 1 and on the other side No. 2
[f. 58v] Wednesday Sept*embe*r 10.[4]

[f. 59r *Pencil and ink landscape, annotated, captioned*] View of Luggila Lake f*ro*m the road com*ing fro*m Blessingtown above it The front ground is all bog. No. 1 is a rocky fine bold hill with large masses of black slate in its $\perp^r$ side and a fine edge of rock. 2 is a body of differ*en*t hills the nearest are young wood the farthest bare rocky and with fern the parts above all are quite boggy. No. 3 consists of 2 hills 1 very rough indeed and the other smooth No. 4 at a very great distance[5]

[1] See SJC, MS U.30 (2), f. 56v; reproduced at p. 122 (Figure 6).
[2] See SJC, MS U.30 (2), f. 61v (p. 126).
[3] Possibly Aghavourk Ford; see SJC, MS U.30 (2), f. 64v (p. 127).
[4] See the diary entry for this date at SJC, MS U.30 (2), ff. 63r–64v (pp. 126–7).
[5] This sketch may have been made on 10 Sept.; see SJC, MS U.30 (2), ff. 63r–64v (pp. 126–7).

[f. 59v *blank*]

[f. 60r *Pencil and ink landscape, annotated, captioned*] View of the water fall at the Entrance of Glin Mackanass [Glenmacknass] which is above 150 feet and falls over a rocky channel. Extremely fine after much rain the rocks above it are fine white spar chiefly and the road runs all along the hillside down to the Barracks. It is defended by a wall near the edge. After falling the water goes to the left of the valley which is a fine rich soil. The sides of the rocks are cut away to make the road[1]
[f. 60v] September 11.

[f. 61r *Ink and pencil sketch of church, cemetery and holly tree against mountain backdrop, captioned*] Curious holly at 7 Churches[2]
[f. 61v] View of 1 of the 7 Churches with a round tower. The roof is ½ covered with ivy 2 walls mark 2 distances and in the front ground is a curious old holly with an old trunk and many fine young branches shooting out from inside[.] Just behind it is one quite dead and white. A rough lofty mountain is in the background. The view is taken in the Church yard between the great Church and the Pillar[3]

[f. 62r *Ink and pencil view of bridge surrounded by trees, annotated, captioned*] View of Ashford Bridge. L[4] Recesses on it
NB. To bring the L side of the Bridge more round and to put in several old cabins and trees among them and to make the Mountain bold.
Friday 12.

[f. 62v *blank*]

[f. 63r *Ink and pencil view of bridge surrounded by trees, annotated, captioned*] Bridge Newry. 21[5]
[f. 63v] Under the L Arch is sun temple on the banks surrounded with wood and the river sides have some fine trees on them to the water edge. The square recess on the bridge has a seat in it and there is one on other side also. Mrs Tighes grounds are beyond the Bridge

[f. 64r *Ink and pencil landscape, annotated, captioned*] View of the Mountain at foot of which are the streams where the Gold mine is[.] The river runs through the valley below the 2 precipices covered with wood and begins at the Mountain in the distance. At the foot of that Mountain is the level and the works[6]
Monday September 15.

[f. 64v *blank*]

---

[1] See SJC, MS U.30 (2), f. 66v (p. 128).
[2] Reproduced at p. 130 (Figure 7).
[3] See SJC, MS U.30 (2), ff. 67v–68v (p. 129).
[4] Refers to shapes drawn on the bridge in the sketch.
[5] See SJC, MS U.30 (2), f. 74v (p. 134). The meaning of '21' here is unclear, as he was in the area on 12 Sept. 1806.
[6] Lee's visit to the mines is described at SJC, MS U.30 (2), ff. 91r–92r (p. 142).

7. SKETCHBOOK, 1806–7

[SJC, MS U.30 (7)]

[*Inside front cover*] The person who finds this Book is requested to return it to Mr Fiott.
Coffys Hotel Killarney
at Swinburnes Hotel, Limerick
Mr Nugents Hatter Grand Parade Cork [*Small ink sketch of crest*]

[f. 1r *Rough pencil sketch of the equestrian statue of King William III on College Green, Dublin*]

[f. 1v *blank*]

[f. 2r *Rough pencil landscape with church tower among low hills; annotated, captioned*] View near Dripsey and Mr Hawks house October 7[1]

[f. 2v *blank*]

[f. 3r *Rough pencil landscape with mountains; annotated, captioned*] View on road to Macroom October 8[2]

[f. 3v *blank*]

[f. 4r *Rough pencil view of mountain and valley; annotated, captioned*] Nearly the same view October 8.

[ff. 4v, 5r *blank*]

[ff. 5v–6r *Rough pencil landscape with mountains; annotated, captioned*] View just beyond on the Right hand side in the Glen October 8.
Autumnal tints on the leaves

[ff. 6v, 7r *blank*]

[ff. 7v–8r *Pencil and ink landscape with tower; annotated, captioned*] View on road near Inchegela[3]

---

[1] See SJC, MS U.30 (3), f. 10v (p. 188).
[2] See SJC, MS U.30 (3), f. 12r (p. 189).
[3] See SJC, MS U.30 (3), f. 13v (p. 191).

14 rock fern and heath
2 4 5 6 7 8 9 10 11 12 13 are different distances of Mountains
Remarkable edge of rocks running across the road in the 2nd distance. October 9.

[f. 8v *blank*]

[f. 9r *Ink view of mountain glen; annotated, captioned*] View on road to Kenmare beyond the Priests Leap October 14[1]

[f. 9v *blank*]

[f. 10r *Ink landscape with hills and cloud; annotated, captioned*] 16 October 3 Mountains (distant) just appearing over the circular ridge of a Mountain just above Kenmare on the road to Killarney[2]

[f. 10v *blank*]

[f. 11r *Pencil and ink mountain view; annotated, captioned*] Entrance to Killarney October 16[.] Back side of Turk[.] Mangerton Mountain[3]

[f. 11v *blank*]

[f. 12r *Ink and pencil view of cabin and tree against mountain backdrop, drawn within portrait frame; captioned*] View from Maurice Fitzgeralds Cabin door October 31. Here we slept one night[4]

[ff. 12v, 13r *blank*]

[ff. 13v–14r *Pencil and ink harbour view; annotated, captioned*] First view of the Harbour of Ventry from the Dingle Road, November 3: 1806.
Bray Head[.] Skelligs[.] Ventry Harbour[5]

[f. 14v *blank*]

[f. 15r *Pencil and ink coastal view, upside-down; annotated, captioned*] Ventry Bay November 3[.] Distant Mountains are in Iveagh[6]

[ff. 15v, 16r *blank*]

---

[1] See SJC, MS U.30 (4), f. 2r (p. 196).
[2] See SJC, MS U.30 (4), ff. 7r–11r (pp. 200–203).
[3] See SJC, MS U.30 (4), ff. 11v–12r (pp. 203–4).
[4] On the Dingle Peninsula; see SJC, MS U.30 (4), ff. 44v–45r (p. 225).
[5] See SJC, MS U.30 (4), ff. 48v–49r (p. 227).
[6] See SJC, MS U.30 (4), ff. 48v–49r (p. 227).

[ff. 16v–17r *Pencil and ink coastal view; annotated, captioned*] First view of the Blasquets from the top of the Eagles Mountains [Mount Eagle] on the road to Trevory and the extremity of the land in that direction November 3: 1806[1]
1 Great Blasquet on which is a signal tower. 2 is a part of the farther island. 3 the rocky island with no soil on it 4. the Northern Isle with a curious reef of rocks on one end. 5 a set of rocks and one island on which is a cottage 6 is the cliff at about 2 miles off from the top of the Mountain whence sketch was taken. Some parts of the cliff are 200 feet high

[ff. 17v, 18r *blank*]

[ff. 18v–19r *Ink and pencil coastal view; annotated, captioned*] View ~~some~~ (somewhere) from Trevory November 5.[2]

[ff. 19v, 20r *blank*]

[ff. 20v–21r *Pencil and ink coastal view; annotated, captioned*] View from the flat on the E side of Dunmore point at the Base of the Mountain [Mount Eagle][3]
1: The Ennistois court Island
2. Constraugh[4] and Sybil Heads[5]

[ff. 21v–22r *Pencil and ink sketch of boat, castle and ruin; annotated, captioned*] View crossing the Ferry at Dungarvan January 17[6]

[ff. 22v–23r *Pencil coastal view; annotated, captioned*] View nearer to the Extremity of Dunmore point from the upper part of the conical Mountain. Upon ascending to the top of the Mountain in the last view, the second distance in the present view appears in front, which is the farthest point of land on the island[.] The whole of the land is the finest turf imaginable. The Cliffs are very steep and many are 70 80 or 100 feet high and no boat could land in any point whatever
1. The great Blasquet
2. Bagnio Island[7]
3. Ennistois court Island [Inishtooskert, *Inis Tuaisceart* (Ir.)]
4. The farthest extremity of Dunmore Point.

[ff. 23v, 24r *blank*]

[ff. 24v–25r *Rough pencil coastal view; annotated, captioned*] View from the very extreme point of rock at Dunmore Point.[8] In front is a remarkable rock and all torn into the most

---

[1] See SJC, MS U.30 (4), ff. 49v–50r (p. 227).
[2] See SJC, MS U.30 (4), ff. 53v–54r (p. 230).
[3] See SJC, MS U.30 (4), ff. 49v–50r (p. 227).
[4] Possibly Lee's rendition of *Ceann Trá*, the Irish name for Ventry.
[5] Sybil Head and Sybil Point, Co. Kerry.
[6] See also sketches at SJC, MS U.30 (7), f. 48v and ff. 51v–52r (pp. 324, 325) and diary entry at SJC, MS U.30 (5), f. 34r (pp. 262–3).
[7] Probably Beiginis.
[8] See SJC, MS U.30 (4), ff. 50v–51r (p. 228).

remarkable forms by the ocean. Beyond this is another rock of a larger size. The sea frequently washes over the greatest part of these rocks and at high water the whole of the rocks where this was drawn are under water. It was necessary to retreat from the spot where I stood at the approach of every wave. These 2 Rocks are to be approached in mild weather and at low water, at the summer low tides, but it is very difficult to get over with even long poles.
1. Great Blasquet
2. Sciligs [Skelligs] } these Is*lands* and Brea [Bray] Head ought to be at least 6 Miles
3. Brea Head further removed on another paper

[ff. 25v–26r *Rough pencil coastal view; annotated, captioned*] View from the top of the ladder at the ~~Light house~~ Signal Tower at the Blasquet Island[1]
1. Trirraught Island [Tearaght Island, *An Tiaracht* (Ir.)] or rock. The most westerly point but inaccessible except in calm summer weather
2. Part of Ennis toisct Is*land*. brought nearer than it sh*ould* be, to shew its situation
3. Ennis vi Killan Is*land* [*Inis Mhic Aoibhleain* (Ir.)]. The most southerly of the Cluster

[ff. 26v–27r *Rough pencil coastal view; annotated, captioned*] Entrance of the Shannon River from the rising ground above Ballingarry[.][2] Ballingarry lies down near No. 1 and there the cliffs are very high and bold. The whole of this part is a bold coast. At No. 2 wh*ich* is on the Clare coast [Loop Head] is a Signal tower and lighthouse not very far asunder. Kerry head lies out to the West of No. 3.

[ff. 27v, 28r *blank*]

[ff. 28v–29r *Rough pencil landscape with mountains and bridge; annotated, captioned*] Bridge between Ardfert and Ballyhagere[3]
1. Are Sand Hills and just on the other side of them within 300 Yds is a fine beautiful strand of Ballyhagan [Ballyheige] Bay and the sea
2. the fine M*ou*nta*i*ns of Tralee wh*ich* is situated somewhere about No. 5, 6 or 8 Miles *fr*om this spot
3 Are the M*ou*nta*i*ns on the promontory tow*ar*ds Dingle. 4 is probably Brandon Hill
It is curious enough that the Sandhills separate the sea and the Bay from this river and just over the river and all along the side of it No. 6 is a large loch [Akeragh Lough] and bogs and marsh of sal*t*water.

[ff. 29v–30r *blank*]

[ff. 30v–31r *Rough pencil landscape with river; annotated, captioned*] Nove*mb*er 21: View up the Shannon between Glyn and Logill,[4] taken near a Cottage on the side of the road, Cottage is on a rising ground

---

[1] See SJC, MS U.30 (4), ff. 51v–52r (p. 229).
[2] See SJC, MS U.30 (5), ff. 3v–4r (p. 235).
[3] Probably Ballymaquin Bridge and Ballyheige.
[4] See SJC, MS U.30 (5), f. 7v (p. 239). The sketch should have been made on 20 Nov.

In the Centre beyond the river is the county of Clare and the Mountains in the distant Land below them and the river, flat and in some places round like the immense back of whales[.] View is high above the river

[ff. 31v–33r *blank*]

[ff. 33v–34r *Rough pencil landscape with river and mountains; annotated, captioned*] November 21. View of a part of the river near Loghill. No. 1 is Loghill Bay. Mountains and flats of Clare form the distance

[f. 34v, 35r *blank*]

[ff. 35v–36r *Rough pencil landscape with low hills and river; annotated, captioned*] November 21. View between Loghill and Askeyton of the Entrance of the channel up to ~~of the~~ Clare and Ennis. Front ground to be made darker considerably.
Ennis lies at the Entrance of the Bog. A great many islands in the channel up to Ennis. the Mountains on the R are all in Clare and on the left of the view is an immense extent of flat country

[f. 36v *blank*]

[f. 37r *Rough pencil sketch of round building surrounded by trees; annotated, captioned*] View of a curious round building behind the Abbey in the Town of Askeyton[1]
Door low. Beautiful vaulted roof with a circular opening.

[ff. 37v–38r *Ink view of city from hill above, with river and surrounding low hills, crossed out; annotated, captioned*] December 30: 1806 View [of Cork] from the N side of the river on the road above that going to Youghal. About ½ Mile from the Bridge. Bank which runs down the river[.] Ships. Sir J.B. Warners Quay and a small part of Cork. 1 442 11m2 44 5-53352 2615-5192 so that I could not see the town, to finish the scetch[2]

[f. 38v *blank*]

[f. 39r *Ink view of city from hill above, with river and surrounding low hills; annotated, captioned*] December 30: View [of Cork] on the road just beyond the last at the corner of a house

[f. 39v *blank*]

[f. 40r *Pencil and ink view of Cork city from hill above, with river and boats; annotated, captioned*] View from the Stone quarries just below the Barrack looking down the river [River Lee]

---

[1] This building was in Adare; see diary entry at SJC, MS U.30 (5), f. 10r (p. 241).
[2] Lee's diary entry for this date does not mention this walk; see SJC, MS U.30 (5), f. 28v (p. 257).

[f. 40v *blank*]

[f. 41r *Two ink sketches of a donkey, side profile and head*] John Fiott Esqu*ire* taken from Life.

[f. 41v *blank*]

[f. 42r *Very rough pencil outline sketch of hill and trees; captioned*] This line is the top of the Next [sketch]

[ff. 42v–43r *Rough pencil landscape with river, houses and trees; captioned, annotated*] Little Island[.] Passage Point[1]

[ff. 43v–44r *blank*]

[ff. 44v–45r *Two pencil and ink sketches of gated entrance with ivy and trees, with detail of the urn on top of the gate; captioned*] View thro*ugh* Mr Spires Lodge Gate of Tivoli. The gate is overhung with ivy wh*ich* hangs down nearly in festoons to the iron rails, there is a fine old arch and a gothic lodge bey*on*d the gate and the Entrance to Mr Penroses seat[2] is also on the L with trees around it thro*ugh* whose branches the river is seen and the Range of shore beyond it. On the top of the gate is an urn[3]

[ff. 45v–46r *Rough pencil and ink view of coast from boat, with town and surrounding hills; captioned, annotated*] Outline of Youghall from the middle of the ferry. Jan*uary* 16:[4]

[f. 46v *blank*]

[f. 47r *Rough pencil and ink view of river with town and surrounding hills; captioned, annotated*] Youghall from Pilltown Hill about 1½ from the ferry. Jan*uary* 16:[5]

[ff. 47v–48r *Rough pencil and ink landscape with low hills; captioned, annotated*] January 16. View from Aglis [Aglish] Hill on road to Waterford[.] Fine cultivated country except on the mount*a*ins in middle

[f. 48v *Pencil and ink view of two mountains and a nearby group of houses, with detail of one section of the view; captioned, annotated*] A fissure in the Mo*u*ntain on the L about 1½ fr*o*m Dungarvan Ferry Jan*uary* 17[6]

---

[1] This sketch may have been made during a walk on 12 Jan. 1807; see SJC, MS U.30 (5), f. 32v (p. 261).

[2] Cooper Penrose of Woodhill; see p. 183, n. 2.

[3] This sketch may have been made on a walk on 12 Jan. 1807; see SJC, MS U.30 (5), f. 32r (p. 260).

[4] Lee had to cross the River Blackwater by ferry before beginning his walk to Clashmore and Dungarvan; see SJC, MS U.30 (5), f. 33v (p. 262).

[5] Pilltown lies between Youghal and Clashmore by Lee's route of 16 Jan. 1807; see SJC, MS U.30 (5), f. 33v (p. 262).

[6] See also sketches at SJC, MS U.30 (7), ff. 21v–22r and ff. 51v–52r (pp. 321, 325) and diary entry at SJC, MS U.30 (5), f. 34r (p. 262).

[f. 49r *Rough outline pencil and ink sketch of low, bare hills; captioned, annotated*] Tops of the dis*tan*t M*o*untains[.] Below this front ground the road descends very much for a great way and depth.

[f. 49v *Rough pencil sketch of harbour and boats; annotated, captioned*] The Quay point and ferry at Dungarvan Jan*ua*ry 17[1]

[f. 50r *Rough pencil and ink outline sketch of low, bare hills; captioned, annotated*] From top of the M*o*untain on the road to Dungarvan. 1 is the point of Youghall and an island laying off that point[.] 2 is a M*o*untain very high at a great distance Jan*ua*ry 26[2]
View of Youghall Point[3]
Cape Island or Ianagappul [Capel Island, *Oileán na gCapall* (Ir.)]

[ff. 50v–51r *Outline ink and pencil view of low hills and coast; annotated, captioned*] View from the top of the M*o*untain wh*i*ch hangs over the plains of Dungarvan and its harbour. 2 Rocks at the point. The M*o*untains in front are at an immense dis*tan*ce and very high for No. 2 appear to be high M*o*untains on descending the M*o*untain[.] Jan*ua*ry 16.

[ff. 51v–52r *Rough, outline ink and pencil sketch of rocky outcrop and waterfall; annotated, captioned*] Jan*ua*ry 17 View up the fissure of a very fine bold Rock scene and a brook rushing down[4]

[ff. 52v–53r *Rough ink and pencil view of valley and river; annotated, captioned*] View from a M*o*untain top to the South of port of Dungarvon [Dungarvan] river.[5] On the Edge of the sea is an old Castle or abbey

[f. 53v *blank*]

[f. 54r *Rough pencil view of low valley and river; annotated, captioned*] View within 50 Yards of the same spot but lower down, looking between the 2 sides of the Glen on the end of Dungarvon and the river and the dis*tan*t M*o*untains beyond wh*i*ch lies Youghall Jan*ua*ry 17.[6]

[ff. 54v–55r *Rough outline ink and pencil view of low hills and distant town; annotated, captioned*] Jan*ua*ry 17. View of Dungarvan from the top of the M*o*untain about 2 Miles[.] In Dungarvon are 2 old towers or Abbeys in ruins[7]

---

[1] Lee left Dungarvan on the morning of 17 Jan.; see SJC, MS U.30 (5), f. 34r (p. 262).
[2] See SJC, MS U.30 (5), f. 33v (p. 262). The date should read 16 January here.
[3] Lee means Knockadoon Head, Co. Cork.
[4] See also sketches at SJC, MS U.30 (7), ff. 21v–22r and f. 48v (pp. 321, 324) and diary entry of 17 Jan. 1807 at SJC, MS U.30 (5), f. 34r (p. 263).
[5] Possibly the view described on 17 Jan. 1807; see SJC, MS U.30 (5), f. 34r (p. 263).
[6] Possibly the view described on 17 Jan. 1807; see SJC, MS U.30 (5), f. 34r (p. 263).
[7] One of these is the Augustinian abbey founded by Thomas Fitzgerald, Lord Offaly, in *c.*1290 and dissolved *c.*1541 (Gwynn and Hadcock, *Medieval Religious Houses*, pp. 295, 299; Moore, *Archaeological Inventory of County Waterford*, p. 162). The other is the early-modern tower house known as McGrath's Castle, a square six-storey building that has since collapsed (Moore, *Archaeological Inventory of County Waterford*, p. 219).

[f. 55v *Rough pencil landscape with a large rock in foreground and low hills in background; annotated, captioned*] No. 2. Continuation of the same view as on the opposite page [f. 56r] Mountains at some distance and all higher very rough surface

[f. 56r *Rough pencil view of 3-arched bridge and surrounding countryside with large rock in foreground; annotated, captioned*] No. 1) View of a Bridge about 4 Miles from Kilmac Thomas on the Dungarvan Side, in a hollow and 2 very remarkable pieces of rock close to it. An old ruined Bridge and farm on top of hill[1]

[ff. 56v–57r *Rough pencil view of low, bare hills and building in foreground; annotated, captioned*] Same view as the other,[2] but from the North. The same Mountains are brought into the Right of this as are in the other

[ff. 57v–58r *Rough pencil and ink landscape with cloud-covered mountain; annotated, captioned*] View about [a] Mile beyond Newtown Mountain, of the Range of Mountains behind it and along whose skirts the road from Dungarvan winds. Mountains were not clear from Clouds but as sun shone on them the edges of them could be discerned, all the parts appear to be Cliffs of white rock and very steep ⊥ʳ precipices[,] very fine white edges like the Eglwsg [Eglwyseg] rocks near Langollen.[3] Very uneven surface and there appear cavities like some craters of volcanoes. The range dwindles off towards Dungarvon
2 Distant is very extensive and wide. 3 is a large Mountain but appears small on account of the immense range. It is at a great distance, perhaps 8 Miles January 18.[4]

[ff. 58v–59r *Rough pencil and ink landscape with cloud-covered mountain in the distance and buildings in the foreground; annotated, captioned*] View near of [*sic*] mill of the same Mountains January 18.
1, 2, 3 Lands not very far off. 4 is about 1½ distant and cultivated. (the rest at a great distance 5, 9 or 10 or 12 miles some parts) 5 is a Mountain at the foot of the others
I never saw the tops of these white Mountains[.] They were always in clouds although the whole of the Sky was blue[.]

[ff. 59v–60r *Neat pencil streetscape with river and medieval tower, Waterford; annotated, captioned*] January 19. View from 1st floor in commercial Building Window, morning too rainy to go out. An old tower is at the corner of the St. The Quay river and country beyond, shops of which several are under the same roof. Bit of the Assembly rooms Tall steeple of the Cathedral. and another old building.[5] Taken from a [dressing?] room window[6]
Mr Powers House on the Hill[7]

[1] See SJC, MS U.30 (5), f. 34r (pp. 262–3).
[2] Lee means the sketch above, at f. 55v.
[3] See SJC, MS U.30 (1), f. 54r (p. 76).
[4] See SJC, MS U.30 (5), f. 35r (p. 263).
[5] Reginald's Tower, Waterford; a circular keep, probably built after 1200 (Moore, *Archaeological Inventory of County Waterford*, p. 215).
[6] See SJC, MS U.30 (5), f. 35v (p. 264).
[7] See p. 158, n. 5.

[f. 60v *blank*]

[f. 61r *Rough pencil sketch of river, riverbank and boat; annotated, captioned*] Curious old rock over the river at Waterford and opposite the E end of the Quay Jan*u*ary 19:[1]

[f. 61v *blank*]

[f. 62r *Rough ink and pencil landscape with river, wooded hills and tower in distance; annotated, captioned*] Jan*u*ary 20. View across the Suire above Carreg [Carrick-on-Suir] of an old castle, old walls along river side at some dist*a*nce from castle, they are ivy topped. M*o*unt*ai*ns behind castle cov*e*red with wood. A Glen
Fine venerable castle with old walls about it[2]

[ff. 62v–63r *Rough pencil and ink landscape with same low hills and tower as in previous sketch; annotated, captioned*] Jan*u*ary 20. An old tower on the R of the river. A fine range of M*o*unt*ai*n tops all strewed with snow[.] Ivy tower[3]
On North side of river, river is close at the Back of a person look*i*ng towards the M*o*unt*ai*n and if a person was on the oppos*i*te side of the river it w*ou*ld form the front of this picture

[f. 63v *blank*]

[f. 64r *Pencil and ink view of cluster of buildings with nearby trees, upside-down on page; annotated, captioned*] Suire side. View of the South side. Some old ivy capt[4] ruins, a wall topped with ivy. Two trees[.] The nearest M*o*unt*ai*ns 1 and 2 form a near Background, But No. 2 goes off a very long way up the river side. 3 are dis*t*ant M*o*unt*ai*ns but were not I believe so high as to be cov*e*red with snow wh*i*ch at this time lay on the tops of the high M*o*unt*ai*ns in the next scetch. All these scetches are not very accurate for the Day was so cold that it was almost impossible to hold the pencil Jan*u*ary 20

[f. 64v *blank*]

[f. 65r *Pencil and ink landscape with low hills and buildings; annotated, captioned*] View from N Side of Suire below Carreg and Clonmel[5]
There is an old ruin of a castle very picturesque, situated at the part where 2 ridges of M*o*unt*ai*ns meet. That on the R is bare and the other is wooded. M*o*unt*ai*ns behind cov*e*red with much snow but parts appear not so
C.[6] Cultivated ground. Declivities and holes on the M*o*unt*ai*ns in dist*a*nce

---

[1] See SJC, MS U.30 (5), f. 35v (p. 264).
[2] See SJC, MS U.30 (5), f. 36v (p. 266); this was one of the five sketches Lee made on that day's walk (see SJC, MS U.30 (5), f. 37r (p. 265).
[3] See SJC, MS U.30 (5), ff. 36v–37r (p. 265); this was one of the five sketches Lee made on that day's walk (see SJC, MS U.30 (5), f. 37r (p. 265).
[4] Capped. This was one of the five sketches Lee made on that day's walk (see SJC, MS U.30 (5), f. 37r (p. 265).
[5] This was one of the five sketches Lee made on that day's walk (see SJC, MS U.30 (5), f. 37r (p. 265).
[6] Refers to a spot in the sketch.

The effect of the Woody Mountain [and] the Bare one. The Old Castle ruins and the Alps behind with snow produced the most beautiful effect.

[f. 65v *Very rough outline pencil sketch; annotated, captioned*] *Vide* large Book[.][1] 2 miles for Lake from *Kilmac*Thomas[2]

[f. 66r *blank, one-third of page torn out*]

[ff. 66v–67r *Pencil and ink view of river, a 3-arched bridge and surrounding buildings and low hills, with detail of tower; annotated, captioned*] Nearest Tower[.] Very perfect. Neat and well finished edges very accurate[3]
View down the river. Taken about 4 Miles from Clonmel. Front ground high and from roadside. Opposite is a Cabin and a bank steep – over which is seen part of a meadow below skirting the river. A new bridge is building and nearly finished. The opposite side is imperfect. River is just seen over the Bridge, and fine arc of Mountains covered with wood diminishes away, and ends between the Cabin and a fine large fairy mound which is in a field behind the Cabin. Two Towers are seen[,] one about ¾ mile off and [the] other [at a] great distance.
3:4 distances 3 very woody. 5 is a flat down where the river runs, high cultivation. Bare Mountains beyond Carreg probably. 7 and 8 different distances. 8 is a distant range of Mountain.[4]
a wall going [behind] the Cabin

[ff. 67v–68v *blank*]

---

[1] This 'large book' has not been located.
[2] This may be one of the five sketches Lee made on that day's walk (see SJC, MS U.30 (5), f. 37r (p. 265).
[3] Possibly one of the towers along the River Blackwater that Lee admired from a distance on 20 Jan. 1807; see SJC, MS U.30 (5), f. 37r (p. 265).
[4] The numbers refer to points in the sketch.

8. SKETCHBOOK, 1807

[SJC, MS U.30 (8)]

[Inside front cover] Mr Smallon. Mr Gaitlands Hotel. Bolton St N° 2[1]
Whoever finds this Book is requested to return it to
Mr Fiott,   Swinburnes Hotel Limerick[2]
   McAvoys Hotel Kildare Street Dublin[3]
   No. 25 Dame Street Dublin
[*Sums of money in pencil, erased but with traces visible, for 10 lines.*]

[f. 1r *No sketch*] Battle of Clontarf fought 23 April 1014 (1014). On Good Friday[4]

[ff. 1v–2r *Pencil sketch of castle and surrounding landscape, with ink annotations*] January 27. Castle Connel Rock.[5] Fine views on the top of it. At the foot of it and about it are large masses of the walls laying about, as if they had been battered down. Road runs at foot of rock. River much flooded. In the Dist*ance* a fine M*ountai*n[.] An old ruined Abbey to the R

[f. 2v *blank*]

[f. 3r *Pencil landscape with village, annotated*] Jan*uary* 27. First view of OBriens Bridge.[6] The water is not the bed of the river but [the] meadow flooded. Dist*ant* M*ountai*ns bare and one part forms a steep hollow conical form. Cultivated land beyond river. White washed cabins with thatched roofs over river. Front ground slopes very much to [the] waters edge. A Mount*ai*n Cabin or hut on the L.

[ff. 3v–4r *Pencil sketch of bridge, annotated*] OBriens Bridge. 14 Arches. N°. 1.[7] A large arch to admit of boats passing. From the side hangs a chain into [the] water and above ~~dn~~ below Bridge are 2 timbers anchored to wh*ich* chain fixed to draw boats thro*ugh* bridge Jan*uary* 27[.] Water falling below bridge a foot nearly.

---

[1] The hotel at 2 Bolton St was in the name of a Thomas Marley in a recent directory (*Wilson's Directory*, p. 159).

[2] Lee stayed at this hotel in Limerick; see SJC, MS U.30 (5), f. 11r (p. 242).

[3] Lee stayed at this hotel when he first arrived in Dublin on 30 Aug. 1806; see SJC, MS U.30 (2), f. 25v (p. 99).

[4] The battle between 'would-be ruler of Ireland', Brian Bórama (see p. 288, n. 11), and the Vikings of Dublin (Lennon, *That Field of Glory*, p. 17).

[5] See SJC, MS U.30 (5), f. 51r (p. 276).

[6] See SJC, MS U.30 (5), f. 51r (p. 276).

[7] Refers to a point in the sketch.

[ff. 4v–5r *Pencil landscape with ink annotations*] View above OBriens Bridge.[1] The Mountains in the distance are barren. The nearer Hills are all in high cultivation and ÷d with hedges and walls etc chiefly pasture. Channel of river runs to the R. but all the rest is flooded January 27

[f. 5v *blank*]

[f. 6r *Pencil landscape, annotated*] January 27. Ruin on E side of Shannon just above OBriens Bridge. No. 1 is the same Mountain as in the last. Cultivated lands and hills[,] Mountain bare. Ruin is in meadow.

[ff. 6v–7r *Three pencil and ink sketches*] Views of the horse bridge on the Bank of the river going up to Killaloe January 27[2]

[ff. 7v–8r *blank*]

[ff. 8v–9r *Pencil and ink landscape with distant village*] January 27. View up to Killaloe.[3] Front ground. A horse bridge and 2 Cabins, one in ruins. Mountains to the right. In the Centre another horse Bridge and at the foot of the Mountain[,] a gents House, a tower of the Cathedral, Town, Ruins of abbey or [*sic*] etc. On the L meadows on river side and beyond them fine cultivated Hills and Mountains in the distance. Quite bare.

[ff. 9v–10r *blank*]

[ff. 10v–11r *Pencil sketch, annotated*] January 27 View of Killaloe Cathedral from the Canal side. 1[4] is a rocky Mountain and round and conical. 2 [is] very distant land. Bridge of 17 Arches.[5] Over [the] Bridge is [a] curious old ruin on an island [Ballina Castle]. Ivy about it. 3 [is] cultivated hills[,] 4 [is] distant Mountain. River very swift and runs over rocks. Bridge straight. Behind [the] Cathedral [is a] Clergymans House and ~~town~~ part of the town and Mountains behind. East window has 3 long windows in it
x Parsons House

[f. 11v *blank*]

[f. 12r *Three pencil sketches, annotated, of cathedral south elevation, corner pillar and base*] January 27. South Window of Cathedral over grown with ivy. The pillars are very perfect and quite neat and not in a ruinous appearance. Scetch of the Corner Pillars of the East Window, which have at the corners round thin pillars with fine regular moulding

[1] See SJC, MS U.30 (5), f. 51v (p. 276).
[2] The two sketches at f. 7r are reproduced at p. 277 (Figure 13).
[3] See SJC, MS U.30 (5), f. 51v (p. 276).
[4] The numbers 1–4, and the letter 'x' in this description refer to points in the sketch.
[5] Lee's error – the bridge, built *c.*1770, had 13 arches (NIAH). The error is repeated at SJC, MS U.30 (5), f. 51v (pp. 277–8).

[ff. 12v–13r *blank*]

[f. 13v *Ink sketch*] January 27. Plan of the tower of the Cathedral

[f. 14r *Two pencil and ink sketches, annotated*] January 27. Oratory of St Molua [Molana] in Killaloe Church. In Top is a window but overgrown with ivy. Fine round arched door and of perfect stone and order

[f. 14v *blank*]

[f. 15r *Three pencil and ink sketches, annotated*] January 27. West End of the same. On each side of the door which is smaller than the other are 2 round pillars, all the mouldings are gothic. Window is Gothic. Whole building is gothic
Nº of Kings buried in this oratory
Cornerpiece of W side 3 round pillars

[ff. 15v–16r *blank*]

[ff. 16v–17r *Pencil landscape with ink annotations*] January 28. View of Cragg [Crag] Mountain. The front ground being clear and the Tops of the Mountains [Slieve Bernagh] but a very thick fog concealing all the centre. The river runs at the foot of these Mountains and would be plainly discernible but for the fog[1]

[ff. 17v–18r *blank*]

[ff. 18v–19r *Pencil landscape with ink annotations*] January 28 View from within 200 yds of the same spot but comprehending part of the river which is seen through the fog. Cragg Mountain is very uneven and with swelling and [cavities?] like the bowels of any animal. River is very wide. A Rock in it
Front ground is a lawn diversified with plantations and weathered trees, ground falling very much to river side. Effect produced by fog very striking. Every part of Mountain seen perfectly clear

[ff. 19v–20r *blank*]

[ff. 20v–21r *Pencil landscape, mountains in fog, with ink annotations*] January 28. View about 1 mile beyond Derry. South View.

[f. 21v *blank*]

[f. 22r *Pencil landscape with ink annotations*] Continuation of the view [on the previous page]

[ff. 22v–23r *blank*]

---

[1] See SJC, MS U.30 (5), f. 52r (p. 278).

[ff. 23v–24r *Pencil landscape with ink annotations*] January 28 View from top of a Hill looking back[.] All the vallies are filled with fog
Part of Lough Derg would be visible but for the fog
B – Barren   C Cultivated   The N⁰ˢ denote the different distances. The Shannon or rather R. shows the course of the river

[ff. 24v–25r *blank*]

[ff. 25v–26r *Pencil sketch of a thatched cabin, with ink annotations*] January 28. View of part of the Lough from a scattered village along the roadside
View of Part of Lough Derg[1]

[ff. 26v–27r *blank*]

[f. 27v *Pencil sketch with ink annotations, from the perspective of sitting at the back of a coach with two people in front*] January 29. Taken at Toomavara (I believe) while Coach stopped opposite a wiskey shop January 29.
1 Wiskey shop
2 Cultivated ground. Much intersected with fences of earth
3 Distant Mountain. Larger swell not so well cultivated
4 Old Hat. 5 New Ditto. 6 Welsh wig[2]
7 Dark brown new coat
8 Old light brown surtout
Poor cabins on roadside

[ff. 28r, 28v, 29r *blank*]

[ff. 29v–30r *Pencil sketch with ink annotations, from the perspective of sitting at the back of a coach with one person in front*] Distant appearance of the Devils Bit January 29, February 2[3]

[f. 30v *blank*]

[f. 31r *Pencil sketch with ink annotations, from the perspective of sitting at the back of a coach with two people in front*] Devils Bit and Distant Mountains. Front ground rounded and cultivated in a great measure
January 29. February 4[4]

[f. 31v *Pencil and ink outline landscape*] Devils Bit

---

[1] See SJC, MS U.30 (5), f. 52r (p. 278).
[2] Numbers 4–8 refer to the clothing and appearance of the two figures in front.
[3] See SJC, MS U.30 (5), f. 55v (p. 281). He travelled by the spot on 29 Jan., so the reason for the reference to 2 Feb. is unclear.
[4] See SJC, MS U.30 (5), f. 55v (p. 281). He travelled by the spot on 29 Jan., so the reason for the reference to 4 Feb. is unclear.

[f. 32r *blank*]

[ff. 32v–33r *Pencil sketch with ink annotations*] Tower at Roscrea January 30 February 4[1]
Taken while horses were changing
Had not enough pencil to put the old castle in. Worne out

[f. 33v *blank*]

[f. 34r *Pencil and ink sketch of a row of cabins along a roadside, annotated*] Lateral continuation of the last
Smoke coming out of the Cabin tops but no chimney

[ff. 34v, 35r, 35v *blank*]

[f. 36r *Pencil and ink sketch, annotated*] Tower at Kildare[2]
~~Taken~~ while watering the Horses January 30
Tower covered with White moss so that the junction of the stone is hardly perceivable

[f. 36v *blank*]

[f. 37r *Pencil sketch of horse and cart with seated figure, annotated*] January 30 Great coat Buttoned in front

[f. 37v *blank*]

[f. 38r *Pencil and ink sketch of towers in flat landscape, with detail of tower window*] S View of Swords Round and Square Towers and ruins of adjacent chapel. The distance is very great beyond the Tower and goes off view flat beyond. On Top of tower is a cross hardly perceivable until examined for[.] Wide open country. No trees except about the river. Swords Village is hid by the rising ground on the Left Nº 1.
February 19: 1807[3]

[ff. 38v, 39r *blank*]

[f. 39v *Pencil and ink landscape with house, annotated*] [*margin:* 1][4] February 18. 2 Views near Old Bridge. Taken from the same spot
View to South West. Cabin in front Ground and field. Thatched House. Mud wall. Beyond are uneven grounds with great nº of scattered trees. Every hedge is marked and the

---

[1] See SJC, MS U.30 (5), f. 55v (p. 281). He passed through Roscrea on 29 Jan., so the reason for the reference to 4 Feb. is unclear. Sketch is reproduced at p. 282 (Figure 14).

[2] See SJC, MS U.30 (5), f. 57v (p. 284).

[3] Lee made this sketch en route back to Dublin from Drogheda, but the diary entry for the day makes no mention of Swords; see SJC, MS U.30 (5), f. 79r (p. 304).

[4] Lee numbered all of his sketches around the site of the Battle of the Boyne, cross-referencing them in his diary. These numbers are given here as marginal notes. The diary entry for this sketch is at SJC, MS U.30 (5), f. 75v (p. 301).

strait ⊥ʳ lines are the trees of which [there are] some in every hedgerow[.] There is one hanging small wood on the hill near a gentleman's house which is surrounded with trees. On that Hill King James is said to have stood and seen the fight below. To the right [is] a bare ridge with 3 or 4 trees on its summit. The lane has trees on each side and up this it is said King William's troops marched after crossing the river which lies under our foreground. Mr Coddingtons House called Old Bridge town[1]

[f. 40r *Pencil and ink landscape with house, annotated, with detail of obelisk*] [*margin:* 2][2]
Spot the same. View North West. End of the same cabin as in the last [sketch]. Below the front ground is seen a part of the Boyne and the pillar erected in commemoration of the Battle. On left of Pillar is a long range of bank which to the river is very steep. Road runs at [the] foot of it below [the] meadow on [the] South of [the] river. The different distances are mostly wood and all thickly interspersed with trees. In the distance appears a range of woods and on an eminence some thing like a tower or signal post. It is Lord — (Cunningham) at Slane Castle
February 18

[ff. 40v, 41r *blank*]

[ff. 41v–42r *Pencil and ink landscape, annotated*] [*margin:* View 3][3] February 18 Near the ford of [River] Boyne. On Left a Bank of Limestone. Covered with fern and grass
The end is bare and white and on it is the Obelisk. River runs round it
Nº 1 is a glen very steep through which King William's army came. He had his cannon on the Height on each side. The 2 lines mark the part where the army crossed the river.
Not the Mr Coddington House in a former but the fathers
Through trees are seen many barns stables etc and part of Mr Coddingtons House
This is a very nasty stream as muddy boggy brook but in Summer it might be better

[f. 42v *blank*]

[f. 43r *Pencil and ink sketch*] [*margin:* View 4][4] February 18 Ford and bridge over which on the opposite side where is a canal. This is not the bridge which is called Old Bridge
Between the bridge and the point opposite the Obelisk the army crossed
Taken from the same spot [as the previous sketch]

[f. 43v *Pencil sketch of obelisk*] believed to be 180 feet high

[f. 44r *Pencil and ink sketch of obelisk, the top of which runs onto f. 43v*] [*margin:* 5][5]
February 18 Pillar commemorating Victory of William 3rd at Battle of Boyne
Base 20 feet Square

[1] Oldbridge House, owned by Henry Coddington, MP (1734–1816) (Gamble, *Society and Manners*, p. 100).
[2] See SJC, MS U.30 (5), f. 75v (p. 301).
[3] See SJC, MS U.30 (5), f. 75v (p. 301).
[4] See SJC, MS U.30 (5), f. 76r (p. 302).
[5] See SJC, MS U.30 (5), f. 76v (p. 302).

Pillar badly proportioned, too thick or not tall enough
I did not see that inscription[1] but am told it is in very large letters

[ff. 44v, 45r *blank*]

[ff. 45v–46r *Pencil and ink landscape, annotated*] [*margin:* 6][2] February 18. Up the river Boyne. Fine rich meadow over the other side of river. Fine gentlemens House Great n° of trees scattered about. Over the river is a canal w*hich* runs alongside of it
From the same spot

[f. 46v *blank*]

[f. 47r *Pencil and ink landscape with cabins and haggard, annotated*] [*margin:* N° 7][3] Glen thro*ugh* w*hich* K*ing* W*illiam's* Army came. Cannon on each side on Top.
View f*rom* within few yds of Obelisk.
N° 1. is steep on both sides only its ridge is seen
Feb*ruary* 18.

[f. 47v *Transcription, originally in pencil and traced over in ink*]
Inscription on the North side of the Pillar in Rom*an* letters.
Sacred to the Glorious Memory
of
King William the third
who on the first of July 1690 passed the river near this place to attack
James the Second at the [head] of a Popish Army advantageously posted on
the South side of it and did on that day by a successful Battle secure to us
and to our posterity our liberty laws and Religion
In consequence of this action James the Second
left this Kingdom and fled to France
This Memorial to our deliverance was erected
on [*sic*] the 9*th* year of the Reign of King George the second
The first stone being laid by Lionel Sackville D*uke* of Dorset
Lord Lieutenant of the Kingdom of Ireland
1736

On the <u>Base</u> of the same side
In perpetuam rei tam fortiter quem <u>feliciter</u> gesta memoriam
HIC publica gratitudinis monumenti fundamen
manibus ipse suis posuit Lionelus Dux DORSETIA
XIII^{mo} Die Aprilis anno 1736[4]

[1] 'BATTLE OF THE BOYNE 1690', on the base of the obelisk, as indicated in the sketch.
[2] See SJC, MS U.30 (5), f. 76v (p. 302).
[3] See SJC, MS U.30 (5), f. 76v (p. 302).
[4] 'In eternal memory of the deeds done by power and good fortune HERE Lionel Duke of Dorset in gratitude has placed the public foundation of the monument with his own hands. 13th day of April in the year 1736.' This inscription was published for the first time in 1776 in Twiss, *A Tour in Ireland*, p. 72.

[f. 48r *Pencil and ink sketch, annotated*] [*margin:* N° 8][1] February 18. S.E. View of Base of Monument and part of the rock on which it stands, It hangs over the river
This spot is nearer to the pillar than 9 in [sketch] N° 3

[f. 48v *Transcription in pencil, repetition of the Latin transcription above at f. 47v*] Below
In perpetuam rei tam fortiter quem feliciter gesta memoriam / HIC publica gratitudinis monumenti fundamen / manibus ipse suis posuit Lionelus Dux DORSETIA / XIII^{mo} Die Aprilis anno 1736
On River Side [of base of obelisk] Battle of the Boyne 1690 (in large letters)

[f. 49r *Ink and pencil sketch, annotated*] Better view of the same [base]. N° 9.[2] February 18. Front ground is separated by a Deep chasm from the rock on which the obelisk is built but appears to have been part of it formerly

[f. 49v *Faded pencil text, illegible*]

[f. 50r *Pencil and ink sketch of male harpist*] February 18. William Cair[3] and Irish Harp
Black Hair[,] Light brown coat, Small hands, round nose
harp 32 Strings
This harp was made by a carpenter who only had a plan in paper to work by drawn by Carr and he after made out the plan plainer for him with chalk on a piece of wood and shewed how the Strings were to be done[.] Body Sally [*Salix cinerea*, rusty willow] other parts ash. It cost him 2½Gs but he was obliged to have a 2[4] head put to it as the other was too straight and a new plate of iron on it for the Keys otherwise it would have only cost 2Gs
It was made before he was blind
A very rough instrument indeed and yet he played very well on it. Blind 2 years. He was at Belfast the year before the rebellion when there was a meeting of the Irish harpers[5]
Iron plate in which the keys are fixed
He is like $\overline{3}\overline{1}\underline{3}\underline{3}\underline{1}\underline{4}$

[f. 50v *blank*]

[f. 51r *Pencil and ink sketch of male harpist*] Not so like as the former [sketch] February 18: 1807

[f. 51v *blank*]

[f. 52r *Pencil and ink profile of male harpist and separate sketch of harp*] Very good profile. Harp inferior to the first [sketch] February 18: 1807
Old Irish harp
32 String

[1] See SJC, MS U.30 (5), f. 77r (p. 302).
[2] See SJC, MS U.30 (5), f. 77r (p. 302).
[3] See SJC, MS U.30 (5), f. 77v (p. 302, n. 8).
[4] Second.
[5] See p. 303, n. 2.

[f. 52v *blank*]

[f. 53r *Three pencil sketches: tree, gate with flag, circular structure*]

[ff. 53v–54r *Pencil and ink sketch of East Gate, Drogheda, and surroundings*][1] February 19. On the R. may be seen the Ships on the Boyne[.] Ground slopes very much down to river (East gate) without the walls.

[ff. 54v–55r *Pencil and ink sketch of East Gate, Drogheda, with detail of top of gate*] January 29.[2] East Tower in Drogheda.
2 Towers and a curtain between them. The whole between the 2 Great towers is hollow and the farthest wall as seen. Except at top. Through the Gateway are seen 2 rows of cabins[.] Ground rises very much to the R of tower and the wall continues on the same spot as the old was, the piece here reproduced is not old but the parts adjoining higher up is old and has the terrace round it

[f. 55v *blank*]

[f. 56r *Ink sketch of base of East Gate, Drogheda*] January 29. Part of the Old Wall to the South adjoining the Gate. Within the walls –
It is built up on arched plan. There are not more than 4 or 5 Arches remaining. The hollow parts are not so deep as here represented

[f. 56v *blank*]

[f. 57r *Pencil and ink sketch of tower and adjoining wall, annotated*] February 19. One of the Towers[3] in the Old Wall which surrounded Drogheda, it is to the North of the Old Gate

[f. 57v *blank*]

[f. 58r *Rough pencil and ink sketch*] Continuation of the Wall
NB. The lower part of the wall is broader than the top and juts out all along. The turrets on some parts may be distinctly seen. The walk which went round is also seen.
Wall broken

[f. 58v *blank*]

[f. 59r *Pencil and ink sketch of tower and surroundings*] Tower in Drogheda[.] Part of an Old Abbey. The Foundation may be easily traced and the building must have been very extensive[.] Tower not sufficiently high

[ff. 59v, 60r *blank*]

---

[1] See SJC, MS U.30 (5), f. 79r (p. 304).
[2] Lee was in Drogheda on 19 Feb. (see SJC, MS U.30 (5), p. 304). The same date applies to the following sketch.
[3] See diary entry at SJC, MS U.30 (5), f. 79r (p. 304).

[ff. 60v–61r *Pencil and ink drawing of approach to Drogheda, with rows of cabins fronted by dung heaps on roadside, annotated*] Entrance of Drogheda from the West, High Ground. On the Left is the river winding beautifully beyond it[,] fine banks scattered over with trees and groves[.] The Abbey and Church are seen in the dist*ance*
New cabins well thatched
Old Cabins generally green at top

[ff. 61v, 62r *blank*]

[ff. 62v–63r *Pencil and ink townscape with ships on the river, annotated*] Drogheda from the South – On the near hill is a House, on the next dist*ance* a Chapel. The woods are those which bound the South side of the river. Steps are up all thro*ugh* the town. Chief part of the town in [*sic*] the opposite side of the river. Some of the chief buildings only put in. The C*hurch*[,] the abby[,] the Gate or Round towers are in former views. On the Left of the road the road sinks very low and thus the tops of the rows of cabins and river are seen. Cabins many under one roof.
Entrance from Dublin after passing thro*ugh* the 2 banks

[f. 63v *blank*]

[f. 64r *Pencil and ink sketch of pillar base*] Octagon
In a field on the roadside about 3 Miles on this side [south] of Drogheda

[f. 64v *blank*]

[f. 65r *Pencil and ink landscape with winding river, annotated*]
[f. 65v] View from road about 3 Miles South of Drogheda, near a bridge, the little stream runs thro*ugh* elegant grounds meandering to the distance, and it is bounded by fine green meadows
M = Meadows. Small copses of wood ~~and wo~~ scattered about, Dist*ant* woods in mass. The view was seen thro*ugh* a hedge wh*ich* formed a screen but was omitted as it wo*uld* have rendered it obscure

[f. 66r *Rough outline pencil sketch of view on approach to Howth, annotated*] View this side [***] ahead an island

[ff. 66v–67r *Rough outline pencil landscape with Dublin and Wicklow Mountains in distance, annotated*] View on this side N of [***]

[f. 67v *blank*]

[f. 68r *Rough outline pencil sketch of Swords round tower and church*]

[f. 68v *blank*]

[f. 69r *Rough outline pencil sketch of cabin with dungheap and pigs*] View of (cabin) in Swords and there are many others like it

APPENDICES

Tis well you wrote it[1]

[f. 69v *blank*]

[f. 70r *Rough outline pencil sketch of two men seated inside an open door, with one man standing outside and another leading a horse and smoking*] An Irish House of Entertainment!!! and of accommod*ation*.
View at 1̄9115̱529̱ 116̱632 631̱5235̱39̄
2 Men were within and one just come out!!! and with his whip under arm before he mounts his horse making all right again and pulling them[2] up. The Horse [*several words crossed out*] of its rider. Hostler [ostler] smoking his pipe[.]
Man of whom there is a full view is fat and with*out* a hat. The others legs and hat are only seen and his nose
At these entertainments the more the merrier in Ireland!![3]

[f. 70v *blank*]

[f. 71r *Very rough pencil sketch of an interior*]

[f. 71v *blank*]

[f. 72r *Rough pencil view of Howth Head in the distance, taken through an arch*] 17 Feb*ruary* H*ill* of How*th* too long – a scale
just thro*ugh* rails are seen a few rocks

[ff. 72v, 73r *blank*]

[ff. 73v–74r *Very rough pencil view of Dún Laoghaire in the distance*] tower martello[4]

[f. 74v *blank*]

[f. 75r *Very rough pencil sketch of harbour and boats*] Dunleary [Dún Laoghaire]

[ff. 75v–92v *blank*]

[f. 93 *Torn out*]

[Inside back cover] Peter Fowlers
Oct*ober* Fowlers 74
Hackney Coach
74

[1] The meaning of this tagline at the bottom of the sketch is unclear. It may be a phrase Lee heard at Swords.
[2] His trousers.
[3] This sketch and note seem to describe a form of public convenience. This may relate to Lee's observations on public latrines made at Cappoquin on 25 Sept. 1806 (see SJC, MS U.30 (2), f. 132v, p. 163) and at Nenagh on 29 Jan. 1807 (see SJC, MS U.30 (5), f. 55r, p. 280). The rough sketch on the following page is of an interior, possibly of the public convenience described here.
[4] See SJC, MS U.30 (5), p. 236, n. 2.

APPENDIX 2

Correspondence of John Lee (né Fiott) Relating to Visits to Ireland in 1806–7 and 1857

1. William Longley[1] to John Fiott, 23 August 1806

London

Dear Fiott,

How goes on your Tour? do your legs last out, or has a poney the honor of bearing you about? Have you learnt "to bide the pelting of the pitiless storms"[2] which have been so numerous, and has the lightning taken no notice of the brass head or foot shall I call it of your umbrella? Do Snowdons lofty summits, the awful, wild and vast forms of Cader [Cadair] Idris, Carnarvon Castle[3] and Conways 'foaming flood'[4] answer your expectations? and do you imagine that after your eye has been accustomed for weeks to rove over so unbounded a variety of romantic scenery, you can look with satisfaction on the tame hills at Totteridge,[5] or endure a glance at the flats of Cambridgeshire? I want an answer to all these questions and to five hundred others of the same sort, and more particularly to know how soon it is likely to be after your return, that the melody of the Welch language and Welch bards will have so far ceased to ring in [your] ears, as to allow you to converse rationally in plain English on what you have seen and heard. As for myself, I am in a populous desert; not a friend, and scarcely an acquaintance in London; I have indeed just now been gratified by the visit of a friend, but it is quite an event. Gipps[6] is on his way from Cambridge into Kent, and is in Town for a few days. If it were not for my weekly visit to the <u>Country</u> ie Hampstead (I venture the term at the hazard of a smile from you for it is to me comparatively the Country) I should soon be possessed by the blue devils, or a fever, or perhaps both. However I hope some time next month to get really into the Country. Private news I have none to tell you. Every day seems pregnant with great public events. The news of today is that the Emperor Francis has made a formal resignation of the Crown of Germany, and is now merely Emperor of Austria.[7] How long

---

[1] (1784–1846), a fellow of St John's College, Cambridge and later a barrister.

[2] From *King Lear*, Act 3, Scene 4, line 29. The correct quote is 'That bide the pelting of this pitiless storm'.

[3] The medieval Caernarfon Castle, which Lee did not visit.

[4] From Thomas Gray's *The Bard: A Pinardic Ode* (1757).

[5] Totteridge Park, Hertfordshire, the ancestral home of Lee's mother, Harriet Lee. Lee inherited the property in 1815 on the death of his uncle and guardian, William Lee Antonie.

[6] Henry Gipps (1786–1832), later curate and vicar in Hereford (Stunt, *Elusive Quest*, p. 208).

[7] Francis II, Holy Roman Emperor, r. 1792–1806. On 6 Aug. 1806, he dissolved the Empire after defeat by Napoleon at the Battle of Austerlitz.

he may retain the latter title no one can say. Bonaparte I conclude will ~~take some~~ take some new titles as that of Emperor of the French is now more than two years old and must sound flat. Perhaps he will be Emperor of Gaul and Germany, Emperor of Rome, or Emperor of the Western Continent. Or as the breed of Emperors has increased of late perhaps he will please to be called by some such title as the Arch Emperor, the Sovereign of Sovereigns, the Father of Europe, the Arbiter of Nations, his illimitable Domination, his preeminent Irresistibility, etc together with all the arrogant titles the Popes used formerly to use, omitting those which had a shew of humility[.]

Lord [La]uderdale[1] is not yet returned, and I hope will not with [*words covered by sealing wax; page torn*] preliminaries, though the opinion of many seems [*words covered by sealing wax*] he will. S*r* J.B. Warren[2] has arrived in the West Ind*ies* [*words covered by sealing wax; page torn*] I fear [*page torn*] far behind Jerome to overtake him. Wednesday it [*words covered by sealing wax*]

This has lain by ever since Saturday, and will probably be a fortnight old when you get it. That it may not be older however I have determined to finish it today. The West India fleet is arrived and the Stocks were rather better yesterday. What however is of more importance to me at present moment than the price of Stocks is that I am going in a few days into the Wild of Kent; my stay there will be quite uncertain perhaps a week, perhaps three weeks or a month. I am almost as much pleased at the prospect of a temporary absence from London as a Schoolboy at the approach of the Holidays. If you wish to write to me you had better (direct) to me at Hampstead whence your letter will be forwarded to me. I leave this at the House of your Uncle[3] who I hope is in Town: or at any rate that he will frank this, that the crime of burthening you with the postage of so unedifying an Epistle may not lie heavy on the conscience of
Yours very sincerely,
Wm Longley.

SJC, Box 1, Doc. 21. Autograph letter, 2 ff.[4]

2. **William Lee Antonie to John Fiott, 28 December 1806**

Colworth

Dear John,
I receiv'd your letter of the 16 In*st* enclos'd to me one for your sister Harriet, the other, for your friend Mr Arrowsmith,[5] which, was left unseal'd and of course I presume, was meant for my perusal – I am the more inclin'd to think so, as it relates to a subject both Mr

---

[1] Page torn here.
[2] Sir John Borlase Warren (1753–1822), naval officer, and commander-in-chief of one of two squadrons sent to seek out French squadrons in the western Atlantic in June–Nov. 1806.
[3] William Lee Antonie (1764–1815), MP for Great Marlow (1790–96) and for Bedford (1802–12) (History of Parliament Online). Brother of John Lee's mother, Harriet Lee of Totteridge Park, he acted as guardian to Lee and his siblings following the deaths of their mother (1794) and father (1797).
[4] Note in Lee's autograph: 'Aug*ust*. 23: 1806. London. *William Lee* / Rec*d*: Clonmel Sep*t* 20'.
[5] Likely Lee's aunt Louisa's husband, Edward Arrowsmith. They lived at Totteridge, and raised the younger Fiott children after the deaths of their parents.

Arrowsmith and myself have written to you upon, and of which, to me, you have taken no notice of the receipt of my letter.

I mean that of your money concerns.

I must first take notice in your letter to Mr *Arrowsmith*. You state that I do "not seem unwilling to allow you leave to pursue your own plans and intentions for some time hence" – My answer to that is, that I can only with common prudence and feeling the situation that you now stand in accord in those plans, so far, as they may and ought to tend to your essential welfare both in regard to Improvement and Economy – I wish to know from you the great advantage you have deriv'd, of either, from your present residence in Ireland and what are your expectations of your continued residence there to go through the remainder of the Country and in the spring to cross over to Scotland?

I perfectly know that travelling over different Country's is a most amusing way of passing the time But without you have a plan in view, for so doing, and without the Means of executing that plan without occurring of great expence when compar'd to the Income of defraying of more expences and above all others at a time when the greatest economy should and must be attended to – I am sure that you will reflect more seriously upon this subject especially when you find that notwithstanding your strict attention to economy you have Bills sent to you to your great surprize, of <u>half as much more</u> as you had suppos'd.

I really should think when you have consider'd well your situation at the present Crisis, that you will think more seriously of attending to the procuring of your Fellowship[1] which, I am still assur'd would be easily obtain'd – Besides, there is your younger Brother[2] who is I am happy to hear to his great Credit improving daily in his education, and I should wish with the consent of his friends that he might be sent to College – The expense of the education is considerable, But as far as I am concern'd I shall think nothing of that, when I reflect that I am endeavouring to assist those Talents which, now appear so promising and if encourag'd a lasting Blessing probably to the Person bestow'd on – I am persuaded that you will feel with Myself the like sentiments and aid as far as in Your power lies, to promote His welfare –

I have had reason to write to His Grace of Bedford[3] by this post[.] I have begg'd to recommend you to His graces protection and favor and stated of your having made a pedestrian tour for (the last) six months over great parts of Ireland –

You will therefore, of course, leave your Card at the Castle, or, follow the forms necessary for an Introduction [at] the first opportunity[4] –

With wishing you many many returns of the season.

Believe me

Yours very sincerely

W Lee Antonie

SJC, Box 1, Doc. 22. Autograph letter, 3 ff.

---

[1] Possibly the Foundress Fellowship that Lee was awarded later, in Apr. 1808, while still holding a Worts Travelling Bachelorship in Scandinavia (summer 1807–June 1809).

[2] Antonie could be referring to any one of Lee's younger brothers.

[3] See p. 297, n. 4.

[4] Lee had an audience with the Lord Lieutenant on 10 Feb. 1807 and dined in his company at Dublin Castle on 21 Feb. 1807; see SJC, MS U.30 (5), ff. 71v, 81r, pp. 297, 305.

APPENDICES

THE MONSTER TELESCOPE
PARSONSTOWN

Figure 15. Illustrated heading of a letter from John Lee to Joseph Bonomi, 14 September 1857, with an engraving of 'THE MONSTER TELESCOPE' at Parsonstown (Cambridge University Library, Add. 9389/2/L/97).

3. John Lee to Joseph Bonomi,[1] 14 September 1857[2]

Gresham Hotel, Sackville Street, Dublin
14 September 1857

My good Sir,
Your letter from Mr Sharpes[3] arrived on the 3rd of this month, the day after the completion of the proceedings of the B. A. of Science,[4] and the day before I set out with a friend Mr Ellis, FRAS,[5] on a tour to Sligo, Mr Coopers Observatory at Mackree,[6] Castlebar and Clifden, Galway, Portumna and to Parsonstown, where we arrived on the evening of the 11th, and saw Lord Rosses[7] Telescopes, and works on Friday, but the weather was very unfavourable for observation, and we returned to Dublin on Saturday night[.]

---

[1] (1796–1878), sculptor and Egyptologist (Meadows, 'Bonomi, Joseph (1796–1878)').

[2] Decorative letterhead, lithograph illustration of 'The Monster Telescope Parsonstown', reproduced above (Figure 15). For more on the context of this letter, see the introduction to this volume (p. 3).

[3] Samuel Sharpe (1799–1881) was an Egyptologist and bible translator with whom Bonomi had collaborated, for example on the 1864 volume, *The Alabaster Sarcophagus*.

[4] The British Association for the Advancement of Science, known as the British Science Association since 2009, was established in 1831 and held annual meetings in various cities in Britain and Ireland. The 1857 meeting was held in Dublin.

[5] William Ellis (1828–1916), Fellow of the Royal Astronomical Society.

[6] Edward Joshua Cooper (1798–1863), astronomer and MP; he established an observatory at Markree castle, Co. Sligo in 1830 (Bohan and Lunney, 'Cooper, Edward Joshua').

[7] William Parsons, 3rd Earl of Rosse (1800–67), of Birr Castle, Parsonstown (Bennett, 'Parsons, William, third earl of Rosse (1800–1867)').

Today I propose to cross to Holyhead with the hope of meeting Mrs Lee[1] and her sister at Chester on the 16 and of proceeding to Manchester on the 17th and to remain there for two or three days –

It is not settled with respect to the Inn at which we may be able to obtain accommodations, but My address on Thursday the 17 will be at the Post office and I shall be obliged to you to favor me with a note of introduction to your brother in Law[2] at the Exhibition[3] and include that we shall be every day at it –

I am pleased with the account of your conference with Colonel Felix[4] and I hope that it will terminate to the benefit of Both Parties –

As the British Association is to meet next year at Leeds – I do not propose to take Mrs Lee, to her death to see the Dukes Museum – as it can be done next year, and I am now limited to time, and wish to be at home at Hartwell on the 25 of this month. –

With my best regards to all with you and to your brother   Believe me
My good Sir
Yours faithfully
J Lee
Joseph Bonomi Esqr

Mr J. Gates was at the association at Dublin. I wish Mr Sharpe had attended [*word blotted*] I hope he will bring some one of his family with him to Leeds[.]

Cambridge University Library, Add MS 9389/2/L/97. Autograph letter, 2 ff.

---

[1] Lee's second wife, Louise Catherine Wilkinson (1830–88).

[2] Bonomi's wife was Jessie Martin (1825–59), daughter of the artist John Martin (1789–1854). Lee probably refers here to Jessie's brother Charles, a portrait painter (Meadows, 'Bonomi, Joseph (1796–1878)').

[3] The Art Treasures of Great Britain Exhibition, held in Manchester in May–Oct, 1857. See Pergam, *The Manchester Art Treasures Exhibition*.

[4] Major Orlando Felix, who travelled extensively in Egypt with Algernon Percy (Lord Prudhoe, 1792–1865), brother of Hugh, Lee's former classmate at St John's (see p. 3).

BIBLIOGRAPHY

Note: Where there is more than one title by the same author, they are listed in chronological order.

MANUSCRIPT SOURCES

Aylesbury, UK, Centre for Buckinghamshire Studies
Lee, John, Correspondence and Papers, D/X720

Bedford, UK, Bedfordshire Archives and Records Service
Antonie, William Lee to John Fiott, undated letter, Unilever Colworth Estate, Sharnbrook fonds, UN494
Hawksley, Reverend John Webster to William Lee Antonie, undated letter, Unilever Colworth Estate, Sharnbrook fonds, UN319

Cambridge, UK, Cambridge University Library
Fiott, John, Documents relating to Worts Bequest, 1808–9, MS Oo.6.96 (19)
Lee, John, Correspondence relating to Joseph Bonomi, 1840–66, Add MS 9389/2/L/77–129

Cambridge, UK, St John's College Library
Lee, John, Diaries and Sketchbooks of Tour from London to Ireland, August 1806–March 1807, MSS U.30 (1–8)
Various Authors, Letters (63) addressed to John Lee (Lee Papers), 1793–1865, Box 1a

London, UK, The British Library, Department of Manuscripts
MSS of the Duke of Northumberland, Letters and Papers, vol. 65, 1808–9, Alnwick Castle, no. 65, 23/1: British Library microfilm no. 311 (Alnwick papers), Letters of John Fiott to Lord Percy, 1808–9
Lee, John, General correspondence, 1809–39, Add MS 47490, ff. 67–241b

London, UK, Lambeth Palace
Lee, John, Correspondence with William Parsons, 3rd Earl of Rosse, 16 March 1864, MS 2879, f. 301

London, UK, National Maritime Museum
Ross, John and Lee, John, Letters Relating to Franklin Search Expeditions and Learned Societies, 1850–56, HAR/301–359

PRINTED PRIMARY AND SECONDARY SOURCES

Abir-Am, Pnina G., and Outram, Dorinda, eds, *Uneasy Careers and Intimate Lives: Women in Science, 1789–1979*, London, 1987.
['An American Gentleman'], 'Tour thro' the South of Ireland', *The Scots Magazine and Edinburgh Literary Miscellany*, 67, 1805, pp. 760–64, 828–31; 68, 1806, 27–31, 175–9.
Anderson, Jocelyn, 'Remaking the Space: the Plan and the Route in Country-House Guidebooks from 1770 to 1815', *Architectural History*, 54, 2011, pp. 195–212.

Andrews, J. H., *Irish Historic Towns Atlas no. 1 Kildare*, Dublin, 1986.

Andrews, Malcolm, *The Search for the Picturesque: Landscape Aesthetics and Tourism in Britain, 1760–1800*, Aldershot, 1989.

Angelomatis-Tsougarakis, Helen, *The Eve of the Greek Revival. British Travellers' Perceptions of Early Nineteenth Century Greece*, London, 1990.

Anglesey, 'Paget, Henry William (1768–1854)', in H. C. G. Matthew and Brian H. Harrison, eds, *Oxford Dictionary of National Biography*, 60 vols, Oxford, 2004; online edn, Jan. 2008. Available at <http://www.oxforddnb.com/view/10.1093/ref:odnb/9780198614128.001.0001/odnb-9780198614128-e-21112> [Accessed 13 January 2018].

Annála Ríoghachta Éireann: Annals of the Kingdom of Ireland, by the Four Masters, from the Earliest Period to the Year 1616, ed. John O'Donovan, 7 vols, Dublin, 2nd edn, 1856; reprinted Dublin, 1990.

The Athenaeum, London, 1828–1921.

Atkinson, A., *The Irish Tourist, in a Series of Picturesque Views, Traveling Incidents, and Observations Statistical, Political and Moral on the Character and Aspect of the Irish Nation*, Dublin, 1815.

Axton, W. F., 'Victorian Landscape Painting: A Change in Outlook', in U. C. Knoepflmacher and G. B. Tennyson, eds, *Nature and the Victorian Imagination*, Berkeley, 1977, pp. 281–308.

Baigent, Elizabeth, 'Bullock, William', in H. C. G. Matthew and Brian H. Harrison, eds, *Oxford Dictionary of National Biography*, 60 vols, Oxford, 2004; online edn, Jan. 2008. Available at <http://www.oxforddnb.com/view/10.1093/ref:odnb/9780198614128.001.0001/odnb-9780198614128-e-3923> [Accessed 15 July 2018].

Baker, Anne Pimlott, 'Catton, Charles, the younger (1756–1819)', in H. C. G. Matthew and Brian H. Harrison, eds, *Oxford Dictionary of National Biography*, 60 vols, Oxford, 2004; online edn, Sept. 2004. Available at <http://www.oxforddnb.com/view/10.1093/ref:odnb/9780198614128.001.0001/odnb-9780198614128-e-4902> [Accessed 13 January 2018].

Barrington, T. J., *Discovering Kerry: Its History, Heritage, and Topography*, Cork, 1976.

Bartlett, Thomas, Dickson, David, Keogh, Dáire and Whelan, Kevin, eds, *1798: A Bicentenary Perspective*, Dublin, 2003,

Barton, Ruth, '"Huxley, Lubbock, and Half a Dozen Others": Professionals and Gentlemen in the Formation of the X Club, 1851–1864', *Isis*, 89/3, 1998, pp. 410–44.

—, '"Men of Science": Language, Identity and Professionalization in the Mid-Victorian Scientific Community', *History of Science*, 41, 2003, pp. 73–119.

Battersea, Constance, *Reminiscences*, London, 1922.

Baugh, Daniel A. and Duffy, Michael, 'Hood, Samuel (1724–1816)', in H. C. G. Matthew and Brian H. Harrison, eds, *Oxford Dictionary of National Biography*, 60 vols, Oxford, 2004; online edn, May 2009. Available at <http://www.oxforddnb.com/view/10.1093/ref:odnb/9780198614128.001.0001/odnb-9780198614128-e-13678> [Accessed 13 January 2018].

Bayly, C. A. and Prior, Katherine, 'Cornwallis, Charles (1738–1805)', in H. C. G. Matthew and Brian H. Harrison, eds, *Oxford Dictionary of National Biography*, 60 vols, Oxford, 2004; online edn, Sept. 2011. Available at <http://www.oxforddnb.com/view/10.1093/ref:odnb/ 9780198614128.001.0001/odnb-9780198614128-e-6338> [Accessed 13 January 2018].

Beauford, William, *A Plan of the City and Suburbs of Cork: According to the Latest Improvements*, London, 1801. Scale approx. 8½ in to 1 mile.

Beaumont, Daniel, 'La Touche, John David', in James McGuire and James Quinn, eds, *Dictionary of Irish Biography*, 9 vols, Cambridge, 2009. Available at <http://dib.cambridge.org/viewReadPage.do?articleId=a4624> [Accessed 13 January 2018].

—, 'Leeson, Joseph', in James McGuire and James Quinn, eds, *Dictionary of Irish Biography*, 9 vols, Cambridge, 2009. Available at <http://dib.cambridge.org/viewReadPage.do?articleId=a4770> [Accessed 13 January 2018].

—, 'Smyth, Arthur', in James McGuire and James Quinn, eds, *Dictionary of Irish Biography*, 9 vols, Cambridge, 2009. Available at <http://dib.cambridge.org/viewReadPage.do?articleId=a8168> [Accessed 13 January 2018].

Beiner, Guy, *Remembering the Year of the French: Irish Folk History and Social Memory*, Madison WI, 2007.

Belsey, Hugh, 'Gainsborough, Thomas (1727–1788)', in H. C. G. Matthew and Brian H. Harrison, eds, *Oxford Dictionary of National Biography*, 60 vols, Oxford, 2004; online edn, Sept. 2017. Available at <http://www.oxforddnb.com/view/10.1093/ref:odnb/9780198614128.001.0001/odnb-9780198614128-e-10282> [Accessed 13 January 2018].

Bennett, Isabel, 'The Archaeology of County Kerry', *Archaeology Ireland*, 1/2, 1987, pp. 48–51.

Bennett, J. A., 'Parsons, William, third earl of Rosse (1800–1867)', in H. C. G. Matthew and Brian H. Harrison, eds, *Oxford Dictionary of National Biography*, 60 vols, Oxford, 2004; online edn, Sept. 2004. Available at <http://www.oxforddnb.com/view/10.1093/ref:odnb/9780198614128.001.0001/odnb-9780198614128-e-21481> [Accessed 1 March 2018].

Bergin, John, 'Sackville, Lionel', in James McGuire and James Quinn, eds, *Dictionary of Irish Biography*, 9 vols, Cambridge, 2009. Available at <http://dib.cambridge.org/viewReadPage.do?articleId=a7892> [Accessed 13 January 2018].

Berkeley, George, 'Description of the Cave of Dunmore', in *The Works of George Berkeley, D.D. Formerly Bishop of Cloyne: Including Many of His Writings Hitherto Unpublished*, ed. Alexander Campbell Fraser, 4 vols, Oxford, 1871, IV, pp. 503–11.

Betham, William, *The Baronetage of England*, 5 vols, London, 1805.

Bickerstaff, Isaac, *The Romp*, London, 1786.

Bickersteth, Robert, 'Query Concerning the Parentage and Pedigree of Joseph Garde, Mayor of Cork in 1830. With a Pedigree of the Garde Family', *Journal of the Cork Historical and Archaeological Society*, 2nd ser., 5, 1899, pp. 200–202.

Bielenberg, Andy, *Cork's Industrial Revolution 1780–1880*, Cork, 1991.

Bingley, William, *North Wales; Including its Scenery, Antiquities, Customs, and Some Sketches of its Natural History; Delineated through all the Interesting Parts of that Country, during the Summers of 1798 and 1801*, 2 vols, London, 1804.

Bohan, Rob, and Lunney, Linde, 'Cooper, Edward Joshua', in James McGuire and James Quinn, eds, *Dictionary of Irish Biography*, 9 vols, Cambridge, 2009. Available at <http://dib.cambridge.org/viewReadPage.do?articleId=a2015> [Accessed 1 March 2018].

Bohls, E. A. and Duncan, Ian, eds, *Travel Writing 1700–1830: An Anthology*, Oxford, 2005.

Bonomi, Joseph, *Catalogue of the Egyptian Antiquities in the Museum of Hartwell House*, London, 1858.

—, and Sharpe, Samuel, *The Alabaster Sarcophagus of Oinemepthah I, King of Egypt, now in Sir John Soane's Museum*, London, 1864.

Bourke, Angela, *The Burning of Bridget Cleary*, New York, 2000.

Bourke, Edward J., *Shipwrecks of the Irish Coast*, I, Dublin, 1994.

Bowen, James, 'Getting into the Archive – the Buildwas Earthquake of 1773: An Earthquake or a Landslip?', Weather Extremes project blog, available at <http://blogs.nottingham.ac.uk/weatherextremes/2014/06/30/getting-into-the-archive-the-buildwas-earthquake-of-1773-an-earthquake-or-a-landslip/> [Accessed 12 January 2018].

Bradley, John, *Irish Historic Towns Atlas no. 10 Kilkenny*, Dublin, 2000.

Breen, Aidan, 'Senán', in James McGuire and James Quinn, eds, *Dictionary of Irish Biography*, 9 vols, Cambridge, 2009. Available at <http://dib.cambridge.org/viewReadPage.do?articleId=a7975> [Accessed 13 January 2018].

de Breffny, Brian, 'The Building of the Mansion at Blessington, 1672', *Irish Arts Review Yearbook*, 1988, pp. 73–7.

Brewer, J. N., *The Beauties of Ireland*, 3 vols, London, 1825.

Brindley, Anna and Kilfeather, Annaba, *Archaeological Inventory of County Carlow*, Dublin, 1993.

Brooks, Alan and Pevsner, Nikolaus, *The Buildings of England: Worcestershire*, New Haven, CT, 2007.

Buckley, Victor M. and Sweetman, P. David, *Archaeological Survey of County Louth*, Dublin, 1991.

Burke, Bernard, *A Genealogical History of the Dormant, Abeyant, Forfeited, and Extinct Peerages of the British Empire*, London, 1866.

Burke, Edmund, *A Philosophical Enquiry into the Origin of our Ideas of the Sublime and Beautiful*, 5th edn, London, 1767.

Burke, John, *A General and Heraldic Dictionary of the Peerage and Baronetage of the British Empire*, 4th edn, 2 vols, London, 1832.

—, and Burke, John Bernard, *A Genealogical and Heraldic Dictionary of the Landed Gentry of Great Britain and Ireland*, 2 vols, London, 1847.

Burke, John Bernard, *A Genealogical and Heraldic Dictionary of the Peerage and Baronetage of the British Empire*, 12th edn, London, 1850.

—, *A Genealogical and Heraldic Dictionary of the Landed Gentry of Great Britain and Ireland, for 1852*, 2 vols, London, 1852.

—, *A Genealogical and Heraldic Dictionary of the Peerage and Baronetage of the British Empire*, 14th edn, London, 1852.

—, *A Genealogical and Heraldic Dictionary of the Peerage and Baronetage of the British Empire*, 15th edn, 8 vols, London, 1853.

Burling, William J., 'Colman, George, the younger (1762–1836)', in H. C. G. Matthew and Brian H. Harrison, eds, *Oxford Dictionary of National Biography*, 60 vols, Oxford, 2004; online edn, Jan. 2008. Available at <http://www.oxforddnb.com/view/10.1093/ref:odnb/9780198614128.001.0001/odnb-9780198614128-e-5977> [Accessed 13 January 2018].

Burton, Janet, and Stöber, Karen, *Abbeys and Priories of Medieval Wales*, Cardiff, 2015.

Buxton, H. W., 'Obituary. John Lee', *Records of Buckinghamshire*, 3, 1866, pp. 215–36.

Byrne, Angela, *Geographies of the Romantic North: Science, Antiquarianism, and Travel, 1790–1830*, New York, 2013.

—, 'Dashing Waves and Dreadful Cliffs: John Lee's Visit to the Blaskets, 1806', *History Ireland*, 24/2, 2016, pp. 24–5.

—, 'Imagining the Celtic North: Science and Romanticism on the Fringes of Britain', in Eleanor Rosamund Barraclough, Danielle Marie Cudmore and Stefan Donecker, eds, *Imagining the Supernatural North*, Edmonton, 2016, pp. 131–47.

—, 'A Previously Unknown Traveller's Account of Kilkenny: John Lee (né Fiott) Visits Dunmore Cave, September 1806', *Old Kilkenny Review: Journal of Kilkenny Archaeological Society*, 69, 2017, pp. 105–13.

Byrne, Patricia, 'Higgins, William', in James McGuire and James Quinn, eds, *Dictionary of Irish Biography*, 9 vols, Cambridge, 2009. Available at <http://dib.cambridge.org/viewReadPage.do?articleId=a4005> [Accessed 13 January 2018].

[Campbell, Thomas], *A Philosophical Survey of the South of Ireland, in a Series of Letters to John Watkinson*, Dublin, 1778.

Carpenter, Andrew, 'Johnson, Esther', in James McGuire and James Quinn, eds, *Dictionary of Irish Biography*, 9 vols, Cambridge, 2009. Available at <http://dib.cambridge.org/viewReadPage.do?articleId=a4291> [Accessed 13 January 2018].

Carr, John, *The Stranger in Ireland: or, A Tour in the Southern and Western Parts of that Country, in the Year 1805*, Philadelphia, 1806.

Casey, Christine, *The Buildings of Ireland: Dublin*, New Haven, CT, 2005.

Catalogue of Theological Books, in the Library of Hartwell House, Buckinghamshire, London, 1860.

Ceadel, Martin, *The Origins of War Prevention: The British Peace Movement and International Relations, 1730–1854*, Oxford, 1996.

The Chronicles of the Sea, London, 1838.

Clarke, Desmond, 'The Library', in James Meenan and Desmond Clarke, eds, *RDS: The Royal Dublin Society 1731–1981*, Dublin, 1981, pp. 75–87.

Clarke, Edward Daniel, *Travels in Various Countries of Europe, Asia and Africa*, 6 vols, London, 1810–23.

—, 'Further Account of Petalite, together with the Analysis of Another New Swedish Mineral Found at Gryphytta, in the Province of Westmania, in Sweden, etc.', *Annals of Philosophy*, 11, May 1818, pp. 365–8.

—, *Travels in Various Countries of Scandinavia; Including Denmark, Sweden, Norway, Lapland, and Finland*, 3 vols, London, 1838.

Clarke, Frances, 'Edwin (Richards), Elizabeth Rebecca', in James McGuire and James Quinn, eds, *Dictionary of Irish Biography*, 9 vols, Cambridge, 2009. Available at <http://dib.cambridge.org/viewReadPage.do?articleId=a2890> [Accessed 13 January 2018].

Clavin, Terry, 'Wingfield, Sir Richard', in James McGuire and James Quinn, eds, *Dictionary of Irish Biography*, 9 vols, Cambridge, 2009. Available at <http://dib.cambridge.org/viewReadPage.do?articleId=a9091> [Accessed 13 January 2018].

Cobb, J., *Paul and Virginia: a Musical Drama*, adapted from J. H. B. de Saint-Pierre, *Paul et Virginie*, Dublin, 1801.

Coleman, James, 'The Castles and Abbeys of the Co. Kerry', *Kerry Archaeological Magazine*, 1, 1908–12, pp. 148–59.

Coleridge, Samuel Taylor and Wordsworth, William, *Lyrical Ballads, with a Few Other Poems*, London, 1798.

Collen, George William, *Debrett's Peerage of Great Britain and Ireland, Revised Corrected and Continued*, London, 1840.

Colman, George the Younger, *The Mountaineers, A Play in Three Acts*, London, 1793.

The Colonial Intelligencer, or, Aborigines' Friend, London, 1847–54.

Concannon, Undine, 'Tussaud, Anna Maria (bap. 1761, d. 1850)', in H. C. G. Matthew and Brian H. Harrison, eds, *Oxford Dictionary of National Biography*, 60 vols, Oxford, 2004; .pdf> [Accessed 12 January 2018].

Connolly, S. J., 'The Catholic Question, 1801–12', in W. E. Vaughan, ed., *A New History of Ireland V: Ireland under the Union 1801–70*, Oxford, 1989, pp. 24–47.

Cooke, George Alexander, *Topographical and Statistical Description of the County of Salop: Containing an Account of its Situation, Extent, Towns, Roads, Rivers …; to which is Prefixed a Copious Travelling Guide … Illustrated with a Map of the County*, London, [1805?].

Cooper, Charles Henry and Cooper, Thompson, *Athenae Cantabrigienses, vol. 2, 1586–1609* (Cambridge, 1861).

Cooper, Thompson, 'Anderson, John (1747–1820)', rev. Anne Pimlott Baker, in H. C. G. Matthew and Brian H. Harrison, eds, *Oxford Dictionary of National Biography*, 60 vols, Oxford, 2004; online edn, Jan. 2008. Available at <http://www.oxforddnb.com/view/10.1093/ref:odnb/9780198614128.001.0001/odnb-9780198614128-e-484> [Accessed 6 August 2018].

Cotter, Eamonn, 'Archaeological and Environmental Heritage at Buttevant, County Cork', 2010. Available at <http://irishwalledtownsnetwork.ie/assets/Buttevant-archaeological-report_ECotter> [Accessed 12 January 2018].

Courtney, W. P., 'Bennet, William (1746–1820)', rev. Alan R. Acheson, in H. C. G. Matthew and Brian H. Harrison, eds, *Oxford Dictionary of National Biography*, 60 vols, Oxford, 2004; online edn, May 2009. Available at <http://www.oxforddnb.com/view/10.1093/ref:odnb/ 9780198614128.001.0001/odnb-9780198614128-e-2115> [Accessed 13 January 2018].

—, 'Winnington, Thomas', rev. M. E. Clayton, in H. C. G. Matthew and Brian H. Harrison, eds, *Oxford Dictionary of National Biography*, 60 vols, Oxford, 2004; online edn, Jan. 2008. Available at <http://www.oxforddnb.com/view/10.1093/ref:odnb/9780198614128.001.0001/odnb-9780198614128-e-29748> [Accessed 15 July 2018].

Croker, Thomas Crofton, *The Keen of the South of Ireland: As Illustrative of Irish Political and Domestic History, Manners, Music, and Superstitions*, London, 1844. Online edn, Sept. 2017. Available at <http://www.oxforddnb.com/view/10.1093/ref:odnb/9780198614128.001.0001/odnb-9780198614128-e-27897> [Accessed 13 January 2018].

Crookshank, Anne, *Irish Sculpture from 1600 to the Present Day*, Dublin, 1984.

Crossman, Virginia, *Politics, Pauperism and Power in Late Nineteenth-Century Ireland*, Manchester, 2006.

Curtin, Nancy J., 'The Transformation of the Society of United Irishmen into a Mass-Based Revolutionary Organisation, 1794–6', *Irish Historical Studies*, 24/96, 1985, pp. 463–92.

Cust, L. H., 'Singleton, Henry (1766–1839)', rev. Robin Simon, in H. C. G. Matthew and Brian H. Harrison, eds, *Oxford Dictionary of National Biography*, 60 vols, Oxford, 2004; online edn, Sept. 2004. Available at <http://www.oxforddnb.com/view/10.1093/ref:odnb/9780198614128.001.0001/odnb-9780198614128-e-25642> [Accessed 13 January 2018].

The Cyclopaedian Magazine and Dublin Monthly Register of History, Literature, the Arts, Science etc., Dublin, 1807–8.

Davies, K. M., *Irish Historic Towns Atlas no. 9 Bray*, Dublin, 1998.

Day, Robert, 'Art Catalogue of the First Munster Exhibition', *Journal of the Cork Historical and Archaeological Society*, 4, 1898, pp. 308–17.

Debrett, John, *The Peerage of the United Kingdom of Great Britain and Ireland*, 9th edn, 2 vols, London, 1814.

Desmond, Adrian, 'Vigors, Nicholas Aylward (1785/6–1840)', in H. C. G. Matthew and Brian H. Harrison, eds, *Oxford Dictionary of National Biography*, 60 vols, Oxford, 2004; online edn, Sept. 2004. Available at <http://www.oxforddnb.com/view/10.1093/ref:odnb/9780198614128.001.0001/odnb-9780198614128-e-28283> [Accessed 13 January 2018].

—, Moore, James and Browne, Janet, 'Darwin, Charles Robert (1809–1882)', in H. C. G. Matthew and Brian H. Harrison, eds, *Oxford Dictionary of National Biography*, 60 vols, Oxford, 2004; online edn, Sept. 2004. Available at <http://www.oxforddnb.com/view/10.1093/ref:odnb/9780198614128.001.0001/odnb-9780198614128-e-7176> [Accessed 26 January 2018].

Dibdin, Thomas, *Of Age Tomorrow: A Musical Entertainment in Two Acts*, Dublin, 1801.

Dickson, David, *Old World Colony: Cork and South Munster, 1630–1830*, Cork, 2005.

—, Keogh, Dáire and Whelan, Kevin, *The United Irishmen: Republicanism, Radicalism, and Rebellion*, Dublin, 1993.

Dictionary of Irish Biography (DIB), 9 vols, Dublin, 2009. Available at <www.dib.cambridge.org> [Accessed 12 January 2018].

Dimond, William, *Adrian and Orilla, or, A Mother's Vengeance: A Play, in Five Acts ... As Now Performing at the Theatre Royal, Covent Garden, with Universal Applause*, London, 1806.

Donlan, Seán P., 'Hayes, Samuel', in James McGuire and James Quinn, eds, *Dictionary of Irish Biography*, 9 vols, Cambridge, 2009. Available at <http://dib.cambridge.org/viewReadPage.do?articleId=a3878> [Accessed 13 January 2018].

Donnell, James, 'An Account of Certain Slate Districts in Ireland, Extracted from Two Reports Drawn up by James Donnell, Esq. Civil Engineer', *Dublin Philosophical Journal, and Scientific Review*, 2, 1826, pp. 164–78.

Downes, Kerry, 'Vanbrugh, Sir John (1664–1726)', in H. C. G. Matthew and Brian H. Harrison, eds, *Oxford Dictionary of National Biography*, 60 vols, Oxford, 2004; online edn, Sept. 2004. Available at <http://www.oxforddnb.com/view/10.1093/ref:odnb/9780198614128.001.0001/odnb-9780198614128-e-28059> [Accessed 13 January 2018].

Dunlop, Robert, 'Lawless, Valentine Browne (1773–1853)', rev. Gerard McCoy, in H. C. G. Matthew and Brian H. Harrison, eds, *Oxford Dictionary of National Biography*, 60 vols, Oxford,

2004; online edn, Jan. 2008. Available at <http://www.oxforddnb.com/view/10.1093/ref:odnb/ 9780198614128.001.0001/odnb-9780198614128-e-16163> [Accessed 13 January 2018].

—, 'Moore, Charles (1730–1822)', rev. Robert T. Stern, in H. C. G. Matthew and Brian H. Harrison, eds, *Oxford Dictionary of National Biography*, 60 vols, Oxford, 2004; online edn, Sept. 2004. Available at <http://www.oxforddnb.com/view/10.1093/ref:odnb/9780198614128.001.0001/odnb-9780198614128-e-19099> [Accessed 13 January 2018].

Eckersley, L. Lynette, 'Townley, James (1714–1778)', in H. C. G. Matthew and Brian H. Harrison, eds, *Oxford Dictionary of National Biography*, 60 vols, Oxford, 2004; online edn, Sept. 2004. Available at <http://www.oxforddnb.com/view/10.1093/ref:odnb/9780198614128.001.0001/odnb-9780198614128-e-27606> [Accessed 13 January 2018].

Egerton, Judy, 'Stubbs, George (1724–1806)', in H. C. G. Matthew and Brian H. Harrison, eds, *Oxford Dictionary of National Biography*, 60 vols, Oxford, 2004; online edn, Sept. 2010. Available at <http://www.oxforddnb.com/view/10.1093/ref:odnb/9780198614128.001.0001/odnb-9780198614128-e-26732> [Accessed 13 January 2018].

—, 'Wright, Joseph (1734–1797)', in H. C. G. Matthew and Brian H. Harrison, eds, *Oxford Dictionary of National Biography*, 60 vols, Oxford, 2004; online edn, Jan. 2008. Available at <http://www.oxforddnb.com/view/10.1093/ref:odnb/9780198614128.001.0001/odnb-9780198614128-e-30044> [Accessed 13 January 2018].

Elliott, Marianne, *Robert Emmet: the Making of a Legend*, London, 2003.

Elliott, Paul, 'The Origins of the "Creative Class": Provincial Urban Society, Scientific Culture and Socio-Political Marginality in Britain in the Eighteenth and Nineteenth Centuries', *Social History*, 28/3, 2003, pp. 361–87.

Ellison, Cyril, *The Waters of the Boyne and Blackwater*, Dublin, 1983.

Engel, Ute, *Worcester Cathedral: An Architectural History*, trans. Hilary Heltay, Chichester, 2007.

Evans, David S., 'Maclear, Sir Thomas (1794–1879)', in H. C. G. Matthew and Brian H. Harrison, eds, *Oxford Dictionary of National Biography*, 60 vols, Oxford, 2004; online edn, May 2009. Available at <http://www.oxforddnb.com/view/10.1093/rcf:odnb/9780198614128.001.0001/odnb-9780198614128-e-17654> [Accessed 13 January 2018].

Evans, Robert, Poyner, David, and Powell, Steve, 'Forest of Wyre Coalfield' in A. Pearce, ed., *Mining in Shropshire*, Telford, 1995, pp. 14–26. Available at <http://www-users.aston.ac.uk/~poynerdr/fowcoal.htm> [Accessed 12 January 2018].

Farquhar, George, *The Beaux' Stratagem*, London, 1707.

Farrelly, Jean, and O'Brien, Caimin, *Archaeological Inventory of County Tipperary Volume 1 – North Tipperary*, Dublin, 2002.

Fénelon, François, *The Adventures of Telemachus*, London, 1699.

Ferrar, John, *An History of the City of Limerick*, 2nd edn, Limerick, 1767.

Fielding, Henry, *The Rehearsal*, London, 1753.

Filippoupoliti, Anastasia, 'Specializing the Private Collection: John Fiott Lee and Hartwell House', in John Potvin and Alla Myzelev, eds, *Material Cultures, 1740–1920: The Meanings and Pleasures of Collecting*, Aldershot, 2008, pp. 53–69.

Fisher, Stuart, *The Canals of Britain: A Comprehensive Guide*, 2nd edn, London, 2012.

FitzGerald, Garret, 'Estimates for Baronies of Minimum Level of Irish-Speaking Amongst Successive Decennial Cohorts: 1771–1781 to 1861–1871', *Proceedings of the Royal Irish Academy*, 84C, 1984, pp. 117–55.

FitzPatrick, Elizabeth, *Royal Inauguration in Gaelic Ireland c.1100–1600: A Cultural Landscape Study*, Woodbridge, 2004.

Flood, William Henry Grattan, 'Henry Eeles, Philosopher and Land Agent', *Journal of the Cork Historical and Archaeological Society*, 2nd ser., 13, 1907, pp. 70–72; 14, 1908, pp. 25–30.

Foster, R. F., *Modern Ireland 1600–1972*, London, 1988.

Fowler, J. Kersley, *Records of Old Times: Historical, Social, Political, Sporting and Agricultural*, London, 1898.

Friedman, Terry, 'Gibbs, James (1682–1754)', in H. C. G. Matthew and Brian H. Harrison, eds, *Oxford Dictionary of National Biography*, 60 vols, Oxford, 2004; online edn, Jan. 2008. Available at <http://www.oxforddnb.com/view/10.1093/ref:odnb/9780198614128.001.0001/odnb-9780198614128-e-10604> [Accessed 13 January 2018].

Fryer, George, *The Poetry of Various Glees, Songs, &c: as Performed at the Harmonists*, London, 1798.

Gamble, John, *Society and Manners in Nineteenth-Century Ireland*, ed. Breandán Mac Suibhne, Dublin, 2011.

Gaughan, J. Anthony, *Doneraile*, 2nd edn, Dublin, 1970.

[A Gentleman of Oxford], *The New Oxford Guide; or, Companion through the University*, Oxford, 1759.

The Gentleman's and Citizen's Almanack ... for ... 1805, Dublin, 1805.

The Gentleman's Magazine: and Historical Chronicle, London, 1736–1850.

Geoghegan, Patrick M., *Robert Emmet: A Life*, Dublin, 2002.

—, 'Crosbie, John', in James McGuire and James Quinn, eds, *Dictionary of Irish Biography*, 9 vols, Cambridge, 2009. Available at <http://dib.cambridge.org/viewReadPage.do?articleId=a2230> [Accessed 13 January 2018].

—, 'Curran, John Philpot', in James McGuire and James Quinn, eds, *Dictionary of Irish Biography*, 9 vols, Cambridge, 2009. Available at <http://dib.cambridge.org/viewReadPage.do?articleId=a2320> [Accessed 13 January 2018].

—, 'Fitzgerald, Maurice', in James McGuire and James Quinn, eds, *Dictionary of Irish Biography*, 9 vols, Cambridge, 2009. Available at <http://dib.cambridge.org/viewReadPage.do?articleId=a3177> [Accessed 13 January 2018].

—, 'Gregory, William', in James McGuire and James Quinn, eds, *Dictionary of Irish Biography*, 9 vols, Cambridge, 2009. Available at <http://dib.cambridge.org/viewReadPage.do?articleId=a3625> [Accessed 13 January 2018].

—, 'Grenville, George Nugent Temple', in James McGuire and James Quinn, eds, *Dictionary of Irish Biography*, 9 vols, Cambridge, 2009. Available at <http://dib.cambridge.org/viewReadPage.do?articleId=a3628> [Accessed 13 January 2018].

—, 'Hitchcock, Robert', in James McGuire and James Quinn, eds, *Dictionary of Irish Biography*, 9 vols, Cambridge, 2009. Available at <http://dib.cambridge.org/viewReadPage.do?articleId=a4029> [Accessed 13 January 2018].

—, 'Jones, Frederick Edward', in James McGuire and James Quinn, eds, *Dictionary of Irish Biography*, 9 vols, Cambridge, 2009. Available at <http://dib.cambridge.org/viewReadPage.do?articleId=a4324> [Accessed 13 January 2018].

—, 'Newenham, Thomas', in James McGuire and James Quinn, eds, *Dictionary of Irish Biography*, 9 vols, Cambridge, 2009. Available at <http://dib.cambridge.org/viewReadPage.do?articleId=a6177> [Accessed 13 January 2018].

—, 'Penrose, Cooper', in James McGuire and James Quinn, eds, *Dictionary of Irish Biography*, 9 vols, Cambridge, 2009. Available at <http://dib.cambridge.org/viewReadPage.do?articleId=a7270> [Accessed 13 January 2018].

—, 'Pery, Edmond Henry', in James McGuire and James Quinn, eds, *Dictionary of Irish Biography*, 9 vols, Cambridge, 2009. Available at <http://dib.cambridge.org/viewReadPage.do?articleId=a7292> [Accessed 13 January 2018].

—, 'Pery, Edmond Sexten', in James McGuire and James Quinn, eds, *Dictionary of Irish Biography*, 9 vols, Cambridge, 2009. Available at <http://dib.cambridge.org/viewReadPage.do?articleId=a7293> [Accessed 13 January 2018].

—, 'Proby, John Joshua', in James McGuire and James Quinn, eds, *Dictionary of Irish Biography*, 9 vols, Cambridge, 2009. Available at <http://dib.cambridge.org/viewReadPage.do?articleId=a7511> [Accessed 13 January 2018].

—, 'Sneyd, Nathaniel', in James McGuire and James Quinn, eds, *Dictionary of Irish Biography*, 9 vols, Cambridge, 2009. Available at <http://dib.cambridge.org/viewReadPage.do?articleId=a8184> [Accessed 13 January 2018].

—, 'Stevenson, Sir John Andrew', in James McGuire and James Quinn, eds, *Dictionary of Irish Biography*, 9 vols, Cambridge, 2009. Available at <http://dib.cambridge.org/viewReadPage.do?articleId=a8295> [Accessed 13 January 2018].

—, 'White, Richard', in James McGuire and James Quinn, eds, *Dictionary of Irish Biography*, 9 vols, Cambridge, 2009. Available at <http://dib.cambridge.org/viewReadPage.do?articleId=a9008> [Accessed 13 January 2018].

— and Quinn, James, 'Newenham, Sir Edward', in James McGuire and James Quinn, eds, *Dictionary of Irish Biography*, 9 vols, Cambridge, 2009. Available at <http://dib.cambridge.org/viewReadPage.do?articleId=a6174> [Accessed 13 January 2018].

[Anon.], *The Georgian Era: Memoirs of the Most Eminent Persons, who have Flourished in Great Britain, from the Accession of George the First to the Demise of George the Fourth*, 4 vols, London, 1834, III: *Voyagers and Travellers; Philosophers and Men of Science; Authors*.

Gibbons, Luke, 'Topographies of Terror: Killarney and the Politics of the Sublime', *South Atlantic Quarterly*, 95, 1996, pp. 23–44.

Gibney, John, 'Meade, Sir John', in James McGuire and James Quinn, eds, *Dictionary of Irish Biography*, 9 vols, Cambridge, 2009. Available at <http://dib.cambridge.org/viewReadPage.do?articleId=a5770> [Accessed 13 January 2018].

Gibson, William H., 'The North and South Moats, Naas', *Journal of the County Kildare Archaeological Society and Surrounding Districts*, 17, 1987–91, pp. 49–58.

Gilpin, William, *Observations, Made in the Year 1772, on Several Parts of England; Particularly the Mountains and Lakes of Cumberland and Westmoreland*, London, 1786.

Goldberg, Gerald Y., *Jonathan Swift and Contemporary Cork*, Cork, 1967.

Goodbody, Rob, *Irish Historic Towns Atlas no. 26 Dublin part III, 1756 to 1847*, Dublin, 2014.

Gott, Richard, *Britain's Empire: Resistance, Repression and Revolt*, London, 2011.

Gray, Thomas, *The Bard: a Pinardic Ode*, London, 1757.

[Greater London Council], *John Joseph Merlin: the Ingenious Mechanick*, London, 1985.

[Green, Rupert], *A Brief History of Worcester; or, 'Worcester Guide' Improved*, 5th edn, Worcester, 1806.

Green, Valentine, *The History and Antiquities of the City and Suburbs of Worcester*, 2 vols, London, 1796.

Greene, John C., *Theatre in Dublin, 1745–1820: A History*, 2 vols, Lanham, MD, 2011.

Grogan, Eoin, and Kilfeather, Annaba, *Archaeological Inventory of County Wicklow*, Dublin, 1997.

Gros, Frédéric, *A Philosophy of Walking*, trans. John Howe, London, 2015.

Grossman, Mark I., 'William Higgins at the Dublin Society, 1810–20: The Loss of a Professorship and a Claim to the Atomic Theory', *Notes and Records of the Royal Society*, 64/4, 2010, pp. 417–34.

Gwynn, Aubrey and Hadcock, R. Neville, *Medieval Religious Houses: Ireland*, London, 1970.

Habakkuk, John, *Marriage, Debt, and the Estates System: English Landownership, 1650–1950*, Oxford, 1994.

Hadfield, Andrew and McVeagh, John, *Strangers to that Land: British Perceptions of Ireland from the Reformation to the Famine*, Bucks., 1994.

Halliday, Paul D., 'Street, Sir Thomas' in H. C. G. Matthew and Brian H. Harrison, eds, *Oxford Dictionary of National Biography*, 60 vols, Oxford, 2004; online edn, Jan. 2008. Available at <http://www.oxforddnb.com/view/10.1093/ref:odnb/9780198614128.001.0001/odnb-9780198614128-e-26660> [Accessed 15 July 2018].

Hanley, H. A., *Dr John Lee of Hartwell, 1783–1866*, Aylesbury, 1983.

Harbison, Peter, 'Early Christian Antiquities at Clonmore, Co. Carlow', *Proceedings of the Royal Irish Academy*, 91C, 1991, pp. 177–200.

Haydon, Colin, 'Johnson, James' in H. C. G. Matthew and Brian H. Harrison, eds, *Oxford Dictionary of National Biography*, 60 vols, Oxford, 2004; online edn, Jan. 2008. Available at <http://www.oxforddnb.com/view/10.1093/ref:odnb/9780198614128.001.0001/odnb-9780198614128-e-14889> [Accessed 15 July 2018].

—, 'Maddox, Isaac (1697–1759), bishop of Worcester' in H. C. G. Matthew and Brian H. Harrison, eds, *Oxford Dictionary of National Biography*, 60 vols, Oxford, 2004; online edn, Jan. 2008. Available at <http://www.oxforddnb.com/view/10.1093/ref:odnb/9780198614128.001.0001/odnb-9780198614128-e-17757> [Accessed 15 July 2018].

[Anon.] *The Heiress: a Comedy in Five Acts. As Performed at the Theatre-Royal Drury Lane*, Dublin, [1786].

The Hibernian Magazine, Dublin, 1771–85.

Highfill, Philip H. Jr., Burnim, Kalman A. and Langhans, Edward A., *Biographical Dictionary of Actors, Actresses, Musicians, Dancers, Managers, and Other Stage Personnel in London, 1600–1800*, Carbondale, 1973.

Hitchcock, Richard, 'Gleanings from Country Church-Yards', *Transactions of the Kilkenny Archaeological Society*, 2/1, 1852, pp. 127–33.

Hoare, Richard Colt, *Journal of a Tour in Ireland, A.D. 1806*, London, 1807.

Hogan, Ita Margaret, *Anglo-Irish Music 1780–1830*, Cork, 1966.

Hogan, Patrick M., '1798 Remembered: Casualties Sustained by Government Forces during the Humbert Episode, August–September, 1798: a Re-Appraisal', *Journal of the Galway Archaeological and Historical Society*, 50, 1998, pp. 1–9.

Holden's Annual London and Country Directory of the United Kingdoms and Wales ... for the year 1811, 3 vols, London, 1811.

Honeyman, Katrina, *Origins of Enterprise: Business Leadership in the Industrial Revolution*, Manchester, 1982.

Hooper, Glenn, 'The Isles/Ireland: the Wilder Shore', in Peter Hulme and Tim Youngs, eds, *The Cambridge Companion to Travel Writing*, Cambridge, 2002, pp. 174–90.

—, *Travel Writing and Ireland, 1760–1860: Culture, History, Politics*, Houndmills, 2005.

Hooper, Steven, *Pacific Encounters: Art and Divinity in Polynesia, 1760–1860*, Norwich, 2006.

Hourican, Bridget, 'Herbert, Henry Arthur', in James McGuire and James Quinn, eds, *Dictionary of Irish Biography*, 9 vols, Cambridge, 2009. Available at <http://dib.cambridge.org/viewReadPage.do?articleId=a3955> [Accessed 13 January 2018].

—, 'Hutchinson, Richard Hely-', in James McGuire and James Quinn, eds, *Dictionary of Irish Biography*, 9 vols, Cambridge, 2009. Available at <http://dib.cambridge.org/viewReadPage.do?articleId=a4181> [Accessed 13 January 2018].

—, 'White, Luke', in James McGuire and James Quinn, eds, *Dictionary of Irish Biography*, 9 vols, Cambridge, 2009. Available at <http://dib.cambridge.org/viewReadPage.do?articleId=a9005> [Accessed 13 January 2018].

Houston, R. A., *The Population History of Britain and Ireland, 1550–1750*, Cambridge, 1992.

Howley, James, *The Follies and Garden Buildings of Ireland*, New Haven, CT, 2004.

Hull, Edward, *Memoirs of the Geological Survey of England and Wales. The Triassic and Permian Rocks of the Midland Counties of England*, London, 1869.

Hurley, Caroline, *Bog of Allen Habitat and Heritage Survey*, Kildare, 2005.

Hutton, William, *Remarks upon North Wales, being the Result of Sixteen Tours through that Part of the Principality*, Birmingham, 1803.

'Introduction: Verner/Wingfield Papers (D2538)', Public Records Office of Northern Ireland, Belfast, 2007 <https://www.nidirect.gov.uk/sites/default/files/publications/verner-wingfield-papers-d2538.pdf> [Accessed 12 January 2018].

James, J. K., *Tourism, Land, and Landscape in Ireland: the Commodification of Culture*, Abingdon, 2014.

Jameson, Robert, *Mineralogy of the Scottish Isles*, 2 vols, Edinburgh, 1800.
Jarvis, Robin, *Romantic Writing and Pedestrian Travel*, Houndmills, 1997.
Johnson, Richard, *The Famous Historie of the Seven Champions of Christendom*, London, 1596/7.
Johnston-Liik, Edith Mary, *MPs in Dublin: Companion to the History of the Irish Parliament 1692–1800*, Belfast, 2006.
—, 'Wolfe, Arthur', in James McGuire and James Quinn, eds, *Dictionary of Irish Biography*, 9 vols, Cambridge, 2009. Available at <http://dib.cambridge.org/viewReadPage.do?articleId=a9105> [Accessed 13 January 2018].
— and Quinn, James, 'FitzGibbon, John', in James McGuire and James Quinn, eds, *Dictionary of Irish Biography*, 9 vols, Cambridge, 2009. Available at <http://dib.cambridge.org/viewReadPage.do?articleId=a3209> [Accessed 13 January 2018].
Jones, Joan, 'Minton, Herbert (1793–1858)', in H. C. G. Matthew and Brian H. Harrison, eds, *Oxford Dictionary of National Biography*, 60 vols, Oxford, 2004; online edn, Sept. 2004. Available at <http://www.oxforddnb.com/view/10.1093/ref:odnb/9780198614128.001.0001/odnb-9780198614128-e-18816> [Accessed 13 January 2018].
Kane, Eileen, 'An Irish Giant', *Irish Arts Review Yearbook*, 1990/1, pp. 96–8.
Kelly, James, '"Drinking the Waters": Balneotherapeutic Medicine in Ireland, 1660–1850', *Studia Hibernica*, 35, 2008–9, pp. 99–146.
—, 'Fitzwilliam, William Wentworth', in James McGuire and James Quinn, eds, *Dictionary of Irish Biography*, 9 vols, Cambridge, 2009. Available at <http://dib.cambridge.org/viewReadPage.do?articleId=a3259> [Accessed 13 January 2018].
—, 'Grattan, Henry', in James McGuire and James Quinn, eds, *Dictionary of Irish Biography*, 9 vols, Cambridge, 2009. Available at <http://dib.cambridge.org/viewReadPage.do?articleId=a3578> [Accessed 13 January 2018].
—, 'Hill, Wills', in James McGuire and James Quinn, eds, *Dictionary of Irish Biography*, 9 vols, Cambridge, 2009. Available at <http://dib.cambridge.org/viewReadPage.do?articleId=a4017> [Accessed 13 January 2018].
—, 'O'Connor, Arthur', in James McGuire and James Quinn, eds, *Dictionary of Irish Biography*, 9 vols, Cambridge, 2009. Available at <http://dib.cambridge.org/viewReadPage.do?articleId=a6580> [Accessed 13 January 2018].
—, 'Ponsonby, George', in James McGuire and James Quinn, eds, *Dictionary of Irish Biography*, 9 vols, Cambridge, 2009. Available at <http://dib.cambridge.org/viewReadPage.do?articleId=a7413> [Accessed 13 January 2018].
—, 'Irish Protestants and the Irish Language in the Eighteenth Century', in James Kelly and Ciarán Mac Murchaidh, eds, *Irish and English: Essays on the Irish Linguistic and Cultural Frontier, 1600–1900*, Dublin, 2012, pp. 189–217.
Kenworthy-Browne, John, 'Nollekens, Joseph', in H. C. G. Matthew and Brian H. Harrison, eds, *Oxford Dictionary of National Biography*, 60 vols, Oxford, 2004; online edn, Jan. 2008. Available at <http://www.oxforddnb.com/view/10.1093/ref:odnb/9780198614128.001.0001/odnb-9780198614128-e-20242> [Accessed 15 July 2018].
Keogh, Dáire, 'The Women of 1798: Explaining the Silence', in Thomas Bartlett, David Dickson, Dáire Keogh and Kevin Whelan, eds, *1798: A Bicentenary Perspective*, Dublin, 2003, pp. 512–28.
Kerrigan, Paul M., *Castles and Fortifications in Ireland 1485–1945*, Cork, 1995.
Killeen, Jarlath, *Gothic Ireland: Horror and the Irish Anglican Imagination in the Long Eighteenth Century*, Dublin, 2005.
Kinsley, Zoë, *Women Writing the Home Tour, 1682–1812*, Aldershot, 2008.
Knight, Joseph, 'Davison [née Duncan], Maria Rebecca', rev. J. Gilliland, in H. C. G. Matthew and Brian H. Harrison, eds, *Oxford Dictionary of National Biography*, 60 vols, Oxford, 2004; online edn, Jan. 2008. Available at <http://www.oxforddnb.com/view/10.1093/ref:odnb/9780198614128.001.0001/odnb-9780198614128-e-7304> [Accessed 15 July 2018].

—, 'Holman, Joseph George (1764–1817)', rev. John Wells, in H. C. G. Matthew and Brian H. Harrison, eds, *Oxford Dictionary of National Biography*, 60 vols, Oxford, 2004; online edn, Sept. 2004. Available at <http://www.oxforddnb.com/view/10.1093/ref:odnb/9780198614128.001.0001/odnb-9780198614128-e-13580> [Accessed 13 January 2018].

Langford, Paul, 'Burke, Edmund (1729/30–1797)', in H. C. G. Matthew and Brian H. Harrison, eds, *Oxford Dictionary of National Biography*, 60 vols, Oxford, 2004; online edn, Oct. 2012. Available at <http://www.oxforddnb.com/view/10.1093/ref:odnb/9780198614128.001.0001/odnb-9780198614128-e-4019> [Accessed 13 January 2018].

Latocnaye, Le Chevalier de, *A Frenchman's Walk through Ireland 1796–7 (Promenade d'un Français dans l'Irlande)*, trans. John Stevenson, [1798] Belfast, 1917.

Leask, Harold G., *Irish Churches and Monastic Buildings I: First Phases and the Romanesque*, Dundalk, 1955.

Lee, John, *Antiquarian Researches in the Ionian Islands, in the Year 1812: Communicated to the Society of Antiquaries*, London, 1848.

[—], *Oriental Manuscripts Purchased in Turkey*, London, 1840.

Leerssen, Joep, 'Owenson, Sydney (Lady Morgan)', in James McGuire and James Quinn, eds, *Dictionary of Irish Biography*, 9 vols, Cambridge, 2009. Available at <http://dib.cambridge.org/viewReadPage.do?articleId=a5972> [Accessed 13 January 2018].

Leet, Ambrose, *A Directory to the Market Towns, Villages, Gentlemen's Seats, and other Notable Places in Ireland*, Dublin, 1814.

Lennon, Colm, *Irish Historic Towns Atlas no. 19 Dublin part II, 1610 to 1756*, Dublin, 2008.

—, *That Field of Glory: The Story of Clontarf from Battleground to Garden Suburb*, Dublin, 2014.

Lewis, Matthew, *Rugantino; or the Bravo of Venice*, London, 1805.

Lewis, Samuel, *A Topographical Dictionary of Ireland*, 2 vols, London, 1837.

Lindsay, Jean, 'Pennant, Richard (*c*.1737–1808)', in H. C. G. Matthew and Brian H. Harrison, eds, *Oxford Dictionary of National Biography*, 60 vols, Oxford, 2004; online edn, Sept. 2004. Available at <http://www.oxforddnb.com/view/10.1093/ref:odnb/9780198614128.001.0001/odnb-9780198614128-e-21859> [Accessed 13 January 2018].

Lloyd, Stephen, 'Cosway, Maria Louisa (1760–1838)', in H. C. G. Matthew and Brian H. Harrison, eds, *Oxford Dictionary of National Biography*, 60 vols, Oxford, 2004; online edn, May 2005. Available at <http://www.oxforddnb.com/view/10.1093/ref:odnb/9780198614128.001.0001/odnb-9780198614128-e-6382> [Accessed 13 January 2018].

Lock, Julian, 'Hough, John', in H. C. G. Matthew and Brian H. Harrison, eds, *Oxford Dictionary of National Biography*, 60 vols, Oxford, 2004; online edn, Jan. 2008. Available at <http://www.oxforddnb.com/view/10.1093/ref:odnb/9780198614128.001.0001/odnb-9780198614128-e-13862> [Accessed 15 July 2018].

Lodge, Edmund, *The Peerage and Baronetage of the British Empire as at Present Existing*, 42nd edn, London, 1873.

Logan, Patrick, *The Holy Wells of Ireland*, Gerrards Cross, Bucks., 1980.

Long, Patrick, 'Fitzgerald, Sir Thomas Judkin', in James McGuire and James Quinn, eds, *Dictionary of Irish Biography*, 9 vols, Cambridge, 2009. Available at <http://dib.cambridge.org/viewReadPage.do?articleId=a3192> [Accessed 13 January 2018].

—, 'Swan, William Bellingham', in James McGuire and James Quinn, eds, *Dictionary of Irish Biography*, 9 vols, Cambridge, 2009. Available at <http://dib.cambridge.org/viewReadPage.do?articleId=a8395> [Accessed 13 January 2018].

—, 'Vereker, Charles', in James McGuire and James Quinn, eds, *Dictionary of Irish Biography*, 9 vols, Cambridge, 2009. Available at <http://dib.cambridge.org/viewReadPage.do?articleId=a8804> [Accessed 13 January 2018].

Lucas, Richard, 'The Cork Directory for 1787', *Journal of the Cork Historical and Archaeological Society*, 72, 1967, pp. 135–57.

Luddy, Maria, 'Whiteboy Support in Co. Tipperary: 1761–1789', *Tipperary Historical Journal*, 8, 1989, pp. 66–79.

Lysaght, Paddy, 'The House of Industry', *Old Limerick Journal*, 3, 1980, pp. 28–30.

MacArthur, C. W. P., 'Mineralogical and Geological Travellers in Donegal 1787–1812', *Donegal Annual*, 39, 1987, pp. 39–57.

Macpherson, James, *Fragments of Ancient Poetry Collected in the Highlands of Scotland*, Edinburgh, 1760.

—, *Fingal, an Ancient Epic Poem composed by Ossian, the Son of Fingal, Translated from the Gaelic Language*, London, 1761/2.

—, *Temora*, London, 1763.

—, *The Works of Ossian*, 2 vols, London, 1765.

Magennis, Eoin, '"A Land of Milk and Honey": The Physico-Historical Society, Improvement and the Surveys of Mid-Eighteenth-Century Ireland', *Proceedings of the Royal Irish Academy*, 102C/6, 2002, pp. 199–217.

Manning, Conleth, 'Ditches at Jigginstown House', *Journal of the County Kildare Archaeological Society and Surrounding Districts*, 17, 1987–91, pp. 226–7.

—, 'The Inscription on the North Cross at Ballymore Eustace, County Kildare', *Journal of the Royal Society of Antiquities of Ireland*, 126, 1996, p. 112.

—, *Rock of Cashel, Co. Tipperary*, Dublin, 2000.

Marshall, David, 'The Problem of the Picturesque', *Eighteenth-Century Studies*, 35/3, 2002, pp. 413–37.

Maunde, John, *The Rural Philosopher; or, French Georgics. A Didactic Poem. Translated from the Original of the Abbe Delille; Entitled l'Homme des Champs*, London, 1801.

Mavor, Elizabeth, *The Ladies of Llangollen: A Study in Romantic Friendship*, London, 1971.

McAlpine, William Henry, *A Catalogue of the Law Library at Hartwell House, Buckinghamshire*, London, 1865.

McBride, Ian, 'Memory and Forgetting: Ulster Presbyterians and 1798', in Thomas Bartlett, David Dickson, Dáire Keogh and Kevin Whelan, eds, *1798: a Bicentenary Perspective*, Dublin, 2003, pp. 478–96.

McCabe, Desmond, 'Kirwan, Walter Blake', in James McGuire and James Quinn, eds, *Dictionary of Irish Biography*, 9 vols, Cambridge, 2009. Available at <http://dib.cambridge.org/viewReadPage.do?articleId=a4593> [Accessed 13 January 2018].

—, 'O'Neill, Arthur', in James McGuire and James Quinn, eds, *Dictionary of Irish Biography*, 9 vols, Cambridge, 2009. Available at <http://dib.cambridge.org/viewReadPage.do?articleId=a6916> [Accessed 13 January 2018].

McCarthy, Muriel, 'Marsh, Narcissus', in James McGuire and James Quinn, eds, *Dictionary of Irish Biography*, 9 vols, Cambridge, 2009. Available at <http://dib.cambridge.org/viewReadPage.do?articleId=a5459> [Accessed 13 January 2018].

McConnell, Anita, 'Clarke, Edward Daniel (1769–1822)', in H. C. G. Matthew and Brian H. Harrison, eds, *Oxford Dictionary of National Biography*, 60 vols, Oxford, 2004; online edn, Jan. 2015. Available at <http://www.oxforddnb.com/view/10.1093/ref:odnb/9780198614128.001.0001/odnb-9780198614128-e-5494> [Accessed 13 January 2018].

McElroy, Martin, 'Tighe, William', in James McGuire and James Quinn, eds, *Dictionary of Irish Biography*, 9 vols, Cambridge, 2009. Available at <http://dib.cambridge.org/viewReadPage.do?articleId=a8562> [Accessed 13 January 2018].

McMinn, Joseph, 'Swift, Jonathan', in James McGuire and James Quinn, eds, *Dictionary of Irish Biography*, 9 vols, Cambridge, 2009. Available at <http://dib.cambridge.org/viewReadPage.do?articleId=a8415> [Accessed 13 January 2018].

McVeagh, John, *Irish Travel Writing. A Bibliography*, Dublin, 1996.

Mead, W. R., 'The Finnish Journey of Dr John Lee in 1808', *Publicationes Instituti Geographici Universitatis Turkuensis*, 164, 2001, pp. 145–52.

—, 'The Mineralogical Collection of Dr John Lee of Hartwell', *Buckinghamshire Archaeological Society Newsletter*, 2001, p. 5.

—, 'Dr John Lee of Hartwell and his Swedish Journey 1807–1809', *Records of Buckinghamshire*, 43, 2003, pp. 9–26.

—, 'A British Visitor to Skåne in 1807', *Geografiska Notiser*, 3, 2004, pp. 161–4.

Meadows, Peter, 'Bonomi, Joseph (1796–1878)', in H. C. G. Matthew and Brian H. Harrison, eds, *Oxford Dictionary of National Biography*, 60 vols, Oxford, 2004; online edn, Sept. 2004. Available at <http://www.oxforddnb.com/view/10.1093/ref:odnb/9780198614128.001.0001/odnb-9780198614128-e-2858> [Accessed 1 March 2018].

Minch, Rebecca, 'Grogan, Nathaniel', in James McGuire and James Quinn, eds, *Dictionary of Irish Biography*, 9 vols, Cambridge, 2009. Available at <http://dib.cambridge.org/viewReadPage.do?articleId=a3658> [Accessed 13 January 2018].

Miss Linwood's Gallery of Pictures, in Worsted, Leicester Square, London, 1822.

The Monthly Mirror, London, 1795–1811.

Mitchell, Leslie, 'Fox, Charles James', in H. C. G. Matthew and Brian H. Harrison, eds, *Oxford Dictionary of National Biography*, 60 vols, Oxford, 2004; online edn, Jan. 2008. Available at <http://www.oxforddnb.com/view/10.1093/ref:odnb/9780198614128.001.0001/odnb-9780198614128-e-10024> [Accessed 15 July 2018].

Moore, Michael, *Archaeological Inventory of County Waterford*, Dublin, 1999.

Morrill, John, 'Cromwell, Oliver (1599–1658)', in H. C. G. Matthew and Brian H. Harrison, eds, *Oxford Dictionary of National Biography*, 60 vols, Oxford, 2004; online edn, Jan. 2008. Available at <http://www.oxforddnb.com/view/10.1093/ref:odnb/9780198614128.001.0001/odnb-9780198614128-e-6765> [Accessed 6 August 2018].

Morton, Thomas, *A Cure for the Heart-Ache, a Comedy, in Five Acts*, Cork, 1797.

Murphy, Arthur, *The Upholsterer*, Glasgow, 1758.

Murphy, David, 'Burke, John', in James McGuire and James Quinn, eds, *Dictionary of Irish Biography*, 9 vols, Cambridge, 2009. Available at <http://dib.cambridge.org/viewReadPage.do?articleId=a1163> [Accessed 13 January 2018].

—, 'Massey, Eyre', in James McGuire and James Quinn, eds, *Dictionary of Irish Biography*, 9 vols, Cambridge, 2009. Available at <http://dib.cambridge.org/viewReadPage.do?articleId=a5501> [Accessed 13 January 2018].

—, 'Ponsonby, William Brabazon', in James McGuire and James Quinn, eds, *Dictionary of Irish Biography*, 9 vols, Cambridge, 2009. Available at <http://dib.cambridge.org/viewReadPage.do?articleId=a7418> [Accessed 13 January 2018].

Murray, Peter, 'The Cooper Penrose Collection', *Irish Arts Review*, 25/2, 2008, pp. 120–23.

Murtagh, Harman, 'General Humbert's Futile Campaign', in Thomas Bartlett, David Dickson, Dáire Keogh and Kevin Whelan, eds, *1798: A Bicentenary Perspective*, Dublin, 2003, pp. 174–87.

Myers, Bernard Samuel, *Encyclopedia of World Art*, 17 vols, New York, 1959–87.

Myrone, Martin, 'Linwood, Mary (1755–1845)', in H. C. G. Matthew and Brian H. Harrison, eds, *Oxford Dictionary of National Biography*, 60 vols, Oxford, 2004; online edn, Oct. 2013. Available at <http://www.oxforddnb.com/view/10.1093/ref:odnb/9780198614128.001.0001/odnb-9780198614128-e-16748> [Accessed 13 January 2018].

Neale, J. P., *Views of the Seats of Noblemen and Gentlemen, in England, Wales, Scotland, and Ireland*, 5 vols, London, 1826.

Nenagh Guardian, 1838– .

Nevin, Monica, 'Vallancey, Charles', in James McGuire and James Quinn, eds, *Dictionary of Irish Biography*, 9 vols, Cambridge, 2009. Available at <http://dib.cambridge.org/viewReadPage.do?articleId=a8781> [Accessed 13 January 2018].

New Scientist, London, 1956– .

Newman, John and Pevsner, Nikolaus, *The Buildings of England: Shropshire*, London, 2006.

Newton, James and Hannah, Gavin, *The Deserted Village: The Diary of an Oxfordshire Rector*, Stroud, 1992.

Ní Cheallaigh, Máirín, 'Going Astray in the Fort Field: "Traditional" Attitudes towards Ringforts in Nineteenth-Century Ireland', *Journal of Irish Archaeology*, 15, 2006, pp. 105–15.

Ní Laoi, Máire, 'Cork' [draft of work in progress] (*Irish Historic Towns Atlas*, ed. H. B. Clarke, Anngret Simms, Raymond Gillespie and Jacinta Prunty, forthcoming), available at <https://www.ria.ie/sites/default/files/cork-gazetteer-ihta.pdf> [Accessed 12 January 2018].

Ní Mhaonaigh, Máire, 'Ua Briain, Domnall Mór', in James McGuire and James Quinn, eds, *Dictionary of Irish Biography*, 9 vols, Cambridge, 2009. Available at <http://dib.cambridge.org/viewReadPage.do?articleId=a8707> [Accessed 13 January 2018].

—, 'Brian Bórama (Bóruma, Boru)', in James McGuire and James Quinn, eds, *Dictionary of Irish Biography*, 9 vols, Cambridge, 2009. Available at <http://dib.cambridge.org/viewReadPage.do?articleId=a0954> [Accessed 13 January 2018].

Nurse, Julia, 'Place, Francis (1647–1728)', in H. C. G. Matthew and Brian H. Harrison, eds, *Oxford Dictionary of National Biography*, 60 vols, Oxford, 2004; online edn, Sept. 2004. Available at <http://www.oxforddnb.com/view/10.1093/ref:odnb/9780198614128.001.0001/odnb-9780198614128-e-22348> [Accessed 13 January 2018].

O'Brien, William, 'Ross Island: The Beginning', *Archaeology Ireland*, 9/1, The Bronze Age Issue, 1995, pp. 24–7.

Ó Ciardha, Éamonn, 'Browne, Sir Valentine', in James McGuire and James Quinn, eds, *Dictionary of Irish Biography*, 9 vols, Cambridge, 2009. Available at <http://dib.cambridge.org/viewReadPage.do?articleId=a1056> [Accessed 13 January 2018].

O'Donnell, Ruán, *The Rebellion in Wicklow 1798*, Dublin, 1998.

—, *Aftermath: Post-Rebellion Insurgency in Wicklow, 1799–1803*, Dublin, 2000.

O'Donovan, John, *Letters Containing Information Relative to the Antiquities of the County of Kerry Collected during the Progress of the Ordnance Survey in 1841*, [Dublin], 1928.

O'Flaherty, Eamon, *Irish Historic Towns Atlas no. 21 Limerick*, Dublin, 2010.

Ó Gráda, Cormac, 'Poverty, Population, and Agriculture, 1801–45', in W. E. Vaughan, ed., *A New History of Ireland V: Ireland under the Union 1801–70*, Oxford, 1989, pp. 108–33.

—, 'Industry and Communications, 1801–45', in W. E. Vaughan, ed., *A New History of Ireland V: Ireland under the Union 1801–70*, Oxford, 1989, pp. 137–57.

O'Hart, John, *The Irish and Anglo-Irish Landed Gentry when Cromwell came to Ireland: or, a Supplement to Irish Pedigrees*, Dublin, 1892.

O'Loughlin, Michael C., *Families of Co. Kerry*, Kansas, 1994.

O'Neill, Francis, *Irish Minstrels and Musicians*, Norwood, PA, 1973.

O'Riordan, Turlough, 'Pike, Mary', in James McGuire and James Quinn, eds, *Dictionary of Irish Biography*, 9 vols, Cambridge, 2009. Available at <http://dib.cambridge.org/viewReadPage.do?articleId=a7339> [Accessed 13 January 2018].

Ó Siochrú, Micheál, 'Roche, Maurice', in James McGuire and James Quinn, eds, *Dictionary of Irish Biography*, 9 vols, Cambridge, 2009. Available at <http://dib.cambridge.org/viewReadPage.do?articleId=a7750> [Accessed 13 January 2018].

O'Sullivan, Muiris, and Downey, Liam, 'Martello and Signal Towers', *Archaeology Ireland*, 26/2, 2012, pp. 46–9.

Ó Tuathaigh, Gearóid, 'O'Connell, Daniel', in James McGuire and James Quinn, eds, *Dictionary of Irish Biography*, 9 vols, Cambridge, 2009. Available at <http://dib.cambridge.org/viewReadPage.do?articleId=a6555> [Accessed 13 January 2018].

Ordnance Survey 6" series, England and Wales, 1843–82. Available at <http://maps.nls.uk/index.html> [Accessed 12 January 2018].

Ordnance Survey 6" series, Ireland, 1829–41. Available at <http://maps.osi.ie/publicviewer/> [Accessed 12 January 2018].

Ousby, Ian, *The Englishman's England: Taste, Travel and the Rise of Tourism*, Cambridge, 1990.

Oxford Dictionary of National Biography (*ODNB*), 60 vols, Oxford, 2004. Available at <www.oxforddnb.com> [Accessed 12 January 2018].

Palmer, Alfred Neobard, 'Notice of the Discovery of Sepulchral Slabs at Valle Crucis Abbey, Denbighshire', *Archaeologia Cambrensis*, 5th ser., 6/21, 1889, pp. 63–7.

Peach, Annette, 'Phillips, Thomas' in H. C. G. Matthew and Brian H. Harrison, eds, *Oxford Dictionary of National Biography*, 60 vols, Oxford, 2004; online edn, Jan. 2008. Available at <http://www.oxforddnb.com/view/10.1093/ref:odnb/9780198614128.001.0001/odnb-9780198614128-e-22174> [Accessed 15 July 2018].

Pennant, Thomas, *Indian Zoology*, n.p., 1769.

—, *A Tour in Scotland*, Chester, 1771.

—, *A Tour in Scotland and Voyage to the Hebrides*, 2 vols, Chester, 1774.

—, *A Tour in Wales MDCCLXXIII*, London, 1778.

—, *Arctic Zoology*, London, 1784–5.

—, *The History of the Parishes of Whiteford, and Holywell*, London, 1796.

Pergam, Elizabeth A., *The Manchester Art Treasures Exhibition of 1857: Entrepreneurs, Connoisseurs and the Public*, Aldershot and Burlington, 2011.

Perkins, Diane, 'Morland, George (1763–1804)', in H. C. G. Matthew and Brian H. Harrison, eds, *Oxford Dictionary of National Biography*, 60 vols, Oxford, 2004; online edn, Sept. 2004. Available at <http://www.oxforddnb.com/view/10.1093/ref:odnb/9780198614128.001.0001/odnb-9780198614128-e-19278> [Accessed 13 January 2018].

Pettifer, Adrian, *Welsh Castles: A Guide by Counties*, Woodbridge, 2000.

Pevsner, Nikolaus, *The Buildings of England: Shropshire*, London, 1958.

Pilbeam, Pamela, *Madame Tussaud and The History of Waxworks*, London, 2003.

Plumptre, Anne, *Narrative of a Residence in Ireland during the Summer of 1814, and that of 1815*, London, 1817.

Postle, Martin, 'Reynolds, Sir Joshua (1723–1792)', in H. C. G. Matthew and Brian H. Harrison, eds, *Oxford Dictionary of National Biography*, 60 vols, Oxford, 2004; online edn, Sept. 2015. Available at <http://www.oxforddnb.com/view/10.1093/ref:odnb/9780198614128.001.0001/odnb-9780198614128-e-23429> [Accessed 13 January 2018].

Potterton, Homan, *Dutch Seventeenth and Eighteenth Century Paintings in the National Gallery of Ireland: A Complete Catalogue*, Dublin, 1986.

Power, Denis et al., *Archaeological Inventory of County Cork*, 4 vols, Dublin, 1997–2000.

Poyner, David and Evans, Robert, 'Survey of Stanley Colliery, Highley and Associated Features', *Shropshire Caving and Mining Club Journal*, 3, 1996, pp. 66–72. Available at <http://shropshirehistory.com/mining/mines/pdf/SCMC%20Journal%201995.pdf> [Accessed 12 January 2018].

Price, Liam, 'The Place-Names of the Barony of Arklow, County of Wicklow. Their Early Forms Collected', *Proceedings of the Royal Irish Academy*, 46C, 1940–1, pp. 237–86.

Prunty, Jacinta, 'Nineteenth-Century Antiquarian Accounts of Medieval and Early Modern Dublin', in Anngret Simms, Alan Fletcher and John Bradley, eds, *Dublin in the Medieval World*, Dublin, 2009, pp. 473–504.

Quarry, John, *A Letter Addressed to ... Thomas ... Lord Bishop of Cork and Ross*, Cork, 1810.

—, *The Rule of Faith, and the Right of Private Judgment Considered. A Discourse*, Cork, 1830.

Quinn, James, 'Bagwell, John', in James McGuire and James Quinn, eds, *Dictionary of Irish Biography*, 9 vols, Cambridge, 2009. Available at <http://dib.cambridge.org/viewReadPage.do?articleId=a0311> [Accessed 13 January 2018].

—, 'Browne, Valentine', in James McGuire and James Quinn, eds, *Dictionary of Irish Biography*, 9 vols, Cambridge, 2009. Available at <http://dib.cambridge.org/viewReadPage.do?articleId=a1052> [Accessed 13 January 2018].

BIBLIOGRAPHY

—, 'Burgh, Thomas', in James McGuire and James Quinn, eds, *Dictionary of Irish Biography*, 9 vols, Cambridge, 2009. Available at <http://dib.cambridge.org/viewReadPage.do?articleId=a1134> [Accessed 13 January 2018].

—, 'Conyngham, Henry', in James McGuire and James Quinn, eds, *Dictionary of Irish Biography*, 9 vols, Cambridge, 2009. Available at <http://dib.cambridge.org/viewReadPage.do?articleId=a9767> [Accessed 13 January 2018].

Radcliffe, Anne, *Observations during a Tour to the Lakes*, ed. Penny Bradshaw, Carlisle, 2014. First published as *Observations during a Tour to the Lakes of Lancashire, Westmoreland, and Cumberland*, London, 1795.

Reid, Stuart, *Armies of the Irish Rebellion 1798*, Oxford, 2013.

Reilly, Ciarán, *The Irish Land Agent, 1830–1860: The Case of King's County*, Dublin, 2012.

Return of Persons Examined and Certified as Qualified by Apothecaries' Hall in Dublin, and Number of Prosecutions, 1791–1829, HC 235 (1829), Sessional papers, XXII(1), London, 1829.

Ritchie, Fiona and Sabor, Peter, eds, *Shakespeare in the Eighteenth Century*, Cambridge, 2012.

Ross, Ian Campbell, 'Sterne, Laurence', in James McGuire and James Quinn, eds, *Dictionary of Irish Biography*, 9 vols, Cambridge, 2009. Available at <http://dib.cambridge.org/viewReadPage.do?articleId=a8285> [Accessed 13 January 2018].

Ryan, Valerie, *The Story of Russborough House*, [Kildare], 2013.

Samuel, Mark and Hamlyn, Kate, *Blarney Castle: its History, Development and Purpose*, Cork, 2007.

Schiötz, Eiler H., *Utlenders Reiser i Norge: En Bibliografi / Itineraria Norvegica: a Bibliography on Foreigners' Travels in Norway until 1900*, Oslo, 1970; supplement, 1986.

Scott, H. M., 'Harris, James (1746–1820)', in H. C. G. Matthew and Brian H. Harrison, eds, *Oxford Dictionary of National Biography*, 60 vols, Oxford, 2004; online edn, May 2009. Available at <http://www.oxforddnb.com/view/10.1093/ref:odnb/9780198614128.001.0001/odnb-9780198614128-e-12394> [Accessed 13 January 2018].

Sharpe, Samuel, *The Triple Mummy Case of Aroeri-Ao: an Egyptian Priest, in Dr Lee's Museum at Hartwell House, Buckinghamshire. Drawn by Joseph Bonomi and Described by Samuel Sharpe: Pub. for the Syro-Egyptian Society of London*, London, 1858.

[Anon.], *Sketch of the Antiquities of the Ancient City of Worcester*, London, [1760?].

Sleater, Matthew, *Introductory Essay to a New System of Civil and Ecclesiastical Topography, and Itinerary of the Counties of Ireland*, London, 1806.

Sloan, Kim, 'Cozens, Alexander (1717–1786)', in H. C. G. Matthew and Brian H. Harrison, eds, *Oxford Dictionary of National Biography*, 60 vols, Oxford, 2004; online edn, May 2007. Available at <http://www.oxforddnb.com/view/10.1093/ref:odnb/9780198614128.001.0001/odnb-9780198614128-e-6546> [Accessed 13 January 2018].

—, 'Cozens, John Robert (1752–1797)', in H. C. G. Matthew and Brian H. Harrison, eds, *Oxford Dictionary of National Biography*, 60 vols, Oxford, 2004; online edn, Jan. 2011. Available at <http://www.oxforddnb.com/view/10.1093/ref:odnb/9780198614128.001.0001/odnb-9780198614128-e-6547> [Accessed 13 January 2018].

Sloman, Susan, 'Barker, Thomas (1767–1847)', in H. C. G. Matthew and Brian H. Harrison, eds, *Oxford Dictionary of National Biography*, 60 vols, Oxford, 2004; online edn, Sept. 2004. Available at <http://www.oxforddnb.com/view/10.1093/ref:odnb/9780198614128.001.0001/odnb-9780198614128-e-1415> [Accessed 13 January 2018].

Smith, Charles, *The Antient and Present State of the County and City of Waterford: Being a Natural, Civil, Ecclesiastical, Historical and Topographical Description thereof*, Dublin, 1746.

—, *The Antient and Present State of the County and City of Cork. Containing a Natural, Civil, Ecclesiastical, Historical and Topographical Description thereof*, 2nd edn, 2 vols, Dublin, 1774.

—, *The Ancient and Present State of the County of Kerry. Containing a Natural, Civil, Ecclesiastical, Historical and Topographical Description thereof*, Dublin, 1774.

Smyth, Jim, *The Men of No Property: Irish Radicals and Popular Politics in the Late Eighteenth Century*, Dublin, 1992.

—, 'Introduction: The 1798 Rebellion in its Eighteenth-Century Contexts', in Smyth, ed., *Revolution, Counter-Revolution and Union*, pp. 1–20.

—, ed., *Revolution, Counter-Revolution and Union: Ireland in the 1790s*, Cambridge, 2000.

Smyth, William Henry, *Descriptive Catalogue of a Cabinet of Roman Imperial Large-Brass Medals*, Bedford, 1834.

Solkin, David H., 'Wilson, Richard', in H. C. G. Matthew and Brian H. Harrison, eds, *Oxford Dictionary of National Biography*, 60 vols, Oxford, 2004; online edn, Jan. 2008. Available at <http://www.oxforddnb.com/view/10.1093/ref:odnb/9780198614128.001.0001/odnb-9780198614128-e-29680> [Accessed 15 July 2018].

Solnit, Rebecca, *Wanderlust: A History of Walking*, New York, 2001.

Sorrell, Mark, 'Pidcock, Gilbert (d. 1810)', in H. C. G. Matthew and Brian H. Harrison, eds, *Oxford Dictionary of National Biography*, 60 vols, Oxford, 2004; online edn, Jan. 2008. Available at <http://www.oxforddnb.com/view/10.1093/ref:odnb/9780198614128.001.0001/odnb-9780198614128-e-73321> [Accessed 13 January 2018].

Speck, W. A., 'James II and VII (1633–1701)', in H. C. G. Matthew and Brian H. Harrison, eds, *Oxford Dictionary of National Biography*, 60 vols, Oxford, 2004; online edn, Oct. 2009. Available at <http://www.oxforddnb.com/view/10.1093/ref:odnb/9780198614128.001.0001/odnb-9780198614128-e-14593> [Accessed 13 January 2018].

Stalley, Roger, *The Cistercian Monasteries of Ireland: An Account of the History, Art and Architecture of the White Monks in Ireland from 1142 to 1540*, London, 1987.

Steele, David, 'Temple, Henry John (1784–1865)', in H. C. G. Matthew and Brian H. Harrison, eds, *Oxford Dictionary of National Biography*, 60 vols, Oxford, 2004; online edn, May 2009. Available at <http://www.oxforddnb.com/view/10.1093/ref:odnb/9780198614128.001.0001/odnb-9780198614128-e-27112> [Accessed 13 January 2018].

Stephens, H. M., 'Duff, Sir James (1753–1839)', rev. Stephen Wood, in H. C. G. Matthew and Brian H. Harrison, eds, *Oxford Dictionary of National Biography*, 60 vols, Oxford, 2004; online edn, May 2008. Available at <http://www.oxforddnb.com/view/10.1093/ref:odnb/9780198614128.001.0001/odnb-9780198614128-e-8169> [Accessed 13 January 2018].

Stevens, George, ed., *The Dramatic Works of Shakespeare Revised*, 9 vols, London, 1802.

Stevenson, John, *Popular Disturbances in England, 1700–1832*, 2nd edn, Abingdon, 1992.

Stokes, George T., ed., *Pococke's Tour in Ireland in 1752, Edited, with Introduction and Notes*, Dublin, 1891.

Stout, Geraldine, 'The Archaeology of County Wicklow', *Archaeology Ireland*, 3/4, 1989, pp. 126–31.

Stout, Matthew, *The Irish Ringfort*, Dublin, 1997.

Strickland, Walter, *A Dictionary of Irish Artists*, 2 vols, Dublin, 1913.

Stunt, Timothy C. F., *The Elusive Quest of the Spiritual Malcontent: Some Early Nineteenth-Century Ecclesiastical Mavericks*, Eugene, OR, 2015.

Sweetman, P. David, Alcock, Olive and Moran, Bernie, *Archaeological Inventory of County Laois*, Dublin, 1995.

Tann, Jennifer, 'Boulton, Matthew', in H. C. G. Matthew and Brian H. Harrison, eds, *Oxford Dictionary of National Biography*, 60 vols, Oxford, 2004; online edn, Jan. 2008. Available at <http://www.oxforddnb.com/view/10.1093/ref:odnb/9780198614128.001.0001/odnb-9780198614128-e-2983> [Accessed 15 July 2018].

Taylor, George, and Skinner, Andrew, *Taylor and Skinner's Survey and Maps of the Roads of North Britain, or Scotland*, London, 1776.

—, *Taylor and Skinner's Survey of the Great Post Roads between London, Bath and Bristol*, London, 1776.

—, *Maps of the Roads of Ireland, Surveyed 1777*, London, 1778.

Thelwall, John, *The Peripatetic, or Sketches of the Heart, of Nature and Society; in a Series of Politico-Sentimental Journals...*, London, 1793.

Thompson, F. M. L., 'Russell, John, sixth duke of Bedford (1766–1839)', in H. C. G. Matthew and Brian H. Harrison, eds, *Oxford Dictionary of National Biography*, 60 vols, Oxford, 2004; online edn, Sept. 2004. Available at <http://www.oxforddnb.com/view/10.1093/ref:odnb/9780198614128.001.0001/odnb-9780198614128-e-24322> [Accessed 13 January 2018].

Topography of London. Facsimile of John Lockie's Gazetteer 1813, London Topograhical Society Publication No. 148, London, 1994.

Townley, James, *High Life Below Stairs: A Farce of Two Acts*, London, 1759.

Tregaskis, Hugh, *Beyond the Grand Tour: The Levant Lunatics*, London, 1979.

Trinder, Barrie Stuart, *The Industrial Revolution in Shropshire*, London and Chichester, 1973.

Tuckey, Francis H., *The County and City of Cork Remembrancer*, Cork, 1837.

Turpin, John, 'The Dublin Society's Figure Drawing School and the Fine Arts in Dublin 1800–1849', *Dublin Historical Record*, 39/2, 1986, pp. 38–52.

Twiss, Richard, *A Tour in Ireland in 1775. With a Map, and a View of the Salmon-Leap at Ballyshannon*, London, 1776.

[Anon.], 'Übersicht von zwanzig Reisen in die Türken', *Jahrbücher der Literatur*, 81–83, 1838, pp. 1–88.

[Anon.], 'Vere, Sir Aubrey de (1788–1846)', rev. Jessica Hinings, in H. C. G. Matthew and Brian H. Harrison, eds, *Oxford Dictionary of National Biography*, 60 vols, Oxford, 2004; online edn, Jan. 2014. Available at <http://www.oxforddnb.com/view/10.1093/ref:odnb/9780198614128.001.0001/odnb-9780198614128-e-7562> [Accessed 13 January 2018].

Veysey, Arthur Geoffrey, ed., *Guide to the Flintshire Record Office*, Mold, 1974.

Victoria County History: Shropshire, X, ed. C. R. J. Currie, Oxford, 1998.

Victoria County History: Shropshire, II, ed. A. T. Gaydon, London, 1973.

Victoria County History: Worcester, III, ed. J. W. Willis-Bund, London, 1913.

Victoria County History: Worcester, IV, ed. J. W. Willis-Bund, London, 1924.

Walker, R. J. B., 'Russell, John (1745–1806)', in H. C. G. Matthew and Brian H. Harrison, eds, *Oxford Dictionary of National Biography*, 60 vols, Oxford, 2004; online edn, Jan. 2015. Available at <http://www.oxforddnb.com/view/10.1093/ref:odnb/9780198614128.001.0001/odnb-9780198614128-e-24321> [Accessed 13 January 2018].

Walker's Hibernian Magazine: or, Compendium of Entertaining Knowledge, Dublin, 1771–1812.

Wallace, Anne D., *Walking, Literature, and English Culture: The Origins and Uses of Peripatetic in the Nineteenth Century*, Oxford, 1993.

Wayman, Patrick A., *Dunsink Observatory, 1785–1985: A Bicentennial History*, Dublin, 1987.

Weinglass, D. H., 'Haughton, Moses, the younger (1773–1849)', in H. C. G. Matthew and Brian H. Harrison, eds, *Oxford Dictionary of National Biography*, 60 vols, Oxford, 2004; online edn, Sept. 2004. Available at <http://www.oxforddnb.com/view/10.1093/ref:odnb/9780198614128.001.0001/odnb-9780198614128-e-12615> [Accessed 13 January 2018].

Wellesz, Egon and Sternfeld, Frederick William, *New Oxford History of Music: The Age of Enlightenment, 1745–1790*, Oxford, 1973.

West, W. A., *A Directory, and Picture, of Cork and its Environs*, Cork, 1810.

Westall, Richard J., 'Westall, Richard (1765–1836)', in H. C. G. Matthew and Brian H. Harrison, eds, *Oxford Dictionary of National Biography*, 60 vols, Oxford, 2004; online edn, Sept. 2004. Available at <http://www.oxforddnb.com/view/10.1093/ref:odnb/9780198614128.001.0001/odnb-9780198614128-e-29106> [Accessed 13 January 2018].

Whelan, Kevin, *The Tree of Liberty: Radicalism, Catholicism and the Construction of Irish Identity 1760–1830*, Cork, 1996.

White, Harry, *Music and the Irish Literary Imagination*, Oxford, 2008.

—, 'Carolan, Turlough', in James McGuire and James Quinn, eds, *Dictionary of Irish Biography*, 9 vols, Cambridge, 2009. Available at <http://dib.cambridge.org/viewReadPage.do?articleId=a1492> [Accessed 13 January 2018].

White, James Grove, *Historical and Topographical Notes, etc., on Buttevant, Castletownroche, Doneraile, Mallow, and Places in their Vicinity*, Cork, 1905.

Wilde, William, 'Tables of Deaths, Containing the Report, Tables of Pestilences, and Analysis of the Tables of Deaths', in *Census of Ireland for the Year 1851*, Part V, Dublin, 1856, pp. 1–362.

Williams, Glanmor, 'Bellot, Hugh', in H. C. G. Matthew and Brian H. Harrison, eds, *Oxford Dictionary of National Biography*, 60 vols, Oxford, 2004; online edn, Jan. 2008. Available at <http://www.oxforddnb.com/view/10.1093/ref:odnb/9780198614128.001.0001/odnb-9780198614128-e-2060> [Accessed 15 July 2018].

Williams, P. B., *A Brief Account of the Abbey of Valle Crucis, near Llan Gollen, Denbighshire*, 2nd edn, Carnarvon, 1830.

Williams, William H. A., *Tourism, Landscape, and the Irish Character: British Travel Writers in pre-Famine Ireland*, Madison, 2008.

—, *Creating Irish Tourism: the First Century, 1750–1850*, London, 2011.

Wilson, David A., *United Irishmen, United States: Immigrant Radicals in the Early Republic*, Ithaca, 1998.

Wilson, William, *The Post-Chaise Companion: or, Travellers' Directory through Ireland [...] To which is Added a Dictionary of Alphabetical Tables Shewing the Distance of All the Principal Cities, Boroughs, Market and Sea Port Towns in Ireland from Each Other*, Dublin, 1786.

Wilson's Dublin Directory, 4th edn, Dublin, 1805.

Windele, John, *Historical and Descriptive Notices of the City of Cork*, Cork, 1840.

Wood, Andy, *Abandoned and Vanished Canals of England*, Stroud, 2014.

Woods, C. J., 'R. R. Madden, Historian of the United Irishmen', in Thomas Bartlett, David Dickson, Dáire Keogh and Kevin Whelan, eds, *1798: A Bicentenary Perspective*, Dublin, 2003, pp. 497–511.

—, *Travellers' Accounts as Source Material for Irish Historians*, Dublin, 2009.

—, 'Colles, William', in James McGuire and James Quinn, eds, *Dictionary of Irish Biography*, 9 vols, Cambridge, 2009. Available at <http://dib.cambridge.org/viewReadPage.do?articleId=a1843> [Accessed 13 January 2018].

—, 'Esmonde, John', in James McGuire and James Quinn, eds, *Dictionary of Irish Biography*, 9 vols, Cambridge, 2009. Available at <http://dib.cambridge.org/viewReadPage.do?articleId=a2945> [Accessed 13 January 2018].

—, 'Keogh, John', in James McGuire and James Quinn, eds, *Dictionary of Irish Biography*, 9 vols, Cambridge, 2009. Available at <http://dib.cambridge.org/viewReadPage.do?articleId=a4514> [Accessed 13 January 2018].

—, 'Musgrave, Sir Richard', in James McGuire and James Quinn, eds, *Dictionary of Irish Biography*, 9 vols, Cambridge, 2009. Available at <http://dib.cambridge.org/viewReadPage.do?articleId=a6121> [Accessed 13 January 2018].

—, 'O'Gorman, James', in James McGuire and James Quinn, eds, *Dictionary of Irish Biography*, 9 vols, Cambridge, 2009. Available at <http://dib.cambridge.org/viewReadPage.do?articleId=a6764> [Accessed 13 January 2018].

Wright, C. J., 'Fitzmaurice, Henry Petty- (1780–1863)', in H. C. G. Matthew and Brian H. Harrison, eds, *Oxford Dictionary of National Biography*, 60 vols, Oxford, 2004; online edn, May 2009. Available at <http://www.oxforddnb.com/view/10.1093/ref:odnb/9780198614128.001.0001/odnb-9780198614128-e-22071> [Accessed 13 January 2018].

Wright, G. N., *A Guide to the County of Wicklow*, London, 1822.

Yeats, Gráinne, *The Harp of Ireland: The Belfast Harpers' Festival, 1792 and the Saving of Ireland's Harp Music by Edward Bunting*, Belfast, 1992.

Young, Arthur, *Six Weeks' Tour through the Southern Counties of England and Wales*, London, 1769.

—, *A Tour in Ireland with General Observations on the Present State of that Kingdom made in the Years 1776, 1777 and 1778*, 2 vols, London, 1780.

Zaring, Jane, 'The Romantic Face of Wales', *Annals of the Association of American Geographers*, 67/3, 1977, pp. 397–418.

Zirpolo, Lilian H., *Historical Dictionary of Baroque Art and Architecture*, Lanham, MD, 2010.

Zuelow, Eric G. E., *Making Ireland Irish: Tourism and National Identity Since the Irish Civil War*, Syracuse, NY, 2009.

WEBSITES

See also under individual authors and titles for works available in print but viewed online.

Archiseek – Irish Architecture website <www.archiseek.com> [Accessed 12 January 2018].

Dictionary of Irish Architects (DIA) 1720–1940 (Irish Architectural Archive) <www.dia.ie> [Accessed 12 January 2018].

Dictionary of Irish Biography (*DIB*), online edition <www.dib.cambridge.org> [Accessed 12 January 2018].

Dictionary of Welsh Biography online <www.yba.llgc.org.uk> [Accessed 12 January 2018].

History of Parliament Online <www.historyofparliamentonline.org> [Accessed 12 January 2018].

'Introduction: Verner/Wingfield Papers (D2538)', Public Records Office of Northern Ireland, Belfast, 2007 <https://www.nidirect.gov.uk/sites/default/files/publications/verner-wingfield-papers-d2538.pdf> [Accessed 12 January 2018].

Irish Archaeology website <www.irisharchaeology.ie> [Accessed 12 January 2018].

Irish Historic Towns Atlas (*IHTA*) website <https://www.ria.ie/research-projects/irish-historic-towns-atlas> [Accessed 12 January 2018].

Irish Walled Towns Network <http://irishwalledtownsnetwork.ie> [Accessed 12 January 2018].

Landed Estates Database (LED), Moore Institute, National University of Ireland Galway. Available at <www.landedestates.nuigalway.ie> [Accessed 12 January 2018].

National Inventory of Architectural Heritage (NIAH) <www.buildingsofireland.ie> [Accessed 12 January 2018].

National Library of Scotland, georeferenced Ordnance Survey 6" series, England and Wales, 1843–82 <http://maps.nls.uk/os/6inch-england-and-wales/index.html> [Accessed 12 January 2018].

National Monuments Record of Wales online database <http://www.coflein.gov.uk> [Accessed 12 January 2018].

National Trust Inventory <www.nationaltrustcollections.org.uk> [Accessed 12 January 2018].

Ordnance Survey 6" series, Ireland, 1829–41. Available at <http://maps.osi.ie/publicviewer/> [Accessed 12 January 2018].

Oxford Dictionary of National Biography (*ODNB*), online edition <www.oxforddnb.com> [Accessed 12 January 2018].

Royal Museums Greenwich collections website <http://collections.rmg.co.uk> [Accessed 12 January 2018].

Shropshire History <shropshirehistory.com> [Accessed 12 January 2018].

Weather Extremes project, University of Nottingham <http://blogs.nottingham.ac.uk/weatherextremes/> [Accessed 12 January 2018].

INDEX

Note: Variant spellings of names and place names are provided in parentheses. Individuals and places that are not positively identified in the text have not been indexed. References to figures and maps are in bold.

Abergele (Abergelly), Conwy, xvii, **26**, 90
Abbeydorney, Co. Kerry, xix, 238
Acaun Bridge, Co. Carlow, xviii, 144, 145n1
Acrefair (Acre Vaser, Acre Vroer), Wrexham, 78, 79
Acton Park, Wrexham, xvii, 85, 85n2
actors,
    Adams, the four Misses, 293, 293n4, 297, 300
    Edwin (Richards), Elizabeth Rebecca (1771?–1854), 296, 296n3
    Gallus, Quintus Roscius (Roscious) (*c*.126–62 BCE), 51n2
    Hitchcock (née Webb), Sarah (d. 1810), 297n6
    Holman, Joseph George (1764–1817), 295, 295n6, 297
    Johnston (née Parker), Nannette, (*fl.* 1797–1807), 296n2
    Talbot, Montague (*fl.* 1807), 295n9, 297, 298
    Walstein, Elizabeth (*fl.* 1807–18), 296, 296n1, 298
Adare (Adair), Co. Limerick: bridge; castle; early and medieval Christian foundations, xx, 240, 241, 241n5, 242, 323n1
agents (for absentee landlords), 140–41, 141n2, 155
Aglish Hill, Co. Waterford, 189, 324
Airy, Sir George Biddell (astronomer, 1801–92), 5
alcohol, 6, 140–41, 145, 155, 166, 175, 176, 188, 195, 214, 219, 228–9, 257, 295
Almer, Captain (*fl.* 1806–7) (Aylmour, Elmor, Elmour), 156, 156n1, 158, 163, 164, 165, 265, 265n1
'Amethyst Cliffs', Co. Kerry, 236n3
Annesley, George, Viscount Valentia (1770–1844), 57n8
antiquarianism, 11, 16–18
Antonie, William Lee (uncle and guardian of John Lee, 1764–1815), 2, 4, 8, 8n2, 76, 103, 297n4, 340n5, 341–2
Apley (Hapley), Shropshire (Salop), xvii, 60, 60n2, 61
Archer, Captain Thomas (*fl.* 1798, of Newtownmountkennedy Cavalry), 115, 115n5
architects,
    Cockerell, Charles Robert (1788–1863), 4

Gandon, James (1742–1823), 17, 100n1, 100n6, 101n3
Ardfert, Co. Kerry, xix, 13, **27**, 234n2, 234n4, 235, 237, 241, 322
Ardmayle (Armaile), Co. Tipperary, 269, 272
Arklow, Co. Wicklow, xviii, **27**, **28**, **30**, **31**, 112, 138, 139, 140, 141, 142, 143, 145
Arrowsmith, Edward (of Totteridge, dates unknown), 341–2
art collections, private, 77–8, 124–5, 260–61
artists and sculptors,
    Barbieri, Giovanni Francesco (also Guercino, 1591–1666), 124n6
    Barker, Thomas (1767–1847), 292n4
    Barry, James (1741–1806), 261n2
    Batoni, Pompeo (1708–87), 124, 124n12
    Borsselaer, Pieter (*fl.* 1664–87), 78n5
    Bowler, T. W. (1812–69), 5–6
    Calvert, Frederick (*fl.* 1807–30), 257, 257n1
    Catton, Charles (the younger, 1756–1819), 291, 291n1
    Copley, John Singleton (1738–1815), 291, 291n3
    Cosway, Maria, Baroness (1760–1838), 291, 291n5
    Cozens, Alexander (1717–86), 291, 291n2, 292
    Cozens, John Robert (1752–97), 291n2
    d'Arthois, Jacques (1613–86), 11, 214n3
    da Correggio, Antonio (1489–1534), 125, 125n7
    de Keysar, William (*fl.* 1683), 101n2
    del Sarto, Andrea (1486–1530), 124, 124n19
    Dolci, Carlo (1616–86), 290n4
    Domenichino (also Domenico Zampieri, 1581–1641), 124n11
    Furini, Francesco (1603–46), 125n3
    Gainsborough, Thomas (1727–88), 290, 290n6, 293
    Giordano, Luca (1634–1705), 124, 124n17
    Grogan, Nathaniel (the elder, *c.*1740–1807), 257, 257n6
    Holbein, Hans (1497/8–1543), 125, 125n12
    Lopez, Gasparo (1650–1732), 124n14

INDEX

Lorrain, Claude (*c*.1600–82), 11, 58n6, 125, 125n11
Maratta, Carlo (also Maratti, 1625–1713), 124n8
Morland, George (1763–1804), 259, 290, 290n9, 291, 292, 292n3
Murillo, Bartolomé Esteban (1617–82), 260n9
Nollekens, Joseph (1737–1823), 46n7
Panini, Giovanni Paolo (1691–1765), 124, 124n9
Phillips, Thomas (1770–1845), 46n5
Place, Francis (1647–1728), 292n2
Poussin, Nicholas (1594–1665), 78, 124, 124n15, 125
Raphael (1483–1520), 260, 260n10, 290n8
Reni, Guido (1575–1642), 78n1, 125n2
Reynolds, Sir Joshua (1723–92), 124, 124n4, 125, 290, 291
Rosa, Salvator (1615–73), 124, 124n21
Roubiliac, Louis-François (1695–1762), 46n3, 83n2
Rubens, Sir Peter Paul (1577–1640), 46, 46n5, 78, 124, 124n7, 125
Russell, John (1745–1806), 290n10
Schedoni, Bartolomeo (1578–1615), 260, 260n8
Shutor (Shuter), Thomas (*fl.* 1725), 50
Singleton, Henry (1766–1839), 290, 290n11
Stubbs, George (1724–1806), 293, 293n1
Teniers, David II (1610–90), 78, 78n4, 124, 125, 125n10
Titian (*c*.1488–1576), 125, 125n4
van Dyck, Anthony (1599–1641), 125n8, 256n7
van Loo (Vanloos), J. B. (1614–70), 50, 50n8
van Rijn, Rembrandt Harmenszoon (1606–69), 125n9
van Ruisdael, Jacob (1628–82), 291n6
Vandyke, Peter (1729–99), 78, 124n5
Veronese, Paolo (1528–88), 125, 125n1
Westall, Richard (1765–1836), 292n1
Wilson, Richard (1712/13–82), 80n2
Wouwerman, Philips (1619–68), 124, 124n20
Wright, Joseph (1734–97), 290, 290n7, 292
Askeaton (Askeyton), Co. Limerick, xx, **27**, 239, 240, 241, 242
Atcham, Shropshire (Salop), xvii, **26**, 69, 70n1, 73, 312
Athassel (Rathassel), Co. Tipperary, 270, 270n5
Atlantic Ocean, 217, 226, 227, 235, 236
Aylesbury, 5
Aylmour, see Almer.

Bagwell, Colonel John (1752–1816), 156, 156n2
Ballinasilloge, Co. Wicklow, xviii, 141
Ballinclare, Co. Kerry, xix, 232, 233
Ballincollig powdermills, Co. Cork, 186n9

Ballingarry Island (Ballengary), Co. Kerry, xix, 235, 236n1, 237, 322
Ballybeg Glen, Co. Cork, 250
Ballyclough, Co. Cork, xviii, **29**, 181, 181n3
Ballyellis, Co. Wicklow, 141
Ballyheige (Ballyhighe), Co. Kerry, xix, **27**, 224, 235, 237
Ballyhooly, Co. Cork, xviii, **29**, 176, 177n1
Ballymagooly (Ballymahooly), Co. Cork, 178
Ballymore Eustace, Co. Wicklow, xviii, **27**, **28**, **30**, **31**, 123, 123n3, 126n2, 309
Ballynamona, Co. Cork, xviii, **29**, 181
Balrothery (Balruddery), Co. Dublin, 304
Baltinglass, Co. Wicklow, **27**, **28**, **30**, **31**, 116, 123
Bandon, Co. Cork, 187, 187n4, 187n5, 189, 191
Bangor, Gwynedd, xvii, **26**, 98
Bantry, Co. Cork, xix, **27**, **30**, 195, 196–7, 198n1
Bantry Bay, Co. Cork, 194, 198, 199n1, 204, 217
barracks,
    Arklow (Co. Wicklow), 140
    Clonmel (Co. Tipperary), 155, 155n4
    Cork, 257, 323
    Drumgoff (Co. Wicklow), 120n1
    Fermoy (Co. Cork), 170–71, 170n5, 174, 174n3, 175
    Glencree (Co. Wicklow), 112n4
    Laragh (Co. Wicklow), 129n1
    Limerick, 243, 243n1
    Prosperous (Co. Kildare), 286n1
Barrigone (Barryowen) well, Co. Limerick, 239
Barry, James Redmond, Viscount Buttevant (no dates), 190n6
Barters, Misses (of Belleview, Cork), 261, 262n1
Basingwerk Abbey, Flintshire, 88, 90
Battersea, Constance, Lady (1843–1931), 5
battles and battlefields,
    Arklow (1798), 138, 139
    the Boyne (1690), 19, **30**, **31**, 301, 334, 335–6
    Clontarf (1014), 329
    Newtownmountkennedy (1798), 115n5
    Trafalgar (1805), 219, 305
    Vinegar Hill (1798), 123
Beeston coal, 55
Belleview, Co. Cork, 261, 261n4
Bellevue Demesne, Co. Wicklow, 113, 114n5
Berkeley, Bishop George (1685–1753), 17
Benthall (Benthal) Edge, Shropshire (Salop), 61, 61n5
Bewdley, Worcestershire, xvii, **26**, 52, 53, 54, 56–7, 58, 311
bills, 53, 61, 73, 75, 76, 77, 81, 83, 85, 90, 90–91, 91, 92, 94, 95, 97, 98, 106, 112, 124, 132, 134, 139, 146, 157, 162–3, 169, 176, 181, 188, 214, 219, 222, 223, 231, 257, 280, 342

Birches, The, (Beeches), Shropshire (Salop): landslip at, 66
Birr Castle, Co. Offaly, 3, 343
Bishop's Court, Co. Kildare, 286n3
Blackrock Castle, Co. Cork, 183n5
Blarney, Co. Cork, xix, **29**, 186, 186n3, 260
Blasket Islands (Blasquets), Co. Kerry, 13n3, **27**, 227, 227n4, 228, 229–30, 321–2
Blenheim Palace park, Oxfordshire, 42n3
Blessington (Blessingtown), Co. Wicklow, xviii, **27**, **28**, **29**, **31**, 116, 120, 121
Blood, Mr (d. 1801, victim of highway robbery), 285, 285n1
Bodnant (Boednod) House, Conwy, 95, 95n1
bogs,
　Annahala (Anahaly), Co. Cork, 190
　Barry's Bog, Co. Cork, 190–91
　bog bursts ('moving bogs'), 272, 272n6
　bog finds, 135, 190–91, 261, 272, 288
　Bog of Allen, 261, 281, 281n7,
　Monaincha (Monela, Mowla), Co. Tipperary, 281, 281n6, 283
　reclamation of, 116, 191, 281, 281n7, 283, 285
　walking over, 120, 128, 190, 218
Bonaparte, Napoleon (1769–1821), 4, 18, 274n2, 341
Bonomi, Joseph (1796–1878, sculptor and Egyptologist), 3, 3n1, 343–4, 343n1
booleying (transhumance), 217, 217n5
Bóruma (Bóruma, Boru), Brian (high-king of Ireland, d. 1014), 278, 278n4, 288, 288n11
Bourchier, Lady (of Worcester, d. 1726), memorial to, 43
Bourchier, John Richard (of Worcester, d. 1728), memorial to, 43
Boydell Shakespeare Gallery, 214n2
Boyle, Lady Katherine (d. 1630), 294n10
Brandon Hill, Co. Kerry, 224, 225, 322
Briain, Domnall Mór Ua (Dermot OBrien) (king of Thomond, d. 1194), 268n2
Bray, Co. Wicklow, xviii, 20, **27**, **28**, **30**, 107, 109, 111, 316
Breidden (Breedon, Brithing) Hill, Worcestershire, 42, 73
brick kilns, 53, 54, 61, 310
Bridgeman, Orlando, 1st Earl of Bradford (1762–1825), 74n2
Bridgnorth (Bridgenorth), Shropshire (Salop), xvii, **26**, 56, 58, 59, 61, 311
British Association for the Advancement of Science, 3, 343, 343n4
Broadway Hill, Worcestershire, xvii, 42
Brodrick, George, 4th Viscount Midleton (1754–1836), 184, 184n2

Brown, Peter (Bishop of Cork and Ross in 1710–35), 192, 192n2
Browne, Mary (Lady Kenmare, no dates), 211n4
Browne, Valentine, 5th Viscount and 1st Earl of Kenmare (1754–1812), 204, 204n2
Browne's Hill House (Browns Walls), Co. Carlow, 145, 145n4
Buildwas (Bildwas), Shropshire (Salop), xvii, 61, 66, 69
Bullock, William (bap. 1773, d. 1849, Liverpool naturalist and antiquary), 52, 52n1, 93
Burganey, Captain John (d. 1798), 115, 115n3, 116
Burgh, Thomas (1744–1810, MP), 298, 298n6, 307n1
Burke, Edmund (1729/30–1797, politician and author), 10, 12, 271, 271n3, 288
Burke, John (1789–1845, priest and political activist), 306n6
Burnham House (Ballingolin), Co. Kerry, 227, 227n1
Burnt Rock promontory, Co. Wicklow, 109, 109n8, 316
Butler, Eleanor (1739–1829), 68, 68n1
Butler, Walter, 1st Marquess of Ormonde (1770–1820), 149, 149n6
Buttevant, Co. Cork, xx, **27**, **29**, 249–50
Byron, Lord (1788–1824), 4

Caergwrle Castle, Flintshire, 85, 85n4, 315, 315n3
Callan, Co. Kilkenny, xviii, 16, **27**, **28**, **30**, **31**, 152–3
Cambridge University, 2, 3, 4, 35, 37–8, 40, 41, 101, 104, 305
Campbell, Thomas (1733–95), 13, 13n5, 104n6, 149n8
canals, England and Wales,
　Chester Canal, 79
　Chester and Ellesmere Canal, 79, 81
　Shropshire Union Canal, 76n10
canals, Ireland,
　Boyne Navigation, 302n2
　Grand Canal, 245n3, 286, 286n7, 300, 300n4, 300n7
　Royal Canal, 300, 300n5
Capel Curig (Cerig), Conwy, xvii, 97, 98
Capel Island (Cape Island, Lanagappul), Co. Cork, 224, 325
Cappoquin, Co. Waterford, xviii, **27**, **29**, 156, 157–8, 161, 163, 164, 168, 170, 229, 339n3
Carlow town, xviii, **27**, **28**, **30**, **31**, 106, 139, 143, 144, 145, 146–7, 148, 163
Carnew (Curnew), Co. Wicklow, 141–2
Carr, Sir John (1772–1832, travel writer), 13, 14, 16, 103n6, 104n1, 133n2, 171n1, 206n2
Carrick-on-Suir (Carreg, Carrig), Co. Tipperary, xx, **27**, **28**, **30**, **31**, 265, 327, 328

INDEX

Carrigacunna (Carreg a hunor), Co. Cork, 177, 177n7

Carrigadrohid (Carrickarudrig), Co. Cork, xix, **29**, 189, 189n4

Carrignacurra tower house, Co. Cork, 191n7

Carrignavar, Co. Cork, xviii, **29**, 181n4

Cashel, Co. Tipperary, xx, **27**, **29**, 266–7, 268, 272, 279

Castell Dinas Bran, Denbighshire, 79, 79n1, 80, 81, 313

Castle Howard, Co. Wicklow, 111n4

Castle Richards, Co. Cork, xviii, 169, 169n1

Castleconnell, Co. Limerick, xx, **29**, 276, 329

Castlehyde, Co. Cork, 176, 176n4

Castlelands tower house and bawn, Co. Cork, 249n3

Castlemaine (Castlemain), Co. Kerry, xix, 232–3

Castlemartyr, Co. Cork, 262, 262n4

Castletown, Co. Laois, xx, 283

Castletownroche, Co. Cork, xx, **29**, 248, 250, 250n4, 299n4

Castletownsend, Co. Cork, 299

Caughley (Cofley), Shropshire (Salop), 60, 61

Caum (Coum), Co. Cork, xix, 189

Cavendish, William, 6th Duke of Devonshire (1790–1858), 164n2

Cefn Mawr, Wrexham, xvii, 81

Chillingworth, Henry (of Holt Castle, d. c.1841), 54, 54n3

Chipping Norton, Oxfordshire, xvii, **26**, 42

Chirk, Wrexham, xvii, 75, 76–8

Clarke, Edward Daniel (1769–1822, traveller and mineralogist), 3, 5, 184n5

Clashmore, Co. Waterford, xx, **29**, 158, 262

Claude glass, 11, 58, 58n6

Clifden, Co. Galway, 3, 343

Cloghane (Clahan), Co. Kerry, xix, 224, 225

Clogheen (Cloghen), Co. Tipperary, xx, 166, 248, 249, 250, 266

Cloghleagh Castle, Co. Cork, 171n3

Clondalkin, Co. Dublin, xx, **28**, **30**, **31**, 286

Clonmel, Co. Tipperary, xviii, xx, **27**, **29**, 155, 156, 157, 158, 170, 262, 265, 266, 272, 273, 274, 327, 328

Clonmore (Klenmore), Co. Carlow, xviii, **28**, 144, 144n3

coal mining,
  coalpits, 69, 77, 78, 79, 85, 88
  collieries, 58, 58n3, 78

Coalbrookdale (Collbrook Dale), Shropshire (Salop), xvii, 21, 57, 59, 62–3, 68
  Darby's (Derby's) ironworks, 62, 62n4,

Coalport, Shropshire (Salop), 60

Cobh (Cove), Co. Cork, xviii, **27**, **29**, 184, 185

coded text, 2, 42, 42n4, 51, 63, 74, 75, 238, 246, 254, 255, 256, 259, 260, 270, 323, 336, 339

Coddington, Henry (1734–1816, MP), 334, 334n1

Coffy (Coffey) (fl. 1805–7, innkeeper), 208, 208n2, 209, 216, 218, 221, 222, 223, 227n4, 231, 260

collecting, 4, 5, 7, 21, 64, 92, 138, 152, 208, 222

Colworth House (Bedfordshire), 2, 341

Connemara, 3

Connor Hill (Cannur, Cunnur), Co. Kerry, xix, 225–6, 227

Conwy, xvii, **26**, 91, 92n2, 93, 95, 142

Conyngham (Cunningham), Henry, 1st Marquess Conyngham (1766–1832), 301, 301n6

Cooper, Edward Joshua (1798–1863, astronomer), 3, 343, 343n6

Cork city and surrounding area, xviii–xix, xx
  Belvelly tower house, 183
  Glanmire (Glandmeir), xviii, xx, **29**, 183, 185, 262
  Haulbowline (Arbolin) Island, xviii, 184
  Hop Island, xviii, 183
  Lapps Island, 183
  Little Island, 183, 324
  Passage West, xviii, **29**, 184, 324
  Rock Island, 184
  Sundays Well, xviii, 185

Cornwallis, Charles, 1st Marquess Cornwallis (1738–1805), 279, 279n3

Cotter, Sir James Laurence, 2nd Baronet (1748–1829), 178, 178n3, 180

Coventry, 4th Earl of, Gilbert (1666–1719), 54, 54n5

Cromwell, Oliver (1599–1658), 78, 178, 178n1

Crosbie, Colonel James (c.1760–1836, of Ballyheigue Castle), 235, 235n6, 236, 237

Crosbie, John, 2nd Earl of Glandore (1753–1815), 234, 234n3

cullum, 158, 159, 160

cultivation of crops,
  clover, 35, 37
  corn, 35, 55, 68, 91, 121, 135, 140, 141, 167, 197, 245, 285, 314
  hops, 36, 55
  oats, 35, 52, 144, 188, 191
  potato, 121, 140, 142, 143, 171, 178, 181, 191, 194, 198, 232, 307
  rapeseed, 285
  Swedish turnip (*rutabaga*, swede), 268
  turnip, 281, 285
  wheat, 52, 143, 191, 285

Curr, John (c.1756–1823, railway innovator), 62, 62n2

Curragh, Co. Kildare, xx, 284, 285

Curran, John Philpot (1750–1817, politician and lawyer), 287, 287n4, 301

currency, xvi, 99, 163, 163n1, 180, 243–4
Cyclopaedian Magazine, 293

Daly (née Maxwell), Lady Harriet (d. 1852), 114, 114n9
dancing, 161, 195, 232, 259, 293, 297
    masquerade at Waterford, 264–5
'Danish mounds', see ringforts (*ráth*).
Darwin, Charles (1809–82), 5, 73n3
Davies, Mutton (of Gwysaney, 1634–84), 86, 86n2, 87n4
de Clare, Richard, 2nd Earl of Pembroke (Strongbow) (1130–76), 99, 99n6, 272n4
deforestation, 166, 177, 193, 211
Delgany, Co. Wicklow, xviii, 114
Delille, Jacques, *l'Homme des Champs* (1800), 119n2
Dent, Edward John (1790–1853, chronometer maker), 6
Derry Castle, Co. Clare, 278
Derrymore, Co. Kerry, xix, 223–4, 232, 233
Devil's Glen, Co. Wicklow, xviii, 111, 133–4
Dingle, Co. Kerry, xix, **27**, 222, 223, 224, 225, 226, 227, 228, 230, 231
disease, 52, 189, 192–3
Doneraile, Co. Cork, xx, **29**, 248–9, 250–1, 271
Doughill (Duhill), Co. Cork, xix, 194
drawing and sketching, 2, 4, 11, 21, 23, 36, 37, 38, **39**, 41n4, 43n4, 44, 46n8, 47, **48**, **49**, 50n5, 52n4, 53n2, 54n2, 55n3, 56n3, 57n7, 60n1, 60n8, 61n2, 64n3, 65, 66, **67**, 69n4, 70n3, 71n1, 76n1, 77n2, 77n3, 79n2, 79n3, 80n4, 81n1, 81n2, 82, 85n3, 85n4, 87n6, 89, 90n1, 91, 92, 94, 95, 96, 106n3, 106n4, 107, **108**, 109n8, 110, 111n1, 114n7, 121, 123n5, 126, 127n3, 128n3, 129, **131**, 134n2, 136n5, 137, 141, 142, 144, 146, **147**, 148, 151, 156, 158, **159**, 164, 167, 168, 171, 174n3, 177, 188n6, 189n3, 191n3, 198, 206n1, 217n1, 225n2, 226n1, 227n2, 227n3, 227n4, 228n1, 229n1, 230n2, 235n1, 235n7, 239n2, 241n7, 247n3, 248n5, 254n2, 259, 260n7, 261, 262n3, 262n5, 262n6, 263n3, 264n1, 264n2, 265, 265n3, 265n5, 265n6, 266, 266n2, 269, 276n4, 276n5, 276n6, 276n7, 278n2, 278n3, 278n6, 278n7, 280n6, 281, 281n1, 281n3, 281n4, **282**, 284n6, 294n, 299, 301, 302, 302n3, 302n4, 302n5, 302n6, 302n7, 302n8, 304n1, 304n2, 304n4, 304n5, 305, 306, 309–39
dress and fashions, 46, 47, 161, 256
Dripsey, Co. Cork, xix, **29**, 188–9, 252, 319
Drogheda, Co. Louth, xx, 19, **27**, **30**, **31**, 301, 302, 304, 337–8
Dromana, Co. Waterford, xviii, 157
Dublin Bay, xvii, 98, 99

Dublin city, xvii, xx, 1, 12, 15, 16, 17, 19, 21, **27**, **28**, **30**, **31**, 99–102, 103–6, 286–300, 304–8, 319, 329, 338, 342n4, 343–4
Duff, Sir James (1753–1839, army officer), 284, 284n
Dundrum, Co. Tipperary, xx, **29**, 271, 275
Dungarvan (Dungarvon), Co. Waterford, xx, **27**, **28**, **29**, 157, 262–3, 321, 324, 325, 326
Dunkerrin, Co. Offaly, xx, **29**, 281
Dunmore Cave, Co. Kilkenny, xviii, 17–18, **28**, **30**, **31**, 149–51
Dunmore Head, Co. Kerry, 228, 230, 321
Dunquin, Co. Kerry, 228–9, 230

Eeles, Henry (1702–81, writer), 157, 157n2
Egypt, 3, 4, 153, 184n5, 274, 344n4
Elizabeth I of England (1533–1603), 288
Ellis, William (1828–1916, astronomer), 3, 343n5
Elmor or Elmour, see Almer
Emmet, Robert (1778–1803, United Irishman), 19, 99, 99n7, 287n4
epitaphs, 44–5, 70–73, 79, 80, 80n4, 82, 82n4, 83, 84–5, 85–7, 206n2
Epps, James (1773–1840, astronomer), 6, 6n7
Esmonde, Dr John (1760?–98, United Irishman), 286n1
Eton College, 35
Evans, John (1723–95, cartographer), 76, 76n9

fairies, 135, 136, 143, 144, 270–71, 326
    punishments for human transgressions, 143, 144, 270–71
'fairy mound', see ringforts
famines, 195, 195n, 246n1
Farming Society of Ireland, 307, 307n
Felix, Major Orlando (1790–1860), 344, 344n4
Fénelon, François, *The Adventures of Telemachus* (1699), 261, 261n5
Fermoy, Co. Cork, xviii, **27**, **29**, 170–71, **172**, **173**, 174, 176, 248
Ferrar, John (of Limerick, c.1735–c.1803), 14, 245, 245n7
ferries, barges and wherries, 46, 52, 52n, 53, 55, 56, 57, 58, 59, 60, 63, 69, 91, 92, 95, 98, 99, 160, 161, 184, 185, 186, 262, 311, 324, 325
Ferris, Captain William, RN (1783–1822), 251, 251n2
Fiott, John, see John Lee.
Fiott, John (father of John Lee, d. 1797), 2
Fiott (née Lee), Harriet (mother of John Lee, d. 1794), 2, 340n5, 341n3
fish and shellfish, 60, 92, 92n2, 98, 98n4, 106, 139, 140, 142, 152, 158, 160, 168, 190, 197, 200, 213, 225, 230, 253, 256, 257, 272

INDEX

fishing, 55, 98, 157, 158, 160, 161–2, 177, 183, 189, 190, 195, 198, 213, 216, 219, 220, 225, 236, 239
Fitzgerald, Maurice, 18th knight of Kerry (1772–1849), 237, 237n9
FitzGibbon, John, 1st Earl of Clare (1748–1802), 276n2, 288n3
Fitzwilliam, William Wentworth, 4th Earl Fitzwilliam (1748–1833), 143, 143n1
Fellowes (Fellows), Captain William D. (*fl.* 1803), 98, 98n5
Flynn (OFlyn), Dennis (*fl.* 1806–7, Cork grocer), 255, 255n2, 257, 262
food and dining, 53, 55, 56, 61, 69, 98, 104, 111, 138, 147, 157, 161, 162, 163, 170, 182, 184, 186, 191, 194, 208, 222, 225, 229, 257
Foljambes of Derby, 171, 171n2, 175, 265
foxhunting, 167, 186
Francis II, Holy Roman Emperor (r. 1792–1806), 340–41, 340n7
funerals (Ireland), 129, 132, 152, 219, 222
  keening, 219, 219n, 222, 238
  wakes, 219, 220–21, 222, 238

game (birds and animals), 189, 190, 229–30, 213, 216, 252, 268
Garde (Gaard, Gard, Grade, Guard, Guarde), Joseph (of Cork, d. 1835), 220, 220n2, 253, 253n2, 254, 255, 258, 259, 260, 261, 262, 287, 300, 300n6, 307
gardens, kitchen gardens, 37, 46, 102, 113–14
general election of 1806, 237
George III of England (r. 1760–1820), 50, 50n12, 68, 68n3
ghosts, 135, 136, 208, 222n2, 270
Giant's Causeway, Co. Antrim, 104, 289
Gillespie (Galespi), William (*fl.* 1806–20, pianist and teacher), 254, 254n1, 258–9, 260
Gilpin, William (1724–1804), 10, 11
Gipps, Henry (1786–1832, curate), 340, 340n6
Glendalough (Seven Churches), Co. Wicklow, xviii, **27**, **28**, **29**, **31**, 111, 129, 129n2, **130**, 135, 318
Golden, Co. Tipperary, xx, **29**, 270, 272
Gore, Captain Robert (*fl.* 1798, of Newtownmountkennedy Cavalry), 115, 115n4, 115n5
Gothic, the, 10–11, 15, 17–19
Gougane Barra (Gogon Barry) Lake and church ruins, Co. Cork, xix, 14, 190, 191, 192–4
Grandison, George, Earl of (d. 1800), 157, 157n3
graveyards, 107, 112–13, 129, 148, 188, 208–9, 222, 234, 236–7, 316
  remains visible at, 188, 209, 234, 237, 249, 270
guidebooks, 13–14, 37, 37n6, 45, 45n5, 73, 73n2

guides, local, 15, 21, 66, 68, 69, 77, 111, 149, 150, 188, 217, 217n4, 235, 236, 287
Gunn (Gun), George (of Mount Kennedy), Co. Wicklow, 115, 115n1

Hacketstown, Co. Carlow, 142, 143, 144
Hartwell House, Buckinghamshire, 2, 4, 5, 6, 10, 21, 344
Henley, Oxfordshire, 11, 36, 37
Herbert, Charles John (of Muckross, 1785–1823), 199, 199n7
Herbert, Henry Arthur (1756–1821, landowner and MP), 237, 237n8, 238
Higgins, William (*c.*1762/3–1825, chemist), 299, 299n2, 300
highway robberies, 74, 74n3, 284–5, 285n1
Hill, Arthur, 2nd Marquess of Downshire (1753–1801), 121, 121n6
Hill, Arundel (of Co. Cork, *fl.* 1806–7), 245, 248, 248n1, 249, 251, 275
Hill, Captain Launcelot (*fl.* 1806–7), 242, 246, 275
HMS *Gloire* (*Glory*), 164, 164n3
Hoare, Richard Colt (1758–1838, travel writer), 12, 13, 14
Hodson (Hodson), Sir Robert (of Hollybrook, Co. Wicklow, 1747–1809), 111, 111n5, 112
Holt, Worcestershire, xvii, 53, 54, 55, 56, 310
holy wells, 15, 15n4, 87, 175–6, 189, 208, 208n1
  Kilmurry (Co. Cork), 189
  St Finian's Well (Co. Kerry), 208, 208n1
  Tobernahulla (Co. Waterford), 175–6
Holycross, Co. Tipperary, xx, 268–9, 268n2, 272
Holyhead, Wales, xvii, **26**, 97, 98, 344
Holywell, Flintshire, xvii, 87n6, 88, 315
Hooker, Joseph Dalton (1817–1911, botanist), 5
Hooker, Sir William Jackson (1785–1865, botanist), 5
Horace, 188, 263, 296n8
Howth (Houth), Co. Dublin, 100, 102, 106, 112, 338, 339
Hughes, Reverend Edward (of Kinmel estate, *fl.* 1786–1806), 90, 90n9
Hume, Captain William (1747–98, politician), 116, 116n3
hunting, 59, 162, 163, 167, 187, 213, 216, 228, 252
Hutton, William (1723–1815), 11

Inchigeelagh (Inchegela), Co. Cork, xix, 191, 319
inns and hotels,
  Blake's Hotel (Cork), 182
  Cantrell's Inn (Nenagh), 12, 278–9, 278n8
  Coffy's Hotel (Killarney), 208n2, 223, 319
  Cross Foxes Inn (Oswestry), 75
  Eagles, The (Ruabon), 81, 83

371

Fitzpatrick's Inn (Nenagh), 280
Gresham Hotel (Dublin), 343
Lynch (Mallow), 180
Marquis of Rockingham Arms (Rathdrum), 134
McEvoy's Hotel (Dublin), 99, 99n2
Moriarty's Inn (Dingle), 231, 231n6
Mr Gaitland's Hotel (Dublin), 329
Mrs Coffy's (Carlow), 148
New Inn (Lismore), 167
New Inn (Nesscliffe), 73, 74
Newtown Inn (Kilmacthomas), 263
Nolan's (Rathnew), 134n8
Quinn's (Bray), 112, 112n1
Red Lion (Wrexham), 81
Rhydlanvair Inn (Rhyd-Lanfair), 97
Rovings public house (Apley), 60, 60n4
Saracen's Head (Bewdley), 56
Star and Garter (Worcester), 43, 46, 52, 53
Swinburne's Hotel (Limerick), 12, 242, 246, 319
Talbot Inn (Atcham), 69, 73
Tontine Inn (Iron Bridge), 59, 60, 66
Wheatsheaf Inn (Kilkenny), 149, 152
Whitehorse Cellar (London), 35, 35n2
York Hotel Tavern (Youghal), 162
industry and manufacturing,
 aqua fortis and vitriol works (Worcestershire), 57
 bacon and pork meat salting and curing, 154, 274
 china manufactories, 21, 47–50, 47n1, **48, 49**
 distilleries, 50–51, 259
 foundries, 55, 55n5
 iron mills, 21, 59, 62
 mills, 90, 98, 132, 154, 177, 186, 189, 247
insects, 54
 aphids, 21, 37, 309
 clover mites (*Bryobia praetiosa*), 54, 54n1
 midges, 118–19
Ireland, people of,
 accent (brogue), 244
 beliefs, see also fairies, 17, 175, 213
 character, 15, 103, 176, 265–6
 children, 95, 127, 146, 178, 195, 232
 cleanliness and dirt, 16, 100, 155, 163, 181, 182, 195, 242, 255
 clothing, 100, 174, 177, 219, 332
 conversations with, 127, 128, 132, 138, 145, 147–8, 153, 165, 166, 169, 176, 182, 187, 188, 201, 223, 225, 231, 240, 244, 246, 263, 266, 267, 268, 270, 271, 273, 274, 275, 279, 280, 283, 284
 food, 126, 147, 191, 194–5, 225, 229–30, 307
 health, see also disease, 126
 housing, 16, 126, 155, 160, 255, 275, 320, 332, 333, 338
Irish Sea, 98, 184n6

Iron Bridge, Shropshire (Salop), xvii, 21, 59–61, 66, 312

James II and VII, king of England, Scotland and Ireland (1633–1701), 19, 187, 187n4, 189, 301, 334, 335
Jameson, Robert (1774–1854, natural historian and geologist), 14
Jephson, Denham (1748?–1813, politician), 155, 155n2, 179, 180
Jigginstown House ruins, Co. Kildare, 285
Johnson, Richard, *The Famous Historie of the Seaven Champions of Christendom* (1596/7), 145, 145n7
Jones, Frederick Edward (1759–1834, theatre manager), 293, 293n6
Judkin-Fitzgerald, Lady Elizabeth (*fl.* 1785–1806), 267, 267n4
Judkin-Fitzgerald, Sir Thomas (1754–1810), 19, 153n6, 154n1, 267, 267n3, 279
Juvenal, 188, 289

Kenmare, Co. Kerry, xix, **27**, 200–201, 203, 216, 223, 320
Kerry Head, Co. Kerry, xix, 235, 236, 237, 322
Kilcrea (Kilcray) Abbey, Co. Cork, xix, 188, 188n3
Kildare town, xx, 284, 284n6
Killaloe, Co. Clare, xx, **27**, **29**, **277**, 278, 278n2, 279, 330, 331
Killarney, Co. Kerry, and surrounding area, xix, 320, 200–222
 Brewsterfield, 214
 chalybeate spring, 206
 Devil's Punch Bowl, 216–18, 221
 Dunloe Castle, xix, 209, 215
 Foiladuane (Philadown), xix, 214, 215, 216, 218, 223
 Gap of Dunloe, xix, 209, 210n1
 Horse's Glen, 218
 Irrelagh Franciscan friary, 208n3, 208–9
 Killaha or Killagh Augustinian priory, 214, 214n5
 Labig Owen, 215
 Lough Erhogh, 217–18
 Lough Garagarry, 216–17
 Lough Guitane, 216
 Lough Managh, 217
 Mangerton, xix, 216, 218, 320
Killarney, Lakes of, 210–14, 221–2
Killavullen (Keilvillar, Killavillin), Co. Cork, xviii, **29**, 177, 178
Killiney (Killaney), Co. Kerry, xix, 224
Kilkenny city, xviii, **27**, **28**, **30**, **31**, 148, 149, 152
Kilmacthomas, Co. Waterford, xx, **28**, 263, 326, 328

INDEX

Kilmalkedar (Keilmicud daw), Co. Kerry, 236–7, 237n1
Kilworth, Co. Cork, xviii, **29**, 147, **172**, 174, 176
Kirwan, Walter Blake (1754–1805, Dublin clergyman), 307, 307n3
Kynaston (Kynnaston), Humphrey (*c*.1468–1534, highwayman), 74, 74n3
Kynnaston cave, Shropshire (Salop), 74

La Surveillante (frigate), 199, 199n1
La Touche family (Dublin bankers), 306, 306n12
lakes (England and Wales),
    Bala Lake (Llyn Tegid), Gwynedd, 79, 79n5
    Harley Lake, 58
lakes (Ireland), see also Gougane Barra, Killarney
    Cappanaboul Lough (Co. Cork), 195, 195n3
    Lough Dan (Co. Wicklow), 117
    Lough Derg (Cos Clare, Galway, Tipperary), 332
    Lough Dromanassa (Droumeneasting) (Co. Cork), 195
    Lough Nahanagan (Co. Wicklow), 135
    Lough Tay (Co. Wicklow), 117
land reclamation, see also cultivation of crops, 191, 197, 198, 250, 281, 281n7, 283, 285
Landaff, Earls of, 267, 267n7
landscape, 2, 10–12, 17, 96–7, 98, 180, 202, 252, 271, 299
Lady Hobart (packet ship), 98n5
languages,
    Irish, 1, 1n2, 15–16, 25, 109, 140n2, 166, 167, 180, 180n2, 187, 210n1, 211n2, 217–18, 217n3, 226, 229, 231, 231n1, 237, 240n3, 249, 255, 255n2, 258, 263, 269, 321n4
    Latin, 45, 153, 188, 244, 255, 264, 269, 294
    Welsh, 1, 16, 24, 77, 78, 83, 92, 95
Latocnaye, Jacques-Louis de Bougrenet, Chevalier de (1767–1823), 190n1, 196n2, 209n1, 211n6, 222n2, 235n3
Latouche (Le Touche), Peter (1775?–1830, of Bellevue, Co. Wicklow), 111, 111n6, 113, 114, 117, 121
latrines, 163, 163n2, 164, 339, 339n3
Lawson, Henry (1774–1855, astronomer), 6, 6n
Lee, John (né Fiott, 1783–1866), **iv**, 2–10, 11–22, 340–44
    self-portrait as donkey, 324
Lee (née Rutter), Cecilia (first wife of John Lee, d. 1854), 6
Lee (née Wilkinson), Louisa Catherine (second wife of John Lee, b. 1830), 6
Leighlinbridge, Co. Carlow, xviii, **28**, **30**, **31**, 148
Lewis, *Topographical Dictionary*, 121n8, 132n3, 133n3, 134n3, 183n6, 272n4
lichen, 90, 127, 202

Limerick city, xx, 10, 14, **27**, **29**, 240–46, 247–8, 249, 275–6, 319, 329
Linnaeus, Carl (1707–78, botanist), 20, 21
    Linnaean taxonomy, 40, 40n6
Linwood, Mary (1755–1845, artist in needlework), 289–93, 289n8
Lisheen, Co. Tipperary, xx, 268, 272, 272n5
Lismore, Co. Waterford, xviii, **27**, **29**, 158, 163, 164, 165, 167, 168, 169
Listowel (Listhowel), Co. Kerry, xix, xx, **27**, 238, 240
literacy, 36, 112, 145, 153, 167, 255, 263
Liúir (Leur) Rocks, Co. Kerry, 228
Liverpool, 52, 85, 92, 93, 94
livestock, 217, 217n5
    bulls, 133–4, 170, 268, 307
    cows, 127, 170, 218, 228, 248, 268, 301, 307
    goats, 117, 138, 142, 170, 171, 192
    pigs, 51, 97, 107, 127, 154–5, 160, 170, 245, 274, 280, 281, 307, 338
    sheep, 210–11, 228, 230, 232, 248, 268, 270, 271, 281, 285, 301, 307
Llangollen, Denbighshire, xvii, **26**, 68, 76, 78–9, 80, 81, 313
Llantysilio (Llandsilio), Denbighshire, xvii, 79n6, 80, 313
Loftus (packet ship), 98n5
Loghill, Co. Limerick, xx, **29**, **30**, 238–9, 322, 323
London, xvii, **26**, 35n2, 154, 340, 341
    comparisons with, 100, 101, 242, 293, 297, 305, 307
Lovers' Leap, Co. Wicklow, xviii, 7, **28**, **30**, **31**, 109–10, 135, 316
Luggala (Luggila), Co. Wicklow, **27**, **28**, **30**, **31**, 111, 317
Luggala Lodge, Co. Wicklow, xviii, 117, 117n1, 127n5
Lyell, Sir Charles (1797–1875, geologist), 5

MacCumhaill, Fionn (Foun Mal Coul), 165, 165n1
Maclear, Sir Thomas (1794–1879, astronomer), 5
Macpherson (McPherson), James (1736–96, author), 255, 255n5
Macroom, Co. Cork, **27**, **29**, 189–90, 319
Maen Achwyfan, Flintshire, 89n2
Magrath (d. 1760, Irish giant), 104n5
Maidenhead, xvii, **26**, 36
Malahide, Co. Dublin, xviii, **27**, **28**, **30**, **31**, 102
Mallow, Co. Cork, xviii, xx, 155n, 176, 178, 179, 181, 251, 299
mammals,
    common rabbit (*Oryctolagus cuniculus*), 90, 150, 177, 198, 229, 230, 268
    deer (*Cervidae*), 41, 81, 179, 198, 271

grey seal (*Halichoerus grypus*): hunting of, 198, 200, 236
stags (*Cervidae*), 202
marble, 21, 91, 120, 126, 128, 148, 150, 151–2, 154, 202, 209
Markree Castle and observatory (Co. Sligo), 3, 343, 343n6
Marlow (Bucks.), xvii, **26**, 35–6, 37
Maryborough (Portlaoise), Co. Laois, xx, **28**, **30**, **31**, 283, 284
Maude, Cornwallis, 3rd Viscount Hawarden (1780–1856), 272, 272n1
Meade, Sir John, 2nd Earl of Clanwilliam (1744–1800), 270, 270n3
Meeting of the Waters, Co. Wicklow, 136, 136n2
Merlin, John Joseph (1735–1803, inventor), 159, 159n1
Methodism, 92, 107, 187n5
Middlemen, see agents
Military Road, Co. Wicklow, 120, 120n1, 128, 132, 317
Millstreet, Co. Cork, xx, **27**, **29**, 251, 252
minerals, 17–18, 21, 22n2, 103–4, 289
  calamine (calomine), 89, 90
  spar, 236, 236n4
mines, see also coal mining
  Benthall Edge (stone, Shropshire), 61
  Cronebane (copper, Co. Wicklow), xviii, 136–8
  Luggala (silver, Co. Wicklow), 120, 143
  Ross Island (copper, Co. Kerry), 204n4, 205, 206–8
  Talargoch (Delargo) (lead, Flintshire), 89–90
Mold, Flintshire, xvii, **26**, 87, 87n1, 87n2, 87n3, 87n5
Monasterevin, Co. Kildare, xx, **28**, **30**, **31**, 284
Moorepark, Co. Cork, xviii, 147, 171n3, 174
Mostyn, Flintshire, xvii, **26**, 88
Mottee Stone, Co. Wicklow, **28**, **30**, **31**, 135, 135n1
Mount Cashell, Earls of, 147, 171, 171n, 266n4
mountains and mountain ranges (Ireland),
  Blackmore (Blackamoor) Hill (Co. Wicklow), 121, 127
  Comeragh Mountains (Co. Waterford), **28**, **29**, 263
  Cronebane (Co. Wicklow), 135, 135n1, 136
  Derrycunihy (Co. Kerry), 213
  Devil's Bit (Co. Tipperary), 281, 332
  Glena (Glenaa, Glenaw) (Co. Kerry), 211, 212, 216, 252
  Glencree (Glan Cree) (Co. Wicklow), 112
  Great Sugar Loaf (Co. Wicklow), **28**, **30**, **31**, 100, 107, 111, 315, 316–17

  Knockmealdown (Knock Meldown, Knockmil down) (Cos Tipperary, Waterford), 15, 157, 165n2
  Little Sugar Loaf (Co. Wicklow), 100, 107, 112, 316
  Luggala (Co. Wicklow), **27**, **28**, **30**, **31**, 111, 117
  Mangerton (Co. Kerry), xix, 216, 218, 252
  Scalp (Co. Wicklow), **28**, **30**, **31**, 106, 111, 112, 113, 315
  Slieve Bloom (Cos Laois, Offaly), 281, 283
  Slieve Mish (Slaighmish, Shlamish) (Co. Kerry), 222
Murchison, Sir Roderick (1792–1871, geologist), 5
Musgrave, Sir Richard, 1st Baronet (1746?–1818), 157, 157n4, 263, 263n5
music and musicians, 99, 102, 176, 211, 253, 254, 255, 257, 259, 262, 302–3
  Arne, Thomas (composer, 1710–78), 258n1
  Belfast Harpers' Festival, 303, 303n2
  Black, Daniel (*c.*1716–96, harper), 303, 303n6
  Bowden, John (d. 1829, composer, violinist and teacher), 253, 253n4, 255n6, 258, 260
  Byrne (O Byrn), Charles (*c.*1712–*c.*1810, harper), 303, 303n7
  Carolan, Turlough (Corillin, Toirdhealbhach Ó Cearbhalláin) (1670–1738, harper), 255, 255n
  Carr (Cair), William (b. 1777, harper), 302, 302n8, 303, 336
  Catch and Glee Club (Cork), 253, 258
  Duncan, James (1747–*c.*1800, harper), 303, 303n11
  Fanning, Charles (*c.*1736–*c.*1800, harper), 303, 303n3
  fiddle, 92, 195, 232, 253, 255, 262
  Handel, George Friedrich (1685–1759, composer), 102, 102n3
  Hempson (Hampton), Denis (1695–1807, harper), 303, 303n9
  Higgins, Hugh (1737–96, harper), 303, 303n5
  Instrumental Music Club (Cork), 255
  Irish harp, 257, 288, 288n, 289, 302–3, 336
  Lynder, Patrick (dates unknown, harper), 303
  Mooney (Moony), Rose (1740–*c.*1798, harper), 303, 303n8
  O'Neill (O Neil), Arthur (1735/6–1816, harper), 302, 302n9, 303
  Quinn (Quin), Patrick (Patric) (b. *c.*1745, teacher at Irish Harp Society), 303, 303n1
  Schwindl (Swindhel), Friedrich (1737–86, composer), 256, 256n1
  songs and singing, 56, 228, 253–4, 243, 258–9, 260, 294, 295
  Welsh harp, 303
  'Williams the Welshman' (dates unknown, harper), 303, 303n4

INDEX

Naas, Co. Kildare, xx, 285–6, 287
Nenagh, Co. Tipperary, xx, 16, **29**, 278n8, 279, 280n3, 339n3
Nesscliffe (Neslip), Shropshire (Salop), xvii, 73
Nesscliffe (Nescliff) Hill, 74
Newcastle, Co. Tipperary, xviii, **29**, 156, 157
Newtownmountkennedy, Co. Wicklow, xviii, **27**, **28**, **30**, **31**, 111, 112, 113, 114, 115, 117, 127, 132
Ninemilehouse, Co. Tipperary, xviii, **28**, **30**, **31**, 153, 157

O'Briensbridge, Co. Clare, xx, **29**, 276, 329, 330
O'Connell (O Connel), Daniel (1775–1847, barrister and politician), 306, 306n8
observatories,
   Birr Castle (Co. Offaly), 3, **343**, 343n
   Cape observatory (South Africa), 5
   Hartwell House (Buckinghamshire), 4, 5, 6
   Hereford, home of Henry Lawson, 6
   Markree Castle (Co. Sligo), 3, **343**, 343n6
Old Bridgetown, Co. Louth, 301, 334
Old Connaught, Co. Wicklow, 106, 107, **108**, 109, 113, 316
'ossified man' (Trinity College, Dublin), 104, 104n6
Oswestry, Shropshire (Salop), xvii, **26**, 73, 75, 76, 77, 85
Ovens caves, Co. Cork, xix, xx, **29**, 187–8, 253
Owennashad (Oun ne sheard, Ouneshead) glen, Co. Waterford, xviii, 185
Owenson, Sydney, Lady Morgan (c.1783–1859, novelist and literary celebrity), 303, 303n10
Oxford, xvii, 21, **26**, 35, 36, 37–42, 43

Paget, Henry William, 1st Marquess of Anglesey (1768–1854), 267, 267n1
Pallas (Pallis), Co. Limerick, xx, 275
Parsons, William, 3rd Earl of Rosse (1800–67), 3, 343, 343n7
peat (turf, fuel), 92–3, 116, 127, 144, 190, 194
   cost of, 116, 127, 201, 240
   cutting of, 120, 127, 127n1, 141, 142, 156, 188, 281n7
pedestrianism, 8–10, 14, 19–20, 21, 97n2, 202, 244n4, 340, 342
Penmaenmawr (Penman mair), Conwy, xvii, 92–3
Pennant, Richard, Baron Penrhyn (c.1737–1808), 97, 97n3
Pennant, Thomas (naturalist, 1726–98), 11, 14, 20, 80n4, 84n3, 88, 88n5, 89n4
Penrose, Cooper (1736–1815), 183, 183n2, 260, 261, 261n2, 324
Percy, Hugh, 3rd Duke of Northumberland (1785–1847), 3, 3n5, 6n5, 344n4
Persius (34–62 CE, Roman poet), 289

Pery, Edmond Henry, 1st Earl of Limerick (1758–1845), 242, 242n8
Petty-Fitzmaurice, Henry, 3rd Marquess of Lansdowne (1780–1863), 200, 200n7, 201
picturesque, the, 2, 10–11, 17, 43, 96, 97, 98, 110, 116, 133, 177, 180, 198, 202, 215, 224, 239, 241, 250, 252, 271, 283, 299, 327
Pidcock, Gilbert (d. 1810, menagerist and showman), 188, 288n8
Pike, Mary (1776–1832, Quaker heiress), 261, 261n7
plays and performances, 43, 51, 162, 258, 293, 295–7, 300
   Bickerstaff, Isaac, *The Romp* (1786), 43, 43n6
   Cobb, J., *Paul and Virginia* (1801), 300, 300n13
   Colman, George the younger, *The Mountaineers* (1793), 300, 300n12
   Dibdin, Thomas, *Of Age Tomorrow* (1801), 293, 293n5
   Dimond, William, *Adrian and Orilla* (1806), 293, 293n2
   Farquhar, George, *The Beaux' Stratagem* (1707), 51, 51n4
   Fielding, Henry, *The Rehearsal* (1753), 162, 162n3
   [Anon.] *The Heiress* (1786), 295, 295n7
   Lewis, Matthew, *Rugantino* (1805), 295–6, 295n8
   Morton, Thomas, *A Cure for the Heart-Ache* (1797), 258, 258n4
   Murphy, Arthur, *The Upholsterer* (1758), 258, 258n, 6
   Townley, James, *High Life Below Stairs* (1759), 297, 297n9, 298n2, 298n5
   Shakespeare, William, *Hamlet*, 162
   Shakespeare, William, *King Lear*, 185, 340n2
   Shakespeare, William, *The Tempest*, 258n1
   Vanbrugh, Sir John, *The Provoked Husband*, 297, 297n5
Plumptre, Anne (1760–1818, travel writer), 101n7, 104n1, 136n2, 289n1
Pococke, Richard (1704–65, traveller and antiquary), 13, 13n, 235, 235n2
Pollahoney, Co. Wicklow, 139, 140, 140n2
population of Ireland, 306, 306n5
Ponsonby, George (1755–1817, Lord Chancellor of Ireland), 121, 121n2
Ponsonby, Sarah (1755–1831), 68n1
Ponsonby, William Brabazon, 1st Baron Ponsonby (1744–1806), 286, 286n3
Pontcysyllte (Pontcysyllty) aqueduct, Wrexham, xvii, 7, 81, 81n3
Poor Law, 152, 152n4
porters (boys for carrying), 21, 127, 134, 135, 135n8, 138, 170, 182, 265
Poulaphouca (Poll a Phuca) waterfall, Co. Wicklow, xviii, 125, 128n2

poverty, 14–16, 37, 59, 74, 100, 106, 139, 145, 152, 152n4, 155, 180, 240, 247n2, 274, 275, 283
Powerscourt, Co. Wicklow, xviii, 12, 109, 109n5, 110, 316
priests (catholic), 136, 138, 147, 152–3, 175, 176, 274, 283, 284–5

Quakers, 183n2, 262, 266
quarries, 64, 75, 81, 157, 167, 177, 198, 238, 280
Quatford, Shropshire (Salop), 61, 311, 312

Radcliffe, Ann (1764–1823, travel writer), 11
railways, 58n2, 61, 62, 62n1, 97
Rathdrum, Co. Wicklow, xviii, 27, **28**, **30**, **31**, 111, 134, 137
rebellion of 1798, 18–20, 99, 104–6, 105n3, 112, 112n4, 115–16, 115n3, 115n5, 116n3, 117–18, 117n3, 120–21, 121n7, 123, 124, 124n2, 127, 138, 138n2, 141, 141n1, 143, 153–4, 154n1, 163, 187, 189, 199, 246n1, 250, 267, 267n3, 273, 274, 283, 284, 284n7, 286, 286n1, 306n9
  battle at the Curragh, 284
  battle of Arklow, 138, 138n2, 139, 140
  battle of Newtownmountkennedy, 115–16
  French landing at Killala, 117–18
  Vinegar Hill, 123
  women in, 127
rebellion of 1803, 18–20, 99, 99n7, 105, 105n4, 287n4
Rhaeadr Dyserth waterfall, Denbighshire, 90, 90n5
ringforts ('Danish mounds', *ráth*), 16–17, 171, 171n1, 270, 275, 328
rivers (England and Wales),
  Severn, 43, 46, 52, 54–5, 56, 57, 59, 59n6, 64, 66, 69, 309
  Thames, 37
rivers (Ireland),
  Awbeg (Obeg) (Co. Cork), 177, 248, 249, 250, 299
  Blackwater (Co. Kerry), 199–200, 201, 204
  Blackwater (Cos Cork, Kerry, Waterford), **29**, 157–8, 169, 170, 177, 248, 299
  Boyne, 302n, 304, 334–5, 337
  Dargle, 109–10, 109n6, 111, 112, 218, 315
  Deel, 239n6, 239n7
  Dripsey, xx, **29**, 188–9, 252, 319
  Flesk, 209n, 214, 216, 220
  Galway (Co. Kerry), 204, 213
  Lee, **29**, 182, 189–90, 252, 323
  Liffey, 100, 101, 125, 317
  Shannon, 235, 235n8, 236, 238–9, 240, 243, 322, 330, 332
  Suir (Suire),

roads, poor quality of, 100, 106, 120, 132, 134, 175, 181, 182, 185, 191, 192, 194–5, 196, 214–15, 224–5, 242
Roman Catholicism, 107, 175
  churches, 147, 205–6, 208, 227
  convents, 206, 254, 256
  catholic emancipation, 306, 306n3
  religious services, 154, 208, 227, 254, 256
Roscrea, Co. Tipperary, xx, **29**, 261, **262**, 333
Ross, John (1777–1856, polar explorer), 4, 9
Ross, Sir James Clark (1800–62, polar explorer), 5
Roundwood, Co. Wicklow, xviii, 20, **28**, **30**, **31**, 111, **131**, 131–2
Royal Oak, Co. Kilkenny, xviii, **28**, **30**, **31**, 148
Russborough House, Co. Wicklow, xviii, 123, 123n1, 124–5, 124n2, 317

St Asaph, Denbighshire, xvii, **26**, 90, 91
St Leger, Hayes, 2nd Viscount Doneraile (1755–1819), 248, 248n3
St Pierre, Mr (*fl.* 1803–7, dancer), 293, 293n3, 297
Sabine, Sir Edward (1788–1883, physicist), 5
Sayers, Richard (of Greenwood, Malahide, no dates), 99, 99n1, 102, 103, 286
Scandinavia, 2, 3, 3n, 6, 7, 8, 184n5, 342
Scotland, 8, 10, 20, 342
seaweed, 160, 228, 236
Seven Churches, see Glendalough
shipwrecks, 98, 102, 199, 199n1, 230, 232
Shrewsbury, Shropshire (Salop), xvii, **26**, 52, 59, 69, 73–4, 75, 76
Sipthorpe or Sibthorpe, Dr Humphrey (1712–97, botanist), 41, 41n1
Skelligs (Sciligs), Co. Kerry, 228, 322
Smith, Charles (1715?–62, apothecary, topographer and writer), 13–14, 14n1, 185n2, 189n2, 196n3, 236n3, 264n5
smoking, 62, 81
soldiers and soldiering, 19, 109, 120–21, **122**, 123, 126, 136, 138, 153–4, 182, 257, 274, 317
solitude, 7, 82, 203
Spike Island, Co. Cork, xviii, 183, 183n4, 184
sports and games, 175
  backgammon, 229
  ball games, 106, 129, 146
  chess, 257
  fives, 144, 144n2
  hockey, 174
  hurling, 174, 174n1
  'mott', 135, 135n2
Stourport, Worcestershire, xvii, **26**, 53, 54, 56, 311
Sterne, Laurence (1713–68, novelist and clergyman), 154, 154n2
sublime, the, 10–12, 97, 199, 203, 213, 252, 263, 276

superstitions, see fairies; ghosts
Swan, Major William Bellingham (1765?–1837), 105, 105n1
Swords, Co. Dublin, 304n5, 333

theatres,
    Cork, 258, 258n5
    Dublin (Theatre Royal), 182n, 253n4, 293n3, 293n4, 293n7, 295–6, 297–8
    Limerick, 246, 246n5
    Tralee, 238
    Worcester, 43
    Youghal, 162, 163
Tighe, William (1766–1816, politician and topographer), 109, 109n4
Tinahely, Co. Wicklow, xviii, **27**, **28**, **30**, **31**, 142, 143, 145
Tinnehinch, Co. Wicklow, 110n1
Toomyvara (Toomavara), Co. Tipperary, xx, **29**, 281, 332
Totteridge Park (Hertfordshire), 2, 6, 9, 340, 340n5, 341n3
tow paths, 311
Tralee, Co. Kerry, xix, **27**, 216, 222–3, 225, 234, 235, 237, 251, 258, 322
travelling scholars, 145–6, 201
Trevory, Co. Kerry, 230–31, 231n2, 321
Tussaud, 'Madame' Anna Maria (*c.*1761–1850), 295, 295n5

Uniacke-Fitzgerald, Robert (1797–1806, MP), 274, 274n1
Union, Act of 1801, 1, 246n6
United Irishmen, 18–19, 99n7, 105n2, 105n3, 105n4, 112n4, 154n1, 198n1, 199, 286n1
Upper Arley, Worcestershire, 61

Vale of Llangollen, Denbighshire, 76
Vallancey (Valencey), Charles (1725?–1812, soldier and antiquary), 184, 184n3

Valle Crucis Abbey, Denbighshire, 80n4, 314, 314n2
Ventry, Co. Kerry, xix, 227, 230, 320, 321n4
Vereker, Charles, 2nd Viscount Gort (1768–1842), 246n6
Villierstown, Co. Waterford, xviii, **29**, 158
Virgil, 188, 263

Warren, Sir John Borlase (1753–1822, naval officer), 341, 341n2
Waterford city, xx, 263, 264–5, 326, 327
weather, 10, 179, 213, 229, 235, 236, 237, 238, 241, 242, 245, 246, 247, 248, 253, 257, 263, 264, 265, 267, 268, 270, 275, 276, 278, 279, 283, 286, 287, 293, 294, 295, 297, 300, 301, 303, 304, 305
White, Luke (*c.*1740–1824, bookseller and politician), 299, 299n6
White, Richard, 1st Earl of Bantry (1767–1851), 197, 197n2
White, Simon (of Bantry, 1768–1838), 196, 196n2, 197, 199n6
Whittington (Wittington), Shropshire (Salop), xvii, 76, 76n7
Whelp (Welp, Wilp) Rock, Co. Wicklow, 121, **122**, 123, 127, 317
Wicklow 'gold rush' of 1775, 112n3, 139, 139n3
Windsor Castle, 35
Wolfe, Arthur, 1st Viscount Kilwarden (1739–1803), 19, 105, 105n4, 286
Worcester, xvii, 21, **26**, 42, 43–51, **48**, **49**, 52, 53, 57, 58, 75, 93, 288, 309, 310n1
Wrekin, xvii, 66, **67**, 68–9, 73, 76
Wrexham, xvii, **26**, 76, 81, 83–5, 87
Wynnstay Park, Powys, xvii, 78, 83, 83n, 315n1

Young, Arthur (1741–1820, agricultural reformer), 11, 14
Youghal (Youghall), Co. Cork, xviii, xx, **27**, **29**, 98n1, 157, 158–63, **159**, 164–5, 185, 262, 264, 323, 324, 325